ROMANTICISM

ROMANTICISM

Critical Concepts in Literary and Cultural Studies

Edited by
Michael O'Neill and Mark Sandy

Volume II
Romanticism and History

Routledge
Taylor & Francis Group

LONDON AND NEW YORK

First published 2006
by Routledge
2 Park Square, Milton Park, Abingdon, OX14 4RN

Simultaneously published in the USA and Canada
by Routledge
270 Madison Avenue, New York, NY10016

Routledge is an imprint of the Taylor & Francis Group

Editorial material and selection © 2006 Michael O'Neill and Mark Sandy;
individual owners retain copyright in their own material

Typeset in 10/12pt Times by Graphicraft Limited, Hong Kong
Printed and bound in Great Britain by MPG Books Ltd, Bodmin, Cornwall

British Library Cataloguing in Publication Data
A catalogue record for this book is available from the British Library

Library of Congress Cataloging in Publication Data
A catalog record for this book has been requested

ISBN 0-415-24722-5 (Set)
ISBN 0-415-24724-1 (Volume II)

M0027089BI

Publisher's Note

References within each chapter are as they appear in the original complete work

CONTENTS

CONTENTS

ACKNOWLEDGEMENTS

The publishers would like to thank the following for permission to reprint their material:

Oxford University Press for permission to reprint Marilyn Butler, 'Godwin, Burke, and Caleb Williams', *Essays in Criticism* 32, 1982: 237–57.

University of California Press for permission to reprint John Barrell, 'Fire, Famine, and Slaughter', *Huntington Library Quarterly* 63, 2000: 277–98. © 2000, by the Henry E. Huntingdon Library and Art Gallery. All rights reserved. Reprinted from *Huntingdon Library Quarterly*.

Studies in Romanticism for permission to reprint Jeffrey N. Cox, 'Keats, Shelley, and the Wealth of Imagination', *Studies in Romanticism* 34, 1995: 365–400.

Cronin, Richard. 'Walter Scott and Anti-Gallican Minstrelsy'. *ELH* 66 (1999), 863–883. © The Johns Hopkins University Press. Reprinted with permission of The Johns Hopkins University Press.

Studies in Romanticism for permission to reprint Jerome J. McGann 'Romanticism and its Ideologies', *Studies in Romanticism* 21, 1982: 573–99.

Oxford University Press for permission to reprint Nicholas Roe ' "A Sympathy with Power": Imagining Robespierre', in *Wordsworth and Coleridge: The Radical Years*, Oxford: Clarendon Press, 1988, pp. 199–233.

Studies in Romanticism for permission to reprint William Keach 'Cockney Couplets: Keats and the Politics of Style', *Studies in Romanticism* 25, 1986: 182–96.

Edinburgh University Press for permission to reprint Nigel Leask '*Kubla Khan* and Orientalism: The Road to Xanadu Revisited,' *Romanticism* 4, 1998: 1–21. www.eup.ed.ac.uk

Studies in Romanticism for permission to reprint Saree Makdisi 'Colonial Space and the Colonization of Time in Scott's *Waverley*', *Studies in Romanticism* 34, 1995: 155–87.

Symbiosis for permission to reprint Fiona Robertson 'British Romantic Columbiads', *Symbiosis* 2, 1998: 1–23.

Cambridge University Press and Helen Thomas for permission to reprint Helen Thomas 'Romanticism and Abolitionism: Mary Wollstonecraft, William Blake, Samuel Taylor Coleridge and William Wordsworth', in *Romanticism and Slave Narratives: Transatlantic Testimonies*, Cambridge, Cambridge University Press, 2000, pp. 82–124. © Cambridge University Press. Reprinted with permission of Cambridge University Press and Helen Thomas.

Cambridge University Press and Alan Richardson for permission to reprint Alan Richardson, 'Of Heartache and Head Injury: Minds, Brains, and the Subject of *Persuasion*', in *British Romanticism and the Science of the Mind*, Cambridge, Cambridge University Press, 2001, pp. 93–113. © Alan Richardson 2001, reprinted with permission of Cambridge University Press and Alan Richardson.

Studies in Romanticism for permission to reprint Tim Fulford and Debbie Lee, 'The Jenneration of Disease: Vaccination, Romanticism, and Revolution', *Studies in Romanticism* 39, 2000: 139–63.

Edinburgh University Press for permission to reprint Alan Bewell, 'Cholera Cured Before Hand: Coleridge, Abjection and the "Dirty Business of Laudanum"', *Romanticism* 4, 1998: 155–73. www.eup.ed.oc.uk

Keats-Shelley Association of America, Inc. for permission to reprint Hugh Roberts, 'Chaos and Evolution: A Quantum Leap in Shelley's Process', *Keats-Shelley Journal* 45, 1996: 156–94.

Studies in Romanticism for permission to reprint Jonathan Bate, 'Living with the Weather', *Studies in Romanticism* 35, 1996: 431–47.

Disclaimer

INTRODUCTION

Volume II Romanticism and History

In much recent criticism of Romantic literature, critics have sought to relate works of literature to contexts of various kinds. In our second volume we offer a range of critical work that reflects this fascination with the interplay between texts and contexts. Sometimes context serves the function of historical background, as in 'old' historicist criticism. But more often it is seen, in a sense associated with 'new' historicism, as bound up with the text, inseparable from its meanings.[1]

Part 3

Contextualism and historicisms

Our first essay in this volume is **Marilyn Butler**'s 'Godwin, Burke, and *Caleb Williams*' (1982). The essay argues that 'politics' is 'central' (21) to William Godwin's novel *Caleb Williams* (1794). It begins with a characteristic tactic of the historicist critic: the provision of an explanatory historical framework, showing how involved Godwin was in contemporary politics at a time of turbulence and repression. Butler demonstrates forcefully 'the dangerous topicality' (23) of the novel, a topicality which, later, Godwin played down, along with many subsequent critics: such critics are dismissed as 'irrationalists' (24). Butler is a polemical critic, fighting against the tendency of commentators to ignore the novel's 'social meaning' (24), and her essay displays the intellectual sharpness typical of her work. She is especially unpersuaded by psychological interpretations that focus (for example) on Godwin's early Calvinist experiences since they are allegedly 'incompatible with his role in radical politics' (24).

Butler puts flesh on the bones of her reading by seeing the novel as 'designed to refute the case for the *status quo* familiarised, above all by [Edmund] Burke' (25) in his *Reflections on the Revolution in France*, Burke commends obedience to authority and reverence for the established social and political order. The strategies adopted by Godwin in *Caleb Williams* undermine such obedience and reverence in perfect accord, so Butler claims, with major themes propounded by Godwin's *Enquiry Concerning Political*

1

Justice. Through the socially corrupt dynamics of the relationship between Caleb Williams and Ferdinando Falkland, Godwin subjects to a critique 'notions of degree and authority within a paternalistic system' (27). In support of this critique, Godwin psychologises Caleb's complex response to his master, Falkland, a response made up of 'inquisitiveness' and 'admiration, even veneration', deliberately employing 'unreliable narrations' to expose the corruptness of Burkean attitudes. Butler remarks tartly that 'most critics' have succumbed to Falkland's 'greatness and attractiveness'; in an attempt to de-glamorise him, she is even prepared to concede that Godwin's characterisation of him results in 'a literary cliché' (29).

Butler makes out a persuasive case for seeing the novel's interest in irrationalism as proceeding from a rational understanding of the impact on human beings of 'social conditions' or 'Things As They Are', as the novel's alternative title has it (31). She points out that the last volume of the novel is less interested in a 'purely personal drama' than in conveying the experience of Godwin and his radical contemporaries, a 'beleaguered intellectual minority . . . who had become singled out as . . . traitors, criminals and outcasts' (32). The general thrust of the novel 're-enacts and even verbally echoes the debate on the merits of the old system conducted since 1790 by Burke and his republican opponents' (33). Butler has no time for the idea of self-division in Godwin, and seeks to demonstrate *Caleb Williams*'s closeness to the tenets of *Political Justice* by showing that the second edition of the latter work contains revisions which show a concern with aristocratic power parallel to that demonstrated by the novel.

Butler's essay shows two traits of much historicist criticism: a mistrust of any interpretation that is not securely grounded in a grasp of the politics of the period, and a conviction that such a grasp can effectively decode details of imaginative works. In our second essay in the volume, ' "Fire, Famine, and Slaughter" ' (2000), **John Barrell** begins by referring, as Butler does, to the power of Burke's *Reflections*, a work which called into question the validity of the imagination for 'radical and loyalist alike' (38). The pivot of Barrell's essay, a new reading of Coleridge's anti-government 1790s poem, 'Fire, Famine, and Slaughter', is his observation that in 1794 the British government charged the leaders of the parliamentary reform with treason, with 'having "compassed or imagined" the king's death' (39).[2] The word 'imagine', drawn from the 'discourses of aesthetics and of psychiatry' (40), finds itself part of political debate, part of the atmosphere of imputed and rejected motives. After all, in a treason trial, as Barrell pithily observes, '*Someone* has been imagining treason' (41).

Barrell's strategy is to show how a word, 'imagination', normally associated with the aesthetic, tugs one into the arena of politics. While the later Coleridge of *Biographia Literaria* may have tried to separate the imaginative from the political, Barrell argues that, in 'Fire, Famine, and Slaughter', the poet had, in fact, been engaged, not just in anti-government polemic, but in 'regicidal imaginings' (44). That he had been (merely) imagining forms the basis of Coleridge's later self-exculpation: 'The very process of imagining Pitt's death', runs Coleridge's apologia on Barrell's account, 'was the means of saving his life; for to imagine his death was at the same time to purge the poet of any malevolent imaginings against him' (48). Although the poem has usually been thought of as attacking the British Prime Minister, William Pitt, Barrell argues that it was aimed at the King. He offers a number of reasons for this view: the poem was signed 'Laberius', the name of a Roman knight who predicted Caesar's death in a pantomime; the threat made by Famine against the 'brood' of the unnamed, four-lettered figure cannot be directed against Pitt since he was childless and famous for 'his total abstinence from sex' (50); the argument used by Coleridge in his later 'Apologetic Preface', that imagining a death prevented the wish from being realised, was used by him in an earlier pamphlet *The Plot Discovered* of 1795; Coleridge's views on the war with France were published in an essay, 'On the Present War', which came furnished with a double epigraph from Statius's the *Thebeid*, one of which alludes to the death of a king (the word 'rex' being replaced by three asterisks in Coleridge's text); the same essay contains a probable reference to a speech by Richard Brinsley Sheridan that refers to 'the *four letters*' which '*form* the title of the despot of Brandenburgh, and of the first Magistrate of this free country' (quoted 52): that is, 'King'. The essay insists on the enmeshing of politics and aesthetics, and draws on a formidable body of contextual detail to drive home its argument.

And yet, for all its force, Barrell's argument is necessarily speculative, and a fascinating feature of historicist criticism of Romantic literature is the alliance to be found in it between the factual and the imaginative. It tries simultaneously to see 'things as they were' and to avoid entrapment within Romantic modes of apprehension. In our next piece, 'Keats, Shelley, and the Wealth of the Imagination' (1995), **Jeffrey N. Cox** revisits a famous exchange of letters between Shelley and Keats in 1820 when, in response to Shelley's invitation to visit him in Italy and advice not to squander his poetic treasures in indistinct profusion, Keats replied that 'an *artist* must serve Mammon – he must have "self concentration" selfishness perhaps' (quoted 59). True to his conviction of the 'importance of groups in culture' (57), and of the centrality in the period of a group of writers linked with Leigh Hunt, Cox reads the younger poet's reply 'as a settling of accounts with a poet whose development paralleled and challenged Keats's own, an attempt to control his personal and poetic relations with Shelley as they had evolved within the Hunt circle' (59). Cox sees a biographical dimension to Keats's insistence on the value of 'selfishness', since Shelley had earlier told Hunt that Keats would be able to raise a loan on Hunt's behalf. Thus, when Keats, alluding to Spenser's account of the Cave of Mammon, counsels Shelley to '"load every rift" of your subject with ore' (quoted 59), he attempts to 'transmute economics into aesthetics'. Keats suggests, according to Cox, that his 'perceived stinginess can . . . be refigured as artistic control and dedication' (62).

Such an emphasis on 'selfishness' is at odds with Keats's theory of Negative Capability. Cox explains this 'selfishness' as 'an inability to commit the self' that has much in common with the contradictions facing liberal capitalism (64). Shelley, for his part, so Cox's argument continues, pondered on the implications of Keats's letter, and his response is evident both in *A Defence of Poetry* and *Adonais*, his elegy for Keats. In *A Defence*, he sets 'Poetry' against 'the selfish principle', equating the former with 'God' and the latter with 'Mammon' (quoted 67), rebutting Keats's attachment to the 'self-concentrated aesthetic object' and replacing it with a force of 'creativity' that precedes and cannot be solely housed by any aesthetic object. Cox claims that this rebuttal squares with Shelley's mistrust of 'paper money as a false substitute for gold' (72). In a comparable way in *Adonais*, Shelley 'seeks the eternal Keats beneath the mask and mantle of his mistaken ideology of Mammon' (75). The supposed self-portrait in the poem is, indeed, a critique of Keats as much as of Shelley, while the close of the poem 'unfurls the wings the Keats of the letter would have bound' in order 'to create an art of magnanimity' (80). The argument is an example of contextual criticism at its most ingenious, dovetailing textual and biographical evidence with great skill.

At its best, as in the pieces we have included, historicist criticism lends precision to literary interpretation and response. Such is the case with our next essay, **Richard Cronin**'s account of 'Walter Scott and Anti-Gallican Minstrelsy' (1999). Cronin is the author of *The Politics of Romantic Poetry: In Search of the Pure Commonwealth* (2000), the introduction to which offers a trenchant and perceptive survey of recent developments in Romantic criticism. Seeking to mediate between historicist criticism and work that has 'maintained the interest in the formal qualities of the poem that characterized the new criticism of the 1950s and 60s', Cronin argues in his book that 'It is through their language that poems most fully engage with their historical moment'. He deftly exposes a tendency of Romantic historicist critics to 'confer a dynamic glamour on one group of writers whilst representing another as crustily antiquated', the former being dubbed 'rebels' or 'radicals', the latter 'reactionaries' in Marilyn Butler's seminal study, *Romantics, Rebels and Reactionaries* (1981). Courteously and wittily he hints at bad faith and sentimentality in the fact that 'critics who live to all appearances sedate and deservedly successful professional lives espouse in their criticism a demand for revolutionary integrity that in its uncompromising rigour would not disgrace Saint-Just'.[3]

In the essay we have included, Cronin uses historicist methods to ensure justice is done to the poetry of Walter Scott, an uncompromisingly Tory figure, but one, who after the antiquarian venture of his collection of ancient ballads, *Minstrely of the Scottish Border* (1802), was able to incorporate a more sophisticated awareness of the 'vital connection' (93) between Scotland's past and present in *The Lay of the Last Minstrel* (1805) and *Marmion* (1808). In both cases, Scott writes historical poems, mediating between the past and the contemporary, a time dominated by the war with Napoleon which could be and was interpreted by the poet as demanding a unity that overrode differences of party and nation. The opening episode of *Marmion*, as Cronin points out, celebrates Pitt and Fox as Britons (not Englishmen) united by the demands of 'the British world' (quoted 100). The essay is subtle on Scott's 'enthusiasm for his military duties as Quartermaster general of the Edinburgh Light-Horse', explaining it as Scott's way of reasserting 'Scottish nationhood' (103), even as he was defending Britain, a concept subsuming national differences.

Cronin allows poetic fictions their right to create and explore imaginary resolutions of conflict. Such resolutions deeply trouble a fascinatingly conflicted and highly significant essay by **Jerome McGann**, 'Romanticism and Its Ideologies' (1982), a lucid summary of the main ideas informing *The Romantic Ideology* (1983). McGann uses his essay to 'bring critique to the Ideology of romanticism'; he warns contemporary critics against 'an uncritical absorption in romanticism's own self-representations' (108). Such an absorption risks a denial of the distance which exists between past cultural achievements and the present, a denial which prevents contemporary culture from seeing romantic works as offering 'present resources by virtue of their differential' (109). Only when we grant this 'differential' will we be in a position to enter into an authentic relationship with romanticism. It is, thus, of vital importance that 'the critic of romantic poetry' should 'make a determined effort to elucidate the subject matter of such poems *historically*' (110).

More ambivalently, McGann half-exempts romantic poetry from the ideology it expresses, seeing this poetry 'as a drama of the contradictions which are inherent to that ideology' and, indeed, as able to adopt a 'critical position toward its subject matter' (108). At times his readings seek to expose Romantic poets as using strategies that erase and displace the facts of history, as in his analyses of Wordsworth's 'The Ruined Cottage', 'Tintern Abbey', and 'Ode: Intimations of Immortality'. Wordsworth's is roundly described as 'a false consciousness' (117) in such works, as he solves the intractable problems of history at an internalised, imaginative level. Yet romantic falsehoods have, for McGann, a way of dramatising historical truth, especially when the poetry is led 'to open itself to . . . acts of self-conscious "reflection" in (and upon) the poetry itself' (122). Romantic poetry is, it turns out, capable of implicit and explicit 'self-criticism': Byron's despair is only what makes his poetry possible; its 'meaning' is the fact that this despair is 'the poetic reflex of the social and historical realities which it is a part of'. McGann draws back from a full-scale Marxist onslaught on romantic poetry as peddling uncritically 'displacements and illusions' (123), a drawing back which gives his essay and *The Romantic Ideology* much of their powerful openness to contradictory interpretation.

The essay is remarkable for its stylish ironies, often deriving from the pointed echoing of famous phrases from the writings of the Romantics, as when, alluding to 'Ode: Intimations of Immortality', McGann lightly mocks the Romantic notion of 'transhistorical' ideas as 'eternal truths which wake to perish never' (125). It is also remarkable for its reluctance fully to hand over the Romantic poets to the merciless insights of the undeceived consciousness. In the end, McGann settles for poetic knowledge as differing from critical knowledge: the latter must unmask, the former must experience. As he puts it, 'Contradictions are *undergone* in romantic poems' (126). The third and final section of the essay takes the case of Byron's poetry, and asserts that 'Like all romantic poetry, Byron's work is deeply self-critical, but only as a drama in which its own illusions must be suffered' (127). It is intriguing to read this account of Byron's poems by one of the poet's major editors and critics, McGann depicting Byron as caught up in the toils of Romantic Ideology, and yet as freeing himself from them as his work clarifies the futility of Romantic illusions.

Imagining is also central to our next essay, a chapter entitled '"A Sympathy with Power": Imagining Robespierre' from **Nicholas Roe**'s *Wordsworth and Coleridge: The Radical Years* (1988). As its sub-title suggests, Roe's book examines and contextualises the writings of Wordsworth and Coleridge in the 1790s when both were at their most sympathetic to the radical hopes embodied in the French Revolution. Roe has a sharp eye for unexpected conjunctions, and he approaches the main theme of the chapter, the impact on Wordsworth and Coleridge of the figure of Robespierre, by suggesting that in the draconian severity of his 1790s policies William Pitt was imitating the Frenchman's methods. Pitt, in fact, turns out to resemble the 'little actor' of 'Ode: Intimations of Immortality' who forever 'cons another part' (quoted 135). John Thelwall, a radical friend of the two poets and the dedicatee of Roe's study, compares the British Prime Minister unfavourably with Robespierre. Coleridge's *The Fall of Robespierre*, written in two days after the execution of Robespierre in 1795, presents Robespierre 'as the heroic rebel undaunted by the ruin brought upon himself' (139).

Compellingly Roe argues that Coleridge and Wordsworth experienced intricate and internalised responses to Robespierre, finding in him 'an alarming, distorted version of themselves' (142). Coleridge, it is claimed, saw Robespierre as driven by a '"horrible misapplication" of imagination during the Terror' (147), a polar opposite to and yet dangerous bedfellow of William Godwin against whose materialist rationalism both poets set their faces. Wordsworth, in his turn, connects Robespierrean Terror and Godwinian rationalism in his account of events in France in *The Prelude*, book 10. Yet Wordsworth was able to survive and live beyond his 'extinction as a Godwinian being' (150) by virtue of the sustenance afforded by

Dorothy Wordsworth and Coleridge. In the character of Rivers in his play *The Borderers*, Roe argues, Wordsworth gives expression to 'Coleridge's perception of the similarities between Godwin's arrogant abstraction and Robespierre's visionary politics' (152). Roe ties together a series of indicators that bear witness to Wordsworth's recognition of the need to move beyond Godwin (and Robespierre): they include a turning towards 'geometric science' (quoted 157), which, in turn, echoes Basil Montagu's ideas about the role of geometry in educating a child (Wordsworth helped to educate Montagu's son); they also include the composition of his 'Lines Left upon a Seat in a Yew-tree' which Roe interprets resonantly as Wordsworth's 'epitaph for a generation of good men like Coleridge and himself who had lost confidence in politics and *Political Justice*, but without discovering a consoling "light / To guide [and chear]"' (157) as they had done. Roe's critical imagination moves with fleetness of foot between text and context in this chapter. He differs sharply from McGann by seeing poetry, not as enmeshed in false consciousness, but as a medium through which political values and beliefs can be consciously crafted and affirmed.

It is important to be aware that some of the best criticism of Romanticism blurs demarcations between different approaches. Our next essay, by **William Keach**, has something in common with the essay by Grant F. Scott included in Volume I as it explores the intersection between context and text in the work of Keats, a poet often thought of until recently as essentially apolitical. In his contribution to a forum on 'Keats and Politics' edited by Susan J. Wolfson in *Studies in Romanticism* (1986), Keach, the author of an especially fine formalist study, *Shelley's Style* (1984), addresses the topic of 'Cockney Couplets: Keats and the Politics of Style'. Keach's point of departure is Lockhart's remark that 'Keats belongs to the Cockney School of Politics, as well as the Cockney School of Poetry' (quoted 164). Lockhart meant to insult, but his insult alerts Keach to the possible 'linking of politics and versification' (164) in the period. Keach resists too straightforward an identification between the freeing up of couplet form in Hunt and Keats, and political liberalism, and his essay is as interesting for the questions it asks about the links between politics and style as for the pondered answers it provides. He observes that Hunt's attitude to the couplet has a conservative as well as radical dimension. But he contends that there is, or may be, an 'anti-conservative impulse' (165) in the poet's avoidance of blank verse, a form associated with the conservatism of Wordsworth's *The Excursion*. And he notes how Byron is prepared to side with Tory reviewers rather than with 'the liberal poetics of Hunt and Keats' (167) in the so-called 'Pope controversy'.

At one stage, Keach asks whether we have 'passed beyond the level at which politics and form intersect' (170). Yet the remainder of his essay argues that, while such an intersection cannot be proved 'theoretically', there is value in 'trying to think about a particular stylistic feature from a historical and political point of view' (171). 'To Autumn' serves as a test-case, a seemingly non-political poem which, viewed in the context of material in the *Examiner* (including a stanza from Shelley's *Revolt of Islam* 'describing a victory feast held by the forces of liberation' (173)), takes on a more politicised appearance. The bees of Keats's first stanza connect, Keach argues, with 'a figurative tradition common in radical political writing' (174). Still, just as he appears to be arguing for a conscious use of political imagery, Keach takes a slightly different tack in his closing paragraphs, and leaves it unclear whether he sees Keats as deliberately writing a political poem or as betrayed into doing so by the suggestions surrounding his images. 'To Autumn', he claims, presents us with an 'idealized, mythologized image ... that fends off but cannot finally exclude a negative historical actuality which Keats was certainly in touch with.' It is the essay's intelligent hesitations, even as it wishes to link 'stylistic instincts' with a 'political dimension' (174), that are especially impressive.

Part 4

Orientalism and post-colonialism

The influence of Edward Said's *Orientalism* (1978), a book analysing the ways in which Occidental writers construct the Orient as an exotic 'Other', has been immense in Romantic studies. The concept of Orientalism offers a new lens through which to view Romantic flights of imagination generally and, particularly, the vogue for Eastern settings and imagery to be found (for example) in Byron's 'Turkish Tales' and satirised by him in *Beppo*. As a representative of this critical interest, we have chosen an essay by **Nigel Leask**, '*Kubla Khan* and Orientalism: The Road to Xanadu Revisited' (1998). Leask seeks to pull his readers away from a widely held view, partly promoted by Coleridge's provision on the poem's first publication in 1816 of a Preface offering the poem as 'a psychological curiosity' (quoted 179), that the poem is about the creation of poetry. His preferred view is that this most 'enigmatic' (179) of poems has covert political meanings which can be reached by 'recovering the lost cultural narrative of the poem's "visionary" elements'. Such recovery will permit the restoration of 'a geopolitical specificity to [the poem's] oriental setting absent in the final, "High Romantic" published version' (the poem was first written in the late 1790s). To this end, Leask ransacks the 'erudite source-hunting' of John Livingston Lowes's *The Road to Xanadu* (1927) while issuing a warning about that work's supposed 'intertextual vertigo and critical impressionism' (181).

Seeking to contextualise the nature of Coleridge's engagement with his oriental materials, Leask takes his cue from Marilyn Butler by seeing Southey's *Thalaba the Destroyer* as an important 'intertext' (182) for 'Kubla Khan'. He briefly flirts with the idea that, whereas Southey attacks 'oriental gardens' as emblems of 'false religious ideologies' that promoted 'mean-ingless wars', Coleridge was 'airing a conservative preference for hedonistic *participation* in Aloadin's narcotic paradise' (183). But further investigation of Coleridge's awareness of 'The politics of the Chinese garden' (189) and its contemporary political resonances leads Leask in the opposite direction; he reads the poem as using the oriental setting of the first thirty-six lines to warn obliquely about Tory oppression.

Leask's most valuable observation is his point that the last eighteen lines, the poem's visionary coda, use a different oriental setting. Instead of intima-tions of 'Oriental despotism', we are given, in this coda, 'an alternative, positive vision of the Abyssinian Maid's "symphony and song"' (190, 191). Leask ingeniously accounts for the waverings and hesitations in the writing as expressive of Coleridge's longing for an uncontaminated, primitivist holy space opposed to 'religious and political establishments'. Building his dome in air, the poet reacts against 'Kubla's paramount control of aesthetic pro-duction' (194). Leask's own reaction is against 'Western orientalism' and 'the discourse of high Romanticism' as he attempts with much argumentative skill 'to reconsider the worldliness of a canonical Romantic text' (195). If this reconsideration smacks more of complicated decoding than patient atten-tion, the historical critic such as Leask is likely to question whether there is, in the end, a fundamental difference between the two critical activities.

Saree Makdisi, in our next piece (1995), brings to bear insights drawn from post-colonialist critical discourse on Scott's novel *Waverley*. The essay's central question is the following: 'how is space, as a fluid and simultane-ously material and political process, produced or re-produced during the process of colonial conquest?' (199). It reads Scott's novel as fascinated by the significance of space, different terrains, real and imaginary, and by the journey taken by its hero and reader through these terrains. At the core of the novel's spatial concerns is the opposition between the Highlands and the Lowlands (and England), an opposition which 'enables . . . a matrix of other essentializing dualisms' (204). As 'essentializing' indicates, Makdisi is suspicious of these dualisms, which serve various encodings of the past and present (the novel is also, he allows, built on a temporal as well as a spatial scheme). He maps the novel's own mappings, suggesting that Colonel Talbot identifies with the Lowlands and England, and with the present, and that, wholly opposed to Talbot, Fergus MacIvor identifies with the Highlands and with a now lost past.

The 'novel's Highland space is fluid', however, and allows for incursions of the past into 'the present of industrializing bourgeois Britain' (206). When Prince Charles Edward leads his Jacobite Rebellion, what is conveyed is 'the Highland *territorialization* of Lowland space' (208), but this implies at best, on Scott's part, regretful sympathy for a 'past' that must be 'exorcized from the present' (210). *Waverley* is concerned, above all, to represent a version of history, in which Hanoverian triumphs over Jacobite and the modern, civilised present defeats the feudal, wild past. Makdisi himself is concerned, first, to identify the novel's characteristic strategies and, second, to point out that its 'imaginary map confronts a representational crisis of its own making'. This crisis has to do with the status of the past, which, to the degree, that it is identified with the Highlands, has had to be 'closed off' (213, 214), just as the hero moves beyond his 'support of Jacobitism' (212). At the same time, however, the novel has also shown the relevance of the Highland past to the present.

Makdisi deals with this 'representational crisis' by adding a further complication: what if ways of viewing the Highland past were, essentially, an invention of the present? His answer is that the Highland past serves a 'symbolic' purpose and becomes a 'contested space' (215). The implication is that the novel contains the grounds for a post-colonial reading that will disrupt the colonial values inscribed in aspects of Scott's imaginary mapping. Certainly Makdisi is clear that the novel itself colonises the 'Jacobite Scottish past', using it for 'the Lowland present' (219), and he argues that the British colonising of the Highlands served as 'a rehearsal of Britain's larger colonial project' (222). He sees *Waverley* as engaged in creating an imaginative distortion of the realities of history. The distortion ensures that the novel's 'colonial vision is never straightforward and unproblematic' (224), but, since it, in effect, elegises a self-created corpse (the Highland past), it retreats from the actuality – the Highland Clearances – of what was happening in the present.

'Imagining America' might be the subtitle of **Fiona Robertson**'s learned and judicious essay on 'British Romantic Columbiads' (1998). She begins with a detail equivalent to the telling anecdote much used by New Historicists, the incomplete nature of William Robertson's *The History of America* (1777), an incompleteness which suggests 'an integrated colonial history which was never to be' (231). Incompleteness shadows the Columbiads ('epics of America' or poems 'recounting the beginning and growth of the United States' (respectively, the *OED*'s and *Webster's Dictionary* definitions, quoted 234, 235)) which are the essay's subject. Robertson is interested in how British Romantic poets imagine a country which was, until the War of American Independence, a colony of Britain, and whose origins are themselves complicated but involve 'Spanish colonial history' (232). In *The Columbiad* (title of revised second version published in 1807) by the American poet, Joel Barlow, there is already the sense of 'a national history which is complex in its elisions and its unexpected confrontations' (236).

Robertson's main exhibits of British Romantic Columbiads are William Bowles's five-book poem *The Spirit of Discovery; or, The Conquest of Ocean*, Robert Southey's *Madoc*, and Samuel Rogers's *The Voyage of Columbus*. All three works display 'an unease with the story of Columbus which emerges at every imagined level of their design'. All three works see the story as making sense 'only as a stage in providential history', a history which had been 'severed' by the 'rebellion of the American colonies' 'from British history' (249). Bowles's poem shows a complicating 'sense of historical irony', telling of the supreme importance in providential history of 'British supremacy' but 'developing', too, a 'contextualising historical narrative which tells of the fall of empires' (239). *Madoc*, in turn, deconstructs the idea of Columbus as the discoverer of America, bestowing that honour on the twelfth-century Welsh prince Madoc. Yet it deconstructs its own deconstruction, according to Robertson, by using details from narratives of Columbus's travels to authenticate its account of Madoc. With regard to 'the rights and wrongs of settlement and possibly of conquest', Robertson asserts, the poem 'leaves many questions unanswered' (244). Samuel Rogers's poem is designed to avoid claims for 'inclusiveness' (246), and sets itself up to be 'a poem of voyaging rather than of vision'. Its narrative complications 'highlight different perspectives on and reactions to Columbus' (246), and the poem's second half places its emphasis on 'discontinuity and failed vision, personal and historical' (248). The essay illustrates how contemporary anxieties shape Romantic-period imaginings about history. If the Romantics were deeply historicist in their creations, as James Chandler argues in *England in 1819* (1998), those historicist creations were affected, as all such creations are, so Romantic historicist criticism argues, by the vantage-point of the present.

The textuality of history is a concern of historicist critics, the idea, that is, that history is not merely a matter of events, but that history is a story or collection of stories, each story telling a further story about the storyteller. In *Romanticism and Slave Narratives: Transatlantic Testimonies* (2000), from which our next article is taken, **Helen Thomas** 'explores the [Romantic] period's cultural productions from a revised historical and ideological context', a revised context that emphasises 'England's participation in the slave trade' (254). Thomas floats the idea that the writings of the first-generation of Romantic-period poets and writers are recognisably 'products of the same historical influences' (255) as slave narratives. She is quick to qualify this idea, pointing to the 'considerable ideological distance' between the two kinds of writing: isolation, a trope in the Romantics' writing, is a literal state in the recountings by slaves of their historical experience. But she claims a connection between the kinds of writing in relation to 'moments of spiritual witness' (256), memory and identity.

The main body of Thomas's chapter comments on the treatment by Wollstonecraft, Coleridge, Wordsworth, and Blake of slavery. Wollstonecraft both opposes slavery and uses abolitionist language in support of her attack on 'gendered inequality' (256). She does leave herself open, however, and here Thomas's own ideological concerns assert themselves, to the charge that she ignores differences in the conditions that existed 'between black slaves and white females' (258). For his part, Coleridge wrote an anti-slavery ode in Greek at Cambridge and launched a brave and passionate onslaught on the slave trade in a lecture given in Bristol in 1795. Thomas finds in Coleridge's account of the Imagination in this lecture a 'minimising' (see 262) of his critique of slavery and, again, one might pause to notice the almost reflex association, after McGann, of references to Imagination with retreat from political actuality. It leads Thomas to make considerable claims for a directly political ballad by Southey, 'The Sailor Who Had Served in the Slave Trade'.

Thomas is persuasive in her reading of Coleridge's conversation poems as making use of 'narratives of spiritual liberation' that centre on 'the concept of the imagination and the individual, rather than the collective self' (268). Her emphasis on narratives of salvation looks ahead to the preoccupations of some pieces included in Volume III of the present work. In her account of Wordsworth, Thomas also finds a pattern of antipathy to slavery combined with 'a discernible severance from ... abolitionist activities'. She detects resemblances between the 'liberationist rhetoric' (276) pervading Words-worth's accounts of his imaginative development in *The Prelude* and slave narratives, but she notes that in his sonnet to Toussaint L'Ouverture, who led a slave rebellion in the French colony of St Domingue, the poet 'avoids any discussion of race' (278) and focuses on natural elements as an image of freedom rather than on a socio-historical analysis. Thomas sees Wordsworth's attitudes, in effect, as another form of that 'displacement' which McGann attacks in *The Romantic Ideology*, and she endorses Mary Jacobus's view that the poet was seeking to buttress the 'fictive representation of the pro-videntially self-shaped mind' (quoted 279). As we have seen in other examples of historicist criticism, Thomas sees Wordsworth's poetry as resisting history. By contrast, she views with undisguised approval the nature of Blake's engagement with 'physical and spiritual enslavement' (289) as revealed in works such as *Visions of the Daughters of Albion*.

Part 5

Science, medicine, and eco-criticism

Explorations of the contextual in recent Romantic criticism have included looking at ways in which Romantic texts reflect and communicate the science and medical knowledge of the period, as well as how they anti-cipate late twentieth-century preoccupations with ecological matters. **Alan Richardson**, the co-editor with **Sonia Hofkosh** of *Romanticism, Race, and Imperial Culture* (1996), a collection of essays on matters addressed in our last section, has emerged as a major commentator on what he calls 'the science of the mind'. In the chapter from his *British Romanticism and the Science of the Mind* (2001) which we have included, he looks at Jane Austen's late novel *Persuasion* in the light of two trends which he sees it as illustrat-ing: a growing emphasis in the period on biological rather than environmental approaches and a 'new psychological appreciation of unconscious mental life and embodied cognition' (302). The early Romantic novel was 'Lockean' (303) in its stress on character as constructed through environmental influences, as is revealed by the upshot of Austen's *Mansfield Park*. But in *Persuasion*, according to Richardson, there are two ways of explaining character: one is 'unabashedly dualistic and in line with orthodox notions of the soul', and allows for the mind to overcome 'bodily discomfort'; the other, illustrated by the change in Louisa Musgrove after her fall from the Cobb and consequent brain injury, aligns 'mental acts with discrete brain functions' (307). Even the characterisation of Anne shows an interest in the 'collision of conscious awareness with unconscious thoughts and feelings' (308). Anne is depicted 'as an emotive, embodied subject, uncommonly reasonable and also uncommonly sensitive' (310) a blend that leads to her experience of 'mental splitting or fragmenting' (311), which, in turn, calls forth from Austen a new, more 'nervous' style and a sense, conveyed through the language, that 'subjectivity seems corporate rather than monologic' (312). Richardson singles out a phrase applied to Louisa in her period of recovery – 'intervals of sense and consciousness' (quoted 317) – as a useful description of Austen's new style of registering experience in the poem, a style influenced by Romantic-era debates about the relationship between mind and brain, and especially able to register the way 'emotional, cognitive, and physiological impulses engage in a complicated dance of action and reaction' (317). Richardson's approach shapes its own 'complicated dance' out of differing but partnered Romantic-period discourses.

In their punningly entitled 'Jenneration of Disease: Vaccination, Romanticism, and Revolution' (2000), **Tim Fulford** and **Debbie Lee** connect Edward Jenner's pioneering work on vaccination, which would ultimately make possible the 'eradication of smallpox' (322), to various central strains in Romantic-period culture and writing. Fulford and Lee demonstrate how Jenner 'attracted the services of romantic poets, who lent their verse to his efforts to create the taste by which his discovery might be enjoyed by the people' (323). As that allusion to Wordsworth suggests, Jenner is seen by Fulford and Lee as a figure in the medical sphere akin to the Romantic poet in the literary sphere. Just as *Lyrical Ballads* was initially regarded as unpalatably levelling in conservative quarters, so Jenner's theories, involving the notion that cattle and men possess 'similar constitutions' (324), triggered considerable 'vaccination anxiety' (325). Jenner fought his corner with vigour, enlisting the support of aristocratic patronage (as Wordsworth would do with the Lonsdale family), and the backing of the popular poet, Robert Bloomfield, who called himself a 'writer of Pastoral poetry, and literally a Cowboy' (quoted 328). Bloomfield's *Good Tidings; Or, News from the Farm* (1804) was dedicated to Jenner. It brings home the horrors of smallpox and extols the virtues of vaccination. Jenner would also receive the support of Coleridge and Southey, poets who believed that 'poetry could be an exaltation of science' (335). Coleridge, typically, offered to pen, but never wrote, a poem in support of vaccination. Southey praised Jenner in terms that reflected his changed political views: vaccination in his later work becomes an image that supports 'his hopes that revolution will be put down' (337). Jenner and the Duke of Wellington are, for Southey, both warriors 'against the miseries which afflict mankind' (quoted 337). Fulford and Lee reveal with much contextual alertness the way in which a medical discourse enters the cultural bloodstream of the period.

A further example of connections made between medicine and Romantic literature occurs in **Alan Bewell**'s ' "Cholera Cured Before Hand": Coleridge, Abjection and the "Dirty Business of Laudanum" ' (1998), an essay which explores 'the middle-class association of the politics of Reform with the cholera epidemic' (345) of 1831–2. Coleridge contributed to the debate with his own 'politico-medical broadside' (347), 'Cholera cured before hand'. In this poem, which adopts for satirical purposes the persona of a 'working-class reformer' (346), Coleridge's language makes clear, according to Bewell, how 'British ideas' about cholera 'conveyed attitudes toward gender, sexuality, vagrancy, and colonial otherness' (350). Coleridge's poem uses techniques of 'disgust' or 'abjection' in order to reconsolidate boundaries being threatened by cholera and its metaphorical twin, reformist politics. So, the working class are admonished to 'Quit COBBET's, O'CONNEL's and BELZEBUB's banners' (351, 352, quoted 352), because cholera was associated with the immigrant Irish poor (Daniel O'Connell being the noted champion of Irish Catholics in the first part of the nineteenth century).

Bewell sees the poem as aimed both at the ruling and the working classes, warning the former and mocking the latter, and as 'an act of abjection' in which Coleridge 'consumes the language of those he disliked in order to spit it out'. This is not so much a question of Coleridge's disliking the working class, Bewell argues, as of his disapproval of the view that they were suitable to 'play a role in governing the nation' (354). The situation is complicated by the fact that opium, from which Coleridge was at the time struggling to free himself, was noted for its 'anti-choleric aspects' (355). Thus, as Bewell notes, Coleridge was caught in a trap capable of being construed in Orientalist terms: 'as he rid himself of one Eastern poison (laudanum), the other Eastern poison (cholera) took its place' (357). For all his poem's satiric dimension, the evidence 'suggest that he believed that he had undergone the state of abjection that he associated with slavery and the working class' (358). Bewell links biographical with political and medical contexts to cast new light on the conflicted nature of Coleridge's politics at this time.

In the final two essays in this volume, we turn our attention to the impact on Romantic criticism of present-day scientific and ecological preoccupations. In the first essay, 'Chaos and Evolution: A Quantum Leap in Shelley's Process' (1996), **Hugh Roberts** reads Shelley's poetic career, and especially *A Defence of Poetry*, in a way that tries to mediate between the poet's supposed idealism and scepticism. Roberts's kind of historicism is drawn from scientific theories of the present, particularly chaos theory, and he rejects ' "political" literary criticism' on account of its tendency to 'read all texts as "typical" expressions of a given socio-political form' (366). Chaos theory, as expounded by Roberts, asserts that 'the limits to our ability to know the world have less to do with epistemology than with the hitherto unsuspected complexity – the "fractal" complexity – of the world itself' (367). Like quantum theory, its basic ideas are 'prefigured', so Roberts following Michel Serres argues, 'in the work of Lucretius' (368). *De Rerum Natura* recognises that 'contingency' is always at work in life. As Roberts puts it, 'Chaotic creativity is a constant process of error becoming essence' (369), or, again, 'A chaotic world is an endlessly destructive one, but it is also an endlessly creative, and endlessly engaging one' (369). One does not, therefore, need either to see Shelley as pursuing a tantalising Absolute that lies beyond language, or to be persuaded that he is forever sceptically 'decentering' truth-claims.

In his essay's third section, Roberts returns to *A Defence of Poetry*, viewed, in its emphasis on the fact that works of art will always remain open to interpretation and that new interpretations will always have about them elements which are, in Shelley's words from *A Defence*, 'unforeseen' and 'unconceived' (370), as anticipating chaos theory. He takes respectful issue with William Keach's view that Shelley's attitude to the endlessness of interpretation is akin to the 'archetypal Romantic-ironic one of celebrating progress over achievement' (371). Drawing on Jacques Derrida to clarify his chaos theory reading of Shelley, Roberts argues that it is wrong to 'think of meaning as something stable'; rather, it 'tends to proliferate endlessly in the promiscuous iterability of the "trace" or "mark" ' (373). Arguably, Roberts risks giving up too quickly on the idea of Shelley's belief in the possibility of stable meaning. But his use of chaos theory and Lucretius illuminates the way in which, for Shelley, 'the literary text never appears twice in exactly the same way'; he offers us a new perspective on Shelley's veil imagery. Shelley's veils are often seen as endlessly pointing beyond themselves to an unreachable ' "real meaning" ', but, for Roberts, they compose 'a perpetually renewed succession of "meanings", each as real as the next' (375).

Roberts also draws on the work of Jean Francois Lyotard, and, in particular, the notion of 'links' (*enchaînements*), to illustrate how Shelley's anticipation of chaos theories permits his poems to serve a coherent political function, as ' "seeds" . . . of some unimaginable future state' (377). In the light of his central argument, he provides an innovative reading of 'The Witch of Atlas', stressing the poem's 'anti-structure', its 'sheer narrativity-without-narrative' (379), its subversion of 'the organic Aristotelian "plot" by being a largely contingent sequence of sheer events' (380). The Witch's 'continuing presence in and response to the world' (389) is an instance of

Shelley's commitment to poetry's agency, complex and undidactic as that agency is conceived by him to be.

Our final piece in Volume II is also concerned with poetry's agency and significance. 'Living with the Weather' (1996) is an essay by **Jonathan Bate** from a special issue of *Studies in Romanticism* on 'Green Romanticism', guest-edited by Bate. The essay is incorporated in Bate's *The Song of the Earth* (2000), a work of eco-criticism that concerns itself with 'why poetry continues to matter as we enter a new millennium that will be ruled by technology'. The book is, Bate continues, 'about the capacity of the writer to restore us to the earth which is our home'.[4] In the essay, Bate writes with lucidity and passion about how Romantic poetry reminds us of 'the earth which is our home'. He begins with Byron's poem 'Darkness', an apocalyptic vision that responds in its vision of an extinguished sun to the eruption of the Tambora volcano in Indonesia in 1815, and observes that Byron, unlike many contemporary critics of Romantic poetry, 'does not set culture apart from nature' (398). Asking about the role of 'romanticism in our age of eco-crisis', Bate then turns an evaluating gaze on the 'ideologically-inflected literary criticism of the 1980s' (398). He sees it as a product of Cold War anxieties, and of an approach that severed culture from nature, and suggests that now 'a New Geographism is replacing the New Historicism' (399).

Bate addresses Keats's 'To Autumn', a text central to modern revaluations of the Romantic. Whereas McGann read the poem as paradigmatic of the Romantic tendency to escape from politics into art, Bate notes that it brings into prominence a Romantic concern with 'weather', with the instability of nature (Bate alludes in this context to chaos theory: see 401). For Bate, it does not do justice to Keats's ode to interpret it as 'an escapist fantasy which turns its back on the ruptures of Regency culture'. Rather, 'To Autumn' reminds us of links between the human and the natural, bonds which are spoken about in the poet's letters of the period, as when Keats writes, 'Now the time is beautiful. I take a walk every day for an hour before dinner and this is generally my walk' (quoted 403). If one retorts that Bate is making a great deal out of mere discussion of the weather, Bate would reply, on the evidence of the letter, that Keats as a consumptive was especially sensitive to the quality of the air and that the ordinariness of the description is precisely its point: we take for granted what is essential for our survival and can easily be damaged. Indeed, the essay quotes near its close a question posed by Serres: 'how can we think *fragility*?' 'To Autumn' celebrates a particularly fine period of weather after several poor summers and autumns. In so doing, it becomes a celebration, such as that offered in Coleridge's 'Frost at Midnight', of 'fragile, beautiful, necessary ecological wholeness' (409).

Bate's eco-criticism is able to harness to its own ends the historicist's alertness to period and the formalist's concern with textual detail. One of the most rewarding passages in the essay demonstrates, by means of close attention to the language of 'To Autumn', the poem's network of suggestions. It 'comes to resemble', Bate asserts, 'a well-regulated eco-system' (404), one that avoids too strong a centre in favour of articulating 'relations'. Though the poem annuls the Cartesian split between self and world, there is mention of the human subject in the poem, the feminised figures of stanza two, but these feminised figures are not the heroines championed by modern critics opposed to 'traditional images of masculinity and femininity'. Instead, they reflect the 'idea of woman's closeness to the rhythms of mother earth' (405). At such a moment, Bate's eco-criticism seems profoundly conservative in its implications, and the longing to conserve experiences of 'a certain kind of being and of dwelling' (406) is a strong impulse (so he argues) in Romantic poetry. Persuasive, contentious, engaged with present and past, Bate's wide-ranging essay brings this second volume to a close; in its re-consideration of feminism, it serves as an appropriate bridge between Volume II and Volume III.

Notes

1 For a useful discussion, see Kenneth R. Johnston, 'New Historicism', in *Romanticism: An Oxford Guide*, ed. Nicholas Roe (Oxford: Oxford UP, 2005), pp. 165–81.
2 See Barrell's full-length study, *Imagining the King: Figurative Treason, Fantasies of Regicide 1793–1796* (Oxford: Oxford University Press, 2000).
3 Richard Cronin, *The Politics of Romantic Poetry: In Search of the Pure Commonwealth* (Basingstoke: Palgrave, 2000), pp. 13, 14, 15.
4 *The Song of the Earth* (London: Picador, 2000), p. ix.

Part 3

CONTEXTUALISM
AND HISTORICISMS

19

GODWIN, BURKE, AND *CALEB WILLIAMS*

Marilyn Butler

Source: *Essays in Criticism* 32 (1982), 237–57.

Where politics appears in English novels, it is commonly at the margins; in *Caleb Williams* it is central. Godwin's most significant creative period was during the political crisis of 1791–6, when a native English radical movement first blossomed, warmed by events across the Channel, and then withered and died in the national crisis of full-scale war with France. He wrote continuously in these years: pamphlets, letters to newspapers, and the two most important books of his career, the treatise *Political Justice* (1793) and the novel *Caleb Williams* (1794). The two books both went into revised second editions by 1796, with *Political Justice* so materially changed that its second edition represents a new political statement.

This body of writing made Godwin the foremost intellectual among English radicals once the post fell vacant with Tom Paine's precipitate departure for France in 1792. Too much knowledge of Godwin's later years makes us pin on him Lamb's tag, 'the Philosopher', as though he was always chairbound and anything but practically dangerous. Despite his emphasis on reason and his disapproval of violence, Godwin was no mere bystander in this brief period when revolution seemed a practical possibility. The hue and cry against Priestley in Birmingham in 1791 and the clamour against Paine in 1792 showed how uncomfortable the role of radical spokesman could become. Godwin defined all the unpleasantness of the position, and yet volunteered for it, when he protested against the loyalist hysteria surrounding Paine's trial *in absentia* in December 1792. In one letter to the *Morning Chronicle* he claimed that those of the reform party were reduced to a state of 'perpetual fear',[1] and in a second letter he complained of the hysteria that made a fair trial impossible:

We all know by what means a verdict was procured: by repeated proclamations, by all the force, and all the fears of the kingdom being artfully turned against one man. As I came out of court, I saw hand-bills, in the most vulgar and illiberal style distributed, entitled, The Confessions of Thomas Paine. I had not walked three streets, before I was encountered by ballad singers, roaring in cadence rude, a miserable set of scurrilous stanzas upon his private life.[2]

In the winter of 1793–4, as he was writing *Caleb Williams*, Godwin visited the two condemned Scottish radicals, Muir and Palmer, who were awaiting transportation to Australia on board the prison hulks in the Thames; in April and May he saw his London radical friend Joseph Gerrald in the same circumstances. On 12 May 1794 Thomas Hardy of the London Corresponding Society, and after him eleven other London radicals, including Godwin's close friend Holcroft, were arrested and charged with treason. At the time radicals believed that, if the twelve were found guilty, many others would follow them into the dock. Godwin nevertheless reacted by dating his provocative Preface to *Caleb Williams* 12 May, the very day of Hardy's arrest, and by alluding in it to the newly devised charge of 'constructive treason'. In October, just before Hardy and the others were brought to trial, Godwin criticised the concept of this offence even more boldly in his *Cursory Strictures on the charge delivered by Lord Chief Justice Eyre to the Grand Jury*, a pamphlet which played a part in obtaining their acquittal.

Godwin was hardly behaving like a theorist though, if he sought martydom through the Preface to *Caleb Williams*; he was saved by his publisher, Benjamin Crosby, who would not print it. The opening to the Preface conveys his anxiety that the reader might miss his contribution to current events: 'The following narrative is intended to answer a purpose more general and important than immediately appears on the face of it'. The novel is designed to explore 'the question afloat in the world respecting Things As They Are', a debate inaugurated by Burke's warm defence of the old order, *The Reflections on the Revolution in France* (1790). The case for change which Godwin previously made philosophically in *Political Justice* is now in *Caleb Williams* to be translated into a more popular language. The real oppressiveness of the order Burke idealised

is a truth highly worthy to be communicated to persons whom books of philosophy and science are never likely to reach. Accordingly it was proposed in the invention of the following work, to comprehend, as far as the progressive nature of a single story would allow, a general review of the modes of domestic and unrecorded despotism, by which man becomes the destroyer of man.

The Preface finally appeared in the second edition of 1795, and in July of the same year, responding to an attack on him in the *British Critic*, Godwin wrote a reply which further amplifies the essentially political purpose of *Caleb Williams*:

> [Your correspondent] presupposes that my book was written 'to throw an odium upon the laws of my country'. But this is a mistake into which no attentive and clearsighted reader could possibly fall. The object is of much greater magnitude. It is to expose the evils which arise out of the present system of civilised society; and having exposed them to lead the enquiring reader to examine whether they are, or are not, as has commonly been supposed, irremediable; in a word, to disengage the minds of men from presupposition, and launch them upon the sea of moral and political enquiry . . . Your correspondent comes nearer the point when he . . . states my object to be: 'the laws of this country, and the mode of their execution'; or rather, as he ought to have stated, *the administration of justice and equity, with its consequences, as it exists in the world at large, and in Great Britain in particular.*[3]

In later years Godwin ceased to emphasise what at the time he had boldly insisted on – the dangerous topicality of his book. His later glosses have to do with its novelistic qualities, and with the method of writing that helped to sustain suspense. The celebrated account he wrote in 1832 of the manner in which he composed the novel (beginning with its thriller-sequence, the hunting of Caleb in Volume III) indicates that he no longer saw his book as dealing with the social and public perspectives of the Enlightenment. Instead, he reinterpreted his own career retrospectively in the aesthetic and private terminology of Romanticism.

Post-Romantic critics have tended to concur with Godwin's later view of his 1790s novel. Leslie Stephen influentially remarked that the moral of *Caleb Williams* eludes its author: 'How about the wickedness of government? The answer must be that it has passed out of sight';[4] 'the reader, unassisted by the preface, would scarcely perceive Godwin's doctrine between the lines'.[5] David McCracken, the book's latest editor, agrees that the Preface has 'by no means an obvious connection with the novel itself'.[6] A. D. Harvey sums up the majority opinion when he separates Godwin's works from one another and from their context, with the novel 'detached from the period of political upheaval in which it was written', so that '*Political Justice* and *Caleb Williams* have very little subject-matter in common'.[7]

Karl Popper once protested at the practice of 'not taking arguments seriously, and at their face value, at least tentatively, but of seeing in them nothing but a way in which deeper irrational motives and tendencies express themselves.'[8] It has been a tendency at least as strong in literary criticism as in other disciplines, and the writers on Godwin's fiction who have attended to his argument[9] have been, for all their weight of evidence, outweighed numerically by irrationalists. Even in the course of a critique sensitively open to nuances from real life and politics, P. N. Furbank insists on the novel's introverted mode. He reads it as 'a highly dramatized symbolical picture of Godwin himself in the act of writing *Political Justice*';[10] at its most political, the action is merely 'a psychological analogue' to revolution and, thus internalized, nearer to Dostoevsky than to Holcroft.[11] For Rudolph E. Storch, however, the very mention of Holcroft in connection with Godwin is a 'critical error';[12] he argues that the novel is a Calvinistic study of the psychology of rebelliousness and the guilt it entails. Falkland comes to stand for Godwin's own father, a Calvinist minister, and for the God of the Old Testament. 'Caleb's curiosity means disobedience . . . It is in fact the Original Sin';[13] the action takes place in a stylized landscape of the mind, and 'the story of *Caleb Williams* has no place in the society of eighteenth-century England'.[14]

Do the proponents of such interpretations realise how extraordinary they are? At the time Godwin insisted on his social meaning, and insisted moreover that the symbolism and stylization of his treatment supported his rational intention, by taking all societies into the critique rather than just England. For Godwin to have written a religious novel, even a novel unwittingly subverted by a religious consciousness, is incompatible with his role in radical politics. The year of *Caleb Williams* was also the year of Paine's anticlerical *Age of Reason*. Godwin noted in his Journal for October 1793, while he was working on *Caleb Williams*, a plan to write a 'treatise on God', which is presumably identical with the project he described elsewhere which would 'sweep away the whole fiction of an intelligent former of the world, and a future state'.[15] During the next two years, Coleridge's indignation with Godwin, as recorded in his Notebooks, reached its height, precisely because he associated Godwin with the atheism then current among English intellectuals. Anti-Godwin propaganda in *The Antijacobin* and in conservative polemical novels in 1797–8 concurs in portraying Godwin as the atheistical philosopher. His erstwhile friends James Mackintosh and Samuel Parr use his irreligion as the cornerstone of their attacks in 1799 and 1800. No-one seems to have sensed any backsliding from the cause of Reason in either *Caleb Williams* or in any other Godwinian writing of the first half of the revolutionary decade.

Storch's notion that Caleb's crime enacts Original Sin is surely a thought that occurs more readily in the late twentieth century than in the late eighteenth: in the post-Freudian era, the idea of the Fall is happily assimilated to a sense of guilt experienced for purely private reasons. It comes as no surprise to find a similar accommodation when a modern critic of Godwin's great opponent, Edmund Burke, investigates the origins of Burke's theological pessimism. Isaac Kramnick explains Burke's conviction of man's fallen nature and the supposed presence in his writing of an irrational sense of guilt as the product of a youthful trauma due to the absence of Burke's father, after which one part of Burke's nature found itself 'worshipping the father, or longing for a father to worship'.[16]

A more historical type of explanation is available for the theme powerfully reiterated in the *Reflections on the Revolution in France*, that man cannot hope to redeem himself through his own efforts and his own fallible reason. Conor Cruise O'Brien, himself a politically minded Irishman, points to the legacy of Irish Catholicism which Burke inherited from both sides of his family. He suggest that Burke's attack on revolution in France was complicated by his suppressed sympathy with resistance in Ireland; in particular, when Burke urged the English to look with favour upon the Catholics now dispossessed in France, he subversively made the case for those Catholics the English themselves had deprived in Ireland.[17] O'Brien's is an analysis which aims to account for Burke's complexity, for his emotionalism and of course for a style profoundly indebted to the scriptures. It helps to show why the *Reflections* were ideologically effective, as history suggests they were. Kramnick's hypothesis cannot do this for Burke, and Storch's remarks on Godwin represent the same difficulty in more acute form. How could a guilt-ridden, God-ridden author make the case for rationalism or radicalism? If Godwin is a tormented Calvinist, must he not also seem an incompetent polemicist? Guilt and fear, God and the Old Testament, are notions necessarily playing a more challenging and difficult part in Godwin's work than in Burke's, so that they cry out for explanation.

Burke and Godwin, living in revolutionary times, adopted strategies that would speak to the educated, uncommitted reader. For modern philosophers writing about *Political Justice*, as for modern critics of *Caleb Williams*, Godwin is the better for not being political. Yet for Godwin himself, as the Preface to *Caleb Williams* makes abundantly clear, both his major books were adversarial, – designed to achieve change and also designed to refute the case for the *status quo* familiarised, above all, by Burke. *Political Justice* has the reputation of rising above polemic to seek an objective (if unreal) blueprint of the just society, but this very appearance of lofty impartiality is dictated by its role as a reply to Burke's *Reflections*. If Godwin appears passionless, it is because Burke appears extraordinarily excited; if Godwin casts his eye forward to a perfect future, it is because Burke has grounded his arguments in an imperfect past. Burke pooh-poohs the insights of modern individualism ('we know that *we* have made no discoveries'), and sonorously alludes to the great men of history, the warriors, the leaders and the poets; he emotively parades such topics as hearth and home, parents, the naturalness of obedience. Burke casts the reader in the role of a small child, dwarfed by the scale of the greater world, and he exploits the language in which the child is instructed, the rhythms of Bible, prayerbook and pulpit, to persuade his reader to respond with the child's implicit obedience.

The main theme of *Political Justice* is that all such lessons are pernicious lies. Society is not naturally virtuous at all. It exercises a strong power, previously little understood, over the lives of individuals. This power operates not merely through political institutions and the law, but through prejudice, prepossession and habit. 'It [government] insinuates itself into our personal dispositions, and insensibly communicates its own spirit to our private transactions.' (I.4)[18] Obedience to authority is thus not a virtue, even in children; it is only by making us believe in obedience, through exhortation, fiction and other devices of imposture, that our governors maintain their position. The virtuous individual models himself not on the child but on the young adult, who, independent of parents, enquires for himself.

Long ago, in his Whiggish polemic writing of the 1780s (for example in *A Defence of the Rockingham Party* (1783)), Godwin had admired Burke as a man who had risen by merit, as a champion of liberty and a truthteller. His fall was therefore all the greater when, as the author of the *Reflections*, he barefacedly set out to defend and sanctify rule by an oligarchy. In a paragraph in his last chapter (to which he appended an obituary of Burke in 1798), Godwin imitated the rhythms of Burke's own celebrated eulogy of Marie Antoinette in order to evoke a similar regret:

'We know . . . that truth will be triumphant, even though you refuse to be her ally. We do not fear your enmity. But our hearts bleed to see such gallantry, talents and virtue employed in perpetuating the calamities of mankind.'

(II.545)

Godwin is seldom so directly personal as this. Yet he does devote about two hundred pages of his treatise (a part of the work on which modern descriptions commonly fail to linger) to such topics as the rival social systems, amongst which the aristocratic system advocated by Burke is clearly the most salient. In Books III to V Godwin considers in turn the characteristics of the monarchical, aristocratic and democratic systems, together with the moral influence of each upon the individual citizen, and upon the relations between governors and governed. Under the monarchical system, virtue, he avers, 'is, in their conception, arrogant, intrusive, unmanageable and stubborn'. (II.56) Monarchy and aristocracy alike have a tendency 'to undermine the values and understandings of their subjects . . . Implicit faith, blind submission to authority, timid fear, a distrust of our powers, an inattention to our own importance and the good purposes we are able to effect, these are the chief obstacles to human improvement'. (II.119) In the crucial chapter V, xv, 'Of Political Imposture', Godwin again alludes specifically to Burke as an upholder of a system of necessary trickery, by which the population must be duped into obedience. In the *Reflections*, says Godwin sardonically, kings and leaders are represented 'independently of their individual character, as deriving a sacredness from their office. They must be accompanied with splendour and veneration'. (II.132) No-one should seek to reduce *Political Justice* to the status of mere polemic reply to Burke, but the core of Godwin's book, – the source of its energy and the main determinant of its rhetoric, – lies in Godwin's conception of it as the ultimate answer to the *Reflections*, the only answer to attack the great issues within the same generous frame of reference to man's history, his culture, his morality, and his personal relationships.

Burke and Burkean rhetoric also recur in *Caleb Williams*. The novel is built round the relationship of two men, Caleb Williams and Ferdinando Falkland, who are 'servant' and 'master' in the words of the first edition, 'secretary' and 'patron' in the second. Commentators agree that this relationship is all-important, even though the direct conflict between the two is reserved mainly for the second of the three volumes. What is less commonly remarked is the degree to which the two characters are not individuals but stereotypes. Instead of entering into unselfconscious intimacy with either, the reader is kept aloof and made aware of the factors that shape the two characters' views of one another, especially the notions of degree and authority within a paternalistic system.

The theme of the first volume is Falkland's past history, as narrated to Caleb by his fellow-servant Collins. The indirect narration establishes the awe Falkland exacts from others as virtually an element of his character. Though Collins leads the story up to the occasion when Falkland was accused of murder, he himself does not believe the charge; he never sees those implications in his tale which are discreditable to his master. Yet Collins's entire story throws a very harsh light on Falkland's class. Falkland, after all, was the competitor and peer of an unpleasant bully, Squire Tyrrel, who hounded down two victims – his cousin, Emily Melville, who, Clarissa-like, was subjected to an attempt to marry her off to a boor, and a local tenant-farmer, Hawkins, whom Tyrrel ruined. Both these victims began by expressing esteem and love for Tyrrel; when both crossed him and proved obstinate, he used the law to imprison and destroy them. Emily and Hawkins stand for the immediate social inferiors of the squirearchy; what happens to them in the first volume, a prolegomena to the main action, is meant to suggest the variety and range of circumstance in which the power of the upper orders can be felt by other citizens.

As a poor female relation in a system strictly given to male primogeniture, Emily has no economic independence, and her family feels little sense of moral obligation towards her. The imprisonment and attempted rape to which she is subjected is obviously an extreme case, but it follows coarse treatment and coercion which must have been very common. Hawkins first offends by declining to vote as another landlord bids him, but he loses

Tyrrel's favour by refusing to let his son Leonard become Tyrrel's servant. Leonard breaks down gates set up on Tyrrel's order, and since he does it at night with his coat turned up, he commits a felony under the 'Black Acts' by which the eighteenth-century gentry maintained their absolute property rights in the countryside. Taken together, these offences by the Hawkinses constitute a rejection of the notion of subservience, which Tyrrel angrily sets out to punish.

As Collins's narrative makes clear, Falkland opposed Tyrrel in the latter's bullying both of Emily Melville and of the Hawkins family. If Tyrrel represents the unacceptable face of the English class system, Falkland is apparently its ornament. His refusal to fight a duel, in his youth in Italy, shows that he is critical of the brutish aspect of 'chivalry'. But in practice Falkland's fastidiousness hardly runs deep. Though he begs Tyrrel to avoid quarrelling with him, he retaliates with interest when Tyrrel strikes him in public. At this insult Falkland reverts to the code of his caste and acts precisely in the manner (so we are told) of the haughtier type of Italian nobleman, when he felt insulted by an opponent he would not deign to meet on the field of honour: he waylays and murders him.

The opening passage of Volume II introduces Falkland and Caleb together in scenes which are closely observed and psychologically complex: this is a different quality of writing from the case-studies of the first volume. Nevertheless, Caleb and Falkland are carefully shown to represent their respective orders. Caleb, on hearing the story of Hawkins, does not share Collins's automatic assumption that Hawkins *must* be guilty of murder or Falkland innocent. Caleb is like Hawkins, another commoner, a man of self-respect and independence. It is unthinkable to Collins, the servant of aristocracy, that a gentleman might be guilty, but the possibility remains for the yeoman Caleb.

While Caleb resembles Hawkins, he also resembles Emily. As an inmate and dependent of Falkland's house, he relates to Falkland much as she did to Tyrrel, and he even recalls her artless, inexperienced character. Just as Emily approached Tyrrel direct, so Caleb tries to deal with Falkland: both give offence by not humbly keeping their distance, not observing the obedience due to rank. Caleb's resemblance to the two victims of Volume I prepares the reader for the strange, yet convincing, emergence of Falkland, formerly the champion of Emily and Hawkins, as the archetypal tyrant of Volumes II and III.

The fascination of the early chapters of Volume II, however, has less to do with archetypes than with Godwin's study of the psychology of his two principals within their respective roles. He ventures an exemplary moralistic dialogue in the Holcroft manner about whether Alexander is a great man or not. In the course of this conversation Falkland is tempted into a number of 'aristocratical' statements which put his supposed benevolence into a curious new light:

'Let me hope that you will become more liberal. The death of a hundred thousand men is at first sight very shocking; but what in reality are a hundred thousand such men more than a hundred thousand sheep? . . . It was necessary to the realising his project that he should pass for a God. It was the only way by which he could get a firm hold upon the veneration of the stupid and bigoted Persians.'[19]

At times it is hard to see in Caleb's conversational tactics anything but a sort of adolescent slyness, a teasing, knowing provocation of a puzzled older man. Caleb oscillates between maddening Falkland with lower-class cynicism about Alexander's nobility, and buttering him up by pretending to despise the commonalty:

I replied: . . . '[The world's] affairs cannot be better than in the direction of the genuine heroes; and, as in the end they will be found the truest friends of the whole, so the multitude have nothing to do, but to look on, be fashioned and admire.'
. . . 'Williams! said he, you instruct me well. You have a right notion of things, and I have great hopes, of you.'

(p. 117)

When after this Falkland accuses Caleb of being a 'base artful wretch' who deals in 'mystery and equivocation', the charge is unfair without being ridiculous in the reader's eyes. Godwin makes Caleb immature, not merely a social inferior and dependant but the essential type of the son. He 'grows' in the course of the novel, without ever being allowed to reach an assured maturity. Godwin maintains his authorial detachment by stigmatizing Caleb's curiosity about his employer's secret as 'inquisitiveness', and by having Caleb stress (as Collins did before him), his admiration, even veneration, for Falkland. It is made to seem to the reader, as apparently to Caleb himself, that in the tussle between veneration and inquisitiveness, the latter is a defect or even a transgression (p. 122). Caleb has no vocabulary to justify what he does; even though he knows Falkland to be guilty of murder, he keeps using Falkland's loaded terminology. Indeed, Falkland exercises a powerful spell over everyone in the world of the novel, as a hero, a 'beneficient divinity', a human being of special value. Unfortunately, he has also exercised it over most critics, who continue to write of Falkland's greatness and attractiveness as though these were objectively established rather than obliquely reflected in the unreliable narrations of Collins and of Caleb.

As a literary achievement, the character of Falkland hardly deserves our high opinion. Gloomy, guilty, the terror of his subordinates, he derives too plainly from Garrick's celebrated Richard III, or Kemble's Coriolanus, or from the period's veneration for Milton's Satan; a literary cliché, he is about to be outdone by Lewis's Ambrosio and Radcliffe's Schedoni, by Scott's Marmion and Byron's Corsair. What subtleties there are in the writing derive from sociological observation, from generalised character-studies of the manners and morals of gentlemen. Falkland's over-valuing of honour and reputation is the characteristic of a type, and it is bluntly stated rather than traced with much refinement – 'This it was to be a gentleman! a man of honour! I was the fool of fame.' (p. 135) More delicately drawn is the unconscious aristocratic hauteur which undercuts Falkland's effort to improve his relations with Tyrrel. (p. 31) Despite his willed benevolence, his role has taught him to be masterful and coercive. Early in the novel, the dying Mr. Clare, a spokesman for some of Godwin's opinions, expresses the Dissenters' abhorrence of seeking to bind another by an oath. As soon as Falkland discovers that Caleb has found out the truth, he tries to swear him to silence. 'I charge and abjure you by everything that is sacred and that is tremendous, preserve your faith!' (p. 136) Thereafter much of Falkland's language is religious – that of a divinity, perhaps, but hardly a beneficent one:

> 'You might as well think of escaping from the power of the omnipresent God, as from mine! If you could touch so much as my finger, you should expiate it – hours and months and years of a torment of which as yet you have not the remotest idea! . . . I have dug a pit for you! . . . Be still! If once you fall, call as loud as you will, no man on earth shall hear your cries.'
>
> (pp. 144–54)

David McCracken and B. J. Tysdahl have pointed out that, in using such language, Falkland alludes to Burke twice over.[20] This Old Testament rhetoric certainly resembles that of the *Reflections*, with its hints of the authority of the Church, and the terrors to be experienced by the Church's disobedient sons. But the rhetoric of terror is accounted for more particularly in another of Burke's books that Godwin knew well, and re-read in the early 1790s, *A Philosophical Enquiry into the Origin of our Ideas of the Sublime and Beautiful* (1756). There Burke holds that terror, the source of the sublime, is the strongest feeling of which the human mind is capable, and it is evoked, characteristically, by contemplating power. Power may be invested in a figure of authority, a master or a king, but ultimately it derives from God; and there is no mistaking the fervour with which Burke sketches the terror inherent in the notion of omnipotence:

> Whilst we contemplate so vast an object, . . . we shrink into the minuteness of our own nature, and are, in a manner, annihilated before him . . . In the Scripture, wherever God is represented as appearing or speaking, every thing terrible in nature is called up to heighten the awe and solemnity of the divine presence.[21]

30

This is a concept not to be underrated by Godwin, who had known the rigours of an equally exigent Christian tradition; yet in the second edition of *Political Justice* Godwin was to declare specifically that Burke's aesthetic doctrines were inadequate, the mere pastimes of 'a man of taste and refinement':

> The sublime and pathetic are barren, unless it be the sublime of true virtue, and the pathos of true sympathy . . . There is no delightful melancholy, but in pitying distress.
>
> (I.447)

Godwin is thus subjecting to critical and satirical analysis the extravagant rhetoric also typical of Falkland.

At the same time, Godwin's own early religious experiences undoubtedly gave him insight into the effect upon an impressionable mind when religious terror of this sort is invoked. Indeed, Godwin never obliterated from his memory the impact religious gloom and rigour had on his adolescence. It is felt in his later novel, *Mandeville* (1817), and most memorably here, in the hold Falkland has over Caleb. Clever and energetic, Caleb longs to become the friend of Falkland and of Falkland's cousin Forester, and is disappointed because both in the end can only think like gentlemen. Yet each relationship is stillborn in any case, because of Caleb's irrational reverence for Falkland, his 'master', an awe which makes him guilty, tongue-tied and impotent. Falkland threatens Caleb terrifyingly, invoking an ancient language of dominance, – temporal authority backed by religion, – and the youthful Caleb withdraws in silence, 'irresolute, overawed and abashed'. (p. 154) It is because he cannot speak to Falkland that he decides to disobey him and run away. Afterwards he comes to see this as a wrong step, because it is dictated by emotion, the rising frenzy in Falkland matched by frenzy in himself. (p. 154) In suggesting that Caleb should have been able to master his emotions, Godwin – as frequently happens in his writing – maps out an ideal plan of behaviour for ideal conditions which are not, as he knows, remotely like the actual ones. Everyone, in this study of 'Things As they Are', behaves irrationally rather than wisely, driven by prepossession, interest or panic. Where the treatise *Political Justice* both analyses the present system and proposes alternatives, the novel *Caleb Williams* confines itself with intensity to the social conditions men are experiencing.

Thus, the quirks and unconscious compulsions of human nature conspire with social conditions to lead these two men, who originally viewed one another with sympathy and mankind with benevolence, to torment and finally to destroy one another. The leading instrument of their mutual aggression is the law, revealed here as un-justice. The courts can sometimes acquit the innocent, but they do not favour the small man's attempt to challenge, and so claim equality with, the great man. Hawkins went to law to challenge Squire Tyrrel, to the latter's glee. (p. 73) Eventually Caleb too challenges Falkland directly in a London magistrate's court, to the indignation of the justice: 'There would be a speedy end to order and good government, if fellows that trample upon ranks and distinctions in this atrocious sort, were upon any consideration suffered to get off'. (p. 276) But the absurdity of Caleb's aspiration to achieve personal equality has already been proved by Falkland's easy manipulation of law to punish rebelliousness:

> I was conducted to the same prison which had so lately inclosed the wretched and innocent Hawkinses. They too had been the victims of Mr. Falkland. He exhibited, upon a contracted scale indeed . . . a copy of what monarchs are, who reckon among the instruments of their power prisons of state.
>
> (p. 177)

The relationship between Falkland and Caleb is, then, a political relationship, unequal despite a cultural tradition ('free and equal in the eyes of the law') that says otherwise; violent and destructive, despite the wish of both men that it should be otherwise.

Most of the characters in the novel are so used to the idea of hierarchy that they only really notice Falkland's behaviour when it is gracious. He can threaten and bully so that Caleb is in danger of his life, but he can also show a lordly compunction to him in prison, for which, absurdly but believably, he expects Caleb to feel grateful. The conventional and virtuous figures in the novel mostly see morality in the same light. Falkland's servants are so convinced of his goodness that they all sincerely abhor Caleb. So does the benign old man who guards him in Liverpool. So, in later editions, does the mother-figure he finds in Wales, Laura.

The last volume indeed becomes a study of the workings of 'imposition' at large, rather than a direct duel between Falkland and Caleb. Falkland no longer needs to lurk melodramatically, a Demon King, behind each of Caleb's misfortunes. 'Things As They Are', the System, ensures that he is hounded as in real life Priestley and Paine had been, and Godwin's friends, the accused in the Treason Trials, afterwards known in Windham's phrase as 'the acquitted felons'. If the whole novel is judged as a purely personal drama, parts of Volume III are a falling off, because Falkland does not appear in them, but the common reaction to the plot is that it intensifies. The explanation for this lies in real-life politics: it is the last volume which conveys the mood of the beleaguered intellectual minority, the frustration, bitterness and fear of marked men, conscious of their own rectitude, who had become singled out as 'constructive' traitors, criminals and outcasts. In its picaresque, unfocused way, less apparently dramatic, yet cumulatively despairing and paranoid, the third volume matches the insight of the other two, while broadening the novel from a closed action which might be read personally to a more open fable of unequivocally political significance.

In general terms, then, *Caleb Williams* is about hierarchy. It shows how the representative relationship of Caleb and Falkland really works, because of the pre-conditioning of the two men and of those about them. More specifically, it re-enacts and even verbally echoes the debate on the merits of the old system conducted since 1790 by Burke and his republican opponents. In *Caleb Williams* the central symbolic moment is the attempt to open the mysterious box, the ark kept in Falkland's private sanctum, an opportunity given to Caleb because of the (revolutionary) fire endangering the house. It is an analogue of the writing of *Political Justice* or the writing of *Caleb Williams*, although the box itself has no literal importance, since there is no one secret, no one piece of evidence, to uncover. Falkland's 'secret' is his evil wish to dominate or to be revered, and it is conveyed everywhere in the text's mimicry of Burkean language, its many moments of sardonic parody, like the near-quotation from *both* the *Reflections* and *Political Justice* with which the character of Falkland is introduced – 'My heart bleeds at the recollection of his misfortunes as if they were my own.' (p. 10)[22] The element of Burke in the portrayal of Falkland has been acknowledged by several of Godwin's most scrupulous and informed critics, including Boulton and Kelly, who do not of course maintain that Falkland 'is' Edmund Burke. Godwin himself avoided much direct mention of his opponent in the treatise and he would not have countenanced a personal caricature in the novel. But just as Peacock evoked the published Coleridge in Mr. Flosky of *Nightmare Abbey*, and Shelley surveyed the output of Wordsworth in *Peter Bell III*, in order to discredit their arguments, so Godwin reviews Burke's career as a political writer through having it re-enacted by Falkland. Volume I of *Caleb Williams*, with its sketch of Falkland's courageous liberal past, his opposition to duelling and to petty tyranny, stands symbolically for Burke's early career on the liberal wing of Whiggism. Falkland falls because, like Burke in Godwin's eyes, he proves not to be the corrector of the system but its dedicated servant, the more fraudulent and the more dangerous because he sees through his own lies.

The close correlation in Godwin's mind between *Political Justice* and *Caleb Williams* is demonstrated, finally, by the textual effects of the latter on the former. Soon after he had published the novel in May 1794, Godwin began work on a series of revisions to *Political Justice* which eventually appear in the second edition dated 1796. He lists, in a Preface, the most substantial of the changes, twelve entirely new-written chapters, and explains some of his amplifications by the need to bring the earlier chapters into line with his later thinking. Three of the complete new chapters in Godwin's list, 'Of Obedience' (III. vi), 'Of forms of government' (III. vii), and 'Of Good and Evil' (IV. xi), together with a number of passages in this part of the treatise (e.g., IV. i; IV. vi; V. xi; V. xv) have been little commented on, probably because they are not readily categorised in terms of politics or political theory. Here Godwin amplifies his discussion of the relations between the classes, and especially, the behaviour of the aristocracy or upholders of existing systems of government.

In keeping with his usual caution, Godwin in contemplating Obedience (III. vi) takes care not to recommend disobedience. 'Government is nothing but regulated force', but it is not wise for the governed to take on a power too strong for them. The citizen's main duty is to try to secure the freedom of his own understanding. 'Obey; this may be right; but beware of reverence.' Godwin contemplates the notion of civic duty propagated in existing society, by Burke above all others:

> To a government, therefore, that talked to us of deference to political authority, and honour to be rendered to our superiors, our answer should be: 'It is yours, to shackle the body, and restrain our external actions; that is a restraint we understand. Announce your penalties; and we will make our election of submission or suffering. But do not seek to enslave our minds . . . you can have no right to extort our deference, and command us not to see, and disapprove of, your errors.'
>
> (I.236–7)

A kind of violence overtakes the language as Godwin contemplates the very Obedience that to a Burke (or a Falkland) constitutes civic virtue.

> When I make the voluntary surrender of my understanding . . . I annihilate my individuality as a man, and dispose of my force as an animal to him among my neighbours, who shall happen to excel in imposture and artifice . . . I am the ready tool of injustice, cruelty and profligacy.
>
> (I.232–3)

The same force sounds in the paragraphs added in 1796 to 'Of Political Imposture' (V. xv), where Godwin contemplates directly the intellectual crime of Burke:

> It may not be uninstructive to consider what sort of discourse must be held, or book written, by him who should make himself the champion of political imposture . . . By whom is it that he intends his book should be read? Chiefly by the governed; the governors need little inducement to continue the system. But, at the same time that he tells us, we should cherish the mistake as mistake, and the prejudice as prejudice, he is himself lifting the veil, and destroying his own system . . . It is not to be wondered at, if the greatest genius, and the sincerest and most benevolent champion, should fail in

producing a perspicuous or very persuasive treatise, when he undertakes so hopeless a task.

(II.139–40)

Thus Burke, as the author of the *Reflections*, the lapsed liberal, the tool of aristocracy and the propagandist of imposture, recurs again and again as the mystifier, the keeper of secrets in *Political Justice*, and as Falkland in *Caleb Williams*. But the figure, part real man, part emblem of the ideological position Burke was now identified with, is more interesting in the second edition of *Political Justice* than in the first, and more interesting in *Caleb Wiliams* than in either. The format of the novel, which treats individuals and their relationships, requires Godwin to study 'imposition' both as the trait of the aristocrat, and, more interestingly still, as the source of guilt and disturbance in the conditioned, vulnerable common man who is imposition's victim. Instead of generalising about how society ought to be, and summarising its present defects, Godwin in *Caleb Williams* enacts coercion, and the impulse to personal liberty, on a private level, and thus uncovers the psychological roots of political behaviour that in the first *Political Justice* philosophic abstraction had tended to conceal. The revisions to the treatise, though more limited, are dictated both by the insights won from the novel and by further thoughtful study of real men suffering actual political oppression. When all Godwin's writing of the 1790s is considered together, including the notebooks, letters and fragments of hard, analytic autobiography, he emerges as a powerful observer of the human psyche, who neither flattered nor simplified his own kind, Caleb's kind. An abrasive, punishing attention to unpleasant realities, rather than utopianism, is the literary characteristic of 'the Philosopher'.

With all its symptoms of fraught times pressing in upon it, *Caleb Williams* finally emerges as an ambitious symbolic study of a political issue big enough to rise above mere topicality. In the early 1790s radicals like Godwin imaged for themselves an unprecedented power to think and act. To achieve it, they had to divest themselves not merely of the *ancien régime* and its institutions, but of the prepossession within their own minds in favour of those institutions – especially their veneration for hereditary leaders, and their vulnerability to the hypnotic rhetoric of paternal authority sanctioned by religion. *Political Justice*, even in its first version, said as much. The power of fiction to generalise through the particular enables *Caleb Williams* to enact metaphorically the relationship between hereditary government and governed. It shows the psychological traumas, the murdering of fathers, which the establishment of a non-hierarchical system would necessarily entail. It is, therefore, a psychological novel, but a psychological novel set in the special conditions of revolution. As such, it has affinities with the writing of Stendhal, Dostoevsky, or Conrad, when they deal with volatile political situations, but it is unlike most novels which have emerged from relatively stable England. In the heady circumstances, there could be no greater warrant of Godwin's integrity than the acknowledgement in his best writing that revolution will not, after all, easily be won; that even the war in the mind has only just started. The greatest of English literary republicans, Milton, wrote his masterpieces as he adjusted to the political failure of *his* revolution. Perfectibility, said Godwin in the second edition of *Political Justice*, does not mean the attainment of perfection, but only the unending capacity to improve. The gritty redefinition, the scaling down of hope, was worked out step by step in the writing of *Caleb Williams*.

Notes

1 Godwin, *Uncollected Writings*, ed. J. Marken and B. R. Pollin (Gainesville, Florida, 1968), p. 113.
2 *Ibid.*, p. 116.
3 Quoted by D. Gilbert Dumas, 'Things As They Were: the original ending of *Caleb Williams*', *Stud. Eng. Lit.*, 6 (1966), p. 583.
4 *Studies of a Biographer*, 2nd ser., 3 (1902), p. 148.
5 *Ibid.*, p. 140.
6 *Caleb Williams*, ed. D. McCracken, Oxford English Novels (1970), p. xii.
7 A. D. Harvey, *E in C* 26 (1976), p. 243, p. 240.
8 Quoted V. Bogdanor, 'Conservatism Psychoanalysed', *Yale Law Journal* 87 (1978), p. 1090. I am indebted to this review-article for the comparison between Kramnick and O'Brien on Burke.
9 These include J. Middleton Murry, *Heaven and Earth* (1938), ch. xix; D. H. Monro, *Godwin's Moral Philosophy* (1953), pp. 207–49; James T. Boulton, *The Language of Politics in the Age of Wilkes and Burke* (1963), pp. 207–49; Gary Kelly, *The English Jacobin Novel, 1780–1805* (1976), pp. 179–208.
10 'Godwin's Novels', *E in C*, 5 (1955), p. 215.
11 *Ibid.*, p. 234.
12 'Metaphors of Private Guilt and Social Rebellion in Godwin's *Caleb Williams*', *ELH* 34 (1967), p. 189.
13 *Ibid.*
14 *Ibid.*, p. 204.
15 C. Kegan Paul, *Godwin: his friends and contemporaries* (1876), 1. 296.
16 I. Kramnick, *The Rage of Edmund Burke: Portrait of an Ambivalent Conservative* (New York, 1977), p. 64.
17 Introduction to Burke, *Reflections on the Revolution in France*, Pelican Books (1968) pp. 34–47; see above, no. 8.
18 Godwin, *Enquiry Concerning Political Justice*, photographic facsimile of 3rd edition of 1798 corrected, ed. F. E. L. Priestley (Toronto, 1946); the sentence quoted first appeared in the 2nd ed. of 1796. Subsequent references in the text are to volume and page in this edition, though the passage cited appeared in the 1st ed. of 1793 unless otherwise stated.
19 Ed. D. McCracken (see above, n. 6), p. 112.
20 D. McCracken, 'Godwin's Reading in Burke', *ELN* 7 (1970), p. 266; B. J. Tysdahl, *William Godwin as Novelist* (1981), pp. 51–2.
21 *The Collected Works of Edmund Burke* [ed. F. Laurence and W. King], 8 vols. (1826), i. 174–5.
22 Cf. above, p. 244.

20

"FIRE, FAMINE, AND SLAUGHTER"

John Barrell

Source: *Huntingdon Library Quarterly* 63 (2000), 277–98.

Lord Grenville, the foreign secretary in the government of William Pitt, was famous for the hugeness of his bottom. In this caricature of 1795, *A Keen-Sighted Politician Warming his Imagination* by James Gillray, he has turned his most famous attribute to a roaring fire while he studies a pamphlet entitled, with a nudge and a wink, "The Fundamental Principles of Government."[1] He is preparing to address the House of Lords, where, the suggestion is, he will speak not with his mouth but his arse. Later in this essay I will return to the association between the fundament, or arse, and the imagination; for the moment I use this image simply to introduce the point that, in the discourses of politics and the law in the 1790s, the faculty of the imagination fell on very hard times. Almost no one but Burke had a good word to say for it; and it was Burke's imagination, as displayed especially in his *Reflections on the Revolution in France* of 1790, that had crystallized the sense that in the discussion of politics, the imagination had no place. In the numerous replies to Burke's *Reflections*, the character of Burke's imagination was qualified by a bewildering range of epithets. It is "fine" and "poetic," "lively" and "vivid," "rich" and "luxuriant," "creative" and "prolific." It is "powerful," "boundless." It is "warm," "glowing," "heated," "combustible," "volcanic." It is "debauched," "libertine," "ungoverned," "distempered," "haunted," "frantic," "wild, malevolent." But the variety of these adjectives conceals a high degree of unanimity among Burke's opponents about the nature both of his own imagination and of the imagination itself.[2]

Virtually without exception, those who reply to the *Reflections* in the early years of the decade, even if they admire Burke's imagination, represent it as inappropriately exercised in a work of political theory. The case is made most powerfully in the most powerful replies—those by Catharine Macaulay, David Williams, Thomas Paine, Mary Wollstonecraft, Joseph

Priestley[3]—but it is made in almost every reply. Repeatedly, the use of the imagination in the *Reflections* is adduced as evidence of a failure on Burke's part to observe the supposedly clear divisions between different forms of cultural and intellectual endeavor: those that are properly undertaken by the imagination, and those that must be pursued by reason, method, and laborious historical inquiry. The "facility" with which ideas are associated in Burke's "lively imagination, "absolved from the laws of vulgar method," disables him from undertaking "the drudgery of close reasoning."[4] The imagination is on the side of sensibility—of passion, even—and is hostile to reason, judgment, understanding. It is infantile, a symptom of intellectual and political immaturity. It is "extravagant" in the literal sense of the word, for the path of reason is straight, direct; but the imagination has a propensity to err, to wander. It is implicitly feminine or effeminate, with a habit of leaping the uncertain boundary between sensibility and sensuality. It is womanish, too, in being easily terrified, the dupe and prey of alarms, horrors, specters, phantoms—"imaginary dangers" that it has itself conjured up. The alarmism of Burke is frequently described as the effect of a "wild," "distempered," "disordered," "deranged," or "diseased" imagination, with the implication that he was mad or infatuated when he wrote the *Reflections*.

"In this battle of books," writes Tom Furniss of the pamphlet war initiated by Burke's *Reflections*, "both sets of antagonists make virtually identical assumptions about the relation between imaginative discourse and reality; while each relies on the persuasive power of visionary rhetoric, each condemns the other for doing so."[5] This is perhaps to overstate the case—few of the participants in the battle, on either side, are quite as "visionary" in their rhetoric as Burke. It is certainly true, however, that in the pamphlets written in the early years of the 1790s to defend the *Reflections*, and usually therefore to attack *The Rights of Man*, the imagination is not much less frequently evoked—and condemned—than it is by the critics of Burke. Those who wrote against the supporters of revolution in general and against Tom Paine in particular tend to argue that to reason on questions of politics from first principles rather than from experience was to make the same use of the imagination as Paine had charged against Burke. The visionary and distorted imagination of Paine is seen to condemn him to inhabit a world no less imaginary than he himself had accused Burke of inhabiting: a world in which "imaginary Systems" of government are supposed capable of redressing "imaginary grievances" or of guaranteeing (by far the most frequent use) "imaginary rights."

The vilification of the imagination, by radical and loyalist alike, continued in the years after the *Reflections* and *The Rights of Man* had ceased to be central to political debate. To radical writers and Opposition M.P.s, Burke's imaginary alarms, his mistaken application of the imagination to the science of politics, became a characteristic of the mentality of all who deplored the revolution in France and defended the unreformed constitution of Britain. To loyalists, not only Paine but also the entire campaign for universal manhood suffrage seemed a kind of disorder or hypochondria of the imagination. And the dangers associated with the imagination became still more salient when, in 1794, the government of William Pitt attempted to suppress the movement for parliamentary reform in Britain by charging its leaders with high treason. They were charged, under the first clause of the medieval law of treason, with having "compassed or imagined" the king's death.

What did this strange clause mean? and what could or might it be taken to mean in 1794? I can begin to explain by pointing out that in English law you cannot be charged with murdering the king or queen. Indeed, you could murder them with perfect impunity, if only you could prove that you had not previously compassed or imagined their death. The fact that you have murdered them is judicially cognizable only as evidence that you had thus compassed or imagined their death, which is the whole crime; and if you have compassed or imagined their death, you have committed high treason, whether or not you have murdered them or made any attempt whatsoever on their life.

The verbs "compass or imagine" in the law of treason both seem originally to have meant "design" or "intend," and since at least the second half of the seventeenth century, indictments for this species of high treason had begun to include words such as "design" or "intend," or "contrive," "devise," "purpose," alongside "compass or imagine"—apparently indicating that the words of the statute were by then thought to be in need of a gloss. By the second half of the eighteenth century, however, legal authorities were repeatedly commenting on the strangeness of using "imagine" in the purposive sense of "intend"—even "design"—at a time when almost every usage of "imagine" and "imagination" seemed to stress the spontaneous, even the involuntary, nature of imagining.

The meaning of "compass," as used in the statute, occurs in no other context except when the word is implicitly borrowed from the statute itself; this meaning of "imagine" was one that the word had retained in only one other context, the King James Bible, where it had long ceased to be generally understood, even by learned commentators. Indeed, the use of "imagine" and "imagination" in the Bible, which might have been expected to lend the legal meaning of the words a degree of stability, probably did the opposite, by supplying lawyers with such ready-made oratorical phrases as "wicked imaginations" and "evil imaginations," whose meaning in the Bible was by then imperfectly understood. In trials of radicals for high treason in the 1790s the lawyers for the Crown frequently use such phrases to attribute a dark and gothic cast of mind to those they are prosecuting. They speak of the "wicked imaginations" in the heart of the traitor, the "desperate imagination" of the supposed revolutionary, and may well have been thought to be accusing the defendants not of intending the king's death but merely of imagining it in the weak sense—by an association of ideas however involuntary.[6] To these lawyers, of course, the legal meaning of "imagine" was clear enough, at least in theory; the difficulty was to preserve that meaning in actual usage, in the heat of courtroom argument. By the 1790s "imagine" and "imagination" were keys that turned the locks of a number of different discourses. Under pressure from a host of other meanings of "imagination"—in the familiar sense of "picturing in the mind," in the discourses of aesthetics and of psychiatry, in controversial political writings—the fence protecting the legal meaning of "imagine" was broken down, and the word lost all definition, a victim of the instability that is liable to occur whenever such a polyvalent term is required to function as a term of art.

Partly, I am suggesting, those charged with the responsibility of describing the crime of imagining the king's death fell victim to the uncontrollably porous nature of all supposedly "closed" discourses. Partly, however, the instability of the word "imagine" seems to have been the result of the deliberate inflection of its, legal meaning with all those meanings supposed to lie outside the discourse of law. The generosity with which the word "imagine' lent itself to figurative and analogical manipulations invited and facilitated a confusion about the nature of the crime of imagining the king's death, a confusion that was differently exploited by prosecuting and defending counsel. The extralegal connotations of the word "imagine" could be exploited by the enemies of the reform movement so as to loosen the notion of what it meant to "devise" or "intend" the king's death; in turn, the accusation of "imagining the king's death" could in one way or another be retorted against the accusers by a similar exploitation of the extralegal meanings of the word.

This development had been prepared for by generations of legal authorities who had extended the law of treason by extending the notions of what it meant to intend, or imagine, the king's death and of what was meant by the "death" thus imagined. Early commentators had defined the treason of imagining the king's death as referring to manifest designs to do something by which the king's life would inevitably be endangered; by the mid-eighteenth century it was represented as referring to manifest designs to do anything at all that might threaten the king's life. By the 1790s it was possible for Crown lawyers to charge defendants with intending the king's death on the grounds that, though they were conscious of no such intention, the king's death, or deposition, or at least a change in his constitutional position, would have been the likely, or at least the possible, outcome of their actions.

This progressive loosening of the meaning of the treason of imagining the king's death was justified as a proper and necessary response to what had become over the centuries a defect in the law. The statute had been framed at a time, it was argued, when it made complete sense to identify the survival of the constitution with the survival of the king. The law therefore

40

took no account of what came to be known as "modern treasons" and had to be extended by construction to catch those who, though having no direct designs on the person of the king, had designs against the constitution that, if successful, would arguably be far more dangerous to the safety of the state than the execution or assassination of a king would be. Equally, however, this extension of the statute by construction was to be deplored, by radical and liberal writers, as an attempt to represent as high treason actions that could be represented as such only figuratively or analogically, only by confusing the king's actual body with his political body, his head with his hat. These actions were, in short, "imaginary treason," treasons imagined not by the defendants but by those who were accusing them.

In the trials for high treason of English and Scots radicals in the mid-1790s, this point was made time and time again. It is as if, once the indictment has released the word into the courtroom, a subject has to be found for it. *Someone* has been imagining treason. The defendant, by pleading not guilty, insists that it is not him; who else, then, can it be but his accusers?—who on the basis of actions that import no apparent intention to kill the king have conjured up an imaginary scene of regicide. The government, whether hysterically or maliciously, has lost all grip on the difference between the spirit of democracy and threats to the king's life. The point was made most economically by Richard Newton, the most economical of caricaturists, in the print *Treason!!!* of 1798,[7] which perhaps reveals its full meaning only when juxtaposed with Gillray's image of Grenville's imagination. John Bull points his own generously rotund imagination at the king's picture and farts; Pitt accuses him of treason—it can only be the treason of imagining the king's death, presumably by asphyxiation. Pitt had, according to Coleridge, no imagination at all, and famously had no bottom: indeed, he was known by satirists as "Mr Bottomless Pitt."[8] But bottomless or not, it is evidently Pitt here who is doing the imagining. In the treason trials, this retort—it isn't me, it's *you* who's doing the imagining—seeks to repel the charge of imagining as intending with a countercharge of imagining as picturing in the mind; it then ushers into the court, and into the newspaper and pamphlet commentary on the trials, the various meanings of "imagine" and "imagination" from writings on aesthetics and psychiatry and from the pamphlet attacks on Burke's *Reflections*. The imagination of the prosecution and the government is under the sway of passion, not of reason; it is wildly associating ideas without end; it is inventing "impossible existences," it is disordered, deranged. The English law is boasted to be "the perfection of reason"; surely then it is inappropriate, ungrammatical, to allow its application to be dictated by the imagination. The imagination that framed the charges is identical with the imagination that has manifested itself in the loyalist alarm; either it is inflamed by imaginary fears, terrified by phantoms of its own creation, or it is foul and malevolent, coolly imagining the death of those it has falsely accused of imagining the king's death.

Arguments like these, and the frequency with which they were made in the mid-1790s, are the signs of a struggle for ownership of the languages of law and politics. In the crisis of the mid-1790s, the word "imagine" became a symbolic trophy that the Opposition in and out of Parliament, the writers of radical pamphlets, the defendants in treason trials and their counsel, repeatedly attempted to wrest from the government, its lawyers and its loyalist supporters, and to use against them. To the defendants in trials for high treason, ownership of the word appeared to bring with it the power to bend and blunt the most dangerous weapon in the armory of the government, the statute by which it hoped the popular movement for parliamentary reform could be destroyed. The arguments I have sketched out helped in the characterization of loyalist alarmism as a disorder of the imagination, a kind of hysteria by which every demand for political change was imagined as a threat to the king. These arguments helped focus attention on the antique language of law and on the need to purge the statute book of ambiguity. For proponents of popular sovereignty they facilitated the accusation that the government was itself imagining the destruction of the democratic part of the constitution and even of the king himself. And these arguments about imagination may need to be understood also as part of the context in which Coleridge developed his account of the poetic imagination.

In a letter to the *Moral and Political Magazine* of the London Corresponding Society written in November 1796, a pseudonymous contributor who signs himself "Paramython" warns his fellow citizens of the dangers of attending "public dinners, free and easy clubs, and other societies wherein singing is introduced as a relaxation from serious business." He has in mind the singing especially of indecent songs and where it might lead:

> Whoever should throw oil on a consuming fire, would, with great justice, be denominated a mad-man; and what name can be more proper for the person who takes the reins of a fiery imagination from reason, to place them in the hands of an inflamed sensibility: yet every one does this, who, by improper discourses raises licentious images in the minds of his hearers, which, by banishing judgment, suffers them to become an easy prey to the inducements of glowing passion. How many of our youth owe their dereliction from virtue to this detestable behavior. Heated by figures, conjured up by the fervor of fancy, and every particle of consideration for future consequences destroyed by the ebullition of the active spirits, they rush heedless into the chambers of the wanton—"Whence without guilt they never more return."[9]

The imagination, escaping the control of judgment, catching fire, heating the figures by which it finds expression, inciting the passions into vicious action—the language here is familiar from loyalist denunciations of licentious radicalism, from radical denunciations of loyalist alarmism, or, as here, from the concern of a radical for the moral purity of the reform societies.

But compare the anxiety of Paramythion with Coleridge's discussion, in *Biographia Literaria*, of how the poetic imagination is manifested in *Venus and Adonis*, and in particular of how Shakespeare's apparently most erotic poem avoids inflaming the sexual appetites of its readers, so that, "though the very subject cannot but detract from the pleasure of a delicate mind, yet never was poem less dangerous on a moral account." For "Shakespeare," Coleridge explains, precludes "all sympathy" with "the animal impulse"

> by dissipating the reader's notice among the thousand outward im-
> ages, and now beautiful, now fanciful circumstances, which form its
> dresses and its scenery; or by diverting our attention from the main
> subject by those frequent witty or profound reflections which the
> poet's ever active mind has deduced from, or connected with, the im-
> agery and the incidents. The reader is forced into too much activity
> to sympathize with the merely passive in our nature. As little can a
> mind thus roused and awakened be brooded on by mean and indis-
> tinct emotion, as the low lazy mist can creep upon the surface of the
> lake, while a strong gale is driving it onward in waves and billows.[10]

The imagination, by this account, is what tames passion rather than what inflames it; the figures it produces are as water, not oil, to the fire. The synthesizing power of the imagination is also a neutralizing agent, which by harmonizing "discordant qualities" disarms them, disarms the passions, of their disruptive force. It does not escape the control of judgment, as Coleridge had explained in the previous chapter, but reconciles it with enthusiasm and vehement feeling, itself remaining under the "irremissive, but gentle and unnoticed controul" of "the will and understanding."[11]

I suggest that one of the numerous origins of the effort, in the second part of *Biographia Literaria*, to "sublimate," as Nigel Leask has put it, the "poetic symbol from the civic or political realm"[12] may be looked for in the arguments about the use of imagination in political discourse and in the quarrels about imagining the king's death, which seem to have helped make the imagination such a dangerous faculty in the mid-1790s. If the imagina-tion was a sublimating and synthesizing power in the *Biographia*, in the political disputes of the 1790s its appearance in political discourse was almost always recognized as a symptom of division—between itself and the faculty of judgment, between words and intentions, between illusion and reality. But the gap between the bad imagination I have been discussing and the good imagination of the *Biographia* was not as great as it appears. At one moment in his life, Coleridge crossed it with a single step; in one instance, at least, the theory of imagination developed by the "mature" Coleridge in the mid-1810s can be shown to have developed directly out of the arguments about regicidal imaginings of twenty years before.

In January 1798, Coleridge published pseudonymously in the *Morning Post* the poem "Fire, Famine, and Slaughter," which he described as a "War Eclogue," and which is set in "a depopulated tract in La Vendée" where the army of the French Republic was mercilessly putting down the remnants of the ill-fated and British-aided Royalist revolt. Ernest Hartly Coleridge suggests that the poem had been written two years earlier, for in both his pamphlet *Conciones ad Populum* of late 1795 and his periodical, the *Watchman*, in early 1796, Coleridge had deplored the bloodshed in La Vendée and Britain's share of the responsibility for it.[13] There is no reason to doubt that the germ of the poem should be traced to that period, but it was probably being revised and added to right up to the date of its publication, for the poem also describes the atrocities of the British army against the Catholics in Ireland, which first became of concern in Coleridge's political writings in the same month as the poem was published.[14] In the column of the *Morning Post* adjacent to Coleridge's poem there appears Arthur O'Connor's "Address to the Irish Nation," in which those atrocities are also described.

The poem recounts a meeting between the three personifications named in its title, which are seemingly based on the three witches in *Macbeth*. All three, it transpires, had been sent there to do their terrible work of destruction by a man whose name is so terrible, so unspeakable, they dare not pronounce it. They are willing only to hint at his identity, each whispering to the others that "Four letters form his name." Toward the end of the poem the three chant in unison:

> He let us loose, and cry'd Halloo!
> How shall I give him honour due?

Famine and Slaughter answer this question in terms suggesting that "he," whoever he is, cannot hope to escape the forces he has so rashly set in motion. "Wisdom comes with lack of food," chants Famine;

> I'll gnaw, I'll gnaw the multitude,
> Till the cup of rage o'erbrim:
> They shall seize him of his brood.

And Slaughter eagerly interrupts to round off the quatrain:

> They shall tear him limb from limb!

Fire pretends to be shocked by the ingratitude of her companions toward a man who ever since the start of the revolution in France has, as she puts in, "richly catered" for them both. Is it fair, she asks, to repay his repeated favors so peremptorily and so treacherously? For her part, she will remain faithful: she will "Cling to him everlastingly!"—offering him perpetual damnation and a death infinitely prolonged in the unquenchable flames of hell.

Within a few years of the publication of "Fire, Famine, and Slaughter," Coleridge's attitude to the French Revolution had undergone a total change, and he was becoming increasingly embarrassed at being reminded of his recent radical past. In 1817 Coleridge republished the poem in the collected edition of his poetry, *Sibylline Leaves*, explaining in an "Apologetic Preface" that he was doing so because it had been attributed at various times to other poets—as David Erdman suggests, to Robert Southey in particular —"and what I had dared beget, I thought it neither manly nor honorable not to dare father."[15] *Sibylline Leaves* had been printed, but not released, in 1815; when it appeared, in July 1817, the preface must have been read as part of the embarrassing controversy provoked by William Hone's unauthorized publication earlier that year of Southey's regicidal and conventionist dramatic poem *Wat Tyler*, written in 1794.[16] Coleridge, in the second of four articles in defense of Southey in the *Courier*, had absolved Southey—now a true blue Tory—from responsibility for the political beliefs expressed in his poem in terms closely borrowed from those in which, in the "Apologetic Preface," he had just excused the radicalism of "Fire, Famine, and Slaughter."[17]

The "Apologetic Preface" is introduced by two epigraphs, one from Ecclesiasticus, the other adapted and misprinted from Claudian's abject but perhaps ironic apology to the prefect Hadrianus, whom in a previous poem Claudian had imagined, if not dead exactly, at least in a perpetual coma.[18] Together these epigraphs represent Coleridge's poem as an impetuous outburst of his youth, one that it would be ungenerous not to forgive. The preface itself is an attempt to justify the poem by recounting a conversation that had taken place, possibly in 1803, at a dinner party attended by, among others, Sir Walter Scott and Sir Humphrey Davy.[19] According to Coleridge, Scott had recited the poem from memory earlier that morning, and was now asked by one of the dinner guests to recite it again. Scott, the preface points out, was "not only a firm and active anti-Jacobin and anti-Gallican, but likewise a zealous admirer of Mr. Pitt, both as a good man and a great Statesman," and by this remark the preface acknowledges, not as if revealing a secret but as if confirming the obvious, that the four letters that spelled, the name of the guilty man—the man whose death the poem had imagined— were *P, I, T, T*. Scott, the preface suggests, must certainly have detested the sentiments of the poem; but as a poet he had been considerably impressed by it and he recited it in such a way as did full justice to its quality. When the recitation was over, however, the host of the party, the scholar and man of letters William Sotheby, suggested to Scott that he had overestimated the poem's merits; and added that even had they been ten times greater than they were, "they would not have compensated," as he put it, "for that malignity of heart, which could alone have prompted sentiments so atrocious": sentiments which, by representing Pitt as an object of detestation, incited the death which the poem had imagined.[20]

To this observation Coleridge was bound to make some kind of reply. One of the company at dinner, Sir Humphrey Davy, "knew, or suspected" the identity of the poem's author,[21] and it would certainly have seemed to him an act of cowardice on Coleridge's part not to engage with Sotheby's judgment or to acknowledge his authorship of the poem. Coleridge did confess himself the author, but not before he had entered an elaborate defense of the eclogue, in which he acquitted himself, at least to his own satisfaction, of having incited Pitt's death, or of ever having entertained any malign sentiments toward him.

In the passage later adapted as part of his defense of Southey in the *Courier*, Coleridge claims that, had he himself just read the poem for the first time, he would have suspected the writer to have been "some man of warm feelings and active fancy," and the poem itself to be the product not of any firsthand knowledge of warfare, but simply of

> his own seething imagination, and therefore impregnated with that pleasurable exultation which is experienced in all energetic exertion of intellectual power; that in the same mood he had generalized the causes of the war, and then personified the abstract and christened it by the name which he had been accustomed to hear most often associated with its management and measures.

Above all, Coleridge tells us, he would have guessed that the minister was present to the poet's imagination only as a kind of poetic counter, without feelings and therefore incapable of suffering—never as "a real person of flesh and blood." Acknowledging at last that he is himself the author of the poem, he avers that, when writing it, he was "far ... from imagining that the lines would be taken as more or less than a sport of fancy"; looking back now to that moment, he is perfectly sure that "there was never a moment in my existence in which I should have been more ready, had Mr. Pitt's person been in hazard, to interpose my own body, and defend his life at the risque of my own."[22]

But these defenses are a kind of epilogue to Coleridge's main attempt to justify the poem, which has involved mounting a defense at once far more and far less radical than this and arguing for a far more thorough dissociation between imagining in the sense of intending and *merely* imagining, in the sense of picturing in the mind or in language. His argument turns on the nature of figurative language and of the imagination that generates it. There is, he argues, a kind of joyousness involved in the invention and development of figurative utterances that is entirely at variance with the intensity of implacable hatred. Poetic imagery dissipates the intensity of the passions; it is, he suggests, something like a polite substitute for swearing, and he compares the "rapid flow" of imagery with "those outré and wildly combined execrations, which too often with our lower classes serve for escape-valves to carry off the excess of their passions, as so much superfluous steam that would endanger the vessel if it were retained."[23] Coleridge had earlier developed a similar argument about the Welsh habit, as he believed it to be, of name calling. In 1794, in an inn at Bala, he had provoked a furious argument by proposing a toast to George Washington. Soon, he wrote Southey, the names "Rogue, Villain, Traitor" were flying back and forth; but this, he explained, "is nothing in Wales—they *make calling one another Liars* &c— necessary vent-holes to the sulphureous Fumes of the Temper!"[24]

In the "Apologetic Preface" he invited the company to imagine a conversation more relevant to the fantasy of Pitt's death. Two sailors claim to harbor a desire to take revenge on one of their shipmates, who had done them some serious wrong. The first produces a highly figurative and foulmouthed account of what he will do, imagining in detail how he will dismember his enemy and devote "every part of his adversary's body and soul to . . . horrid phantoms and fantastic places." The second is much more laconic and literal, as if taking a morbid pleasure in the contrast between the intensity of his desire for revenge and the matter-of-fact language in which it finds expression; for "all deep feelings of revenge," Coleridge assures us, "are commonly expressed in a few words, ironically tame and mild." "I'll tickle his pretty skin!" says the second sailor. "I won't hurt him! oh no! I'll only cut the —— to the liver!"[25] "I dare appeal to all present," Coleridge continues,

> which of the two they would regard as the least deceptive symptom of deliberate malignity? nay, whether it would surprise them to see the first fellow, an hour or two afterwards, cordially shaking hands with the very man the fractional parts of whose body and soul he had been so charitably disposing of; or even perhaps risking his life for him?[26]

In short, Coleridge is maintaining that the figurative language of "Fire, Famine, and Slaughter" is decisive evidence to establish that it does not mean what it says; that the very fact that he had imagined the death of Pitt in the figurative language of poetry proves that he had nourished no desire to see Pitt dead. "Could it be supposed, though for a moment," he argues, "that the author seriously wished what he had thus wildly imagined," the poem would be entirely indefensible. But surely "the mood of mind . . . in which a Poet produces . . . such vivid and fantastic images" is most unlikely to coexist, is even incompatible with, "that gloomy and deliberate ferocity which a serious wish to *realize* them would pre-suppose." To desire or to intend the death of Pitt is so different an activity of mind from imagining his death, in the wildly figurative language of poetry, that to do either virtually precludes doing the other. "There is," wrote Burke in 1791, developing his favorite theme of regicide in his *Appeal from the New to the Old Whigs*, "a boundary to men's passions when they act from feeling; none when they are under the influence of imagination." Not so, Coleridge may be thought of as replying: men are dangerous only when they speak their cold desires without the aid of warm figures—exercising "a perpetual tautology of mind in thoughts and words, which admit of no adequate substitutes," and speaking with "that sort of calmness of tone which is to the ear what the paleness of anger is to the eye."[27]

In both the "Apologetic Preface" and the discussion of *Venus and Adonis* in *Biographia Literaria*, passion is the passive antagonist of the active fancy and imagination—and not much if anything in either place is staked on the difference between fancy and imagination, for the nature of both discussions requires that whatever is true of the fancy is true in spades of the imagination. Passion, Coleridge explains, is a state of restless inactivity that, "if not precluded . . . by a constitutional activity of fancy and association," will become morbid, brooding, threatening. By contrast, nothing very terrible need be apprehended from what we merely fancy, merely *imagine*. "These violent words," writes Coleridge, comparing his poem with passages by Jeremy Taylor and Shakespeare, are "mere bubbles," the productions of a "skipping spirit, whose thoughts and words reciprocally ran away with each other."[28] Indeed, the real burden of the "Apologetic Preface" is that Coleridge has nothing to apologize for. It is true, Coleridge says, that he had "wildly imagined" Pitt's death; but the wildness of that act of imagining was the wildness of the poet considered as the antithesis of the wildness of the political activist. The very process of imagining Pitt's death was the means of saving his life; for to imagine his death was at the same time to purge the poet of any malevolent imaginings against him. To read the poem, similarly, is to be dissuaded from any desire to kill him. Not only is what we imagine not what we intend; what we imagine becomes the opposite of what we intend, by the very process of imagining it.

In June 1795, however, in a lecture on the slave trade given a few months before "Fire, Famine, and Slaughter" may have first been conceived, Coleridge had offered a very different account of the imagination. God has given us the faculty of imagination, he then wrote, to enable us to imagine a future better than the present, and to stimulate us to attain it. Imagination, by this account, is not itself a purposive, an intentional, faculty; but it does exist, as Coleridge puts it, to revivify "the dying motive within us"; it is what animates us to turn objects of aspiration into objects of intention.[29] If we were to interpret the imaginings in "Fire, Famine, and Slaughter" in terms of this version of the imagination, it would become a quite different poem from the one Coleridge later defended; not one that speaks the opposite of what we desire, or that magically removes the motive to realize our fantasies, but one that, by imagining an end to the war, stimulates us to take the murderous step—the assassination of Pitt—supposed to be necessary to achieve it.

The "Apologetic Preface," by contrast, is an attempt to take the politics out of the imagination by voiding the imagination of all connection with intention or desire, and so by making poetry, even poetry on political subjects, something that inhabits a quite other universe of discourse from politics itself one characterized not by conflict but by harmony. As if to underline this, the preface goes on to recapitulate its implied comparison of Scott with Coleridge by a more elaborate discussion of Taylor and Milton. Opposites in politics, Scott and the Coleridge of 1798 are at one in the belief that the products of the imagination transcend the most violent political differences. Both Taylor and Milton imagined the elaborate torture of their political and religious enemies in hell, but because both (merely) imagined it, neither intended it; ideological opposites, as poets they too were at one. By 1817 and the *Wat Tyler* controversy, the separation of poetry from politics, so strenuously contended for earlier, had become for Coleridge so self-evident that it was absurd to question it. "Who in the Devil's Name," Coleridge asked the editor of the *Courier*, "ever thought of reading poetry for any political or practical purposes till these Devil's Times that *we* live in?"[30]

Those reading Coleridge's impassioned self-defense in 1817, however— even more so those who first heard it, if we believe that his words in the "Apologetic Preface" are indeed "substantially the same" as in the spoken conversation—will certainly have heard in it the echo of the much more familiar, and thoroughly political, argument whose language it was equally certainly alluding to.[31] The account of the imagination that Coleridge offers in his own defense can be seen as one that emerged directly out of the political crisis, and the crisis in the history of the imagination, that I began by describing. If the argument really was "substantially the same" as the original spoken defense, the "Apologetic Preface" may record his first thoroughgoing attempt to put the imagination at the service of a conservative politics by representing it as elevated above the merely political and as having nothing to do with desire and intention. I want to conclude, however, by proposing that this attempt is much more closely connected to the arguments of the mid-1790s than I have so far suggested; and that what was driving the attempt was more than a desire to disavow a fantasy of the death of the prime minister. The "Apologetic Preface" was also disavowing a fantasy of the death of the king. The clues are everywhere, in the poem itself and in Coleridge's contemporary political writings. I will discuss them in ascending order of persuasiveness, the weakest first.

1. The poem, like a few other poems of Coleridge's published about this time, is signed "Laberius." The Laberius he had in mind was no doubt Decimus Laberius, a Roman knight and writer of pantomime who owed his fame to one incident in his life. In 45 B.C. Julius Caesar, then dictator, compelled Laberius to perform one of his pieces on the public stage, though to do so would be to forfeit his rank. Laberius reluctantly complied, but used the occasion to protest against the loss of liberties under Caesar's rule, and apparently to predict Caesar's death: "Needs must he fear, who makes all else adread." Later that day he added:

> None the first place for ever can retain—
> But, ever as the topmost round you gain,
> Painful your station there and swift your fall.[32]

Radical and Opposition writers seem generally to have seen Sejanus as Pitt's Roman prototype, but their view of Pitt as dictator, anxious not to seem too anxious to get his hands on the Crown, fits the character of Caesar perfectly well. In a speech of December 1794, the radical orator John Gale Jones made the comparison a paragraph or two before accusing Pitt of being "the Prime Mover and instigator of the massacres of Paris, Toulon, and La Vendee,"[33] and it would not be surprising if many other examples could be found. But to the satirists George III was Caesar too: to the old Etonian radical blackmailer Charles Pigott, for example; and to John Wolcot, who repeatedly satirized the sheer ordinariness of the king by hailing him, in large block capitals, as "CAESAR" or "GREAT CAESAR."[34]

2. The punishment Famine threatens against the four-letter villain includes seizing him "of his brood." We can take "brood" to mean no more than "kind" or "like," and read Famine as threatening to deprive Pitt of his ministers or other supporters. But if we take the more usual and more literal sense of the word, "progeny," the point of the threat appears to be that the multitude will lay violent hands on the villain's family, on his children; and this raises an intriguing question. Pitt had no children; but, more to the point, to suggest that he had, in radical and Opposition circles of the 1790s, would have been to suggest what was widely believed to be impossible. Pitt was famous for his apparent indifference to women and his total abstinence from sex: radical satirists in the mid-1790s remarked on his "maiden coyness"; described him as "Prettygirlibus indifferentissimus"; compared the childless minister with the philoprogenitive king; and linked all this to a presumed preference for masturbation.[35] His sexual abstinence, which his supporters represented as a virtue, was widely satirized by radicals as the result of a physiological deficiency: as well as having no chin and no bottom, Pitt, it was pretended, had no genitals. There is, for example, a political squib of 1795 that describes the imagined death of Pitt; the report on the autopsy notes that the marks of "sexual distinction . . . were not easily to be

discerned."[36] The notion that Pitt had fathered a "brood" would have been like suggesting, as in the 1940s lyrics sung to the tune of *Colonel Bogey*, that Goebbels, who had no balls, had children of his own. The king, however (who could be accused as plausibly as Pitt of instigating the war with France), had fathered nine sons and six daughters; and in late 1795 Coleridge had drawn elaborate attention to the clause in the Treasonable Practices Bill that proposed to make it high treason to imagine the death not only of the king and the Prince of Wales but also of any of the king's heirs and successors.

3. Indeed, the whole issue addressed in the "Apologetic Preface"—what it means to "imagine" the death of Pitt—is brought forward at a time when the notion of "imagining" a death could not avoid recalling the arguments about imagining the king's death in the 1790s. But the point is more than a matter of general context. The structure of argument in the preface, by which Coleridge acknowledges that he has imagined Pitt's death but disavows "any serious wish to *realize*" it, evidently repeats that of the argument he had developed in his pamphlet *The Plot Discovered* of late 1795, where, attacking the provision of the Treasonable Practices Bill, he defends writers who, in recommending republican government, thereby imagine the deposition (and death, for in law it comes to the same thing) of one of the king's "distant successors," and denies that they ever dream of seeing it "realized," except under conditions that remove all guilt from the desire and its fulfillment.

4. Coleridge had first published his thoughts on the war with France and the revolt in La Vendée in an essay, "On the Present War," which had appeared in the pamphlet *Conciones*. The pamphlet begins with a prefatory "Letter from Liberty to her dear Friend Famine." The essay on the war has a double epigraph, two untranslated passages from Statius's epic poem the *Thebaid*, which describes the war that broke out between the two sons of Oedipus when Eteocles refused to honor the agreement he had made with his brother Polynices that each should reign for alternate years. The first epigraph is from a speech made to Eteocles by an ambassador sent to Thebes by his brother; it denounces the war Eteocles has let loose as "unholy," and it describes that war in terms that closely anticipate those used by Coleridge elsewhere in the essay to describe the civil war in La Vendée. The second epigraph is from a speech made by a former adherent of Eteocles, who has now deserted his cause. It warned the king, just as Coleridge would warn the instigator of the war with France in "Fire, Famine, and Slaughter," that he would deserve the same death as he had inflicted on his enemies and their families. In Statius, this sentence ends with an ironic address to the king, "bone rex," "worthy king"; in the epigraph, Coleridge omitted the last word, replacing it with three asterisks. It may be that the point of this omission was to leave room for the reader to squeeze the four letters of Pitt's name into the space vacated by the

word "rex." But it may equally have been to avoid a charge of seditious libel, for had Coleridge included that word, he would have been imagining the king's death in what I have called the weak sense; and if it is for this reason that the king's name is unspeakable in *Conciones*, so it may be in the poem. But the effect of the omission in the epigraph is of course to call attention to what is omitted, and to invite the knowledgeable to discover, in this imagining of Eteocles's death, an imagining of the death of George III, and in connection with the same events in France as are described in "Fire, Famine, and Slaughter."[37]

5. Finally, at the end of the same letter to the editor of the *Courier* in which he ridiculed the attempts of Southey's enemies to find politics in poetry, Coleridge suddenly found politics in Southey's own *Wat Tyler*. The poem, he suggested, "seems nothing but a string of servile plagiarisms from the Speeches of the *Opposition* Party from 1792 to the Peace of Amiens."[38] A similar plagiarism lies concealed in "Fire, Famine, and Slaughter." In the essay introduced by the epigraphs from Statius, Coleridge quotes a passage from a speech of January 1795 by the great dramatist and political orator Richard Brinsley Sheridan. It concerns the absurdity of supposing that the radical societies, with their tiny armory and war chest, could have launched an insurrection against "the armed Force and established Government of Great-Britain," and it appears to be quoted from the *Morning Chronicle*, which offered a far fuller version of Sheridan's speech than any other newspaper. The *Chronicle*, at this time Coleridge's preferred source of news, was in the process of publishing his "Sonnets on Eminent Characters," including the sonnet to Sheridan, which also appeared in January. In the *Chronicle* version of his speech, Sheridan goes on to argue that a love of liberty is not the same as republicanism and that it is perfectly possible to combine hatred of despotism with reverence for George III. "I am not to be misled by *names*," he declared; "I regard not that the *four letters* are the same which *form* the title of the Despot of Brandenburgh, and of the first Magistrate of this free country."[39] This sentence, in a speech Coleridge knew and admired, appears to be the origin of the four-letter conceit in "Fire, Famine, and Slaughter"; and in Sheridan's speech the "four letters" are *K, I, N, G*. They may still, in the poem, be intended to form the name "Pitt"; but if so, only by an act of erasure that, like the asterisks in the place of "rex," reveals what it pretends to conceal: that behind the fantasy of Pitt's death is a fantasy of regicide.

The conclusion seems to me irresistible. Coleridge may well have thought of "Fire, Famine, and Slaughter" as a poem in which the death that is imagined is Pitt's death, but somewhere in the penumbra of the poem, whether Coleridge recognized it or not, whether or not he knew he knew it, though it's hard to believe he did not, lies the imagined corpse of the king, too. In 1795 Coleridge described Burke's *Reflections* as a "magnificent

Mausoleum, in which he has interred his honest fame."[40] One point of elaborating, in the "Apologetic Preface," the theory of imagination by which he denies having intended Pitt's death—denies indeed any connection between poetry and politics—was to erect a tomb, inscribed with the name of the prime minister, beneath which could be interred, in hugger mugger, the body of George III.

The papers for the 1790s of the Treasury Solicitor in the Public Record Office in London are full of reports of imaginings of the king's death or damnation (which must be preceded by his death). These explosive outbursts, some perhaps more or less faithfully reported, some certainly fabricated by false witnesses, have survived in the historical record as traces of the epidemic of disloyalty that true Britons believed was rampaging through the nation. But their appearance in the reports of legal proceedings, and among legal papers concerned with intended prosecutions for "seditious words," is evidence also of an epidemic of loyalist alarmism in those years, characterized by much the same symptom, a ready disposition to imagine the king's death, but vicariously, by imagining that others were imagining it. The regicidal imaginings of loyalists were of course partly factitious, as radical pamphleteers frequently pointed out; they were part of an attempt to silence demands for parliamentary reform by representing them as a threat to the constitutional position of the king and therefore to his life. But the regicidal outbursts of radicals were no doubt also in part provoked by the fact that loyalists in the 1790s were apparently so sensitive to any apparent or imaginary threat to the king's life. However calculated and calculating the phenomenon of alarmism sometimes seems to be and sometimes certainly was, the tendency of loyalists to make the king's safety so much the focus of their anxieties invited both active reformers and the merely disaffected to recognize that here was their most tender, their most vulnerable spot; that their sensitivity on this topic was apparently so great because it was inseparable from a guilty knowledge that they participated in—that it was impossible for them not to do so—the very imaginings they were so anxious to punish in others.

"Damn the King and Country too!" cursed William Francis, an Essex innkeeper, in May 1794; "if the French come I wonder who the Hell would not join them?" "Damn the King and Queen!" cursed Edward Swift of Windsor a fortnight later; "they ought to be put to Death the same as the King and Queen of France were. . . . Damn and bugger the King and all that belong to him! . . . Damnation blast the King! I would as soon shoot the King as a Mad dog." The following month a wealthy Oxford Street coachmaker, Jonathan Panther, announced, in language more decorous but no less bloodthirsty, that he wished the heads of all the kings in Europe, and all the royal family, were cut off. "And if I had an opportunity of being their executioner," he continued, "and washing my hands in their blood, I would be contented to have my own hand cut off that instant." In February 1795, Peter Cox, a Cornish miner, drank Tom Paine's health and "perdition to all the Kings of the earth"; no sooner had he done so than "his jaw became locked, and he died on the spot, in the most excruciating torments. He left a pregnant wife, and four helpless infants behind him."[41]

"Fire, Famine, and Slaughter," I am arguing, is a polite and disguised descendant of these plebeian regicidal imaginings, these provocatives to alarmism, that so preoccupied the authorities in the mid-1790s. And the theory of imagination developed in the "Apologetic Preface," and even in the second volume of *Biographia Literaria*, by which Coleridge attempts to sever all connection between poetry and politics, between imagining and intending, must be seen as having in part originated as a disavowal of the poem's ancestry.

Notes

1 No. 8659 in Dorothy George, *Catalogue of Satires in the British Museum*.
2 For full citations on these brief quotations, readers are referred to the introduction to my book *Imagining the King's Death, 1793–1796: Figurative Treason, Fantasies of Regicide* (Oxford, 2000).
3 [Catharine Macaulay], *Observations on the Reflections of the Right Hon. Edmund Burke, on the Revolution in France, in a Letter to the Right Hon. The Earl of Stanhope* (London, 1790); [David Williams], *Letters to a Young Prince, by an Old Statesman*, 5th ed. (London, 1790); Paine, *Rights of Man* (1791, 1792, numerous editions); Mary Wollstonecraft, *A Vindication of the Rights of Men, in a Letter to the Right Honourable Edmund Burke* (London, 1790); Joseph Priestley, *Letters to the Right Honourable Edmund Burke, occasioned by his Reflections on the Revolution in France* (1791), 3d ed. (Birmingham, 1791).
4 *Short Observations on the Right Hon. Edmund Burke's Reflections* (London, 1790), 10; James Mackintosh, *Vindiciae Gallicae* (London, 1791), vii; Wollstonecraft, *Vindication* 132, 67, and see 3, 19; and Macaulay, *Observations*, 93.
5 Tom Furniss, *Edmund Burke's Aesthetic Ideology: Language, Gender, and Political Economy in Revolution* (Cambridge, 1993), 257.
6 *State Trials*, 33 vols., comp. T. J. Howell (London, 1811–26), 24:133, 209, 271.
7 George 9188.
8 For "Mr. Bottomless Pitt," see the broadside *A New Tragedy, entitled Another Campaign* ([London, 1795]), first published in the *Telegraph*, 16 July 1795. The phrase refers to Pitt's natural home (in Hell); to his lack of any ideological baggage, and hence of sound principles ("bottom"); to his inscrutability and talent for political intrigue ("Deep Will"); to his capacity for alcohol; to his extravagance in pursuing the war (throwing money into a bottomless pit); but also, more literally, to his physique.
9 *Moral and Political Magazine* 1 (November 1796): 264–65.
10 Coleridge, *Biographia Literaria*, vol. 7 of *The Collected Works of Samuel Taylor Coleridge*, gen. ed. Kathleen Coburn, ed. James Engell and W. Jackson Bate (London and Princeton, N.J., 1983), 2:22; henceforward cited in the text as *CC*.
11 *CC* 7; 2:16–17.

12 Nigel Leask, *The Politics of Imagination in Coleridge's Critical Thought* (London, 1988), 160.

13 *The Complete Poetical Works of Samuel Taylor Coleridge*, ed. Ernest Hartley Coleridge, 2 vols. (Oxford, 1912) 1:237n; see Coleridge, *Conciones ad Populum. Or, Addresses to the People* ([Bristol], 1795), 13, 46; and *Watchman, CC*, vol. 2, ed. Lewis Patton (London and Princeton, N.J., 1970), 213.

14 The essay on Ireland of 9 March 1796 in *Watchman, CC* 2:75–77, is concerned with the persecution of Catholics by the "Orange Boys"; military persecution seems not to be discussed until the articles "Ireland and La Vendée," *Morning Post*, 17 January 1798 (attributed to Coleridge by David Erdman); Coleridge, *Essays on his Times, CC*, vol. 3, ed. David Erdman (1978), 11–12; and "Lord Moira's Letter," *Morning Post*, 20 January, *CC* 3, 1:13–17.

15 Coleridge, *Sibylline Leaves* (London, 1817), 98, 88; Erdman in *CC* 3, 3:270.

16 Robert Southey, *Wat Tyler; a Dramatic Poem. A New Edition* (London, 1817).

17 Compare *CC* 3, 2:458–59, with *Sibylline Leaves*, 95–96; and see Hazlitt's withering attack on Coleridge's *Courier* articles in "*The Courier* and *Wat Tyler*," *The Complete Works of William Hazlitt*, ed. P. P. Howe, 21 vols. (London, 1930–34), 7:196, noting that Southey had himself published a poem apparently in praise of king killing, an inscription "For the Apartment in CHEPSTOW-CASTLE where HENRY MARTEN the regicide was imprisoned Thirty Years"; see *Poems by Robert Southey* (Bristol and London, 1787), 59–60.

18 Ecclesiasticus 19:16; the epigraph from Claudian is made up of lines 6–8 and 12 of the "Apology to Hadrian"; see *Claudian*, ed. and trans. Marice Platnauer, 2 vols. (London and Cambridge, Mass., 1963), 2:196–99; for the insulting epigram for which it apparently apologizes, see 2:196–97. Both poems had been made famous by Gibbon's discussion of them at the end of chapter 30 of *The Decline and Fall of the Roman Empire*.

19 The date is suggested by E. H. Coleridge in *Complete Poetical Works*, 1097n.; that some such conversation took place at some time is confirmed by Scott in a letter of 1830; see *The Letters of Sir Walter Scott*, ed. H. J. C. Grierson, 12 vols. (London, 1932–37), 11:442.

20 Coleridge, *Sibylline Leaves*, 89–90.

21 Ibid., 89.

22 Ibid., 95–97.

23 Ibid., 91–93.

24 *Collected Letters of Samuel Taylor Coleridge*, ed. Earl Leslie Griggs, 6 vols. (Oxford, 1956–71), 1:89.

25 Coleridge, *Sibylline Leaves*, 91–93.

26 Ibid., 93.

27 Ibid., 91–93; *The Works of the Right Honourable Edmund Burke*, new ed., 14 vols. (London, 1815–22), 6:239.

28 Coleridge, *Sibylline Leaves*, 91–95.

29 Coleridge, *Lectures 1795 on Politics and Religion*, in *CC*, vol. 1, ed. Lewis Patton and Peter Mann (1971), 235; for a similar early account of the imagination, see *CC* 2:131.

30 Coleridge, *Sibylline Leaves*, 94–95, 98–107; *Collected Letters*, 4:713, quoted in Leask, *Politics of Imagination*, 158.

31 Coleridge, *Sibylline Leaves*, 91.

32 William Smith, *A Dictionary of Greek and Roman Biography and Mythology*, 3 vols. (London, 1880), 2:695.

33 John Gale Jones, *Sketch of a Speech delivered at the Westminster Forum, on the 9th, 16th, 23rd, and 30th Mar. 1795* (London, 1795), 41–42.

34 [Charles Pigott], *The Jockey Club; or a Sketch of the Manners of the Age, part the Third*, 2d ed. (London, 1792), 19; "Peter Pindar" [John Wolcot], *Liberty's Last Squeak* (London, 1795), 9; *The Convention Bill, an Ode* (London, 1795), 7; and, preeminently, *The Royal Tour, and Weymouth Amusements* (London, 1795), where the appellation is scattered everywhere.

35 See *Mustapha's Adoration . . . Part II, No. II. More Wonderful Wonders!!!* ([London], [1794 or 1795]), first published in the *Courier*, 15 December 1794; and [Robert Merry], *Wonderful Exhibition!! Signior Gulielmo Pittachio* ([London], [1794]), first published in the *Courier*, November 28, 1794, where Pitt, a showman, in the absence of female performers, advertises that he "will indulge the Company with a Solo on the Viol d'Amour." See also the caricature *The Apotheosis of the Virgin in Breeches* (London, 8 June 1802); George 9872.

36 *A Faithful Narrative of the Last Illness, Death, and Interment of the Rt. Hon. William Pitt* (London, [1795]), 10.

37 Coleridge, *Conciones*, 4–6, 56; *Statius*, trans. J. H. Mozley, 2 vols. (London and Cambridge, Mass., 1928), 1:429, 455–57.

38 *Collected Letters*, 4:714.

39 Coleridge, *Conciones*, 50–51; *Morning Chronicle*, 6 January 1795.

40 Coleridge, *An Answer to "A Letter to Edward Long Fox, M.D."* (Bristol, [1795]), in *CC*, 1:332.

41 For Francis, see Public Record Office, London, *Treasury Solicitor's Papers*, 11\1071\3238; after a petition signed by his neighbors and the local vicar, Francis, who was known to be loyal and had spoken his words when drunk, was not prosecuted. For Swift, see *Treasury Solicitor's Papers*, 11\944\3433; Swift was imprisoned for a year (see Clive Emsley, "An Aspect of Pitt's 'Terror': Prosecutions for Sedition during the 1790s," in *Social History* [1981]: 179). For Panther, see *Caledonian Mercury*, 27 October 1794; the case was dismissed. For Cox, see *True Briton*, 2 March 1795.

21

KEATS, SHELLEY, AND THE WEALTH OF IMAGINATION

Jeffrey N. Cox

Source: *Studies in Romanticism* 34 (1995), 365–400.

On August 12, 1820, Keats left the household of Leigh Hunt, where his ill health had brought him on June 23: a letter from Fanny Brawne had been mishandled, and Keats—though he would apologize shortly to Hunt for his "lunes"—decided he could not stay in the rather chaotic Hunt home any longer. On the same day as this uproar, Keats received another, more famous letter; as he would write to his sister on August 13, "Yesterday I received an invitation from Mr Shelley, a Gentleman residing at Pisa, to spend the Winter with him." On July 27, 1820, Shelley had sent from Pisa what Donald Reiman has called "probably the best known [letter] that Shelley ever wrote." Directed to John Keats care of Leigh Hunt at the office of the *Examiner*, the letter invited Keats, who had been ordered to Italy by his doctors, to join Shelley. Shelley's friends the Gisbornes had seen Keats at Hunt's and had written to Italy about the younger writer's illness. The Gisbornes carried Keats's reply, dated August 16, back to Italy along with Keats's volume of 1820, both of which were left with Claire Clairmont sometime around October 10. Hunt would write to Shelley on August 23 that Keats "is sensible of your kindness."[1]

Shelley's offer and Keats's reply constitute perhaps the most famous two-letter correspondence in literary history,[2] but this exchange will only be understood if it is seen in the context of the complex interactions within the set of artists and intellectuals around Leigh Hunt. The centrality of this circle has received too little attention, as generations of Keats and Shelley scholars have sought to protect their poets from too close identification with the "King of Cockaigne," an interesting example of the power and persistence of the "anti-romantic ideology" and its assault on the radical "Cockney Poets."

We need to affirm in general terms the importance of groups in culture, as, first, establishing the social nature of cultural objects and, second, as representing the real ground upon which individuals come to share in a more widely diffused ideology; but this need is particularly great in the study of the movement we call romanticism. The scene of writing in many conventional accounts of romantic poetry finds the poet in isolation, standing on the mountaintop, waking from a dream, or drowsing beneath a tree listening to a nightingale. Leigh Hunt, however, offers a socialized scene of writing in his poem "Poetry and Politics" (1811). He depicts himself writing not in splendid isolation, alone with nature, but at a desk in the city surrounded by historical and political texts. While he might long for a tête-à-tête with his muse, he finds his writing shaped by many pressures: by economic concerns, as "The Devil who comes for copy" waits for him to finish the journalism he writes to earn his bread; by political worries, as he remains aware that the government watches, ever ready to prosecute anything it can label seditious or libellous; even by physical pressures, as exhaustion, headaches, and the "Blue Daemon" of depression threaten to overtake him. His writing is shaped as much by editors' pens and government writs as it is by some internal muse. For Hunt and for poets such as Shelley and Keats who entered his circle, poetry was a social activity in an immediate way, as they wrote for the highly politicized *Examiner*, as they penned occasional verse to one another, and as they participated in sonnet-writing contests. In fact, the relations between Keats and Shelley were always mediated through this circle into which they both first came in the fall of 1816 when Hunt was to praise them along with John Hamilton Reynolds as the rising "New Poets" (*Examiner* 1 December 1816: 761–62). They knew each other as members of a coterie, especially after Keats decided not to become too close to Shelley so that "I might have my own unfettered scope" (Letter to Benjamin Bailey, 8 October 1817, *Letters* 1.170). They were brought together in this final exchange of letters again through the mediation of Hunt.

This context is important, for it helps to explain the nature of Keats's often-cited reply, as well as that of Shelley's oblique response in the *Defence of Poetry* and in the portrait of Keats in *Adonais* to which I will turn later. Keats acknowledges Shelley's offer while doubting his own ability to act upon it. Most of the letter, however, is devoted to a critique of Shelley's verse, a response to various comments Shelley had made on Keats's poetry, from the two poets' first meetings through Hunt at Hampstead in 1816 up to the letter Keats is answering. Keats's observations on Shelley—which have been seen as "trenchant," as a "famous" and "merited reproof," and as "critical wisdom"[3]—are worth quoting in full:

> I am glad you take any pleasure in my poor Poem [*Endymion*];— which I would willingly take the trouble to unwrite, if possible, did I care so much as I have done about Reputation. I received a copy of the Cenci, as from yourself from Hunt. There is only one part of it I am judge of; the Poetry, and dramatic effect, which by many spirits now a days is considered the mammon. A modern work it is

said must have a purpose, which may be the God—an *artist* must serve Mammon—he must have "self concentration" selfishness perhaps. You I am sure will forgive me for sincerely remarking that you might curb your magnanimity and be more of an artist, and "load every rift" of your subject with ore. The thought of such discipline must fall like cold chains upon you, who perhaps never sat with your wings furl'd for six Months together. And is not this extraordina[r]y talk for the writer of Endymion? whose mind was like a pack of scattered cards—I am pick'd up and sorted to a pip. My Imagination is a Monastery and I am its Monk—you must explain my metap^{cs} to yourself. I am in expectation of Prometheus every day. Could I have my own wish for its interest effected you would have it still in manuscript—or be but now putting an end to the second act. I remember you advising me not to publish my first-blights, on Hampstead heath—I am returning advice upon your hands. Most of the Poems in the volume I send you have been written above two years, and would never have been publish'd but from a hope of gain; so you see I am inclined to take your advice now.

(Letters 2.322–23)

I want to suggest that this letter is not so much a wise reproach to Shelley —a "telling criticism of Shelley's hortatory bent" as Aileen Ward puts it (368)—as a settling of accounts with a poet whose development paralleled and challenged Keats's own, an attempt to control his personal and poetic relations with Shelley as they had evolved within the Hunt circle.

The Keats who received Shelley's invitation was a man with very little control over his life. He was dying and knew it. He was desperately in love with Fanny Brawne and could do nothing about it. He was also in serious financial difficulties. All of these troubles surface in the letter. The reference to his illness and expected death is the clearest, as he predicts he will not live to join Shelley. Any direct mention of Fanny Brawne would have been lost upon Shelley; Shelley did not know anything about her, Keats, of course, having kept secret his engagement even from friends such as Hunt.[4] Still, one wonders about the image of Keats's imagination as his monastery and of himself as a monk: is this a statement of his faith in his art or an ironic commentary upon his inability to have a full sexual life, his forced cloistering from the world of the senses? As Keats says, "you must explain my metaph[ysics or metaphor] to yourself."[5]

The financial references are the most insistent, riddling his central discussion of the nature of poetry with fiscal terms and images. Keats's use of economic imagery in his letter might have been inspired by Shelley's reference in his invitation to the "treasures" of *Endymion* that Shelley felt had been "poured forth with indistinct profusion" resulting in "the comparatively few copies which have been sold" (*Letters* 2.221). Or perhaps it was Keats's recent rereading of Spenser to mark passages for Fanny Brawne (*Letters* 2.302) that brought the image of Mammon to mind. This is not, of course, the only place where such images appear in Keats; the use of economic imagery in Keats's later poetry has been powerfully addressed by critics such as K. K. Ruthven, Kurt Heinzelman, and Marjorie Levinson.[6]

However, by the time Keats received Shelley's letter, finances were for him less the subject of figuration than of literal figuring, as he found himself in debt following his brother George's visit in January of 1820. George needed to raise money for his family and his financial ventures in the United States. To his credit, George did manage to force their guardian Abbey to clarify some issues and received the rest of his own inheritance and his share of Tom's estate, for a total of approximately 300 pounds. He needed more, however, and thus he apparently asked Keats to lend him his share of Tom's money.[7] While George would later deny that he had done anything improper,[8] several of Keats's statements and the observations of such witnesses as Charles Armitage Brown, Fanny Brawne, and Keats's publisher John Taylor lead one to believe that George at the very least took advantage of his brother's willingness to help him and his family.[9] According to Taylor, George left Keats with 70 pounds, which could not even cover Keats's immediate debts of 80 pounds, with another 70 pounds of debt not taken into account at that point.[10] Keats found himself forced to borrow from Brown and Taylor. Increasingly ill, he was taken in first by the Hunts and then by the Brawnes. When the doctors told him that summer that he must voyage to Italy, he was faced not only with a long trip fighting his disease but the extreme difficulty in funding such an excursion in the first place. Hunt and others would try to help. Shelley's letter is his offer of assistance.

Keats could not have been surprised by Shelley's generous letter, which he told Brown was "of a very kind nature" (*Letters* 2.231). Shelley's generosity was well-known among his circle of friends, the person he had tried to help most being Leigh Hunt. The Hunts' financial problems are notorious, and Leigh Hunt's inability to handle money appears to be one of the things that bothered Keats about his mentor and benefactor. Hunt was an incessant borrower, and Shelley had been one of his main sources of income. As Hunt himself tells us in his *Autobiography*, "the princeliness of his disposition was seen most in his behavior to another friend, the writer of this memoir, who is proud to relate, that with money raised by an effort, Shelley once made him a present of fourteen hundred pounds, to extricate him from debt" (323).

As Hunt notes, "I was not extricated," and Shelley continued to try to find the means to help his friend. The large loan was made to Hunt at the end of 1816. In a letter to Hunt of 3 August 1817, Shelley was again trying to fix Hunt's finances, trying to secure him a loan: "In fact I should imagine among your intimate friends nothing could be more easy than to arrange a loan on the terms and in the manner that I suggested. Your Brother I do not doubt will or can do nothing. But there is Keats, who certainly *can*, and Alsager, from whom I should expect much" (*Letters* 1.550). He goes on to say, however, that Hunt will probably need to rely upon the poet-financier Horace Smith. This letter suggests that Shelley and Hunt believed that Keats had the means to help a friend, that he simply did not want to, that unlike Shelley with his princely magnanimity, Keats was too self-concentrated, selfish perhaps.

These tangled financial relations are, I believe, the subtext for Keats's discussion of poetry in his letter to Shelley. Shelley's suggestion that Keats lacked generosity will, of course, meet with disagreement from Keats scholars who have seen him as a model of caring, generous behavior.[11] Whether he was in fact generous or not, there is still the indication that Shelley and Hunt, perhaps mistaken about Keats's financial situation, doubted Keats's willingness to aid his friend; and we do know that Keats did not like being in debt or feeling a sense of obligation that would limit his freedom. Charles Cowden Clarke gives an interesting account of perhaps another Shelley invitation to Italy (though Clarke may simply be misremembering dates) that confirms this sense of a tension between Shelleyan generosity and economic independence and Keatsian concerns over money and freedom: "When Shelley left England for Italy, Keats told me that he had received from him an invitation to become his guest, and, in short, to make one of his household. It was upon the purest principle that Keats declined this noble proffer, for he entertained an exalted opinion of Shelley's genius . . . he also knew of his deeds of bounty. . . . Keats said that in declining the invitation his sole motive was the consciousness, which would be ever prevalent with him, of his being, in its utter extent, not a free agent, even within such a circle as Shelley's—he himself, nevertheless, being the most unrestricted of beings." Again, Keats's brother George later asserted, after reading in Hunt's *Lord Byron and Some of His Contemporaries* of John's having housed with the Hunts and the Brawnes, that "no Man who ever lived was more impatient at being under an obligation than John"; John was, he wrote, "more magnanimous in conferring than in receiving a benefit, he felt too impatient of obligations."[12]

Keats may well have felt impatient in the summer of 1820, residing with Hunt, contemplating accepting help from Shelley. Cowden Clarke and George insist upon Keats's sense of independence, and independence of several sorts can be considered the theme of Keats's struggles to find his place within the Hunt circle, as he sought to escape the label of Hunt's student or worked to stay aloof from Shelley.

In the letter to Shelley, Keats wants to declare his poetic independence, but he knows of his financial dependence. Unable to match Shelley's princely financial status, Keats displaces his problems with gold into theorems about poetry's "realms of gold." This attempt to transmute economics into aesthetics is perhaps clearest in his suggestion that Shelley "curb his magnanimity"; Shelley, he says drawing on Spenser, needs to "be more of an artist, and 'load every rift' of your subject with ore." This passage on Shelley's magnanimity is sometimes taken to refer to Shelley's poetic productivity and sometimes to Shelley's "passion for reforming the world,"[13] but surely it is also a suggestion that Shelley stop loaning his money to a Hunt or a Godwin, that Shelley be less of the magnanimous prince Hunt admired, perhaps even that Shelley worry more about his poetry than about acting magnanimously towards Keats himself. Moreover, Keats seeks to convert Shelley's financial magnanimity into poetic prodigality, and thus Keats's own perceived stinginess can then be refigured as artistic control and dedication.

Keats's comments on *The Cenci* again rely upon economic images: "There is only one part of it I am judge of; the Poetry, and dramatic effect, which by many spirits now a days is considered the mammon. A modern work it is said must have a purpose, which may be the God—*an artist* must serve Mammon—he must have 'self-concentration' selfishness perhaps." We need to be alive to the polemical inversion of Christ's words Keats offers here. The Gospels record the phrase about God and Mammon in two different places. In Matthew, they occur within the Sermon on the Mount (5:24), where Jesus says that one must lay up spiritual treasures in God's heaven rather than seeking Mammon's rewards on earth; in Luke, they come as a gloss on the parable of the dishonest steward (16:1–13) and again act as a warning to those who would concentrate on gain in this world. Spenser uses Mammon in the episode Keats echoes as a summary figure for the pursuit of worldly goods. Keats wants to contrast poetry's internal formal riches with poetry's interests in the world, but he does so by invoking a biblical opposition between worldly wealth and spiritual interests. Keats's argument that the artist must be of Mammon's party offers an inversion of religious language and conventional morality that Keats might have expected to appeal to the religious skeptic in Shelley, whom Keats had seen engage in religious disputes with Haydon and to whom Hunt had dedicated his sonnets "On the Degrading Notions of Deity," perhaps written in a contest with Keats's own "Written in Disgust of Vulgar Superstition."[14] Keats would seem to be playing with biblical injunctions against worldly wealth to establish his credentials as a freethinker, speculating apart from convention.

Conventions are not, however, all he would be free of; Keats wants to assert poetry's absolute independence, arguing that art must serve its own internal, presumably formal ends rather than some extra-poetical purpose or cause. However, this claim for art's self-contained freedom is complicated by the financial imagery Keats invokes. For the Hunt circle, artistic independence was tied to freedom from certain kinds of economic dependence. We may feel that any involvement with the cash nexus is compromising, that disinterestedness gives way to financial interest as soon as one finds oneself within a capitalist economy. The Hunt circle—whose organ the *Examiner* had as its motto Pope's claim, "Party is the madness of many for the gain of a few"—defined themselves against men such as Wordsworth and Southey who they felt had become dependent upon the government for their income. As John Kinnaird has argued, the Hunt circle's attacks on the Lake Poets' "apostasy" are based more on their surrender of economic independence than on a change in political conviction. We can see such charges in Hazlitt's doggerel lines on Wordsworth's appointment as Stamp-Distributor, where Wordsworth who once "Scorn'd service purchased by rewards" and thus was able to talk "of Milton and of Freedom" is now seated in "*silent* state" having taken the bait from "Favour's golden hook."[15] Byron's dedication to *Don Juan* attacked "Lakers in and out of place" (6); and, noting that "Wordsworth has his place in the Excise," Byron asks Southey about his status as poet laureate and his political conversion: "You have your salary; was't for that you wrought" (45–46).[16] In "An Exhortation"—which Shelley sent to the Gisbornes and Hunt in the late Spring of 1820 and which he called "a kind of excuse for Wordsworth" (8 May 1820, *Letters* 2.195)—Shelley compares chameleons who "feed on light and air" with poets who are nourished by "love and fame": "Where light is, chameleons change: / Where love is not, poets do: / Fame is love disguised: if few / Find either, never think it strange / That poets range." However, he goes on to exclaim, "Yet dare not stain with wealth or power / A poet's free and heavenly mind" (1–2, 14–20).[17] We may doubt the independence of men of inherited wealth such as Shelley or of those who tried to earn a living through their writings such as Hunt, but at the time the Hunt circle felt there was a significant difference between the source of their money and that of those such as Wordsworth and Southey whom they saw as party poets. The Hunt circle felt they owed no interest to any interest.

Keats's epistolary assertion of poetic independence reads somewhat oddly against this context. The Hunt circle sought to avoid compromising economic entanglements so that they would be free to pursue their ideological goals in their poetry. Keats asserts that one must eschew ideology—"purpose"—for poetry, but he does so in the name not of Apollo but of Mammon. His goal seems less pure poetry than better sales. Shelley had written to Keats that *Endymion* did not sell because it was too profusely poetic. Keats responds that Shelley's poetry fails because it is not poetic enough, that it is too controversial, ideological. Keats knew from his experience with *Endymion* how politics could influence the reception of poetry, and thus he might wonder whether it was partisan politics rather than profuse poetry that hindered the sales of *Endymion*. Keats's call for a poetry where every textual rift is filled with the imagination's ore strikes me less as a declaration of art's independence than a recognition, coming with debt, that his art had to serve the market, Mammon. As he says to Shelley at the end of the letter, he would not have published his 1820 poems "but from a hope of gain." The astonishing feature of the letter is that Keats, recognizing that circumstances forced him to write for money, attempts to construct a powerful theory of poetry that links together art-for-art sake doctrines and profitability: if one gives up prodigal politics for formal gems, one will strike it rich, poetically and financially.

Keats, ever tough-minded, follows his argument and imagery to their logical conclusion: if Shelleyan magnanimity threatens art, then the artist must be self-concentrated, selfish perhaps. Shelley's willingness to give of himself, to care about and connect with others, to place some purpose above personal gain or reputation or even his art—this is now found to be a flaw in the poetical temperament. Keats writes later in the letter, "And is not this extraordinary talk for the writer of Endymion?"—presumably indicating that he recognizes the lack of artistic discipline in his own earlier work. But it is extraordinary talk in another way, for *Endymion* is a poem which, in one of Keats's favorite passages (see *Letters* 1.218–19), uses what he calls his "Pleasure Thermometer" to explore "Richer entanglements, enthralments far / More self-destroying, leading, by degrees, / To the chief intensity: the crown of these / Is made of love and friendship" (1.798–801).[18] Keats had always seemed to identify the poet as one who is not self-concentrated, who in fact has no self, a position he set forth most famously in differentiating himself from the "wordsworthian or egotistical sublime":

> As to the poetical Character itself, (I mean that sort of which, if I am anything, I am a Member; that sort distinguished from the wordsworthian or egotistical sublime; which is a thing per se and stands alone) it is not itself—it has no self—it is every-thing and nothing—It has no character—it enjoys light and shade; it lives in gusto, be it foul or fair, high or low, rich or poor, mean or elevated—It has as much delight in conceiving an Iago as an Imogen. What shocks the virtuous philosop[h]er, delights the camelion Poet.
> (Letter to Woodhouse, 27 October 1818, *Letters* 1.387–88)

If much of Keats's late work can be viewed, in Paul de Man's words, as "an attack on much that had been held sacred in the earlier work"[19]—with "The Fall of Hyperion" offering a subjective reworking of the purportedly objective "Hyperion," with "Lamia" deconstructing the union of truth and beauty found in "The Eve of St. Agnes," or with the 1819 poem to Fanny Brawne unwriting, as de Man suggests, the Nightingale ode—then Keats's letter to Shelley can be read as a repudiation of the entire line of epistolary speculation that marks Keats's great letters on the poetic character.

Or more precisely, Keats faces here the contradiction in his theory of the poet's selflessness, a contradiction which de Man locates in a failure to confront the self but which I would suggest lies in an inability to commit the self. The "camelion poet" delights in everything because it delights in no one thing greatly. It has no character, because it has never inscribed itself in the world, never impressed itself on others by making choices, taking stands: it may play roles—whether Imogen or Iago—but never establishes a firm identity. Keats's poet must refuse purpose, for as a camelion the poet must have the total psychic mobility celebrated in Keats's "Fancy": "Ever let the Fancy roam, / Pleasure never is at home" (1–2). Keats had perhaps felt that this psychological independence embraced selflessness, but in the letter to Shelley he admits the self-concentration, selfishness, in this attempt to exist without purpose: what looked like an attempt to exist without a self is revealed as an inability to conceive of an other important enough to stop the fancy's roaming. Keats's camelion poet becomes Shelley's poet as chameleon, who "ranges" because he cannot find a binding love. The irony, intentionally in Shelley's "Exhortation" and perhaps unconsciously in Keats's letter, is that— just as the abstractly independent individual of classical liberal thought finds himself determined by his place within the market—so does the man of self-concentrated independence find that his freedom lies in a hoarding of the self's resources that is determined by a financial situation over which he has no final control. Mammon is the appropriate tutelary spirit for Keats's letter, because the individual supposedly free of the God of ideological commitment is still bound by economic need; the idea of "pure" poetry "liberated" from purpose is a marketing strategy driven by "a hope of gain."

Shelley did not read Keats's letter unmoved. Keats was already much on Shelley's mind as he and his Italian circle anticipated Keats's arrival in the autumn of 1820. Claire Clairmont followed Shelley in reading *Endymion* at this time. Percy, Mary, and Claire all read Keats's 1820 volume after it arrived in early October. In the following months, Shelley issued several queries about Keats and apparently tried to contact him after his arrival in Italy.[20] While *Adonais*, begun in April 1821, is the best known of Shelley's responses to Keats, there were others, such as the unsent letter defending Keats's poetry to Gifford written in November 1820 and a draft dialogue on Keats's poetry written perhaps in October 1820 upon reading Keats's volume or perhaps in late January or early February 1821 as Shelley moved toward writing the *Defence of Poetry*.[21] Keats was clearly present before Shelley as representing one form of modern poetry when the *Defence* was begun during the Spring of 1821. Moreover, Shelley first came to know about and to read Peacock's *Four Ages of Poetry*, spurring his writing of the *Defence*, at the same time as he was grappling with Keats's letter and the 1820 volume; it is significant that both letters to Peacock about his attack on poetry contain praises of *Hyperion* (*Letters* 2.244, 262). *The Defence of Poetry* is, among other things, part of Shelley's ongoing meditation on Keats.

While it has repeatedly and correctly been said that Shelley would never have written the *Defence* without the stimulus of Peacock's essay, I would suggest that the *Defence* would have been written differently had it not been for the stimulus of Keats's letter; for Shelley's essay is not only a defense of poetry but also an attack upon the principle of self-concentration that Keats had embraced. Shelley's most direct response to Keats comes, as Fred L. Milne has noted, at the end of Shelley's discussion of the notion of utility, a placement which suggests Shelley's attempt to return Keats's notion of art to a social and economic context.

Shelley accuses thinkers such as Peacock of having too narrow a notion of utility, "one of banishing the importunity of the wants of our animal nature, the surrounding men with security of life, the dispersing the grosser delusions of superstition, and conciliating a degree of mutual forebearance among men as may consist with the motives of personal advantage" (500–501).[22] In other words, Peacock has identified utility with the forward movement of liberal capitalism, with its technological advances, its tolerant, enlightened religious views, and its *laissez faire* ideology. The problem Shelley has with this notion of utility is that it does not attend to "first principles," it does not care about pleasure in its "highest sense"; it celebrates minor alleviations of man's suffering without transforming his state. Sounding not unlike Marx and Engels of the *Communist Manifesto*, Shelley argues in his *Philosophical View of Reform*,[23] one of the precursor texts for the *Defence* from which he draws material, that liberal capitalism has replaced a feudal and superstitious past with the brutal rule of the rich; the "calculating" notion of utility enables those in power to develop technology and expand the economy without being concerned over the effect these transformations have upon those who do the work. The theory of utility is merely an ideological mask for the glorification of the cash nexus.

Shelley's account of the economics of selfishness has its roots in his own writing as far back as the note to *Queen Mab*, "And Statesmen Boast of Wealth," where he argues that all "real wealth" arises from labor but that labor is exploited "not for the necessities, not even for the luxuries of the mass of society but for the egotism and ostentation of a few of its members." He could also draw upon a line of communitarian critiques of capitalist ideology that includes Hazlitt's *Essay on the Principles of Human Action* and Robert Owen's *Observations on the Effect of the Manufacturing System*.[24] Hunt's *Examiner* also repeatedly attacked what it saw as the worst aspect of the post-Napoleonic reaction, "The Spirit of Money-Getting," defined by Hunt in 1816 in language parallel to Shelley's in the *Defence*: "The interest of the few is substituted for those of the many; till by degrees the social virtues are displaced by absolute vices; and instead of turning superfluety to its true glory, and doing justice to those who want, the sum total harmony between man and man consists in not irritating those who possess . . . an egotism of the worst species takes the place of the old healthy varieties of character" (13 March 1816). While Shelley joins with Hunt and others in their concern with what he calls "this matter of fact and money loving age" (*Letters* 2.242), the phrasing of his argument is finally determined by Keats's letter which he echoes at the close of the section on utility:

The cultivation of those sciences which have enlarged the limits of the empire of man over the external world, has, for want of the poetical faculty, proportionally circumscribed those of the internal world; and man, having enslaved the elements, remains himself a slave. To what but a cultivation of the mechanical arts in a degree disproportioned to the presence of the creative faculty, which is the basis of all knowledge, is to be attributed the abuse of all invention for abridging and combining labour, to the exasperation of the inequality of mankind? From what other cause has it arisen that the discoveries which should have lightened, have added a weight to the curse imposed on Adam? Poetry, and the principle of Self, of which money is the visible incarnation, are the God and the Mammon of the world.

(503)

Following upon Keats's play upon biblical language and alluding to Genesis 3:19, Shelley defines Adam's loss of paradise as a fall into labor. The human project is to redeem man from this fall, but the narrow definition of utility pursued under capitalism, while revolutionizing the technical means of production, leads only to greater disparities of wealth, a greater alienation of those who work, and an ironic enslaving of mankind to material things even as the material world is conquered. We have, Shelley claims, the material means to create an earthly paradise, but we lack the moral vision to do so.

Shelley's complex attack—which most clearly targets the oppressors of the people and the utilitarian would-be reformers—is also a covert riposte to Keats. For Shelley, Keats's identification of the imagination with the self plays into the hands of the utilitarians who wish to reject the imagination. Keats enters the *Defence*, disguised through the unattributed echo, as the poet of the self, as a worshipper of a demonic parody of Christianity in which Mammon, the god of the unholy and ghostly principle of self, is incarnated in its earthly representative, money.[25] Keats had sought to transmute his personal financial problems into empowering poetic maxims, but despite this attempted displacement his financial imagery had revealed that what he offered was an alliance between poetry and the principle of self. He did so to protect his poetry from what he wanted to see as extra-poetic demands (and, perhaps, to protect his poetry in its "monastery," to use his image, from the self-destroying enthralments of Fanny Brawne). Shelley insists upon the ideological implications of Keats's private and poetic choices; in other words, Shelley insists here, as he does throughout the *Defence*, on the ties between poetry, politics, and material or technological conditions. Behind Shelley's analysis here is what we would now call the crisis in representation, a crisis that for Shelley has economic, political, and poetic configurations.

The importance here of the idea of representation to Shelley is revealed in the draft version of his echo of Keats: "Poetry is the representation of the benevolent principle in man, as [gold] [property] is the representation of the selfish principle: they are the God and the Mammon of the world. . . ."[26] Shelley's shift from "representation" to "incarnation" strengthened his play upon religious terminology but masked a key issue, an issue that is raised again however by his substitution of money for either gold or property.

Shelley alludes here to a very lively contemporary debate over a very practical form of representation: the use of paper currency to represent gold specie. Ever since the 1797 Bank Restriction Act—passed to meet a crisis brought on by the need to send money overseas to support forces arrayed against Napoleon and by a run on the county banks—the Bank of England had made payments through paper currency. Everyone assumed that this practice would come to an end with the victory over Napoleon, but in fact the government continued to restrict payment with precious metals until Peel established the return of gold payments in 1823. Shelley had attacked the use of paper currency and the connected enlargement of the national debt in the *Philosophical View of Reform*. In Shelley's view, the public debt is a system for transferring income from the laboring segment of the population to those who (1) opposed liberty in America and France, (2) profited by the huge government expenditures to prosecute "liberticide wars," and (3) will reap even larger profits from the interest due them as lenders to the government. The government borrowed money from the rich to pay the rich for goods in order to fight liberty, and now it will pay back to the rich interest raised through taxes on everyone.[27]

Connected with this economic shell game, in Shelley's view, is the debasing of the currency through the printing of paper currency, and here Shelley makes explicit the issue of representation: "All great transactions of personal property in England are managed by signs, and that is by the authority of the possessor pressed upon paper, thus representing in a compendious form his right to so much gold, which represents his right to so much labour." Shelley argues here as he had in *Queen Mab* that labor is the source of all value. Precious metals would seem to be an easy and accurate way to represent labor, but Shelley already sees difficulties: "The precious metals have been from the earliest records of civilization employed as the signs of labour and the titles to an unequal distribution of its produce." The intervention of a system of representation already alienated labor and made it susceptible to exploitation, as is most clearly seen, Shelley argues, when the government debases specie through alloy, thus robbing people of a just payment for their work. But as Shelley notes, paper currency is "a far subtler and more complicated contrivance of misrule." Paper currency is a representation of a representation, and it is issued to obscure the gap between the sign and the signified, between the purported value of the paper bill and the labor it purchases: people work just as hard but they are paid in a bill worth a fraction of that labor's value. England's monetary system is based upon a corrupt and debased form of representation.[28]

When paper money ceases to represent labor, it comes to represent or incarnate the "principle of self"; that is, this false sign is overdetermined, operating overtly as a debased representation of labor and covertly as the incarnation of selfishness and greed. Shelley was not alone, of course, in attacking paper money. For example, in 1797, Gillray had attacked the suspension of cash payments in such prints as *Midas, Transmuting all into Gold Paper*, and Cobbett issued his *Paper against Gold* in 1815. Perhaps closest to Shelley is William Hone in his satiric "Bank Restriction Note" of 1819.[29]

Hone also sees paper money as the incarnation of an oppressive system, though his focus is on the link between the rise of paper currency and the imposition of the death penalty. Hone parodies a Bank of England note, decorating his currency with a picture of Britannia eating her children, a pound sign made from a noose, and a series of men and women being hanged. The face of the note proclaims that "I Promise to Perform, During the Issue of Bank Notes, easily imitated, and until the Resumption of Cash Payments, or the Abolition of the Punishment of Death, for the Govr and Comp.^a of the Bank of England. J. Ketch." Hone's "Bank Restriction Barometer" which was issued with the Bank Note helps to explain his series of references to forgery and hanging. The Barometer tracks the good effects for the nation that would accrue from a return to payments in gold and indicates the horrors that will follow from the "Disappearance of the Legal Gold Coin" and the issuing of paper notes by the Bank of England and the county banks; "Paper Accommodation," the Barometer indicates, creates "False Credit, Fictitious Capital, and Mischievous Speculation," but more importantly for Hone, the very ease with which the bills can be counterfeited leads to the "Frequent and useless inflictions of the barbarous Punishment of Death" against those who are tempted into forgery. Hone argues that the Bank Note should represent specie; but—as it is involved in only fictional credit and capital—it in fact represents the oppressive system that keeps in place the public debt and paper currency, a system upheld through the imposition of the death penalty. Shelley almost certainly knew of Hone's parody from a description in the *Examiner*. In *Oedipus Tyrannus; or, Swellfoot the Tyrant*, Shelley's satire on the Queen Caroline affair, he makes the same connection between paper money and capital punishment. The interestingly named Mammon, Arch-Priest of Famine, disinherits his son, Chrysaor (=Gold ore), for having argued for "public faith / Economy, and unadulterate coin"; he entails his estate upon his daughter "Banknotina" and marries "her to the gallows" (i.i.201–2, 206–7). Like Hone, Shelley sees money incarnating or representing not labor but the principle of self, the guiding principle behind the existing economic, social, and political system.

Representation also obscures the "first principle" of government, betraying the people to the principle of self. For Shelley, as Michael Scrivener has argued, the first principle of government is self-government, an anarchist's vision of a society that governs itself from below, without the intervention of a system of representation.[30] However, Shelley as a practical reformer supports a system such as that in the United States where there is "no false representation." The problem with England is that its system of representation is corrupt or rotten. In Shelley's *Philosophical View of Reform*, governments are to be judged by how closely they approximate an ideal in which each individual would stand for him or herself, just as the economic system is most just when labor stands for itself. Once a system of representation is introduced, the first principle (what Shelley calls "actual" representation) is abandoned, but one can still have a good government ("virtual" representation) based on reasonable ratios of representation just as one can have a sound financial system based upon just ratios between labor and gold. As paper debases the currency, so have developments in England—mainly increases in the "unrepresented multitude" which changed the ratio of those represented to those not represented from 1 to 8 in 1641 to 1 to 20 in 1688 to 1 to "many hundreds" in 1819—diluted representation so as to make it "false": "The number therefore of those who have influence on the government, even if numerically the same as at the former period, was relatively different. And a sufficiently just measure is afforded of the degree in which a country is enslaved or free, by the consideration of the relative number of individuals who are admitted to the exercise of political rights" (Shelley, "Philosophical" 234, 242). Shelley wants to go beyond complaints about "rotten boroughs" to make an argument for universal man suffrage; and he makes it clear that the corruption of the system that leads to this demand is not just a matter of statistics but also of historical shifts in power. When Parliament and the lords who controlled it stood against royal power in the seventeenth century, it sided with the people and was thus the "virtual" if not a "legal and actual" representative of the will of the people. But with the ascension of William III, an alliance was made between the aristocrats and the throne so as to make "the Crown the mask and pretence of their own authority. At this period began that despotism of the oligarchy of party, and under colour of administering the executive power lodged in the king, represented in truth the interests of the rich" (Shelley, "Philosophical" 243). The system of political representation, like the economic system, has been so distorted from its first principle that it comes not to represent the people but only the wealthy and their ideology, the principle of self.

But what of poetry? In Keats's letter, Shelley would seem to be the poet of representation, serving a God outside of poetry, while Keats embraces the formal first principles of art. That is, Keats might argue that his art-for-art's-sake theory defended poetry against its devaluation within a theory of representation that subordinates art to something prior to art, something art merely re-presents. In surveying the problem of representation, W. J. T. Mitchell has argued that such "formalist or 'abstract' theories of art have provided the most fundamental challenges to representational models in the modern era. . . . Formalism emphasizes the representational means and manner—the materiality and organization of the 'signifier' or representational object. . . ."[31] For Keats, Shelley has devalued his art by serving the God of ideological argument when he should be concerned only with formal qualities, with "the Poetry and dramatic effect." Shelley's response in the *Defence* is that art is not an object to be hoarded like Mammon's money nor is it a static representation of a pre-existing signified; rather it is labor, the activity of imagining, creating. Where Keats would emphasize the aesthetic object, Shelley celebrates the act of creation.[32]

As we have seen, Shelley, in revising the passage echoing Keats, consciously dropped a phrase that would have posited poetry as a representative parallel to money: "Poetry is the representation of the benevolent principle in man." It is important that he kept the notion of money incarnating or representing the self while he altered the status of poetry from being a representative of another power to being itself a "first principle," a God to stand against the Mammon of money and selfhood. Shelley's analysis of representation finally leads him to place poetry—or, more exactly, the imagination of which poetry is a particular instance—prior to representation. Peacock had argued that poetry began as a trade which "like all other trades, takes its rise in the demand for the commodity, and flourishes in proportion to the extent of the market."[33] Its trade was flattery of the powerful and its commodity a representation of the ideas and accomplishments of those who rule. In its "golden age," poetry had at least represented all of the ruling culture's ideas, but as history, religion, politics, and philosophy separated themselves off from poetry, it was left with the purely ornamental and sentimental task of evoking the glories of past days; the end of poetry's decline might very well be a purely decorative art, bereft of all content, serving only Keats's Mammon of formalism. Throughout the *Defence*, Shelley works to protect the imagination from a series of such reductive formulations that turn it into a representation of something else—a shadow of the truths perceived by reason, a reflection of prophetic insights, a mere ornamental recollection of the past, insignificant next to central cultural forms such as science and law.

Citing Tasso on the parallel between the poet and the creating God, Shelley argues that the imagination—like labor or self-governance—does not re-present but constitutes, creates. Immediately following the passage on poetry and the mammon of self, Shelley cites the functions of poetry as "two-fold: by one it creates new materials of knowledge, and power and pleasure; by the other it engenders in the mind a desire to reproduce and arrange them according to a certain rhythm and order which may be called the beautiful and the good" (503). Poetry creates and orders. It provides truth, beauty, and the good. Poets "are not only the authors of language and of music, of the dance and architecture and statuary and painting: they are the institutors of laws, and the founders of civil society and the inventors of the arts of life and the teachers, who draw into a certain propinquity with the beautiful and the true that partial apprehension of the agencies of the invisible which is called religion" (482). Poetry does not represent anything, not even benevolence; it is represented by other things—by individual works of art, by philosophy, by religion, by human institutions, by benevolent acts. Peacock would render poetry the representation of an external, prior culture and then a mere echo of such a representation. Keats appears in his letter as a poet who is forced to accept the Peacockian assertion that poetry can no longer represent the world and insists that instead art should merely represent itself, should merely reflect back upon its own means. And, of course, Keats also sounds like Peacock's earliest poet, plying his trade with "a hope of gain." In Shelley's view, Keats has made a false idol out of art, worshipping the image rather than the real activity that lies behind it. Just as paper currency comes to replace gold, so does Keats's self-concentrated aesthetic object replace creativity, betraying poetry to the principle of self. Standing against Peacock and Keats, Shelley argues that poetry is creative of all culture. Like Vico or Marx, Shelley believes that man makes his own history; he would stress that he does so through acts of imaginative labor.

Poetry is even the true path to the self to which Keats would seem to be turning. For Shelley, self-concentration is ultimately self-defeating: the self can only be approached through imagining the other. As the analysis of Greek drama in the *Defence* makes clear, one discovers oneself through the other in which one sees the "internal type of all that he loves, admires, and would become" (490), that is an inner vision that ironically represents all that one is not; as he puts it in the preface to *The Cenci*, "the highest moral purpose aimed at in the highest species of the drama, is the teaching the human heart, through its sympathies and antipathies, the knowledge of itself" (240). *The Cenci*, to which of course Keats was responding in his letter, is Shelley's greatest examination of what occurs when one does not come to the self through the other, through one's sympathies and anti-pathies for things outside of oneself, but instead turns inward to what Shelley calls in the play "self-anatomy" (ii.ii.110). Serving the Mammon of the self as Cenci does, one does not only destroy others in the pursuit of money; ironically, one can never come to understand oneself properly. Serving the God of poetry, however, one comes to learn that "The great secret of morals is Love; or a going out of our nature, and an identification of ourselves with the beautiful which exists in thought, action, or person, not our own" (487); the poet is capable not only of reimagining the world but of imagining a self that is something more than what one already is, of imagining what the self is not.

This approach to the self through the other is central to Shelley's politics as well as to his morals—or, rather, as a Godwinian, there is an equation between the political and the moral. Shelley is concerned with the central political/moral values of the revolutionary age. If Peacock and the utilitarians valued liberty most—a liberty defined by free enterprise and by freedom of the individual, as long as the latter does not interfere with the freedom of others or of enterprise—Shelley argues for greater equality of wealth and, most importantly, celebrates fraternity, the fraternity he revealed at a cosmic level in *Prometheus Unbound*, that he found as the secret of morals in the *Defence*, and that he wanted to believe could be incarnated in the various real human circles of which he had been a part. The Keats who had once turned from Shelley and from the Hunt circle and who in his letter embraces the self stands behind the *Defence* as the representative of a mode of poetry that must be rejected. Where Keats may have seen his arguments in his letter to Shelley as poetical—one must concentrate upon form rather than message—or personal—one must make money and not be prodigal—Shelley insists that the personal and poetical are political, that Keats's embrace of self-concentration and of art as self-contained precious object are linked through the principle of self with oppressive economic and social arrangements that arise through a perversion of representation.

Of course, Shelley's more renowned pronouncement on Keats was not such hidden criticism but the elegy *Adonais*. Such a melange of praise and censure marks Shelley's attitude towards Keats during 1820–1821: defending "Hyperion" to Peacock and others, he criticized the rest of the 1820 volume. The most violent representation of this mixed opinion occurs in a draft dialogue about Keats's book, where one speaker praises the epic fragment while the other calls Keats's poetry "a new knot of abortions engendered by vanity upon idleness." Shelley even opens his preface to *Adonais* with a typically divided assessment of Keats that focuses on the issue of his fame as a poet:

> It is my intention to subjoin to the London edition of this poem, a criticism upon the claims of its lamented object to be classed among the writers of the highest genius who have adorned our age. My known repugnance to the narrow principles of taste on which several of his earlier compositions were modelled, prove, at least that I am an impartial judge. I consider the fragment of *Hyperion* as second to nothing that was ever produced by a writer of the same years.
>
> (390)[34]

Not only do we hear here Shelley's repeated division of Keats's work—between those written on "narrow principles of taste" and "Hyperion"—but he also indicates that he feels the need to make a prose argument for the survival of Keats's poetry. This prose argument was never made; *Adonais* itself, after interring what is dead in Keats's poetry, works to establish Keats as "among the writers of the highest genius." More than that, however, *Adonais* is an investigation of what is dead and what is alive or creative in modern, that is, post-Wordsworthian poetry. Whatever the claims in *Adonais* about personal immortality, it is clearly concerned with poetry's survival, with the defense of poetry in the age of reaction. As Michael Scrivener has suggested, *Adonais* is part of Shelley's defense of poetry being mounted in 1821 against what he saw as a variety of reductive visions of the role of the poet (250–56).

Adonais, thus, needs to read in the context of the *Defence* and of Shelley's response to Keats during 1820 and 1821. Stuart Curran has made the vital argument that *Adonais* is a systematic response to Keats's 1820 volume, pointing in particular to Shelley's reworking of the "Ode to a Nightingale" within the elegy and to his use of "Hyperion" to represent what Shelley values in Keats's poetry.[35] We need to remember that when Shelley first read Keats's 1820 volume, he did so sensitized by Keats's letter to the presence of a poetry of self-concentration. Critics have been puzzled by Shelley's lack of response to the great odes and the narrative poems, but with the letter as preface the Nightingale ode's turn from possible imaginative engagement to the "sole self" or "Isabella"'s portrait of self-involved desire might very well have struck Shelley as representing a false poetry of the self just as the "Ode on a Grecian Urn" or even "To Autumn" might have seemed to him to embrace the formalism of Mammon. Within the opening movements of *Adonais*, as Shelley emphasizes Adonais' mortality, we also get several allusions to what Shelley finds mortal in Keats's poetry, his poetry of self; there are references to the Nightingale ode (as well as to the ode "To Autumn"), to the inward-turned Isabella, and to the myths of Echo and Narcissus which Keats had used in "I stood tiptoe upon a little hill" (*Adonais* 145, 116–17, 47–48, 127–44). The "Hyperion" fragment, however, clearly appeared to Shelley as an epic of sympathy and creative engagement, a poem with a vision akin to his own *Prometheus Unbound* to which he links *Hyperion*.[36]

This use of the Nightingale ode and "Hyperion" to define Keats's work— as when Shelley links Keats's poetry to the lyric nightingale and the epic eagle (145–47) or again when he defines the range of Keats's poetry as extending "from the moan / Of thunder, to the song of night's sweet bird" (371–72)—is interesting for it is found throughout the response to Keats by Shelley's Pisan circle. For example, Gisborne, in a letter to the Reverend Colonel Finch (30 May 1821) lamenting Keats's death, mentions only two poems, commenting on "his inimitable Ode to a Nightingale" and praising "Hyperion" as an "unequalled modern production" that "announces the full maturity of the richest poetic genius" (Gisborne also already seems to believe that Keats was killed by "critical malignity").[37] Even more striking is Leigh Hunt's *Indicator* review of Keats's volume (2 and 9 April 1820) which uses the same two poems in its second part to define Keats's range: the Nightingale ode is quoted in full and "Hyperion" is praised. Interestingly enough, the review also mentions Milton's "Lycidas," one of Shelley's models for *Adonais*, and discusses Keats's ill-health in relation to the harsh reviews he has received. One is tempted to find the seed of *Adonais* in Hunt's review, to find Hunt mediating between the two other poets one more time.

Given Shelley's multilayered reaction to Keats, we are not surprised to find that *Adonais* opens with a double vision of the dead poet: "he is dead" and yet "till the Future dares / Forget the Past, his fate and fame shall be / An echo and a light unto eternity" (1.7–9). The opening stanzas restate the dual vision of the dead poet in a number of ways. In the second stanza, Urania is found at the moment of the poet's death "in her Paradise" while an echo "Rekindled all the fading melodies" that were his poems. Stanza three tells us again that he is dead and yet asks "wherefore" do we cry, "For he is gone, where all things wise and fair / Descend." In fact, we are reminded in the next stanza that Milton died, "but his clear Sprite / Yet reigns o'er earth." This image of Milton has a corresponding passage in the *Defence*, where the immortality of Milton's and Dante's poetry is contrasted with the perishable ideological masks they were forced to wear: "The distorted notions of invisible things which Dante and his rival Milton have idealized, are merely the mask and the mantle in which these great poets walk through eternity enveloped and disguised" (498). *Adonais* seeks the eternal Keats beneath the mask and mantle of his mistaken ideology of Mammon.

In a sense, the entire poem—which ends with Adonais in "the abode where the Eternal are" (495)—works out the double fate set forth in this opening section. The *Defence* expresses a similar idea in a passage that evokes Keats: "Even in modern times, no living poet ever arrived at the fulness of his fame; the jury which sits in judgement upon a poet, belonging as he does to all time, must be composed of his peers: it must be impanelled by Time from the selectest of the wise of many generations. A poet is a nightingale, who sits in darkness and sings to cheer its own solitude with sweet sounds; his auditors are as men entranced by the melody of an unseen musician, who feel that they are moved and softened, yet know not whence or why" (486). The jury of poetic peers that Shelley envisages here is a key to the argument of *Adonais*: from the early evocation of Milton and of those who struggle for "Fame's serene abode" (45) through the convocation of poet-mourners in stanzas 30–35 and the account of "inheritors of unfulfilled renown" such as Chatterton, Sidney, and Lucan (stanza 45) to the image of the abode of the Eternal that closes the poem, Shelley seeks to define the survival of Keats within a community of poets. This community is an idealized version of the real circle of writers of which Keats had been a part and to which Shelley had alluded in the draft of his preface: one version reads, "The offence of this poor victim seems to have consisted solely in his intimacy with Leigh Hunt M.ʳ Hazlitt & some other of the enemies of despotism & superstition"; again, Shelley writes of having met Keats "at my friend Leigh Hunt's."[38] It is community—the group as mediator between isolated author and abstract audience—that will save the poet from the lack of fame that Shelley's "An Exhortation" argues leads to the poet's self-betrayal to power and wealth.

It is isolation—the lack of fame—that threatens Keats and modern poetry. This isolation has two sites: in the corrupt community created by "despotism and superstition," by false systems of government, finance, and thought, by false systems of representation; and in the work of the poets of the "egotistical sublime" and the principle of self. In *Adonais*, corrupt society is embodied in the figure of the critic, one of the preface's "literary prostitutes," one who serves power and money and who corrupts language to "insults" and "slander" (391);[39] such critics are "herded wolves, bold only to pursue; / The obscene ravens, clamorous o'er the dead; / The vultures to the conqueror's banner true, / Who feed where Desolation first has fed, / And whose wings rain contagion" (244–48). Interestingly, the critic will be denied fame: "Live thou, whose infamy is not thy fame! / Live! fear no heavier chastisement from me, / Thou nameless blot on a remembered name! / But be thyself, and know thyself to be!" (325–28). A destroyer of community and its bonds of language and love, the critic is finally left with only himself, with "Remorse and Self-contempt" (331)—these being along with Hate Shelley's deadly sins to be counteracted by his cardinal virtues of "Love, Hope, and Self-esteem" ("Hymn to Intellectual Beauty" 37).

The corrupt society which speaks through the critic threatens modern poetry, as seen in its attempted destruction of Adonais. The danger, however, is not only that the poet may be silenced but that he may either sell his poetic soul for fame or remain in solitude and quietude, creating the poetry of self-concentration. *Adonais* continues an argument that Shelley had begun as early as his sonnet "To Wordsworth" and had continued in "An Exhortation" and *Peter Bell the Third*. As these three poems suggest, this problem is connected in Shelley's mind with the career of Wordsworth. In *Adonais*, Shelley extends his criticism of Wordsworth to a concern about modern poetry, including his own, by creating a composite Wordsworthian-Keatsian-Shelleyan poet of the self in what has often been regarded as an embarrassing self-portrait of Shelley as poet-mourner. The purpose of this "self-portrait" is not self-pity but an analysis of the principle of self in modern poetry.

Stanzas 31 to 34 have been misread as autobiography. Responding to the hostility this passage has generated, recent defenders of the poem have argued for the abstractness of the portrait, finding not Shelley but the nineteenth-century philosophical poet or the archetype of the young poet doomed to death; Stuart Curran has stressed the identity between Shelley with his "partial moan" (290) and Keats in this passage.[40] What these readings suggest is that we have a generalized, composite portrait here, one in marked contrast to the clearly identifiable depictions of Byron, Moore, and Hunt.

The presence of Keats in this supposed self-portrait of Shelley is particularly intense: the "pardlike Spirit" of line 280 echoes the Nightingale
ode with its "Not charioted by Bacchus and his pards" (32); "A Love in
desolation masked;—a Power / Girt round with weakness" (281–82) seems to
invoke both the stanza in the Nightingale ode where a reductive vision of
life is offered in which we are ruled by "The weariness, the fever, and the
fret," "Where Beauty cannot keep her lustrous eyes, / Or new Love pine at
them beyond to-morrow" (23, 29–30), and the world of the fallen Saturn of
"Hyperion," who asks, "Who had power / To make me desolate" (102–3);
the frail form's head is bound in flowers—"pansies overblown, / And faded
violets, white, and pied, and blue" (289–90)—reminiscent of the Nightingale
ode's "Fast fading violets" (47) as well as of the "Ode to Psyche"'s "cool-
rooted flowers, fragant-eyed, / Blue, silver, white, and budded Tyrian" (14);
the references to Bacchus's ivy (290–91) seem to echo the description in
Endymion (IV.193–211) of Bacchus and his "crew" (a word used in line 295
of *Adonais*) where Bacchus carries an "ivy-dart," that is here transformed
into "a light spear topped with a cypress cone, / Round whose rude shaft
dark ivy tresses grew" (292–93), with the "dart" reappearing as the "hunter's
dart" that strikes the "herd-abandoned deer" (297). Internal echoes also
support our sense that Keats/Adonais is present here: the "pardlike Spirit"
is described as "a dying lamp, a falling shower, / A breaking billow;—even
whilst we speak / Is it not broken? / On the withering flower / The killing sun
smiles brightly" (285–86), words which recall an early account of Adonais,
who as "the loveliest and the last, / The bloom, whose petals nipt before
they blew / Died on the promise of the fruit, is waste; / The broken lily lies
—the storm is overpast" (51–54). Again, while some find autobiography
in Shelley's description of the "frail form" as "companionless" (272), as
"neglected and apart" (296), Keats, who confronted illness and death with
only Severn by his side, would seem a more likely candidate than Shelley
alive among his Italian circle of friends and loved ones.

While the identification between Shelley and Keats in this passage is usually read as a prelude to Shelley's desire to follow Keats at the poem's close,
I believe that what is identified here is the weakness in their poetry, in all
modern poetry. This point becomes clearer if we also uncover the presence
of Wordsworth in this passage, for then it becomes clear that the "frail
Form" is a portrait of a false Wordsworthian-Keatsian-Shelleyan poet of
the self who is opposed to the Hyperion-Prometheus poet of sympathy and
engagement who writes *Adonais*. Evocations of Wordsworth have been noted
by several critics, particularly in Shelley's image of the Actaeon-like destruction of the poet: "he, as I guess, / Had gazed on Nature's naked loveliness,
/ Actaeon-like, and now he fled astray / With feeble steps o'er the world's
wilderness, / And his own thoughts, along that rugged way, / Pursued, like
raging hounds, their father and their prey" (274–79). In annotating this
passage, Anthony Knerr mentions Shelley's vision of Wordsworth as Peter

Bell who "touched the hem of Nature's shift, / Felt faint—and never dared uplift / The closest, all-concealing tunic" (IV.53–55) (Knerr 84). Ross Woodman has suggested the link between this passage and *Alastor* with its assault upon the Wordsworth of *The Excursion*.[41] The Wordsworthian poet of the egotistical sublime—like the Keats in a Shelleyan reading of the Nightingale ode and like part of Shelley himself—flees from the truth revealed in nature into the self. *The Excursion*—to which Mary Shelley's response was "much disappointed. He is a slave"[42]—challenged the younger romantic poets by revising Wordsworth's own early embrace of nature as now a turn from society and particularly from social change, for the "unexpected transports of our age" have brought about a "loss of confidence in social man" (*The Excursion* IV.261–62). In their differing ways, *Alastor* and *The Revolt of Islam*, *Endymion*, and *Childe Harold III* are responses to *The Excursion*, attempts to attack the "egotistical sublime" and to discover a renewed hope for the future. Shelley continues to worry whether he and his fellow poets have escaped the Wordsworthian trap or whether like the "frail Form" they reveal a "branded and ensanguined brow, / Which was like Cain's or Christ's" (305–6); the question raised is whether the modern poet must either be a martyr to a repressive society or an apostate to poetry, serving the Mammon of power and money like the critic upon whom the poem calls down "the curse of Cain" (151).

The other mourners oppose this problematic figure with Byron, Hunt, and Moore standing against the Wordsworthian poetry of the self (and draft versions of the preface and of the poet-mourners section would have added Hazlitt and Horace and James Smith, that is, other members of the Hunt circle[43]). Cameron and Knerr have stressed the political allegiances of the mourning Byron, Moore, and Hunt; they are clearly not present because of their attitudes towards Keats, since of the three only Hunt was his supporter.[44] Byron is here, Knerr notes, as "the leading liberal poet of the age" and as the clearest example of the poet who, rather than retreating inward, has turned outward, becoming in *Adonais* the "Pythian of the age," able to destroy his conservative opponents (248–51). Hunt appears as one of the opponents of "despotism & superstition" in the draft of Shelley's preface and one of the writers—along with Godwin, Hazlitt, and Bentham—who Shelley in the *Philosophical View of Reform* hoped would bring about profound political change through their work.

Keats had, of course, been subject to political attacks because of his connections with Hunt and "Cockney poetry," and *Adonais* would be assaulted for the same reason: *Blackwood's* (December 1821: 696–700) labeled the elegy as "Cockney" and found that it was weak flattery forced upon the public by the "*Pisan* triumvirate" of Shelley, Byron, and Hunt; the *Literary Gazette* (8 December 1821: 772–73) assaulted the poem and its subject, contending that Keats was a "radically presumptuous profligate," "made presumptuous chiefly by the treacherous puffing of his cockney fellow gossips and profligate in his poems merely to make them saleable. . . . For what is praise of cockneys but disgrace, or what honourable inscription can be placed over the dead by the hands of notorious libellers, exiled adulterers, and avowed atheists," the attacks being levelled at Hunt, Byron, and Shelley. Clearly reviewers saw *Adonais* as part of the radical work of the Pisan circle with its planned organ, *The Liberal*; Shelley's conservative opponents understood the presence of Hunt and Byron in the poem. Moore seems the odd figure in this group, until we remember Shelley's dedication of *Peter Bell the Third* to Moore in his incarnation as Thomas Brown, Historian of the Fudges, or Hazlitt's review of *The Fudge Family in Paris* in *The Yellow Dwarf* (25 April 1818), where Moore is praised as "the poet and the Patriot. He is neither a coxcomb nor a catspaw,—a whiffling turncoat, nor a thorough-paced tool, a mouthing sycophant, 'a full solempne man,' like Mr. Wordsworth,—a whining monk, like Mr. Southey,—a maudlin Methodistical lay-preacher, like Mr. Coleridge."[45] Like Hazlitt, Shelley links Moore to the liberal party of poets standing in opposition to Southey, Coleridge, and Wordsworth.

Adonais seeks to rescue Keats from a Wordsworthian poetry of self-concentration and to place him within the Pisan circle to which Shelley had invited him. The poem argues that Keats does not belong with a syco-phantic tool such as Wordsworth but with Milton, "Who was the Sire of an immortal strain, / Blind, old, and lonely, When his country's pride, / The priest, the slave, and the libericide, / Trampled" (30–33). Keats does not belong with the laureate Southey ("A heart grown cold, a head grown grey in vain" 358) but with Chatterton, destroyed by the society that praised the apostate. Keats's peers are Sidney who "fought / As he fell and as he lived and loved / Sublimely mild" (401–3), and Lucan, killed by the tyrant Nero, not Coleridge, writing lay sermons to protect the status quo. Jerome McGann has called Keats's 1820 volume a "great and (politically) reactionary book" which sought "not to enlist poetry in the service of social and political causes—which is what Byron and Shelley were doing—but to dissolve social and political conflicts in the mediations of art and beauty."[46] Shelley, confronted with Keats's espousal of the Mammon of formalism and the turn to the self, might have agreed; but in "Hyperion"—the poem that perhaps as Ruthven has argued works through Keats's anxieties about money, that perhaps as Sharp has argued offers a vision of political reform, that perhaps as Watkins has contended sets forth "republican or libertarian principles"[47]— Shelley saw something else. The poet of *Endymion* might be easily defeated by the hostile world of bought critics. The poet of the Nightingale ode might be tolled back to the sole self of Wordsworthian quietist isolation. But the poet of "Hyperion" was ready to create a poetry of magnanimous and imaginative self-sacrifice, to "die into life," as Adonais does in Shelley's poem where "He is made one with Nature" (370), where "He is a portion of the loveliness / Which once he made more lovely" (379–80). The poet of

"Hyperion" belongs with Byron, Moore, and Hunt, with Hazlitt and Horace Smith, with Shelley. *Adonais* returns Keats to the circle of liberal writers of which the Hunt circle in London and the Shelley circle in Pisa were particular embodiments. They are the city of poets on earth and, like Keats, seek "the abode where the Eternal are."

The poet of *Adonais* is also ready to die into life: "What Adonais is, why fear we to become?" (459). The end of *Adonais* offers the poetry that Shelley promises in the *Defence* against the principle of self. Shelley unfurls the wings the Keats of the letter would have bound to create an art of magnanimity, an art that places his rival before himself as a beacon in eternity. The astounding close of Shelley's poem should be read as an embodiment of Shelley's poetry of creativity, a poetry that does not re-present any given of the self or the world but strives to envision anew. The last four stanzas, in the words of the *Defence*, make "us the inhabitants of a world to which the familiar world is a chaos" (505); that is, they imagine a world ordered beyond present understanding, and thus not reducible to present meanings, Platonic, Christian, or otherwise. Shelley, the skeptic, may find that "Rome's azure sky, / Flowers, ruins, statues, music, words, are weak / The glory they transfuse with fitting truth to speak" (466–68). But Shelley still believes in the Light, Beauty, Benediction and Love (478–85) that will forever remain beyond the reach of poetry. The "deep truth is imageless, " but it is the task of the poet to quest through newly minted images into those depths, to offer "mirrors of the gigantic shadows which futurity casts upon the present" (508).

Harold Bloom has called the poem's final lines "this great but suicidal stanza," finding in it "the sepulcher of a humanist and heroic quest":[48]

> The breath whose might I have invoked in song
> Descends on me; my spirit's bark is driven,
> Far from the shore, far from the trembling throng
> Whose sails were never to the tempest given;
> The massy earth and sphered skies are riven!
> I am borne darkly, fearfully, afar:
> Whilst burning through the inmost veil of Heaven,
> The soul of Adonais, like a star,
> Beacons from the abode where the Eternal are.
>
> (487–95)

Instead, I believe, we find Shelley committing himself to this quest even unto death. Beginning with Shelley's friend John Taaffe, critics have heard Dante's *Paradiso* (Canto II.1–9) echoed here, but I think we should hear another moment in Dante, that of Ulysses' last voyage, where the questor leaves behind all known shores to challenge the limits placed on man. Shelley offers one last inversion, for the breath that drives him here is not

God's punishing whirlwind as in Dante but the power of poetry, and where Ulysses and his crew are destroyed approaching Mount Purgatory, Shelley and his circle are still borne—even if "darkly, fearfully"—towards the paradise of poets. They will not get there alone: it is Shelley who has placed Keats/Adonais in the abode of the Eternal, and it is Keats who will lead Shelley there. Shelley's community of poets—dedicated to defeating the Mammon of the closed self and the closed text—inhabit the city of poetry on earth.

Adonais and *The Defence of Poetry*, along with *Peter Bell the Third* and other works of this period in Shelley's life, share a goal of wresting control of the definition of poetry in the post-revolutionary age, of protecting the wealth of the imagination from its degraders. Peacock and the utilitarians would dismiss the wealth of the imagination in favor of money-getting. Popular poets such as Barry Cornwall offered what Shelley saw as "trash" in pursuit of sales. Wordsworth and the Lakers had sold their imaginative power. We are used to hearing Shelley's rejoinder to Peacock or his satirical response to Wordsworth; we can locate comments on Cornwall in the letters. But I think it was Keats who finally was seen as posing the greatest danger and thus required the most vigorous response. For Keats too claimed to be defending poetry, but in seeking to defend art from ideology he separated it from commitment, finally from the real human problems he confronted daily. In the letter to Shelley, he essentially argues for a poetry "all breathing human passion far above." Victorian readers of Keats and their inheritors often embraced this Keats of urn-like, self-concentrated art. For Shelley, the isolation of the poetic from the political betrayed not only political purpose but also the poetic and the personal to the principle of self. Shelley, defending what he felt was the true wealth of the imagination against false systems of representation and defending the Keats of "Hyperion" against the Keats of self-concentration, demanded a different kind of poetry and sought to portray a different Keats, a Keats who belonged with Byron, the "Pythian of the age," and Moore, singer against Ireland's "saddest wrong," and Hunt, enemy of "despotism & superstition," and Shelley, the magnanimous poet of *Adonais*.

Notes

1 In June of 1820, Keats was living at 2 Wesleyan Place in Kentish Town, near to Leigh Hunt's lodgings at Mortimer Terrace. Keats came to Hunt's on June 22 after a serious hemorrhage, where he found that Hunt himself was ill. Still, the Hunts insisted on Keats moving in with them the next day. Mrs. Maria Gisborne also visited the Hunts on June 22 and saw the ill Keats. Keats remained with the Hunts until August 12, when Mrs. Hunt—being otherwise occupied—gave a letter from Fanny Brawne to the maid to deliver to Keats; the maid, who left the next day, gave the letter to one of the Hunts' boys, who broke the seal, provoking an outbreak from Keats that lead him to move to Well Walk and the Brawne household. Keats's letter of apology to Hunt is dated 13 August 1820, *The Letters of John Keats*, ed. Hyder Edward Rollins (Cambridge, MA: Harvard UP,

1958) 2.316. His letter to Fanny Keats about Shelley's offer is also dated 13 August 1820, *Letters* 2.313–14; he also wrote to Charles Brown on 14 August 1820, commending both Shelley's offer and Hunt's help, *Letters* 2.320–21. His letter to Shelley is dated 16 August 1820, *Letters* 2.322–23. Shelley's letter to Keats is dated 27 July 1820, *The Letters of Percy Bysshe Shelley*, ed. Frederick L. Jones (Oxford: Clarendon, 1964) 2.220–21. Mrs. Gisborne recounts her meeting with Keats at Hunt's house in her journal entry for Friday, 23 June 1820, *Maria Gisborne & Edward E. Williams, Shelley's Friends: Their Journals and Letters*, ed. Frederick L. Jones (Norman: U of Oklahoma P, 1951) 35–36; she mentions Keats's move to the Hunt household in her entry for Wednesday, 28 June 1820, and notes that Keats was "under a sentence of death from Dr. Lamb" in the entry for Wednesday 12 July 1820; the story of Keats's departure from the Hunt household, received from Mrs. Hunt, is told in the entry for Sunday, 20 August 1820, *Gisborne & Williams* 37, 40, 44–45. John Gisborne's letter to Shelley concerning Keats's health is not extant. The Gisbornes' arrival in Italy and delivery of the volume and letter to Claire Clairmont can be reconstructed from Shelley's letters to the Gisbornes, 11 October 1820, to Marianne Hunt, 29 October 1820, and to Claire Clairmont, 29 October 1820, *Letters* 2.55, 239–40, 241–44. Richard Holmes places the delivery on 11 October; *Shelley: The Pursuit* (New York: E. P. Dutton, 1975) 613. Hunt mentions Keats's residing with him in his *Autobiography* (Oxford: Oxford UP, 1928) 331, and his remark on Keats's response to Shelley's letter (along with the information that Keats's letter and volume were sent with the Gisbornes) is found in the postscript of his letter to Shelley, 23 August 1820, *The Correspondence of Leigh Hunt*, ed. Thornton Hunt (London: Smith, Elder and Co, 1862) 1: 158. Reiman's comment on Shelley's letter comes in his essay on "Keats and Shelley: Personal and Literary Relations," in Vol. v of *Shelley and his Circle 1773–1822*, ed. Donald H. Reiman (Cambridge, MA: Harvard UP, 1973): 413. For accounts of Keats's life during this period, see Walter Jackson Bate, *John Keats* (Cambridge, MA: Harvard UP, 1964) 644–53; Robert Gittings, *John Keats* (London: Heinemann, 1968) 394–405; and Aileen Ward, *John Keats: The Making of a Poet* (New York: Viking P, 1963) 357–73.

2 Shelley appears to have written two other letters to Keats after he arrived in Italy. In William Sharp, *The Life and Letters of Joseph Severn* (London: Sampson Low, Marston & Company, 1892), we learn from Severn that while he was in Naples Keats "received a letter from Shelley, then in Pisa, urging him to come northward, and be the guest of him and his wife; a most generous letter, and the second he had received from that fine poet and noble man" (63). There is also a cancelled beginning of a letter to Keats in Shelley's letter to Claire Clairmont of 18 February 1821 (*Letters* 2.610), which Jones speculates did not reach Severn in Rome until after Keats's death. Only the letter to Keats in London of 27 July 1820 survives.

3 Ward 367; Peter Quennell, *Byron in Italy* (London: Collins, 1941) 250; Douglas Bush, *John Keats: His Life and Writings* (New York: Macmillan, 1966) 191.

4 Charles Armitage Brown, for example, indicates that Keats wished to keep his relationship with Fanny Brawne a secret. Keats may have told Hunt during the summer of 1820, however. Hunt later offered this reminiscence in talking about Hampstead: "It was from a house on the eastern part of the heath that Keats took his departure to Italy. Melancholy as it was, and the more so from his attempt to render it calm and cheerful, it was not the most melancholy circumstance under which I saw him there. I could not hinder him one day from going to visit the house, in which, though he himself ill and weak, he attended with such exemplary affection his younger brother that died. Dead almost himself by

that time, the circumstance shook him beyond what he expected. The house was in Well Walk. You know the grove of elms there. It was in that grove, on the bench next the heath, that he suddenly turned upon me, his eyes swimming with tears, and told me he was 'dying of a broken heart.' He must have been wonderfully excited to make such a confession; for his was a spirit lofty to a degree of pride. Some private circumstances pressed on him at the time; and to these he added the melancholy consciousness, that his feeble state of health made him sensible of some public annoyances, which no man would sooner otherwise have despised. His heart was afterwards soothed where he wished it to be; and when he took his departure for Italy had hope, or he would hardly have gone. Even I had hope.—My weaker eyes are obliged to break off. He lies under the wall of Rome, not far from the remains of one, who so soon and so abruptly joined him. Finer hearts, or more astonishing faculties, never were broken up than in those two. To praise any man's heart by the side of Shelley's is alone an extraordinary panegyric" (*Wishing Cap Papers* [Boston: Lee and Shephard, 1873] 238–39). This passage, which of course links Keats to Shelley once again, covers all the difficulties besetting Keats—his health, his love for Fanny Brawne, his problems with reviewers, and perhaps even his financial woes (the "private circumstances" that "pressed on him at the time").

5 Gittings transcribes the incomplete word as "metap^{cs}" and offers "metaphysics" as a reading; Ruthven offers "metaphor" as a reading in "Keats and *Dea Moneta*," *SiR* 15 (Summer 1975): 453 n. 10.

6 See Kurt Heinzelman, "Self-Interest and the Politics of Composition in Keats's *Isabella*," *ELH* 55 (Spring 1988): 159–93; Marjorie Levinson, *Keats's Life of Allegory: The Origins of A Style* (Oxford: Basil Blackwell, 1988); and K. K. Ruthven, "Keats and *Dea Moneta*" 445–59.

7 Jack Stillinger, "The Brown-Dilke Controversy," *Keats-Shelley Journal* 11 (1962): 39–45.

8 George Keats, Letter to C. W. Dilke, 10 April 1824, in *The Keats Circle: Letters and Papers 1816–1878*, ed. Hyder Edward Rollins (Cambridge, MA: Harvard UP, 1948) 1: 276–81.

9 Charles Armitage Brown was the harshest critic of George's actions; see his letter to C. W. Dilke, 6 September 1824, *The Letters of Charles Armitage Brown*, ed. Jack Stillinger (Cambridge, MA: Harvard UP, 1966) 182–85, where he quotes John as saying that his "brother did not act rightly in leaving him so." Fanny Brawne wrote to Fanny Keats that John had told her "George ought not to have done this" (*Letters of Fanny Brawne to Fanny Keats, 1820–1824*, ed. Fred Edgcumbe [New York: Oxford UP, 1939] 34). Keats's publishers Taylor and Hessey wrote to George Keats, 17 February 1821, concerning his knowledge of Keats's lack of money, saying "Before he left this country he had no money left in his possession as you know" (*Keats Circle* 1: 102). See also, Stillinger, "Brown-Dilke Controversy."

10 Taylor, Letter to Michael Drury, 19 February 1821, *Keats Circle*, 1: 217–20. See also, Edmund Blunden, *Keats's Publisher: A Memoir of John Taylor* (1936; rpt. London: Jonathan Cape, 1940) 81–86.

11 See, for example, Ronald A. Sharp in "Keats and the Spiritual Economies of Gift Exchange," *Keats-Shelley Journal* 38 (1989): 66–81. Sharp quotes Woodhouse, for example, who wrote to Taylor, "I wish [Keats] could be cured of the vice of lending—for in a poor man it is a vice" (in Keats, *Letters* 2.151). Of course, Shelley makes two different assumptions: first, that Keats is not poor, and second, that he does not like to lend. Sharp is finally interested in a kind of spiritual generosity, in which Keats's works are seen as a gift to posterity. However, the

instances of economic language from Keats's poetry that he cites—such as "And can I e'er repay the friendly debt" (from the verse epistle to Charles Cowden Clarke 77) or "repay her scorn for scorn" (from "On Fame" 13)—strike me as being more concerned with debt and repayment than with gift giving. There seems little doubt that Keats disliked being in debt; it is less clear whether he entered into the spirit of gift exchange. Perhaps we can resolve this tension through Cixous' analysis of the Realm of the Proper and the Realm of the Gift. Keats's "self-concentration," his concern about having his "own unfettered scope," his worries about repayment all suggest his entanglement in the Realm of the Proper, where property is important, where self-identity is sought. See Cixous, "Castration or Decapitation?" trans. Annette Kuhn, *Signs* 7 (1981): 50.

12 Charles and Mary Cowden Clarke, *Recollections of Writers* (New York: Charles Scribner's Sons, 1878) 150–51. George Keats to C. W. Dilke, 12 May 1828, *Keats Circle* 1: 314.

13 See Kenneth Muir, "Shelley's Magnanimity," in *Essays on Shelley*, ed. Miriam Allon (Totowa, NJ: Barnes & Noble, 1982) 125–43.

14 Haydon recounts the debate on Christianity—opened by Shelley's comment, "As to that detestable religion, the Christian"—in *The Autobiography and Memoirs of Benjamin Robert Haydon 1786–1846*, ed. Tom Taylor (New York: Harcourt Brace, 1926) 1: 253–55. The two poems by Hunt were published in *Foliage* (1818) together with other sonnets, such as "The Cricket and the Grasshopper" from the sonnet contests of 1816–1817. Tom Keats wrote on the draft of "Written in Disgust of Vulgar Superstition," "Written by JK in 15 minutes," almost surely indicating that it was created in one of these contests; its date—either 22 or 24 December 1816 (interestingly, either a Sunday or Christman Eve)—place it in the middle of Keats's most intense involvement with the Hunt circle.

15 John Kinnaird, *William Hazlitt: Critic of Power* (New York: Columbia UP, 1978) 102–3.

16 Byron, "Dedication," *Don Juan*, Volume v of *Complete Poetical Works of Byron*, ed. Jerome J. McGann (Oxford: Clarendon, 1986).

17 "An Exhortation," in Shelley, *Poetical Works*, ed. Thomas Hutchinson, rev. G. M. Matthews (Oxford: Oxford UP, 1970) 579.

18 Keats, *Complete Poems*, ed. Jack Stillinger (Cambridge, MA: Harvard UP, 1978). All quotations from Keats's verse will be from this edition; line numbers will be given in the text.

19 Paul de Man, "Introduction," *The Selected Poetry of Keats* (New York: New American Library, 1966) xxvii.

20 Claire Clairmont indicates in her journal for 26 and 27 September 1820 that she was reading Keats's *Endymion*; by the fifteenth of October, she is reading "Isabella," on 8 November she is reading "Lamia" and on 10 November she reads "Hyperion" (*The Journals of Claire Clairmont 1814–1827*, ed., Marion Kingston Stocking [Cambridge, MA: Harvard UP, 1968] 178–79, 184–85). As was indicated before, the Gisbornes brought the 1820 volume together with Keats's letter to Claire on 10 or 11 October 1820. Mary Shelley's journal tells us that on 17 October 1820 "Shelley goes to Leghorn, and returns very late," and presumably on that trip he retrieved the volume and letter from Claire; on 18 October, he reads Keats's "Hyperion" aloud, and on 19 October, Mary Shelley reads Keats's poems (*The Journals of Mary Shelley*, ed. Paula R. Feldman and Diana Scott-Kilvert [Oxford: Clarendon, 1987] 1: 139). Shelley writes to Marianne Hunt on 29 October 1820 concerning his opinions of Keats's volume and also requests information about him (*Letters* 2.239–40); he praises "Hyperion" in a

letter to Peacock, 8 November 1820 (*Letters* 2.244). Shelley may have returned the volume to Claire Clairmont when he accompanied her to Florence on 20 October 1820 (*Journals* 1: 179); in any event, he knows by 15 November 1820 that she has enjoyed both "Hyperion" (which she read on the 10th) and *Prometheus Unbound* (*Letters* 2.596). On Shelley's inquires after Keats, see n. 2.

21 For the unsent letter to Gifford, see *Letters* 2.251–53. The dialogue on Keats is in Bodleian Ms. Shelley adds. e. 8, transcribed in Neville Rogers, *Shelley at Work* (Oxford: Clarendon, 1956) 257, in Fred L. Milne, "Shelley on Keats: A Notebook Dialogue," *English Language Notes* 13 (June 1976): 278–84, and in *Shelley's Pisan Winter Notebook (1820–1821): A Facsimile of Bodleian MS. Shelley adds. e. 8*, ed. Carlene A. Adamson, Vol. 6 of *The Bodleian Shelley Manuscripts* (New York: Garland, 1992). Milne dates the dialogue with Shelley's reading of Keats in October 1820, but Rogers argues that it was written in late January or early February 1821 as Shelley was preparing to write the *Defence* (*Shelley at Work* 257). On Shelley's divided attitude towards Keats, see Christine Gallant, *Shelleys' Ambivalence* (New York: St. Martin's P, 1989), esp. 147–48.

22 All quotations from *The Defence of Poetry* are taken from *Shelley's Poetry and Prose*, ed. Donald H. Reiman and Sharon B. Powers (New York: Norton, 1977); page numbers will be give in the text. On the *Defence* and particularly on its links to *Adonais*, I have found particularly useful John W. Wright, *Shelley's Myth of Metaphor* (Athens: U of Georgia P, 1970); P. M. S. Dawson, *The Unacknowledged Legislator: Shelley and Politics* (Oxford: Clarendon, 1980) 99, 210–58; and Paul Fry, "Shelley's *Defence of Poetry* in Our Time," in *Percy Bysshe Shelley: Modern Critical Views*, ed. Harold Bloom (New York: Chelsea House, 1985) 159–85.

23 *A Philosophical View of Reform* (1819–1820) in *Shelley's Prose or The Trumpet of a Prophecy*, ed. David Lee Clark (Albuquerque: U of New Mexico P, 1954), esp. 242–47. For a good discussion of Shelley's essay, see Terence Allan Hoagwood, *Skepticism and Ideology: Shelley's Political Prose and Its Philosophical Context from Bacon to Marx* (Iowa City: U of Iowa P, 1988).

24 Shelley's note to *Queen Mab* is to Section v.93–94; in *The Poems of Shelley*, Vol. 1, ed. Geoffrey Matthews and Kelvin Everest (New York: Longman, 1989): 364–65. Hazlitt's *An Essay on the Principles of Human Action* (1805) appears in *The Complete Works of William Hazlitt*, Centenary Edition, Vol. 1, ed. P. P. Howe (London: J. M. Dent and Sons, 1932); Heinzelman has called the essay "a response to the heuristic construct that came to be called 'economic man,'" in "Self-Interest and the Politics of Composition in Keats's *Isabella*" 162. Owen's *Observations on the Effect of the Manufacturing System* (1815), in *A New View of Society and Other Writings* (New York: J. J. Dent, 1927), argues that with the rise of the commercial classes, commerce comes to define the national character and that "the governing principle of trade, manufactures, and commerce is immediate pecuniary gain, to which on the great scale every other is made to give way. All are sedulously trained to buy cheap and to sell dear; and to succeed in this art, the parties must be taught to acquire strong powers of deception; and thus a spirit is generated through every class of traders, destructive of that open, honest sincerity, without which man cannot make others happy, nor enjoy happiness himself" (122).

25 While I believe Shelley is responding directly to Keats, his language would also have had resonance within the political discourse of the day. See, for example, Howard Fish's *The Wrongs of Man* (London: Sherwood, Neely, and Jones, 1819), where greed and selfishness have undermined all values: "Honour,—religion,—equity, and shame, / Are now, alas! but symbols, but a name" (12), and where, as

in the *Defence*, Mammon comes to represent this rise of money-getting: "On all let EXECRATION fix her seal, / Who meanly at the shrine of MAMMON kneel" (10).

26 Fanny Delisle, *A Study of Shelley's "A Defence of Poetry": A Textual and Critical Evaluation* (Salzburg, Austria: Institut für Englische Sprache und Literatur, 1974) 1: 138. The cancelled lines are found in Bodleian Ms. Shelley d. 1, f. 34 v rev. top.

27 *Philosophical View of Reform*, esp. 249–50. The *Examiner* frequently addressed the issue of the debt, the Sinking Fund, and currency; see, for example, the issues for 12 January and 23 February 1817. In his *Autobiography*, Hunt recounts an episode at Hampstead when Shelley came to him "with a deep, though not melancholy, interest in his face"; "I thought he was going to speak of some family matter, either his own or mine, when he asked me, at the close of an intensity of pause, what was 'the amount of the national debt'" (325).

28 *Philosophical View of Reform* 243–44. Walter Benn Michaels has addressed the issues surrounding paper money, the gold standard, and representation in *The Gold Standard and the Logic of Naturalism*, The New Historicism: Studies in Cultural Poetics, Vol. 3 (Berkeley: U of California P, 1987), esp. 139–80. See also, Georg Simmel, *The Philosophy of Money*, trans. Tom Bottomore and David Frisby (London: Routledge & Kegan Paul, 1978). It is interesting to note that Peacock would later write his *Paper Money Lyrics* (1825 or 1826, published 1837), which include satiric slaps at Southey, Wordsworth, and Coleridge.

29 On Gillray's prints, see M. Dorothy George, *English Political Caricature 1793–1832* (Oxford: Clarendon, 1959) 2: 28–29. William Cobbett, *Paper against Gold and Glory against Prosperity, or, An account of the rise, progress, extent, and present state of the funds and of the paper-money of Great Britain* (London, 1815). Hone's satire, engraved by Cruikshank, was issued under the pseudonym "Abraham Franklin," *Bank Restriction Barometer; or, Scale of effects of banknote system and payments in gold* (London, 1819). The Note but not the Barometer is reproduced in Frederick Wm. Hackwood, *William Hone: His Life and Times* (1912; rpt. New York: Burt Franklin, nd), between 200 and 201. Shelley would most likely have known of Hone's Note from the *Examiner* which described the Note on 17 January 1819: 58. Hackwood tells us the Note was published 26 January 1819 (and it was advertised as published that day in the *Times*), which suggests that Hunt saw an early version of the Note. Hackwood offers a sketch of the Note dated 12 January. Hunt would seem to have known of the Note at the time of its creation, which suggests closer ties between Hunt and Hone (perhaps through Hazlitt) than we might have suspected.

30 See Michael Henry Scrivener, *Radical Shelley: The Philosophical Anarchism and Utopian Thought of Percy Bysshe Shelley* (Princeton: Princeton UP, 1982) 212, 210–18, 3–76.

31 W. J. T. Mitchell, "Representation," in *Critical Terms for Literary Study*, ed. Frank Lentricchia and Thomas McLaughlin (Chicago: U of Chicago P, 1990) 76.

32 Shelley's view might be considered to be close to what Mitchell identifies as "expressionism": "Expressionism generally posits an unrepresentable essence (God, the soul, the author's intention) that is somehow manifested in a work. . . . The aesthetic object does not 'represent' something, except incidentally; it 'is' something, an object with an indwelling spirit, a trace in matter of the activity of the immaterial" (16). However, this expressionist theory still posits something prior to the art work that, under this theory, it does not represent but somehow embodies. For Shelley, what the art object offers does not exist prior to the creative act; he is concerned with neither representation nor expression but creation, the work in art not the work of art.

33 Peacock, *The Four Ages of Poetry*, in Vol. 8 of *The Works of Thomas Love Peacock*, Halliford Edition, ed. H. F. B. Brett-Smith and C. E. Jones (London: Constable & Co., 1934): 4.

34 The transcription of the dialogue is from Milne, "Shelley on Keats," 278–79. For the text of *Adonais*, see *Shelley's Poetry and Prose*; line numbers will be given in the text.

35 Stuart Curran, "*Adonais* in Context," in *Shelley Revalued: Essays from the Gregynog Conference*, ed. Kelvin Everest (Totowa, NJ: Barnes and Noble, 1983) 165–82.

36 The two poems are mentioned together in Shelley's letters to Peacock, 8 November 1820, to Claire Clairmont, 18 November 1820 ("I am happy that the 'Hyperion' and 'Prometheus' please you"), and to Byron, 4 May 1821 (*Letters* 2.244, 250, 289).

37 John Gisborne, letter to Finch, 30 May 1821, in Elizabeth Nitchie, *The Reverend Colonel Finch* (New York: Columbia UP, 1940) 86–87.

38 Bodleian notebook e. 20 fol. 9 Recto and 10 Recto. There is an interesting parallel to and perhaps influence on Shelley's conception of Keats and a society of poets in a response to Keats's death in *The Gossip* of 14 April 1821, entitled a "Posthumous Epistle," supposedly a letter from Laurence Sterne sent from Elysium, where Keats is met by Chatterton and Kirke White (who is mentioned in cancelled drafts of Shelley's preface); Southey is attacked under the nickname given to him by Hone, "Dr. Slop." Walter Peck believes Shelley had seen the *Gossip* piece; see *Shelley: His Life and Work* (1927; rpt. New York: Burt Franklin, 1969) 2: 218.

39 The economic imagery surrounding the description of the critic is insistent. In a draft of the preface, Shelley wrote that the critic "pr(os)tituted his soul for twenty pounds per sheet" and that reviewers "with some rare exceptions are in general a most stupid & malignant race; and as a bankrupt thief turns thief taker in despair, so an unsuccessful author turns critic"; Bodleian Ms. Shelley e.20, fol. 1r, 5r, transcribed in *Shelley's "Adonais": A Critical Edition*, ed. Anthony D. Knerr (New York: Columbia UP, 1984) 184–88. Shelley also referred to the payment of reviewers in his unsent letter to Gifford defending Keats, where he writes that the critic who attacked Shelley himself "has doubtless the additional reward of a consciousness of his motives, besides the 30 guineas a sheet or whatever it is that you pay him" (November 1820, *Letters* 2.251).

40 For attacks upon the passage as self-indulgent autobiography see, for example, Edward E. Bostetter, *The Romantic Ventriloquists* (Seattle: U of Washington P, 1963) 213–14; and Milton Wilson, *Shelley's Later Poetry: A Study of His Prophetic Imagination* (New York: Columbia UP, 1959) 2–5. For arguments that the passage offers a generalized portrait of the poet, see, for example, Carlos Baker, *Shelley's Major Poetry: The Fabric of a Vision* (Princeton: Princeton UP, 1963) 243–45; Roswith Riese-von Freydorf, "Die Gestalt des Letzten Hirten— Ein Selbstportrait Shelleys?" (*Adonais* xxxi–xxxiv)," in *Versdichtung der Englishen Romantik*, ed. Teut Andreas Riese and Dieter Riesner (Berlin: E. Schmidt, 1968) 294–316; Timothy Clark, *Embodying Revolution: The Figure of the Poet in Shelley* (Oxford: Clarendon, 1989); and Stephen C. Behrendt, *Shelley and His Audiences* (Lincoln: U of Nebraska P, 1989) 252–55. See also, Curran, "*Adonais* in Context" 174–75.

41 Ross Woodman, *The Apocalyptic Vision in the Poetry of Shelley* (Toronto: U of Toronto P, 1964) 159–78.

42 Mary Shelley, *Journals* (14 September 1814) 1.15. For *The Excursion*, see Wordsworth, *Poetical Works*, ed. Thomas Hutchinson, rev. Ernest de Selincourt (New York: Oxford, 1936).

43 We have already seen the link to Hazlitt in the draft of the preface. Horace and James Smith, best known for their satiric *Rejected Addresses*, appear in Bodleian Ms. Shelley e.9, p. 15, transcribed in Knerr, *Shelley's "Adonais"* 156: "And two brothers followed him / And [mimicked] in a quaint & solemn song."

44 Kenneth Neill Cameron, *Shelley: The Golden Years* (Cambridge, MA: Harvard UP, 1974) 436; Knerr 83, 87–88.

45 Hazlitt, "The Fudge Family in Paris," 25 April 1818, reprinted in *Political Essays, With Sketches of Public Characters* (1819), in *Complete Works* 7: 287–97.

46 Jerome J. McGann, *Beauty of Inflections* (Oxford: Clarendon, 1988) 53.

47 Ruthven, esp. 456; Ronald Sharp, *Keats, Skepticism, and the Religion of Beauty* (Athens: U of Georgia P, 1979) 114–58; Daniel Watkins, *Keats's Poetry and the Politics of the Imagination* (London: Associated UP, 1989) 88.

48 Harold Bloom, *Visionary Company* (rev. ed. New York: Cornell UP, 1971) 350.

22

WALTER SCOTT AND ANTI-GALLICAN MINSTRELSY

Richard Cronin

Source: *English Literary History* 66 (1999), 863–83.

In Scott's continuation of the ballad *Thomas the Rhymer*, the Rhymer tells the story of Tristram, and his audience is moved:

> Then woe broke forth in murmurs weak:
> Nor ladies heaved alone the sigh;
> But, half ashamed, the rugged cheek
> Did many a gauntlet dry.[1]

The gauntlet distinguishes the audience within the poem from Scott's contemporary readership—medieval knights, it seems, wore gauntlets at their evening entertainments rather than the kid gloves favored by gentlemen at the beginning of the nineteenth century—but in their susceptibility to pathos the two audiences merge. Fashions may change, but feelings remain the same. Hence Scott's confidence that his collection of ancient ballads, *Minstrelsy of the Scottish Border* (1802), will be appreciated by the modern reader, that the "fragments of the lofty strain" that he has worked so hard to recover might "Float down the tide of years" (*T*, 288) to awaken in his readers sympathetic emotions that would unite them with those who had listened to the ballads centuries ago. It is a precarious faith—though a faith, however sophisticated, on which all historical fiction ultimately depends— and its precariousness reveals itself clearly enough in Scott's stanza.[2] His knights shed tears of which they are only "half ashamed," as if they already dimly glimpse a culture in which a man might wear his tears with pride, as a badge of his cultural attainment. Scott's knights inhabit at once a thirteenth-century castle and an Edinburgh drawing room of the later eighteenth century: the "tide of years" that separates them from their modern readers has shrunk to a stream so narrow that they can nonchalantly stand astride it.

Scott, it is agreed, made sentimental additions even to the authentic ballads in his collection, and re-wrote lines to accommodate them to contemporary taste. A couplet from *The Dowie Dens of Yarrow* is adjusted to meet a modern demand for more finished pathos:

> A better rose will never spring
> Than him I've lost on Yarrow.

> A fairer rose did never bloom
> Than now lies cropp'd on Yarrow.[3]

But it is the presentation of the ballads rather than their emendation that works most powerfully to integrate the traditional material with the society that Scott was addressing. The ballads are prefaced by an introduction of more than a hundred pages and buttressed by five appendices, in which Scott applies to his traditional materials the methods of historical scholarship that had been developed only during the previous fifty years. He fixes in print poems many of which, until his publication of them, had survived only by oral transmission, and, in addition, he applies to them a scholarly method distinguished above all by its respect for the written document. So he adds to his introduction a letter from Surrey to Henry VIII, passages from the memoirs of Sir Robert Carey, and an indenture terminating a feud between the Scotts and the Kers. Individual ballads are furnished with an editorial apparatus that refers whenever possible to written documents. A typical example is *Johnnie Armstrong*, a ballad which is preceded in Scott's edition by a preface of eight pages offering an account of the career of the historical Armstrong, and followed by an appendix of two pages in which Scott transcribes a "Bond of Manrent" given by Armstrong to the Warden of the Western Marches. The most extreme example is *The Souters of Selkirk*, a song of only twelve lines occupying a single page, but preceded by an introduction of thirteen pages and followed by two pages of explanatory notes.

One effect of Scott's editorial labors is to bestow on the ballads a value quite independent of their literary merit. He presents the ballads in a manner designed to appeal not solely, nor even primarily, to a literary taste but to a taste for the antiquarian. The affectionately mocking and self-mocking representations of antiquarians so common in Scott's novels has secured our awareness of the fashion for antiquarianism in the later eighteenth and early nineteenth centuries, but the harmless eccentrics depicted by Scott, obsessive in their enthusiasm for the long ago, obscure one obvious enough aspect of the cult. The antiquarian object is distinguished not by any enhanced aesthetic value, but by an enhanced economic value. A better guide to this are the booksellers who continue to offer to the public "second-hand and antiquarian books," a phrasing by which they distinguish their stock into two categories: books the value of which has been reduced by their having been previously owned, and books which, by virtue of the same fact, have acquired an enhanced value. Scott's *Minstrelsy* transforms ballads freely passed from speaker to speaker around cottage fires on the Scottish Borders into luxury items, items available only to book-buyers of some means—the original two volumes of the *Minstrelsy* sold for a guinea. James Ballantyne's printing of the volumes works in tandem with Scott's editorial work to secure this effect. Typefaces elegantly distinguish the ballads from the editorial matter, and the ballads themselves are displayed with an opulent disregard for economy, no more than eighteen lines to the page, so that the one hundred and thirty-four lines of *Johnnie Armstrong* occupy eight pages of the first volume.

In its sentimentalism, in its antiquarianism, and in its scholarship, *Minstrelsy of the Scottish Border* is a characteristic product of the Edinburgh in which Scott was educated, and where, as a young man, he worked. It is fitting that the most important stimulus to antiquarian research in the later eighteenth century came from the improved road system that allowed scholars to extend the area of their investigations, because the growth of commerce, of which the activities of a man such as Macadam were both a cause and an effect, itself generated the surplus capital that made possible the cultivation of refined hobbies such as antiquarianism.[4] It was that same burgeoning of commerce that transformed the Scottish universities by creating a demand for professional men, not just ministers of the church, but doctors and, most important of all, lawyers such as Scott himself. It was commerce, too, that supported the new respect for the written word, for in commerce the written contract supersedes the spoken agreement, a fact of which Scott, whose father's official designation was Writer to the Signet, and who, during his apprenticeship to his father, accustomed himself to covering in one sitting a hundred and twenty pages in his own swift, easy hand, could scarcely have been ignorant. Sentimentalism might seem important as offering an antidote to the economic motives prevailing in such a society. It seemed so to Burns, who denied that "the man whose mind glows with sentiment" could ever "descend to mind the paltry concerns about which the terrae-filial race fret, and fume, and vex themselves."[5] But in truth, sentimentalism, which locates ethical value not in principles of conduct but in the play of the individual's emotional responses to the plight of his fellows, is a moral system precisely adapted to a commercial society.[6] The sentimental man responds always as an individual, and if he responds in concert with others, like Scott's knights when all together they raise their gauntlets to wipe away a tear, then this can never be more than a happy coincidence. The sentimental can only ever form themselves into accidental communities. The sentimental pressure towards individualism is so strong that its representative hero becomes increasingly defined by his eccentricity, as a Parson Yorick or Uncle Toby. If the sentimental man's distinctive emotional state is to be tearful, his most distinctive action is to give money. He gives money because he has it to give, and he gives it in response to a sudden pressure of sympathetic emotion.[7] Hence, his charities, because they are performed in response to an emotional pang rather than in accordance with a rule of conduct, can never threaten the economic individualism on which a commercial society is founded.

In *Minstrelsy of the Scottish Border*, Scott, one might say, re-makes ballads that had until then circulated freely amongst a community of speakers by converting them into items that could be sold. Scott's scrupulously kept annual accounts allowed Lockhart to determine that for the sale of the first edition of the *Minstrelsy*, Scott's half-share of the profits yielded him £78.10, and he was able to sell the copyright to subsequent editions to Longman for £500.[8] Such information reveals the startling disparity between the society within which Scott's volumes were designed to circulate and the society out of which the ballads themselves were produced, which was regulated by an economy that Scott himself liked to characterize in an anecdote concerning his grandfather's great-great-grandfather, Auld Watt of Harden, husband of the beautiful "Flower of Yarrow." When the last stolen English bullock had been consumed, the Flower of Yarrow would place on her husband's table a dish containing nothing but a clean pair of spurs, a signal to him that it was time he and his men rode out on a raid into England to replenish the castle's supplies.[9] In publishing *Minstrelsy of the Scottish Border*, Scott took a collection of ballads which celebrated the exploits of those living within a subsistence economy founded on theft and circulated them within an economy powered by surplus capital and founded on trade. It was a combination piquant enough to secure the success of the volumes, but Lockhart is surely wrong to point to it as the achievement on which the whole of Scott's subsequent career was founded.[10] The combination may be piquant, but it remains inert, for the two societies are related only by their difference.

The difference between Scotland's present and its past was obviously important to Scott. His biographers have done no more than recognize this when they fashion Scott's youth, as biographers will, into a sequence of emblematic moments—the childhood divided between his father's genteel, pious house in Edinburgh and the border farm at Sandy-knowe where his grandmother enthralled him with tales of Watt of Harden, Wight Willie of Aikwood, and Jamie Telfer of the fair Dodhead; or the days spent in his father's office refreshing himself amidst "the barren wilderness of forms and conveyances" by devouring "like a tiger . . . every collection of old songs or romances that chance threw in [his] way."[11] It was Scott's sense of this difference, after all, that enabled him to maintain at once a staunch Hanoverian patriotism that expressed itself most comfortably in a cultivation of the civic virtues and a sentimental Jacobite nostalgia, rival impulses that powered his first novel and led him towards the principle of organization on which his achievement in fiction is founded. But difference, by itself, could never have served this purpose. Had Scott been content with a simple relish of the difference between the past and the present he would have remained like one of his own antiquaries, a charming, harmless eccentric. It is at the moment that he found a vital connection between the two that he became a historian and a writer of historical fiction, and that moment is documented by his poems. It was in *The Lay of the Last Minstrel* (1805) that Scott first succeeded in expressing his awareness that the interest of historical fiction lies not in the past, but in the past's relation to the present, and it was in that poem, too, that he first discovered the device through which this awareness manifests itself in fiction, the device that Lukács has named, in a phrase borrowed from Hegel, "the necessary anachronism."[12]

Scott recalls his discovery in his characteristic manner, modestly and casually. The *Lay* was all but finished when a friend suggested to him that "some sort of prologue might be necessary to place the mind of the hearers in the situation to understand and enjoy the poem," and, in response, Scott "introduced the Old Minstrel, as an appropriate prolocutor, by whom the lay might be sung, or spoken."[13] The old minstrel tells his tale to the Duchess of Buccleuch. She has mourned the death of Montrose and survived to see the Stuarts restored to the throne and banished once again. The minstrel entertains her with a tale of her ancestor, the widow of Sir Walter Scott of Buccleuch, of how the widow was reconciled to the marriage of her daughter to Lord Cranstoun, who belonged to a family with whom the Scotts were at feud. The minstrel is himself the representative within the poem of the young Walter Scott, who wrote his poem at the suggestion of his noble kinswoman (who was herself to become Duchess of Buccleuch) and dedicated it to her husband. As Lockhart notes, a system of "arch allusions" runs through all the framing passages of the lay, which allows Scott to register his gratitude for the hospitality and the patronage he has received from the house of Buccleuch.[14] But the allusions work, too, to interweave within the poem three generations of the Buccleuch family, stretching from the middle of the sixteenth century to the end of the seventeenth and up to the present. The poem does not simply tell the story of a sixteenth-century border conflict: it includes the lapse of centuries that separates Scott from his material, and in doing so it decisively distinguishes *The Lay of the Last Minstrel* from the modern imitations of old ballads that Scott included in the third volume of his *Minstrelsy*. The invention of the old minstrel is an indication that Scott has found a new subject, his own belatedness.

Scott's minstrel is an anachronism, a product of sixteenth-century Scottish culture who has survived improbably into the time of the Hanoverian settlement. His role is as a mediator between Scott, who writes at the beginning of the nineteenth century, and the writers of the sixteenth-century border ballads whose subject matter Scott appropriates. The minstrel tells his tale to the Duchess of Buccleuch and her ladies, and their role too is mediatory. He is a warrior poet, but he responds to his audience of women with a tale which celebrates martial exploits and yet subordinates the theme of war to the theme of love. Warmed by the women's presence, and by their wine, he belies his own account of his abilities and sings a hymn in praise of the power of love. The women arouse in him, too, a new tenderness, so that his pride in his son, who died bravely in battle, is complicated by a father's grief. The fierce sixteenth-century border widow, whose business in life it is to defend her castle and to uphold the pride of her clan, must be violently persuaded that pride must yield to love: she is a sorceress, an embodiment of unnatural and threatening female power who must be forced into the proper mold of womanhood. But in her seventeenth-century successor, also a widow and a patriot, pride has given way to pathos, the chivalric obligation to uphold the honor of the family name has been modified into the obligation of politeness.

Scott invented his minstrel as the source of a deliberately anachronistic language, a mediating language that has "caught somewhat of the refinement of modern poetry, without losing the simplicity of the original models."[15] The texture of the poem becomes a palimpsest, inviting its reader to reconstruct its history. It can include a celebrated passage of picturesque description, such as the ruins of Melrose Abbey seen by moonlight, but for Scott the description is completed only when he registers Deloraine's indifference to its beauty: "Little reck'd he of the scene so fair."[16] The sixteenth-century moss-trooper's indifference inscribes in the text the centuries that separate Deloraine from the contemporary taste for the picturesque. Scott offers his reader a picture which is to be enjoyed but also understood as itself an item of cultural history.

The largest difference between Scott and his minstrel is that the minstrel speaks or sings, whereas Scott writes his poem. Between them stretch the centuries that have elapsed as Scotland passed from an oral to a literary culture. The minstrel accompanies his poem with a harp, while Scott prefers the detailed historical notes with which he furnishes his poem. Again the difference is allowed to infiltrate the text, the first three cantos of which are dominated by a book—the book in which the wizard, Michael Scott, has recorded his spells. The book of spells achieves a mighty presence in the poem, a presence only underlined by its negligible role in the poem's plot. One of the reasons Deloraine is given the mission to collect the book from the wizard's grave is that he would be quite unable to read it—"Letter nor line know I never a one" (L, 6). When the illiterate Deloraine rides back from Melrose to Branksome Hall with the book tucked close to his chest, he becomes a living emblem of the poem in which he appears, the true subject of which is the difference between the society Scott writes about and the society that he writes within, between a society that trusts in "gramarye" and a society that confines its trust to grammar.

Lukács was right to claim *Waverley* (1814) as the first historical novel, but Scott was able to write it because he had already written the first historical poem, and he went on, in *Marmion* (1808), to refine his invention. For Lukács the enabling condition of Scott's invention was the revolutionary conflict throughout Europe which had been inaugurated by the French Revolution. Lukács's thesis gains its strength from his insistence on the need to identify the political and economic circumstances that produced Scott's achievement, but in his choice of which circumstances to adduce he leaves himself vulnerable. He is forced to present Scott as a man who wrote in ignorance of the import of his own novels. His Scott is a reactionary legitimist who somehow managed to achieve a truly realistic mastery of his materials despite the fact that this realism was "in conflict" with his "personal views and prejudices."[17] It is notorious that Lukács writes on the assumption that Scotland is a district of England, and the correction of that error has resulted in the most persuasive modification of Lukács's argument. David Brown contends that Scott's historical understanding has its foundation not in the condition of Europe, but in the specific condition of Scotland, a nation that had lost its independence in 1707 and had failed to reassert it despite two rebellions. The rapid development of historical studies in Scottish universities, according to Brown, was a direct consequence of this. The need to recover a sense of national identity impelled Scots in the later eighteenth century to develop a new understanding of the nature of historical process.[18] Brown's argument has obvious advantages over Lukács's. It can be shown that Scott was exposed to this newly developed historical understanding while a student at Edinburgh, and that he was deeply influenced by it. By contrast, his contact with revolutionary ideas seems to have been negligible. But Lukács's argument has one striking advantage over Brown's. Scott—and in this it is only Byron of all his contemporaries who can be compared with him—was a peculiarly European figure: his novels were very quickly translated into the major European languages and became the most significant models in the development of the novel all over Europe, from Russia to France. It seems somehow inappropriate to locate the ground of this achievement in the conditions peculiar to one, small European nation. But it may be that Brown's and Lukács's arguments are not as inconsistent as they seem.

Scott's earliest reference to the *Lay* is in a letter to Ellis, when he mentions that he is working on a long poem, "a kind of romance of Border chivalry, in a light horseman sort of stanza."[19] He was later to acknowledge that he had adopted his stanza after hearing Coleridge's *Christabel* recited, but Scott's stanza has a galloping momentum that Coleridge's entirely lacks.[20] Lockhart helpfully suggests that the stanza may have something to do with "the circumstances under which the greater part of the original draft was composed."[21] In the autumn of 1802, Scott was carrying out his duties as Quarter-master of the Edinburgh Light-Horse, who were in camp at Musselburgh. This was a volunteer force, and Scott had himself been the prime mover in its formation in 1797 as a response to the threat of French invasion. It was surely his service in the Light-Horse that prompted Scott to describe the *Lay* as written in "a light horseman sort of stanza." It seems more than a coincidence that the years of Scott's significant poetic achievement —the years in which he compiled the *Minstrelsy* and wrote his first three narrative poems—coincided with those years in which there were recurrent invasion alarms. During this period Scott devoted himself to his duties as a cavalryman with just as much enthusiasm as he pursued literature and his legal profession. Scott may be self-mocking when he describes himself as "a complete hussar," but it is characteristic of Scott to mock himself when he is at his most serious.[22] Scott's friend, Skene, suggests the connection between Scott's military enthusiasm and his love of border ballads. Unable to serve on foot because of his lameness, Scott, Skene remarks, "had seen nothing for it but to raise the spirit of the moss-trooper" and set about the formation of the Edinburgh Light-Horse.[23] From 1797 and for the greater part of the first decade of the nineteenth century, the professional and cultural life of Edinburgh went in tandem with a quite different kind of activity. Edgar Johnson vividly describes the summer of 1803: "Drums and bugles sounded above the rumble of drays in the street; the evening quiet was broken by the pop of muskets and the thunder of the volley."[24] It is out of this coincidence that Scott's narrative poetry was born. He was no longer an Edinburgh lawyer who delighted to recall in his daydreams a lost time of moss-troopers, border raids, and clan feuds. The commercial ethos of Edinburgh and the warrior ethos of the Borders in the sixteenth century were no longer related only by their difference: there was a vital association between them that was visibly and dramatically evident in the everyday texture of Edinburgh life.

In *Marmion* the introductory epistles confess Scott's distance from the centers of power. Four letters are written from Ashestiel in the Ettrick Forest compared to only one from Edinburgh, and at Ashestiel Scott represents his life as pastoral, devoted to country sports, his children, and memories of his own childhood. He offers his readers "an old romance," a tale sheltered from the urgencies of contemporary life, a tale that appeals less to men than to boys, and to the nostalgia that grown men feel for their boyish passions.[25] His poem is characterized by its distance from "heroic song" (*M*, 114) and the freedom it allows him from the discipline of the "classic poet" (*M*, 115). The letters offer a definition of romance which associates the genre with the country rather than the city, with the childish rather than the adult, and with play rather than work. In writing such a poem, Scott acts like his own King James, exchanging his business dress for a suit of Lincoln green and retreating from his professional duties into the greenwood. But the epistles fit oddly with the poem that they introduce and interrupt, for *Marmion* is "A Tale of Flodden Field," and if the subtitle agrees with the epistles in modestly disclaiming that the poem is any more than a tale, it nevertheless identifies its subject as the greatest military disaster in the history of Scott's nation. There is an odd discrepancy between the confession of a playful refusal of seriousness and the choice of theme, a disparity that the very first epistle, addressed to William Stewart Rose, works into the fabric of the poem. With his usual modesty Scott represents Nature as teaching him his unworthiness for the "high theme" (*M*, 92) that he had once aspired to:

> Meeter, she says, for me to stray
> And waste the solitary day,
> In plucking from yon fen the reed,
> And watch it floating down the Tweed.
> (*M*, 92)

This is the aimlessly pastoral activity that Scott aligns with his own modest poetic ambition, the telling of a "legendary lay" (*M*, 92). But at once he is prompted to a defense of such legends:

> They gleam through Spenser's elfin dream,
> And mix in Milton's heavenly theme;
> And Dryden in immortal strain
> Had raised the Table Round again,
> But that a ribald King and Court
> Bade him toil on to make them sport.
> (*M*, 92)

Spenser, Milton, and Dryden were, Scott claims, dedicated to the romance tradition, but they also constitute, for Scott, the great line of England's national poets. The argument has turned so completely that Dryden's distraction from romance is described in exactly the same terms as Scott's devotion to it, as a retreat from serious labor to "sport."

The "high theme" of which Scott protests his unworthiness was given him by the death of Britain's two great statesmen, Pitt and Fox, and his letter begins as a memorial to their greatness. But Scott finds himself inadequate to his mighty subject:

> It will not be—it may not last—
> The vision of enchantment's past:
> Like frostwork in the morning ray,
> The fancied fabric melts away;
> Each Gothic arch, memorial-stone,
> And long, dim, lofty aisle are gone;
> And lingering last, deception dear,
> The choir's high sounds die on my ear.
> (*M*, 92)

The great patriotic theme dissolves to make way for the romance, the "tale," that Scott will tell, but as it dissolves it reveals that it was itself a romance, a Gothic church like his own Melrose Abbey, and subject, like all the visions of romance, to dissolve in the hard light of day. Scott's opening epistle begins by rigorously distinguishing the "high theme" of patriotic poets from the idle predilection for romance, a stern attention to the momentous present from the whimsical devotion to things that have long since passed away, and having established the distinction the poem works to confuse it. So does the tale that follows.

Marmion, the poem's central character, takes the place of the last minstrel by himself embodying the "necessary anachronism" on which Scott's historical fiction depends. Marmion is a rational man of the eighteenth century, one who accepts that "Nature's laws" (*M*, 131) have made redundant any appeal to "superhuman cause" (*M*, 131), and, simultaneously, a man prompted by an inn-keeper's tale to arm himself in the middle of the night and ride off to do battle with an "Elfin Foe" (*M*, 123). Marmion is Ralph de Wilton's rival for the hand of Lady Clare de Clare, but Marmion woos her not for love but for her land. It is avarice that prompts him to rid himself of his mistress Constance, the runaway nun. His is dastardly behavior, but behavior that aligns him as nearly with the villain of the novel as with the dishonorable knight of romance, with Jane Austen's Henry Crawford as closely as with Mordred. He defeats Wilton in a trial by combat, but only after incriminating him by planting forged letters in his possession. Again the effect is to make him straddle the gap between chivalric notions of dishonor and contemporary notions of criminality.[26] Forgery, after all, was the most distinctive crime of the first decades of the nineteenth century, a crime ushered into prominence by Pitt's decision to finance the war against Napoleon by massively increasing the supply of paper money. Marmion dies bravely fighting at Flodden Field, and a monument to him is erected in Lichfield Cathedral (a monument that stood, Scott tells us, until the cathedral was despoiled during the Civil War), but the tomb in Lichfield cathedral never contained Marmion's body, for after the battle his corpse was confused with another body, and Marmion was interred in the "nameless grave" (*M*, 169) dug for an ordinary Scottish peasant. Even in death Marmion is allowed to glide between the centuries, between a war such as that fought at Flodden and the new kind of war inaugurated by Napoleon, mass war, of which the characteristic memorial is not the tomb built to house the remains of a hero, but the grave of the unknown soldier. In death Marmion still plays out his role as the necessary anachronism, an anachronism that can make the connection between Flodden Field and Austerlitz.

Scott's time of poetic creativity—the years when he wrote his first three narrative poems and secured his place as the supreme poet of Britain, the "Monarch of Parnassus" to whom Byron declared himself a humble subject —coincided with the Napoleonic wars.[27] This is unsurprising, for the war with France constituted the historical moment at which Scott's antiquarian love of old ballads coincided with the demands of the present.[28] It was a moment that Tennyson was to rediscover some fifty years later. Maud's "passionate ballad," her "martial song like a trumpet's call," provokes at first only a weak nostalgia, tears for the difference between a time when men marched merrily "to the death for their native land" and a present "so sordid and mean," but the outbreak of the Crimean War brings into connection the well-kept meadow in which Maud sings and the long-ago battles she sings of, fusing them into the "blood-red blossom of war."[29] It is a point that was once obvious enough: it prompted Lockhart to pay tribute to the significance of Scott's poetic achievement by hailing him as "the 'mighty minstrel' of the Antigallican war," a description that has the added merit of offering an explanation of why, after Waterloo, Scott's fame was so quickly eclipsed by Byron's.[30] *Childe Harold* won its astonishing popularity by offering the most complete expression of a new national mood: it is the first post-war poem.

Unlike his greater contemporaries, Scott did not waver in his political allegiances throughout the war years. He remained a Tory and a fiercely partisan one, who viewed the war against Napoleon with uncomplicated enthusiasm. But whereas his Toryism had once found occasion to express itself only in outbreaks of patriotic hooliganism, as when he went to the theater in Edinburgh armed with a cudgel for the express purpose of leading an attack on a group of Irish radicals who were intent on drowning out any attempt to sing the national anthem, the war allowed him to present his conservatism in its most dignified guise, as an expression of national purpose within which mere party political differences were subsumed.[31] So, in the opening epistle of *Marmion*, Scott's eulogy on the dead Pitt is extended to embrace Fox, in life Pitt's great opponent, but in death his brother. Fox had at the last participated in the Whig ministry that continued Pitt's policy of war against France, and Scott seizes on that fact as evidence of Fox's redemption: it allows him to cast aside "partial feeling" and "Record that Fox a Briton died" (*M*, 91).[32] Pitt and Fox in life opposed each other, but Scott supplements their antagonism by allowing them each a generous sense of the other's honor and greatness. Pitt and Fox become the prototypes of all those noble enemies that people Scott's fiction, differing in their principles but alike in their greatness of spirit. In writing his memorial to them Scott found the rhetoric that was to serve him equally well when Vich Ian Vohr confronted Colonel Talbot or when the Lionheart spoke with Saladin, a rhetoric that confers on his historical novels their rare generosity of spirit. But it was a rhetoric that was born out of war, and out of Scott's recognition that in war allegiance to a party must be subsumed within allegiance to a nation, that his own identity as a Tory must be subsumed within his identity as a "Briton."

It is significant that Pitt and Fox are celebrated by Scott as Britons rather than as Englishmen. Between them, they represent something more than just England: they embody what Scott calls "the British world" (*M*, 91). Robert Crawford has argued that the invention of British literature, that is, of a literature that included but was not comprehended by Englishness, was a distinctively Scottish achievement. For Crawford, *Waverley*, with its central figure who travels from England and discovers in his travels the quite different life of the neighboring kingdom, is the crucial text. Scott may have been anticipated by Smollett in a novel such as *Humphrey Clinker* (1771), and he may have been indebted, as he himself acknowledged, to Maria Edgeworth's Irish novels, but the publication of *Waverley* marks for Crawford the decisive moment when the idea of an English literature gave way to an idea of British literature.[33] But if Smollett's *Humphrey Clinker* is one of *Waverley*'s precursors, Scott's own *Marmion* is another, for already in *Marmion* Scott's concern is to discover for both the English and the Scots a common identity that both nations might acknowledge without any requirement that the one subordinate itself to the other. Scott's English and Scots readers are invited to recognize themselves as "Britons" and citizens of "the British world."

It may seem that Scott chose an odd subject for a poem dedicated to the idea of Britain, England, and Scotland not in harmony, but at war. But in Scott conflict becomes an occasion for mutual compliment. In *The Lay of the Last Minstrel*, the English Howard marches against the Lady of Branksome, but the two forces agree to resolve their differences by single combat rather than in battle, and as soon as the decision is taken the hostile armies mingle in gruff good fellowship:

> The hands the spear that lately grasp'd,
> Still in the mailed gauntlet clasp'd,
> Were interchang'd in greeting dear.
>
> (*L*, 32)

Scott claims that such sudden transitions were characteristic of Border society, and it may be so, but they serve a wider rhetorical purpose. They transform the long history of war between England and Scotland into a lover's quarrel, the fierceness of the conflicts proving only the earnestness of the mutual attachment. Marmion, when he looks down on the Scottish camp spread over the plain, is so struck with admiration that he quite forgets his peace-keeping mission:

> For, by St George, were that host mine,
> Not power infernal or divine
> Should once to peace my soul incline,
> Till I had dimm'd their armour's shine.
> In glorious battle-fray.
>
> (*M*, 134)

100

And when Marmion rides into the Scottish camp, his admiration is returned:

> Fast ran the Scottish warriors there,
> Upon the Southern band to stare,
> And envy with their wonder rose,
> To see such well-appointed foes.
>
> (*M*, 138)

Each nation's soldiers serve as the other's appreciative audience. Scott, as it were, reviews the wars between nations through the ethical system that governed his own Edinburgh schoolyard, where a bout of fisticuffs served only as the prelude to the frank handshake that instituted a lifelong friendship. It may be a naive, though benign, understanding of international relations, but it is crucial to Scott's wider purpose, for it establishes the centuries of intermittent warfare between Scotland and England as a history that, far from threatening the union of the two nations, secures it.

By the time that Scott began to write the economic integration of Scotland and England was well advanced. The publication history of *Marmion* itself serves to indicate this. Constable, the Edinburgh publisher, bought the copyright before he had seen a line of the poem—indeed, before much of it had been written—for the unprecedented sum of a thousand guineas. But he immediately decided to secure the cooperation of London publishers, which he achieved by selling a quarter share of the copyright to William Miller and another quarter to the young John Murray.[34] The publication of *Marmion* became a tripartite venture in which London and Edinburgh shared the risk equally, and in this it was just one of countless commercial transactions that linked the capitals of the two nations. Throughout his career, Scott depended on the economic ties between Scotland and England to secure his phenomenal literary earnings. But Scott did not welcome so kindly other kinds of integration. In 1807, for example, he was not only engaged in the composition of *Marmion*, but also busy organizing opposition to the Whig government's attempts to reform the Scottish legal system by bringing it into conformity with English practice. When Jeffrey, who as a Whig supported the reform, good-naturedly complimented Scott on a spirited speech he had made on the matter, he was shocked by the intensity of Scott's response. "No, no," he said to Jeffrey —"it is no laughing matter, little by little, whatever your wishes may be, you will destroy and undermine, until nothing of what makes Scotland Scotland shall remain." Scott turned his face away, and Jeffrey noticed, when the two walked on together, that Scott's face was streaming with tears.[35] Taken together, the two stories represent well enough the coincidence in Scott of a thorough-going acceptance of the Union, in particular of its economic benefits and of the political stability that the Union had secured, and a passionately sentimental desire to preserve all that was distinctive in the Scottish national identity.

Scott had arrived early at both of these positions, but as a young man the Scottish patriotism that expressed itself in the cultivation of Jacobite sentimentality could exist only in inert contradiction to the loyal Hanoverian practice of his everyday life. It required some external stimulus to force the two aspects of Scott's identity into creative combination and make possible, for example, the most famous lines of Scott's old minstrel:

> Breathes there a man, with soul so dead,
> Who never to himself hath said,
> This is my own, my native land!
>
> (L, 39)

The minstrel's land is Scotland, "Caledonia," and for him Scotland is defined in opposition to the "Southern land" (L, 39) of England. England may be generous to minstrels, but he scorns it, preferring poverty in the Ettrick hills and the free winds of Scotland even though they "chill [his] wither'd cheek" (L, 39). But the English generosity that the minstrel spurns, Scott reciprocates, for he allows the minstrel's patriotic sentiment to blow south across the border, until it becomes an expression of the passionate nationalism that united all of Britain in its war against Napoleon.

After the defeat of the '45, the English government had passed in quick succession a series of measures designed to extirpate Scotland's nationhood. The Disarming Act of 1746, the third such act of the century, banned not only the carrying of arms but the wearing of all distinctive forms of Highland dress. English soldiers garrisoned in the Highlands had instructions to arrest anyone wearing the plaid. The Heritable Jurisdictions Act was designed to destroy the common law practices on which the clan system was founded. An attempt to impose the English legal system on Scotland in its entirety was averted, but only narrowly. The status of Scotland, an equal partner in the Union of 1707, was reduced to that of an occupied colony.[36]

As a colony, Scotland had, of course, flourished remarkably. The foundation of the *Edinburgh Review* in 1802 conveniently marks the point at which Scotland's cultural preeminence within Britain became indisputable even by the English. By then, Glasgow was already the second city of the empire. It was an achievement that Scott was particularly well placed to recognize, because he was, himself, one of its products. But his Scottish patriotism could not have allowed him to ignore the truth that whatever Scotland's achievements, they were the achievements of a nation that had been for half a century ruled by its neighbor—hence the Jacobite attachment that Scott preserved from his childhood until long after he had become an active member of the Edinburgh legal profession, upholding in all his professional activities the settlement enforced on Scotland by the victors of Culloden.

This is the context in which Scott's enthusiasm for his military duties as Quarter-master general of the Edinburgh Light-Horse needs to be understood. When his troops mustered, he was taking part in something that had not been seen in Scotland since the '45, Scots in arms, preparing for the defense of their own nation against invasion. The demands of the war effort meant that Scotland was left to its own defense. In the midst of one invasion scare Scott dashed off a letter in which he noted that nothing stood in the way of Napoleon, should he land in Scotland, but Scottish volunteers. The tone of his letter is not at all fearful, it is jubilant.[37] Scott's joy in his soldiering, an enthusiasm that struck some of his friends as ridiculous, marks his sense that he and his fellow volunteers were not just offering their services for the defense of Britain, but were seizing the opportunity to reassert Scottish nationhood.

In each of his first three narrative poems, Scott describes a gathering of the clans, and on each occasion his verse swells with the pressure of patriotic sentiment. When Marmion views the Scottish camp, he sees a "martial kingdom's vast array" (M, 133):

> For from Hebudes, dark with rain,
> To eastern Lodon's fertile plain,
> And from the southern Redswire edge,
> To farthest Rosse's rocky ledge;
> From west to east, from south to north,
> Scotland sent all her warriors forth.
>
> (M, 133)

These moments are thrilling precisely because they escape mere nostalgia. They are occasions on which Scotland's past intersects with its present. In March 1804, the beacon fires were lit in Kelso, the message passed from hill to hill, and all through Scotland men seized their arms and made for their meeting-places. Again in 1806 the beacon-fires were lit. Scott was holidaying over the border, and he rode the 100 miles to Musselburgh in twenty-four hours.[38] On both occasions the invasion warnings proved false, but for Scott the gatherings they brought about had symbolic importance: a conquered, disarmed, and garrisoned nation was proclaiming itself once again a "martial kingdom," and it was as a reflex of that reborn national confidence that Scott found his own creative talent. He was freed in *Marmion* to tell the tale of Scotland's greatest military defeat, and in his first novel he could tell the story of its most recent military disaster, because he had discovered a way to be both a British and a Scottish poet. Napoleon, or so it seemed to him, had resolved the contradiction between the two terms.[39] The war against France had made possible for every Scotsman the proud sentiment that in *The Heart of Midlothian* (1818) he allows the Duke of Argyll to express to the Queen: "My sword, madam, like that of my fathers, has always been at the command of my lawful king, and of my native country—I trust it is impossible to separate their real rights and interests."[40]

In 1825, at the very end of Scott's career, Hazlitt identified him in *The Spirit of the Age* as a writer who cultivated a nostalgia for the past in order to escape from a present that he found distasteful. Hazlitt's judgement is inherently implausible. It is hard to fathom how a man might become what Hazlitt acknowledges Scott to be, "the most popular writer of the age," by virtue of his refusal to speak to that age of any of the things that concerned it.[41] But Hazlitt's essay is in any case inconsistent. He admires Scott's novels and hates his politics, and, since the novels are rather obviously political, he can rescue himself from self-contradiction only by claiming that their politics is of the past, and has no connection with the present time. But this is a desperate stratagem, and Hazlitt is reduced at the last to arguing that Scott's novels may entertain when they are impotent to persuade: "Is he infatuated enough, or does he so doat and drivel over his own slothful and self-willed prejudices, as to believe that he will make a single convert to the beauty of Legitimacy, that is, of lawless power and savage bigotry?"[42] This is strident enough to suggest that Hazlitt has not quite lost sight of the fact that for almost twenty years Britain had been governed in obedience to principles that for him are no more than "slothful and self-willed prejudices," that in 1825 they seemed as firmly embedded as ever, and that in Scott's poems and later his novels they are given their most powerful and beguiling expression.

It was the war against Napoleon that prompted Scott first to develop a rhetoric in which difference, the difference pre-eminently between the Scots and the English, could be celebrated as the ground of a higher unity, the condition of the strong union between all of its peoples that was demanded of the nation in its war against the French. But when peace came, that rhetoric did not become obsolete. Scott turned from poetry to the novel at the moment when the stability of Britain was no longer threatened by a foreign nation but by divisions within itself, and the rhetoric that Scott had devised in his poems, when transferred to the novel, proved versatile enough to accommodate the new threat. The novels survey bitter ideological conflicts—between Jacobite and Hanoverian, Christian and Saracen, Cavalier and Roundhead, peasant and aristocrat—with a calm and disinterested tolerance, but that tolerance is not, as Hazlitt would have us believe, in contradiction to Scott's political beliefs, but their most seductive expression. He writes within a nation that, in the post-war years, seemed ever more fiercely divided, and delivers the smiling wisdom that its divisions are the source of its strength, and the mark of its broad humanity.

Notes

1 Scott included *Thomas the Rhymer*, which he believed to be an authentic work of the legendary Thomas of Ercildoun, together with his own continuation of it in the second volume of *Minstrelsy of the Scottish Border* (London: Cadell and Davies, 1802). This quotation is on page 291 of *Minstrelsy*. Hereafter, *Thomas the Rhymer* will be cited parenthetically in the text by page number and abbreviated *T*.

2 Lukács was the first critic to dispute the notion that Scott represented human nature as independent of history. Scott for him is the first historical novelist precisely because he was able to overcome "the greatest obstacle to the understanding of history," which lay in "the Enlightenment's conception of man's unalterable nature" (*The Historical Novel* [1933], trans. Hannah and Stanley Mitchell [London: Merlin Press, 1962], 28). This view has become standard amongst Scott's critics, but Lukács himself fails to sustain it, or rather he is able to sustain it only by introducing another category, the "human," which he can represent as existing outside the historical process within which "character" has its being. Hence, he is able both to recognize and to celebrate the "human greatness" of Scott's characters (see for example 51, 56).

3 This and other examples are given by Edgar Johnson in *Sir Walter Scott: The Great Unknown*, 2 vols. (London: Hamish Hamilton, 1970), 1:205–6. The extent of the freedom that Scott allowed himself in the transcription of ballads is discussed by his modern editor. See *Minstrelsy of the Scottish Border*, ed. T. F. Henderson, 4 vols. (Edinburgh: Oliver and Boyd, 1932).

4 On the relationship between road building and antiquarian research, see Stuart Piggott, *Ruins in a Landscape: Essays in Antiquarianism* (Edinburgh: Edinburgh Univ. Press, 1976), 122–24. In Scotland, the Wade roads offered for the first time access by carriage to the Highlands. The Wade roads, it is important to note, were not built solely, nor even primarily, for commercial reasons, but to facilitate the garrisoning of the Highlands in the wake of the '45.

5 Robert Burns to John Murdoch, Lochlea, 15 January 1783, in *The Complete Letters of Robert Burns*, ed. James A. Mackay (Ayrshire: Alloway Publishing, 1987), 55.

6 On this, see John Mullan, *Sentiment and Sociability: The Language of Feeling in the Eighteenth Century* (Oxford: Clarendon Press, 1988). The sentimental man, according to Mullan, "relies on feeling, indulges benevolence, and yearns for sociability," but his yearning is doomed to be unfulfilled, for the sentimental novel creates the man of feeling as "a species only by being an exception—a simple soul in an unsentimental world" (146).

7 Harley, in Scott's favorite sentimental novel, *The Man of Feeling*, is typical of such novels in his benevolence, and typical, too, in his inability to explain the principles that direct his generosity. When approached by an old man who excites pity by his poverty, but discourages the donor by being evidently roguish, Harley finds that "Virtue held back his arm," but "a younger sister of virtue's, not so severe" loosens his fingers, and he drops a shilling as alms (Henry Mackenzie, *The Man of Feeling*, ed. Brian Vickers [London: Oxford Univ. Press, 1970], 22–23).

8 J. G. Lockhart, *Memoirs of the Life of Sir Walter Scott*, 5 vols. (Edinburgh: Robert Cadell; London: John Murray and Whittaker, 1837), 1:343, 379–80.

9 Lockhart, 1:67.

10 Lockhart, 1:381–82.

11 From Scott's own memoir of his early life, in Lockhart, 1:46.

12 Lukács, 61–63. The necessary anachronism works to "clarify and underline" the relationship between the past and the present.

13 Scott, from the "Introduction to the Edition of 1830," in *The Poems of Sir Walter Scott*, ed. J. Logie Robertson (Oxford: Oxford Univ. Press, 1904), 53.

14 Lockhart, 2:24. The system of allusions is well explicated by Nancy Moore Goslee (*Scott the Rhymer* [Lexington: Univ. Press of Kentucky, 1988], 22–24). Goslee's book is the most authoritative and suggestive account of Scott's poetry yet published, and I am indebted to it.

15 Scott, from his short introduction to the first edition of the *Lay* (1805), in *Poems*, 1.

16 Scott, *The Lay of the Last Minstrel*, in *Poems*, 8. Hereafter the *Lay* is cited parenthetically in the text by page number and abbreviated *L*. Goslee usefully notes that these lines are spoken by the minstrel to "his late seventeenth-century audience but also to Scott's own early nineteenth-century one. For both, though not for Deloraine, the abbey was in ruins" (34).

17 Lukács, 31.

18 David Brown, *Walter Scott and the Historical Imagination* (London: Routledge and Kegan Paul, 1979), 195–99. Brown argues for the decisive influence on Scott of the Scottish school of "philosophical" history, to which he would have been introduced by Dugald Stewart, who lectured to him at university in Edinburgh. The seminal works of this school were the lectures delivered by Adam Smith at Edinburgh University in the 1750s and 1760s, Adam Ferguson's *An Essay on the History of Civil Society* (1767), and John Millar's *Origin of Ranks* (1771). Scott's own *Essay on Chivalry*, first published in 1818, is itself sufficient to indicate his affiliation with this school.

19 Scott to Ellis. Quoted in Johnson, 1:197.

20 For Scott's acknowledgement of the influence of *Christabel*, see the "Introduction to the Edition of 1830," in *Poems*, 52–53.

21 Lockhart, 1:243.

22 Lockhart, 1:349.

23 Lockhart, 1:258.

24 Johnson, 1:212.

25 Scott, *Marmion*, in *Poems*, 93. Hereafter *Marmion* is cited parenthetically in the text by page number and abbreviated *M*.

26 The unheroic nature of Marmion's criminality was noted disapprovingly even by reviewers who admired the poem and by Lockhart, who thought *Marmion* was Scott's greatest poetic achievement. It is an incongruity that continues to strike modern readers. Goslee, for example, notes "the unchivalric nature of Marmion's crime—a crime that uses writing" (42).

27 Byron wrote on Scott's presentation copy of *The Giaour*, "To the Monarch of Parnassus from one of his subjects" (Johnson, 1:462).

28 Scott's recognition of this may be deduced from his decision to publish at the very end of the third volume of *Minstrelsy of the Scottish Border* his own "War-Song of the Royal Edinburgh Light Dragoons":

> To horse! To horse! The standard flies,
> The bugles sound the call;
> The Gallic navy stems the seas,
> The sound of battle's on the breeze,
> Arouse ye, one and all!

29 Alfred Lord Tennyson, *Maud* (1855), Part 1, lines 160–72 and Part 3, line 53, in *The Poems of Tennyson in Three Volumes*, ed. Christopher Ricks (London: Longman, 1987), 2:533, 2:584.

30 Lockhart, 2:155. Lockhart even claims that Jeffrey's lukewarm review of his friend's poem was prompted by his recognition that *Marmion* was the poem that "first annouced him in that character": Scott "had put the trumpet to his lips, and done his part, at least, to sustain the hope and resolution of his countrymen in that struggle from which it was the doctrine of the Edinburgh Review that no sane observer of the times could expect anything but ruin and degradation." It is revealing of the manner in which war transforms the nature of ideological difference that, despite this, Lockhart can insist that "feelings of political partisanship find no place in this poem."

31 The story of Scott at the theater in Edinburgh is from Johnson, 1:102.

32 Lockhart records that it was the Tory, Lord Abercorn, who prompted Scott to add his eulogy of Fox. Abercorn may even have written the lines himself (2:154–55).

33 Robert Crawford, *Devolving English Literature* (Oxford: Clarendon Press, 1992), 16–44.

34 Johnson, 1:262. One of Scott's concerns in *Rob Roy* is to trace through the developing relationship between Jarvie's Glasgow trading house and the large London house of the Osbaldistones the origin of this economic interdependence.

35 Lockhart, 2:110–11.

36 For a summary of these measures, see Bruce P. Lenman and John S. Gibson, *The Jacobite Threat—England, Scotland, Ireland, France: A Source Book* (Edinburgh: Scottish Academic Press, 1990), 239–41.

37 On 14 October 1803, Scott wrote to George Ellis: "God has left us entirely to our own means of defence, for we have not above one regiment of the line in all our ancient kingdom. In the meanwhile we are doing our best to prepare ourselves for a contest, which, perhaps, is not far distant" (*The Letters of Sir Walter Scott*, ed. H. J. C. Grierson, 12 vols. [London: Constable, 1932], 1:204).

38 Lockhart, 2:71–72.

39 In his *Life of Napoleon Buonaparte*, Scott on several occasions implies the efficacy of the Napoleonic wars in realizing the idea of Britain, as when he remarks on the evident superiority in raw courage that the British soldier displays over his French counterpart: "The Guards supplied by the city of London, may be contrasted with a regiment of Irish recruited among their rich meadows, or a body of Scotch from their native wildernesses," but "all are found to exhibit that species of dogged and desperate courage, which, without staying to measure force or calculate chances, rushes on the enemy as the bull-dog upon the bear" (*The Prose Works of Sir Walter Scott* [Edinburgh: Robert Cadell; London: Whitaker, 1835], 12:284).

40 Scott, *Heart of Midlothian*, chap. 37.

41 William Hazlitt, *The Spirit of the Age*, in *The Complete Works of William Hazlitt*, ed. P. P. Howe, 21 vols. (London and Toronto: J. M. Dent, 1932), 11:57.

42 Hazlitt, 65.

23

ROMANTICISM AND
ITS IDEOLOGIES

Jerome J. McGann

Source: *Studies in Romanticism* 21 (1982), 573–99.

The subject of the present essay is the ideology of the romantic tradition as it appears in the literary work of the early nineteenth century in England (the so-called Romantic Period). My interest in this subject grows out of my academic work, and in particular out of a desire to arrest a process which I have observed in my immediate experience as well as in the scholarly traditions which have helped to shape that experience. That is to say, the present work proposes a new, *critical* view of romanticism and its literary products. To realize this aim necessitates a critique of the scholarly and critical traditions which have delivered these subjects into our hands. The ground thesis of this study is that the scholarship and criticism of romanticism and its works are dominated by a Romantic Ideology, by an uncritical absorption in romanticism's own self-representations.[1]

Consequently, my aim in this paper is to bring critique to the Ideology of romanticism and its clerical preservers and transmitters, and to bring a measure of exposition to the works of the romantic poets. These works are deeply involved with and affected by the ideologies of romanticism, and they have even been used, by the priests and clerics of romanticism (in whose number I must, alas, include myself), to perpetuate those ideologies. My own view—it follows Heine—is that romantic poetry incorporates Romantic Ideology as a drama of the contradictions which are inherent to that ideology. In this respect romantic poetry occupies an implicit— sometimes even an explicit—critical position toward its subject matter. The works of romantic art, like the works of any historical moment, "transcend" their particular socio-historical position only because they are completely incorporated to that position, only because they have localized themselves. In this fact we observe that paradox fundamental to all works of art which is best revealed through an historical method of criticism: that such works transcend their age and speak to alien cultures because they are so completely true to themselves, because they are time and place specific, because they are—from our point of view—*different*. Works of the past are relevant in the present, it seems to me, precisely because of this difference.

This is why the past and its works should be studied by a critical mind in the full range of their pastness—in their differences and their alienations (both contemporary and historical). To foster such a view of past works of art can only serve to increase our admiration for their special achievements and our sympathy for what they created within the limits which constrained them—as it were, for their grace under pressure. Even more importantly, to emphasize the differentials which separate the present from the past serves to diminish the confusion which follows from an uncritical process of identification. Such a confusion, it seems to me, has been too much a part of the academic view of our past literature for too long a time. This is particularly the case with the academic criticism of romanticism, whose ideology continues to be translated and promoted, and whose works continue to be taught and valued for that ideology. I have tried in this essay to arrest that process of reification: on the one hand, to situate romanticism and its works in the past in order to make them present resources by virtue of their differential; and, on the other, to free present criticism from the crippling illusion that such a past establishes the limits, conceptual and practical, of our present and our future.

I

At the beginning of his great work *Critique of Taste*[2] Galvano Della Volpe quotes Goethe's assertion "that 'the highest lyric is decidedly historical', and that if for instance you tried 'to separate the mythological and historical elements from Pindar's Odes' you would find that 'you had cut away their inner life altogether'" (p. 25). Della Volpe endorses this historical and incipiently sociological view of poetry, and he uses it to prepare his readers for his own "rapid sociological reading of Sophocles' *Antigone*" (ibid.). This exemplary act of interpretation initiates his entire *Critique* and stands as his first illustration of the principle which he argues throughout his book with so much variety and force: that the "poetry" of poems is historical, its time and place specific. The tragic pathos of Sophocles' play is inseparable from its circumstantial origins, both material and ideological; consequently, the critical analysis of the play must ground itself in an historical scholarship.

Della Volpe argues his position with a series of brilliant readings of poems chosen from various languages, periods, and social structures. The most telling of these analyses are those which focus on different sorts of nineteenth and twentieth century poems. The critical task which he has set for himself in this situation is, first, to mark out those differentials clearly, and second, to show that their particular poetic force is inseparably linked to the special—indeed, to the unique—historical character of the different works. Della Volpe has shrewdly chosen his examples from the past two centuries because his argument means to attack the entire Kantian and romantic-based tradition of criticism and aesthetics. That is to say, Della Volpe chooses to examine a series of poems which were produced in a period dominated by Kantian and romantic concepts of poetry, but he analyzes the poems from an historical and sociological vantage. His program is set forth explicitly toward the beginning of his book: to replace an Idealist and romantic aesthetic with a materialist and historical one.

Della Volpe's book is a critique in the general field of the philosophy of art. As such, its exercises in literary criticism, though excellent in themselves, do not elaborate a materialist method of literary criticism. They practise such a method in order to critique a certain philosophy of art, not to demonstrate the operations of the method. In what follows, then, I want to adopt the general orientation which Della Volpe has proposed but shift the focus from aesthetics to critical method. I am particularly interested in such a method as it must be applied to poems written in the romantic tradition, for one of the recurrent conceptual presuppositions of such poems —one of the recurrent conceptual arguments which they will make from time to time—is that poets, poems, and the poetic Imagination are transcendent. From the point of view of critical method, the following interesting problem presents itself: in what ways do romantic poems create the illusion that they are themselves historically and socially transcendent? To answer such a question demands that we develop and employ a critical method that can show how poetry may be the vehicle of certain conceptual illusions (the false consciousness of its ideology) without at the same time having its productive value vitiated by its attachment to those illusions. The method, in short, must be able to distinguish the illusions of poetry from the illusions of ideology.

We begin by forcing the critical act to attend to the specific referential patterns which appear in specific poems. These references may be factual or cognitive, but in all cases they will be historically and socially specific. In the case of romantic poems, we shall find that the works tend to develop different sorts of artistic means with which to occlude and disguise their own involvement in a certain nexus of historical relations. This act of evasion, as it were, operates most powerfully whenever the poem is most deeply immersed in its cognitive (i.e., its ideological) materials and commitments. For this reason the critic of romantic poetry must make a determined effort to elucidate the subject matter of such poems *historically*: to define the specific ways in which certain stylistic forms intersect and join with certain factual and cognitive points of reference. Rather than speak of the method in such general terms any longer, however, let me take up some concrete examples. I shall concentrate initially on some poems by Wordsworth, principally because his works—like his position in the Romantic Movement in England—are normative and, in every sense, exemplary.

II

Let me commence with "The Ruined Cottage,"[3] partly because it is a great poem, and partly because its structural methods for dealing with substantive issues are so clear. In his Fenwick note Wordsworth says that the work was based upon incidents and conditions which he had himself observed in 1793 in the southwest of England. The information is to an extent supererogatory since no one reading the story when it was first published in 1814, still less if it had been read earlier in a manuscript version, would have been unaware of the context in which the tragic events are embedded.

Margaret's husband Robert is a weaver and the poem focuses upon the precarious state in which this cottage industry found itself in the late eighteenth and early nineteenth-century. Two bad harvests coupled with "A worse affliction . . . the plague of war" (l. 136) bring Robert's family to the point of ruin, as he becomes one among those "shoals of artisans" who

> Were from their daily labor turned away
> To hang for bread on parish charity,
> They and their wives and children.
>
> (ll. 154–57)

Eventually Robert joins the army in a pathetically incompetent and misplaced effort to free his family from their economic plight. Robert disappears in the gulf of war while his wife and child are left to the beautiful slow-motion narrative of their painfully slow-motion demise.

I have myself re-narrated these well-known details because the strategy of Wordsworth's poem is to elide their distinctiveness from our memories, to drive the particulars of their tragedy to a region that is too deep either for tears or for what Wordsworth here calls "restless thoughts" (l. 198). Margaret's cottage is gradually overgrown and "ruined" when "Nature" invades its neglected precincts. This—the poem's dominant and most memorable process—finally comes to stand as an emblem of the endurance of Nature's care and ceaseless governance, just as it glances obliquely at the pathetic incompetence of individual, cultural, and institutional efforts to give stability to human affairs. Not England, not Robert's social and economic institutions, not even Robert by himself can afford protection against "A time of trouble." Margaret's cottage will collapse under their "neglect," which Wordsworth sees as inevitable, indeed, as a function of the social *rerum natura*.

This gradual collapse of the cottage into what Wordsworth calls, in his characteristic form of romantic wit, Nature's "silent overgrowings" (l. 506), has yet another analogue, however, in the poem's narrative method itself. To read Wordsworth's re-telling of this pitiful story is to be led further and further from a clear sense of the historical origins and circumstantial causes

111

of Margaret's tragedy. The place of such thoughts and such concerns is usurped, overgrown. Armytage, poet, and reader all fix their attention on a gathering mass of sensory, and chiefly vegetable, details. Hypnotized at this sensational surface, the light of sense goes out and "The secret spirit of humanity" emerges:

> I stood, and leaning o'er the garden gate
> Reviewed that Woman's suff'rings, and it seemed
> To comfort me while with a brother's love
> I blessed her in the impotence of grief.
> At length [towards] the [cottage I returned]
> Fondly, and traced with milder interest,
> That secret spirit of humanity
> Which, 'mid the calm oblivious tendencies
> Of nature, 'mid her plants, her weeds and flowers,
> And silent overgrowings, still survived.
>
> (ll. 497–506)

Margaret's devotion, love, and fidelity to her house speak to Wordsworth's "restless" narrator from beyond the grave and transfer his allegiance from "The Party of Humanity" to its secret spiritual replacement. "The Ruined Cottage" aims to effect a similar translation of attention and commitments in the reader:

> . . . what we feel of sorrow and despair
> From ruin and from change, and all the grief
> The passing shews of being leave behind,
> Appeared an idle dream that could not live
> Where meditation was. I turned away
> And walked along my road in happiness.
>
> (ll. 520–25)

"The Ruined Cottage" is an exemplary case of what commentators mean when they speak of the "displacement" that occurs in a romantic poem. An Enlightenment mind like Diderot's or Godwin's or Crabbe's would study this poem's events in social and economic terms, but Wordsworth is precisely interested in preventing—in actively countering—such a focus of concentration. The displacement is reproduced in the poem's transformation of Wordsworth's 1793–94 world—including the social and political discontents which dominated his life at that time—into the changed world of 1797–98, when he began to write the poem in the exuberant atmosphere of Racedown and Alfoxden. Wordsworth himself becomes a poetic narrator, and the focus of his original feelings of dislocation are displaced from France and the Bishop of Llandaff to the more homely and immediate discomforts of the walking tourist (ll. 18–26). In such circumstances, the story of Margaret produces in the narrator a sense of shame and humility before a great suffering, and an overflow of sympathy and love for the sufferer rather than, as in 1793–94, a sense of outrage, and an overflow of angry judgment upon those whom Wordsworth at the time held accountable for helping to maintain the social conditions which generated a surplus of social evil.

I shall have more to say about the poetic significance of these erasures and displacements in a later part of this essay. Here I am interested in the fact of the displacement, and in the extent to which—including the manner in which—it is brought about. In works like "The Ruined Cottage" and the Salisbury Plain poems we are kept in a direct contact with the particular social circumstances with which these works are concerned. Nevertheless, James Butler is right to say that "*The Ruined Cottage* is not a work of social protest,"[4] a fact about the poem which appears in the process of attenuation that I have been remarking upon. Yet the character and extent of the displacement in "The Ruined Cottage" is quite different—is far less extreme —from what we may observe in "Tintern Abbey."

Here the temporal displacement is at once more exact and yet less clear, more specific and yet not so easy to understand. The "Five Years" of which the poem speaks delimit on the one hand Wordsworth's trip to Salisbury Plain and North Wales in the summer of 1793, and on the other his return visit, particularly to the abbey, on July 13, 1798. In the course of the poem not a word is said about the French Revolution, or about the impoverished and dislocated country poor, or—least of all—that this event and their conditions might be structurally related to each other. All these are matters which had been touched upon, however briefly, in "The Ruined Cottage," but in "Tintern Abbey" they are further displaced out of the narrative.

But not entirely displaced. As in "The Ruined Cottage," these subjects are present in the early parts of the poem, only to be completely erased after line 23. But their presence is maintained in such an oblique way that readers —especially later scholars and interpreters—have passed them by almost without notice. Recently Marjorie Levinson, in a brilliantly researched and highly controversial polemic, has redrawn our attention to the importance of the date in the subtitle, and to the special significance which Tintern Abbey and its environs had for an informed English audience of the period.[5] Her argument is complex and detailed and neither can nor need be rehearsed here. Suffice it to say—and to see—that Wordsworth situates his poem (and his original experience) on the eve of Bastille Day. Secondly, the force of lines 15–23 depends upon our knowing that the ruined abbey had been in the 1790s a favorite haunt of transients and displaced persons —of beggars and vagrants of various sorts, including (presumably) "female vagrants." Wordsworth observes the tranquil orderliness of the nearby "pastoral farms" and draws these views into a relation with the "vagrant dwellers in the houseless woods" of the abbey. This relation contains a startling, even a shocking, contrast of social conditions. Even more, it suggests an ominous social and economic fact of the period: that in 1793 no great distance separated the houseless vagrant from the happy cottager, as "The Ruined Cottage" made so painfully clear. Much of Wordsworth's poem rests on the initial establishment of this bold image of contradiction, on the analogous one hinted at in the subtitle's date, and on the relation between them which the poem subtly encourages us to make. It was, of course, a relation which Wordsworth himself made explicit in his *Letter to the Bishop of Llandaff*.

But like "The Ruined Cottage," "Tintern Abbey's" method is to replace an image and landscape of contradiction with one dominated by "the power / Of harmony" (ll. 47–48). So in 1798 he observes the ruined abbey and its environs "with an eye made quiet" by such power. He sees not "the landscape [of] a blind man's eye" (l. 24)—not the place of conflict and contradiction which he now associates with his own "blind" jacobinism of 1793—but an earlier, more primal landscape which he explicitly associates with his childhood. This last is the landscape which does not fill the eye of the mind with external and soulless images, but with forms of beauty through which we can "see into the life of things" (l. 49) to penetrate the surface of a landscape to reach its indestructible heart and meaning:

> a sense sublime
> Of something far more deeply interfused,
> Whose dwelling is the light of setting suns.
> (ll. 95–97)

This famous passage defines Wordsworth's sense of "the life of things" which lies beneath the external "beauteous forms." The lines have transcended ordinary description altogether, however, and replaced what might have been a picture *in* the mind (of a ruined abbey) with a picture *of* the mind: a picture, that is—as the pun on the preposition makes clear—of the "mind" in its act of generating itself within an external landscape. Wordsworth narrates that act of replacement in four magnificent lines of verse:

> And now, with gleams of half-extinguish'd thought,
> With many recognitions dim and faint,
> And somewhat of a sad perplexity,
> The picture of the mind revives again:
> (ll. 58–61)

The abbey associated with 1793 fades, as in a palimpsest, and in its disappearing outlines we begin to discern not a material reality but a process, or power, exercising itself in an act of sympathy which is its most characteristic feature. No passage in Wordsworth better conveys the actual moment when a spiritual displacement occurs—when the light and appearances of sense fade into an immaterial plane of reality, the landscape of Wordsworth's emotional needs.

That Wordsworth was himself well aware of what his poem was doing is clear from the conclusion, where he declares himself to be a "worshipper of Nature" (1. 152) rather than a communicant in some visible church. Whereas these fade and fall to ruin, the abbey of the mind suffers no decay, but passes from sympathetic soul to sympathetic soul—here, through all the phases of Wordsworth's own changing life, and thence from him to Dorothy as well, whose mind: "Shall be a mansion for all lovely forms" (1. 140). Dorothy is, of course, the reader's surrogate just as Tintern Abbey's ruins appear, on the one hand, as a visible emblem of everything that is transitory, and on the other as an emotional focus of all that is permanent.

At the poem's end we are left only with the initial scene's simplest natural forms: "these steep woods and lofty cliffs / And this green pastoral land-scape" (ll. 157–58). Everything else has been erased—the abbey, the beggars and displaced vagrants, all that civilized culture creates and destroys, gets and spends. We are not permitted to remember 1793 and the turmoil of the French Revolution, neither its 1793 hopes nor—what is more to the point for Wordsworth—the subsequent ruin of those hopes. Wordsworth displaces all that into a spiritual economy where disaster is self-consciously transformed into the threat of disaster ("*If* this / Be but a vain belief," ll. 49–50; my italics), and where that threat, fading into a further range of self-conscious anticipation, suddenly becomes a focus not of fear but of hope. For the mind has triumphed over its times.

Thus the poem concludes in what appears to be an immense gain, but what is in reality the deepest and most piteous loss. Between 1793 and 1798 Wordsworth lost the world merely to gain his own immortal soul. The greatness of this great poem lies in the clarity and candor with which it dramatizes not merely this event, but the structure of this event.

This part of my argument can be briefly concluded. The processes of elision which I have been describing reach their notorious and brilliant apogee in the "Intimations Ode," a work which has driven the philologic-ally inclined critic to despair. In this poem all contextual points of reference are absorbed back into the poem's intertextual structure. The famous "pansy at my feet," the one tree of many, the timely utterance: readers have sought long and in vain to specify the references of these passages. Perhaps we glimpse a metaphoric afterimage of the Bastille in "Shades of the prison-house"—but perhaps not. The poem generalizes—we now like to say mythologizes—all its conflicts, or rather resituates those conflicts out of a socio-historical context and into an ideological one. "We in thought will join your throng." This is the famous process of internalization which is at once the ode's central problem and its final solution as well.

The problem is clearly presented in stanza IV when Wordsworth acknowledges his belief that "all the earth is gay" (l. 29). The pattern in the first four stanzas is to set a contrast between all that Wordsworth can "hear," which the poem associates with his belief in and feelings of universal joy, and all that Wordsworth can and cannot see. These latter things, which Wordsworth associates initially with loss, induce in him a sense of fear and anxiety. The contrast establishes a distinction between a world of the indefinite and the unseen on the one hand, and world of visible particulars on the other. "The things which I have seen I now can see no more"; the catalogue in stanza II is itself not a record of immediacies, but a recitation of generalities recalled from particular past experiences, as the very heterogeneous character of the items shows. And the unadorned presentation of these memory-mediated particulars explains that the flight of the visionary gleam is a function of the loss of immediacy.

In short, the poem's problem emerges when Wordsworth recognizes that his sense of a universal joy—his insight into the life of things—has resulted in his loss of the concrete and particular:

> —But there's a Tree, of many, one,
> A single Field which I have looked upon,
> Both of them speak of something that is gone:
> The Pansy at my feet
> Doth the same tale repeat:
>
> (ll. 52–56)

Scholars who have labored to identify that tree and the "single field," and to locate the spot where Wordsworth observed the pansy, have followed the poet's own futile quest. These things are gone, and Wordsworth fears—despite his own reiterated convictions—that their departure will signal the passage of "the glory and the dream" as well.

As "The Ruined Cottage" and "Tintern Abbey" have already shown, the disappearance of such particulars occurred as part of a strategy of displacement. But where these earlier poems involved dramatizations and enactments of the strategy's discovery, the "Intimations Ode" is a study of its character and, finally, a justification and embodiment of its operations. The ode begins with a fearful sense that the immediate and concrete experience has disappeared into the mists of consciousness and memory. It concludes, however, with the reiterated conviction that: "The thought of our past years in me doth breed / Perpetual benediction:" (ll. 135–36). Immediacy is "fugitive" and impermanent, but not so the consciousness of all that is fugitive. Wordsworth therefore lifts a final "song of thanks and praise" for the activity of displacement itself, for the moments of loss. In the ode, objective history has disappeared. The poem annihilates its history, biographical and socio-historical alike, and replaces these particulars with a record of pure consciousness. The paradox of the work is that it embodies an immediate and concrete experience of that most secret and impalpable of all human acts: the transformation of fact into idea, and of experience into ideology.

Its pathos is a function of that paradox. For Wordsworth's poem does not actually transcend the evils it is haunted by, it merely occupies them at the level of consciousness. That Wordsworth's is as well a false consciousness needs scarcely to be said, nor is it an indictment of the poem's greatness that this should be the case. The work completes and perfects the tragic losses of Wordsworth's life and times. Had he merely "yielded up moral questions in despair" (*The Prelude*, XI.305) his case would have been pitiful. Wordsworth went on to struggle further with those problems and to arrive at what he believed was their solution. What he actually discovered was no more than his own desperate need for a solution. The reality of that need mirrored a cultural one that was much greater and more widespread. Wordsworth transformed both of these realities into illusions. The process began with the displacement of the problem inward, but when he went on to conceptualize his need, as we observe in the ode, the pity of Wordsworth's situation approaches tragic proportions. Indeed, it is a very emblem of the tragedy of his epoch, for in that conceptualization Wordsworth imprisoned his true voice of feeling within the bastille of his consciousness. Wordsworth made a solitude and he called it peace.

This idea that poetry, or even consciousness, can set one free of the ruins of history and culture is the grand illusion of every romantic poet. The idea has been inherited and reproduced in the cultural support systems—principally the academy—which have followed in the wake of the Romantic Movement. In English and American culture, this idea has descended to us largely through the lines of thought which have developed out of the work of Coleridge and Hegel. As a consequence, academicians and literary commentators have turned what Blake once called "poetic tales" into "forms of worship." In current terms (or perhaps "jargon"), the ideology of romanticism has undergone a process of cultural reification. Today the scholarship and interpretation of romantic works is dominated by an uncritical absorption in romanticism's own self-representations.

That my own work on Byron cannot escape the criticism of such a judgment now seems to me very clear. My interest in Byron was triggered years ago largely because he seemed so different from the other romantics. The differences were marked out by criticism itself, which preferred to set Byron aside, or to treat his work as marginal to the central projects of romanticism. And of course Byron is in many ways a figure who covets the stance of an "outsider," and who presented himself as "the enemy within," the gadfly and critic of his own age and culture.

Without minimizing the differential which Byron represents, I would say now that my initial enthusiasm for Byron's self-representations misled my critical judgment. The poetry of the Romantic Movement, from its earliest to its latest transformations, is marked by extreme forms of displacement and poetic conceptualization whereby the actual human issues with which the poetry is concerned are resituated and deflected in various ways. I have already described an instance of this process in some poems by Wordsworth. Let me extend the discussion at this point to take up the work of the later romantics, whose antithetical position toward certain crucial aspects of the early romantics can sometimes lead one to misconceive the critical nature of their work.

III

I will begin by way of Shelley and his enthusiasm for the Greek revolution. On this topic one of his greatest critics has written:

> The most encouraging and significant event on the continent, Shelley felt, was the beginning, in 1821, of the revolutionary war of the Greek people, significant because it represented the first major cracking of the Metternich system, and hence a culminating point in the historical evolution of the forces of liberty. It is in this perspective that he treats the Greek revolution in "Hellas" putting into flaming lyrical verse the same concept of historical development we have already noted in his prose.[6]

But *Hellas*—that "classic English statement of Philhellenism," as Richard Holmes has rightly said—is, like *Prometheus Unbound*, "almost entirely visionary and mystic" in its formulation.[7] Furthermore, although Cameron represents the Greek revolution as a significant crack in the structure of the Holy Alliance, it was far from being that. Rather, it represented the beginning of the end of the Turkish Empire and the definitive triumph of European imperialism—at the head of which was England in world history. Shelley's philhellenism, like Byron's, was a nostalgic attachment to their image of a human civilization.

> We are all Greeks. Our laws, our literature, our religion, our arts have their root in Greece. But for Greece—Rome, the instructor, the conqueror, or the metropolis of our ancestors, would have spread no illumination with her arms, and we might still have been savages and idolaters; or, what is worse, might have arrived at such a stagnant and miserable state of social institution as China and Japan possess.
>
> The human form and the human mind attained to a perfection in Greece which has impressed its image on those faultless

productions, whose very fragments are the despair of modern art, and has propagated impulses which cannot cease, through a thousand channels of manifest or imperceptible operation, to ennoble and delight mankind until the extinction of the race.[8]

These ideas are typical philhellenist illusions[9] and, as such, were open to a political exploitation by Europe's imperialist powers, as well as a poetical exploitation by writers like Shelley and Byron. In Byron, however, philhellenist idealism assumed emotional forms that were quite different from what we see in Shelley. Byron's early work, for example, generates a despair which is normally marked by a cynical recoil:

5.

Or burst the vanish'd Hero's lofty mound;
Far on the solitary shore he sleeps:
He fell, and falling nations mourn'd around;
But now not one of saddening thousands weeps,
Nor warlike-worshipper his vigil keeps
Where demi-gods appear'd, as records tell.
Remove yon skull from out the scatter'd heaps:
Is that a temple where a God may dwell?
Why ev'n the worm at last disdains her shatter'd cell!

6.

Look on its broken arch, its ruin'd wall,
Its chambers desolate, and portals foul:
Yes, this was once Ambition's airy hall,
The dome of Thought, the palace of the Soul:
Behold through each lack-lustre, eyeless hole,
The gay recess of Wisdom and of Wit.

(*CHP*, Canto II)[10]

In the later work the despair normally appears either as the comic pathos typified in the Haidee episode of *Don Juan*, for example, or the stoical pathos of a poem like "On This Day I Complete My Thirty-Sixth Year." In all instances, however, Greece is a poetic resort, an Ideal against which the insufficiencies of the political and cultural present can be measured and judged. Greece was Byron's most important "unreached paradise" and, therefore, the focus of his deepest despair: "Fair Greece, sad relic of departed worth! / Immortal, though no more; though fallen, great. . . ." (*CHP* II, st. 73). A set of contradictions in itself, Byron's Greece became the catalyst which separated out whole patterns of contradictions in a world Byron spent so much of his life observing.

In this situation we can begin to see how Byron's idealisms were to become in his verse a vehicle for critical analysis. His poetry has often been an object of suspicion because it cultivates moods of despair. But as Baudelaire was the first to appreciate fully, Byron's despair, along with the entire range of his negative emotions, is the source of his greatness as a poet and his importance for the (programmatically hypocritical) reader. Byronic Despair is the reflex of an Ideal attachment in precisely the same way that Shelleyan Hope is the reflex of his Idealism. This is the structure which governs their ideological commitments. When we look at their poetical works we find that Shelley's Hope (the Ineffectual Angel) assumes various futurist modes, and that Byron's Despair (Mad Bad Lord Byron) appears in corresponding sets of sensationalist forms (in every sense). In each case the poetry develops the specific patterns of emotional and intellectual contradictions which define what is valuable in their work.

The poetical myth of his life, which Byron invented, is a convenient entrance into his works. Disheartened by his world and his own inability to alter its force or circumstance, Byron creates in his poetry a drama of the disillusioned existence. Its desperation appears in an escapist gesture of a special sort: not into the future, or into art, but into the flux of everything which is most immediate, a flight into the surfaces of poetry and life, the dance of verse, the high energy of instant sensations and feelings (whether of pleasure or pain makes no difference). In poetry this sometimes appears as the effort to break free of language altogether in order to achieve an unmediated set of responses:

> 108.
> There is the moral of all human tales;
> 'Tis but the same rehearsal of the past,
> First Freedom, and then Glory—when that fails,
> Wealth, vice, corruption,—barbarism at last.
> And History, with all her volumes vast,
> Hath but *one* page,—'tis better written here,
> Where gorgeous Tyranny had thus amass'd
> All treasures, all delights, that eye or ear,
> Heart, soul could seek, tongue ask—Away with words! draw near,
>
> 109.
> Admire, exult—despise—laugh, weep,—for here
> There is such matter for all feeling . . .
> (*CHP*, Canto IV)

At other times it appears as the effort to plunge into the verbal medium itself, to make the flow of language the encompassing totality of immediate experience. Byron's famous "spontaneity"—what Swinburne called his

ROMANTICISM AND ITS IDEOLOGIES

"sincerity and strength"—is a poetic style which covets verbal immediacy, and *Don Juan*'s digressive manner is its exemplary form. The mediations of language are destroyed by turning language into an environment for sensations and feelings. The first twelve stanzas of Canto XIV of *Don Juan* reflect upon this sort of poetic style:

7

But what's this to the purpose? you will say.
   Gent. Reader, nothing; a mere speculation,
For which my sole excuse is—'tis my way,
   Sometimes *with* and sometimes without occasion
I write what's uppermost, without delay;
   This narrative is not meant for narration,
But a mere airy and fantastic basis,
To build up common things with common places.

8

You know, or don't know, that great Bacon saith,
   "Fling up a straw, 'twill show the way the wind blows";
And such a straw, borne on by human breath,
   Is Poesy, according as the mind glows;
A paper kite, which flies 'twixt life and death,
   A shadow which the onward Soul behind throws:
And mine's a bubble not blown up for praise,
But just to play with, as an infant plays.

12

I think that were I *certain* of success,
   I hardly could compose another line:
So long I've battled either more or less,
   That no defeat can drive me from the Nine.
This feeling 'tis not easy to express,
   And yet 'tis not affected, I opine.
In play, there are two pleasures for your choosing—
The one is winning, and the other losing.

This hedonism of the imagination—it characterizes all three of the later romantics, as Arthur Henry Hallam was soon to observe—is what Byron calls "The grand antithesis" to everything in his life and world which seems debased (*Don Juan*, Canto XV, st. 2). His poetic escape into immediacy is an aesthetic and critical move for "seeing matters which are out of sight" (ibid.):

I

Ah!—What should follow slips from my reflection:
   Whatever follows ne'ertheless may be

As apropos of hope or retrospection,
  As though the lurking thought had follow'd free.
All present life is but an Interjection,
  An "Oh!" or "Ah!" of joy or misery,
Or a "Ha! ha!" or "Bah!"—a yawn, or "Pooh!"
Of which perhaps the latter is most true.

(*Don Juan* xv.1)

A latent cynicism and despair—the "lurking thought" behind these lines—sharpens the verse to a fine edge. Byron's attack upon the Europe of Napoleon, Metternich, and Castlereagh is made possible because he agrees in his poetry to "become what he beholds." His abandoned and sensational poetry is the reflex of the civilization which created the necessity for such a style of life and art. The poetry triumphs in its hedonism, however, whereas the objective world which it mirrors merely suffers and inflicts. The difference is a function of the reflexive (in both senses) capacity of verse. The poetry supplies a reflection of the world (as we commonly say), but the image is generated from the poetry's "reflex" or response to that world and its own act of observation. In this way the poetry draws itself into the world it is "reflecting." The process forces the poetry to become what it beholds, to translate its observations (via the images) into equivalent emotional signs, and finally to open itself to further acts of self-conscious "reflection" in (and upon) the poetry itself.

A paradox lies at the heart of Byron's sensationalism which we can begin to approach through Shelley. In his "Defense of Poetry" Shelley attacked his age for its selfishness and calculation on the one hand, and on the other for the refusal of its people to reflect upon the meaning of their forms of life:

> We have more moral, political, and historical wisdom, than we know how to reduce into practice; we have more scientific and economical knowledge than can be accommodated to the just distribution of the produce which it multiplies. The poetry in these systems of thought, is concealed by the accumulation of facts and calculating processes. . . . Our calculations have outrun conception; we have eaten more than we can digest. The cultivation of those sciences which have enlarged the limits of the empire of man over the external world, has, for want of the poetical faculty, proportionally circumscribed those of the internal world; and man, having enslaved the elements, remains himself a slave.[11]

When Shelley in another part of this passage urges his readers to imagine what they know, his plea is for an act of sympathetic and critical reflection. The fool persists in his folly to gain wisdom, and poetry is an especially useful vehicle for such a project.

The subject of Byron's poetry is the world which Shelley had in mind in the passage above. This is the environment which they, along with their contemporaries, were "doomed to inflict or bear" (*CHP* III, st. 71). The grand illusion of romantic *ideology* is that one may escape such a world through imagination and poetry. The great truth of romantic *work* is that there is no escape, that there is only revelation (in a wholly secular sense):

> The race of life becomes a hopeless flight
> To those that walk in darkness: on the sea,
> The boldest steer but where their ports invite,
> But there are wanderers o'er Eternity
> Whose bark drives on and on, and anchored ne'er shall be.
>
> (*CHP* III, st. 70)

What is most stirring about this great passage is the "lurking thought" of pity and despair. Imagination and poetry do not offer a relief and escape but a permanent and self-realized condition of suffering, a Romantic Agony. The "hopeless flight" of "those that walk in darkness" is not removed when that flight becomes an eternal one; on the contrary, the hopelessness is raised to a pitiful and tragic level precisely because the Pilgrim of Eternity no longer has any illusions about the human world he sees, no longer has any illusions about himself. The Romantic Imagination does not save, it offers, like Keats's Moneta, a tragic understanding. And for the romantic poet, the best and worst knowledge it brings is the critique of the ideology upon which romantic poetry is itself founded. The judgment which it passes upon its world is therefore always justified—if it is to be justified at all—by the depth of the poetry's self-criticism. This is necessarily the case since romantic poetry places the individual at the determining center of the human world.

Like Shelley's meliorism and Keats's aestheticism, Byron's despair is not a philosophic but an experiential datum. We are gripped by Byron's work through the medium of this despair, which becomes an ethical category only after it has first been seized as an aesthetic one. This is why Byron's poetic despair must not be a cause for our critical valuations of his poetic work: despair is not the meaning of his poetry, it is its condition of being, and the poetic reflex of the social and historical realities which it is a part of.

What is true of Byron's work is true of romantic poetry in general. It is a poetry of ideas, of Ideals, and—ultimately—of Ideology, which is why displacements and illusions are its central preoccupations and resorts. Consequently, its greatest moments of artistic success are almost always those associated with loss, failure, and defeat—in particular the losses which strike most closely to the Ideals (and Ideologies) cherished by the poets in their work.

In Keats these moments are typically related to the apparent failures of poetry and the imagination:

> Adieu! the fancy cannot cheat so well
>   As she is fam'd to do, deceiving elf.
> Adieu! adieu! thy plaintive anthem fades
>   Past the near meadows, over the still stream,
>   Up the hill-side; and now 'tis buried deep
>   In the next valley-glades:
>   Was it a vision, or a waking dream?
>   Fled is that music:—Do I wake or sleep?
>   (ll. 73–80)[12]

Of course, Keats's "fancy" has not failed him at all, it has simply refused to submit to the final ideological appropriation which the poem itself had proposed. The displacement efforts of romantic poetry, its escape trails and pursued states of harmony and reconciliation—ultimately, its desire for process and endless self-reproduction ("something evermore about to be")—are that age's dominant cultural illusions which romantic poetry assumes only to weigh them out and find them wanting.

In no poem are all these illusions exposed more terribly than in Keats's epistle commonly known as "To J. H. Reynolds, Esq.," and particularly in the great and famous passage toward the conclusion (ll. 74–105). The passage needs to be recalled in full because of its gradual movement of self-revelation. The experience of Imagination first draws Keats into a malaise of doubt (ll. 74–82), then into a positive experience of immediate dissatisfaction (ll. 82–85), and finally into a terrible vision of what, in his epoch, it would mean for something to be evermore about to be—of what is entailed in the ideology of growth and process:

>   I was at home,
> And should have been most happy—but I saw
> Too far into the sea; where every maw
> The greater on the less feeds evermore:—
> But I saw too distinct into the core
> Of an eternal fierce destruction
> And so from happiness I far was gone.
> Still am I sick of it: and though to-day
> I've gathered young spring-leaves, and flowers gay
> Of periwinkle and wild strawberry,
> Still do I that most fierce destruction see,
> The shark at savage prey—the hawk at pounce,
> The gentle robin, like a pard or ounce,
> Ravening a worm.—
>   (ll. 92–105)

This is the displaced image from "Nature" which represents, and reflects upon, the conditions of life in the world Keats knew. Organic growth and the ideology of process are here graphically analyzed as the illusions which the cultural institutions of the age developed. These illusions attempt to disguise the horror entailed in the maintenance and reproduction of the social structures—of the human life—Keats knew, to hide from the recognition of horror.

The poetics of romanticism supposed that in a dark time the eye might begin to see into the One Life through the Imagination, which would establish a "standard law" for the self-destructive world of one's experience. In making this supposition the poetry became what it beheld: it assumed to itself the most advanced ideology of its culture and it suffered, as a result, the contradictions of such an assumption, the meaning of the ideology. Romantic poetry pursued the illusions of its own ideas and Ideals in order to avoid facing the truths of immediate history and its own Purgatorial blind. Its triumph, and Keats's odes demonstrate this fact as well as any work produced in the period, is discovered when the pursuit is thwarted and interrupted, and finally broken.

When reading romantic poems, then, we have to remember that their ideas—for example, ideas about the creativity of Imagination, about the centrality of the Self, about the organic and processive structure of natural and social life, and so forth—are all historically specific in a crucial and paradoxical sense. In the Romantic Age these and similar ideas are represented as transhistorical—eternal truths which wake to perish never. The very belief that transcendental categories can provide a permanent ground for culture becomes, in the Romantic Age, an ideological formation— another illusion raised up to hold back an awareness of the contradictions inherent in contemporary social structures and the relations they support. As far as romantic poetry is concerned, this General Ideology informs all its work as an implied and assumed premise which takes various forms specific to the particular writers and their circumstances.

Ideas and ideology therefore lie at the heart of all romantic poetry. Its entire emotional structure depends upon the credit and fidelity it gives to its own fundamental illusions. And its greatest moments usually occur when it pursues its last and final illusion: that it can expose or even that it has uncovered its illusions and false consciousness, that it has finally arrived at the Truth. The need to believe in such an achievement, either immediate or eventual, is deeply romantic (and therefore illusive) because it locates the goal of human pursuits, needs, and desires in Ideal space. When Manfred, at the opening of his play, condemns his entire life's pursuit with the maxim "The tree of knowledge is not that of life" he lays open the heart of romantic darkness. His manner of doing so remains, however, profoundly romantic, as we see clearly in the drama's patterns of absolutes and ultimatums. Manfred's last cherished illusion is that he has no illusions

125

left, that he has cleared his mind of its cant and finally knows the whole truth: "that nothing could be known" (*Don Juan* VII, st. 5).

Later scholars and readers have often absorbed the ideological commitments which these works themselves first made. A typical example of such an absorption will take the following form. The critic will trace out a pattern of "poetic development" which will show (say) Keats's or Byron's progress from certain interesting but undeveloped ideas, through various intermediate stages, to conclude in some final wisdom or "achievement."[13] In Keats criticism we recognize this as the twice-told tale of his movement from a testing and tentative commitment to the idea of the creative "fancy" to the final truths which center in ideas like "negative capability" and in poems like "To Autumn." But the fact is that Keats's aesthetic ideas were in constant flux, and they have, in any case, a purely circumstantial relation to the development of his artistic skill or the production of his artistic work. Ideas and Ideology are important for Keats's work because they help to define the concrete and specific character of different poems, and because they help to provide those poems with the terms (the images) in which their emotional dramas are played out. For Keats's poetry, the idea of negative capability is no more advanced *as an idea* than is the idea of the creative fancy. Rather, it locates a certain (as it were) psychological stage of Keats's poetic career, a special focus for the agony and strife of the human hearts he studied. Out of the advancement and the critique of this and similar ideas Keats was able to fashion some of his greatest works; at the same time, the idea itself has been frequently debased in its critical representation. Literary criticism too often likes to transform the critical illusions of poetry into the worshipped truths of culture.

Romantic poetry presents its contradictions at the level of consciousness and as ideology, and the revelation of the contradictions takes the typical form of an immediate experience. Contradictions are *undergone* in romantic poems, necessarily, because the ideology which informs their styles involves the supreme illusion of the transhistorical privilege of poetry and the creative imagination. This is why romantic poets like Keats appear to suffer in and through their work, and why Keats could call a reading of *King Lear* "the fierce dispute / Betwixt damnation and impassion'd clay" ("On Sitting Down to Read *King Lear* Once Again," ll. 5–6). The writing and the reading of poetry in a romantic style involves the emotional experience of contradiction at the level of consciousness and in the form of romantic ideology. This is what Shelley's famous passage on the nature of romantic experience *means*:

> Most wretched men
> Are cradled into poetry by wrong,
> They learn in suffering what they teach in song.
> ("Julian and Maddalo," ll. 544–46)

126

Shelley's presentation of the tensions and contradictions which typify romantic poems seems preferable to the formulations of much contemporary criticism, because Shelley's verse has fewer illusions about the truths it speaks of. Famous passages like the one just quoted should remind us that in romantic poems the tensions and contradictions appear as experiences to be undergone, as a drama of suffering. Furthermore, the power of such a drama has little to do with the "delight" of a happily discovered truth.[14] On the contrary, it is either an awesome and fearful experience before which one "trembles like a guilty thing surprised," or it is the terrible knowledge of "those to whom the miseries of the world / Are misery, and will not let them rest" ("The Fall of Hyperion," ll. 148–49). Romantic poets, insofar as they are like men speaking to men, are no different from most human beings, and do not find much pleasure in having their most cherished illusions unmasked, and themselves left at the edge of defenselessness. The literary criticism of romantic works will justify itself, therefore, when it is seen to have followed the example of the poetry itself.

IV

I should like to conclude this essay with an illustrative case from Byron, partly because I have been to some extent responsible for perpetuating certain misconceptions about his work, and partly because Byron's late achievements can sometimes appear to have transcended his own romantic illusions. The "poetic development" of Byron which I argued in *Fiery Dust* now seems to me a most misleading critical formulation.

Like all romantic poetry, Byron's work is deeply self-critical, but only as a drama in which its own illusions must be suffered. To achieve this effect requires, therefore, that the illusions be embraced and advanced. So it is with Byron. From his earliest to his latest work he cherished the idea (or the hope) that he could stand above or beyond the contradictions of his age: not merely a "grand Napoleon of the realms of rhyme" (*DJ* xi, st. 55) but a superb *Citoyen du Monde* who could survey, as from "a tower upon a headlong rock" (*CHP* iii, st. 41), the world of dispute and turmoil below. The grand and pitiful illusion reached its most extreme form in *Don Juan*, where Byron sought to establish his self-sufficiency and power through a comic panorama of the world's folly, evil, and self-deceptions. His last resort from his own illusions was to declare that he was the most disillusioned of mortals—the *Être Suprême* of human detachment who could at last take God's laughter over from Milton.

The romanticism of *Don Juan* appears as the repeated collapse of this assault upon detachment. The failures of love, the fragility of whatever seems most to be cherished (beauty, innocence, courage, justice), the persistence of surplus evils like indifference, cruelty, war, religion, and state power:

all these things drove Byron out of his disillusioned fastnesses and retreats to suffer the conflict of his feelings. One immediately recognizes such eventualities in the stories of Julia and Haidée, in Byron's rage at his age's special thrones (the Church) and principalities (the States), in his horror at the power of circumstances over human beings (the shipwreck of Canto II) and the blind persistence of cruel practices (the Siege of Ismail). But most moving of all, perhaps, is Byron's loss of detachment in the English cantos. From Canto XI to the poem's interrupted conclusion Byron returns to the world of Regency England where his own fame was born. It is, of course, the easiest of targets for Byron, whose knowledge of that "paradise of pleasure and ennui" (*DJ* XIV, st. 17) was intimate and wide. So his satire unrolls itself in a splendid variety of styles which extend from the broadest ironic humor to the most subtle comic revelations, such as in Canto XVI when Juan descends to breakfast after his night encounter with the ghost of the Black Friar.

The comedy and satire of the English cantos, however—so cool and so urbane—rests upon a series of contradictory emotional involvements which threaten to break through at any point, and which do so repeatedly. We observe such a moment at the outset of the English cantos, in Canto XI, where Byron's art of memory stirs up a range of complex and contradictory emotions. In stanzas 55–63, for example, when Byron surveys the recent history of English poetical fashions, his status as the world-famous expatriate bard permits him to assume an amused pose of unruffled detachment. As he begins his commentary on the literary scene of that tight little island Byron seems all coolness and superiority.

<blockquote>

55

In twice five years the "greatest living poet,"
  Like to the champion in the fisty ring,
Is called on to support his claim, or show it,
  Although 'tis an imaginary thing.
Even I—albeit I'm sure I did not know it,
  Nor sought of foolscap subjects to be king,—
Was reckoned, a considerable time,
The grand Napoleon of the realms of rhyme.
</blockquote>

Ensconsed in the treasure-house of such brilliant and witty poetry,[15] Byron can smile at his own folly from a throne of self-assurance. But as the period of his memory shifts between the present and the recent past, between 1814 and 1822, the tone also slips and shifts.

<blockquote>

56

But Juan was my Moscow, and Faliero
My Leipsic, and my Mount Saint Jean seems Cain:
</blockquote>

128

"La Belle Alliance" of dunces down at zero,
    Now that the Lion's fall'n, may rise again:
But I will fall at least as fell my hero;
    Nor reign at all, or as a *monarch* reign;
Or to some lonely isle of Jailors go
With turncoat Southey for my turnkey Lowe.

Here the larger truth begins to emerge, that Byron is still deeply involved, emotionally, in the pursuit of that "imaginary thing." His comparison of this ridiculous pursuit to a pugilist's ambition—the quest for the championship of poetry, as it were—underscores his consciousness of the absurdity of these things. That it is all ludicrous, even pathetic, is very clear; that he has not given any of it over is, however, no less apparent, to himself and us alike. Byron's poetic awareness that his own assumed detachment is actually no more than a new form of desired superiority drives his verse into a dazzling sequence of stanzas whose most remarkable feature is their complex emotional shifts and contradictions.

62

This is the literary *lower* Empire,
    Where the Praetorian bands take up the matter;—
A "dreadful trade," like his who "gathers samphire,"
    The insolent soldiery to soothe and flatter,
With the same feelings as you'd coax a vampire.
    Now, were I once at home, and in good satire,
I'd try conclusions with those Janizaries,
And show them *what* an intellectual war is.

63

I think I know a trick or two, would turn
    Their flanks;—but it is hardly worth my while
With such small gear to give myself concern:
    Indeed I've not the necessary bile;
My natural temper's really aught but stern,
    And even my Muse's worst reproof's a smile;

Such are Byron's illusions—thoroughly to be despised, but never to be forsaken. Stanza 63 is perhaps especially remarkable. Here Byron closes out this part of his digression and appears to recover some of his initial detachment. In reality, the pose has only been further unmasked and the reader is left to wonder at the depth and persistence of Byron's self-deceptions.

This is the drama of romantic poetry where one becomes what one beholds, where education must be suffered through, where every poet is an

Appolyon who must be pierced with his own weapon. The splendid stanzas toward the conclusion of Canto XI, where Byron raises up a series of Pictures from the Gone World of 1814, reinforce and culminate the significance of the canto which introduces the final long episode of *Don Juan*.

76

> "Where is the world," cries Young, "at *eighty*? Where
>   The world in which a man was born?" Alas!
> Where is the world of *eight* years past? *'Twas there*—
>   I look for it—'tis gone, a Globe of Glass!
> Cracked, shivered, vanished, scarcely gazed on, ere
>   A silent change dissolves the glittering mass.
> Statesmen, chiefs, orators, queens, patriots, kings,
> And dandies, all are gone on the wind's wings.

78

> Where's Brummell? Dished. Where's Long Pole Wellesley?
>   Diddled.
>   Where's Whitbread? Romilly? Where's George the Third?
> Where is his will? (That's not so soon unriddled.)
>   And where is "Fum" the Fourth, our "royal bird"?
> Gone down it seems to Scotland to be fiddled
>   Unto by Sawney's violin, we have heard:

What, we wonder, is Byron doing in this lament over the passage of such a world, whose triviality he sees perfectly well? Is this what we should expect from the Pilgrim of Eternity? Is this the place, as Heine might say, to lament the Regency?

The answer, of course, as we are all aware, is "yes." This is the place, and this is precisely what we must expect, for the pilgrim shuffles along through this passage as surely as he marched across Italy. The pathos, even the tragedy, of his progress is perhaps more profound here in *Don Juan* than it was in *Childe Harold's Pilgrimage*. For here the whole truth emerges with an almost unbearable clarity: that whenever Byron says "I have not loved the world, nor the world me" (*CHP*, Canto III, st. 113) he is uttering a desperate and piteous lie. The truth is that he has loved it much too long and far too well, and that in this love his illusions (which are part of his loves) have always been threatened with collapse. Byron's poetry is born in the conflict of love and illusion, in the contradictions which are a necessary part of that conflict.

Here at the end of Canto XI the pity of those contradictions approaches a tragic level because here we see that Byron's illusion of detachment is utterly imaginary.

79

Where is Lord This? And where my Lady That?
  The Honourable Mistresses and Misses?
Some laid aside like an old opera hat,
  Married, unmarried, and remarried: (this is
An evolution oft performed of late).
  Where are the Dublin shouts—and London hisses?
Where are the Grenvilles? Turned as usual. Where
My friends the Whigs? Exactly where they were.

80

Where are the Lady Carolines and Franceses?
  Divorced or doing thereanent. Ye annals
So brilliant, where the list of routs and dances is,—
  Thou Morning Post, sole record of the pannels
Broken in carriages, and all the phantasies
  Of fashion,—say what streams now fill those channels?

He has triumphed over nothing, been superior to nothing—not even to that "Globe of Glass" the Regency, or all those "Lady Carolines and Franceses."[16] Rather, Byron has been in love and he has loved what vanishes. Here at the outset of the final movement of *Don Juan* he parades before us the touching tableau of his emotional commitments, and all those butterflies he has loved and hated, sought and scorned. Their images arrest our attention and focus our sense of the contradictions involved in this poetry.

What is easiest to miss in this passage, however, is Byron's greatest love of all, the deep truth to which he has been committed but which has always remained imageless in his, as in all, romantic poetry. That is to say, what we can miss are Byron's romantic illusions, the ideas and the ideologies which lead him into a disclosure of his world's contradictions by tempting him to believe that that they can be transcended in imaginative thought, "our last and only place / Of refuge" (*CHP*, Canto IV, st. 127). In the end Byron's poetry discovers what all romantic poems repeatedly discover: that there is no place of refuge, not in desire, not in the mind, not in imagination. Man is in love and love's what vanishes, and this includes—finally, tragically—even his necessary angels.

Notes

1 This essay has been culled from several different sections of a newly completed book on English Romanticism where the topics are handled in greater detail. A series of recently published or soon to be published essays take up the critical and methodological issues in relation to particular authors and topics which have seemed to me especially important. See, for example, "Keats and the Historical Method in Literary Criticism," *Modern Language Notes* 94 (1979), 988–1032;

"The Text, the Poem, and the Problem of Historical Method," *New Literary History* 12 (1981), 269–88; "The Anachronism of George Crabbe," *English Literary History* 48 (1981), 555–72; "The Meaning of the Ancient Mariner," *Critical Inquiry* 8 (Autumn, 1981), 35–67.
2 Galvano Della Volpe, *Critique of Taste* (London: New Left Books, 1979), trans. Michael Caesar.
3 My text for this poem is James Butler's critical edition, *The Ruined Cottage and The Pedlar* (Ithaca, N.Y.: Cornell U. Press, 1979). The most comprehensive discussion of the poem can be found in Jonathan Wordsworth's *The Music of Humanity* (New York: Harper and Row, 1969).
4 *Ibid.*, p. 4.
5 Marjorie Levinson, "Insight and Oversight: A Reading of 'Tintern Abbey,'" unpublished manuscript essay.
6 From K. N. Cameron's "The Social Philosophy of Shelley," reprinted in Donald H. Reiman and Sharon Powers, eds., *Shelley's Poetry and Prose* (New York: W. W. Norton 1977), p. 516. All extracts from Shelley are taken from this edition.
7 Richard Holmes, *Shelley. The Pursuit* (London: Dutton, 1974), p. 617.
8 From the "Preface" to *Prometheus Unbound*.
9 The critical analysis of European philhellenism has yet to be made. But much excellent work has been produced describing this phenomenon. See Terence Spencer, *Fair Greece, Sad Relic* (London: Weidenfeld and Nicholson, 1954); William St. Clair, *That Greece Might Still Be Free* (Oxford: Oxford U. Press, 1972); and Harry Levin, *The Broken Column* (Cambridge, Mass.: Harvard U. Press, 1931).
10 The *Childe Harold* references are cited from *Lord Byron. Complete Poetical Works*, ed. Jerome J. McGann (Oxford: Clarendon Press, 1980), Vol. 2; the *Don Juan* passages are taken from *Byron's Don Juan. A Variorum Edition*, ed. T. G. Steffan and W. W. Pratt (Austin, Tex.: U. of Texas Press, 1957).
11 *Shelley's Prose*, ed. David Lee Clark (Albuquerque, N.M.: U. of New Mexico Press, 1954), p. 286.
12 My Keats texts are all taken from *The Poems of John Keats*, ed. Jack Stillinger (Cambridge, Mass.: Harvard/Belknap, 1978).
13 From my own point of view, this critical representation is most to be deplored in a book like *Fiery Dust. Byron's Poetic Development* (Chicago: U. of Chicago Press, 1968); and see below, section IV, for further discussion.
14 I have in mind here some of the most common formulations to be found in recent academic criticism. These matters are taken up in detail in the book from which this essay has been put together.
15 The wit of such passages—they are characteristic of Byron's poem—is a function of the interplay between certain crucial puns (like "imaginary" and "foolscap subjects") on the one hand, and a series of specific social and historical references on the other. The brilliance of such verse requires that the reader be able to enter and share in this social consciousness which the poem calls up.
16 For readers not familiar with Byron's life, I should point out that the phrase "the Lady Carolines and Franceses" is peculiarly pointed, since it deliberately sets forth a cultural generalization that is based upon the highly particular experience of one person. In his own amatory relations with Lady Caroline Lamb and Lady Frances Wedderburn Webster Byron finds a means for seeing poetically into the essential life of an entire age, and of establishing a trenchant view into its cultural formations.

24

'A SYMPATHY WITH POWER': IMAGINING ROBESPIERRE

Nicholas Roe

Source: *Wordsworth and Coleridge: The Radical Years* (Oxford: Clarendon Press, 1988), pp. 199–233.

Wordsworth's 'hymn of triumph'

> O friend, few happier moments have been mine
> Through my whole life than that when first I heard
> That this foul tribe of Moloch was o'erthrown,
> And their chief regent levelled with the dust.
>
> (*P*. x. 466–9)

So Wordsworth tells Coleridge of his feelings when he heard of the death of Robespierre in summer 1794, while crossing the Leven Sands. 'Great was my glee of spirit, great my joy', he recalls. Coleridge's reaction to the news was different. He immediately collaborated with Southey on a tragedy, *The Fall of Robespierre*, and he continued to explore Robespierre's character and motives in his political lectures of 1795. Coleridge's interest in Robespierre was shared by John Thelwall, and both agreed that William Pitt wanted Robespierre's political acumen. Coleridge went further, though, and used Robespierre as a foil in his developing idea of the imagination during 1795–6. When he wrote about Robespierre's death in *The Prelude* Wordsworth knew that Coleridge had not shared his feelings at the time, and that his friend's complex response to the Jacobin leader was ultimately of the greatest importance to himself.

As remembered in Book Ten, Robespierre perished 'by the might | of [his] own helper', in confirmation of Wordsworth's own vision of cyclical and self-consuming violence,

> 'Year follows year, the tide returns again,
> Day follows day, all things have second birth'
>
> (x. 72–3)

—hence his 'hymn of triumph', his sense of personal vindication: '"Come now, ye golden times" | Said I.' But the 'golden times' did not come immediately. France did not recover the revolutionary idealism of former years, and no longer provided a model for political and social change in Britain. Despite his 'hymn of triumph' and apparently renewed confidence in the future, the Terror marked the end of Wordsworth's belief in revolution as a means to political and social regeneration. Between 1794 and 1795 he found compensation in *Political Justice*, until that too led him to the 'moral despair' recalled in Book Ten.

In *The Prelude* Wordsworth claims that

>   then it was
> That thou, most precious friend, about this time
> First known to me, didst lend a living help
> To regulate my soul.
>
>   (x. 904–7)

Coleridge and Wordsworth first met at Bristol in late August or September 1795, but they had no obvious mutual influence until two years later. Nevertheless, Wordsworth deliberately presents Coleridge as a redeeming figure in Book Ten, the successor to his schoolmaster and poetic mentor, William Taylor, whose grave Wordsworth visited on the day he had heard of Robespierre's execution back in August 1794. When Wordsworth reminded Coleridge of that day, he did so in the knowledge that Robespierre's downfall was a threshold to their early meetings and mutual commitment to poetry in June 1797. Looking back, his 'hymn of triumph' over Robespierre was also an anthem to the 'golden times' at Racedown and Alfoxden, then three years in the future.

'Excess of glory obscured': Robespierre, Pitt, and Godwin

Many years after the French Revolution, William Godwin looked back to the time when he had 'blazed as a sun in the firmament of reputation' as the author of *Political Justice*. For Godwin 1794 was memorable not for the Terror in France and the execution of Robespierre, but for the treason trials in London, 'an attempt to take away the lives of men by a constructive treason, & out of many facts no one of which was capital, to compose a capital crime—the name of the man in whose mind the scheme of this trial was engendered was Pitt—'.[1] He was recalling the moment when his demolition of the charge of 'constructive treason' in *Cursory Strictures* had enhanced his notoriety and made him a hero of the reform movement. In Book Ten of *The Prelude* Wordsworth also remembers the government's 'attempt to take away the lives of men' by perverting the forms and rule of law. 'Our shepherds', he says,

> at that time
> Thirsted to make the guardian crook of law
> A tool of murder
>
> (x. 645–7)

—and this memory, in turn, recalls his nightmare dreams of the massacres at Paris earlier in Book Ten,

> Such ghastly visions . . . of despair,
> And tyranny, and implements of death . . .
>
> (x. 374–5)

The implied similarity between the British 'tool of murder' and French 'implements of death' was deliberate. Unlike Godwin, Wordsworth did not believe that the scheme of the treason trials had been 'engendered' in Pitt's mind. Pitt had no capacity for originality; he was an imitator, and a foolish one at that,

> Though with such awful proof before [his] eyes
> That he who would sow death, reaps death, or worse,
> And can reap nothing better, childlike longed
> To imitate—not wise enough to avoid.
>
> (x. 648–51)

The 'awful proof' Wordsworth had in mind was the violent repression in France, which culminated in Robespierre's death on 28 July 1794. In spite of this example the British government had persisted in 'composing a capital crime', as Godwin put it, and charged the reformists with treason. In Book Ten, Wordsworth draws a direct analogy between the 'unjust tribunals' of Paris and those at the Old Bailey, and also implies that by 'sowing death' like Robespierre the British government would have risked a similar downfall.

Wordsworth's recollection of the treason trials in *The Prelude* was written during August 1804, exactly ten years after the event. The date is important, for his portrayal of Pitt and his government as imitators of Robespierre has a curious link with work on the last seven stanzas of 'Ode'—'Intimations'— in spring of the same year. In stanza seven of his 'Ode' Wordsworth had described the four-year-old child's restless urge to imitate, 'fit[ting] his tongue'

> To dialogues of business love or strife
> But it will not be long
> Ere this be thrown aside
> And with new joy and pride
> The little actor cons another part

Filling from time to time his humourous stage
With all the persons down to palsied age
That Life brings with her in her Equipage
As if his whole vocation
Were endless imitation.[2]

(ll. 97–107)

The child's 'joy and pride' at adopting a succession of adult roles is ironic, for the 'earnest pains' of his imitation hasten the loss of his own childhood and draw him to the 'prison-house' of adult life. In *The Prelude*, Book Ten, though, Wordsworth's 'little actor' is William Pitt; his wilful 'conning the part' of Robespierre leads—literally—to the prison-houses of Newgate and the Tower. The child in the 'Ode' impatiently throws aside one 'part' to adopt another, innocently aware that he is at strife with himself. Pitt, on the other hand, had only one vocation: to imitate the man whose execution should have stood as a warning example,

Though with such awful proof . . . childlike longed
To imitate—not wise enough to avoid.

The idea of Pitt as a perverse child is peculiar to Wordsworth in 1804, but he was not alone in interpreting the British repression as an imitation of the Terror in France. Besides recalling the child from 'Intimations', the passage from *The Prelude*, Book Ten, was almost certainly influenced by Wordsworth's reading of *Conciones* and also, perhaps, by John Thelwall's *Tribune*. In 1795 Coleridge and Thelwall agreed that Pitt was in every way inferior to Robespierre; furthermore, their attitudes to Robespierre himself also closely coincided.

On 23 May 1795 the *Tribune* contained Thelwall's third lecture on 'The Prospective Principle of Virtue', which drew upon his reading of *Political Justice*. Wordsworth was in London at this time and, given his friendship with Godwin and his democratic politics, he may well have been among the audience at Beaufort Buildings when Thelwall made a sustained 'comparison between the character of Robespierre and the immaculate minister of this country' (*Tribune*, i. 254). Thelwall argued that the arrests of 1794, the suppression of Habeas Corpus, the charges and trials were a policy of terrorism copied from the French, in the hope of suppressing all opposition to the government. 'I will ask you', Thelwall said,

what might have been the situation of this country, if the late prosecutions had succeeded? . . . who knows, when you once begin a system of massacre, and especially *legal* massacre, for opinion, where you can stop? I do not believe that *Robespierre* meditated, in the first instance, those scenes of carnage into which he at last was plunged. . . . I have strong suspicions in my mind, that, if they had touched the life of an individual who stood at the bar of the Old Bailey, the gaols of London (and we all know we have abundance) would have been as crammed as ever the prisons of Paris were, even in the very dog-days of the tyranny of Robespierre.

(*Tribune*, i. 258)

Since Thelwall's life had depended on the outcome of 'the late prosecutions' his suspicions were understandable, and were shared by others as well. The government had been frustrated by the acquittals at the Old Bailey, and Thelwall developed his argument further by attacking Pitt as an unsuccessful imitator of Robespierre. He outlined their political characters, but to the disadvantage of

> that Minister who, without the energy of Robespierre, has all his dictatorial ambition; who, without the provocations which Robespierre and his faction experienced, has endeavoured, vainly endeavoured, to carry into execution the same system of massacre for opinion, of sanguinary prosecution for proclaiming truth, of making argument High Treason, and destroying every individual who dared to expose his conduct, or oppose his ambitious views.
>
> (*Tribune*, i. 254)

Thelwall damns Pitt for endeavouring to execute a 'system of massacre for opinion', and—ironically enough—for failing to succeed in his ambition. At the same time, he almost acquits Robespierre who had introduced his system of terror after 'provocations'. The provocation Thelwall had in mind was the European coalition against France, which he believed had encouraged the leaders of the republic to adopt extreme and violent policies. In *The Prelude* Wordsworth makes an identical point,

> And thus beset with foes on every side,
> The goaded land waxed mad
>
> (x. 311–12)

—and at the end of his lecture 'On the Present War' in *Conciones* Coleridge takes the argument full circle by identifying Pitt, not Robespierre, as ultimately responsible for the Terror in France:

> It was a truth easily discovered, a truth on which our Minister has proceeded, that valour and victory would not be the determiners of this War. *They* would prove finally successful whose resources enabled them to hold out the longest. The commerce of France was annihilated . . . Immense armies were to be supported . . . Alas!

Freedom weeps! The Guillotine became the Financier-General.—
That dreadful pilot, Robespierre, perceived that it would at once
furnish wind to the sails and free the vessel from those who were
inclined to mutiny.—Who, my Brethren! was the cause of this guilt,
if not HE, who supplied the occasion and the motive?

(*Lects. 1795*, p. 74)

One month after Britain joined the war against France the patriot
armies under General Dumouriez were defeated at Neerwinden in Holland,
while the simultaneous rebellion in the Vendée put the republic at risk
from within. Coleridge's analysis of the financial ruin caused by maintaining
large armies at a time when war sapped commerce and trade was insightful.
Throughout 1793 inflation and the shortage of goods meant that prices
rose steeply, adding in turn to unrest at Paris and elsewhere in the country.
In response, the National Convention sought to consolidate the powers of
central government. Representatives were sent to the armies and into the
provinces to bolster revolutionary enthusiasm, recruit soldiers, and root
out counter-revolutionaries. The Revolutionary Tribunal was set up at Paris,
and on 6 April the Committee of Public Safety was established to direct
executive government and policy. As Coleridge indicated, the machinery
through which the Terror was implemented was set up in spring 1793 as
a response to threats inside, and from outside, the republic. He had substantial grounds for his claim that, by maintaining a war of attrition against
France, Pitt had in fact supplied the 'occasion and the motive' for the
Terror. In 1795 Coleridge and Thelwall agreed that Robespierre had been
'provoked' into violence. At the same time, their need to condemn the
repressive policies of the British government led both to compare Pitt unfavourably with Robespierre. Like their analyses of the immediate causes
of the violence in France, their perceptions of Robespierre's character and
motives are also strikingly similar.

Robespierre's execution was first reported in the London *Times* on 16
August.[3] Six days later Southey wrote to Horace Bedford telling him that,
with Coleridge, he had written 'a tragedy upon [Robespierre's] death in the
space of two days' (Curry, i. 72–3). This 'tragedy' was *The Fall of Robespierre*,
and Southey continued his letter by giving his 'opinion of this great man',
whom he believed had been 'sacrificed to the despair of fools and cowards':

Coleridge says 'he was a man whose great bad actions cast a
dis[astrous] lustre over his name.' He is now inclined to think with
me that the [actions?] of a man so situated must not be judged by
common laws, that Robespierre was the benefactor of mankind and
that we should lament his death as the greatest misfortune Europe
could have sustained . . .

(Curry, i. 73)

Coleridge's idea of Robespierre during 1794–5 was more complex than Southey suggests; in none of his surviving writings does he hail Robespierre as 'the benefactor of mankind', although he may have done so in conversation. Southey's letter does, however, anticipate Coleridge's dedication to the play where he says that he has 'endeavoured to detail . . . the fall of a man, whose great bad actions have cast a disastrous lustre on his name' (*CPW* ii. 495). In the opening speech of the play, Robespierre is described as

> Sudden in action, fertile in resource,
> And rising awful 'mid impending ruins;
> In splendor gloomy, as the midnight meteor,
> That fearless thwarts the elemental war
>
> (*CPW* ii. 496)

—and just visible through the gloom is Milton's 'dread commander' in *Paradise Lost*

> above the rest
> In shape and gesture proudly eminent
> Stood like a tower; his form had yet not lost
> All her original brightness, nor appeared
> Less than archangel ruined, and the excess
> Of glory obscured . . .
>
> (i. 589–94)

Robespierre's awful stature recalls Satan's towering presence, his 'disastrous lustre' the obscured glory of the fallen archangel. Rather than seeing Robespierre as 'the benefactor of mankind' as Southey had done, Coleridge presents him as the heroic rebel undaunted by the ruin brought upon himself. Like Satan he retains traces of his 'original brightness' in his resourcefulness and swiftness to action. Despite the obvious debt to Milton, *The Fall of Robespierre* reveals Coleridge's genuine interest in Robespierre's character and motives, subsequently explored with greater insight in his lectures of 1795. There is also evidence that the similarity between Coleridge's and Thelwall's ideas of Robespierre may have been influenced by Thelwall's reading of the play, providing a first instance of the mutual awareness that developed during 1795.

In late September 1794 five hundred copies of *The Fall of Robespierre* were published at Cambridge by Benjamin Flower. At least 125 copies were sent to London, one hundred to Kearsley the bookseller, and twenty-five to George Dyer (*CL* i. 117). Dyer was a friend of Thelwall's and may have sent a copy to him in the Tower. This would explain what appear to be echoes of Coleridge's play in Thelwall's lecture 'On the Prospective Principle of Virtue':

Robespierre had a soul capacious, an imagination various, a judgement commanding, penetrating, severe. Fertile of resources, he foresaw, created, and turned to his advantage all the events that could possibly tend to the accomplishment of his designs. The mind of Pitt is barren and inflated, his projects are crude, and his views short sighted.

(*Tribune*, i. 259)

Thelwall's lecture develops Coleridge's idea of Robespierre as 'Sudden in action, fertile in resource', into a Machiavellian hero who turns all to his advantage. Thelwall's purpose was to present Pitt in a relatively unfavourable light and he did so by stressing Robespierre's resourceful energy and the quality of his mind. Where Robespierre was vital and creative, Pitt's mind was 'barren and inflated', lifeless and flatulent. Where Robespierre could foresee and manipulate events to his advantage, Pitt was myopic and his politics inept. 'Having viewed these facts,' Thelwall concluded, 'it is impossible to doubt which of these characters we must prefer.'

This lecture was delivered and published in London during May 1795, some eight months after the publication of *The Fall of Robespierre* and almost a year after the death of Robespierre himself. Three months previously, in February 1795, Coleridge had delivered 'three political Lectures' at Bristol (*CL* i. 152). One of these was his *Moral and Political Lecture*, published in February and later expanded to form the 'Introductory Address' to *Conciones* which was published the following December. One of Coleridge's major additions in his 'Introductory Address' was a history of the different factions that had recently held power in France. Like Thelwall, Coleridge emphasizes Robespierre's ruthlessness, but he was also concerned to explore his motives:

Robespierre . . . possessed a glowing ardor that still remembered the *end*, and a cool ferocity that never either overlooked, or scrupled, the *means*. What that *end* was, is not known: that it was a wicked one, has by no means been proved. I rather think, that the distant prospect, to which he was travelling, appeared to him grand and beautiful; but that he fixed his eye on it with such intense eagerness as to neglect the foulness of the road.

(*Lects. 1795*, p. 35)

In the 'Introductory Address' the Machiavellian politician turns visionary, and Coleridge implies that Robespierre might have redeemed himself had his 'grand and beautiful' prospect ever been realized. This idea of Robespierre was probably influenced by Coleridge's reading of his speeches to the National Convention, from which he had already drawn material for *The Fall of Robespierre*. In his major speech on political morality, delivered

5 February 1794, Robespierre defended the original ideals of the French Revolution but countenanced violence as a means of ensuring the rights of man. 'What is the objective toward which we are reaching?' Robespierre asked, and then declared the aim of the Revolution to be 'The peaceful enjoyment of liberty and equality; the reign of that eternal justice whose laws are engraved not on marble or stone but in the hearts of all men, even in the heart of the slave who has forgotten them or of the tyrant who disowns them'.[4] In reaffirming the principles of 1789 Robespierre also defined the 'distant prospect' to which Coleridge refers in his 'Introductory Address'. But within minutes of advocating the 'peaceful enjoyment of liberty and equality', Robespierre claimed that, only by 'sealing our work with our blood, we may witness at least the dawn of universal happiness— this is our ambition, this is our aim'.[5] He then described the 'goadings' and 'provocations' the republic had endured from its enemies:

> Externally all the despots surround you; internally all the friends of tyranny conspire; they will conspire until crime is deprived of all hope. It is necessary to annihilate both the internal and external enemies of the republic or perish with its fall. Now, in this situation your first political maxim should be that one guides the people by reason, and the enemies of the people by terror. . . . Terror is only justice that is prompt, severe, and inflexible; it is thus an emanation of virtue . . .[6]

Robespierre's speech vindicates Coleridge's idea of his contradictory motives, 'His cool ferocity that persuaded murder, | Even whilst it spake of mercy' (*CPW* ii. 516). The abstract bases of Robespierre's 'maxim'— 'reason', 'justice', 'virtue'—also correspond to those of *Political Justice*,

> the philosophy
> That promised to abstract the hopes of man
> Out of his feelings

—and for Coleridge in 1795 this abstraction from human nature was the fundamental weakness of Godwin's system. As I suggested in Chapter 4, an identical realization on Wordsworth's part was one contributing factor in the dissolution of his own faith in *Political Justice*. By invoking 'reason' and 'justice' to excuse terrorism, therefore, Robespierre is another ancestor of Rivers who attempts a similar rational justification of murder in *The Borderers*. In *The Prelude* Wordsworth further identified Robespierre's politics with Godwin's philosophy by using the Terror as an extended and internalized metaphor for the misguided Godwinian 'reasonings' which preceded his work on *The Borderers* in 1796—a point to which I shall return shortly.

Robespierre's 'great bad actions' did not merely challenge Coleridge's and Wordsworth's allegiance to the French Revolution. As Coleridge realized, and as Robespierre's speech shows, the *'end'* that he had in view was true to the ideals of 1789 which had been shared by all good men since. Those ideals were betrayed, though, by the *'means'* he had adopted to realize them. Both Coleridge and Wordsworth discovered in Robespierre an alarming, distorted version of themselves. Although the Terror ceased with Robespierre's death, his shadow endured long afterwards, to be reincarnated by Wordsworth in 1796–7 as Rivers. Coleridge's self-recognition in Robespierre had a formative influence on his idea of imagination in 1795, and ultimately contributed to the 'living help' he was able to offer Wordsworth in 1797.

Coleridge and the politics of imagination

During 1794 the 'rules of political justice' offered Wordsworth and some of his Cambridge contemporaries certainty and guidance at a time when all seemed tending to 'depravation'. As editor of the *Philanthropist* Wordsworth conceived himself as a Godwinian sage and prophet, propagating Godwin's philosophy of necessary progress and passivity to 'establish freedom with tranquillity' (*EY*, p. 124). In 1795 Coleridge assumed an identical role, but for him the only 'gentle words' that might prevent violent revolution were those of religion:

> In that barbarous tumult of inimical Interests, which the present state of Society exhibits, *Religion* appears to offer the only means universally *efficient*. The perfectness of future Men is indeed a benevolent tenet, and may operate on a few Visionaries, whose studious habits supply them with employment, and seclude them from temptation. But a distant prospect, which we are never to reach, will seldom quicken our footsteps, however lovely it may appear; and a Blessing, which not ourselves but *posterity* are destined to enjoy, will scarcely influence the actions of *any*—still less of the ignorant, the prejudiced, and the selfish.
>
> (*Lects. 1795*, pp. 43–4)

Like Thelwall, Coleridge realized that Godwin had neglected the means to achieve his vision of perfectibility. Religion, however, offered the certainty of 'an infinitely great revolution hereafter', simultaneously the establishment of a just society and the promised millennium. This, he believed, might serve as a popular restraint—'Rest awhile | Children of Wretchedness!'—which was exactly how Wordsworth and Thelwall responded to *Political Justice* between 1794–5. But the function of religion was not limited to a palliative for misery. It also comprised a genuine alternative to the bogus prospect of perfection offered by the 'studious visionaries' of the Philomathean Society, the 'dim-eyed Sons of Blasphemy' with whom Wordsworth was connected in 1795. Coleridge's means of attaining that 'distant prospect' was a function of his idea of benevolence, which provided the impetus to progress and perfectibility that he believed *Political Justice* lacked.

In his defence speech to the university court in May 1793, William Frend had listed the principal 'articles of his creed' as a unitarian dissenter. 'We may boast of our knowledge of and acquaintance with god,' Frend had said,

> we may confound every gainsayer on the terms of our salvation, yet, if we neglect the principle of universal benevolence, our faith is vain, our religion is an empty parade of useless and insignificant sounds. That every christian is bound to entertain sentiments of universal benevolence, to love his fellow creatures of every sect, colour or description, is the third grand point of my faith.
>
> (*Account*, pp. 89–90)

For Frend, 'universal benevolence' was the reconciling expression of faith and the foundation of his hope for salvation. From present human love he construed the terms of future regeneration, and this complex idea of benevolence was inherited and developed by Coleridge after 1794. It underlies his idea of Pantisocracy as a *'center'* from which restoration might proceed by assimilation and expansion, and this process was reinforced by Hartley's belief that 'vice originates not in the man, but in the surrounding circumstances' (*Lects. 1795*, p. 12).[7] On these grounds Coleridge could offer a necessary and Christian alternative to Godwin in his 1795 lectures. Ultimately, though, Frend's definition of benevolence as an expansive and regenerative power lies behind Coleridge's evolving idea of imagination during the same year. The contemporary political context and the awful figure of Robespierre were to prompt Coleridge's reformulation of 'the third grand point of [Frend's] faith' in the restless, progressive faculty of imagination.

'It is melancholy to think', Coleridge wrote to George Dyer on 10 March 1795,

> that the best of us are liable to be shaped & coloured by surrounding Objects—and a demonstrative proof, that Man was not made to live in Great Cities! Almost all the physical Evil in the World depends on the existence of moral Evil—and the long-continued contemplation of the latter does not tend to meliorate the human heart.—The pleasures, which we receive from rural beauties, are of little Consequence compared with the Moral Effect of these pleasures —beholding constantly the Best possible we at last become ourselves the best possible. In the country, all around us smile Good and Beauty—and the Images of this divine καλοάαγαθόν are miniatured on the mind of the beholder, as a Landscape on a Convex Mirror.
>
> (*CL* i. 154)

143

Dyer had written complaining of 'languor' and 'illiberal feelings' caused by living in London, drawing Coleridge's comments on the necessary influence of 'surrounding Objects' to moral good or evil. 'God love you, my very dear Sir!', Coleridge continued, 'I would that we could form a Pantisocracy in England, and that you could be one of us!—The finely-fibred Heart, that like the statue of Memnon, trembles into melody on the sun-beam touch of Benevolence, is most easily jarred into the dissonance of Misanthropy' (*CL* i. 155). Coleridge's image of mind as the 'Convex Mirror' of a Claude glass is passive and reflective: the 'finely-fibred Heart', though 'easily jarred', is vital and responsive to 'the sun-beam touch of Benevolence' and becomes a power to moral good in itself. This letter to Dyer reveals Coleridge moving on from the essentially mechanical 'leading idea' of Pantisocracy, 'to make men necessarily virtuous by removing all motives of Evil', to discover a living principle of amelioration in the workings of the 'heart' that he would later attribute specifically to the imagination. This development was also shared by George Dyer early in 1795, and suggests a considerable mutual influence during these months.

Dyer's *Dissertation on the Theory and Practice of Benevolence* was published in March 1795, and contains passages strikingly akin to Coleridge's thinking at this time:

> The GOOD MAN from the appearances of nature derives tender affections, generous principles, and humane conduct. From the glowing and variegated scenes around him he derives something which warms his heart, and throws a smile over his countenance. The imbecility of the beings, to whom by his very nature he is related, does but strengthen his heart, and when he takes a gloomy view of things, the exertions of benevolence raise his spirit. The good man thus acquires universal tenderness.[8]

One might easily mistake this for a passage from one of Coleridge's lectures or letters of 1795. Given Coleridge's friendship with Dyer since August 1794, their correspondence and familiarity with each other's publications, the parallels between the two are perhaps not surprising. Both were concerned to redefine the possibility of progress in a non-political context; Dyer appropriates the contemporary liberal label 'The GOOD MAN' to this end, discarding politics for the benevolent tendency to good in 'the appearances of nature'. A comparable development appears in Coleridge's discussion of 'thinking and disinterested Patriots' in his *Moral and Political Lecture* and the 'Introductory Address' to *Conciones*.

Coleridge's patriots were the reformists Joseph Gerrald, Thomas Muir, Thomas Fysshe Palmer, and Maurice Margarot, all of whom had been tried for sedition during 1793–4 and transported to Botany Bay. In his *Moral and Political Lecture* Coleridge was silent about their political activities as members of reformist societies, and principally concerned to define his ideal of progressive 'intellect':

> These are the men who have encouraged the sympathetic passions till they have become irresistible habits . . . Accustomed to regard all the affairs of man as a process, they never hurry and they never pause; theirs is not that twilight of political knowledge which gives us just light enough to place one foot before the other; as they advance, the scene still opens upon them, and they press right onward with a vast and various landscape of existence around them. Calmness and energy mark all their actions, benevolence is the silken thread that runs through the pearl chain of all their virtues. Believing that vice originates not in the man, but in the surrounding circumstances; not in the heart, but in the understanding; he is hopeless concerning no one . . .
>
> (*Lects. 1795*, p. 12)

The reference to 'sympathetic passions' and the origin of vice in circumstances recall Coleridge's theory of Pantisocracy in 1794; the 'vast and various landscape' corresponds to Dyer's 'glowing and variegated scenes' in his *Dissertation*. Coleridge differs importantly from Dyer, however, in emphasizing onward 'process' and 'advance' within this vibrant landscape; his patriots 'press right onward', he says, with 'calmness and energy' and 'benevolence' as their guiding principle. But, like Godwin in *Political Justice*, Coleridge lacks for the moment any motive to this progress beyond his assertion that true patriots are 'Accustomed to regard the affairs of man as a process'. The patriot 'looks forward with gladdened heart to that glorious period when Justice shall have established the universal fraternity of Love', Coleridge claims, and then adds,

> These soul ennobling views bestow the virtues which they anticipate. He whose mind is habitually imprest with them soars above the present state of humanity, and may be justly said to dwell in the presence of the most high. Regarding every event even as he that ordains it, evil vanishes from before him, and he views with naked eye the eternal form of universal beauty.
>
> (*Lects. 1795*, p. 13)

Here, the working of 'Justice' to 'universal fraternity' is in fact less significant than the patriot's happy anticipation of that state. The emphasis is less on immediate fulfilment than aspiration. The patriot 'looks forward with gladdened heart', his foresight is 'soul ennobling', soaring above quotidian existence to participate 'in the presence of the most high'. Coleridge starts in the twilight world of 'political knowledge' to end with a vision of God, viewing 'with naked eye the eternal form of universal beauty'.

In February 1795 Coleridge followed Price, Priestley, and Frend in identifying political and social regeneration with divine revelation, but he also located the revolutionary motive to progress within the visionary power of the individual mind. At this moment, though, he wanted philosophical support for his claims, as the *Critical Review* pointed out: 'he has not stated, in a form sufficiently scientific and determinate,' the reviewer noted, 'those principles to which, as he expresses it, he now proceeds as the most *important point*' (*Lects. 1795*, p. 2). One of Coleridge's overriding concerns hereafter would be to identify religious and philosophic grounds for certainty, and in *Religious Musings* he would marshal the 'systems' of Hartley, Berkeley, and Priestley to this end. But the *Critical Review* had in fact pin-pointed a fundamental weakness in Coleridge's visionary politics. Ultimately, visionary revelation—'Regarding every event even as he that ordains it'—is not philosophically or rationally 'determinate'. By translating revolutionary 'process' as a function of that revelation, therefore, Coleridge abandoned possible certainty of proof and this disability was one reason for his failure to supply Wordsworth with any coherent philosophic framework for *The Recluse*. More immediately fruitful, however, was his identification of imagination as the focus of his hopes for the amelioration of mankind. A crucial factor in doing so was Coleridge's self-perception in Robespierre.

In their various lectures during 1795 Coleridge and Thelwall both presented Robespierre as a man of vision, although their purposes in doing so were ultimately different. Thelwall claimed Robespierre had a 'capacious' soul, a 'varied' imagination, and that Pitt was in every way his inferior. Coleridge would have agreed, but he found the paradoxes of Robespierre's character and motives equally fascinating. Where Thelwall was content to describe, Coleridge was concerned to analyse. Thelwall's Robespierre was of political significance only, but Coleridge's Robespierre had a direct bearing on his thinking about imagination in 1795. Coleridge's earliest definition of imagination comes at the beginning of his *Lecture on the Slave Trade*, delivered 'by particular desire' on 16 June 1795. 'To develope the powers of the Creator', Coleridge says,

> is our proper employment—and to imitate Creativeness by combination our most exalted and self-satisfying Delight. But we are progressive and must not rest content with present Blessings. Our Almighty Parent hath therefore given to us Imagination that simulates to the attainment of *real* excellence by the contemplation of splendid Possibilities that still revivifies the dying motive within us, and fixing our eye on the glittering Summits that rise one above the other in Alpine endlessness still urges us up the ascent of Being, amusing the ruggedness of the road with the beauty and grandeur of the everwidening Prospect. Such and so noble are the ends for which this restless faculty was given us—but horrible has been its misapplication.
>
> (*Lects. 1795*, pp. 235–6)

This passage foreshadows the definitions of primary and secondary imagination in *Biographia Literaria*, but its seminal significance lies in its immediate implications in 1795 rather than in anticipating Coleridge's position twenty years later. In 'the contemplation of splendid Possibilities that still revivifies the dying motive within us' Coleridge recalled his 'soul ennobling views' that 'bestow the virtues which they anticipate' in *A Moral and Political Lecture*. There, however, he had lacked any explanation for that attainment and his most significant development in his *Lecture on the Slave Trade* was to define imagination as the progressive and God-given power that 'stimulates' to excellence through 'contemplation of splendid Possibilities'. The imagination emerges as the faculty that sustains the dying motive to progress 'up the ascent of being' to reveal—in the end—'the eternal form of universal beauty'. It was this translation of 'splendid Possibilities' from revolutionary politics to the 'restless faculty' of mind that offered Coleridge a counterbalance to disappointment through years when Wordsworth—who had made a parallel investment of hope in *Political Justice*—suffered a period of despair. That transition, in turn, was conditioned by Coleridge's insight into Robespierre's 'horrible misapplication' of imagination during the Terror.

By the end of 1796 Coleridge had identified the cause of Robespierre's downfall in his lack of patience. 'Permit me', Coleridge wrote to John Thelwall on 17 December 1796, 'as a definition of this word to quote one sentence from my first Address, . . . "Accustomed to regard all the affairs of Man, as a Process, they never hurry & they never pause." In his not possessing *this* virtue, all the horrible excesses of Robespierre did, I believe, originate' (*CL* i. 283). Coleridge's definition of patience comes from his discussion of 'thinking and disinterested Patriots', with whom he evidently identified himself, in his 'Introductory Address' and *A Moral and Political Lecture*. Like Robespierre these patriots were distinguished by their foresight and vision, but also for the restraint which he had not possessed. 'Calmness and energy mark all their actions', Coleridge had said in February 1795, while their visionary and progressive intellects identify them as prototypes of his elect in 'Religious Musings',

> Who in this fleshly World . . .
> Their strong eye darting thro' the deeds of Men
> Adore with stedfast unpresuming gaze
> Him, Nature's Essence, Mind, and Energy!
> And gazing, trembling, patiently ascend
> Treading beneath their feet all visible things
> As steps, that upward to their Father's Throne
> Lead gradual . . .
>
> (ll. 52–9)

Robespierre, in comparison, was too presumptuous. He might have belonged among the elect but for the impatience which betrayed his own vision and usurped God's providence. His imagination had slipped the control of love, which alone could have reconciled Robespierre's efforts to the 'distant prospect' he had in view and avoided the excesses of the Terror. As it was, Robespierre remained unregenerate, a patriot manqué, a damaged version of Coleridge himself. In the 'Introductory Address' Robespierre appears as a grotesque parody of the 'disinterested Patriots' and the elect, divided against himself and his country. 'His dark imagination was still brooding over supposed plots against freedom', Coleridge said, '—to prevent tyranny he became a Tyrant—and having realized the evils which he suspected, a wild and dreadful Tyrant. . . . he despotized in all the pomp of Patriotism, and masqueraded on the bloody stage of Revolution, a Caligula with the cap of Liberty on his head' (*Lects. 1795*, p. 35).

Coleridge drew this passage from the first act of *The Fall of Robespierre*. In the 'Introductory Address' the theatrical metaphor works to highlight the contradictory fragments of Robespierre's political personality, a tyrant ruling in the name of liberty. Coleridge coined a new word—'despotize', meaning to act the part of a despot—to define the split in Robespierre's psyche which he attributed to impatience, equivalent for Coleridge to a lack of faith.[9] Not surprisingly, Coleridge found a similar dislocation in *Political Justice*, 'a book which builds without a foundation, [and] proposes an end without establishing the means' (*Lects. 1795*, p. 164), whereas Robespierre 'remembered the *end*' but was unscrupulous about the '*means*' adopted to achieve it (*Lects. 1795*, p. 35). Robespierre's politics and Godwin's philosophy failed to 'develope the powers of the Creator' and were inevitably self-defeating. Robespierre rushed headlong to attain his 'distant prospect', and the spectacle horrified and fascinated Coleridge. At the other extreme was 'dim-eyed' Godwin, the 'studious visionary' who denied the existence of God and passively awaited the triumph of political justice in 'a distant prospect, which we are never to reach'. Coleridge's perception of an underlying similarity between Robespierre and Godwin fed his doubts about the moral effects of *Political Justice* and its popularity among reformists. His deepest fear, I think, was that Godwin's abstract and unprincipled philosophy might lead to political and social breakdown, and ultimately to violence like that witnessed in France. As it turned out, *Political Justice* had a restraining effect upon the reform movement late in 1795, and Coleridge's worries never became a reality. But they did have an imaginative fruition in Wordsworth's *Borderers* and later on in *The Prelude*, Book Ten.

In Book Ten Wordsworth recalls the 'miserable dreams' that he experienced during the Terror:

> Such ghastly visions had I of despair,
> And tyranny, and implements of death,

> And long orations which in dreams I pleaded
> Before unjust tribunals, with a voice
> Labouring, a brain confounded . . .
>
> (x. 374–8)

His night-visions of despair and confusion before those 'unjust tribunals' subsequently reappear in Wordsworth's recollection of his Godwinian speculations about society and human nature. 'Thus I fared', he says,

> Dragging all passions, notions, shapes of faith,
> Like culprits to the bar, suspiciously
> Calling the mind to establish in plain day
> Her titles and her honours . . .
>
> (x. 888–92)

Here Wordsworth is prosecutor, judge, and defendant, divided against himself over the 'bar' of self-inquisition. He is endlessly prevented from reaching a verdict,

> by reasonings false
> From the beginning, inasmuch as drawn
> Out of a heart which had been turned aside
> From Nature by external accidents,
> And which was thus confounded more and more,
> Misguiding and misguided
>
> (x. 883–8)

—in exactly the way that Coleridge believed Robespierre had been confounded by the means he had adopted to save France. With the republic threatened with invasion and rebellion, he had been pushed into terrorism to protect the Revolution: 'And thus beset with foes on every side', Wordsworth says in Book Ten, 'The goaded land waxed mad' (x. 311–12). A little later in the same book, Wordsworth again connects the Terror with his Godwinian thinking by using identical language to define his intellectual confusion. '[M]y mind was both let loose,' he recalls, 'Let loose and goaded'— and the deliberate link with the 'goaded land' is confirmed by these being the only two usages of in 'goaded' in Wordsworth's poetry. 'I took the knife in hand', he continues,

> And, stopping not at parts less sensitive,
> Endeavoured with my best of skill to probe
> The living body of society
> Even to the heart.
>
> (x. 872–6)

149

The guillotine has become a surgeon's knife, and the surgeon is Wordsworth himself performing a grotesque anatomy by vivisection upon the 'living body of society', as Robespierre had sought to purge the internal enemies of France and 'seal our work with our blood'. Through a series of deliberate and striking verbal parallels the madness of the 'goaded land' is internalized as the self-consuming disturbance of Wordsworth's mind,

> now believing,
> Now disbelieving, endlessly perplexed
> With impulse, motive, right and wrong
> (x. 892–4)

—until he 'Yielded up moral questions in despair', bringing ruin upon himself as Robespierre had done. However, Wordsworth's extinction as a Godwinian being carries an intimation of future restoration in its echo of Matthew 27: 50, 'Jesus, when he had cried again with a loud voice, yielded up the ghost'—but the resurrection was to follow. For Wordsworth in *The Prelude* despair gives way to Dorothy's healing presence, Coleridge's friendship, and, under their influence, his own reincarnation as a poet:

> 'Come now, ye golden times',
> Said I, forth-breaking on those open sands
> A hymn of triumph . . .

Book Ten of *The Prelude* imaginatively associates Robespierre's politics with Godwin's philosophy, Wordsworth's confused Godwinian self with the author of the Terror: both 'by the might | Of their own helper [were] swept away' (x. 548–9). Wordsworth wrote this section of *The Prelude* in 1804, but it apparently insists that some realization of the deathly potential of *Political Justice* originally contributed to his moral 'despair'. Moreover, the very nature of that despair seems to have fostered Wordsworth's subsequent receptivity to Coleridge's ideas when they met in June 1797.

In *The Prelude* Wordsworth confounds Robespierre with Satan, 'Chief regent' of the 'foul tribe of Moloch', the serpent that marred the Revolution with violence. But his effort to damn Robespierre momentarily relaxes at one point where he admits that even during the 'rage and dog-day heat' of the Terror he had found

> Something to glory in, as just and fit,
> And in the order of sublimest laws.
> And even if that were not, amid the awe
> Of unintelligible chastisement
> [He] felt a kind of sympathy with power—
> (x. 412–16)

Wordsworth's 'kind of sympathy with power' ironically resembles his 'ready welcome' for *Political Justice* in 1794 as a means to prevent the 'scourge' of violence afflicting Britain (*EY*, p. 124). In *The Prelude* he recalls Godwin's philosophy as an 'unimpeachable' power

> To look through all the frailties of the world,
> And, with a resolute mastery shaking off
> The accidents of nature, time, and place,
> That make up the weak being of the past,
> Build social freedom on its only basis:
> The freedom of the individual mind,
> Which, to the blind restraint of general laws
> Superior, magisterially adopts
> One guide—the light of circumstances, flashed
> Upon an independent intellect.
>
> (x. 820–9)

The 'resolute mastery' and magisterial guidance recall Wordsworth's confident assertion of the 'rules of political justice' in his letter to Mathews of 8 June 1794 (*EY*, p. 124). Four months before Wordsworth wrote that letter, in his speech on political morality Robespierre had made an equally sweeping claim for 'virtue and equality' which he identified as the 'soul of the republic'. Robespierre too had 'shaken off' the frailties of feeling and other 'accidents' of human nature, to present republican virtue as 'a compass to direct you through the tempest of the passions and the whirlwind of the intrigues that surround you. You have the touchstone with which you can test all your laws, all the propositions that are laid before you'.[10] Moments later Robespierre used that 'touchstone' to justify his ruthless equation of terrorism with justice. In *The Prelude* Wordsworth presents *Political Justice* as a similar touchstone, 'to the blind restraint of general laws | Superior': where Robespierre had openly advocated the use of violence, Wordsworth hints darkly at the similar end to which Godwinian rationalism tended. He does so by defining Godwin's philosophy,

> —the light of circumstances, flashed
> Upon an independent intellect

—in words taken from the mouth of a man who would persuade murder. As is well known, these lines originally appeared in *The Borderers* where Rivers congratulates Mortimer for killing Herbert:

> You have obeyed the only law that wisdom
> Can ever recognize: the immediate law
> Flashed from the light of circumstances

151

Upon an independent intellect.
Henceforth new prospects ought to open on you,
Your faculties should grow with the occasion.
(Osborn, p. 210, III. v. 30–5)

However, the 'new prospects' and growing 'faculties' contingent upon
Rivers's 'immediate law' ironically also correspond to the 'ever-widening
Prospect' and restlessly progressive faculty of imagination in Coleridge's
Lecture on the Slave Trade. The anti-Godwinian thrust of Wordsworth's
irony in *The Borderers* lies in the conditional 'ought to open', 'should
grow', and in the immediate context of the play where no 'prospect' appears
except a mutual bond in guilt. In the character of Rivers Wordsworth
had, in fact, realized Coleridge's perception of the similarities between
Godwin's arrogant abstraction and Robespierre's visionary politics. By
working through his doubts about Godwin and political revolution in
The Borderers, Wordsworth effectively cleared his mind of the intellectual
debris of the previous five years. When he completed his play in spring
1797, he was ready to respond to the help and guidance Coleridge could
now bring him. The nature of that help and of Wordsworth's receptivity
to it are revealed, perhaps unexpectedly, by Wordsworth's renewed
interest in mathematics sometime in 1796 and in his portrait of a
misanthropic solitary in 'Lines left upon a Seat in a Yew-tree', which was
composed between April and June 1797 just before Coleridge arrived at
Racedown.

Mathematics, the 'lost man', and Coleridge's 'living help'

What then remained in such eclipse, what light
To guide or chear? The laws of things which lie
Beyond the reach of human will or power,
The life of Nature, by the God of love
Inspired . . .
(*P.* xi. 96–100)

Wordsworth's memory of the 'despair' to which *Political Justice* led him is
also a recollection of self-discovery and renewal that would lead to his
emergence as poet and friend of Coleridge. As I suggested in Chapter 5,
his dissatisfaction with Godwin can be dated from his months in London in
1795; rather than culminating in a single moment of crisis and breakdown,
the process of disillusion extended well over a year and was accompanied by
Wordsworth's search for a philosophical alternative to Godwinian rationalism. In *Prelude* Book Ten this need led Wordsworth, initially, to a return
upon his Cambridge self and a revived interest in mathematics. 'I lost | All
feeling of conviction', he recalls in *The Prelude*,

                          and, in fine,
          Sick, wearied out with contrarieties,
          Yielded up moral questions in despair,
          And for my future studies, as the sole
          Employment of the inquiring faculty,
          Turned towards mathematics, and their clear
          And solid evidence.
                                        (x. 897–904)

The 'evidence' he had in mind was the objective certainty offered by 'the elements | Of geometric science' (vi. 136–7) as a counterpoise to Godwin's legacy of intellectual and moral confusion. Wordsworth's recourse to mathematics at this moment was, literally, a return to basics but it was also the start of his self-reconstitution as a poet. The significance of mathematics in this process is revealed in his recollected fondness for such studies in *Prelude*, Book Six. 'I had stepped | In these inquiries but a little way', he recalls there, but had found 'Enough to exalt, to cheer me and compose' (vi. 137–8, 141). In what follows he explains the power of geometry to sustain and calm, in a passage that has important implications for his post-Godwinian self of 1796. 'I meditated', Wordsworth says,

          Upon the alliance of those simple, pure
          Proportions and relations, with the frame
          And laws of Nature—how they could become
          Herein a leader to the human mind—
          And made endeavours frequent to detect
          The process by dark guesses of my own.
          Yet from this source more frequently I drew
          A pleasure calm and deeper, a still sense
          Of permanent and universal sway
          And paramount endowment in the mind,
          An image not unworthy of the one
          Surpassing life, which—out of space and time,
          Nor touched by welterings of passion—is,
          And hath the name of, God. Transcendent peace
          And silence did await upon these thoughts
          That were a frequent comfort to my youth.
                                        (vi. 143–59)

Here, geometry is recalled as an analytical science of 'Proportions and relations' that correspond with 'the frame | And laws of Nature'. In establishing such certainty, though, geometry also offered intellectual stimulus—'a leader to the human mind'—in Wordsworth's 'meditation' and 'dark guesses of [his] own'. Furthermore the sense of 'permanent and universal sway' afforded by geometry as a manifestation of the mind's 'paramount endowment', constituted an image of transcendent order and power which 'hath the name of, God'. Wordsworth was writing Book Six in spring 1804, and at that moment presented the geometric intellect as correspondent to the 'paramount endowment' assumed by imagination in Book Thirteen, to perceive 'an under-presence, | The sense of God' (xiii. 71–2). The source of his identification of geometry with the visionary imagination can be traced eight years earlier in Wordsworth's 'turn towards mathematics' in 1796, which offers an emergent parallel with Coleridge's experience immediately before his meeting with Wordsworth at Racedown. The evidence, oddly enough, appears through Wordsworth's friendship with Basil Montagu after 1795.

Wordsworth first met Basil Montagu 'by an accident' in London early in 1795; they spent 'some months together' before Wordsworth left for Bristol in August, and Montagu subsequently considered his meeting with Wordsworth 'the most fortunate event of [his] life'.[11] Wordsworth helped Montagu out of certain 'wild' habits, and subsequently took Basil Montagu, Junior, to Racedown leaving his father free to develop his legal career. Their early friendship was encouraged by a mutual admiration for *Political Justice*, although Montagu's personal acquaintance with Godwin apparently dated from July 1795 and flourished during the following autumn and winter after Wordsworth's departure. Godwin's diary shows him to have been frequently in Montagu's company at this time, often with Francis Wrangham and William Mathews present too. Like Wordsworth, Montagu seems to have attended the Philomathean society, Godwin noting on 23 February 1796 'tea Montagu's . . . Philomaths, property' (GD vii), and he sent Wordsworth the second edition of *Political Justice* in March. When Wordsworth visited London the following June, he stayed in Montagu's chambers, and renewed his acquaintance with Godwin on at least four occasions (*EY*, p. 170n.).

By mid-1796, however, Wordsworth's enthusiasm for *Political Justice* had cooled; he told Mathews in March that Godwin's 'second preface' was 'a piece of barbarous writing' and that he had not been encouraged to read any further (*EY*, p. 170). Montagu, on the other hand, seems to have remained a firm Godwinian until summer 1797 when he visited Wordsworth and Coleridge at Stowey (Reed, p. 204). At this time he told Azariah Pinney he no longer agreed 'with Mr. Godwin . . . that all men are Benevolent & Wise & that restrictions are useless':

> If man be benevolent & wise: it certainly is unnecessary that there should be Promises, Gratitude, Restraints, Law, Religion &c: But he is short sighted & selfish, & without these restraints he is a Monster—It is a specious system, it is addressed to the most flattering of the passions: & is not easily refuted, because it requires some knowledge of human nature . . .[12]

154

Montagu's revised opinion of Godwin in 1797 coincided exactly with Wordsworth's and Coleridge's, and undoubtedly reflected their influence. He might well have been thinking of Rivers when he described man 'without restraints' as 'a Monster'; Coleridge had criticized Godwin's ignorance of human nature in his 1795 lectures, and the same realization had fed Wordsworth's doubts about *Political Justice*. Finally, in defining *Political Justice* as 'a specious system . . . addressed to the most flattering of the passions', Montagu anticipates Wordsworth's memory of Godwin's 'flattering dream' in *The Prelude*. Given Wordsworth's and Coleridge's bearing upon Montagu's 'fluctuating opinions on Morals' in 1797, it is significant that among his papers are some sheets that elaborate connections between geometry and imagination. These appear to date from 1796–7 and may possibly represent some 'mathematical' collaboration between Wordsworth and Montagu during these two years, perhaps on Wordsworth's visit to London in June 1796 or Montagu's short stay at Racedown in March 1797 (Reed, pp. 182–5, 194).

Wordsworth's account of 'geometric science' in *The Prelude*, Book Six, anticipates the visionary imagination in Book Thirteen and, ultimately, Coleridge's 'primary imagination' in *Biographia*. Basil Montagu's manuscript scheme for the 'Proper Mode of teaching Geometry' and its relation to the developing imagination of a child, is perhaps closer to Coleridge's idea of 'Creativeness by combination' in his *Lecture on the Slave Trade* and to the 'secondary imagination' in *Biographia*. 'If I am to imagine', Montagu writes,

> *or form an image*, by putting things together in my mind, in an arrangement different from that in which I have beheld them, & thus create a whole which I have not seen, out of parts which I have seen; the distinctness of the original conceptions will be equally subservient to this process. By appealing in this manner to his senses, & making him feel the firmness of the ground on which he treads, one might probably instruct a boy, at an early age, in the elements of Geometry, so as rarely to give him disgust, & frequently great satisfaction.[13]

Montagu argues that geometry would foster 'distinct & deep . . . impressions of sense' in the child, which in turn would feed the imagination or 'power of abstraction'. His theory corresponds to Wordsworth's memory in *The Prelude*, Book Six, that geometry encouraged his own efforts 'to detect | The process by dark guesses of [his] own', leading him also to a sense of 'universal sway'. Although there is no certain evidence to connect Montagu's papers on geometry with Wordsworth's 'turn towards mathematics', their mutual concern with what Montagu termed 'the irresistible force of Mathematical Evidence' suggests its likelihood. Possibly Wordsworth and Montagu were both interested in young Basil's education, and the best method of teaching him mathematics. For both Wordsworth and Montagu, though, the significance of geometry lay in establishing fundamental impressions from which the imaginative 'process' could begin. In outline at least this foreshadows Wordsworth's portrait of the early years of his Pedlar:

> deep feelings had impressed
> Great objects on his mind with portraiture
> And colour so distinct that on his mind
> They lay like substances & almost seemed
> To haunt the bodily sense. He had received
> A precious gift for as he grew in years
> With these impressions would he still compare
> All his ideal stores, his shapes & forms
> And being still unsatisfied with aught
> Of dimmer character he thence attained
> An *active* power to fasten images
> Upon his brain & on their pictured lines
> Intensely brooded even till they acquired
> The liveliness of dreams.
>
> (Butler, p. 341)

Wordsworth substitutes 'deep feelings' for Montagu's 'deep . . . impressions of sense', but the progression from a formative 'substantial impression' to an '*active* power' is essentially the same. As Jonathan Wordsworth says, *The Pedlar* is Wordsworth's most confident statement of the philosophy of One Life, and reflects Coleridge's influence in providing 'a philosophical basis for his response to Nature' (*MH*, pp. 200–1). In doing so Coleridge gave Wordsworth creative access to his own experience; but when he subsequently wrote about the growth of the Pedlar's mind he seems to have drawn upon his idea of the geometric intellect to provide a coherent pattern for that development, while discarding the framework of mathematical theory.

In the Second Book of *The Two-part Prelude*, Wordsworth's concern was to emphasize a comparable continuity and unity of progression in his own mind, and he contrasts the 'false distinctions' created by analytical reason:

> But who shall parcel out
> His intellect by geometric rules,
> Split like a province into round and square? . . .
> Thou, my friend, art one
> More deeply read in thy own thoughts, no slave
> Of that false secondary power by which
> In weakness we create distinctions, then
> Believe our puny boundaries are things

> Which we perceive, and not which we have made.
> To thee, unblinded by these outward shews,
> The unity of all has been revealed . . .
>
> (*1799*, ii. 242–4, 249–56)

Wordsworth's hymn of thanks to his friend and philosophic guide represents a reaction from his mathematical self of 1796, rejecting geometric rules as reductive and divisive and celebrating the revealed 'unity of all'. But, although he presents that self as misguided in *The Two-part Prelude*, his development between 1796 and 1798 suggests the contrary, and that his recourse to mathematics had prepared his receptivity to Coleridge's thinking in the first place.

The Prelude, Book Six, and Montagu's 'Mode of teaching Geometry' indicate that Wordsworth's renewed interest in mathematics had two immediate effects. One was to regain the 'clear | And solid evidence' which Godwinian abstraction had denied him, and was effectively a return upon his own experience and senses, 'making him feel the firmness of the ground on which he [trod]'. Secondly, in those 'elements | Of geometric science' he rediscovered a 'guiding light' for his own 'dark guesses' or insights, now allied once more 'with the frame | And laws of Nature' as 'the rules of political justice' had not been. In this respect mathematics reinforced Dorothy's influence in maintaining a 'saving intercourse | With [his] true self', and that of 'Nature's self' in reviving 'the feelings of [his] earlier life' (x. 914–15, 924). Although not mentioned as such in *The Two-part prelude*, or in Book Ten of the 1805 poem, Wordsworth eventually recognized that geometry held a redemptive possibility, a paradigm of the visionary and creative powers of his own imagination. In 1796 geometry was Wordsworth's intellectual bridge from Godwin to One Life, a further redefinition of revolutionary possibility in the relation of mind to nature. Coleridge enabled Wordsworth to move on from this point, to reformulate his revolutionary and Godwinian solicitude for man as a corollary of his own visionary fondness for nature. Wordsworth's recognition of this potential, just before Coleridge's arrival at Racedown, appears in his 'Lines Left upon a Seat in a Yew-tree'. This poem is also an epitaph for a generation of good men like Coleridge and himself who had lost confidence in politics and *Political Justice*, but without discovering a consoling 'light | To guide [and] chear' as they had done.

The reclusive solitary in Wordsworth's 'Lines' is a study of disappointment exacerbated by a simultaneous awareness of possible—but unattainable—fulfilment:

> —He was one who own'd
> No common soul. In youth, by genius nurs'd,
> And big with lofty views, he to the world

Went forth, pure in his heart, against the taint
Of dissolute tongues, 'gainst jealousy, and hate,
And scorn, against all enemies prepared,
All but neglect: and so, his spirit damped
At once, with rash disdain he turned away,
And with the food of pride sustained his soul
In solitude.—Stranger! these gloomy boughs
Had charms for him; and here he loved to sit,
His only visitants a straggling sheep,
The stone-chat, or the glancing sand-piper;
And on these barren rocks, with juniper,
And heath, and thistle, thinly sprinkled o'er,
Fixing his downward eye, he many an hour
A morbid pleasure nourished, tracing here
An emblem of his own unfruitful life:
And lifting up his head, he then would gaze
On the more distant scene; how lovely 'tis
Thou seest, and he would gaze till it became
Far lovelier, and his heart could not sustain
The beauty still more beauteous. Nor, that time,
Would he forget those beings, to whose minds,
Warm from the labours of benevolence,
The world, and man himself, appeared a scene
Of kindred loveliness: then he would sigh
With Mournful joy, to think that others felt
What he must never feel: and so, lost man!
On visionary views would fancy feed,
Till his eye streamed with tears. In this deep vale
He died, this seat his only monument.

(ll. 12–43)

Like the royalist officer in *Prelude*, Book Nine, the 'lost man' is self-consumed and ruined by his arrogance and 'contempt', and this issues in a sort of diseased paralysis. The officer's sword

> was haunted by his touch
> Continually, like an uneasy place
> In his own body

(ix. 162–4)

—but never drawn from its scabbard. Similarly, the 'Yew-tree' solitary is haunted by his own frustrated powers of intellect and vision, nourishing a 'morbid pleasure' in discovering 'emblem[s] of his own unfruitful life'. Both soldier and solitary are harmless brothers of Rivers in *The Borderers*, the

158

disgruntled intellectual who expresses his contempt in murderous conspiracy. It would be wrong, though, to regard the recluse in 'Lines' simply as a victim of Godwinian rationalism, a desiccated intellect. The poignancy of his isolation stems from his awareness of a genial possibility that is withheld:

> lifting up his head, he then would gaze
> On the more distant scene; how lovely 'tis
> Thou seest, and he would gaze till it became
> Far lovelier, and his heart could not sustain
> The beauty still more beauteous.

His heart responds to the beauteous scene but cannot escape its own solipsism, remaining a 'sordid solitary thing', wanting the power to 'sacred sympathy' of 'Religious Musings'. He is an inarticulate visionary who has withdrawn from 'the world' to exist in a limbo between the potential politics had once seemed to hold and an alternative communion he cannot attain:

> Nor, that time,
> Would he forget those beings, to whose minds,
> Warm from the labours of benevolence,
> The world, and man himself, appeared a scene
> Of kindred loveliness: then he would sigh
> With mournful joy, to think that others felt
> What he must never feel: and so, lost man!
> On visionary views would fancy feed,
> Till his eye streamed with tears.

For George Dyer in 1795, the 'GOOD MAN' had derived 'tender affections, generous principles, and humane conduct' from 'the appearances of nature', a regenerate harmony of 'man, nature, and society' that also harks back to Paine's democracy of 'kindred' in *The Rights of Man*. 'There is no time', Dyer says in his *Dissertation*,

> in which we range with so much advantage to ourselves through the walks of creation, as that, in which we contemplate the character of Benevolence. In whatever point of the universe we take our stand, and to whatever spot we turn our eyes, how fertile and glowing the landscape! In a system so contrived, that one part sheds its influence on, and promotes the harmony of, the other, this cannot be otherwise: There is a kind of voice that speaks through the universe.[14]

Between 1795 and 1796 Coleridge was to offer Dyer's benevolent access to universal harmony as the One Life of 'Religious Musings', Dyer's 'kind of voice' as the omnipresence of God:

'Tis the sublime of man,
Our noontide Majesty, to know ourselves
Parts and proportions of one wond'rous whole:
This fraternises man, this constitutes
Our charities and bearings. But 'tis God
Diffused through all, that doth make all one whole . . .

(ll. 135–40)

Wordsworth's 'lost man' in his 'Lines Left upon a Seat in a Yew-tree' cannot attain this benevolent and fraternizing knowledge of 'God | Diffused through all'. He is similarly unable to connect 'the labours of benevolence' with a transcendent communion in One Life, which was central to Coleridge's and Dyer's political thought and also recalls Frend's defence speech back in 1793: 'if we neglect the principle of universal benevolence, our faith is vain, our religion is an empty parade of useless and insignificant sounds'. For Coleridge in June 1795 'the principle of universal benevolence', the knowledge of 'one wond'rous whole', was a prerogative of the imagination. In Wordsworth's 'Lines' the visionary power appears as a function of 'fancy', although in the didactic conclusion to the poem—possibly added later— Wordsworth identifies 'the holy forms | Of young imagination' as a corrective to his solitary's intellectual pride. One should, perhaps, be careful not to overstress parallels in Coleridge's and Wordsworth's thinking about the politics of imagination and nature between 1795 and 1797, but the similarities are often insistent. As Jonathan Wordsworth pointed out some time ago in *The Music of Humanity*, 'That Coleridge should have evolved a philosophical belief which Wordsworth assimilated is perhaps not very surprising. That he should also have been the first to portray the central Wordsworthian mystical experience is quite extraordinary' (*MH*, p. 193).

It is equally surprising, too, that just before Coleridge's visit to Racedown Wordsworth should have reached a point where he was in need of precisely the intellectual and philosophic guidance that Coleridge could bring him. Coleridge's 'living help' recollected in *The Prelude*, Book Ten, was to provide a vocabulary and philosophy that enabled Wordsworth to articulate his own 'visionary views' as his misanthropic recluse could never do. In giving Wordsworth imaginative access to his own 'mystical experience', Coleridge also allowed him to reconstitute the revolutionary hopes he had first experienced in France during 1792 in the relation of his own mind to

The life of Nature, by the God of love
Inspired

(xi. 99–100)

—and specifically in the act of self-communion celebrated by Coleridge at the end of 'France, an Ode':

Yes! while I stood and gaz'd, my temples bare,
And shot my being thro' earth, sea, and air,
Possessing all things with intensest love,
O Liberty, my spirit felt thee there!

These final lines of Coleridge's 'Ode' are his most confident assertion of the One Life as a redemptive possibility that might replace his former hopes that France would 'compel the nations to be free'. His act of participation and possession is also personal and private, an act of faith. Nevertheless, it was this belief that was to provide the philosophical basis for *The Recluse* as first planned by Coleridge and Wordsworth in spring 1798. Their mutual certainty at this moment explains Wordsworth's initial confidence in the scheme: 'I know not any thing which will not come within the scope of my plan', he told James Webbe Tobin on 6 March (*EY*, p. 212). 'The Ruined Cottage' and 'Pedlar' doubtless made up the '1300 lines' of verse Wordsworth claimed to have completed towards *The Recluse* at this moment. But in 1798 Wordsworth came rather closer to his idea of *The Recluse* as a poem that would reconcile 'Nature, Man, and Society' in a very different work: 'Tintern Abbey'.

Notes

1 A-S Dep. c. 531.
2 Quoted from the text in J. Curtis, *Wordsworth's Experiments with Tradition: The Lyric Poems of 1802* (Ithaca and London, 1971), 167.
3 N. Ascherson (ed.), *The French Revolution; extracts from 'The Times', 1789–1794* (London, 1975), 114–15.
4 P. Beik (trans. and ed.), *The Documentary History of Western Civilisation: The French Revolution* (London, 1971), 278 [cited hereafter as Beik].
5 Beik, p. 279.
6 Beik, p. 283.
7 See Chapter 3 above.
8 Dyer, *Dissertation*, p. 19.
9 See my note, 'Robespierre's Despotism and a word Coined by Coleridge', *N&Q* (Aug. 1981), 309–10.
10 Beik, p. 281.
11 DC MS A/Montagu B/26. 'Basil Montagu's Narrative of the Birth and Upbringing of his son.'
12 Basil Montagu to Azariah Pinney, undated letter watermarked 'Russell & Co 1797', BUL, Pinney Papers, Domestic Box R/3, Miscellaneous papers of Basil Montagu. Montagu refers to his 'residence at Alfoxden', which could be his visit of July–Aug. 1797, or more likely his extended stay the following Nov.–Dec., which would mean the letter was probably written early in 1798. In either case, though, his revised opinion of Godwin dates from summer 1797.
13 BUL, Pinney Papers, Domestic Box R/3. The sheets of comments on the teaching of maths and geometry, undated but watermarked 'E&P1796.' The writing is all in Montagu's hand.
14 Dyer, *Dissertation*, p. 15.

Abbreviations

Account	William Frend, *An Account of the Proceedings in the University of Cambridge against William Frend, M.A.* (Cambridge, 1793).
A-S Dep.	Abinger-Shelley papers, in the Bodleian Library.
Bod.	Bodleian Library, Oxford.
CC	*Collected Coleridge* (Bollingen Series 75; Princeton, NJ, 1969–).
CL	*The Collected Letters of Samuel Taylor Coleridge*, ed. E. L. Griggs (6 vols; Oxford, 1956–71).
CPW	*The Complete Poetical Works of Samuel Taylor Coleridge*, ed. E. H. Coleridge (2 vols; Oxford, 1912).
CUL	Cambridge University Library.
Curry	*New Letters of Robert Southey*, ed. K. Curry (2 vols; New York and London, 1965).
EY	*The Letters of William and Dorothy Wordsworth*, ed. E. de Selincourt, 2nd edn, *The Early Years, 1787–1805*, rev. C. L. Shaver (Oxford, 1967).
GD	William Godwin's MS Diary, in the Abinger-Shelley Deposit at the Bodleian Library.
Lects. 1795	S. T. Coleridge, *Lectures 1795 on Politics and Religion*, ed. L. Patton and P. Mann, *CC* i (Princeton, NJ, 1971).
Osborn	William Wordsworth, *The Borderers*, ed. R. Osborn (Cornell Wordsworth Series; Ithaca, NY, 1982).
P.	William Wordsworth, *The Prelude* (1805); see note on texts.
Reed	M. L. Reed, *Wordsworth: The Chronology of the Early Years, 1770–1799* (Cambridge, Mass., 1967).
Tribune	John Thelwall, *The Tribune* (3 vols; London, 1795–6).

A note on texts

All references to *The Prelude* will be to William Wordsworth, *The Prelude, 1799, 1805, 1850*, ed. J. Wordsworth, M. H. Abrams, and S. Gill (New York, 1979). Quotations will be from the 1805 text unless designated *1979* or *1850*. I have occasionally cited an additional abbreviation, *P.*, to identify quotations from the 1805 *Prelude* where this may not be evident from the context.

Unless indicated otherwise, quotations from Wordsworth's poetry will be from *The Poetical Works of William Wordsworth*, ed. E. de Selincourt and H. Darbishire (5 vols; Oxford, 1940–9), and quotations from Coleridge's poetry will be from *Poems*, ed. J. Beer (London, 1973). Poems by Wordsworth and Coleridge published in *Lyrical Ballads* will be quoted from the text in *Lyrical Ballads, 1798 and 1800*, ed. R. L. Brett and A. R. Jones (London, 1963).

25

COCKNEY COUPLETS: KEATS AND THE POLITICS OF STYLE

William Keach

Source: *Studies in Romanticism* 25 (1986), 182–96.

The focus of this paper—Keats's couplet writing in the *Poems* of 1817 and in *Endymion* of 1818—may seem less than inviting if you take the dim view of this poetry that still prevails. But the conspicuous influence of Leigh Hunt, together with the Tory attacks on Keats's "Cockney style" largely provoked by that influence, make it possible to reconstruct a more detailed political context for this poetry than for any other text or moment in Keats's career. I should acknowledge straightaway that the political implications of Keats's "Cockney style" have been recognized before by (among others) John Hayden, Theodore Redpath, and most recently Jerome McGann.[1] What I want to do is explore one aspect of those implications more intensively, speculating along the way about the difficulties as well as the possibilities of doing so. And I want to suggest that whatever you think about the couplets in *Sleep and Poetry* or *Endymion*, the critical questions they encourage aren't entirely dissolved in Keats's later stylistic achievements. McGann is right, I think, to say that "the significance of this Cockney style . . . is not very widely recognized,"[2] especially (I would add) its significance for Keats's own subsequent development.

In late July 1818, on a visit to Scotland, Benjamin Bailey dined at the house of Bishop George Glieg, his future father-in-law, and there met John Gibson Lockhart, one of the main contributors to the new magazine recently founded by the Tory publisher and bookseller William Blackwood.[3] In August, Bailey wrote to Keats's new publisher, John Taylor, about this meeting:

> [Lockhart] abused poor Keats in a way that, although it was at the
> Bishop's table, I could hardly keep my temper. I said I supposed

then [Keats] would be attacked in Blackwood's. He replied "not by *me*"; which would carry the insinuation he would by some one *else*. The objections he stated were frivolous in the extreme. They chiefly respected the *rhymes*.[4]

As it turned out, of course, Lockhart—and possibly his cohort John Wilson—did attack Keats in *Blackwood's Magazine*, in the last of a series of abusive articles begun in October 1817 on the "Cockney School of Poetry." For "Z," as the *Blackwood's* reviewers signed themselves, Keats's rhyme in his 1817 and 1818 volumes wasn't a frivolous matter at all. It epitomized the corruption of what *Blackwood's* called "the Cockney school of versification, morality, and politics":

> . . . this romance is meant to be written in English heroic rhyme. To those who have read any of Hunt's poems, this hint might indeed be needless. Mr Keats has adopted the loose, nerveless versification, and Cockney rhymes of the poet of Rimini.[5]

Lockhart's implication is clear: Keats's loose liberal couplets are the stylistic analogue of the loose liberal politics he had imbibed from Hunt. Near the end of the review Lockhart quotes twenty-two lines (exactly half of them enjambed) from Keats's denunciation of those "who lord it o'er their fellow-men / With most prevailing tinsel"[6] at the beginning of Book III of *Endymion*. He introduces this quotation by saying: "We had almost forgotten to mention, that Keats belongs to the Cockney School of Politics, as well as the Cockney School of Poetry."[7]

The same linking of politics and versification marks John Wilson Croker's attack on *Endymion* in the arch-Tory *Quarterly Review*:

> —At first it appeared to us, that Mr. Keats had been amusing himself and wearying his readers with an immeasurable game at *bouts-rimés*. . . . He seems to us to write a line at random, and then he follows not the thought excited by this line, but that suggested by the *rhyme* with which it concludes. There is hardly a complete couplet inclosing a complete idea in the whole book.[8]

For Croker, Keats's Cockney couplets are an affront to the orthodoxy of the closed Augustan couplet and to the social and moral traditions it symbolizes. Croker's reference to the game of *bouts-rimés*, although it doesn't exactly fit the compositional process he thinks he sees in Keats, is politically significant. Addison had defined the game in attacking its eighteenth-century vogue in one of his *Spectator* essays (No. 60) on forms of "False Wit": "They were a List of Words that rhyme to one another, drawn up by another Hand, and given to a Poet, who was to make a Poem to the Rhymes in the same Order that they were placed upon the List."[9] That this game was still fashionable in Regency society is evident from Byron's delightfully macaronic couplet in Canto 16 of *Don Juan*, where we hear about the Duchess of Fitz-Fulke's taste in poetry: "But of all verse, what most ensured her praise / Were sonnets to herself, or 'Bouts rimés'" (St. 50).[10] In accusing Keats of playing at *bouts rimés*, Croker insinuates that this low-born London "neophyte" of Leigh Hunt is abusing Pope by taking seriously a parlor game with which his aristocratic betters merely while away their time on country weekends. Like *Blackwood's* "Z," Croker ridicules other features of Keats's Cockney style as well: the meter, the diction, the erotic imagery. But it is the "Cockney rhymes" that most obviously betray what these Tory reviewers see as Keats's inseparable poetical and political vices.

Keats was caught up, then, in a squabble between Tory traditionalists, for whom the balanced and closed Augustan couplet had become something of a cultural fetish, and the liberal reformers who set out to establish "a freer spirit of versification," as Hunt says in the Preface to *The Story of Rimini*,[11] along with a freer society. So far this picture of the politics of Keats's "Cockney style" seems to be fairly predictable—but that's because it's still misleadingly simple.[12] Consider, for instance, the political ramifications of Hunt's developing the couplet, not blank verse, as an antithesis to what he saw as the monotonous regularity of "Pope and the French school of versification" (Preface, *The Story of Rimini*). Hunt's effort to reform the heroic couplet is an exact image of his reformist politics. There is a general formulation in Hunt's essay "What is Poetry?" that could characterize his ideal society almost as easily as his ideal couplet: "Poetry shapes this modulation into uniformity for its outline, and variety for its parts, because it thus realizes the last idea of beauty itself, which includes the charm of diversity within the flowing round of habit and ease."[13] Hunt loves "the flowing round of habit and ease" that marks the couplet as long as it is internally varied, diverse. And there is an undeniably conservative impulse in his desire, as he says in the Preface to the second edition of *The Feast of the Poets*, "to bring back the real harmonies of the English heroic, and to restore to it half the true principle of its music,—variety."[14]

But there may also be a specifically political anti-conservative impulse in Hunt's—and initially Keats's, before the unCockney Miltonic experiments of the first *Hyperion*—avoidance of blank verse. For by 1817–1818, blank verse had come to be inevitably associated with Wordsworth, whose political conservatism Hunt frequently criticized even as he made efforts to align himself with Wordsworth's power as a poet of nature.[15] We should note in this regard that when the *Blackwood's* review defends Pope against Keats's attack on "rocking Horse" couplets in *Sleep and Poetry*, it does so by proclaiming that "to deny [Pope's] genius, is just as absurd as to dispute that of

Wordsworth, or to believe in that of Hunt."[16] Hunt and Keats may not have shared Shelley's judgment that the author of *The Excursion* was "a slave"[17] (Shelley himself countered *The Excursion* in *Alastor* by taking on its verse form as well as its argument), but their staying away from blank verse may have had a political motivation all the same. It was in the summer of 1818— the summer of the *Blackwood's* and *Quarterly Review* attacks—that Keats tried to visit Wordsworth at Rydal Mount, only to hear that he was out campaigning for the Tory Lowthers against the reformer Henry Brougham in the Westmoreland elections.[18]

While Keats praises Wordsworth in that section in *Sleep and Poetry* on the current state of English verse, he does so as part of a performance that suggests anything but a writer naive about or unaware of the politics of style. It's not just that 28 of the 49 lines in these two verse paragraphs are enjambed, in open defiance of the closed couplets savored by the likes of Croker. At several points Keats's couplets mock by mimicking the poetic conventions under scrutiny:

> with a puling infant's force
> They sway'd about upon a rocking horse,
> And thought it Pegasus. Ah dismal soul'd!
> (185–87)

The rhythm of "They sway'd about upon a rocking horse" rocks childishly along in satirical harmony with the rhyme ("infant's force"/"rocking horse"), and then comes to an abrupt halt at the medial full-stop after "And thought it Pegasus."[19] Keats knew what he was about in attacking Pope's couplets with couplets of his own devising:

> But ye were dead
> To things ye knew not of,—were closely wed
> To musty laws lined out with wretched rule
> And compass vile: so that ye taught a school
> Of dolts to smooth, inlay, and clip, and fit,
> Till, like the certain wands of Jacob's wit,
> Their verses tallied. Easy was the task:
> (193–99)

Here Keats flouts the "wretched rules" of Augustan verse formally as well as argumentatively by refusing to pause grammatically for four consecutive line-endings (the doubly unstopped "rule"/"school" couplet is an act of open unruliness)—until he moves into the mincing steps of "to smooth, inlay, and clip, and fit," where he prosodically parodies the process he names. It was shrewd of Byron, in what would have been the first of his contributions to the "Pope controversy," to attack Keats's attack on Pope by referring sarcastically to Mr. Keats's "new 'Essay on Criticism.' "[20] Byron recognized Keats's polemical exploitation of making "The sound . . . seem an Echo to the sense" (*Essay on Criticism* II.365), and he knew that Keats learned to do that sort of thing from Pope himself.

Byron's response to Keats's parody of Pope's couplets suggests just how complicated and even contradictory the politics of style can become. He first mocks Keats's mockery in "Some Observations upon an Article in *Blackwood's Magazine*," a rambling piece written in March 1820 and sent to Murray for immediate publication (Murray held it back, however, and did not publish it until 1833).[21] The *Blackwood's* article in question, published in August 1819, had nothing directly to do with Pope—it was a moralizing denunciation of Byron's private life as reflected in *Don Juan*. Byron thought the *Blackwood's* piece to have been authored by John Wilson,[22] who the previous summer had very likely collaborated in the attack on Hunt and Keats. So Byron's initial denunciation of Keats's writing appears as part of his assault on the same Tory magazine that had first derided Keats's "Cockney rhymes." The ironic political crossings get even more intricate. Byron dedicated his unpublished "Observations" to Isaac Disraeli, who just four months later defended Pope in a long review of two competing editions of Joseph Spence's *Anecdotes* and of William Lisle Bowles's *The Invariable Principles of Poetry* in *The Quarterly Review*,[23] which had of course published Croker's savaging of *Endymion*. It was Disraeli's review that elicited Byron's first public entry into the "Pope controversy" (the first, that is, since *English Bards and Scotch Reviewers*). "They support Pope I see in the Quarterly," he wrote to Murray. "Let them Continue to do so. . . ."[24] In his *Letter to *********[John Murray] . . . on the Rev. W. L. Bowles's Strictures on the Life and Writings of Pope* (March 1821), Byron sides openly with the *Quarterly*'s position in the "Pope controversy." In his *Second Letter* on the same subject (also written in March 1821 but not published until 1835), Byron has another go at Keats (or "Ketch," as he now calls him)—this time as part of a condescending dismissal of "my friend Leigh Hunt" and what "some one has maliciously called the 'Cockney School.' "[25]

Byron's willingness to side with the Tories in the "Pope controversy" against the liberal poetics of Hunt and Keats reflects interestingly on the politics of his own couplet style. As Peter Manning has recently shown in two excellent articles on the political context and significance of *The Corsair*,[26] Byron's writing appealed strongly to reformist and even to radical readers. Conrad's "anti-authoritarian" and "anarchic" behavior led to his being invoked as the type of Jeremiah Brandreth, one of the leaders of the Pentridge uprising of June 1817, and to a popular prose adaptation of *The Corsair* by the radical publisher William Hone. Byron himself had indicated his own ties to the reformist Whigs in the dedicatory letter to Thomas Moore which prefaced the first edition of *The Corsair* in 1814. By referring to "The wrongs of your own country" and "the magnificent and fiery spirit of her sons,"[27] Byron reaffirms his passionate appeal for Catholic emancipation in his second speech before the House of Lords (21 April 1813).[28] At the same time, as Manning demonstrates, there was much about *The Corsair* that contradicted its oppositional implications and made it appeal to conservative bourgeois readers: the volume's expensive production, the learned epigraphs and notes, the urbane authorial voice adopted in those notes and in the letter to Moore—and the versification, which Byron advertises as "the best adapted measure to our language, the good old and now neglected heroic couplet."[29]

The couplets of *The Corsair* provide a striking contemporary contrast to Keats's Cockney couplets in *Sleep and Poetry* and *Endymion*. Enjambment is rare; only two lines in the poem's opening 42-line section, for example, aren't strongly end-stopped. Croker could have found in Byron's couplets just what he missed in Keats's: "a complete couplet inclosing a complete idea." And the relation between couplet form and idea in *The Corsair* is politically suggestive. Consider the couplet that begins the opening song of Conrad's pirates: "'O'er the glad waters of the dark blue sea, / Our thoughts as boundless, and our souls as free,'" (I.1–2). Conrad and his followers may have "thoughts" that are "boundless" and "souls" that are "free," but the couplet which celebrates this spirit is neither—it is as carefully bounded and closed as a couplet from *The Essay on Man*. An even more arresting instance of the way in which Byron's heroic couplets check—and also give contrasting point to—the poem's appeal to a restless, rebellious energy appears later in this opening section, as the pirates distinguish their lives on the open sea from "him who crawls enamoured of decay": "'While gasp by gasp he faulters forth his soul, / Ours with one pang—one bound—escapes controul.'" (I.31–32). "Escapes controul" comes sharply up against the controlling closure of a full-stop. Manning's work on *The Corsair* helps us see that however anti-authoritarian and anarchic Byron's hero may be, he performs within stylistic terms as familiar and congenial to genteel Regency readers as Keats's Cockney couplets were strange and rebarbative.

Keats knew what he wanted to do in his 1817 Cockney couplets, and he knew how far beyond the "flowing round of habit and ease" characteristic of Hunt's liberal reform couplets he wanted to go. The *Blackwood's* review is right, given its basic assumption, to assert that "the defects of [Hunt's] system are tenfold more conspicuous in his disciple's work than in his own"[30] Tenfold may be an exaggeration, but anyone interested in the statistical evidence for just how much further Keats went than Hunt in breaking the metrical and grammatical conventions of the Augustan couplet can look such evidence up in the studies of M. R. Ridley and W. J. Bate.[31] Hunt himself had complained about the excesses of Keats's couplet experiments in his *Examiner* review of the 1817 *Poems*:

Mr. Keats' . . . fault, the one in his versification, arises from . . . contradicting over-zealously the fault on the opposite side. It is this which provokes him now and then into mere roughness and discords for their own sake, but not for that of variety and contrasted harmony.[32]

Keats's friend John Hamilton Reynolds had made much the same complaint a few months earlier in his unsigned review for the progressively liberal *Champion* (9 March 1817).[33] In fact the liberal reviewers, though quite favorably disposed towards Keats's early poem, had almost as many reservations about the couplets as their Tory counterparts. P. G. Patmore in *The London Magazine* (April 1820) praised the "freedom, sweetness, and variety" of Keats's rhythms in *Endymion* but admitted that "the verse frequently runs riot, and loses itself in air."[34]

Such responses ought to make us ask to what extent, and in just what ways, the stylistic choices and performances of the 1817 and 1818 volumes *are* political choices and performances. The broad relevance of a highly politicized context to Keats's early style is clear, but no one would want to argue that his extravagant experiments in couplet writing are in themselves expressive of political convictions more radical and anarchic than those of liberals like Hunt. If anything, Keats's stylistic extravagance might appear to be radically anti-political in its tendency to produce lines which, as Hunt said in 1832 of the more disciplined couplets of *Lamia*, "seem to take pleasure in the progress of their own beauty."[35] We seem to have arrived at a point where the explanatory usefulness of the political context for Keats's early couplet style breaks down. Or perhaps both that context and Keats's stylistic response to it are only complicating themselves beyond the level at which we usually work when we look at what McGann refers to as "the specific ways in which certain stylistic forms intersect and join with certain factual and cognitive points of reference."[36]

As a way of pushing on speculatively at this point, I want to turn to another moderately liberal reviewer, Francis Jeffrey, writing belatedly about *Endymion* in the August 1820 number of *The Edinburgh Review*. Jeffrey sees that if Keats is playing at *bouts rimés* in the couplets of *Endymion*, he is doing so in a distinctive and at least potentially fruitful way:

A great part of the work indeed, is written in the strangest and most fantastical manner than can be imagined. It seems as if the author had ventured every thing that occurred to him in the shape of a glittering image or striking expression—taken the first word that presented itself to make up a rhyme, and then made that word the germ of a new cluster of images—a hint for a new excursion of the fancy—and so wandered on, equally forgetful whence he came, and heedless whither he was going, till he had covered his pages with an interminable arabesque of connected and incongruous figures, that multiplied as they extended, and were only harmonized by the brightness of their tints, and the graces of their forms.[37]

Some of Jeffrey's response is vaguely generalizing, but the part that's worth holding onto for the moment is the suggestion that Keats allows himself to be led (and also misled) by the rhyme as it generates a need for connection and development, as it provokes and then gives unexpected shape to figurative elaborations. At times in *Endymion* and in the 1817 volume, Keats seems to be doing just this, and with an air of self-delighting curiosity as to the consequences. There is an extraordinary moment in "I Stood Tip-toe" when Keats wanders off into a day-dream occasioned by the couplet that precedes it:

> Were I in such a place, I sure should pray
> That nought less sweet might call my thoughts away,
> Than the soft rustle of a maiden's gown
> Fanning away the dandelion's down:
>
> (93–96)

He follows this figure for four more couplets before reluctantly letting her depart:

> And as she leaves me may she often turn
> Her fair eyes looking through her locks auburne.
>   What next? A tuft of evening primroses,
> O'er which the mind may hover till it dozes;
>
> (105–8)

The genial audacity of that "What next?" is winning in its way—it's hard not to read it as Keats's exclamation about having gotten by with a rhyme like "turn"/"auburne," as well as an indication that he is letting himself be surprised by what turns up next.

The serious critical issue here is the extent to which Keats is willing to let the pressures and possibilities of rhyming, and thus of contending with arbitrary phonetic and semantic convergences, shape the development of his poem. Is this an issue with political implications, amenable to historical and political understanding? Or have we passed beyond the level at which politics and form intersect? It's one thing to accept, say, P. N. Medvedev's principle that "A linguistic form is only real in the concrete speech performance, in the social utterance,"[38] or David Simpson's insistence "on the historical grounds of [a] play of possibilities rendered into language."[39] It's quite another to make good on McGann's claim that "Only by reading [Keats's Cockney poetry] in a sharply specified historical frame of reference are we able to see . . . and hence to describe precisely not merely the abstract *characteristics*, but the felt *qualities* of its poetic structure."[40] Some of those "felt *qualities*," as we have seen, yield amply to being understood "in a sharply specified historical" and political "frame of reference." But what about the quality Jeffrey felt in observing that Keats often allows the first rhyme-word in a couplet to become "the germ of a new cluster of images— a hint for a new excursion of the fancy"?

One initial response to these questions ought to be that they can't be settled theoretically, simply as points of principle. The degree to which historical and political circumstances are precisely useful in understanding matters of style, or the level at which they cease to become useful, isn't decidable in advance of our actually trying to think about a particular stylistic feature from a historical and political point of view. With this in mind, I want to look briefly at rhyme-induced figurative "excursions" from Keats's later poetry. That such "excursions" grow out of the sort of verbal opportunism in Keats's "Cockney style" that upset Tory and liberal reviewers alike was demonstrated years ago by Kingsley Amis, in the inaugural volume of *Essays in Criticism*. Amis complained that Keats's "hopelessly inadequate" rhyming of "my sole self" and "deceiving elf" in the last stanza of "Ode to a Nightingale" has its origin in one of the Cockney couplets of *Endymion*, when the narrator laments "The journey homeward to habitual self! / A mad-pursuing of the fog-born elf" (ii.276–77).[41] Readers more interested than Amis apparently was in Keats's broodings about the self as a construct at once deceiving in its significance and yet hauntingly persistent may find that the rhyming precipitation of "elf" out of "self" (it's like a miniature of Blake's "spectre" and "emanation"), far from being "hopelessly inadequate," is intrinsic to Keats's thinking through the issue of poetic subjectivity. His attitude towards the self, as reading Hazlitt helps us see, is implicitly political in deep and complicated ways. Instead of trying to draw those implications out within the confines of this paper, however, I want to turn to another example which raises more immediate questions about the politics of style and impinges directly on the debate provoked by McGann's political reading of "To Autumn."

Here are the last seven lines of the poem's opening stanza, beginning with the second of that stanza's opulent infinitive clauses:

> To bend with apples the moss'd cottage-trees,
>   And fill all fruit with ripeness to the core;
>   To swell the gourd, and plump the hazel shells
>   With a sweet kernel; to set budding more,
> And still more, later flowers for the bees,
> Until they think warm days will never cease,
>   For summer has o'er-brimm'd their clammy cells.
>   (5–11)

171

In this stanza of "To Autumn," where all is made to feel so inevitable, we feel an inevitable resistance to recognizing that anything as overtly arbitrary as the exigencies of rhyme could be involved in generating that culminating image. Yet the "bees" in "their clammy cells" are there in part to rhyme with "cottage-trees" and "hazel shells." And these very rhymes appear in *Endymion*, in Cockney couplets like the ones attacked by *Blackwood's* and the *Quarterly*:

> Just when the light of morn, with hum of bees,
> Stole through its verdurous matting of fresh trees.
>
> (III.419–20)

> And gather up all fancifullest shells
> For thee to tumble into Naiads' cells,
>
> (I.271–72)

It's plausible to think that Keats was led to the "cluster of images" that concludes the first stanza of "To Autumn" by, among other concerns, the suggestive pressure of rhyme, and by his recalling his own Cockney versification. But is there anything political about his being thus led?

As David Bromwich points out, Keats had already used a reference to bees to distinctive political effect in "Robin Hood" (1818), where it is followed in rhyming position by an aggressively Cockney couplet linking "honey" to "money." We know from a letter to Bailey shortly after his moving to Winchester that however pleased Keats may have been with this quiet retreat into solitude, the class-based slurs on his Cockney writing were still very much in his mind: "One of my Ambitions is . . . to upset the drawling of the blue stocking literary world" (14 August 1819).[42] And as both Bromwich and Paul Fry remind us, Keats was avidly keeping up with the current political turmoil in the country. He had gone back to London from Winchester for a few days (to try to arrange financial help for his brother George in America) just in time to see Orator Hunt's tumultuous return from Manchester and Peterloo. The *Examiner*'s reports on Peterloo, which Keats read during his Winchester stay, provide a dark backdrop to the "Season of mists and mellow fruitfulness" celebrated in "To Autumn." The number for Sunday, 5 September—the last number Keats would have seen before his trip to London—contains a particularly important linking of the month's political and literary significance. Following a series of letters reporting on the aftermath of Peterloo, including letters from Henry Hunt himself on his Manchester trial, and immediately following a piece entitled "Return of the Killed and Wounded at Manchester. Letter from Mr. Pearson," is an entry called "Calendar of Nature. (From the Literary Pocket-Book.) September." This item begins with the September stanza from the procession of the months in Spenser's Mutability Cantos (*The Faerie*

Queene VII.vii.38), a stanza that contains iconographical details to which Keats was clearly responding in "To Autumn."[43] Even more suggestive, however, are the details in the *Examiner*'s gloss on Spenser's stanza:

> The poet still takes advantage of the exuberance of harvest and the sign of the Zodiac in this month, to read us a lesson on justice.
>
> Autumn has now arrived. This is the month of the migration of birds, of the finished harvest, of nut-gathering, of cyder and perry-making. . . . The swallows . . . disappear for the warmer climates, leaving only a few stragglers behind, probably from weakness or sickness. . . .
>
> September, though its mornings and evenings are apt to be chill and foggy, and therefore not wholesome to those who either do not or cannot guard against them, is generally a serene and pleasant month, partaking of the warmth of summer and the vigour of autumn. . . . The feast, as the philosophic poet says on a higher occasion . . .[44]

Here the *Examiner* quotes a Spenserian stanza from Shelley's *The Revolt of Islam* (Hunt's extended enthusiastic review of the poem had appeared in February and March 1818) describing a victory feast held by the forces of liberation. The stanza is slightly misquoted to make it fit with the *Examiner*'s prose:

> The feast is such as earth, the general mother,
>   Pours from her fairest bosom, when she smiles
> In the embrace of Autumn. To each other
>   As some fond parent fondly reconciles
> Her warring children, she their wrath beguiles
>   With their own sustenance; they, relenting, weep.
> Such is this festival, which from their isles,
>   And continents, and winds, and oceans deep,
> All shapes may throng to share, that fly, or walk, or creep.
>
> (v.lv.2209–2307)

Is this Autumn's "lesson on justice," this image of a momentary natural bounty that "beguiles" the "wrath" of people previously oppressed? Hunt had not quoted the stanza in his review of Shelley's poem, but his summary of this phase of the narrative is pertinent: "a festival is held at which *Cythna* presides like a visible angel, and every thing seems happiness and security. The Revolters however are suddenly assailed by the allies of the tyrant; and the fortune of the contest is changed."[45]

All this contextual material may seem remote from Keats's bees in "To Autumn," but the *Examiner*'s quoting of Shelley suggests one way in which it may be pointedly relevant. When in his "Song to the Men of England" (1819) Shelley asks the "Bees of England" why they allow "these stingless drones" to "spoil / The forced produce of your toil" (the "spoil"/"toil" rhyme, incidentally, appears in the stanza from Spenser quoted in the *Examiner*), he is drawing upon a figurative tradition common in radical political writing of the later eighteenth and early nineteenth century.[46] True, Keats's imagery has an important Virgilian source, as editors have pointed out: even the rhyme-word "cells" has its antecedents in the "cellas" of Virgil's famous simile.[47] But knowing this doesn't preclude our thinking politically about Keats's image. After all, Virgil's early summer image ("aestate nova") of Dido's subjects joyfully laboring to build Carthage has complicated political resonances of its own, resonances carried over but transformed in Keats's early autumnal image of worker-bees whose momentary abundance makes them "*think* warm days will never cease" (my emphasis), and whose "o'er-brimm'd . . . cells" are disturbingly "clammy." A reader in 1819–1820 familiar with popular political pamphlets and songs might have found Keats's image of laboring bees political in ways that no blue stocking would have approved of.

I'm not arguing that all references to bees in romantic poems ask to be read politically, or that Keats's stylistic habits led him deliberately to focus his own and his readers' attention in these lines on the living conditions of real English gleaners in the autumn of 1819. But I am arguing that here as elsewhere, "To Autumn" presents us with an idealized, mythologized image of culminated and therefore death-set fruition that fends off but cannot finally exclude a negative historical actuality which Keats was certainly in touch with. His writing cannot free itself, entirely from either the political reality or the political language that both McGann and Fry, in opposite ways, insist that he wants to avoid.

My larger point is that even at a level of performance where the specific political context of Keats's Cockney couplets ceases to be immediately instructive, the stylistic instincts encouraged and shaped by that context may produce writing with an important though momentarily suppressed political dimension. If our engagement with the "richer entanglements" of Keats's poetry is going to expand to include a fresh sense of that political dimension, we will need to make ourselves newly alert to the ways in which acts of writing and reading may be subject to historical and political circumstances quite remote from a poem's immediate field of reference.

Notes

1 John O. Hayden, *The Romantic Reviewers, 1802–1824* (London: Routledge, 1969) 188–96; Theodore Redpath, *The Young Romantics and Critical Opinion 1807–1824* (London: Harrap, 1973) 418–21; Jerome McGann, "Keats and the Historical Method in Literary Criticism" *MLN* 94 (1979): 996–99.

2 McGann, "Keats and the Historical Method" 996.

3 Walter Jackson Bate, *John Keats* (Cambridge, Mass.: Harvard U P, 1963) 366–67.

4 *The Keats Circle: Letters and Papers 1816–1878*, ed. Hyder Edward Rollins (Cambridge, Mass.: Harvard U P, 1948) 1: 34.

5 "Cockney School of Poetry, No IV," *Blackwood's Edinburgh Magazine* 3 (August 1818): 522.

6 All quotations are from *The Poems of John Keats*, ed. Jack Stillinger (Cambridge, Mass.: Harvard U P, 1978).

7 "Cockney School of Poetry" 524.

8 "Art. VII.—*Endymion: A Poetic Romance*. By John Keats," *The Quarterly Review* vol. 19, no. 37 (April 1818): 205–6.

9 *The Spectator*, ed. Donald F. Bond (Oxford: Clarendon, 1965) 1: 256.

10 All quotations of *Don Juan* are from *Byron's "Don Juan": A Variorum Edition*, ed. Truman Guy Steffan and Willis W. Pratt (Austin: U of Texas P, 1957).

11 (London: J. Murray; W. Blackwood; Cumming, 1816) xv. Subsequent quotations are from this edition. In "The Return of the Enjambed Couplet" (*ELH* 7 [1940]: 239–52, Earl Wasserman argued that Hunt's and Keats's originality in opening up the closed Augustan couplet had been exaggerated, that "the versification of Keats and Hunt is . . . the fulfillment of a movement that had its beginnings in the last quarter of the eighteenth century" (251).

12 We need to remember here that a majority of the reviewers of both Keats's early volumes were encouraging. See Hayden, *The Romantic Reviewers* 188, 190.

13 "An Answer to the Question What is Poetry? Including Remarks on Versification," *Imagination and Fancy* (New York: Wiley and Putnam, 1845) 2.

14 (London: Gale and Fenner, 1815) 32.

15 See P. M. S. Dawson, "Byron, Shelley, and the 'new school,'" *Shelley Revalued: Essays from the Gregynog Conference*, ed. Kelvin Everest (Totowa, N.J.: Barnes, 1983) 89–108, esp. 91–101.

16 "Cockney School of Poetry" 520.

17 *Mary Shelley's Journal*, ed. Frederick L. Jones (Norman: U of Oklahoma P, 1947) 15.

18 Bate, *John Keats* 349–50.

19 Douglas Bush notes that the source of Keats's image here is Hazlitt's "On Milton's Versification" (1815): "Dr. Johnson and Pope would have converted his [Milton's] vaulting Pegasus into a rocking-horse" (John Keats, *Selected Poems and Letters* [Boston: Houghton, 1959] 312).

20 "Some Observations Upon an Article in *Blackwood's Magazine*," Appendix IX in *Byron's Works: Letters and Journals*, ed. Rowland E. Prothero (London: John Murray, 1898–1901) IV: 493.

21 See note 20 above and Leslie A. Marchand, *Byron: A Biography* (New York: Knopf, 1957) II: 845 and note.

22 Prothero, *Letters and Journals* IV: 474, refers to Byron's letter to Murrary of 10 December 1819 (see IV: 385 and note in Prothero's edition). Leslie Marchand, *Byron's Letters and Journals* (Cambridge, Mass.: Harvard U P, 1976) VI: 257n. says, "It is still a question as to whether John Wilson wrote the review."

23 Vol. 23, no. 46 (July 1820): 400–34.

24 *Byron's Letters and Journals* VII: 217 (4 November 1820). Bowles's own preference for the open, enjambed couplet is an aspect of the "Pope controversy" that doubtless exacerbated Byron's antipathy to Bowles as it did his antipathy to Keats. See Wasserman, "The Return of the Enjambed Couplet" 248–49.

25 Prothero, ed., *Letters and Journals* Appendix III, V: 588.
26 "Tales and Politics: *The Corsair, Lara,* and *The White Doe of Rylstone,*" *Salzburger Studien zur Anglistik und Amerikanistik* 13 (1980): 204–30; and "The Hone-ing of Byron's *Corsair,*" chapter 6 in *Textual Criticism and Literary Interpretation,* ed. Jerome McGann (Chicago: U of Chicago P, 1985) 107–26.
27 Quotations of *The Corsair* are from vol. III of *The Complete Poetical Works,* ed. Jerome J. McGann (Oxford: Clarendon, 1981). The references to Byron's Preface are on III: 148.
28 See Manning, "Tales and Politics" 209.
29 *Complete Poetical Works* III: 149.
30 "Cockney School of Poetry" 522.
31 M. R. Ridley, *Keats' Craftsmanship: A Study in Poetic Development* (London: Methuen, 1963) 241–49 and 305, Note J, and Walter Jackson Bate, *The Stylistic Development of John Keats* (New York: Humanities, 1945) 19–28, 147–55.
32 6 and 13 July 1817, reprinted in Redpath, *The Young Romantics and Critical Opinion* 455–56.
33 Reprinted in Redpath, *The Young Romantics and Critical Opinion* 451–52.
34 Vol. 1, no. 4: 383.
35 *The Poetical Works of Leigh Hunt* (London: Edward Moxon, 182) xxxvi–xxxvii.
36 "Romanticism and its Ideologies," *SiR* 21 (1982): 576.
37 *The Edinburgh Review* vol. 34, no. 67 (August 1820): 204–5.
38 P. N. Medvedev/M. M. Bakhtin, *The Formal Method in Literary Scholarship: A Critical Introduction to Sociological Poetics,* trans. Albert J. Wehrle (Baltimore: Johns Hopkins U P, 1978) 122. This passage is quoted by McGann in "Keats and the Historical Method" 990.
39 "Criticism, Politics, and Style in Wordsworth's Poetry," *Critical Inquiry* 11 (1984): 67.
40 "Keats and the Historical Method" 996–97.
41 "The Curious Elf: A Note on Rhyme in Keats," *EIC* 1 (1951): 189–92.
42 *The Letters of John Keats,* ed. Hyder Edward Rollins (Cambridge, Mass.: Harvard U P, 1958) 2:139.
43 Helen Vendler emphasizes the influence of the Mutability Cantos on "To Autumn" in *The Odes of John Keats* (Cambridge, Mass.: Harvard U P, 1983) 242–43. She mentions the September stanza in passing but says nothing about its appearance in *The Examiner.*
44 No. 610 (5 September 1819): 574.
45 No. 527 (1 February 1818): 76.
46 See P. M. S. Dawson, *The Unacknowledged Legislator: Shelley and Politics* (Oxford: Clarendon, 1980) 50–51. The quotation is from *Shelley: Poetical Works,* ed. Thomas Hutchinson, corrected by G. M. Matthews (Oxford: Oxford U P, 1970).
47 References are to *Aeneid* I.430–36 in the Loeb Classical Library edition (Cambridge, Mass.: Harvard U P, 1934).

Part 4

ORIENTALISM AND POST-COLONIALISM

26

KUBLA KHAN AND ORIENTALISM: THE ROAD TO XANADU REVISITED

Nigel Leask

Source: *Romanticism* 4 (1998), 1–21.

Coleridge's *Kubla Khan* has teased generations of critics, according to the customary inverse logic that the more enigmatic and elliptical the poem, the more loquacious the interpreters. The unusual lack of reference to *Kubla Khan* in Coleridge's copious journals and letters of the late 1790's increases the uncertainties surrounding its exact dating and conception.[1] One aspect of the poem seems beyond dispute: despite Coleridge's disclaimer in the 1816 Preface that his fragmentary 'Vision in a Dream' was presented to the public rather 'as a psychological curiosity, than on the grounds of any supposed *poetic* merits',[2] it represents a highly self-conscious and highly-structured poetic achievement. Even Hazlitt, whose review of the 1816 volume in which it was first published was of the opinion that *Kubla Khan* 'only shews that Mr Coleridge can write better *nonsense* verses than any man in England' admitted as much when he added 'it is not so much a poem but a musical composition' (*Poems*, p. 500). The poem's formal achievement is well summarised by J. R. de J. Jackson; '[a] regular iambic framework is used to set off variants, and the entire poem is marked by alliteration and elaborate assonance that reaches back in subtlety to Milton. There is a sense of incantatory elevation throughout'.[3] Reaching any sort of consensus about the poem's meaning has been problematical, however, although recent critical orthodoxy might be summed up by Jerome McGann's conclusion (in *The Romantic Ideology*) that *Kubla Khan* is concerned with 'the poetical faculty itself, and [its] central problem . . . that the faculty might lose its potency . . . its concrete symbols deliberately forego any immediate social or cultural points of reference in order to engage with its audience at a purely conceptual level.'[4]

McGann's conclusion is based on the form of the poem's first publication in 1816, the Preface of which famously describes the poet's unconscious, drugged conception of two to three hundred lines of poetry and his transcription of 'the present fragment', interrupted by the 'person on business from Porlock', apparently developing the theme of the poem's final 18 lines, or 'coda'. That is to say, Coleridge's thwarted desideratum in the Preface of 'finish[ing] for himself what had been originally, as it were, given to him' reiterates the poet/visionary's subjunctive wish to revive the Abyssinian Maid's 'symphony and song'. In this respect, and inasmuch as the poem and Preface together work out a theory of (unconscious) creativity through the ironic indirection of the Romantic fragment poem, Coleridge is justified in denominating his poem 'a psychological curiosity'. As K. M. Wheeler sums up: 'the Preface distances the reader from the specific imagery and content of the poem by explicitly focusing his attention upon the poem as an instance of poetic creation . . . away from factual details and concern for their accuracy, toward structural properties, narrative voices, and the relation of the preface to the verse'.[5]

What if, however, we imagine the poem as it stood *before* the addition of the 1816 Preface, or even the short after-note of the 'Crewe Manuscript' with its account of the poem's composition 'in a sort of Reverie brought on by two grains of Opium, taken to check a dysentery . . . in the fall of the year, 1797'?[6] Back in 1953, Elizabeth Schneider (p. 78) suggested that we should take Coleridge's account of the poem's drugged, unconscious composition with a pinch of salt given its highly-organised form and structure. Led to doubt the claims of the 1816 Preface's account of 'dream-composition', we might then seek gradually to disentangle an earlier version of *Kubla Khan*, product of the climacteric and political 1790's, from the poem published by Coleridge the celebrated 'man of letters' and conservative public moralist in 1816. Without the apologetic Preface, and shorn of the textual changes which we know Coleridge had made to the Crewe Manuscript version by 1816, the 'specific imagery and content' of the poem might then assume much more importance than they do in the final published version. By comparing this earlier version with the published text of 1816 we might better understand how a conservative Coleridge – author of the *Statesman's Manual* and the *Biographia Literaria* – subjected the poetry of his early, youthful radicalism to a revisionary process similar to that which McGann has dubbed 'the Romantic Ideology'.

To resituate *Kubla Khan* in the intellectual climate of the late 1790's is also to discover a context of literary *orientalism* rather different from that associated with the 1816 poem. The opium-inspired vision of the latter is closer to the orientalist dreams of Thomas De Quincey, in particular to the paranoid opium dream of a composite orient recounted in *The Confessions of an English Opium Eater* (1822). I have elsewhere discussed the double valency of opium in this period; at once a staple *commodity* of Britain's oriental empire and (at least in the writing of De Quincey and Coleridge) a psychotropic technology for viewing the Orient as a 'synchronic essence'.[7] Coleridge's 1816 Preface to *Kubla Khan*, by focusing readerly attention on the agency of the drugged imagination as a syncretizing power, erases the geopolitical distinction between the poem's constituent *topoi*. Kubla Khan and the Abyssinian Maid, Xanadu and Mount Abora are condensed by a kind of drug-induced poetical dreamwork into an 'essentialised' Orient. Elinor Shaffer in *Kubla Khan and the Fall of Jerusalem* eloquently sums up the poem's 'dream-work' in terms of the 'higher' Bible Criticism, with its notion of mythological syncretism; 'the poem's "piecing out" from a diversity of culturally uprooted mythologies . . . creat[es] a unity of superimposed, overlapping images whose not quite exact correspondence sets their edges shimmering and revives each nation's failing gods into authentic universal life'.[8]

In the introductory comments to their recent volume *Romanticism, Race, and Imperial Culture 1780–1834*, editors Alan Richardson and Sonia Hofkosh note a common tendency of critical studies of Romantic syncretism (from Jonathan Livingston Lowes's *The Road to Xanadu* (1927), to Elinor Shaffer's book cited above) to 'celebrate the sublime contraction of the "four quarters of the globe" into a free-standing work of imagination, a testament to the "imperially present" mind of the romantic artist rather than the discursive presence of the Empire in the seemingly autonomous literary work'.[9] In the light of these strictures, my essay will explore how the 'dreamlike orient' of *Kubla Khan* might look *without* the strictures of the 1816 Preface, placed back into the context of Coleridge's geopolitical interests in the late 1790's. For by recovering the lost cultural narrative of the poem's 'visionary' elements we might restore a geopolitical specificity to its oriental setting absent in the final, 'High Romantic' published version. In order to revisit Coleridge's oriental settings, I will return to Jonathan Livingstone Lowes's contention, worked out in over 600 pages of erudite source-hunting in *The Road to Xanadu*, that *Kubla Khan* (amongst other poems) was inspired by Coleridge's wide reading in the literature of travel.[10]

A note of caution needs to be sounded here, however, in order to avoid the sort of intertextual vertigo and critical impressionism which blight Lowes's study, and which, as Richardson and Hofkosh suggest (p. 2), were perhaps instrumental in preventing it from 'stimulating a global approach to canonical British Romanticism long ago'. Verbal echoes alone are insufficient evidence of source material unless backed up by plausible contexts; for, as Schneider indicated (p. 120), 'the literature of England for some years before and after 1800 was honeycombed with caverns and bursting at the seams with fountains, springs, cataracts, rills, and "meanderings", not to mention also chasms and fragrant groves'. Cognisant of this warning, I revisit the terrain of Lowes' *Road to Xanadu* with some caution, attempting to contextualise some of the travel-narratives which he cited as sources, and also suggesting some important omissions from Lowes's reconstruction of Coleridge's reading list. In addition to reconsidering the significance of *Purchas His Pilgrimage*, the *named* seventeenth-century source for *Kubla Khan*, I will discuss two contemporary travelogues as being of particular importance to Coleridge's poem: Sir George Staunton's *An Authentic Account of an Embassy from the King of Great Britain to the Emperor of China . . . taken from the papers of . . . the Earl of Macartney* (1797), and James Bruce's approximately 3,000-page epic *Travels to Discover the Source of the Nile* (1790). I will argue that not the syncretic links between the poem's two oriental 'settings', China and Abyssinia, but rather a cultural contrast dependent upon their abrupt *juxtaposition*, determines the geopolitical meaning of *Kubla Khan*, a meaning virtually suppressed in the 1816 published version of the poem.

Marilyn Butler has suggested that Coleridge's medieval and orientalist poetry of the 1790's has more in common with Southey's writings in the same period than with those of Wordsworth, despite the fame of their collaborative *Lyrical Ballads*.[11] In these years Southey was at work in his 'laboratory of cultures'[12] seeking to fulfil a boyhood aspiration of writing narrative poems based upon the mythologies of diverse cultures; Welsh, Norse, Zoroastrian, Arabic, Hindu, Peruvian, Mexican. This was part of a politico-theological project – influenced by the French ideologues Constantin Volney and Charles Dupuis – of describing a world-revolution in which egalitarian rationalism would smash the idols of priestcraft and tyranny. In 1799 Southey collaborated with Coleridge on a poem in hexameters about Mahomet whom he described as an idol-breaker and liberator of Mecca from the Koreish.[13] Fragments by both Southey and Coleridge survive, although the poem was never completed; Coleridge's is particularly suggestive with its image of Mahomet as scourge of 'the blasphemous rites of the Pagan / And idolatrous Christians' (*Poems*, p. 309, ll. 4–5) who had corrupted primitive Christianity, as well as for the manner in which lines 11–14 echo the imagery of *Kubla Khan* lines 19–25. But by far the most important Southeyan context for Coleridge's poem is *Thalaba the Destroyer*, published in 1801 as fruit of Southey's extensive reading in the contemporary archive of orientalism. *Thalaba* continues the politico-theological critique of *Madoc* and *Mahomet*; in Butler's words, 'Thalaba is a Bedouin herdsman, a nomad, a man without landed property who descends as an iconoclast on Baghdad and other corrupt cities of the plain, imposing by force their return to an ideal republican simplicity' (p. 143).

Critics like Lowes, Butler and Schneider have all found an important intertext for *Kubla Khan* in books 6 and 7 of *Thalaba*, where Southey's hero enters and destroys the false earthly paradise of the oriental magician Aloadin (see SPW, pp. 262–74) Accepting Schneider's late, 1799–1800 dating of the poem, Marilyn Butler (p. 148) speculates that it was Southey's

'work-in-progress' *Thalaba* which first introduced Coleridge to the catalogue of oriental gardens in Purchas and the early travel-writers, as well as
prompting 'the unexplained transition from Cathay to Abyssinia' in *Kubla
Khan* which 'occurs naturally in Southey's note [to book 7]'. Southey's long
footnote quotes a passage from Purchas's *Pilgrimes* in which the young men
who have been seduced into Aloadin's false paradise are furnished with
'fruits, pictures, rills of milk, wine, honey, pallaces, and beautiful damosells,
richly attired' (SPW, p. 272). These young men, drugged by Aloadin or 'the
Old Man of the Mountain', are then forcibly removed from the garden and
promised a return ticket only on condition of carrying out various acts of
political murder as 'hashishim', or assassins. This was a legend which served
radical Southey well as an allegory of false religious ideologies with their
promises of heavenly rewards for death in meaningless wars. In contrast,
Butler (p. 152) suggests that Coleridge's version of Aloadin's garden in
Kubla Khan, emptied of its stupefied inmates, implies that the garden 'has
no function except to give pleasure to its solitary maker', evidence that by
1799 (or thereabouts) Coleridge's political quietism and aestheticism had
stolen a march on revolutionary activism. Although Butler never makes the
point explicitly, it seems also possible by the logic of this reading that
the inspired poet/visionary in the coda of *Kubla Khan* is identifiable with
one of Aloadin's stupefied 'assassins', yearning to be readmitted to the
paradise of false consciousness. Beyond quietism, according to this reading
Coleridge might be seen to be (rather perversely) airing a conservative
preference for hedonistic *participation* in Aloadin's narcotic paradise rather
than identifying with Southey's revolutionary idol-smasher Thalaba. In
many ways Marilyn Butler's seems the most fruitful context yet offered
for reading the '1790's' *Kubla Khan*, although in my view it does mean
accepting too early a date for Coleridge's drift to political quietism or even
conservatism. Moreover, a close reading of the Odoricus passage quoted in
Southey's footnote reveals that Aloadin's paradise was actually overthrown
by the Tartars,[14] so it would seem an odd decision on Coleridge's part to
represent the 'Old Man of the Mountains' as a Tartar emperor. In what
follows I will offer another suggestion, whilst at the same time accepting
Butler's argument that there is an important link between the politico-
theological radicalism, footnotes and oriental setting of Southey's *Thalaba*
and Coleridge's *Kubla Khan*.

COLERIDGE AND CHINESE GARDENING

One important contribution to understanding Coleridge's striking
juxtaposition of Kubla and the inspired visionary of the poem's coda was
John Beer's suggestion that the two figures exemplify Coleridge's distinction
between 'commanding' and 'absolute' genius theorised in chapter two of
Biographia Literaria.[15] Whereas 'absolute geniuses' 'rest content between

thought and reality, as it were in an intermundium of which their own living spirit supplies the *substance*, and their imagination the ever-varying *form*',[16] Coleridge theorises 'commanding genius' in terms of the creativity of political despots 'impressing their preconceptions on the world without': 'These in tranquil times are formed to exhibit a perfect poem in palace or temple or *landscape-garden*; . . . But alas! in times of tumult they are the men destined to come forth as the shaping spirit of Ruin, to destroy the wisdom of ages in order to substitute the fancies of a day, and to change kings and kingdoms, as the wind shifts and shapes the clouds' (I, pp. 32–3 italics mine). Kubla Khan, layer-out of the paradisal garden in lines 1–36 of Coleridge's poem also embodies the whirlwind-like power of Tartar world conquest and as such perfectly embodies 'commanding genius'. (Within two generations, starting with the election of Kubla's grandfather Ghengis to the Khanate in 1206, the Tartars had conquered virtually the whole Asian landmass, excepting the 'peninsulas' of Indo-China, Arabia, India and Western Europe). In a notebook of 1802, about the time that Napoleon created himself Consul for life, Coleridge wrote; 'A *Throne* the [earth-moving fulcrum] of Archimedes – Poet Bonaparte – Layer out of a World-garden –'.[17] The final phrase here, which chimes with the later account of the commanding genius as landscape-gardener, provides another hint for understanding Kubla's garden in the first 36 lines of Coleridge's poem. I am *not* suggesting here that the 'early' Kubla be read as an allegory of Napoleonic despotism, unlikely in view of the poem's date. But the notebook entry explicitly links up landscape-gardening and political tyranny in a manner quite distinct from Aloadin's oriental garden in *Thalaba*.

One aspect of the poem's topography which has been constantly acknowledged without, as far as I am aware, having being adequately examined, is the fact that the first 36 lines of *Kubla Khan* represent a landscape garden; in other words an artificial rather than a natural landscape. A striking feature of Coleridge's source (Marco Polo's account of Kubla Khan included in Purchas) is his account of the Tartar Emperor as a gardener.[18] Yet the Khan's gardens at the imperial palace in Khan-Bhalik (Beijing) and his summer palace at Shang-tu (Purchas' 'Xamdu', Coleridge's 'Xanadu') are more in the nature of hunting grounds than the sort of garden described in Coleridge's poem; 'fertile Meddowes, pleasant springs, delightful streames, and all sorts of beasts of chase and game'.[19] In striking contrast, Kubla's garden as evoked by Coleridge's poem seems closer to the eighteenth-century European orientalist conception of the Chinese garden or 'jardin anglo-chinois'. Remarkably, the enormous body of source studies of Coleridge's poem, in part led off the trail by the 1816 Preface, seem to have missed the most obvious, literal fact that *Kubla Khan* is a poem about the garden of a Chinese Emperor. The fact that poem was purportedly written in 1797, the same year as the first published account of the Earl of Macartney's failed Embassy to the court of the Chinese emperor Qianlong in 1793–4, and that Chinese affairs and Chinese gardens were very much 'in the news' gives an additional resonance to Coleridge's orientalist topos.

So what would Coleridge have understood by a Chinese garden? Earlier writers like Sir William Temple, Joseph Addison, Horace Walpole, and Oliver Goldsmith (in *The Citizen of the World*, 1762), had developed an aesthetic of Chinese gardening which marks one of the most influential 'orientalisms' in eighteenth-century European culture.[20] China was still largely closed to European trade – with the exception of the port of Canton – and the continuing strength of the Manchu dynasty (in contrast with the faltering Mughal dynasty in India) would exclude European empire-builders until the first Opium War of 1839–42. Nevertheless, Chinese aesthetics made a considerable impact on European garden styles, architecture and decorative arts, collectively described as *chinoiserie*. The definitive account of Chinese gardening was produced by Sir William Chambers in his *Dissertation on Oriental Gardening*, published in 1772 with an extremely fulsome dedication to George III. Chambers's Tory politics were embodied in his disdain for 'raw' nature and his imperialising desire to transform its paltry surface: developing Goldsmith's idea of the 'sublime' and 'beautiful' sections of the Chinese garden (as well as his own personal observation made during an early visit to China), Chambers divided the aesthetic of the Chinese garden into three categories, the pleasing, the terrible, and the surprising.[21] These seem to correspond to the structure of the garden landscape of Xanadu represented in the first 36 lines of Coleridge's poem.

Chambers described the 'pleasing' section of the Chinese garden as adorned by fragrant shrubs and blossoming trees, winding waterways with ornamental bridges, dotted with ornamental pavilions. The *Dissertation* specifies a domed-shaped pavilion called 'Miau Ting', or the 'Halls of the Moon' where the 'Chinese princes retire, with their favourite women' (*Dissertation*, pp. 30–1). This section seems to correspond to lines 6–11 in *Kubla Khan*, the 'gardens bright with sinuous rills' surrounding the Khan's pleasure dome. The description of the Chinese aesthetic of 'terror' is the most striking and memorable section of Chambers's book, however, with its 'deep vallies inaccessible to the sun . . . impetuous cataracts . . . blasted and shattered [trees], [ruined buildings] . . . gibbets, crosses, wheels, and the whole apparatus of torture, are seen from the roads . . . temples dedicated to the king of vengeance, deep caverns in the rocks, and descents to subterraneous habitations' (*Dissertation*, pp. 36–7). The aesthetic of 'surprise' (really an adjunct of 'terror', for both are influenced by Burke's celebrated theory of sublime astonishment as formulated in his 1757 *Philosophical Enquiry into the Origin of our Ideas of the Sublime and Beautiful* as much as any first-hand report of Chinese emblematic gardening), finds the quaking garden-tourist deep in gloomy valleys, 'on the banks of dull moving rivers, whose shores are covered with sepulchral monuments', where he is surprised by 'colossal figures of dragons', 'repeated shocks of electrical impulse, with showers of artificial rain, or sudden violent gusts of wind . . . the earth trembles under him'. He is shaken by terrifying noises, bulls roaring, the shouts of tortured men, the croaking of ravenous birds, thunder, cannon shots 'and all the noise of war' (*Dissertation*, pp. 38–40). Whole rivers are precipitated from mountain tops, where they 'foam and whirl amongst the rocks, till [they] . . . bury themselves in the gloom of impenetrable forests. In another place, the waters burst out with violence from many parts, spouting a great number of cascades; which, through various impediments, at last unite, and form one great expanse of water' (*Dissertation*, p. 74).

To read this harrowing aesthetic obstacle-course as a source for *Kubla Khan*'s 'deep romantic chasm' (with its 'mighty fountain', wailing women and 'ancestral voices prophesying war'), is to incorporate the sublime as well as the beautiful into the aesthetic design of the Khan's Chinese garden, rather than presuming that the romantic chasm disrupts its superficial charms. For Coleridge the *entire* landscape of the poem's 36 lines, for all its aesthetic potency, is massively contrived, quite literally 'a miracle of rare device' (1.34) woven from apparently irreconcilable elements of nature; 'A sunny pleasure dome with caves of ice!' (1.36). This is also to suggest that the psycho-sexual agency of Alph, the sacred river, might not be quite as redemptive as most critics have supposed. The libidinal energy of the sacred river rising in the Khan's garden according to my reading figures the futile power of Tartar conquest which ultimately squanders itself in the barren, torpid, 'sunless sea'. A footnote to Book 6, stanza 12 of Southey's *Thalaba* (in a passage of the poem which, as Schneider pointed out, is particularly rich in echoes of *Kubla Khan*) offers an additional clue to the possible identity of this world-conquering river; 'The Whang-ho . . . i.e. the Yellow River, rises not far from the source of the Ganges, in Tartarian mountains west of China, and having run through it with a course of more than six hundred leagues, discharges itself into the eastern sea. It hath its name from the yellow mud which always stains its water' (SPW, p. 264). The enigmatic Alph may have a more literal, historical referent than critics have supposed, for the Yellow River (the modern Hwang-ho) was, like the Yangtze-kiang, closed to European navigation and commerce, one of the prohibitions which the British Government sought unsuccessfully to overturn by sending the Earl of Macartney's embassy to the Chinese emperor in 1793. Coleridge has of course considerably foreshortened the course of the river in his microcosmic garden empire, but both Chambers's 'dull, moving rivers', (*Dissertation*, pp. 38–40) and Southey's yellow, stained 'Whang-ho' with its Tartarian origin seem plausible sources for the river Alph's meandering, mazy motion and its tumultuous descent into the 'sunless' or 'lifeless ocean' of the partially land-enclosed Yellow sea.

As far as I am aware, only one critic, J. R. de J. Jackson, has noted (in passing) the links between Chambers's *Dissertation on Oriental Gardening*

186

and Coleridge's *Kubla Khan*, plausibly suggesting that Coleridge may have read the extracts from the *Dissertation* anthologised in Vicesimus Knox's *Elegant Extracts* (Jackson, pp. 47, 311). Jackson does not however comment on the fact that the *Dissertation* had rapidly stirred up a bitter political controversy, satirised by the Whig landscape poet William Mason (aided by Horace Walpole) in *A Heroick Epistle to Sir William Chambers* in 1773, which effectively and comically linked Chambers's account of Chinese gardening to political tyranny and the Tory politics of the Court party. The politics of Chambers's *Dissertation* is an important factor in reconstructing radical Coleridge's notion of the ideological valency of Chinese gardening.[22] But a more immediate context for *Kubla Khan*, and one which reheated the twenty-year old polemic around Chinese gardening, was the publication in 1797 of Sir George Staunton's *Authentic Account of an Embassy from the King of Great Britain to the Emperor of China . . . taken from the papers of the Earl of Macartney*, accompanied by a lavishly illustrated volume of maps and prints, most of them the work of the expedition's painter William Alexander. As mentioned above, Macartney's embassy aimed to persuade the Emperor to allow a British resident to settle in Beijing and to loosen the tight regulations limiting foreign trade to the single port of Canton. Lavish presents were showered on the 82-year old Emperor Qianlong by the embassy – as much a trade mission as a diplomatic expedition, accompanied by scientists, linguists and artists numbering 94 members in all, and costing the East India Company a grand total of £78,000 – but it ultimately foundered on the fact of Macartney's refusal to 'Kow-tow' to the instransigent Emperor. A further account of the embassy by Macartney's secretary Sir John Barrow, *Travels in China*, was published in 1804 and appreciatively reviewed by Robert Southey in the same year.[23]

In the course of narrating the vicissitudes of the Macartney embassy, Staunton's *Authentic Account* gave extensive descriptions of the Chinese Emperor Qianlong's gardens at Yuen-min-yuen in Beijing and his summer palace at Zhe-hol (or 'Gehol') in Tartary. 'Every thing seemed to be avoided which betrayed a regularity of design',[24] wrote Staunton, confirming the Chinese garden aesthetic as understood by Chambers and other eighteenth-century European commentators. A particular symbolism was attached to Qianlong's decision to receive the embassy at his summer palace of Zhe-hol, north-west of the Great Wall in Chinese Tartary, rather than in the capital Beijing. (Kubla's summer palace as described in Coleridge's source Purchas was also situated north of the Great Wall in Chinese Tartary, at Shan-tu, or 'Xamdu' or 'Xanadu'; see *Pilgrimage*, p. 472.) Staunton (II, p. 268) pointed out that the Emperor Qianlong did not regard himself as Han Chinese, but rather as a Manchu Tartar, claiming direct descent from Kubla Khan, thirteenth-century conqueror of China; Qianlong was apparently obsessed by this Tartar lineage, which was reflected in the symbolism of his court. When the Embassy finally arrived at Gehol, they were impressed by the wild mountain scenery of Chinese Tartary, but above all by the Garden of Ten Thousand Trees at the Royal Palace at Zhe-hol, where the Emperor received Macartney's suite on the 14th September, 1793. In Alexander's coloured engraving of the reception, the Emperor is seen approaching his white, dome-shaped Tartar tent (or 'yurt') borne on a litter, whilst Macartney approaches from the bottom right in his robes of office. The day following the reception, Macartney, Staunton and a number of other British diplomats were entertained in the Imperial gardens by the Grand Vizier, described in the *Authentic Account* (II, pp. 246–8).

Macartney's appreciative account of this turn around the Zhe-hol gardens was published in Barrow's *Travels in China* in 1804 (Barrow himself had remained in Beijing, but had the Earl's permission to publish this section of his journal), and is of especial interest given that the Earl was an accomplished landscape gardener. 'Had China been accessible to Mr ["Capability"] Browne and Mr Hamilton', he wrote, 'I should have sworn they had drawn their happiest ideas from the rich sources, which I have tasted this day . . . I have been enchanted by scenes perfectly similar to those I have known [in England], to the magnificence of Stowe, the softer beauties of Woburn, and the fairy-land of Paine's Hill'.[25] Although Macartney is dismissive of the accuracy of Sir William Chambers's *Dissertation on Oriental Gardening*, it seems to have provided him with a framework for understanding the layout of Gehol (Barrow's rendering of Zhe-hol). Whilst the eastern section of the gardens corresponded to Chambers's aesthetic of pleasing beauty, the western section figured the sublime of terror; 'in many places immense woods, chiefly oaks, pines and chestnuts, grow upon almost perpendicular steeps . . . these woods often clamber over the loftiest pinnacles of the stony hills, [or] descend with a rapid sweep, and bury themselves in the deepest vallies'. Here ruined banqueting halls and monasteries overlook 'a cataract tumbling from above, raging with foam and rebounding with a thousand echoes from below, or silently engulphed in a gloomy pool, or yawning chasm' (p. 132). Macartney's enthusiasm for the sublime features of Gehol maps onto the landscape of Coleridge's *Kubla Khan* more closely than many of the sources urged by critics (note for example the distinctive use of the word 'rebounding' here, and in line 21 of *Kubla Khan*). But although *written* in 1793–4 it wasn't published until 1804, so couldn't have been seen by Coleridge before he wrote his poem. Staunton (whose account on the other hand Coleridge *could* have read)[26] had more to say about the Imperial Gardens in Beijing, Yuen-min-yuen, than Gehol, but struck a more disapproving, critical note than Macartney in his description of the politics of the Chinese garden; 'mountains and vallies, lakes and rivers, rude precipices and gentler slopes, have been produced where nature did not intend them . . . this world, in miniature, has been created at the command, and for the pleasure of one man, but by the hard labour of thousands' (II, 303). One notable feature of Yuen-ming-Yuan was a powerful mechanical fountain constructed in the 1750's by a Jesuit missionary, Fr. Michel Benoist (see 'Case Study', p. 517). The Chinese garden described here by Staunton symbolises oriental despotism; in this light it is perhaps ironic that Staunton's son the pioneer Sinologist Sir George Staunton, who had accompanied the Embassy as a young page, later sought to recreate Gehol in the grounds of his estate at Leigh Park in Hampshire, which he bought in 1820.[27]

It was however Barrow rather than Staunton who provided the source material on Tartar gardening for the eighth book of Wordsworth's *Prelude*, completed in 1805:

> . . . tract more exquisitely fair
> Than is that paradise of ten thousand trees,
> Or Gehol's famous gardens, in a clime
> Chosen for widest empire, for delight
> Of the Tartarian dynasty composed
> (Beyond that mighty wall, not fabulous,
> China's stupendous mound) by patient skill
> Of myriads and boon Nature's lavish help.
> Scene linked to scene, and evergrowing change,
> Soft, grand, or gay! with palaces and domes
> Of pleasure spangled over, shady dells,
> For eastern monasteries, sunny mounds
> With temples crested, bridges, gondolas
> Rocks, dens and groves of foliage taught to melt
> Into each other their obsequious hues . . .[28]

Wordsworth, whose allusion to 'domes of pleasure' seems to echo Coleridge's unpublished *Kubla Khan*, here picks up Staunton and Barrow's political critique of Chinese gardening as a product of oriental tyranny, in contrast to 'the paradise where I was reared' in the Lakeland mountains. The politics of the Chinese garden emerging from the Chambers/Mason controversy and the recent Macartney travelogues, superimposed on the traditional Biblical topos of the false paradise, maps out the ideological terrain of Coleridge's *Kubla Khan* more closely than Aloadin's garden in Southey's *Thalaba*. Coleridge's poetic rendering of a Chinese imperial garden seems to be tempered by the ominous words attached to the second edition of Sir William Chambers's *Dissertation*, which envisaged England itself as an immense Chinese Garden, and George III a sort of western Qianlong. Chambers hailed Britain as 'an empire transformed into a splendid Garden, with the imperial mansion [Windsor] towering on an eminence in the centre, and the palaces of the nobles scattered like pleasure-pavilions amongst the plantations', finding that such a Tory vision 'infinitely surpasses any thing that even the Chinese ever attempted; yet vast as the design appears, the execution is certainly within your reach'.[29]

THE ABYSSINIAN MAID

In his 1804 review of Barrow's *Travels in China* Southey commented that, in the last 250 years at least 'Europe has been progressive in all the arts of life, while China has stood still'.[30] Anticipating the aggressive sinophobia of Thomas De Quincey and many other commentators around the time of the first Opium War of 1839–42, Southey here analyses the 'patriarchal system of parental authority', the quintessence of Chinese despotism, in which 'the son is the slave of the father, the subject is the slave of the emperor' (p. 79). Harking back to the jacobinical mood of his hero Thalaba's destruction of Aloadin's false paradise, Southey (taking issue with the Tory Barrow) wishes for the 'radical destruction' of the Chinese empire by European-style social revolution, for, 'we have not, like [Mr Barrow], that horror of the enlightened doctrines of the rights of man' (p. 81). A similar judgement on Kubla's dynasty might seem to underlie Coleridge's poem, as I have been arguing, although the resolution offered in *Kubla Khan*'s 18-line epilogue seems strikingly different from Southey's revolutionary desideratum for China.

As we saw above, the politico-theological target of Southey and Coleridge's poems in the 1790's was the idolatry of false religion and the act of political liberation in such poems was represented as a smashing of the idols.[31] Coleridge's 1799 poetical fragment *Mahomet* insisted that the Prophet Mahomet's shortcomings were balanced by the fact that he 'crush'd the blasphemous rites of the Pagan / And idolatrous Christians. – For veiling the Gospel Of Jesus, / They, the best corrupting, had made it worse than the vilest' (*Poems*, p. 309, ll. 4–6). Although the theme of idolatry is not manifestly present in *Kubla Khan*, it is strongly evident in Coleridge's cited source, *Purchas his Pilgrimage*. In Purchas's account of Kubla (based on Marco Polo's *Travels*), immediately after the lines describing the garden of 'Xamdu', the emperor is described, at the behest of his 'Astrologers or Magicians' 'pour[ing] forth with his owne hands the milke of [the Royal] Mares in the ayre, and on the earth, to give drinke to the Spirits and Idols which they worship' (*Pilgrimage*, p. 472). In the paragraph that follow (p. 473), Kubla is shown to be completely at the mercy of these devilish Priests or 'Bachsi' 'delud[ing] the people with opinion of their sanctitie', his whole temporal power-structure organised around their idols. Moreover the Bachsi, like other Tartars, appear to be addicted to usury, sodomy and cannibalism. By extension, Kubla's garden, and the tradition of Chinese gardening upon which Coleridge draws in the first part of the poem, symptomizes the Khan's *political* idolatry, imposing on nature in order to wield unlawful political power. Oriental despotism, idolatry and gardening can be taken here to represent English 'Old Corruption', the configuration of monarchy, priesthood and aristocracy which was the target for Coleridgean polemic in the 1790's, symbolised by the landscape gardens of Chambers, Capability Brown, and Repton.

What is just as remarkable as *Kubla Khan*'s implicit links with Coleridge and Southey's politico-theological critique of idolatry, however, is the extent to which the poem's 18-line coda now *differs* in mood and content from the Southeyan programme of revolutionary destruction. As I have argued, the Khan's despotism is manifest in the aesthetic idolatry of 'laying out a world-garden' in contradistinction from the kinds of social allegory associated with Southey's poems. But rather than implementing a Thalaban programme of destruction, Coleridge's second fragment shifts from the negativity of the 'world-garden' to an alternative, positive vision of the Abyssinian Maid's 'symphony and song'. Critical readings of the poem have tended to stress the unity of the two parts of *Kubla Khan*, lines 1–36 and the 18-line 'coda', summed up by K. M. Wheeler's comment (p. 138) that 'the maid's song and Kubla's dome are distinct, but are then mysteriously brought together both when we realise that the 'second' vision may imply that the song of the maid is about the dome, and when the visionary says that he will build the dome with the song of the maid'. Without rejecting such undeniable continuities, a contextual reading of the poem needs however to take seriously the specificity of the two diverse 'oriental' settings if it is to avoid the syncreticist conclusion that 'all of Asia is present in one spot: all realism whatsoever about locations and distances falls away' (see Shaffer, p. 165).

In point of fact the coda *is* marked by a strong cultural allusion which focuses its visionary lyricism in a particular – and distinct – geopolitics. The coda belongs to Abyssinia just as the first 36 lines belong to Xanadu; and the Maid's song is of 'Mount Abora' (in the earlier Crewe Manuscript, 'Mount Amara'), *not* Xanadu. Now Abyssinia, in striking contrast to idolatrous Tartary, connoted an ancient Christian culture, whose customs and religious practices had recently been evoked for European readers with all the dramatic force of personal witness in James Bruce's *Travels to Discover the Source of the Nile* (1790). By juxtaposing the source of the visionary's inspiration and his wish to 'revive' it in imagination with Kubla's landscape garden, haunted as it is by intimations of war and mortality, Coleridge sets up a counterpoint between two quite different cultural *topoi* at the same time as comparing and contrasting different modes of aesthetic experience. Above all, the Abyssinian Maid's visionary song and the 'poet's' ecstatic response to it seem to work as an antistrophic rebuke to the Khan's aesthetic idolatry (i.e. the 'jardin anglo-chinois'), a juxtaposition which gets somewhat obscured by subsequent textual alterations and by the addition of the 1816 Preface.

In the seventeenth and eighteenth centuries Abyssinia had become the focus of theological polemic after the publication of the Lutheran divine Hiob Ludolf's *Historia Aethiopica* in 1681. Ludolf claimed, against the Portuguese Jesuits who had sought converts and political influence in the region throughout the seventeenth century, that the Abyssinian Church represented a pure primitive Christianity uncontaminated by Roman Catholic doctrine. A similar view was implied in Samuel Johnson's 1735 translation of Father

Jerome Lobo's *Voyage to Abyssinia* (celebrated as a source for Johnson's 'Abyssinian Tale', *Rasselas*). Although Lobo's account was severely censured by the anti-Catholic Bruce, it did emphasise the primitive vigour of Abyssinian worship, and above all the importance or devotional singing; 'No country in the world is so full of churches, monasteries, and ecclesiasticks, as Abyssinia; it is not possible to sing in one church or monastery without being heard in another . . . They sing the psalms of David, of which as well as the other parts of the Holy Scriptures, they have a very exact translation in their own language' (p. 53). Bruce had brought back with him a copy of the apocryphal Book of Enoch, which described how the sons of God fell in love with the daughters of men, giving birth to a race of giants who plagued the world until destroyed by Noah's flood. This seemed to provide the key to an early Gnostic strain of Christianity, and we have it on record that both the doctrines of the primitive Christian church and the Gnostic canon were of great interest to the Unitarian Coleridge in the 1790's, whose writings in this period are a sustained critique of the idolatrous 'corruptions of Christianity'.

Seen in its Abyssinian context, the coda takes on a new meaning in relation to the first 36 lines of the poem. Much ink has been spilt by critics on the significance of 'Mount Abora', a name which doesn't correspond to any known site in Abyssinia or elsewhere.[32] The discovery of the Crewe MS cast some light on the mystery, for 'Abora' was seen in the earlier version to have been 'Amara' (apparently 'Amahra' was the original, deleted form, Shaffer, p. 103), one of the major provinces of Abyssinia described by Bruce as 'a very mountainous country, full of nobility; the men are reckoned the handsomest in Abyssinia, as well as the bravest'.[33] It was also the site where the Abyssinian dynasty had confined heirs to the throne prior to their succession in an attempt to prevent usurpation and rebellion, a legend upon which Johnson had based his account of Prince Rasselas's 'Happy Valley'. Coleridge's change from 'Amara' to 'Abora' seems motivated by more than a poet's concern for internal sound-patterns; as Marjorie Levinson has suggested, such changes 'suggest the author's general concern [in 1816] to liberate the poem from its historical and literary sources'[34] As most commentators have pointed out, the Abyssinian 'Mount Amara' also featured in Milton's *Paradise Lost*, book 4 lines 280–284: 'where Abassin kings their issue guard, / Mount Amara – though this by some supposed / True Paradise – under the Ethiop line / By Nilus' head, enclosed with shining rock, / A whole day's journey high'.[35] I believe that it is however necessary to read this Miltonic allusion rather carefully, if we are not to be led off on a false trail which would identify Mount Amara with the false paradise, thereby skewing the underlying meaning of the poem's contexts by enforcing a superficial link between the Abyssinian Maid's song and Xanadu.[36]

The Miltonic resonance of 'Mount Amara' doubtless aroused Coleridge's interest in the location in the first place, although his reading of Purchas would have led him back to Milton's own source for his allusion: chapter 5, book 7 of *Purchas's Pilgrimage*, baldly entitled 'Of the Hill Amara'. Here is another instance of Coleridge mapping a contemporary travel account (Bruce's *Travels*) onto an earlier, renaissance source in Purchas, just as I argued above that he mapped the near-contemporary texts of Staunton and Chambers onto Purchas's account of Kubla's Tartar garden. Purchas's chapter described how in ancient times 'before the Raigne of the Queene of Saba'[37] the high, dome-like Mount Amara was the seat of pagan temples to the Sun and Moon. Despite Milton's emphasis however, Mount Amara only seems to have represented a false paradise in ancient times. Its modern theological significance would rather seem to lie in the fact that it symbolised the conversion of Abyssinia from pagan idolatry to Christianity, and the transformation (after the fourth century AD) of the pagan temples into Christian churches. Purchas's Mount Amara was also the site of the Monastery of the Holy Cross, furnished with a wonderful library containing manuscripts of the Books of Enoch, Abraham, Solomon and Job. After the Fall of Jerusalem, it also became the repository of a wealth of Rabbinical texts (*Pilgrimage*, p. 845). The library on Mount Amara was just the sort of place which the young Unitarian Coleridge, immersed in the new Bible criticism and struggling to distinguish 'primitive' Christian doctrine from later Trinitarian chaff, might well have conjured over in a visionary moment. Moreover, as a putative source of the Nile, Purchas's Mount Amara might symbolise, given the imagistic parallelism with 'Alph the Sacred River' in *Kubla Khan*, a source of uncontaminated primitive Christianity, its fructifying influence upon the Egyptian desert contrasting with the Alph's unprofitable descent into the 'sunless sea'.

Bruce's account of contemporary Abyssinia would, of course, have been a corrective to any facile Unitarian idealisation of Abyssinian Christianity, for it is often described as a place of nightmarish cruelty as well as of romantic fascination and primitive devotion. Coleridge cited Bruce's *Travels* in his 1795 poem *Religious Musings*[38] and dubbed him the 'prince of travellers'. As Lowes (pp. 337–46) indicated, Bruce's text seems also to have exerted a powerful influence on *Kubla Khan*, although I would qualify his claim by arguing that this influence is limited to the geopolitics of the coda rather than to fugitive verbal parallels with the 'mighty fountain' at lines 17–24 or other aspects of the poem's imagery. The powerful erotic interest of Bruce's narrative and especially his portrait of his royal patroness Ozoro Esther ('most lovely and amiable of women', III, p. 544) is surely discernible in Coleridge's almost feverish evocation of the 'Abyssinian Maid' and her 'symphony and song'. Bruce's lonely and romantic journey to the remote and mountainous Christian kingdom of Abssyinia – a land frequently described by Bruce as flowing (quite literally) with milk and honey – is internalised in the poet/visionary's inner journey in *Kubla Khan*'s coda, as the travel narrative is troped into a dream. Bruce's *Travels* was obsessed with accurately describing and evoking the unknown kingdom of Abyssinia (and particularly the fountains of the Nile which the Scots traveller claimed to have 'discovered'), given that his veracity had been universally questioned following his return to Britain in 1774. This seems to find an echo in the subjunctive mood of Coleridge's visionary; 'Could I revive within me / Her symphony and song, / To such a deep delight 'twould win me, / That with music loud and long, / I would build that dome in air' (ll.41–6). 'Weav[ing] a circle round him thrice' was exactly what the British public had *not* done to Bruce, instead simply adding his name to the long list of 18th century 'travel-liars'.[39] Troping Bruce's literalist claims for readerly credit into a visionary 'dome in air', Coleridge seeks to replace universal scepticism with poetic faith, thereby mirroring his evolving defence of Christian revelation as visionary spirituality rather than rational acquiescence. The Abyssinian Maid and her song of Mount Amara thus symbolise a pure, primitive Christian spirituality deeply threatening to the religious and political establishments against which Coleridge throughout the 1790's had waged an unremitting war. Coleridge's eroticised response to oppression ('to such a deep delight t'would win me' l. 44) represents a stark contrast to Southey's revolutionary programme, the stoic and masculinist republicanism of *Thalaba the Destroyer* and other poems. In response to Kubla's paramount control of aesthetic production, Coleridge's visionary wishes neither to 'decree' nor destroy but to *build* his dome in air, like the *Biographia*'s 'absolute genius', 'rest[ing] content between thought and reality, as it were in an intermundium of which [his] own living spirit supplies the *substance*, and [his] imagination the ever-varying *form*' (I, p. 32).

That Coleridge seems rather rapidly to have shrugged off the seduction of the Abyssinian Maid is suggested by his dismissive reference to a similar visionary maid as 'a watery idol' in line 83 of his poem entitled 'The Picture', written in 1802. As if to underline his recantation, he then went on to make a point of quoting lines 91–100 of 'The Picture' in his 1816 Preface to *Kubla Khan*, in which the disturbed surface of the pool becomes a mirror as 'the fragments dim of lovely forms / Come trembling back' (ll.98–9). This has generally been taken to refer to a wished-for 'completion' of *Kubla Khan*, left in fragmentary form after the interruption of the person from Porlock. However, given that 'The Picture' goes on to describe how the visionary maid whom the poet had formerly imagined to be reflected upon the water (the 'watery idol') is absent from its recomposed mirror surface, the quotation of these lines in the Preface to *Kubla Khan* might rather be taken to refer specifically to the illusionary nature of the Abyssinian Maid and her song of Mount Amara. Both the 1802 'The Picture' and the 1816 Preface *to Kubla Khan* might thus be read as slightly embarrassed recantations of the idealised Ozoro Esther and the eroticised primitive Christianity associated with the Abyssinian Maid in his original draft of the poem. An increasingly orthodox Coleridge now represents 'oriental' Christian primitivism as yet another form of idolatry.

In *Kubla Khan* the sort of allusions which I have been discussing of course remain submerged, absorbed in the textual compression of the poem, their context lost in the obscurity of its pre-publication existence and in the ideological controversy of the late 1790's. The relationship between the contemporary travel narrative and the romance-epic of the 1790's and 1800's is made manifest in the footnote documentation of Southey's narrative poems written in these same years. But the absence of any such explicit documentation in Coleridge's condensed, elliptical and self-conscious poetic productions of the same period should not be read as detracting from their abiding contextual importance. If imagination, in Coleridge's mature thought – in the *Biographia*, or the 1816 redaction of *Kubla Khan* – has been relocated in an 'intermundium' of the inner spirit, it has been at the cost of cutting loose from its point of origin in the politico-theological polemic and the travel-narratives so widely read by the poets in the late 1790's. The ongoing prestige both of Western orientalism (in Edward Said's sense) and the discourse of high Romanticism are dependent upon the powerful syncretising and unifying impulse of Coleridgean 'absolute genius'. In examining the geopolitics of some of Coleridge's sources I have sought to resist these impulses in order to reconsider the worldliness of a canonical Romantic text.

Notes

1 John Beer suggests that the 'various notes on Kubla Khan and the Tartars' contained in the *Notebooks* represent material for a continuation of the poem, supporting Coleridge's assertion that the poem was unfinished. See *Coleridge the Visionary* (London: Chatto and Windus, 1970), p. 275. Coleridge's published Preface and note to the Crewe MS claim that it was composed in the summer or fall of 1797, E. H. Coleridge preferred the summer of 1798 in his 1912 edition of Coleridge's *Complete Poetical Works* for Oxford University Press (p. 295), and more recently Elizabeth Schneider, in her study *Opium, Coleridge and Kubla Khan* (1953: rpt. New York: Octagon Books, 1966), argued for later composition in 1799 or even May or June, 1800 (p. 154). The poem was clearly in manuscript circulation by October 1800, when Mary 'Perdita' Robinson referred to both its Tartar and 'Abyssinian' sections in her 'Lines to the Poet Coleridge'. My connection here of *Kubla Khan* with Staunton's *Authentic Account* (1797) makes the earlier date marginally more probable. *Kubla Khan*'s allusions to Southey's *Thalaba* (1801) are clearly not to the published poem, but rather to manuscript drafts or notes which Southey's 1837 Preface claimed the poet had been working on since 1796, and which Coleridge could of course have seen. (*Southey's Poetical Works, Complete in One Volume*, (London 1876), p. ix, hereafter SPW.) Beyond that, my interpretation must unfortunately remain agnostic concerning the poem's exact date of composition.

2 *Samuel Taylor Coleridge: Poems*, ed. by John Beer (London: Everyman, 1993), p. 203. Beer's edition usefully contains parallel texts of the Crewe MS of *Kubla Khan* and the published 1816 version. Hereafter *Poems*.

3 J. R. de J. Jackson, *Poetry of the Romantic Period* (London: Routledge and Kegan Paul, 1980), p. 46, hereafter Jackson.

4 Jerome J. McGann, *The Romantic Ideology: A Critical Investigation* (Chicago and London: Chicago University Press, 1983) pp. 100–1.

5 Kathleen M. Wheeler, *'Kubla Khan* and the Art of Thingifying' (1981), in *Romanticism: A Critical Reader*, ed. by Duncan Wu (Oxford: Blackwell 1995), pp. 123–150; p. 123.

6 *Poems*, p. 206. The Crewe manuscript, containing a number of textual discrepancies from the 1816 version, was only discovered in 1934, and its date is uncertain: although John Beer speculates that it was 'apparently written down soon after the time of composition', his own admission of the 'retrospective quality' of the note would rather seem to suggest a later date. Cf *Poems*, pp. 201–2.

7 Nigel Leask, *British Romantic Writers and the East: Anxieties of Empire* (Cambridge University Press, 1992), pp. 170–228.

8 Elinor Shaffer, *'Kubla Khan' and the Fall of Jerusalem: The Mythological School in Biblical Criticism and Secular Literature 1770–1880* (Cambridge University Press, 1975), p. 142.

9 *Romanticism, Race and Imperial Culture, 1780–1834*, ed. by Alan Richardson and Sonia Hofkosh. (Bloomington and Indianapolis: Indiana University Press, 1996), p. 2.

10 Jonathan Livingstone Lowes, *The Road to Xanadu: A Study in the Ways of the Imagination* (1927: rpt. London: Pan Books, 1978).

11 Marilyn Butler, 'Plotting the Revolution: The Political Narratives of Romantic Poetry and Criticism' in *Romantic Revolutions: Criticism and Theory*, ed. by Kenneth Johnston *et al.* (Bloomington and Indianapolis: Indiana University Press, 1990), pp. 133–157; p. 142.

12 Javed Majeed, *Ungoverned Imaginings: James Mill's 'The History of British India' and Orientalism* (Oxford: Clarendon University Press, 1992), p. 53.

13 See *Robert Southey's Common-Place Book, Fourth Series Original Memoranda, etc.*, ed. by J. W. Warter (London: Brown, Green, and Longmans 1851), p. 19.

14 SPW, p. 272. The identification made by Schneider (p. 141) and Butler (mentioned above) of a putative leap from 'Cathay to Abyssinia' in Southey's footnote, with the abrupt geographical transition in *Kubla Khan*, is likewise problematical. The account of Aloadin's garden in Purchas (cited in Southey's note) locates it in N. E. Persia, and Odoricus situates his garden in 'Melistorte', both Western – rather than Eastern – Asian settings. Mandeville's version of the 'Old Man of the Mountains' story takes place in 'Ye Yle of Pentexoire, that is, the Lond of Prestre John' (SPW, p. 272). The identification of Prester John with Abyssinia made by late medieval Portuguese geographers had by the eighteenth century been refuted, most prominently in Joachim Legrand's 'Dissertation on Prester John', appended to his redaction of Jerome Lobo's *Voyage to Abyssinia*, translated by Samuel Johnson in 1735. The account of Genghis Khan's defeat of the Asian Christian monarch Prester John in Marco Polo's *Travels* was on the other hand well known, and translated in Coleridge's source Purchas. There seems therefore little hard evidence for any supposed shift from China to Abyssinia in Southey's note. See Samuel Johnson, *A Voyage to Abyssinia (Translated from the French)*, ed. by Joel J. Gold, vol. xv of the *Yale Edition of the Works of Samuel Johnson* (New Haven and London: Yale University Press, 1985), pp. 190–207.

15 John Beer, *Coleridge's Poetic Intelligence* (London and Basingstoke: Macmillan, 1977), pp. 115–6.

16 S. T. Coleridge, *Biographia Literaria*, ed. by James Engell and W. Jackson Bate, 2 vols (Princeton and London: Princeton University Press 1983), I, 31–3.

17 *The Notebooks of Samuel Taylor Coleridge*, ed. by Kathleen Coburn *Volume 1 1794–1804* (New York, Princeton and London: 1957–), entry 1166.

18 *Purchas his Pilgrimage, or Relations of the World and the Religions observed in all Ages and Places discovered, from the Creation into this Present* (1613: London, 1617), p. 472. See also Purchas's *Hakluytus Posthumus, or Purchas His Pilgrimes* (1625), 19 vols (Glasgow: J. MacLehose and Sons, 1906), XI, p. 231. Cf Lowes, pp. 328–9 on the links between Purchas's two books in the conception of Coleridge's poem.

19 *Purchas his Pilgrimage*, p. 472.

20 See A. O. Lovejoy, 'The Chinese Origin of a Romanticism' in *Essays in the History of Ideas* (1940: rpt. New York: Capricorn Books, 1960) pp. 99–135 for an overview.

21 William Chambers, *A Dissertation on Oriental Gardening* (1772) hereafter, *Dissertation* William Mason, *An Heroic Epistle* (14th ed., 1777) and *An Heroic Postscript* (8th ed., 1774), with an intro. by John Harris (England: Gregg International Publishers Ltd., 1972), p. 35.

22 For an illuminating account of Mason, Chambers, and the politics of the Chinese garden, see Stephen Bending's 'A Natural Revolution? Garden Politics in 18th Century England', forthcoming in *Refiguring Revolutions*, ed. by Steven Zwicker and Kevin Sharpe.

23 *Annual Review*, 3, 1804 (London 1805), 69–82. For a recent collection of essays on the Macartney embassy, see *Ritual and Diplomacy: The Macartney Mission to China 1792–4*, ed. by Robert A. Bicker (London: British Association for Chinese Studies, 1993).

24 Sir George Staunton, *An Authentic Account of an Embassy from the King of Great Britain to the Emperor of China . . . taken from the papers of . . . the Earl of Macartney*, 2 vols (London: 1797), II, 245.

25 John Barrow, *Travels in China* (London: 1804), p. 130.

26 I have been unable to find any direct evidence for Coleridge's first-hand knowledge of Staunton's book, but given intense contemporary public interest, Coleridge's well-attested love of travel accounts, and the practical concerns of Thomas Beddoes and Josiah and Tom Wedgwood with the outcome of the Macartney Embassy (a crate of Wedgwood's ceramics was amongst the samples of English manufactured produce presented to the Emperor by the 'trade mission'), it was very much part of his intellectual milieu in the mid-1790's. See J. L. Cranmer-Byng and Trevor Levere, 'A Case Study in Cultural Collision: Scientific Apparatus in the Macartney Embassy to China, 1793', *Annals of Science*, 38(1981), pp. 503–525; 505, hereafter 'Case Study'.

27 Mavis Batey, *Regency Gardens*, (Bucks.: Shire Publications, 1995), pp. 41–2.

28 1805 text, book 8, lines 121–135, W. Wordsworth *The Prelude, A Parallel Text*, ed. by J. C. Maxwell (Harmondsworth: Penguin, 1971), pp. 302–4.

29 Sir William Chambers, *An Explanatory Discourse, by Tan Chet-qua, of Quang-chew-fu*, pub. with the 2nd edition of Chambers's *Dissertation* (London: 1773), pp. 133–4. Cited in Bending, 'A Natural Revolution?'

30 *Annual Review*, 3 (1804), (London 1805), 69.

31 Simon Jarvis had argued for the importance of the notion of idolatry in the poetry of Wordsworth around the same time; see his essay 'Wordsworth and Idolatry', forthcoming in *Studies in Romanticism*.

32 Lowes p. 341 speculated that 'Abora, might be based on two Abyssinian rivers mentioned by Bruce, 'Abola' and 'Astaboras', before presciently suggesting that 'Abora' in fact stood for 'Amara' (the Crewe manuscript, which would confirm this suggestion, had not yet come to light)'. H. W. Piper suggests another river in *The Singing of Mount Abora* (London: Associated University Presses, 1987), p. 63, but this doesn't eliminate the difficulty that 'Abora' is a 'Mount' and not a river.

33 James Bruce, *Travels to Discover the Source of the Nile, in the years 1768, 1769, 1770, 1771, 1772, 1773, and 1774*, 5 vols (Edinburgh: 1790), III, 255.
34 Marjorie Levinson, *The Romantic Fragment Poem: A Critique of a Form* (Chapel Hill and London: University of N. Carolina Press, 1986), p. 100.
35 *John Milton: Complete English Poems, Of Education, Areopagitica*, ed. by Gordon Campbell (London: Everyman, 1993), p. 230.
36 Schneider, p. 25, for example, assumes this to be the case.
37 *Pilgrimage*, p. 844. Lowes comments that this chapter in Purchas 'is one of the most memorable purple patches in the book, and nobody who knew the *Pilgrimage* would be likely to forget it' [p. 343].
38 *Poems*, p. 87. Cf Lowes p. 123 for Coleridge on Bruce.
39 See Perey Adams, *Travellers and Travel Liars 1660–1800* (New York: Dover Publications, 1980), pp. 210–20 for an account of the sceptical reaction to Bruce's claims.

27

COLONIAL SPACE AND THE COLONIZATION OF TIME IN SCOTT'S *WAVERLEY*

Saree Makdisi

Source: *Studies in Romanticism* 34 (1995), 155–87.

A. Introductory

It would be only a small exaggeration, I think, to say that the images that many of us associate with the Scottish Highlands have their origins in Walter Scott's first novel, *Waverley*. Scott started writing *Waverley* in 1805, though he dropped it for several years and only completed it in 1814. The novel, which is set mostly in Scotland during the Jacobite Rebellion of 1745, not only presented to its nineteenth-century readers a romanticized view of the Jacobite rebels and their leader, Bonnie Prince Charlie; it offered, virtually for the first time, an altogether new series of images and representations of the Scottish Highlands. Beginning with *Waverley*, in other words, Sir Walter Scott's image of the Highlands has in cultural terms virtually taken over from and supplanted "the real thing," by which I mean something stronger than that Scott's representation has precluded other views of the Highlands.

For this raises the question, not simply of what that "real thing" was or is, but rather of how today's Highlands were brought into being *as* a reality— or as a set of at once material and symbolic realities—at a certain specifiable moment in the violent cultural history of the United Kingdom. The question that lies at the heart of my interest in *Waverley* is this: how is space, as a fluid and simultaneously material and political process, produced or re-produced during the process of colonial conquest? Or, to what extent can the violent and productive process of colonialism be understood as *spatial*—as a process not merely involving the coding and recoding of conquered territories and peoples, but the virtual reinvention of the colonized territory as a space that can be put to use in various ways? Moreover, if we do want to understand colonialism as a spatial operation, can we see the

199

resistance to colonial rule in spatial terms, as an anti-hegemonic attempt to either limit or to contest the hegemonic territorializations undertaken in colonialism? The answers to these questions may depend on the extent of the spatial project undertaken in any given historical instance of colonization. But—even given that this may be a matter of degree or extent—what is for me the most urgent question here is this: what happens to a people, a history, a culture, that falls victim to a colonial project whose objective is not only to exploit its victims, but to dispossess them and claim *all* of their land in order to re-encode it, re-name it, to literally re-write it and re-invent it? What happens to the history of such a dispossessed people? And what, finally, are the relationships between the material processes of such spatial reinventions and broader cultural ones? To what extent does symbolic production play a role in the endless creation of space? With these questions in mind, what I want to argue in the present essay is that Scott's *Waverley* contributed not only to the invention of a new Highland reality, but also to the construction and colonization of a Highland past to go with it.

B. Mapping the past

1

Having arrived at the border of the Scottish Highlands, Edward Waverley arrives at a symbolic border dividing one world from another, and one epoch from what is posited as the next. The village of Tully-Veolan, and with it the great estate of the Baron of Bradwardine, lies in the shadow of the Highlands, which during Edward's approach "had appeared a blue outline in the horizon, but now swelled into huge gigantic masses, which frowned defiance over the more level country that lay beneath them."[1] As Edward enters the village, he becomes increasingly aware of the proximity of the border, and of the fantastic charge that this proximity carries with it, and his forward movement in space seems to take him ever backwards in time. "The houses seemed miserable in the extreme, especially to an eye accustomed to the smiling neatness of English cottages. They stood, without any respect for regularity, on each side of a straggling kind of unpaved street, where children, almost in a primitive state of nakedness, lay sprawling, as if to be crushed by the hoofs of the first passing horse" (74). The frowning mountains pose a limit to this movement in time, just as they do to movement in space: a limit that the novel posits only in order for it to be transcended, as Waverley leaps beyond it and into a space of cultural otherness. For this border is also one between cultures and nations, and although even here on *this* side of the border there prevails a sense of poverty, wretchedness and "backwardness," we are still on the firm ground of the knowable, a ground symbolically defended from the predatory raids of Highland *caterans* by the loopholes and arrowslits of the baronial estate. Beyond the dim line of the mountains, however, not even the awkward and broken English of the border region is spoken, and if the Lowlanders of the border resemble Italians and the folk "of Minerva," the people beyond are scarcely assimilable to such reassuring European (even Southern European) standards.

Edward Waverley is, of course, immediately tempted to venture into the unknown. And, as if in answer to Edward's inquiry "whether it was possible to make with safety an excursion into the neighboring Highlands, whose dusky barrier of mountains had already excited his wish to penetrate beyond them," Evan Dhu Maccombich makes his appearance: the first appearance, indeed, of a Highlander in the novel:

> . . . the door suddenly opened, and, ushered in by Saunders Saunderson, a Highlander, fully armed and equipped, entered the apartment. Had it not been that Saunders acted the part of the master of ceremonies to this martial apparition, without appearing to deviate from his usual composure, and that neither Mr Bradwardine nor Rose exhibited any emotion, Edward would certainly have thought the intrusion hostile. As it was, he started at the sight of what he had not yet happened to see, a mountaineer in his full national costume. The individual Gael was a stout, dark young man, of low stature, the ample folds of whose plaid added to the appearance of strength which his person exhibited. The short kilt, or petticoat, showed his sinewy and clean-made limbs; the goatskin purse, flanked by the usual defences, a dirk and a steel-wrought pistol, hung before him; his bonnet had a short feather, which indicated his claim to be treated as a Duinhéwassel, or sort of gentleman; a broadsword hung upon his shoulder, and a long Spanish fowling-piece occupied one of his hands.
>
> (144)

Evan Dhu serves as Waverley's (that is, the novel's as well as the character's) guide into the Highlands and into the imaginary terrain of the past. With his strength and rugged features, his air of indomitability, and above all the latent violence expressed through his layers of weaponry ("the usual defences"), he appears here as a representative figure: more than a spokesman, he is a personification of the Highlands. His "claim" to be treated as a "sort of gentleman," a claim which in the narrator's view is clearly misplaced, is really backed up not by the feather in his bonnet, but by his broadsword and rifle. And while his "national costume" makes him a fit national representative, the novel establishes the represented nationality not as British, nor even as Scottish, but as Highlander ("mountaineer") and Gaelic.

Thus, the novel re-launches itself and begins anew, as Waverley leaves behind the relative safety of Tully-Veolan and pushes into the vast and rugged Highlands of Scotland. When Waverley awakens on his first full day in the mountains, in the cave of the robber Donald Bean Lean, he emerges to find himself on the "wild and precipitous shores of a Highland loch, about four miles in length, and a mile and a half across, surrounded by heathy and savage mountains, on the crests of which the morning mist was still sleeping" (145). His Lowlander and English standards of measurement cannot mean much here, though, and rather than assimilating the surroundings, such standards are overwhelmed by the "heathy"—which suggests both *heathen* and *healthy*—savagery of the mountains. In his tour, Waverley appropriates the rugged landscape of the Scottish Highlands. But Waverley is an Englishman, a gentleman and an officer in the service of the Hanoverian king, intruding on the Jacobite and Gaelic heartland of Scotland; thus, as James Kerr points out, Waverley's tourism "is not a politically innocent activity."[2]

The novel begins to "slip" in between its invented background of landscape and its equally invented (that is, produced rather than reproduced) background of Highland Nature, culture, and society. Earlier, while pausing in the border region before entering the Highlands, the narrator tells us that the Lowland borderers—the people themselves—somewhat "resembled Italian forms of *landscape*" (75; my emphasis). Once the novel has gained the fastnesses of the Highlanders, particularly the domain of clan Vich Ian Vohr, distinctions between natives and landscape collapse altogether, and Waverley begins to consume the culture and activity of the Highlands just as he had already consumed their landscape. In other words, people and land are reduced not only to one another, but to the level of aesthetic objects to be taken in and consumed by the eager eye of the "tourist:" the character, the narrator—and the reader.[3] It is an alienated consumption, however; and just as Waverley can appreciate the wildness of the Highland scenery only to the extent that he is charmed by (or afraid of) it, he can enjoy the great clan feast and other cultural events only to the extent that he feels a revulsion towards them and towards the clansmen themselves.[4]

While sitting on the banks of the loch outside Bean Lean's lair, Edward finds himself reflecting on his romantic situation "on the banks of an unknown lake, under the guidance of a wild native, whose language was unknown to him, on a visit to the den of some renowned outlaw" (138). Indeed, just as *Waverley* had established a comparison—as if to establish points of reference for the reader—between the Lowland borderers and Greeks and Italians, the novel continually compares the Highlanders not just to their "wild" surroundings, but to the natives of Africa and America, India and the Orient.[5] The narrator reinforces this comparison, on the one hand by repeatedly denying that his is anything like an Oriental tale:

Mine is an humble English post-chaise, drawn upon four wheels, and keeping his Majesty's highway. Such as dislike the vehicle may leave it at the next halt, and wait for the conveyance of Prince Hussein's tapestry, or Malek the Weaver's flying sentry-box.

(63)

On the other hand, however, the novel repeatedly dredges up Oriental and Orientalist allusions, including a passing reference to Flora in her capacity as a "dragoman" (the corrupted English version of the Arabic word for an interpreter and guide for foreigners in the Arab lands of southwest Asia) as she interprets the Gaelic language and folklore of the Highlands for Waverley—and for the reader (see 174). The cumbersome notes about the Highlands and Scotland, as well as those addressing the history of the 1745 Jacobite Rebellion, add to the novel's exaggerated exoticism, in the same way as the notes to an Oriental tale amplify not only its own variety of the exotic but also its claims to authenticity.[6]

Edward Waverley's tour of the imaginary terrain of the Highlands also involves a kind of time-traveling, in which the movement from Lowlands to Highlands is a movement back in time (so that, with his contrary movement, Evan Dhu appears in Tully-Veolan as little short of a ghost from the past, just as the *cateran* raids on the Lowlands are like vestigial hauntings from bygone days). In other words, the novel's leap into the Highlands of "sixty years since"—expressed in spatialized terms as an incursion into the Jacobite and Gaelic heartland—is also registered as an imaginary leap "backwards" in time to the space of a previous epoch. Just as the novel, then, is a spatialized "reclamation" of the imaginary terrain of the Highlands, it also reclaims the past through inventing "authentic" Highland cultures and traditions. Here, however, Scott's novel is caught up in the various movements in late eighteenth- and early nineteenth-century Scotland literally to invent the traditions of a mythic Highland "past." Indeed, Scott, a founding president of the Celtic Society of Edinburgh, was a major figure in these movements, which included Macpherson's Ossian (who has a Welsh equivalent in Iolo Morganwg), and also the creation of "traditional" patterned clan tartans and kilts (these were first developed—by an Englishman—in the 1720s, and firmly established only *after* the 1745 Rebellion).[7]

2

The imaginary map that underlies and sustains Waverley's tour—the "ground" on which the narrative is written, and towards which all referentiality is directed—involves the simultaneous creation and re-presentation of an imaginary terrain. It has been argued that, "whatever fictional gloss may be applied, when he is writing of Scotland, and especially of his own Border region, Scott is recording, not inventing; his vision grows out of an objective world, a place of time and the senses."[8] On the contrary, however, the novel's complex and fluid architectonic of space simultaneously constructs *and* presupposes its own conditions of existence. It does so, in the first instance, by positing a rigid dualistic structure of space, through which the narrative is channeled. This involves an opposition between the Highlands, on the one hand, and the Lowlands and England on the other. The Highlands-Lowlands opposition enables (and simultaneously rests upon) a matrix of other essentializing dualisms: thus, superimposed on this dualistic structure is an opposition between the fanciful and the realistic, the wild and the tame, the unknown and the known, the threatening and the reassuring, the turbulent and the level, the violent and the peaceful, the noble and the mundane, the heroic and the quotidian, the youthful and the mature. Other historical, symbolic, and political dualisms are similarly inscribed: feudal against modern; myth against Enlightenment; Jacobite against Hanoverian; revolutionary against counter-revolutionary; Catholic against Protestant; sympathies with France against anti-French sentiment; anti-Unionist against Unionist.

Waverley's map of Scotland is also a map of time, for the opposition between Highlands and Lowlands is temporally and historically coded as an opposition between past and present. That is, the novel's Highland space does not just open up into the past, and into the archaic trappings and rituals of (an invented) tradition; it is the spatialization of the past and of this tradition. At the same time, it is the temporalization of the Highlands, registering, merging, coupling, linking, relentlessly identifying the Highlands with the past. *Waverley*'s Highland space is, indeed, a Wordsworthian "spot of time." It is a *fluid* spot of time, one that can extend itself like the arms of an amoeba to enwrap and claim other areas; and one that can, conversely, be beaten back so that it can lose its hold over areas that it had once held firmly in its grip. Written retrospectively from the standpoint of the narrative's future (i.e., Scott's present), the novel maps out the Highlands as a space that *was once* unknown, that *was once* feudalistic, that *was once* violent, romantic, wild, inhabited by myth; the Highlands are reduced to a turbulent, but, for Scott, colorful and attractive albeit dangerous past, associated with the Jacobites, with feudalism, masculinity, backwardness, a hierarchical class-structure, Catholicism, and of course anti-Unionism. On the other hand, *Waverley* presents the identity of the Lowlands as true and valid not only for the past, but for the present as well as for the future.[9] The Lowlands plus England—in other words, the modernizing core of Great Britain as opposed to the Celtic peripheries of Wales, Ireland and Scotland—are thus situated and constructed as the spaces that *were then, still are, and will forever be* peaceful, rational, scientific, enlightened, known, and civilized; this civilizational core, in other words, is associated with Protestantism, progress, rationality, Unionism, capitalism, a fluid notion of class-mobility, and finally with what is for Scott a supremely necessary but nevertheless uninspiring and even boring "feminine" domesticity. Coextensive with the overarching *spatial* opposition between Highlands and Lowlands is an overarching *temporal* opposition between past and present.[10]

The novel's map of space and time is supplemented with characters who serve as markers of the map's coordinates. Each character, with the exception of Edward Waverley himself, stakes out, marks, and defends a certain slice of the novel's symbolic terrain, and hence a certain political, social, temporal, and historical position.[11] Edward is the exception; he alone can move through and between the novel's variegated terrains and territories: he is the explorer, the adventurer, the traveler who in his movements ties these symbolic territories together; for as other characters move, they necessarily stake out new terrain, so that the novel's imaginary map moves with them. Edward—the lone hero, the monadic traveler—is the only character who has neither a territorial identification nor a territorial limitation. The other characters are spread out in association with the territorial identifications allowed for by the imaginary map's dualistic epistemology, with the two extreme positions being held by Fergus MacIvor, on the one hand, and Colonel Talbot, on the other.

Talbot is the voice of the present. An officer and a gentleman, an Englishman, a Unionist, a Hanoverian, his territorial identification is with the Lowlands and England. His position is solidly reinforced, justified, validated and relentlessly proved correct by the narrator and the narrative, for Talbot does not just speak for rationality, progress, Englishness, justice (he "reminds" us all that "of all nations, the English are least bloodthirsty by nature" [424]), he speaks as well, of course, for the unity of the kingdom and nation. He speaks for what is correct and logical for and in the novel's own present: a correctness and logic inevitably validated by *Waverley*'s retrospective narration, so that his "prophecies" are by definition "self-fulfilling." Talbot is instrumental in showing Waverley the hopelessness of his situation as a Jacobite, and in providing help for his escape: an escape which the novel, as a prototypical *Bildungsroman*, defines as growth and maturity that are themselves enabled by Talbot's interventions.[12] But he is also the signpost for and spokesman of the present and the future; his pronouncements on and judgments of the Highlands, Fergus, the Jacobites, the Baron, and the future of the United Kingdom are indistinguishable from the judgments and pronouncements of the narrator himself.[13]

At the other pole of this opposition stands Fergus MacIvor. Despite his Parisian upbringing, "few men," we are told, "were more attached to ideas of chieftainship and feudal power" than Fergus MacIvor, Chief of the Clan of Ivor, Vich Ian Vohr (153). Indeed, his education has not changed his essential quality as a Highland *laird*, nor, in the novel's terms, could it have. Instead, for the most part it merely adds a gloss, a fine veneer that at first makes Fergus more "palatable" as a character, although it gradually and subtly undermines his position by reinforcing the notion that no amount of Continental education and manners could improve upon his stubbornly and immutably Highland mentality and physiognomy. Fergus is a perfect specimen of the species, plucked from what the narrator identifies as an ideal historical moment:

ORIENTALISM AND POST-COLONIALISM

Had Fergus MacIvor lived Sixty Years sooner than he did, he would, in all probability, have wanted the polished manner and knowledge of the world which he now possessed; and had he lived Sixty Years later, his ambition and love of rule would have lacked the fuel which his situation now afforded. He was, indeed, within his little circle, as perfect a politician as Castruccio Castrucani himself. He applied himself with great earnestness to appease all the feuds and dissensions which often arose among other clans in his neighborhood, so that he became a frequent umpire in their quarrels. His own patriarchal power he strengthened at every expense which his fortune would permit, and indeed stretched his means to the uttermost, to maintain the rude and plentiful hospitality, which was the most valued attribute of a chieftain. For the same reason, he crowded his estate with a tenantry, hardy indeed, and fit for the purposes of war, but greatly outnumbering what the soil was calculated to maintain.

(157)

Found neither Sixty Years too soon nor too late, then, Fergus is the perfect embodiment not only of the Highland *laird*, but of the precise moment of the novel's historical setting "Sixty Years" since, or in other words 1745: one of the many crucial turning-points for the history of Britain, and perhaps *the* crucial moment in the history of the Highlands. (As the description of the clan makes clear with its ominous Malthusian language of population and resources, there are "too many" people for "too little" land; the events of 1745, which are chronicled by the novel, laid the historical pre-conditions for the events which were clearing the Highlanders off their land as Scott was writing his novel.) Fergus, of whom the narrator confides that "we should term him the model of a Highland Chieftain," represents, like the Highland space which he personifies, the past (170). That is, just as he speaks for the Highlands, identifies the standpoints and positions of the Highlands (with its myths and legends, its romanticism and feudalism, its violence and instability, its Jacobitism and revolutionism) and defends the Highlands, he speaks for, identifies and defends the hopelessly beleaguered past spatialized in and through the Highlands.

Waverley thus territorializes its political, historical, temporal and chronological oppositions and dualisms, inscribing them onto its imaginary dualistic map of Highlands and Lowlands. As I have already suggested, however, the novel's Highland space is fluid: it and its associations are capable of movement out of and away from the Highlands "properly" speaking—just as, ultimately, the Highlands can be purged of these associations. In these terms, the Jacobite Rebellion of 1745 figures in the novel as an eruption of this imaginary Highland space into the imaginary space of the Lowlands and England; or, put differently, it is an eruption of the past into the present of industrializing bourgeois Britain; both spatially, in the Highlander's brief incursion into the Lowlands and down into England as far as Derby; and textually, in their arrival, through the novel, into the world of 1814 Scotland (or, Sixty Years later . . .).

3

The army and followers of Prince Charles Edward Stuart—Bonnie Prince Charlie—thus storm into *Waverley*'s Lowlands like a horde of ghosts issuing forth from the past. The novel emplots the rise and fall of the final Jacobite Rebellion of 1745 "as it actually happened" sixty years previously (although it sometimes restricts historical events to the background in its emplotment of the events of the Rebellion into a diachronic "story").[14] The rebellion's vague beginning in the Highlands, where the Prince had landed with a force of half a dozen men, is transcoded into the novel in equally vague and uncertain terms.[15] It moves quickly from being a barely "audible" background murmur—with the passing glimpse at strange movements and gatherings of people, of horses, of weapons—to the highest pitch of an attempted revolution, into which the novel's characters, including its distinctly English hero, Edward Waverley, are suddenly drawn. By the time Edward has joined the movement, however, the Jacobites have already taken over cosmopolitan Edinburgh, and are planning for their future campaigns from there. After winning the important battle at Prestonpans (or Gladsmuir), they collect themselves and begin the long march to London, reaching as far south as Derby. Suddenly the tide begins to turn, and just as the novel tracks the beginning of the revolt in a sudden switch in tempo, it transcodes the movement's demise in the same terms. The withdrawal back to the Highlands—against the wishes and counsels of many, including Fergus—takes place very quickly, and soon the Jacobite army, its morale having collapsed, is in full retreat, thinning and dissolving as it breaks up during the march back north. Finally, the rearguard, including Edward himself, are caught up by the forward dragoons of the British army and scattered in a skirmish near Clifton. Thus Edward is once again isolated from the full movement of "history," which recedes into the background whence it had issued. Indeed, the Jacobite rebellion ends as it had begun—in the novel's background. The news from faraway Culloden[16] enters the narrative and reaches Edward only as disembodied information.

Until its final annihilation at Culloden, whatever terrain is held by the Jacobite army under Prince Charles Edward during its doomed campaign in *Waverley* is quickly invested with the spatial forces and assemblages of the Highlands. Colonized by Highland rituals, feasts, dancing and singing, and of course by the Highland army itself, such territories effectively *become* Highland space (space understood, of course, not as an inert material given, but as a fluid political process). In other words, places reclaimed by Jacobitism, as a political movement in support of an absolute monarchic line whose "rights" had been "usurped" by the modernizing forces of nascent parliamentary democracy after 1688, are effectively reclaimed as sites of tradition and feudalism and are overlaid with rituals harking back to a mythic Highland past.[17] When Edward first meets Prince Charles, in the palace at Edinburgh, the palace has been reactivated as a site of tradition-alism, as if the past had been brought back to life in the dreams of the present—or, rather, as if the past had been reborn as a spatial enclave, a violent spatial eruption into the present.[18] Indeed, the feudal ritual of homage to the Prince performed by the Baron of Bradwardine—and ridiculed by the novel in a chapter entitled "rather unimportant"—is presented precisely as the reemergence of the past in the present. The only account of the ritual is in a Gazetteer which is "quoted" by the novel:

> "Since that fatal treaty [i.e., the 1707 Act of Union] which annihilates Scotland as an independent nation, it has not been our happiness to see her princes receive, and her nobles discharge, those acts of feudal homage, which, founded upon the splendid actions of Scottish valour, recall the memory of her early history, with the manly and chivalrous simplicity of the ties which united to the Crown the homage of the warriors by whom it was repeatedly upheld and defended. But on the evening of the 20th, our memories were refreshed with one of those ceremonies which belong to the ancient days of Scotland's glory. . . ."
>
> (355–56)

Apart from these charmingly archaic rituals, which are confined to the nobles in the palace, it is the presence of the Jacobite army in Edinburgh that profoundly enforces the Highland *territorialization* of Lowland space. The army's encampment is repeatedly described from the vantage point of "present-day" Edinburgh, as though it were being superimposed on an 1814 map of the city; or as though the novel's imaginary spatial flows could invade and even occupy the space of the present, thus militarily occupying 1814 Edinburgh by claiming a certain space on its imaginary map.[19] The Highland army's appearance in the Edinburgh of 1745 is described as though a Highland host were actually descending on the Edinburgh of Scott's own time—that is, as the ghostly apparitions of the "primitive" existence of the past. Indeed, it is above all the army that represents the eruption of the past into the present, for, apart from the vanguard (made up of the sympathetic Lowland-Jacobite gentry's tiny cavalry) it is overwhelmingly composed of "the common peasantry of the Highlands":

> Here was a pole-axe, there a sword without a scabbard; here a gun without a lock, there a scythe set straight upon a pole; and some had only their dirks, and bludgeons or stakes pulled out of hedges.

The grim, uncombed and wild appearance of these men, most of whom gazed with all the admiration of ignorance upon the most ordinary production of domestic art, created surprise in the Lowlands, but it also created terror. So little was the condition of the Highlands known at that late period, that the character and appearance of their population, while thus sallying forth as military adventurers, conveyed to the south-country Lowlanders as much surprise as if an invasion of African Negroes or Esquimaux Indians had issued forth from the northern mountains of their own native country. It cannot therefore be wondered if Waverley, who had hitherto judged of the Highlanders generally from the samples which the policy of Fergus had from time to time exhibited, should have felt damped and astonished at the daring attempt of a body not then exceeding four thousand men, and of whom not above half the number, at the utmost, were armed, to change the fate, and alter the dynasty, of the British kingdoms.

(324)

This Highland *levée en masse*, this army of the people, effectively brings the people of the Highlands (in Scott's own time a people being burned off their land and scattered to the winds) into a direct and terrifying confrontation with the people of Edinburgh. This encounter takes place at two simultaneous spatio-temporal levels; for it is a confrontation between the Highland Jacobite and Lowland Hanoverians of 1745, and also symbolically between the forgotten Highlands of the early nineteenth century and the Lowlands trying to forget them. It is also, fundamentally, a confrontation between two different social formations (so that the Highlanders can be compared to Eskimos and Africans), and indeed the confrontation between the two armies at Gladsmuir is described as a confrontation between the "primitive" and the modern, "each admirably trained in its own peculiar mode of war" (332).[20] Thus the disorganized and "primitive" Highland *levée* is pitched against the well-equipped British army, with its rationalized detachments and regiments, its squadrons and dragoons, its lines of battle, its artillery and infantry. The battle itself is quite brief, and the clans overwhelm the British army:

The English infantry, trained in the wars in Flanders stood their ground with great courage. But their extended files were pierced and broken in many places by the close masses of the clans; and in the personal struggle which ensued, the nature of the Highlanders' weapons, and their extraordinary fierceness and activity, gave them a decided superiority over those who had been accustomed to trust to their array and discipline, and felt that the one was broken and the other useless.

(340)

The Highlanders' success is of course only temporary, and they are ultimately beaten back into the dark recesses of history in *Waverley*'s background, so that their temporary eruption into the space of the present is contained and even reversed. The past is thus exorcized from the present.

4

Just as the eruption of the Highlands is spatialized in *Waverley*, this exorcism is also expressed in spatial terms, first as the containment of the eruption of the Highlanders into the Lowlands, and then as the political, military, economic and symbolic colonization and pacification of the Highlands themselves. Historically, and at the "overtly" political level, this process involved the containment of the Jacobite rebellion, and ultimately the Hanoverian victory at Culloden, where Prince Charles' forces were finally vanquished, and with them whatever hopes the Highland people may have had in the Jacobite movement. But this process in *Waverley* involves more than the Hanoverian reclamation of the Jacobite territories, which in any case—from the Highlands and Edinburgh south to Derby—are quickly recaptured by the forces of the (Hanoverian) state. Rather, expressed *through* this spatialized movement over the novel's imaginary terrain, there is the symbolic "resolution" of the dualistic structure underlying *Waverley*. Thus, inscribed in the containment and then the rollback of the Highland space, there is not only the victory of Hanoverian over Jacobite, but also the modern over the feudal, the civilized over the wild, the counter-revolutionary over the revolutionary, the "feminine" domestic over the "masculine" adventurous, and so forth—including the victory of the present over the past. In other words, the defeat of the Jacobite Rebellion is expressed spatially in the shift of the symbolic border between Highlands and Lowlands. If *Waverley* is an historical narrative, it narrates history through spatializing it, or rather through producing historically-inscribed space as a "background" upon which the novel's own narration and plot can take place: a background inscribed with a version of history which it has itself written. *Waverley* thus produces its own historical "context."[21] The novel's spatial movements are historical flows channeled through an imaginary terrain of its own construction.

In constructing its historical and imaginary-geographical background, the novel also establishes its own politicized contour lines, of which the symbolic border between Highlands and Lowlands is of crucial symbolic significance. For if, at the beginning of the novel, the border between Highlands and Lowlands defines a boundary between different spaces and times, this border is afterwards set in motion, like a shoreline during the sweep of the tide. By the end of the novel, the borderline has been pushed back out of sight, the "old" Highlands are cleansed of their associations, and what had been the old border region—in the novel's imaginary map, Tully-Veolan—has been relieved of the proximity of the old Highland space.

Tully-Veolan, especially the great estate of the Baron of Bradwardine, is therefore used in the novel as an exemplary space, in which the novel's larger spatial—and political—movements and flows can be represented. For the Highland shadow which had once darkened the village is lifted by the end of the novel. Moreover, the Baron's own status as a feudal lord (a status enabled and sustained by the proximity of the Highlands) is revoked, and he is reduced to the status of *Mr* Bradwardine—disarmed, like the Highland chiefs, and stripped of his Heritable Jurisdiction over land and tenantry. That he is allowed to retain his estate at all is due solely to the intervention of the benevolent Colonel Talbot; but even then the quasimagical restoration of his property (which had been demolished by the Hanoverian army) can only take place once its ownership has passed through Talbot's hands. Indeed, this passage of the estate's ownership through Talbot enables a purification of the association of the old space. Having *once been* the center of a feudal estate, it is now merely a grand country house in the English tradition, and the Baron is astonished upon his return:

> All seemed as much as possible restored to the state in which he had left it when he assumed arms some months before. The pigeon-house was replenished; the fountain played with its usual activity; and not only the Bear who predominated over its basin, but all the other Bears whatsoever, were replaced on their several stations, and renewed or repaired with so much care, that they bore no tokens of the violence which had so lately descended upon them. While these minutiae had been so heedfully attended to, it is scarce necessary to add, that the house itself had been thoroughly repaired, as well as the gardens, with the strictest attention to maintain the original character of both, and to remove as far as possible, all appearance of the ravage they had sustained.
>
> (484)

Talbot immediately congratulates the Baron, adding that "your family estate is your own once more in full property, and at your absolute disposal, but only burdened with the sum advanced to repurchase it, which I understand is utterly disproportioned to its value" (487). The estate's sudden physical restoration is allowed by the pacification of the site's previous symbolic significance; indeed, its precise restoration, down to the last of its minutest details, suggests not so much that it had ever actually changed, but rather that its space had been symbolically and politically cleansed by an almost ritualistic passage through the modern economic system of the market. That is, the condition of possibility for the return (or the spatial reinvention) of Tully-Veolan to the person who was, after all, its original and "rightful" owner, is the commodification of its space and the obectification of its value—its sole burden being the mortgage which financed its repurchase from the past.

At the same time, the dark spell of the Highlands has been lifted from Tully-Veolan, so that the Highland line—and with it the threat of *caterans* and other raiders from the past—has been pushed back into an unbridgeable distance. Indeed, the novel does not return to the Highlands, it does not allow for the preservation of Highland space. On the contrary: once the eruption from the past has been contained, the Highlands cease to exist as a spot of time. Once the possibilities of this spot have been closed, once it has been cleansed, it is gone forever, and its imaginary terrain must be un-imagined, or rather, re-imagined in an altogether new spatial configuration (to which Scott returns in his next novel, *Guy Mannering*, set a decade or two after the Forty-Five). It cannot be transformed in *Waverley* itself.

As for the Highlanders themselves, they are trapped in their space: a space which was only ever accessible from the outside by those—notably Waverley himself—whose origins are on the outside. In other words, if the Highland space is a spot of time, it is one that can only be entered from the outside, and one that can only be left behind again, as it closes shut for the last time, by an outsider. For this spot of time allows access to another time, another mode of life and of society, whose members are apparently incapable of movement to a different time and a different mode of social and political organization. Fergus and Flora (despite their gloss of Continental taste and manners), Callum, Evan Dhu: none can make the transition from Highlands (feudalism, wilderness, the past) to Lowlands (the present and the future). Their evolution—or, more precisely, their modernization—is inconceivable as such.

Thus the Highland space produced in *Waverley* cannot be transformed: like those Natural bowers which appear so often in Wordsworth's poetry, it can be either preserved in its original state of difference, accessible through the magic of a spot of time, or else utterly destroyed in a "fall" into the modern; in either case, modernization amounts less to a transformative process than to a spatio-temporal annihilation and reinvention. The novel's imaginary map of the Highlands is not, strictly speaking, a map of *the* past, but rather a map of a possible past, an imaginary past that is forever spatially (and temporally) different and distinct. It is a past that can never become present because it cannot be modernized *and* remain identical to itself—it is necessarily anti-modern.

The novel, as a prototypical *Bildungsroman*, does however allow for the *ontogenetic* transformation of Edward Waverley himself. For it chronicles his growth and development from the immaturity and romance of youth to the steady rationality of adulthood. Politically, this development is coded in terms of Edward's maturation from his support of Jacobitism and its emotional and unrealistic claims to the throne, to a sober and independent outlook more congenial to Talbot and the Hanoverian and Unionist standpoint. That is, the novel directly equates his early affiliation with the Jacobite cause with an emotional and intellectual—as well as a political —immaturity. His gradual move away from the cause (which he effects without actually betraying his friends) is consonant with his emotional and intellectual growth and maturation under the guidance of Talbot. More generally, however, the novel equates Jacobitism with immaturity, emotion, irrationality and even romantic fancy (embodied by Bonnie Prince Charlie himself); and Unionism with rationality and maturity.[22] Thus, although Waverley is shown to be the only character capable of movement from one position to the other, even at his early stage he is capable of rational insight, feeling "inexpressible repugnance at the idea of being accessory to the plague of civil war." Indeed,

> whatever were the original rights of the Stuarts, calm reflection told him, that, omitting the question of how far James the Second could forfeit those of his posterity, he had, according to the united voice of the whole nation, justly forfeited his own [in 1688]. Since that period, four monarchs had reigned in peace and glory over Britain, sustaining and exalting the character of the nation abroad, and its liberties at home. Reason asked, was it worth while to disturb a government so long settled and established, and to plunge a kingdom into all the miseries of civil war, for the purpose of replacing upon the throne the descendants of a monarch by whom it had been willfully forfeited?
>
> (222)

That Edward does join the Jacobites is due partly to his emotional reaction at being (with his father) falsely accused of treason by the government, and partly to the romantic allure of the Bonnie Prince Charlie. Moreover, his attraction to the Jacobite cause is overlaid with his attraction to the Highlands and to Fergus—both, as I have already argued, embodiments of Jacobitism, feudalism, masculinity, and so forth.[23]

Here, however, the novel faces an impossible representational somersault, for *Waverley*'s Highlands do not and cannot enter the present: they remain a space apart. That is, with Edward's maturity evolving with the unfolding of the novel's plot, *Waverley*'s imaginary map confronts a representational crisis of its own making. For the Highland space does not and cannot become modern in the novel's own representational framework, and Edward must leave it behind. *Waverley*'s Highland space is established as the space of the past, although the novel has brought "the past to life as the prehistory of the present" (Lukács 53). It repeatedly establishes the links between certain historical events or developments (including spurious Malthusian claims about the overpopulation of the Highlands, as well as the abolition of the Highland chiefs' heritable jurisdictions) and their ramifications and implications for the future (that is, Scott's own present). Yet, once the past has been closed off, the novel is unwilling to acknowledge the impact of these historical developments. The space of the past cannot enter the present, even though the novel has already traced lines of present historical development "back" into the Highlands.

C. Mapping the present

1

Waverley does not quite close off all references to the Highlands, however, for even in the relentless present that closes in at the end of the novel, there does remain one aperture into the Highlands. This is the portrait of Edward and Fergus:

> It was a large and spirited painting, representing Fergus Mac-Ivor and Waverley in their Highland dress; the scene a wild, rocky, and mountainous pass, down which the clan were descending in the background. It was taken from a spirited sketch, drawn while they were in Edinburgh by a young man of high genius, and had been painted on a full-length scale by an eminent London artist. Raeburn himself (whose Highland Chiefs do all but walk out of the canvas) could not have done more justice to the subject; and the ardent, fiery, and impetuous character of the unfortunate Chief of Glennaquoich was finely contrasted with the contemplative, fanciful, and enthusiastic expression of his happier friend. Beside this painting hung the arms which Waverley had borne in the unfortunate civil war.
>
> (489)

The full-scale painting, hanging on a wall of the freshly reconstructed manor house in Tully-Veolan, appears as a window to the outside world, to the Highlands lying beyond the walls of the estate. But, as a window, it directs the viewer's gaze to the past; as a symbolic production, in other words, it draws attention to itself and away from other windows allowing views of the present Highlands (views which the novel itself does not access), it intervenes and intercedes between the viewer and the space of the present. As an imaginary production, it disrupts the referentiality of the "real" Highlands and claims this referentiality for itself.

Yet the novel does not claim the portrait's view of the past as an "accurate" representation. On the contrary, it emphasizes the artificiality of its reconstruction of the past. The portrait involves the final assembly of several prefabricated parts. The usual premise for the production of a portrait—the subject's presence—is here not only unfulfilled, it is at several

removes from the artist who assembles the images. For the portrait, produced and assembled by "an eminent London artist," is based upon a sketch
of Waverley and Fergus taken (by an altogether different artist, "a young
man of high genius") while they were in Edinburgh. The London artist combines elements of the Edinburgh sketch with "typical" Highland scenery,
"a wild, rocky and mountainous pass," down which a clan, also as part of
the background, is charging. The portrait thus consciously and artificially
re-produces a past (from which it is alienated both because of its distance
and its fictiveness) by appropriating it.[24] Its claim to "authenticity" is based
upon this appropriation of a past that had never "really" existed, this
automatic and even tautological "seizure" of an imaginary terrain by virtue
of having invented it. Whether such a past had or had not "really" existed
does not matter as much as the fact that it has been claimed as a symbolic
space. Once it has been claimed and mapped out, it "becomes" real: that is,
it takes on political, cultural and symbolic significance on its own terms.[25] It
also becomes a contested space. The portrait's invention of the past is in this
sense an allegorical restatement of *Waverley*'s own production of the past,
of the space of the past (the Highlands), and of the narration of the past (its
version of the history of the Forty-Five). Alongside the portrait hang Edward
Waverley's weapons from the "unfortunate" civil war and the revolution
whose rise and fall the novel has documented. *Waverley* thus not only
spatializes the past as the Highlands: it reifies the past and ossifies history,
commodifying both and presenting them as museum-piece images and
aestheticized icons for consumption in and for the present and the future.

2

What, then, of the Highlands in the novel's own present? Although *Waverley*
is an historical novel, it remains self-reflexive about its own (and its reader's)
standpoint in the present and the future. It is "aware" of what is happening
outside its own pages as it is being written, and it draws these events into
itself, textualizing them and sometimes simultaneously rewriting the present
as the past.[26] But, despite its obsession with the Highland past, and despite
its many commentaries on the Lowland British present, it has virtually
nothing to say about the present-day Highlands.

The Highlands are blank spots on the novel's imaginary map of the
present. They are blank not only because they are neither scene nor seen, but
because they have been cleansed, drained of significance and signification. The
novel's present-day Highlands have been emptied out, darkened, silenced, and
written over as the space of the past. The events of the present, the terrain
of the present, the people of the present—who were being cleared off their
land and forced at bayonet-point either to bogs on the wild coasts of Ross
and Sutherland or to the farthest reaches of the far-flung British empire—
are neither heard, nor seen, nor is their presence registered. Their presence

is, rather, almost entirely written off and written over in *Waverley*'s textual repression of the Highland present. The novel removes the people of the Highlands from its own pages and from its imaginary production of *their* space just as they were being removed in a more literal, concrete, material and abjectly miserable way from their land, from their ancestral homes, from the glens of their clans, all of which were quickly being claimed, purged and reinvented by politicians, by economists, by Lowland and English sheepfarmers, and by artists, poets, musicians, and writers, not least Sir Walter Scott himself.

What does it mean, then, to say that Walter Scott and *Waverley* participate in the history of the spatial reclamation of the Scottish Highlands? How can a work of fiction help to produce historical and geographical realities? The reclamation and reinvention of the Highlands took place in a number of simultaneously textual *and* contextual registers or discourses. The two overlapping and mutually-determining narrative fields that I am pointing to here are, on the one hand, the material re-production and re-utilization of the physical terrain of the Highlands during the Clearances; and, on the other, what we can call—by way of an *apposition* rather than an *opposition* to that process—the imaginary creation of a new Highland reality, a new history, a new series of images and associations, to cover over and replace the old ones as they were being literally wiped off the geophysical and cultural map of the United Kingdom. And it is in this register that I think *Waverley* can be usefully located, even though it defies any traditional encapsulation as a textual event distinct from a contextual "background."

Waverley claims the referentiality of the Highland present by laying claim to its past; that is, it claims the right to narrate and represent (or not to narrate, not to represent) its present by having narrated and represented its past. But this past is also the past of the Lowlands: the relationship of Highlands to Lowlands, as I have already suggested, is that of the past to the present. In other words, in its assertion of the new national identity of Great Britain, the novel needs to associate a distinctly Scottish nationalism with the past, and hence it needs to translate what it has so far identified as (invented) Highland "traditions" into, more generally, *Scottish* "traditions." *Waverley*'s "postscript, which should have been a preface," or in other words a present which has been retrieved and saved from a consignment to the past, is worth quoting at length.

> There is no European nation which, within the course of half a century, or little more, has undergone so complete a change as this kingdom of Scotland. The effects of the insurrection of 1745—the destruction of the patriarchal power of the Highland chiefs— the abolition of the heritable jurisdictions of the Lowland nobility and barons—the total eradication of the Jacobite party, which, averse to intermingle with the English, or adopt their customs, long

continued to pride themselves upon maintaining the ancient Scottish traditions and manners—commenced this innovation. The gradual influx of wealth, and extension of commerce, have since united to render the present people of Scotland a class of beings as different from their grandfathers as the existing English are from those of Queen Elizabeth's time. The political and economical effects of these changes have been traced by Lord Selkirk with great accuracy. But the change, though steadily and rapidly progressive, has, nevertheless, been gradual; and like those who drift down the stream of a deep and smooth river, we are not aware of the progress we have made, until we fix our eye on the now distant point from which we have been drifted.—Such of the present generation who can recollect the last twenty or twenty-five years of the eighteenth century, will be fully sensible of the truth of this statement;—especially if their acquaintance and connections lay among those who, in my younger time, were facetiously called "folks of the old leaven," who still cherished a lingering, though hopeless, attachment to the house of Stuart. This race has now almost entirely vanished from the land, and with it, doubtless, much absurd political predjudice— but also many living examples of singular and disinterested attachment to the principles of loyalty which they received from their fathers, and of old Scottish faith, hospitality, worth, and honour.

(492)

The sense of urgency underlying the novel's postscript (or preface) is derived from the imminent disappearance of the last vestiges of what the novel identifies as the "ancient Scottish traditions and manners." The eradication of these manners and customs is due, in the novel's scheme of history, to "the gradual influx of wealth, and extension of commerce," and at the same time to the annihilation of the clan system in the Highlands, as well as of the heritable jurisdictions of the border regions' gentry. These developments, in turn, were enabled by the victory of the Hanoverian state over the Jacobites of the Forty-Five, and hence to the "total eradication of the Jacobite party." Thus, in the novel's political and historical terminology, the eradication of the Highlands' social formation stands for the eradication of a now outmoded *Scottish* national-historical bloc. And if the dying remnants of the previous social formation, exemplified by and embodied in the Jacobites, are unwilling to mingle with the English, it is due not merely to their retention of an archaic Scottish nationalism, but to the identification of commerce and wealth—that is, modernity—with England and the English. Here the narrator's own Scottishness is stretched to its limits; but in comparing the development of "the present people of Scotland" to that of the people of England since the time of Elizabeth, the narrator is registering the fusion of the two nationalities into a new and emerging nationalism, the newly invented "imagined community" of the United Kingdom of Great Britain.[27]

The "modern people of Scotland," mingling and gradually fusing with the English, are thus distinguished by the novel from those dying holdovers from the days of Jacobitism, with their "old Scottish faith, hospitality, worth, and honour," as well as their "absurd political prejudice." The latter (especially the Highlanders) are unable to adapt and to evolve: an evolution which is, nevertheless, experienced by the former—the modern Scots—who can look back not only at the past, but at the remnants of the past in the present, in order to see how much they themselves have changed. Here the novel deploys, once again, a spatial figuration for time: "the change, though steadily and rapidly progressive, has, nevertheless, been gradual; and like those who drift down the stream of a deep and smooth river, we are not aware of the progress we have made, until we fix our eye on the now distant point from which we have been drifted." It is only through identifying a certain spatial location with the past that "we," who are privileged to have "*been* drifted," can measure the temporal span of "our" drift by measuring the distance between us and those who are not so privileged, or who are incapable of "progress," however "gradual."

Waverley thus qualifies somewhat its earlier stance against modernization by granting it as a privilege rather than an inevitability. Its spatialized metaphor of a river representing a "stream of time" anticipates both later nineteenth-century views of evolution as well as later metaphorical uses of a river as the expression of slow and gradual, yet inexorable, progress.[28] Johannes Fabian has pointed out how this temporal scheme, codified through such new disciplines as anthropology, lay at the heart of the Victorian colonial project, so that "all living societies were irrevocably placed on a temporal slope, a stream of Time—some upstream, others downstream. Civilization, evolution, development, acculturation, modernization (and their cousins, industrialization, urbanization) are all terms whose conceptual content derives, in ways that can be specified, from evolutionary Time."[29] But if Scott's novel invents this metaphor, it does so not by placing all societies on the same "stream of time," as the post-Darwinian Victorian anthropologists would do, but by placing some societies and individuals on the stream, while leaving others fixed to the banks of the river, from which they cannot move or progress—although "we" can measure "our" progress by our distance from them. Such immobile and "ahistorical" societies, and their remnants in the present, are thus reduced in this historical evolutionary scheme to spatialized temporal reference points for those capable of movement and progress. They remain as museum pieces for the appreciation and self-comprehension of those who are supposed to have left them behind.

The Highland past—and hence its present—are thus appropriated by *Waverley* as the prehistory of the Scottish element of the British *jetztzeit*. In being consigned to the prehistory of the (historical) "present people of

Scotland," the Highlanders and the vanishing remnants of the "ancient" and Jacobite Scottish past are stripped of their own historicity, and left stranded on the banks of the river of Time. In other words, their history, and hence their space, is colonized by the novel; it is taken over and used for and by the Lowland present. Indeed, what Hugh Trevor-Roper and others have identified as the invention of Highland "traditions" involved not only the "artificial creation of new traditions, presented as ancient, original and distinctive," but also the process by which these supposedly Highland traditions—the philabeg or kilt, the bagpipes, the clan tartans—were offered to Lowland Scotland and ultimately adopted by the Lowlanders as *their* own traditions (*The Invention of Tradition* 16). What had originally been devised as purely Highland traditions thus become appropriated as the traditions of the whole Scottish nation, which the Scots needed to wean themselves of in order to fully assimilate into the Union with England; or, rather, which the Lowland Scots could keep as the quaint museum-piece relics from their past, once they had been disinfected and emptied of any political and nationalist content.[30]

The final subjugation of the Highlands, enabled, as the postscript hints, by the results of the Forty-Five, took place at once in the military, economic, and political pacification and colonization of the Highlands; in the symbolic purification of the political content of supposedly Highland traditions— leaving only their emptied-out and hence reusable forms; in the temporal colonization of the history of the Highlands; and in the spatial colonization of the Highlands, that is, in the colonization of the signifying and productive capacity of its imaginary terrain. Georg Lukács has argued that Scott "was able to portray objectively the ruination of past social formations, despite all his human sympathies for, and artistic sensitivity to, the splendid, heroic qualities they contained. Objectively, in a large historical and artistic sense; he saw at one and the same time their outstanding qualities and the historical necessity of their decline" (Lukács 55). Yet Lukács, for all his claims of Scott's supposed "objectivity," is unable or unwilling to see that these supposedly "past" social formations were not at all "past" in Scott's own time: that they were being finally eradicated and destroyed only in the early nineteenth century, and not—as *Waverley* pretends—immediately after 1745.

3

The aftermath of the 1745 Jacobite Rebellion did, however, establish the historical preconditions for what happened later in the eighteenth century, and on into the nineteenth. The great highlands of western and northern Scotland, following the defeat of the clans at Culloden, were opened up to a process of colonization. Immediately after Culloden, several acts of legislation were passed by the British Parliament to facilitate the colonization of the Highlands, with particular reference to the re-division of its space, which lay now under direct military rule.[31] Thus the old feudal and clan property

divisions and inscriptions were erased as the Highlands were (spatially) literally, materially, politically, economically, socially and culturally redrawn
and rewritten, in a manner often anticipatory of the enclosure process in
England, though on a larger scale and usually through more brutal methods
(see J. D. Mackie 266–315). The Highlands were looked upon as a wilderness requiring pacification and improvement; as early as 1748, for instance,
the Society for the Propagation of Christian Knowledge could say of the
Highlanders that they "were not quite civilized," and even that they were
"wild and barbarous" (quoted in Richards 80–81). Indeed, the first acts of
legislation designed to pacify the Highlands concerned not only directly
political and military issues—such as the disarmament of the clans (1747),
the abolition of heritable jurisdictions (1747), and the confiscation of
lands belonging to clans or to Lowland gentry sympathetic to the Jacobites
(1746)—but, all-importantly, cultural concerns. Thus, for instance, in a
measure used very effectively during the subjugation of Wales and Ireland
(not to mention India and elsewhere), cultural forms such as the bagpipes
and kilt were banned in 1747, as one of the provisions of the Disarmament
Act (despite the fact that the kilt had only been invented in the 1720s—
indeed, it was this act that suddenly justified the kilt's claims to cultural
authenticity, if not political potency).[32]

By the early 1780s, the Highlands had been sufficiently pacified for the
ban on the kilt to be lifted (1782), and even for the confiscated Jacobite
properties to be returned to their previous owners (1784), an event that
Waverley anticipates by a few decades in the case of the Bradwardine estate.
The basis of the Highland social structure—the clan system—had been
destroyed by the disarming acts and the destruction of the old system
of land tenure. Indeed, just as the British, following the trial of Warren
Hastings, and through the Permanent Settlement Act, completely destroyed
India's indigenous structure of land-ownership (by transforming the
zamindars from revenue-collectors for the Mughal provincial governors to
private landlords in the capitalist sense), they destroyed the old Highland
land-tenure system, replacing it with the legal and juridical structures of
private property sustaining capitalism.[33] Under the old system, the clan chief
granted *tacks*, or leases, on the clan's property. These leases were held by
his closest supporters, his tacksmen, who officered the clan "army" and
recruited companies from their own subtenants; rents were paid in kind or
in service. Having, with his clan, been disarmed, the chief no longer needed
officers or fighters; and, the land having been transformed into his own
private property, his clan ceased being his "people" in the feudal sense,
and became tenants in the capitalist sense. Thus, as John Prebble argues,
"having ceased to be a king in his own glens, having lost by Act of Parliament the power of 'pit and gallows' over the clan, he slowly realized that
he needed paying tenants, not officers."[34] Not only were the clanspeople
too impoverished to pay leases, but the returns that the landlord could gain

from their subsistence economy were paltry compared to what returns would be made possible by large-scale "improvement," especially given the lucrative option of leasing land to English sheepfarmers.

Ultimately, sheep proved to be more profitable than the clanspeople. Under the authority of the new landlords, and enforced by the power of the state, the Highlanders were forced off their land in great Clearances that swept northern and western Scotland during the late eighteenth and early nineteenth centuries: up to a third of Scotland's population was thus uprooted and dispossessed.[35] Two of the earliest clearances, in 1782, involved land and people in Balnagowan and Glenquoich—both names that appear in altered form in *Waverley*, most notably in that Fergus MacIvor is the chief of *Glennaquoich*. The first large-scale clearance, however, took place in 1784, on the lands of Alistair Macdonnel of Glengarry, a close friend of Sir Walter Scott, with the help of the Duchess of Sutherland (also a friend of Scott), one of the most zealous "improvers," and—with cruel and bitter irony—the founder of the so-called Society of True Highlanders.[36] The Clearances, justified by a discourse of "improvement," then accelerated through the Year of the Sheep (1792)—during which, in what proved to be the last major act of Highland resistance, the people of Ross revolted and drove the Lowland and English Cheviot sheep off their land, until the local landlords brought in the 47th Regiment of the Black Watch and suppressed them—and on to the Year of the Burnings (1814), by which time the Clearances had reached full pitch, and during which people were literally burned out of their homes by order of the Duchess of Sutherland.

> This person, who had been well instructed in economics, resolved, when she succeeded to the headship of the clan, to undertake a radical economic cure, and to turn the whole county of Sutherland, the population of which had already been reduced to 15,000 by similar processes, into a sheep-walk. Between 1814 and 1820 these 15,000 inhabitants, about 3,000 families, were systematically hunted and rooted out. All their villages were destroyed and burnt, all their fields turned into pasturage. British soldiers [actually they were Irishmen of the 21st Foot Regiment, still bitter at the participation of Sutherland troops in the suppression of the 1798 revolt in Ireland! (Prebble 67)] enforced this mass of evictions, and came to blows with the inhabitants. One old woman was burnt to death in the flames of the hut she refused to leave [she was, according to witnesses, too weak to leave, and none of her family was present to save her (Prebble 79)]. It was in this manner that this fine lady appropriated 794,000 acres of land which had belonged to the clan from time immemorial.
>
> (Marx 891)[37]

Unlike the enclosure movement in England, however, the Highland Clearances were not only justified by an ideology of improvement, but by a discourse of colonialism, in whose terms the victims of the clearances—the Highlanders—could only be capable of "improvement" once their old way of life had been annihilated; or, in other words, once their space had been cleansed of its otherness and absorbed into the world-system of the British empire, once the Highlands had ceased being a neutral zone and had been locked into this economy as a subdued peripheral region.[38] Thus, and in addition, the Highlands' cultural associations with Ireland had to be entirely purged before their de facto union with Britain could be achieved. Indeed, an observer of the Highlands' colonial transformation in the wake of Culloden wrote in 1746: "it is remarkable that, in some districts bordering upon the Highlands, where within memory the inhabitants spoke the Irish language, wore the Highland dress, and were accustomed to make use of Arms, upon the accidental [sic] introduction of industry, the Irish language and Highland dress gave way to a sort of English, and lowland Cloathing; the Inhabitants took to the Plough in place of Weapons; and, tho' disarmed by no Act of Parliament, are as tame as their Low Country neighbors" (quoted in Richards 106). At a certain political level, the subjugation and colonization of the Highlands represented not only the conquest of a previously wild and unruly revolutionary zone, but also the reclamation of this zone from the cultural influence of Ireland, or in other words a cultural revolt against Ireland. Hugh Trevor-Roper notes that, from at least the fifth century onwards, western Scotland was "always linked rather to Ireland than to the Saxon Lowlands," and even that the Scottish Highlands were, culturally, politically and linguistically, long seen as a colony of Ireland (Trevor-Roper 15).[39] In other words, the Highlands had been one of those spaces referred to by Blake as the "spaces of Erin."[40] The colonization of the Highlands involved not only the appropriation of their territory (both material and symbolic), but the draining-away of their Irish influence, through which what had been culturally a part of Ireland was purged of its Irishness.

To this extent, the British colonization of the Highlands, and their political and cultural annexation after 1745 (only in name had they become part of Great Britain following the 1707 Union with Scotland), anticipated the official annexation of Ireland itself some fifty years later. *Waverley*'s re-emplotment of the rise and fall of the 1745 Jacobite Rebellion, and ultimately its claim on the Highlands, is in this sense not only a symbolic reenactment of the demise of Ireland after 1800, but a spatialized allegory of the colonization of a space of Irishness—a space of Otherness—both outside and inside Ireland "proper."[41]

Beaten, subdued and ultimately colonized, the Highlands became a site not only for the rehearsal of the multitudinous practices of "improvement," which would become more general throughout Britain in the nineteenth century, but also a site for the rehearsal of Britain's larger colonial project:

an imaginary zone in which the spatial processes of colonial penetration and development were practiced on a small scale before being brought to bear on much of Africa and Asia. The languages of improvement and of colonization are brought together by the man directly responsible for the Sutherland Clearances, James Loch, in the conclusion to his *Account of the Improvements on the Estates of the Marquess of Stafford*:

> *First:* Nothing could be more at variance with the general interests of society and the individual happiness of the people themselves than the original state of Highland manners and customs.
>
> *Second:* The adoption of the new system, by which the mountainous districts are converted into sheep pastures, even if it should unfortunately occasion the emigration of some individuals is, upon the whole, advantageous to the nation at large.
>
> *Third:* The introduction of sheep farms is perfectly compatible with retaining the ancient populations in the country.
>
> *Fourth:* The effect of this change is most advantageous to the people themselves; relieving them from personal services, improving their industrious habits, and tending directly to their rapid increase and improvement.
>
> *Lastly:* The improvements . . . have had constantly for their object the employment, the comfort, the happiness of every individual who has been the object of removal; and that there is no single instance of any man having left this country on account of his not having had a lot provided for him; and that those who have gone have been induced to do so by the persuasion of others, and not from themselves, and that in point of numbers they are most insignificant.
>
> (quoted in Prebble 106–7)

The improvement offered by the Clearances, in other words, is offered not only for the land and its owners, but for the people being cleared off the land. Using the same proto-evolutionary and utilitarian language that would later be used to justify the colonization of India (particularly after India passed from the East India Company to the Crown in 1858), improvers like Loch were arguing that the people could be transformed and improved through the transformation and improvement of their space. This is (partly) why Michael Hechter and others have insisted that "the incorporation of the Celtic Periphery into England can, with the partial exception of Cornwall, be seen to be imperial in nature, rather than national."[42]

Waverley does not so much reorder the various "narratives" surrounding the Clearances as it suppresses them, partly by using a discourse of nationalism to describe a colonial process (as in the Postscript), and partly by writing over the Clearances in drawing blank its imaginary map of the

Highland present.[43] Yet references to the Highland present do leak out of the novel's politicized unconscious. It uses the same Malthusian language to describe the Highlands' overpopulation as was being used to justify the clearances, and it contains dark hints as to what would happen to the High-lands after the failure of the Forty-Five. The disarmament act enters the narrative, as do the abolition of heritable jurisdictions and the confisca-tion of property—all of which were instrumental to the Clearances—only in reference to Tully-Veolan, and the novel carefully isolates these issues from the Highlands "proper" as they fade from view. However, Fergus MacIvor's dying wish to Edward is that he take care of the clan in their time of need; and the novel mentions that Edward "amply redeemed" his pledge, which can only mean that the clan must have desperately needed his help, for which the memory of his name lives on—not in the minds of the clanspeople, but in "their glens."

Waverley's colonial vision is never straightforward and unproblematic; its will to colonize the Highlands is partially undermined by its claims to a sentimental Jacobitism, to the trappings and rituals of a mythic Highland past. While the Highlands were being, in *Waverley*'s own present, cleaned of their otherness and brought symbolically into the present by being colonized, the novel wants to negate this process—while at the same time it is nevertheless forced to acknowledge it—and insist on their retention of a charge of Difference and Otherness. While the efforts at colonization and improvement were sustained by a colonial discourse of discipline, industry, and progress, *Waverley* counters these with a nationalist discourse and a pre-evolutionary view of Difference: one which rejects the possibility of transmutation, transformation and development. Thus the novel wants to preserve the Highlands as a site of otherness; but the cost for this—a cost paid neither by the novel nor by its reader—is that their present cannot be admitted into the novel as a presence. *Waverley* thus simultaneously acknowledges the historical transformation of the Highlands, and negates this transformation by keeping the Highland space intact as the space of the past. In other words, it keeps the Highlands "alive" (in the past) by symbolically "killing" them (in the present).

Waverley can only cling to the Highlands as a site of difference and otherness to the extent that it can negate its loss of otherness, its fall from difference to sameness. The novel's Highlands are not only parts of Blake's "space of Erin"; rather, their claim to be parts of the space of Erin is enabled by their being—like the spaces of Erin—what Robert Gleckner terms a "residuum of 'unfallenness'" (Gleckner 312). For, even though they are consigned to the past, *Waverley*'s Highlands have not yet fallen: they are held in suspense, forever on the brink of their calamitous fall from difference.

A commentator on the subjugation of Ireland in the late eighteenth century wrote: "The husbandman must first break the ground before it be made capable of good seed: and when it is thoroughly broken and manured, if he do not forthwith cast good seed into it, it will grow wild again, and bear nothing but weeds. So a barbarous country must first be broken by a war, before it will be capable of good government; and when it is fully subdued and conquered, if it be not well planted and governed after the conquest, it will often return to the former barbarism" (quoted in Hechter 76). Although *Waverley* acknowledges the colonization of the Highlands, and, extending the above metaphor, its implantation with the "seeds" of modernity and of the present, the novel refuses to map the "actual" modernization of the Highlands (in which, as I have been trying to suggest, it "actually" participated). The colonization of the Highlands amounts to their symbolic "implantation" with the seeds of the present social order of capitalist modernity. Yet this "implantation" does not involve the fundamental transformation of the colonized space as such or on its own terms: it involves an appropriation and clearing-away of this space as a site in which modernity can then be planted by force. Modernity, in this historical schema, is not something that can be achieved by the colonized themselves: it is something that must be implanted *in* them as a germ, to work its own way out and into the flow of "history," to alter its "host" society beyond all recognition. Hence this process does not exactly involve the *transformation* of anti-modernity into modernity, or the transformation of an anti-modern society into a modern one. Rather it involves the annihilation of one form of society (the anti-modern) and its replacement by another (the modern). For, ultimately, modernity—that teleological discourse of progress, of evolution, of process—turns out to be more about the sudden replacement of one state of being by another than about a gradual development; modernization as a process needs, therefore, to be understood as in some sense identical to modernity itself, rather than as process *leading towards* modernity.[44] The beginning of the process of modernization, in other words, implies its "end" as well; for modernity is a process that, paradoxically, "leads" only to itself. As for those who, like *Waverley*'s Highlanders, are "shown" to be "incapable" of modernization —their fate is shown to be "inevitable": outside history and beyond even the margins of modernity, they end up serving merely as immobile place-markers along the banks of the river of time.

Notes

This essay is adapted from a chapter in a book-length study of imperialism and modernity in British romanticism, which is presently being prepared for publication. Previous and shorter versions of this essay were presented as lectures at the University of Iowa and Carnegie-Mellon University. I would like to thank Robert Gleckner, Marjorie Levinson, Fredric Jameson, Kenneth Surin, Barbara Herrnstein Smith, James Chandler, Rebecca Karl and Cesare Casarino for their helpful and productive criticisms of earlier drafts of the essay.

1 Sir Walter Scott, *Waverley* (1814; Harmondsworth: Penguin, 1983) 73.
2 James Kerr, *Fiction Against History: Scott as Storyteller* (Cambridge: Cambridge UP, 1989) 24. Tourism is *never* politically innocent, so that this is, I think, a difference of degree rather than of kind.
3 Just as workers and landscape are reduced to aestheticized background objects in other kinds of tours: see John Barrell, *The Dark Side of the Landscape: The Rural Poor in English Painting, 1730–1840* (Cambridge: Cambridge UP, 1980).
4 "The bagpipers, three in number, screamed, during the whole time of dinner, a tremendous war-tune; and the echoing of the vaulted roof, and clang of the Celtic tongue, produced such a Babel of noises, that Waverley dreaded his ears would never recover from it" (164).
5 See, for example, 56, 63, 91, 83, 139, 174 and 324.
6 One result of this arrangement in an Oriental tale is the sense that the exoticism of the Orient cannot be approached simply by reading what is supposed to be an Arabic or Turkish (or Indian, or Chinese) text. Rather, the Orient fundamentally requires the mediation of the Orientalist, who alone is capable of understanding all of its complexities and dangers, and of communicating his or her understanding to other Europeans. This is precisely the effect of the enormous weight of the notes at the end of William Beckford's *Vathek* and each of Byron's Turkish tales, for these notes do not convey useful information about this or that detail of Oriental culture as much as they convey a sense of the "vast complexity" of the Orient to the sheltered European reader. Because each noted reference in the main body of an Oriental tale necessarily brings up a dozen other references, the overall effect of the notes is not to clarify things, but rather to make them more obscure—and hence to reinforce the need for the intervention of the knowledgeable or informed authority figure (the Orientalist).
7 See Hugh Trevor-Roper, "The Invention of Tradition: The Highland Tradition of Scotland," in *The Invention of Tradition*, eds. Eric Hobsbawm and Terence Ranger (Cambridge: Cambridge UP, 1983). He says that "the whole concept of a Highland culture and tradition is a retrospective invention," developed after the 1707 Union with England, against which it was a protest. Also see the Introduction to Bernard Bailyn and Philip Morgan, eds., *Strangers Within the Realm: Cultural Margins of the First British Empire* (Chapel Hill: U of North Carolina P, 1991) 27.
8 James Reed, *Sir Walter Scott: Landscape and Locality* (London: The Athlone P, 1980) 6.
9 Hence the novel contrasts the ahistorical essences of the Highlands with the historically-constructed identity of the Lowlands.
10 Though, as I will discuss more fully later on, the Highlands are the spatialized past that cannot enter or become the future. They remain immutably past.
11 This is one way in which the novel uses characters to embody social or historical positions. See Georg Lukács, *The Historical Novel*, trans. Hannah and Stanley Mitchell (Lincoln: U of Nebraska P, 1962) 33–39.
12 "The character of Colonel Talbot dawned upon Edward by degrees" (366); indeed, Edward's appreciation of the Colonel is in a mutually-determining relationship with his own gradual maturation and development. The other proper English gentlemen (and officers) in the novel—notably Melville, Morton and Gardiner (given Scott's benediction in the Notes as "a good Christian and gallant man")—hold the same "correct" attitudes as Talbot. As characters, they are virtually indistinguishable from one another, since their propriety, justice, warmth, loyalty and generosity fade into and blend with one another, just as the selfishness, crudeness, and fanaticism of some of the Highlanders—principally

Evan Dhu, Callum Beg, and Fergus in his "Highland" mode—make each also indistinguishable from the others.

13 See, for instance, 366, 387, 424, and especially 463, where Talbot pronounces judgment on Fergus' fate: "Justice . . . which demanded some penalty of those who had wrapped the whole nation in fear and in mourning, could not perhaps have selected a fitter victim. He came to the field with the fullest light upon the nature of his attempt. He had studied and understood the subject. His father's fate could not intimidate him; the lenity of the laws which had restored to him [after the 1715 Jacobite revolt] his father's property and rights could not melt him. That he was brave, generous, and possessed many good qualities, only rendered him the more dangerous; that he was enlightened and accomplished made his crime the less excusable; that he was an enthusiast in the wrong cause only made him the more fit to be its martyr. Above all, he had been the means of bringing many hundreds of men into the field who, without him, would never have broken the peace of the country." Talbot's assessment and the historical assessment of the narrator in the opening and closing chapters of the novel are not only exactly the same, they even *sound* the same in tone, phrasing, and emphasis. From the Unionist/Hanoverian standpoint, Talbot is historically "correct" to point to the "lenity" of the laws following the 1715 revolt; and indeed after the Forty-Five, the Highland chiefs were stripped of their hereditary jurisdictions (and hence of their ability to bring fighters into the field), and ultimately transformed into landlords in the capitalist sense: a process which led to the great Clearances, whose full ramifications were being felt in Scott's own time.

14 See Hayden White, *Metahistory: The Historical Imagination in Nineteenth-Century Europe* (Baltimore: Johns Hopkins UP, 1974) 7–11. Emplotment, he says, "is the way by which a sequence of events fashioned into a story is gradually revealed to be a story of a particular kind."

15 Prince Charles had, with French assistance, attempted a proper invasion in 1744, but a violent storm scattered his fleet and ended that attempt. Having financed his own operation, he returned to western Scotland on 25 July 1745, in a small boat with seven men (of whom three were Irish, and one more a Macdonald from Ulster), to begin his attempt to topple the British government in the name of his father (James viii of Scotland/iii of England) and the House of Stuart. For more on the Jacobites, see J. D. Mackie, *A History of Scotland* (London: Pelican, 1978) 221–82; Christopher Haigh, ed., *The Cambridge Historical Encyclopedia of Great Britain and Ireland* (Cambridge: Cambridge UP, 1990) 197–222; and Christopher Hill, *Reformation to Industrial Revolution* (Harmondsworth: Penguin, 1969) 213–38.

16 The battle of Culloden (16 April 1746) marked the end of the Forty-Five rebellion, and the final collapse of Jacobitism. Charles was spirited away by Flora Macdonald to the Isle of Skye, and thence to France, where he died in exile. His followers at Culloden suffered heavily; over a thousand were killed in the battle; a further 120 were executed afterwards; 1,000 were transported; and 700 others disappeared.

17 Thus the novel exaggerates the identification between Highlands and Jacobitism, since the latter stood for much more than the former. Indeed, this identification is merely the result of the defeat of the House of Stuart during and after 1688 in all of Britain, the Highlands merely being one of their last areas of support. But the novel collapses Jacobitism into the Highlands, so that the one becomes the other. It also collapses anti-Unionism into Jacobitism.

18 "Unaccustomed to the address and manners of a polished court, in which Charles was eminently skilful, his words and his kindness penetrated the heart of our

hero, and easily outweighed all prudential motives. To be thus personally solicited for assistance by a Prince, whose form and manners, as well as the spirit which he displayed in this singular enterprise, answered his ideas of a hero of romance; to be courted by him in the ancient halls of his paternal palace, recovered by the sword which he was already bending towards other conquests, gave Edward, in his own eyes, the dignity and importance which he had ceased to consider as his attributes" (295).

19 When Waverley "had surmounted a small craggy eminence, called St Leonard's Hill, the King's Park, or the hollow between the mountain of Arthur's Seat, and the rising ground on which the southern part of Edinburgh is now built, lay beneath him, and displayed a singular and animating prospect. It was occupied by the army of the Highlanders, now in the act of preparing for their march . . ." (321).

20 Gladsmuir is the Highlanders' name for the battle on 21 September 1745, which the English called Prestonpans, after the nearby town (southeast of Edinburgh).

21 See Fredric Jameson, *The Political Unconscious* (Ithaca, NY: Cornell UP, 1981) 81–82.

22 Thus, defending Edward from charges of treason, one of the novel's spokesmen for the rational present (Morton) says that "He whom ambition, or hope of personal advantage [i.e., Fergus], has led to disturb the peace of a well-ordered government, let him fall a victim to the laws; but surely youth [i.e., Edward], mis-led by the wild visions of chivalry and imaginary loyalty [i.e., Prince Charles], may plea for pardon" (252).

23 At the same time, *Waverley* chronicles not only the growth and maturity of its hero, but the growth and maturity of the British nation away from what it posits as the irrationality of its "past." The 1707 Act of Union was a necessary and beneficial act, in the novel's view. The Highlands and their people pay the price for being the "immature" area away from which the nation had to develop, or, put differently, the space that had to be sacrificed in order to achieve the unity of the nation. The novel, as Lukács suggests, uses personal feelings and attractions to express political attachments. Waverley's homoerotic attraction to Fergus, a supplement to his attraction to Flora, thus expresses his attachment to the Jacobites. His drift away from Flora and Fergus and his growing fondness for Rose express his gradual move away from Jacobitism. The homoerotic supplement to his attraction to Rose is Talbot himself, Waverley's "true" father-figure (since his own has had little to do with him). The novel's politicized sexual dynamics lead Waverley toward an Oedipal "crisis" which it suppresses.

24 "Unreserved alienation is thus unreserved representation. It wrenches presence absolutely from itself and absolutely re presents it to itself" (Jacques Derrida, *Of Grammatology*, trans. G. C. Spivak [Baltimore: Johns Hopkins UP, 1976] 296).

25 It is precisely in these terms that the invention of a Highland (or any other) tradition does not necessarily lose its "authority" and "authenticity" for being a forgery. On the contrary, it becomes a powerful political reference and referent.

26 As, for instance, its concerns with revolution have to do not only with the Jacobite Rebellion of 1745, but also the revolutionary situation in Britain in the early nineteenth century.

27 See Benedict Anderson, *Imagined Communities: Reflections on the Origin and Spread of Nationalism* (London: Verso, 1983).

28 Good colonial examples of this are the Thames and the Congo in Conrad's *Heart of Darkness*; a good postcolonial instance of writing this theme "back to the empire" is the river Nile in al-Tayyeb Saleh's *Season of Migration to the North*, which is in some ways a counter-narrative of the European voyage of exploration into the unknown.

29 Johannes Fabian, *Time and the Other: How Anthropology Makes its Object* (New York: Columbia UP, 1983) 17.

30 A similar occurrence took place in Wales at about the same time, with the reinvention of the bardic meeting or *eisteddfod*, Druidism, and so forth. See Prys Morgan, "From a Death to a View: The Hunt for the Welsh Past in the Romantic Period," in *The Invention of Tradition* 43–100. But if Wales and Scotland had been colonized by England and annexed into a Union with it long before the romantic period (1536 and 1707, respectively), Ireland was still facing the process of this incorporation, for its Act of Union with England was only legislated in 1800.

31 Much of the post-45 legislation explicitly used the language of colonialism, calling, for instance, for "the better civilizing and improving the Highlands of Scotland, so preventing disorders there in future." Quoted in Eric Richards, "Scotland and the Uses of the Atlantic Empire," in *Strangers Within the Realm: Cultural Margins of the First British Empire* 111.

32 See Trevor-Roper 22. Indeed, earlier legislation to pacify the Highlands, after the Fifteen, had proscribed the Irish longshirt which had originally been worn by the inhabitants. The kilt was invented by Thomas Rawlinson, an Englishman.

33 See Eric Wolf, *Europe and the People Without History* (Berkeley: U of California P, 1982) 239–52; J. D. Mackie 280–81; Karl Marx, *Capital*, vol. 1, trans. Ben Fowkes (New York: Vintage, 1977) 877–96. The French did precisely the same thing in Algeria later in the 19th century, destroying the old Berber and Arab family-property system and replacing it with the private ownership of land.

34 John Prebble, *The Highland Clearances* (London: Penguin, 1963) 14.

35 Compare this to the Dutch murder or eviction of the inhabitants of various East Indian islands, such as Banda, to make room for spice plantations worked by a few natives and supervised by even fewer Europeans. See Wolf 237–39.

36 See Prebble 139–44; also see Christopher Harvie, "Scott and the Image of Scotland," in *Patriotism: The Making and Unmaking of British Identity*, ed. Raphael Samuel (London: Routledge, 1989) 189.

37 Also see Prebble 49–115; Mackie 289–91. After her clan's outcries against their eviction, the Duchess, then in London, wrote to a friend: "I hope to be in Scotland this summer, but I am uneasy about a sort of mutiny that has broken out in one part of Sutherland, in consequences [*sic*] of our new plans having made it necessary to transplant some of the inhabitants to the sea-coast from other parts of the estate. The people who are refractory on this occasion are part of Clan Gun, so often mentioned by Sir Robert Gordon, who live by distilling whisky and are unwilling to quit that occupation for a life of industry of a different sort which was proposed to them. London is more full and gay, if possible, than usual. A great many foreigners from Russia, etc., *parlant bon anglais-russe*" (quoted in Prebble 65).

38 See Homi Bhabha, "The Other Question: Difference, Discrimination and the Discourse of Colonialism," in Francis Barker, *et al.*, eds., *Literature, Politics & Theory* (London: Methuen, 1986) 148–72.

39 The invention of the Highland "tradition," he goes on, had not only to do with the retrospective invention of cultural form and their presentation to the Lowlands, but also with a cultural revolt against Ireland, a usurpation of Irish culture.

40 See Robert Gleckner, *Blake and Spenser* (Baltimore: Johns Hopkins UP, 1985) 311–18.

41 *Waverley* can be read as a narrative of the colonization of Ireland, in addition to being a "map" of the colonization of the Highlands and of the suppression of insurgency in Britain. There are several—hardly surprising—connections between

the 1745 Jacobite Rebellion and the doomed 1798 revolution in Ireland (although the Forty-Five arose out of the 1707 Union of Scotland and England, and the 1798 rebellion *led to* the 1800 Union of England and Ireland, as a better means of controlling the Irish). There are strong connections between the United Irishmen, one of the movements involved in the 1798 rebellion, and Jacobitism in general (partly through the UI's articulation of Defenderism, which is itself caught up with Irish Catholicism and Jacobitism). But there are also striking connections between the revolutionary situations in Scotland (1745), Ireland (1798), and *Waverley*'s Britain (1805–14), in the underlying British fear in all three contexts (as was the case during the American Revolution) of French involvement, and ultimately the involvement of the French Revolution. Also the United Irishmen had strong connections to an English revolutionary organization (not surprisingly called the United Englishmen), who were actively involved in the 1797 Mutiny in the Royal Navy's Channel and North Sea Fleets at Spithead and the Nore.

42 Michael Hechter, *Internal Colonialism: The Celtic Fringe in British National Development, 1536–1966* (Berkeley: U of California P, 1975) 65. Hence his use of the term "internal colonialism."

43 In relentlessly using the same language of nationalism and national development as Scott uses in *Waverley*, Georg Lukács not only overlooks the colonial—rather than national—incorporation of the Highlands into the United Kingdom: he ruthlessly consigns the novel to English (not even British) literature, arguing in the course of his discussion of "English reality" and "English development," that "it is no accident that this new type of novel arose in England" (31, 54). It seems to me, on the contrary, that it is no coincidence that this historical novel arose not at all in England, but in Scotland (with Walter Scott) and Ireland (with Maria Edgeworth).

44 I discuss the significance and contemporary relevance of such an understanding of modernity in "'Postcolonial' Literature in a Neo-Colonial World: Modern Arabic Culture and the End of Modernity," in *Boundary* 2 (Spring 1995).

28

BRITISH ROMANTIC
COLUMBIADS

Fiona Robertson

Source: *Symbiosis* 2 (1998), 1–23.

In his preface to *The History of America* (1777), William Robertson describes the development of the Spanish colonies in the Americas following Columbus's voyages of exploration as 'not only the most splendid portion of the American story, but so much detached, that it forms a perfect whole by itself, remarkable for the unity of the subject'.[1] In contrast, he argues, the story of the British colonies in North America is unresolved and untellable. As the War of Independence progressed, Robertson's planned philosophical history was left in a state of permanently suspended animation, with fragments (Books 9 and 10) of his accounts of Virginia and New England appearing posthumously in 1796, edited by his son.[2] The unresolved status of British North America shadows the declared unity of the narrative of Spanish conquest, which in turn comes to seem like a prelude to a fuller account, an integrated colonial history which was never to be. As a significant intellectual and imaginative resource for British writers of the Romantic period, Robertson's *History of America* has never fully attained the recognition it deserves. Arguing that '[o]ur false ideas of the Americans have done us infinite mischief', the English translator of J. P. Brissot de Warville's *New Travels in the United States of America [in 1788]* cites as a major authority for these ideas the misconceptions 'mounted among the heavy armed cavalry of Robertson. Under such able commanders [the others are all French: the Encyclopædists, Cornelius De Pauw, and the Abbé Raynal], who could doubt of their doing execution?'[3] The impact of the descriptions and analyses in *The History of America*, especially the reinforcement of eighteenth-century 'stadial history' in the account of the Native Americans in Book 4 and the narratorial voice by which an assumed European cultural authority is registered and sustained, can be felt in works as various as Book 3 of *The Excursion*, the closing scenes of *The Heart of Midlothian*, and *Gertrude of Wyoming*. Perhaps as potent as these aspects of *The History of America* is its status as prelude and (ultimately) fragment, its awareness of the untellable which is the ironic product of its own historical moment.[4] Readers take from it not only a unified or narratorially unifiable story but also an artificial division between 'completed' Spanish colonial history (with all the political convenience such a notion implies) and a British colonial history to which no pattern can yet be assigned.

Robertson's *History* also brought British readers closer to a long tradition of prose narratives relating to Christopher Columbus, including the mariner's own frequently-translated *Letter* (1493), the narrative of his lieutenant Diego Mendez and the biography purportedly written by his illegitimate son Hernando Colón, and the *Historia de las Indias* (begun in 1523) of the Dominican Bartolomé de las Casas, which includes a digest of Columbus's lost journal from the first voyage; as well as the major historical narratives of the Spanish royal historian Gonzalo Fernández de Oviedo (*Historia general y natural de las Indias*, 1547), Francisco López de Gómara (*Historia general de las Indias*, 1552), José de Acosta (*Historia natural y moral de las Indias*, 1590), and Antonio de Herrera y Tordesillas (*Historia general*, 1610, 1615). To these might be added the host of works by later explorers and commentators ranging from Bernal Díaz del Castillo and Hernán Cortés to Voltaire and the Abbé Raynal, whose perspectives on the Americas entailed more or less explicit assessment of the role and legacy of Columbus. In retelling the story of Columbus, Robertson persuasively fixed for later readers an image which had gained in currency throughout the eighteenth century. This is the image of Columbus as 'a modern before his time', as Anthony Pagden has expressed it in an important assessment of the development of Columbus from Christian explorer inspired by God, to ideas-led inventor of America, to the man of scientific vision celebrated by Alexander von Humboldt.[5]

There is one group of poems to which the creation of a unified Spanish colonial history and a revised and consolidated image of Columbus in Robertson's *History of America* is especially significant. Not usually considered as a group, British Columbiads of the Romantic period are curiously placed historically, politically, and generically, telling the story of European exploration and settlement in a context which Robertson's *History* could not encompass. They show how writers of a nation which had lost its colonies in North America imagined the early colonial history of another, rival, nation. They bear the imprint, especially in their treatment of maritime history, of Britain's war against Spain and Spain's colonies from 1796 to 1808: for, as may be seen in competing accounts of the discovery of the Americas in Elizabethan England, territorial and political disputes in the 1790s and 1800s made the representation of Columbus a sensitive matter.[6] More intriguingly still, British Romantic tales of Columbus find ways of expressing Robertson's sense of writing in an historical vacuum even when the outcome of revolution in British America had become abundantly clear. This essay refers to an international range of epic Columbiads and smaller-scale poems about Columbus, but its central interest lies in three interrelated British poems: William Bowles's *The Spirit of Discovery; or, the Conquest of Ocean* (1804), Robert Southey's *Madoc* (1805), and Samuel Rogers's *The Voyage of Columbus* (1812). In different ways all these poems resist their subject-matter and respond to what I identify below as key structural and narratorial problems in the tale of Columbus as well as to difficulties in accounting for him intellectually, historically, and nationally.

The term 'Columbiad', made current by its use in the title of the epic poem published by the celebrated French salonist and poet Marie Anne Fiquet du Boccage in 1756, is now most frequently associated with works by American writers and most frequently traced back to Joel Barlow's ten-book national epic *The Columbiad* of 1807 (the revised version of the nine-book *The Vision of Columbus*, 1787, which was an important influence on Volney and Blake). Columbiads were a literary endeavour central to early literature of the United States, although they have not always been accorded this status in representations of its history.[7] Creating a heroic narrative of the history of the nation, on a classical model, was important to writers in the newly independent United States in the same way and for many of the same reasons that classical models shaped the art and rhetoric of early republicanism. Epics such as Timothy Dwight's *The Conquest of Canäan* (1785) fashion links between American history and the foundation-stories of other nations, caught between claims for exceptionalism and the move to be part of a broader inclusive Christian history. Barlow's works (sharply defined for modern readers by Stuart Curran as radically disruptive of epic convention)[8] are concerned not so much with the deeds of Columbus as with the vision vouchsafed to the imprisoned Columbus of the future of the continents he did not know he had discovered. The vision compensates for the bitterness of the aftermath of his voyages and in so doing both concedes his place in the history of the Americas and limits his significance. It is noticeable that the British work most famously indebted to Barlow, Blake's *America*, misses out altogether the Columbus element in the continents' history. In his attention to British colonial power Blake presents the heroes of American independence on their own terms as fathers and founders, not as usurpers or as suppressors of earlier traditions. The literary relationship between Barlow and Blake is long-established: less frequently noted is the impossibility, for Blake, of including Columbus at the heart of American genealogy.

Du Boccage's 1756 *La Colombiade, ou la foi portée au nouveau monde*, dedicated to Pope Benedict XIV, unequivocally fixes the nature of its subject and the challenge this presents to the artist: 'Ce nouvel Ulysse méritoit sans doute un autre Homère'.[9] Other Columbiads are less certain of Columbus's centrality and rather less keen to confer on him the qualities of Ulysses or any other comparable hero. A shift away from Columbus is observable in the American Richard Snowden's *The Columbiad, or, A Poem on the American War* (Philadelphia, 1795), while a more traditional line is taken by the British schoolmaster and cleric James L. Moore in his twelve-book poem of 1798, *The Columbiad: An Epic Poem on the Discovery of America and the West Indies by Columbus* (printed by the Rivingtons for a price which scandalised Southey, 15 shillings). Like *La Colombiade*, Moore's *Columbiad* focuses closely on the tale of Columbus's four voyages, but it is more equivocably poised between remaining an epic of Columbus and becoming an epic of Columbia. Moore carefully separates British from Spanish colonial iniquities. The description given by Raphael to Columbus of the future of the American continents sharply contrasts the Spanish south and the British north; while God discourses on the moral difference between Spanish and British explorers, declaring that 'One nation, well belov'd and long caress'd, / Shall here transplant her sons, supremely bless'd' and conveniently declaring it to be his purpose that the American wilderness should be cultivated.[10] When the time comes in Book 7 for the American colonies to declare independence, Columbus reacts with horror at the idea of dissension between peoples joined by language, religion, and habit. The oddities of Moore's epic, most notably perhaps the way in which Columbus is given by God and by the Spirit of the Orinoco insights into the history not of Spanish or Portuguese but of British America, reveal a contradictory subject-matter, a tale of Columbus awkwardly metamorphosing into a tale of Columbia. The ending of Moore's *Columbiad* is assertively upbeat, focusing on praise for the mariner and his satisfaction with his own deeds. For Joel Barlow, in contrast, discovery becomes less a European event than an American beginning. As Terence Martin has stated in a brief but suggestive essay, Du Boccage and Moore present the 'discovery' of the Americas in European terms, emphasising the consequences of discovery for the cultures of France and Britain. In contrast, according to Martin, Barlow's *Columbiad* offers a vision 'protean and all-encompassing', a vision generated by decline and death rather than by triumphant conquest.[11] The shift in emphasis for the American market is nowhere clearer than in the revision of Barlow's *The Vision of Columbus* (dedicated to Louis XVI) to *The Columbiad* of 1807 (dedicated to Robert Fulton).

As the contrast between Barlow and Moore begins to show, even those early poems which grant the story of Columbus full-length epic treatment differ significantly in the importance they attach to the mariner himself. It is perhaps fitting, therefore, that the literary term 'Columbiad' should have been the subject of considerable critical redefinition ever since. In current usage there is even some transatlantic slippage, for it is defined rather differently in the major current British and North American dictionaries. In the second edition of the *Oxford English Dictionary* a Columbiad is described simply as 'an epic of America'. *Webster's Third New International*

Dictionary, however, defines it both more narrowly and more inclusively as 'any of certain epics recounting the beginning and growth of the United States; also any epic with similar subject matter'. By analogy with the *Aeneid* or the *Lusiad*, most readers would expect it to be an epic, focusing on the supposed or recorded deeds of Columbus, which tells of the foundation of a nation. Recent critical evocations of the term Columbiad have challenged its assumed parameters, however, and in ways which offer new insights into the poems to be discussed in this essay. The clearest example of this is the scholarship relating to so-called Black Columbiads. Claiming the narrative of Olaudah Equiano in 1789 as the paradigm of this genre, recent studies reappraise the term in the context of the African diaspora, exploring the meaning of 'discovery' and the evolution of a new 'American' identity for slave journeys to European settlements in the New World.[12] In this usage a Columbiad has become more inclusively 'the poetical name for the journey to the New World', and within possible Columbiads the kind specifically concerned with Columbus is identified as 'a journey not of dreaming and freedom but of calculation and enslavement'.[13] Another approach to the Columbiad is broader still, using the term to refer to 'the Dream of America, the material and spiritual promise that from the outset attracted people to the New World'.[14] Radical writers of the twentieth century who are now seen to be subverting and redirecting traditional Columbiads have been described as 'simultaneously foreground[ing] the gender and racial issues concealed in the traditional version of a dream articulated and enacted primarily by white men' (Shulman 24). The tales of Columbus produced by the three British writers examined in this essay, however, show that such issues were far from lurking unquestioned in much earlier works.

I have already suggested that the story of Columbus presents the writer in whatever genre with certain structural and narratorial difficulties, and that these are further complicated by problems in accounting for him intellectually, historically, and nationally. The claim for narrative unity made by Robertson is an obvious starting-point. Southey's review of James L. Moore's 1798 *Columbiad* for the *Critical Review* begins with the objection that Columbus's discoveries, 'important as they have proved to mankind, do not form a proper subject for an epic poem. They want the unity which such a work requires.'[15] The only event of American history which possesses such a unity, Southey suggests, is the conquest of Mexico, 'which, in the hands of a Spaniard of sufficient genius, might be formed into a noble poem' (*Quarterly Review* 23: 66). (Southey tellingly assumes that the writer should have an appropriate national identity.) The question of unity also troubled Barlow, who gives the difficulty of composing 'a regular Epic Poem' on the discovery of America as the reason for his decision to present it as a 'vision' in the introduction to *The Vision of Columbus* in 1787.[16] By 1807, when the extensively revised second version of this work, *The Columbiad*, was published, Barlow had reflected further on the disjunction between his subject and the epic form. In a preface preceding the original introduction he now presents his work as an explicitly republican poem and expands on the ideological reasons for his rejection of traditional epic. But he also has grander notions of his poem as a founding-text of 'America's' (that is, the United States') nationhood. It is, he now insists, 'a patriotic poem; the subject is national and historical [. . .] But most of the events were so recent, so important and so well known, as to tender them inflexible to the hand of fiction.'[17] He had also reimagined the poem's audience, expanding the opening sentence of the introduction to read: 'Every circumstance relating to the discovery and settlement of America, is an interesting object of enquiry, *especially to the great and growing nations of this hemisphere, who owe their existence to those arduous labors*' (1807 addition in my italics: *Columbiad* 1). It is not only the storyteller but also the readership which unites the story of one explorer to the story of the foundation of a nation he never envisaged. Both versions of Barlow's epic present Columbus as the lost opportunity of the New World, as the benefactor whose moral ownership of the Americas has literally been erased in their name (in an expanded section of the introduction Barlow in 1807 dismisses Amerigo Vespucci as 'one of his followers, a man of no particular merit': *Columbiad* 18). Barlow's two Columbiads present readers with a vision *of* Columbus in two distinct senses: with Columbus as vision, an occasion for a historical panorama of a continent out of his control; and also as its lost and slighted origin. It is both rhetorically and politically convenient to have one lost origin (that of the spiritual hero) replace another (that of the natives of the Caribbean and of South America). Barlow's two poems construct a national history which is complex in its elisions and its unexpected confrontations; but one of its key moves is to institute Columbus as already a displacement and echo of the fate of the indigenous peoples he described.

The second structural feature to which all the Columbiads considered here respond, though not all in the same way, is closely related to this sense of Columbus as displacement (or, as Otto B. Heim has suggested, Derridean supplement)[18] Columbus's achievements may be regarded either as triumphant fulfilments of an intellectual pattern, a grand navigational conjecture, or as accidents which more closely resemble disruptions in the narrative scheme. The tension is resolved in different ways in different accounts of Columbus, but with Robertson's *History of America* standing as primary authority for British readers the most common emphasis in the late eighteenth century fell on the interpretation of Columbus as a scientific visionary; a visionary, moreover, at war with the prejudices of his own times. Anthony Pagden notes one artistic possibility opened up by such a view when he comments that for Robertson, 'the history of Columbus's initial rejection at the hands of the Genoese, the English, the Portuguese and even, at first, the Spanish, made his personal biography an ideal subject for metaphorical transformation' (Pagden 100). That is, reason may be shown to triumph over the systems of belief and custom prevalent in any particular age and culture. If one sees Columbus in personal rather than metaphorical terms, however, the artistic possibilities of his story are just as complex and various. The conclusion of Washington Irving's *History of the Life and Voyages of Christopher Columbus* (1828) presents an image of the mariner which transforms the idea of the discovery-as-accident into far richer artistic material:

> What visions of glory would have broke upon his mind could he
> have known that he had indeed discovered a new continent, equal
> to the whole of the old world in magnitude, and separated by two
> vast oceans from all the earth hitherto known by civilised man![19]

Bruce Greenfield points out in an innovative discussion of Irving's biography that the narrative of Columbus is full of dramatic irony for the modern reader, who understands the lands 'discovered' in terms which are quite different from those available to their discoverer; but this irony also presents problems for works focusing on the supposed heroism of the man himself.[20] One solution is to make Columbus a kind of artist, governed by inspiration even when he fails to recognise what he has created. Hence Irving's Columbus, 'capable of [. . .] enthusiastic soarings of the imagination' (Irving 346), is a subtly different creature from Robertson's combination of rational enquiry and 'the ardent enthusiasm of a projector (*History of America* 1: 66). Irving's account of Columbus as a man of 'ardent and enthusiastic imagination' and 'poetical temperament' brings his image distinctly closer to Shelley's evocation of poets at the close of *A Defence of Poetry* as 'hierophants of an unapprehended inspiration, the mirrors of the gigantic shadows which futurity casts upon the present, the words which express what they understand not'.[21] As Bruce Greenfield comments: 'The idealizing of Columbus's character offers the possibility of an ideal discovery yet to be made, and in this sense readers of Irving's biography are offered Columbus as a symbol of America's ultimate potential and a focus for renewed hope and effort' (Greenfield 130).

The distinctions necessary to a discussion of Columbus as imaginative material are complex, and they vary in emphasis from text to text. Columbus is construed as an idealised origin but he is also separated from the sequential narrative of the whole pattern of colonisation. He is a man of imagination who is not responsible for the consequences of his imaginings; and who cannot imagine the future, or believe it when he is shown it in vision (as in Moore's *Columbiad*). Columbiads seek both to identify Columbus as the originator of American history and to separate him from it, presenting him as humanitarian and wise and thereby distinguishing him from the subsequent actions of his followers and imitators. All the poetical tales of Columbus considered in this essay include some attempt to mark Columbus's voyages as historically distinct from what was to follow; all attest in some way to the need to preserve Columbus's life-story as the alternative it seems to be in Barlow's introduction to *The Columbiad*. They are works of historical irony, with an avowed double vision which is further complicated by Britain's often equivocal response to the United States in the early period of its independence.

All three of the British Columbiads explored in this essay were conceived or partly written in the late 1790s. None of them finds it possible to broach the subject of Columbus as unabashedly as had Moore's maligned *Columbiad*. The first to be published, William Bowles's five-book poem of 1804, *The Spirit of Discovery; or, The Conquest of Ocean*, claims the imminence of the other two as its reason for swerving from the story of Columbus. As Bowles states, one key part of the work as originally envisaged had been crowded out by rumours of other competitors:

> It was at first intended that the Poem should consist of six books; one book being assigned to Da Gama, and another to Columbus. These have been compressed; which I was the more inclined to do, as the great subject of the DISCOVERY OF AMERICA is in the hands of such poets as Mr. SOUTHEY and Mr. ROGERS.[22]

Like Robertson's *History of America*, though for different reasons, Bowles's account avoids a full rehearsal of the story it claims to have planned to tell. Despite this declared reason for avoiding extended treatment of the subject of Columbus, it is apparent from internal evidence that the subject posed serious problems for Bowles's poem, the purpose of which is to trace discovery while asserting the eventual irrelevance of discovery 'when the SUPREME DISPOSER's plan shall have been completed, THEN THE EARTH, which has been explored and enlightened by discovery and knowledge, shall be destroyed' (*Spirit of Discovery* xi). The question of America haunts its presentation of such confident progress.

The Spirit of Discovery is organised historically but is preoccupied by an anxiety about the coherence of its materials. Beginning with a section called 'The Vision of the Ark', Bowles traces maritime history through the Egyptians and Phoenicians, Babylonians and Alexandrians, and through the discoveries of new trade routes via the Cape of Good Hope and across the Atlantic to the Americas. As Bowles's cautious preface makes clear, this ambitious work is especially concerned to find or to assert principles of connection, historical and poetical: '*carelessness of arrangement*' is the central anxiety of the preface (*Spirit of Discovery* xxii). One of the principal connecting ideas, however, is persistently elided; and here the decision not to expand the Columbus section begins to seem more symptomatic than accidental. The first vision of America, in Book 1, is given to Noah by the spirit of Destruction, who vows to wreak vengeance for the salvation of the Ark by making similar vessels the agents of disaster and inhumanity:

> Then saw the just man in his dream what seem'd
> A new and savage land: Huge forests stretch'd
> Their world of wood, shading like night the banks
> Of torrent-forming rivers [. . .]
>
> (*Spirit of Discovery* 11)

Amid this scene a father and child are idyllically viewed, until the con-
querors' ships appear:

> Before their fiery tubes the natives fall,
> Happy erewhile nor dreaming ill; nor long
> Ere the great sea for many a league is ting'd,
> While corpse on corpse, down the red torrent roll'd,
> Floats, and the inmost forests murmur 'Blood'.
>
> (*Spirit of Discovery* 12)

Despite its adoption of the natives' untaught perception ('fiery tubes' is a
commonplace analogy for the ships' guns in historical accounts of Columbus, including Robertson's), the Angel's speech quickly moves to justify the
loss of this Edenic scene. Noah, appalled by the scene of blood, seeks
reassurance, and is given the conventional explanation that these apparent
innocents in fact harbour the principles of false religion which will be overthrown by the spread of Christian truth. The savage is to be '[r]eclaim'd
by gradual intercourse, his heart / Warm'd with new sympathies' (*Spirit of
Discovery* 22). Long before the poem's introduction of Columbus, the fate
of the American natives calls forth its most strident assertions of divine
providence.

The greatest complication in *The Spirit of Discovery* is its underlying
sense of historical irony. The poem assumes British supremacy in the scheme
of providence while at the same time developing a comparative contextualising historical narrative which tells of the fall of empires. Within this
narrative the American sections of the poem are a constant, uneasy, under-
mining presence. The closing section of Book 2 and the Epode on the Fall
of Acre celebrate British maritime supremacy specifically in contrast to the
older and now lost supremacy of Tyre. Tyre, once glorious, has regressed,
while an island once savage reprises its heroic role:

> Meantime the farthest isle, cold and obscure,
> Whose painted natives roam'd their woody wilds,
> From all the world cut off, that wond'ring mark'd
> Her stately sails approach, now, in her turn,
> Rises a star of glory in the West—
> ALBION, the WONDER OF THE ILLUMIN'D WORLD.
>
> (*Spirit of Discovery* 63)

The key elements—natives, wonder, conquest by sea—strikingly parallel the account of Europeans landing in their New World, and the historical logic is, precisely as British commentators were to realise during naval victories by the United States in the 1812–14 war, that the conquered nation will in turn conquer. At the beginning of Book 3 Bowles voices his anxiety that Britain will be supplanted by some island she has discovered, but Australia is the wild possibility he suggests (an idea repeated in Book 5, 196). The apparent extravagance of the idea allows any possibility of supremacy by a closer rival to be dismissed as soon as it is envisaged. There is an extra complication in the parallel to be drawn between the savages of ancient Britain and those of the Americas, however. The painted natives of Britain are the ancestors of those now in power, temporarily bowed to the conqueror but not lastingly subjugated. Not so the natives of America. It is this difference which allows Bowles to keep his account of America strictly within the bounds of the providential history his poem celebrates. As a result, the parallel between ancient British and American peoples and their possibly equally grand imperial futures is subsumed, albeit awkwardly and incompletely.

When Bowles introduces Columbus himself, therefore, key elements in his history have already been defused. The emphasis which remains falls on the visionary aspects of discovery. In a passage crowded with variants of gaze and vision, land seems to appear, then fades, is compared to a mirage and to 'the pensive dream / Of poor imagination' (*Spirit of Discovery* 163). The first sight of land is reserved not for the watchman but for the captain, which allows the geographical discovery to be allied explicitly with spiritual revelation for the natives, just as it had been in Columbus's own accounts. The gaze is returned by the 'gazing natives' while the narrative veers to consider how these peoples can be descended from the same stock as the rest of the world. By a curious sleight of hand this allows Bowles to end the account of Columbus with a paean to British venture in the shape of Drake's circumnavigation and to celebrate another Englishman, Cook, whose North American expedition of 1778 had clarified current thinking about the migration of tribes from Asia to America. (Cook is the heaviest loss Bowles recognises when he asks whether discovery has had evil consequences: first, he suggests, is the slave trade and the ravagement of Peru and Mexico; next, the victims of shipwreck; finally, the explorers killed by savages or lost like Perrouse.) Book 5 proceeds to consider 'the change of mighty empires' and the falls of the empire of Catholicism and the civilization of savages. Bowles asks Britain to reflect on its own social morality, to consider its part in the plunder of the east and the enslavement of Africa, and to face its domestic evils, its grim cities and the threat of atheism. The closing image, however, is of world harmony: 'the chief / Whose hatchet flash'd amid the forest gloom, / Who to his infants bore the bleeding scalp / Of his fall'n foe, shall weep unwonted tears!' (*Spirit of Discovery* 204). The notes to Book 5 are driven by the desire for connection, for proof that 'Every accession of knowledge from the East, and from the West, tends to confirm the Mosaic history' (*Spirit of Discovery* 214). To this end Bowles quotes an account of tribal tradition about the origins of the world, taken from Sir Alexander Mackenzie's *Voyages from Montreal, on the river St. Laurence, through the Continent of North America, to the Frozen and Pacific Oceans, in the years 1789 and 1793* (1802). Mackenzie's account interests him not because of the differences it describes but because they are capable, at least in this brief extract, of being assimilated to the narrative proposed by Christian history.

The Spirit of Discovery presents readers with a Columbus who is kept marginal to a tale to which the moral and social consequences of his voyages are pressingly pertinent, and which spill out to challenge the whole purposive direction of the work. At first sight, the swervings in Southey's *Madoc* are even more extreme. The epic which Southey expected to be 'the greatest poem [he] should ever produce' is in one sense an anti-Columbiad, a rejection of Barlow's vision of the early history of his country.[23] In another sense it is the first Columbiad to anticipate modern definitions of the form as the poetical name for the journey to the New World. Southey's epic denies Columbus's status as the discoverer of a continent, upholding instead the then-fashionable claims of the twelfth-century Welsh prince, Madoc, an inspirational figure for Welsh national feeling and for antiquarian debate in the 1790s and early 1800s.[24] In doing so, Southey disrupted the received national narrative of America so fundamentally that Timothy Dwight attacked him in his 1815 pamphlet *The United States and England; being a Reply to the Criticism on Inchiquin's Letters, contained in the Quarterly Review for January 1814* as one who had 'meditated a most serious injury against the reputation of the New World, by attributing its discovery and colonization to a little vagabond Welsh prince' (Southey xi). There are few better demonstrations of the extent to which Columbus's character and virtue had become both a synecdochic guarantor of the new national history he was seen to have initiated and a displacement of it. Discovery seems to become just a little more contentious when claimed by anybody else. Southey clearly recognised his disruptive Columbiad as an alternative history and drew attention to the challenges it posed for American identity. He prominently quotes Dwight's attack on the poem in his own later edition of the work, for example. And this was not his only or his most teasing display of self-unravelling, as I hope to show. Many authors quote their most acerbic critics in introductions of their own choosing. Southey's attention to Dwight, however, serves as a coda to a principle which is fundamental to the construction of *Madoc*, and which considerably complicates any reader's response to it.

For *Madoc* is a repudiation of Columbus which parades the experiences of Columbus as its avowed source and authority. Although Southey's poem offers many swervings from the implications of the retold Columbus story, notably all its emphases on Madoc as a sharer, a brother, someone who discovers new land not singly but in company with Cadwallon in the other ship, it relies heavily on accounts of Columbus and later travellers, from which its weighty notes quote extensively. (Southey is especially indebted to Herrera.) The effect is strangely to deconstruct the very myth the poem promotes. At the top of the page the reader encounters Madoc seeing, subduing, converting; while at the bottom of the page the historical authorities presented by the poet's alter ego, the annotator, are a constant reminder that these things happened not to Madoc but to Columbus. As a result, the notes, especially in the second half of the poem ('Madoc in Azltan'), are essentially subversive of the poem's construction of its tale. Walter Scott, writing about *Madoc* in a letter of September 1806 to Anna Seward (who was an enthusiastic admirer of Southey's tale, as Southey's introduction records, with a not altogether becoming show of embarrassment), ponders the transfer of historical detail which Southey had made:

> Also I cannot give up my objection that what was strictly true of Columbus becomes an unpleasant falsehood when told of some one else. Suppose I was to write a fictitious Book of travels I would certainly do ill to copy exactly the incidents which befel Mungo Park or Bruce of Kinnaird. [. . .] Could any one bear the story of a second city being taken by a wooden horse[?][25]

Scott goes unerringly to the heart of the matter. The context in which he raises the question of Southey's strange tactics is also strikingly relevant. Most of this letter to Anna Seward is taken up with a discussion of the authenticity of Ossian, a subject on which Scott had strong views backed up by considerable scholarship. He does not directly raise the question of the invention of national tradition, but it informs the whole discussion. Ossian, in fact, provides an unexpected key to Southey's alternative epic of the founding of a nation. To think of bards and their audiences and to ask of *Madoc* 'who hears? who reads?' helps to open up the way in which Southey extends the ethical and ethnic questions raised in Bowles's tentative, elliptical *Spirit of Discovery* into a more audacious (though still far from explicit) interlinking of native traditions, Welsh (/British) and American.

The shadow of Ossian is appropriate to a major aspect of the meanings of *Madoc*: the significance of bardic utterance and the insistence on story itself as utterance, as a communication within a particularised social and political setting. Southey's Madoc tells his tale of discovery to an identifiable audience, the court of the Welsh king David, and his description of the first encounter with the natives significantly unites his wondering listeners and the wondering natives—a wonder from which the Romantic-period reader is eternally divided:

> To the shore
> The natives throng'd; astonish'd, they beheld
> Our winged barks, and gazed with wonderment
> On the strange garb, the bearded countenance
> And the white skin, in all unlike themselves.
> I see with what enquiring eyes you ask
> What men were they? [. . .]
> And while they eyed us grasp'd their spears, as if,
> Like Britain's injured but unconquer'd sons,
> They too had known how perilous it was
> To let a stranger, if he came in arms,
> Set foot upon their land.
>
> (Southey 324)

Although narratee and reader are separated by their ethnographic and historical knowledge in passages like this, they are in one respect closely allied. In his address to a Welsh audience which he fears has allowed or will soon allow strangers to dominate his native land, Madoc parallels the Welsh and the native peoples of the Americas. His account, meanwhile, has an added meaning for the Romantic-period reader envisaged by Southey, who has an entirely different perspective on the historical ironies of Madoc's account. As a result, Madoc's tale of discovery has a political and social purpose within the poem, which Madoc manipulates. As Madoc says, 'our crimes / Have drawn this dolorous visitation down!': 'The House that is divided in itself, / How should it stand?' (Southey 337). Southey's contemporaries might reflect on the applicability of this warning to their own situation. Southey the annotator extends this process: one footnote to Bede, for example, parallels the feelings of the native Americans converted to Christianity to those of ancient Britons in the same situation (Southey 335). In other words, the story of discovery is demonstrably within the poem a directed account, and serves a comparable function outside it as a warning against national division.

The parallels found in Madoc's account of his first encounter with the natives of the Americas are present throughout the poem, though they are often more subtle than in this scene of prophetic admonition. *Madoc* interlinks two stories of the migration of a people: the emigration of the Welsh followers of Prince Madoc and the events leading up to the Aztecs' decision to leave their original country and to settle in what was to become the Mexican empire. Although the narrative fine of the poem presents these two peoples as enemies (the Aztecs are first subdued by Madoc's forces, swear friendship, then betray this trust and are again defeated), a more complex version of conquest is given by the underlying similarities between the two migrations. Certain customs of the Welsh and the American peoples are paralleled, such as their concern about the sanctity of ancient burial sites. Even more fundamentally, their societies are threatened by the same basic evil, betrayal within the family. The story of Welsh migration begins in fratricidal conflict, while the downfall of the Aztecs, though more complicated, has two roots, one the ambition of the young warrior Amalahta to usurp his mother's power and the other the ambition of the priests of the Aztecs to restore the idols of their ancestral religion.

Another grand migration shadows these two main movements of great peoples, however; and this aspect of the poem becomes familiarly auto-biographical. Southey dated his interest in the Madoc story from 1789, and began the first poetic version of the work in 1794. Rewriting began in 1797 and lasted for about two years; Southey returned to it in 1803–4, when substantial changes were made.[26] Early in its history Southey planned to make Madoc into a version of Manco Capac, first Inca ruler of Peru (and a significant figure in Barlow's *Vision of Columbus*), an identification which would have made Pantisocratic social revisionism central to his Welsh epic.[27] The changes to different states of the poem disguise its most potent personal and political context. The version published in 1805, in which Madoc settles in North America instead of in Peru, is more concerned with the defeat of the corrupt Aztecs than with the establishment of a political alternative. Even so the context of pantisocracy is significant biographically and politically, as Paul Muldoon assumes in *Madoc: A Mystery* (1990). Madoc journeys west specifically to escape the conflict which has beset his native land. His companion Cadwallon explains their aim:

> [...] that there
> Might manly courage, manly wisdom find
> Some happy isle, some undiscovered shore,
> Some resting place for peace
> [...] Oh that my soul
> Could seize the wings of Morning! soon would I
> Behold that other world, where yonder sun
> Speeds now, to dawn in glory!
>
> (Southey 321)

Cadwallon/Coleridge in tow, Madoc sails away from a country of corrupted power in which he foresees Welsh ruin at the hands of the Plantagenets with whom David has rashly allied himself, and initiates for his people what is recognisably the allure of emigration, the chance to start afresh.

As an exploration of the rights and wrongs of settlement and possibly of conquest, *Madoc* leaves many questions unanswered. Some answers, perhaps, are given implicitly: Madoc is troubled by the future he foresees in which the Welsh have been colonized by the English, and the language in which his tale is written marks the victory of the dominant nation. This irony is implicit in the scenes in which, like all discovery-narratives, *Madoc* explores the tensions between the two languages of the Welsh explorers and the American natives. In this subtle way the poem records the outcome of the events it describes. In other ways, however, it leaves outcomes uncertain. The end of the poem does not raise the question of the future for Madoc and his people in America. As a historical force they simply fade away at the end of the narrative, which is shaped conventionally on one great battle allowing the Welsh to triumph at the poem's end but surely not to triumph historically. The point about Columbiads is that they allow one to imagine a continuous reach of history forward to the present. This quality links the otherwise disparate works of Du Boccage, Moore, Richard Snowden, and Barlow. *Madoc* gives readers instead a broken line, leaves the future of the Welsh Indians silent, hints at intermarriage but in the parallel love stories at the end has the native one end in a double death and the imported Welsh one end in happiness. The emphasis is not, as a result, on interchange but on stasis, on a Welsh contingent not mingled but eternally stranded. In these ways Southey's poem, in factual respects so dependent on accounts of Columbus and later voyagers, implicitly undoes the historical thread on which they depend and which their retelling promotes. The subversive footnotes turn out not to be clumsy but instead to offer a key to the poem's self-unravelling as well as to its simultaneous unravelling of the enormous cultural implications of the Columbus story. There are of course counter-currents, such as the poem's extensive use of imperial prospect passages claiming the land, and the use of a whole range of conventions about the representation of Amerindians from alcohol-craving to blood sacrifice. But although these factors point to Southey's acceptance of colonial conquest in the spirit of Enlightenment progress, I differ in my reading of the poem from Marilyn Butler, who has described the 1805 published version as 'a frank, very urgent justification of colonialism as a move entirely for the native's own good'.[28] The narrative line is more equivocal than that in part because it is so crowded with alternatives and with tales which end variously. This makes the poem less assertively expansionist than Butler suggests. Nor is it quite enough to say as Nigel Leask does that whether poems such as *Madoc* deal with the orient or the occident the political message is much the same.[29] True, the issues raised are closely interlinked and in the case of the slave trade they are interdependent. The crucial difference about America for British writing is that this is an empire *lost*, and that in the process of losing it Britain had been imaged to herself as the oppressor not the saviour of other peoples.

The difference between eastern and western colonialisms is essential to an understanding of a third Romantic Columbiad. Samuel Rogers's *Voyage of Columbus* enjoys a limited repute in studies of Romantic orientalism because of its significance for Byron's eastern tales, especially *The Giaour* (which is dedicated to Rogers). Nigel Leask brackets it with poems by Beddoes, Landor, Campbell, and Thomas Moore which establish 'an ideal of rational colonialization and free trade against the belligerent opportunism and monopolist commercial policy of late eighteenth-century British imperialism' (Leask 25). This reading is broadly true to the poem's political leanings, but the manner of Rogers's explorations in colonial history greatly complicates the matter. Rogers began work on *The Voyage of Columbus* sometime before 1797 but the poem was not printed until 1810 and not published until 1812. It was known in private circles long before this: in a letter to Rogers of October 1809 Scott hopes 'your little jewel the Columbiad is at length to be drawn out of the portfolio and given to the press' (*Letters* 2: 251). The sense of diminished scale, of 'littleness', is significant. The poem's title disavows inclusiveness, rejecting four voyages to attend to only one, and no vision is presented to Columbus although one of a typically truncated kind is related by the narrator in the final canto. This is to be a poem of voyaging rather than of vision. Its preface proclaims it to be a relic of a much longer narrative, written in the Castilian language by a companion of Columbus on his first voyage, although this identity is undermined by its supposed translator, who declares in a footnote that 'its style and manner are evidently of an after-time'.[30] He seems to have in mind someone such as Bernal Díaz who completed his 'True History' of the conquest in old age, but the frame allows for interpolations from different periods. It also requires active interpretation from the reader (being 'sudden in its transitions, and full of historical allusions; leaving much to be imagined by the reader': Rogers 233). The translator supports and expands the narrator's account with references to other authorities, mainly Spanish, and by declaring his own views in the preface is able to preserve a double perspective on 'the deep tragedy of America' and the spiritual enlightenment of Columbus as an individual, 'a person of extraordinary virtue and piety, acting under the sense of a divine impulse' (Rogers 233, 234).

The Voyage of Columbus consists of twelve brief cantos, with frequent elisions and several framing devices. In addition to the translator's preface, a poem 'Inscribed on the Original Manuscript' presents the narrator as an isolated poet-monk in the Convent of La Rábida; there are footnotes (as well as endnotes added after the first edition), one of which jokes at the narrator's expense ('The author seems to have anticipated his long slumber in the library of the Fathers': Rogers, 250); a preface to the second edition which abandons the pretence of the poem's monkish origins; an Argument which militates against the fragmentary design by giving a linear account of the poem's action; and a concluding section which purports to be a transcription of two leaves in another hand, consisting of ballad stanzas interspersed with a prose account of a supposed visit to La Rábida by Cortés and Pizarro. For a fragment-poem of this length this is an elaborate frame, and its effect is to highlight different perspectives on and reactions to Columbus, complicating the narrative of his companion, who sees him consistently as a man divinely inspired and morally spotless. As the preface to the second edition suggests, moreover, this is a fragment which may compensate for a perceived gap in Spanish literature:

> No National Poem appeared on the subject; no Camoëns did honour to his Genius and his Virtues. Yet the materials, that have descended to us, are surely not unpoetical; and a desire to avail myself of them, to convey in some instances as far as I could, in others as far as I dared, their warmth of colouring and wildness of imagery, led me to conceive the idea of a Poem written not long after his death, when the great consequences of the Discovery were beginning to unfold themselves, but while the minds of men were still clinging to the superstitions of their fathers.
>
> (Rogers 239–40)

The transitional historical period imagined here allows Rogers to introduce a more flamboyant demonic superstructure than is usual in Columbiads. Columbus's purpose is opposed by a congress of Evil Spirits, false gods who hold sway in unconverted America, and they fly vampire-like to possess Columbus's sailors, who mutiny. Implicit in the narrator's account in consequence is the unusual idea that the Americas were the initiators of aggression and that Columbus, to quote the Argument, 'restore[d] order'. At the same time, the frame draws back from anything other than 'poetical' validation of such a superstition. In a revealing comment, however, Rogers speculates that a 'belief in the agency of Evil Spirits [. . .] even yet seems almost necessary to enable us to clear up the Darkness, / And justify the ways of God to Men' (Rogers 240). As with the summative Argument, some aspects of the poem suggest continuities between past and present interpretations of the consequences of discovery which are more than merely fragmentary.

An extended view of these continuities of perspective is given in the cantos describing Columbus's, and the narrator's, early experiences among the natives of the Caribbean. Here, the narratorial perspective of the poem is central to its effect. At the end of Canto 11 the narrator recalls the scenes of native community with their central focus, the Indian maiden Cora, youngest of her people:

> That night, transported, with a sigh I said
> "Tis all a dream!'—Now, like a dream, 'tis fled;
> And many and many a year has passed away,
> And I alone remain to watch and pray!
> Yet oft in darkness, on my bed of straw,
> Oft I awake and think on what I saw!
> The groves, the birds, the youths, the nymphs recall,
> And CORA, loveliest, sweetest of them all!
>
> (Rogers 288–9)

As if to compensate for the aggression of the ruling evil spirits of the Americas, the natives themselves are presented as benevolent figures, likened, traditionally enough, to wood-nymphs and figures from romance. The narrator lingers on Cora, but this likewise is traditional, a reflection of the natives as peaceable, malleable, childlike and female, a transmutation of 'innocent' desire. Cora represents the future of her people, but everything about her depiction registers incipient loss, even as the narrator must bring her back in the gaze of memory. (The name Cora is usually thought to have been invented—after the Greek *Kore* ('maiden' but also associated with Persephone)—by James Fenimore Cooper but instead the naming of the dark heroine of *The Last of the Mohicans* should be understood as an allusion to Rogers's poem.) In contrast to the narrator's gaze, the gaze of the natives themselves is severely restricted. Cora herself, when given an anachronistic telescope through which to look, trains it not on the imaginative future which is the true perspective of the poem, but on her lover in his canoe. In a Keatsian moment 'lost in wild amaze, / [She] Gazes again, and could for ever gaze!' (Rogers 282). The only native with a more complex gaze is the seer Cazziva, who sees Columbus and flees (wrongly, the narrator chides: 'to other eyes' are the riches of the new lands to be revealed, as the guilty last canto, 'A Vision', insists). Nigel Leask suggests a parallel between the narrative of *The Voyage of Columbus* and the French Revolution, with Cora as an embodiment of the innocent continent about to be betrayed (Leask 31). In this perceptive but Eurocentric reading Cora is Rogers's way back to his experiences in early revolutionary Paris. As with Southey's *Madoc*, it is not ultimately very rewarding to view Romantic writings about the Americas as an adjunct to Orientalism, and Rogers was well known in his own time for his pro-American sympathies and his active and influential promotion of American literature.[31] Cora is indeed a sentimental link between the narrator (not Rogers) and the reader, but like the lovers of Keats's Grecian Urn she is preserved in her prelapsarian state. Like so much else in *The Voyage of Columbus* she is a stage, a fragment, kept separate from the narrative of history.

Much of the second half of *The Voyage of Columbus* is darkened by the narrator's decline, his anxiety about failing to do justice to the memory of a Christ-like Columbus, and by presages of 'the deep tragedy of America'. The emphasis falls on discontinuity and failed vision, personal and historical. Columbus has died, the full extent of his achievements unrecognised, the narrator is old and frail, and the Americas have become 'a prison-house, full of sights of woe' betrayed by 'dogs of carnage' (Rogers 294). The final canto asserts that these wrongs will eventually be righted, and the Americas ruled again by the God who sent Columbus to save them. The providential pattern is similar to that of Bowles, but, unlike Bowles, Rogers does not try to assert British righteousness at the expense of criminalising the Spanish. Nor is a flattering image of British political, legal, or commercial custom used as the basis for American self-determination. If this seems to bring Rogers closer to the dark images for which Terence Martin praises Barlow, however, it ought also to be emphasised that *The Voyage of Columbus* offers no more comfortable continuities to the United States than it does to Spain or Britain. *The Voyage of Columbus* with all its mannered hesitancies offers little settling-place for irony, at least historical irony of the kind that would provide a level of implied commentary on the three hundred years separating Columbus's voyage from its publication in this form. The narrative of Columbus, his discovery and the part this plays in God's plan for humanity, are strangely but deliberately fragmented, cut off from the historical context on which the frame-narrative seems to insist.

The three British Columbiads examined here suggest an unease with the story of Columbus which emerges at every imagined level of their design, from narrative superstructure to local detail. For Bowles, America challenges the working out of God's plan, and Columbus edges into the margins of a celebration to which he might have been made central. Southey disputes Spanish victory altogether and reclaims the Americas for the Welsh. Rogers frames his poem as fragmentary and claims that it is governed by the perspective of an earlier age. The Columbus story for all three writers makes sense only as a stage in providential history. But the rebellion of the American colonies had severed this history from British history. The same severance—now actualised—which had troubled Robertson continues to affect the shape which can be discerned from, or imposed upon, both British and Spanish colonial history. British rewritings of the Columbus story in the Romantic period differ from Barlow's *Columbiad* in proposing not continuity between Columbus and the future development of the Americas but varieties of disjunction. They are responding, with fewer nationalist inhibitions perhaps than may be discerned in the comparable and contemporary United-States accounts of the founding of Columbia, to a fundamental difficulty in integrating Columbus to linear histories of his imagined land.

Notes

1 William Robertson, *The History of America*, 2 vols. (London: W. Strahan, 1777), 1: vi. Robertson makes this claim while also criticising the 'excess of caution' with which Spain has continued to try to keep its actions in the Americas secret from other nations: he refers to his being refused access to the *Archivo* of Simancas (1: ix), the records of which were to be opened to Washington Irving in the 1820s. The most striking contrast to Robertson's division between Spanish and British colonial history in the Americas is the account of both given in the revised edition of Raynal's *Historie philosophique des . . . deux Indes* in 1780.

2 *The History of America, Books IX. and X. Containing the History of Virginia to the Year 1688; and of New England to the Year 1652* (London, 1796); the Advertisement (1: iii–vii) by Robertson's son William tells of the destruction of many papers during his last illness and describes the survival of the present fragments from an earlier period, corrected and revised as usual by the historian.

For an analysis of the planned contrasting of Spanish and British histories and the reasons for Robertson's first suspending and later abandoning his integrated project see Jeffrey R. Smitten, 'Moderatism and History: William Robertson's Unfinished History of British America', in *Scotland and America in the Age of the Enlightenment*, ed. Richard B. Sher and Jeffrey R. Smitten (Edinburgh: Edinburgh University Press, 1990), 163–79, and Karen O'Brien, *Narratives of Enlightenment: Cosmopolitan History from Voltaire to Gibbon* (Cambridge: Cambridge University Press, 1997), 151–66, esp. 161–3.

3 Translator's Preface to J. P. Brissot de Warville, *New Travels in the United States of America, Performed in M. DCC. LXXXVIII*, 2nd edn., 2 vols. (London: J. S. Jordan, 1794, 1797), 1: x–xi.

4 David Armitage comments that 'history itself overtook Robertson's *History* and condemned it to live as but a fragment of his great design': 'The New World and British Historical Thought: From Richard Hakluyt to William Robertson', in *America in European Consciousness, 1493–1750*, ed. Karen Ordahl Kupperman (Chapel Hill and London: University of North Carolina Press, 1995), 52–75 (69). On Robertson's reinforcement of stadial history (the argument that society develops in stages) see O'Brien, 132–6.

5 Anthony Pagden, *European Encounters with the New World: From Renaissance to Romanticism* (New Haven and London: Yale University Press, 1993), 89–115 (100). The literature relating to the Elizabethan geographical writings of Hakluyt, Ralegh, Sir George Peckham, John Dee, and others, is extensive; but see particularly John T. Juricek, 'English Territorial Claims in North America under Elizabeth and the Early Stuarts', *Terrae Incognitae* 7 (1975), 7–22, and, for the part played by the Madoc story, Gwyn A. Williams, *Madoc: The Making of a Myth* (London: Eyre Methuen, 1979), 31–67.

6 Nanora Sweet has recently analysed aspects of what she sees as a triangulation of political, commercial, and literary practices in Britain, Spain, and South America in the early nineteenth century, concentrating on the period after the Spanish War of Independence in 1808, in '"Hitherto closed to British enterprise": Trading and Writing the Hispanic World circa 1815', *European Romantic Review* 8 (1997), 139–147 (139).

7 Early United States' narratives of the continent's discovery are invisible, for instance, in the fourth edition of the *Norton Anthology of American Literature* (New York and London: Norton, 1994), which begins with Columbus, demonstrating the extent to which he still shapes American history. Dwight is excluded altogether, and Joel Barlow represented only by 'The Hasty Pudding' and 'Advice to a Raven in Russia'. Barlow's two versions of the Columbus story are mentioned only as being practically unreadable today.

8 Stuart Curran, *Poetic Form and British Romanticism* (New York: Oxford University Press, 1986), 170–2. See also J. P. McWilliams Jr., *The American Epic: Transforming a Genre* (Cambridge: Cambridge University Press, 1989), 54–63.

9 *La Colombiade, ou la foi portée au nouveau monde* (Paris: Desaint and Saillant, 1756), vii.

10 James L. Moore, *The Columbiad: An Epic Poem on the Discovery of America and the West Indies by Columbus. In Twelve Books* (London: F. and C. Rivington, 1798), 6: 185–7. An attempt to revive interest in Moore's work was made during the Quincentenary of Columbus's arrival in the Caribbean, in the brief preface to a series of extracts from the work: Richard Gander, *The Columbiad: An Epic Poem for the Quincentenary of 1992. Adapted from James Moore's Original Work of 1798* (Hertford: for the Author, 1992). Moore was Master of the Free Grammar School in Hertford from 1788 to 1806.

11 Terence Martin, 'Three Columbiads, Three Visions of the Future', *Early American Literature* 27 (1992), 128–32 (131). Martin writes shrewdly of the poetic effects of situating Columbus amid the European wreck of his fortunes: 'In this [Barlow's] poem, Europe has failed Columbus, who is (almost by that fact) absolved from crimes against the native population and vindicated (virtually reconstituted) by the evolution of history' (132).

12 See the wide-ranging collection of essays *The Black Columbiad: Defining Moments in African American Literature and Culture*, ed. Werner Sollors and Maria Diedrich, Harvard English Studies 19 (Cambridge, Mass. and London: Harvard University Press, 1994), which includes analyses of the work of William Wells Brown, Frank Webb, W. E. B. Du Bois, Zora Neale Hurston, and Toni Morrison, among many others, and of topics ranging from *Casablanca* to the Black Arts movement.

13 Christopher Mulvey, 'The Fugitive Self and the New World of the North: William Wells Brown's Discovery of America', in *The Black Columbiad* 99–111 (99).

14 Robert Shulman, 'Subverting and Deconstructing the Dream: The Radical Voices of Le Sueur, Herbst, and Wright', in *Deferring a Dream: Literary Sub-Versions of the American Columbiad*, ed. Gert Buelens and Ernst Rudin, International Cooper Series in English Language and Literature (Basel, Boston, Berlin: Birkhäuser Verlag, 1994), 24–36 (24).

15 Review of *The Columbiad*, *Critical Review*, 2nd ser., 23 (1798), 66–8 (66).

16 Joel Barlow, *The Vision of Columbus; A Poem in Nine Books* (Hartford: Hudson and Goodwin for the Author, 1787), xx.

17 Joel Barlow, *The Columbiad: A Poem* (Philadelphia: C. and A. Conrad; Baltimore: Conrad, Lucas, 1807), v. For the differences between Barlow's two Columbiads, see Emory Elliott, *Revolutionary Writers: Literature and Authority in the New Republic, 1725–1810* (New York: Oxford University Press, 1982), and John Bidwell, *The Publication of Joel Barlow's 'Columbiad'* (1983; Worcester, Mass.: American Antiquarian Society, 1984).

18 Otto B. Heim, 'Supplement to the Voyage of Columbus: Literary Voyages of (Un-) Discovery in the South Pacific', in *Deferring a Dream* 48–75.

19 Washington Irving, *A History of the Life and Voyages of Christopher Columbus*, 4 vols. (London: John Murray, 1828), 4: 61.

20 Bruce Greenfield, *Narrating Discovery: The Romantic Explorer in American Literature, 1790–1855* (New York: Columbia University Press, 1992), 123.

21 Irving 4: 58; *Shelley's Poetry and Prose*, ed. Donald H. Reiman and Sharon B. Powers (New York and London: Norton, 1977), 508.

22 William Lisle Bowles, *The Spirit of Discovery; or, The Conquest of Ocean. A Poem, in Five Books: with Notes, Historical and Illustrative* (Bath: printed by R. Cruttwell; and sold by Cadell and Davies and J. Mawman, London, 1804), viii and xxii; Bowles suggests a link between the plan and the subject of his poem by referring to it as 'my *circum-navigation*', xi. References to this poem and to Southey's *Madoc* and Rogers's *The Voyage of Columbus* are to page numbers, no line numbers being given in the originals.

23 *The Poetical Works of Robert Southey* (London: Longman, Brown, Green, and Longmans, 1844), x. Southey's letters testify to his belief over several years that *Madoc* would be his central poetic achievement, 'my opus magnum' as he described it in January 1804: *New Letters of Robert Southey*, ed. Kenneth Curry, 2 vols. (New York and London: Columbia University Press, 1965), 1: 348.

24 See Prys Morgan, 'From a Death to a View: The Hunt for the Welsh Past in the Romantic Period', in *The Invention of Tradition*, ed. Eric Hobsbawm and Terence Ranger (1983; Cambridge: Cambridge University Press, 1992), 43–100, esp. 83–5.

Southey's work is a surprising omission from Gwyn Williams's study, which makes a single reference to it as 'his interminable and intolerable epic poem *Madoc*' (Williams 189).

25 *The Letters of Sir Walter Scott*, ed. H. J. C. Grierson *et al.*, 12 vols. (London: Constable, 1932–7), 1: 325.

26 See Lynda Pratt, 'Revising the National Epic: Coleridge, Southey, and *Madoc*', *Romanticism* 2 (1996), 149–63.

27 Lynda Pratt comments: 'for Southey, *Madoc* (1797–9) was a poem with immense cultural significance. [. . .] *Madoc* was intended to engage at every level with cultural change and displacement: at a thematic level, with the replacement of the old Aztec civilisation of blood sacrifice by a theistic system based upon brotherly (and sisterly) love; and at a formal / generic one, with the transformation of the old martial epic, embodied in the fierce colonialism of Aztec society with its exaltation of the warrior as hero, into the new epic of intellect, liberty and peace' (160). Mark Storey also places *Madoc* in the context of Pantisocracy in *Robert Southey: A Life* (Oxford: Oxford University Press, 1997), 55–6, 77, 172–7.

28 Marilyn Butler, 'Welsh Nationalism and English Poets 1790–1805', unpublished paper quoted by Nigel Leask, *British Romantic Writers and the East: Anxieties of Empire* (Cambridge: Cambridge University Press, 1992), 26.

29 Leask 25. *The Voyage of Columbus* 'duplicates the strategy of the hoax poem' but its charade is not very serious, concludes Marjorie Levinson in her discussion of Rogers in relation to *The Giaour* in *The Romantic Fragment Poem: A Critique of a Form* (Chapel Hill and London: University of North Carolina Press, 1986), 116.

30 *Poems, by Samuel Rogers* (London: Edward Moxon, 1839), 233.

31 Rogers's influence as a supporter of American letters and friend of American writers is described in Joseph J. Firebaugh's essay 'Samuel Rogers and American Men of Letters', *American Literature* 13 (1942), 331–45. Washington Irving was a friend from 1822; Rogers knew his 1828 *Columbus*, which, according to Thomas Moore, he considered 'rather *long*' (cited by Firebaugh 336).

29

ROMANTICISM AND ABOLITIONISM: MARY WOLLSTONECRAFT, WILLIAM BLAKE, SAMUEL TAYLOR COLERIDGE AND WILLIAM WORDSWORTH

Helen Thomas

Source: *Romanticism and Slave Narratives: Transatlantic Testimonies* (Cambridge: Cambridge University Press, 2000), pp. 82–124, 289–97.

Over the past two decades the concept of Romanticism as an homogenised 'project' has been rigorously challenged from both sides of the Atlantic. Leading representatives of Romantic criticism have presented sophisticated critiques of the established hierarchy of the Romantic 'canon' and have applied illuminating deconstructive and poststructuralist analyses of Romantic literature; others have provided lucid interdisciplinary accounts of Romanticism in terms of class, gender and new historicism.[1] As a result, Romanticism is no longer perceived as simply a 'European phenomenon', informed solely by the political and philosophical legacy of the French Revolution and the German Empire. The ahistorical, close readings provided by New Criticism gave way to a study of Romanticism within the context of a history of ideas informed by western liberalism. Paul de Man's deconstructive approach offered a way of reading that resisted 'authoritarian complacency' or a belief in 'timeless truths' and highlighted the inevitable failure of Romanticism's rhetoric of conscious intent and self-representation.[2] Work focusing upon eighteenth-century concepts of sexuality and representations of gender by scholars including Mary Jacobus, Anne Mellor, Marjorie Levinson and Helen Vendler revisited this rhetoric of 'failure' and enlarged the scope of Romantic Studies in terms of feminist literary history.[3] As Mary Favret and Nicola Watson have indicated, Romanticism's increased identification with critical theory prompted interest in new areas of previously excluded material and concerns, including medical treatises, political pamphlets, conduct books and Jacobin novels.[4] Jerome McGann's *Romantic Ideology* (1983) registered a critical shift in Britain and America in its critique of the isolation of the self-conscious Romantic poet from the agents of 'real history' and cultural materialism. According to McGann, the role of the critic of Romantic poetry is to 'make a determined effort to elucidate the subject matter of such poems historically: to define the specific ways in which stylistic forms intersect and join with factual and cognitive points of reference'.[5] More recent critical essays (including those anthologies edited by Alan Richardson and Sonia Hofkosh, and by Tim Fulford and Peter Kitson) have extended the study of Romanticism to the wider contexts of colonialism, education, racial policy, imperialist practice and international trade.[6] This critical interest in the material conditions and sociopolitical constructs within and against which Romantic authors and poets were placed, has brought about an important revaluation of the literature produced during the period 1770 to 1830. In addition to these more recent investigations, this book explores the period's cultural productions from a revised historical and ideological context. Romanticism is analysed in terms of its connection with eighteenth-century dissent and enthusiasm and the use of the discourse of the spirit by leading Romantic figures is examined in the context of abolition and the emergence of literary expressions of liberation, identity and self-consciousness. In its application of some of the major strands of postcolonial, cultural and poststructural theory, this study relocates the Romantic era within a highly complex period that witnessed both the culmination of England's participation in the slave trade and the emergence of pervasive theories of racial difference, alongside the most vigorous spate of abolitionist demands.[7] Indeed, prominent blacks such as Ottobah Cugoano and Olaudah Equiano (discussed in Chapters 6 and 8), in many instances had friends, associations and acquaintances in common with the Romantics such as Thomas Clarkson, Granville Sharp and James Ramsay.[8] By highlighting the relation between the use of the discourse of the spirit employed by Romantic writers, including Wordsworth, Coleridge and Blake, and the uncanonical eighteenth-century dissenting figures discussed in Chapter 2, this study proposes an analysis of eighteenth-century spiritual discourse popularised by radical dissenting Protestantism and contained within the prophetic, confessional and abolitionist works published in both America and England at this time. Moreover, in its relocation of Romanticism within such a context, this chapter prepares the groundwork for an important juxtaposition between Romantic writing and the auto-biographical narratives by African slaves published in England; a juxtaposition which not only locates a point of cultural contact between two disparate cultures (Africa and the west) but identifies a significant translation and subsequent fusion of African epistemology with Christian ideology and its expression.

The discourse of the spirit employed within a selection of works by the first generation Romantic poets, Coleridge, Wordsworth and Blake, suggests that the language of radical dissenting Protestantism played a major role in the development of Romantic poetry. Together with the radical liberationist demands contained within Mary Wollstonecraft's texts, these works indicate Romanticism's heterogeneous interaction with liberationist and, at times, abolitionist ideology. With their emphasis on spiritual discourse, epiphanic moments of 'divine' witness and actual and figural concepts of 'captivity' and 'emancipation', these texts demonstrate an intricate relationship with the literary framework appropriated by the slave narratives. In a sense, therefore, these seemingly disparate literary movements may be seen as products of the same historical influences. However, whilst the works by the Romantics and the slaves determined an inscription of a self-authorised sociohistorical self, they prescribed two very different kinds of literary enterprise and motives, and were intended for radically different audiences. Whereas the language of radical dissenting Protestantism provided the Romantics with convenient tropes of metaphorical captivity and liberation, the narratives by the slaves registered the very real experience of transportation and enslavement and carried with them overt political messages of emancipation.

With the exception of the poems included in the *Lyrical Ballads* first published in 1798, the Romantic poems discussed below were originally exposed to a relatively small audience comprised of close friends and acquaintances, including Charles Lamb, Dorothy Wordsworth and Robert Southey.[9] Wordsworth's two-part *Prelude*, transcribed in December 1799, was not published until 1974; the *Prelude* of 1805 remained a manuscript until 1926 and the *Prelude* of 1850 was not printed until ten weeks after Wordsworth's death on 23 April 1850.[10] Similarly, the manuscript version of Coleridge's *Letter to Sara Hutchinson* differed significantly from the published version, *Dejection: An Ode*, and was not published until 1963.[11] Blake's single bid for public recognition, a one-man exhibition in 1809, proved a total failure; only when he was in his sixties did he attract a small group of painters to serve as an audience for his work.[12] In contrast, the slave narratives were on the whole aimed at a wider audience as a means of providing financial support for their authors and advancing abolitionist ideology. Many of their works were immensely popular and were reissued in numerous editions and under various titles throughout Great Britain and America during the seventy years or so following their publication.[13] One other major difference between the production and consumption of the works by the slave narrators was economic: most slave narratives were published by subscription; buyers were committed to paying something towards the book prior to its publication. As a consequence, the subscription lists which preceded the texts functioned as a means of promotion and credibility and often included the names of socially and politically prominent figures, members of the aristocracy, key abolitionists and bluestocking authors. The texts themselves, often edited or rewritten by dissenting editors and philanthropists, attracted a wide spectrum of readers who welcomed the narratives' adventurous plots, their 'conversion' frameworks and their pro-abolitionist ideology.

Therefore, whilst it is true that the writings by slaves and the Romantics employed similar tropes of liberation and spiritual discourse, it is also clear that a considerable ideological distance separated them. In the works of the Romantics, the trope of isolation and/or alienation tended to be at most a temporary, fairly domestic, 'literary' device which established the poets' sense of election, isolation and subsequent reassimilation into society. For the slaves however, the narrative tropes of 'captivity' and 'liberation' designated actual rather than figurative traumatic processes of cultural severance and estrangement, an experience shared by many thousands of other slaves by virtue of their removal from their native lands, their transportation across the Atlantic to the plantations of the West Indies and America and (for a significant few) their subsequent journeys to the slave-trading ports of England and their reemergence as identities in the diaspora. For the slave narrators, the discourse of the spirit described a process by which the slave's former cultural self was redetermined within the parameters of Christian ideology and expression. This reconfiguration of identity involved a delicate negotiation in which cultural *alterity* was inscribed and contained within the popularised discourse of radical dissenting Protestantism. For both the Romantics and the slave narrators, however, the 'non-linguistic' moments of spiritual witness provided cryptic paradigms of liberationist, and some-times abolitionist, ideology wherein the concept of memory inaugurated a complex discourse of identity configuration within a literary framework.

MARY WOLLSTONECRAFT: FEMINISM AND ABOLITIONISM

If they are really capable of acting like rational creatures, let them not be treated as slaves.[14]

On the margins of canonical Romanticism, yet highly significant in its rela-tionship with Romanticism's paradigms of liberationist ideology, the work of Mary Wollstonecraft provides an invaluable link between the discourse of racial and gendered inequality in its employment of abolitionist rhetoric. Published by Johnson, the same publisher of works by William Blake and John Stedman, Mary Wollstonecraft's *Vindication of the Rights of Men* (1790) and *Vindication of the Rights of Woman: With Strictures on Political and Moral Subjects* (1792) provide key components in the development of liberationist discourse in the context of colonial and slave ideology. Written as a repudiation of Edmund Burke's defence of the monarchy and the aristocracy contained within his *Reflections on the Revolution in France*,

Mary Wollstonecraft's *Vindication of the Rights of Men* identified the inalienable right to liberty as a necessary prerequisite to the creation of a society based upon the principles of reason and justice. Wollstonecraft's text denounced Burke's three main hypotheses: that all legal and political authority should be derived from the past; that the alliance between the church and civil government was a condition of civil society; and that the class system, as determined by property ownership, was 'natural'.[15] It condemned Burke's unashamed conservatism and denounced slavery as an atrocious and inhuman traffic that contravened 'every suggestion of reason and religion'.[16] Likewise, Wollstonecraft defined the slave trade as a pernicious cause of spiritual deterioration, a trade which fed 'upon human flesh' and consumed the 'very soul' of society.[17]

> But is it not consonant with justice, with the common principles of humanity, not to mention Christianity, to abolish this abominable inveterate mischief . . . If it [Parliament] gloriously dared to shew the world that British senators were men: if the natural feelings of humanity silenced the cold cautions of timidity . . . and all men were allowed to enjoy their birth-right – liberty.[18]

Wollstonecraft's *Vindication of the Rights of Men* concluded with an utopian vision of land redistribution, the new 'Eden' that would be achieved if large estates were divided into smaller farms. Such a concept had informed the millenarian prophetic writings of the New Jerusalem, including those by Richard Brothers, and indeed the more extreme demands of slaves, maroons and radical abolitionists. A rather more philosophical justification was given within William Godwin's. *Enquiry Concerning Political Justice* (1793).[19] In that text, Godwin (later Wollstonecraft's lover and the source of Wordsworth's anxiety in Book XI of the *Prelude*) prophesied society's inevitable but peaceful progression, achieved by equal land distribution and the eradication of government. Such radical notions of land redistribution must have haunted English absentee landlords and plantocratic owners, especially in the wake of recent slave rebellions in the colonies and parliamentary debates on abolition.

Published in the year following the successful insurrection by slaves in the French colony of St Domingue, Wollstonecraft's *Vindication of the Rights of Woman: With Strictures on Political and Moral Subjects* (1792) hinged upon a discourse of property rights.[20] In this text, Wollstonecraft identified the condition of women with that of the oppressed slaves and further emphasised the morally undesirable effects of sexism/slavery upon slaveholders and husbands: 'They [women] may be convenient slaves, but slavery will have its constant effect, degrading the master and the abject dependent'.[21] Wollstonecraft emphasised the violation of the 'sacred rights of humanity' effected by women's subordination and placed a significant stress on the enforced sexual abuse suffered by female slaves at the hands of their plantocratic masters: 'Is one half of the human species, like the poor African slaves, to be subject to prejudices that brutalise them?'[22] According to Wollstonecraft, 'marriage', in the form that it existed in England in 1792, was a form of legal slavery not dissimilar to that endured by Africans in the British West Indies. In legal and sociopolitical terms, a wife could not own property, bring legal suits, or expect guaranteed custody of her own children.[23] Hence Wollstonecraft's discussion of female subjugation rested fundamentally upon the dynamics of emancipatory and abolitionist discourse. Economic and psychological dependence had, according to Wollstonecraft, deprived women of their rights to liberty and autonomy:

> Liberty is the mother of virtue, and if women are, by their very constitution, slaves, and not allowed to breathe the sharp invigorating air of freedom, they must ever languish like exotics, and be reckoned beautiful flaws in nature.[24]

A woman's value, she argued, was judged not in terms of her spiritual or intellectual capacities, but upon her external and reproductive potential – a process not dissimilar to the way in which a slave's value was assessed. This subjugated women to the 'pride, sensuality and desire' of their tyrants and confined them to a perpetually dependent state of childhood and ignorance: 'Taught from their infancy that beauty is woman's sceptre, the mind shapes itself to the body, and, roaming round its gilt cage, only seeks to adorn its prison'.[25] If instead, she argued, a woman's understanding was 'emancipated' from its condition of servitude, then claims advocating her biological and rational inferiority would be overturned: rational education would lead to rational love and egalitarian marriages based upon companionship rather than purely sexual desire.[26]

Wollstonecraft's *Vindication of the Rights of Woman* therefore strategically correlated tenets of emancipation with concepts of social freedom and intellectual stimulation. In addition, her text radically suggested that given the conditions of women's/slaves' servitude, their cunning methods of rebellion and independence were, in a sense, justified: 'Women, it is true, obtaining power by unjust means, by practising or fostering vice, evidently lose the rank which reason would assign them, and they become either abject slaves or capricious tyrants'.[27] Similarly, in her *Historical and Moral View of the Origin and Progress of the French Revolution* (1794), Wollstonecraft argued that the deprivation of natural, equal, civil and political rights established a dichotomy between 'tyrants and slaves' and forced otherwise respectable individuals to resort to theft, 'atrocious robberies and murder'. Such a pernicious hierarchy, she suggested, would always result in volatile, 'always terrible', insurrection.[28]

However, her parallel between black slaves and white females was not unproblematic, especially when one considers the complex nature of the power relationships between white colonial mistresses and their female slaves, vividly described in Mary Prince's *History of Mary Prince* (1831) and Moses Roper's *Narrative of the Adventures and Escape of Moses Roper, from American Slavery* (1837).[29] In terms of structure and content, Wollstonecraft's work represented a strategic detachment from any overt relation to autobiographical or 'spiritual' discourse and advanced instead an effective rational, objective rhetoric. Indeed, her account of the *Interesting Narrative* by Olaudah Equiano in the *Analytical Review* of May 1789, suggested that the slave's rendition of his conversion to Methodism was 'rather tiresome' and that his narrative should have concluded with his acquisition of freedom.[30] Thus, whereas Wollstonecraft's work promoted a liberationist schema in terms of gender, her texts remain resolutely detached from the mode of discourse popularised by radical dissenting Protestants and emancipatory ideology. Conversely, the poetical works by Wollstonecraft's contemporary, Samuel Taylor Coleridge, prescribed narratives of 'emancipation' wherein the influence of the dynamics of spiritual discourse were barely concealed. Coleridge's work extended the abolitionist and evangelical design, established by William Cowper, into the public forum as demonstrated by his *Lecture on the Slave Trade*. His poems, especially those referred to as the 'conversation poems', maintained the personalised, autobiographical framework of conversion narratives, yet proffered a significantly revised version of both the confessional motif and the discourse of the spirit.

COLERIDGE'S BITTER SWEET 'LECTURE ON THE SLAVE TRADE'

On 16 June 1795, Samuel Taylor Coleridge delivered his *Lecture on the Slave Trade* at the Assembly Coffee House at the Quay in Bristol, one of England's major slave-trading ports. The text of the *Lecture* was subsequently printed in a condensed and revised form in the fourth issue of the poet's short-lived journal, *The Watchman*, on 25 March 1796.[31] Given that the height of abolitionist protest occurred during the period 1789–1792 and was followed by a climate of suspicion and fear under the Pitt government, Coleridge's lecture took place at a time when 'abolitionism' had begun to lose respectability.[32] Seven years earlier, in March 1788, in the same city, Wesley had preached his famous sermon on the immorality of slavery at the New Room in Bristol. In 1792, three years prior to his *Lecture*, Coleridge, then still at Cambridge, had been awarded the Browne Gold Medal for his 'Ode on the Slave Trade', a poem which had invoked Nemesis to send punishment to those who were 'sated with the persecution' of a miserable people.[33] Coleridge may well have read Blumenbach's 'On the Varieties of Mankind' (1775), a text which repudiated claims which suggested that blacks and whites were two distinct species (see Chapter 5), as three years after the delivery of this *Lecture on the Slave Trade*, Coleridge went to study under Blumenbach in 1798–1799.

The day before the delivery of the *Lecture*, Coleridge consulted the Bristol Library's copy of Clarkson's *Essay on the Impolicy of the African Slave Trade* (1788) and Carl Bernhard Wadstrom's *Essay on Colonization, Particularly Applied to the Western Coast of Africa, with Some Free Thoughts on Cultivation and Commerce* (1794), along with notes gathered by his friend and colleague, Robert Southey, from Antony Benezet's *Some Historical Account of Guinea* (1781).[34] Clarkson's text referred to the work of the female slave, Phillis Wheatley (discussed in Chapter 7 below), as an example of 'African intellectual potential' and provided a synopsis of her life as a slave and extracts from three of the poems included in her poetical volume, *Poems on Various Subjects* (1773), a 'Hymn to Evening', a 'Hymn to Morning' and 'Thoughts on Imagination'.[35] Wheatley's work had also been celebrated in the long poem, *The Female Advocate* (1774) by Mary Scott, the Unitarian poet and in Mary Deverell's 'On Reading the Poems of Phillis Wheatley', a poem in the latter's *Miscellanies in Prose and Verse* (1781) which described Wheatley as a representative of 'a race divine; / Like marble that in quarries lies conceal'd'.[36] Coleridge's text may also have been influenced by the testimonial narratives delivered at abolitionist gatherings by former slave-traders and African slaves alike, as well as by denunciations of the trade contained within published narratives, including Ottobah Cugoano's pamphlet of 1787 and Olaudah Equiano's (Gustavus Vassa's) autobiographical text of 1789. In his two-volume *Essay on Colonization*, which contained the now famous cross-section of a typical slave ship, Wadstrom had denounced the trade as an 'European iniquity' which had hindered the superior benefits of colonisation:

> Thus Asia and America became the principal theatres of the ambition and avidity of the Europeans; and happy had it been for Africa if they had so continued. But it is distressing to recollect the rapid progress of European iniquity among the simple and untutored nations inhabiting the other quarters of the world . . . It was soon found that the aborigines of the former [America] could not endure the toils imposed on them by their new masters . . . Here commenced the *Slave-trade*.[37]

For Wadstrom, the slave trade, 'that scourge of the human race which has kept down a great part of the Africans in a state of anarchy and blood', had not only impeded the expanding forces of civilisation within Africa, but had prevented plantocratic merchants from 'countenancing the colonisation of that continent'.[38] Wadstrom's text thus proposed commercialisation of Africa as an alternative to the transportation of West African slaves to the West Indies. During his *Lecture on the Slave Trade*, Coleridge advanced a critique of the trade in terms of its creation and maintenance of unnecessary, or 'artificial wants'. He defined the produce of others' labour, such as the 'Sugars, Rum, Cotton, log-wood, cocoa, coffee, pimento, ginger, indigo, mahogany, and conserves' imported from the colonies, as a major source of the nation's miseries and vices.[39] If, argued Coleridge, English consumers were to confine their wishes to the 'actual necessaries and real comfort of Life', all causes of complaint and iniquity would be removed: 'What Nature demands Nature everywhere amply supplies – asking for it that portion only of Toil, which would have been otherwise necessary, as Exercise'.[40] Coleridge criticised government policy concerning the slave trade, higlighting the fact that the import duties of such 'slave' produce contributed a substantial amount to the government's revenue.[41] Paradoxically, however, it was precisely the marketing of such 'artificial wants' which had precipitated the increasing popularity of coffee houses throughout Britain, including that in which Coleridge's own lecture took place.

Nevertheless, Coleridge's text developed a narrative which juxtaposed the development of a spiritual capacity with the gratification of 'bodily' wants. Composed in the same year as the *Lecture*, Coleridge's *Six Lectures on Revealed Religion* (1795) had established a critique of the defects of the established Church and its clergy, and cited psychological evidence of truth as offered by David Hartley's *Observations on Man* (1749).[42] Likewise, his *Lecture* prioritised the transcendental potential of the mind and its pilgrim-age towards an 'ever-widening prospect': 'the mind must enlarge the sphere of its activity'.[43] By fusing, perhaps unknowingly, Joseph Addison's principal ideas of the imagination stated in *The Spectator* (21 June 1712) and Mark Akenside's blank-verse poem, *Pleasures of Imagination* (1744), Coleridge's text advanced a prototype of liberationist ideology subtly synchronised with a diluted (or indeed, muted) form of spiritual discourse and individual autonomy:

> To develope the powers of the Creator is our proper employment – and *to imitate Creativeness* by combination our most exalted and self-satisfying Delight. But we are progressive and must not rest content with present Blessings. Our Almighty Parent hath therefore given to us Imagination that stimulates to the attainment of *real* excellence by the contemplation of splendid Possibilities that still revivifies the dying motive within us, and fixing our eye on the *glittering Summits* that rise one above the other in *Alpine endlessness* still urges us up the ascent of Being, amusing the ruggedness of the road with the beauty and grandeur of the *ever-widening Prospect*.[44]

In the condensed form of the *Lecture on the Slave Trade* which appeared in the *Watchman* one year later, Coleridge made explicit man's dependence upon this faculty of the imagination in determining his position upon the Great Chain of Being: 'But Providence which has distinguished Man from the lower orders of Being by the progressiveness of his nature, forbids him to be contented. It has given us the faculty of the *Imagination*'. In so doing,

Coleridge minimised his critique of slavery, or indeed the slave trade, and advanced instead the metamorphic translation of the discourse of the spirit into Romantic ideology's concept of the 'imagination'. As far as his criticism of the 'pestilent invention' of 'unreal wants' was concerned, Coleridge's analysis of the trade implied that without the demand for luxurious goods, the problem of London's poor would be eradicated. His lecture hence presented a shift in focus away from the plight of the African victims and highlighted instead the fate of those English citizens who, 'unwary or in greater distress', had been tricked into employment on board a slave-trading vessel. By prioritising the deplorable 'loss of liberty' encountered by these slave-trading seamen and their horrific experience amidst the 'unwholesomeness of the climate' of both the African continent and the middle passage, Coleridge's text relocated the traumatic experience of slavery onto the hardships suffered by locals:

> From the brutality of their Captain and the unwholesomeness of the Climate through which they pass, it has been calculated that every Slave Vessel from the Port of Bristol loses on an average almost a fourth of the whole Crew – and so far is this Trade from being a nursery for Seamen, that the Survivors are rather shadows in their appearance than men and frequently perish in Hospitals after the completion of the Voyage.[45]

Coleridge's endeavour to avoid too direct a reference to the trade, alongside the omission from the published text of his vehement attack on the Pitt administration, reflected both the growing suppression of anti-state criticism in the 1790s and the continued reverberations of the public response to the St Domingue slave insurrections of 1791–1892. Yet the transcript of the original (now lost) manuscript of the *Lecture on the Slave Trade* by E. H. Coleridge suggests that the contributions made by Coleridge's colleague, Robert Southey, to the text strategically differed from Coleridge's focus on luxury and the sufferings of England's poor.[46] Drawing heavily on Benezet's account of his voyage to the coast of Guinea and the reports by the Dutch traveller, William Bosman, Southey's contribution to the narrative focused on the slaves themselves and presented a sexualised (and somewhat titillating) account of the slaves' experience during the Middle Passage, possibly in an attempt to heighten his audience's sympathy:

> The wretched slaves . . . are examined *stark naked male and female*, and after being marked on the breast with a red hot iron, with the arms and names of the company or owner, who are the purchasers; they are *thrust promiscuously* into the ship – when on board they are always fettered with leg-shack[l]es and handcuffs, two and two – right and left – they lie in a crowded and cramped state, having neither their length nor breadth.[47]

These intertextual, co-editorial relations between Southey and Coleridge, and indeed between their work and Newton's *Authentic Narrative* were reinforced in Southey's 'The Sailor Who Had Served in the Slave Trade' (1790), a poem not dissimilar to Coleridge's ballad poem, 'The Rime of the Ancient Mariner' (1798). Based on the story of a dissenting minister in Bristol who discovered a sailor in a perplexed state of mind, Southey's and Coleridge's poetical compositions reworked the autobiographical narrative of the conscience-haunted sailor in Newton's text. Yet whereas in Coleridge's text, direct references to the slave trade were removed, in Southey's account, these were foregrounded and specified.[48] Thus whilst Coleridge's 'Rime of the Ancient Mariner' describes the journey of a guilt-ridden sailor who seeks forgiveness for his involuntary killing of an albatross, Southey's 'Sailor' relates the tale of his journeying on board a 'Guinea-man' towards the slave coast, the capture of a cargo of 300 negro slaves and their refusal to eat. One of these enslaved Africans, a 'woman sulkier than the rest', is singled out by the captain of the ship, who orders the sailor to 'tie her up' and flog her to death in front of the crew and the other captives. Her body is flung overboard and Southey's sailor, traumatised, repeatedly revisits the scene in his conscience:

> I saw the sea close over her,
>   Yet she was still in sight;
> I see her thrashing every where;
>   I see her day and night.[49]

The sailor's efforts to purge himself of guilt culminate in a moving confessional account of his cruel treatment of a female slave, an account similar to that found in the *Interesting Narrative* (1789) by the ex-slave, Olaudah Equiano (discussed in Chapter 8 below).[50] The casting of black slaves overboard into the Atlantic, whether healthy or dying, was not a rare occurrence; the most infamous example being that which occurred on board the slave ship *Zong*. During its return voyage to England in 1781, a debilitating illness wiped out a significant number of slaves on board. In an effort to recover the slavers' initial investment via the legal insurance provision for slaves 'irretrievably' lost at sea, 133 healthy slaves were cast overboard at the orders of Luke Collingwood, the *Zong*'s captain.[51] In court (*Gregson v. Gilbert*), the owners of the *Zong* pleaded successfully that the slaves' presence had endangered the water supply. As the note at the end of 'The Sailor' suggests, Southey felt that such accounts of inhumane treatment 'ought to be made as public as possible'. This was precisely the motivation behind the actions of the ex-slave, Olaudah Equiano, who, in March 1783, informed Granville Sharp of the *Zong* incident.[52] Sharp's initial response was to pursue the prosecution of the *Zong* sailors themselves. Although Sharp abandoned this approach, it was, in a sense, continued within the poems produced by Coleridge and Southey. In Coleridge's poem, however, specific identification of the slave trade as a 'sin' is absent; the unmotivated killing of the albatross is mitigated by the involuntary blessing of the slimy serpents of the sea. Indeed in both poems, deliverance is granted, or at least secured, by the respective mariners' pleas for forgiveness. Nevertheless, the issue of forgiveness on a scale that implicates the error at the heart of Britain's legal and economic practice, is not, and indeed could not be addressed so long as slaves were considered as forms of property.

Taking his cue from William Fox's famous pamphlet, *A Short Account of the African Slave Trade, and an Address to the People of Great Britain on the Propriety of Abstaining from West Indian Sugar and Rum*, Coleridge's *Lecture on the Slave Trade* proposed abstinence from slave-grown produce, 'sweetened with the Blood of the Murdered', as an effective means of achieving a cessation of the trade – a method which he considered preferable to the circulation of petitions by what he termed 'the vanity of pretended Sensibility': that is, well-educated philanthropic females.[53] Yet Coleridge's concluding inflammatory lines daringly correlated the volatile insurrections and 'justified rebellions' of West Indian slaves in the colonies with the desperate plight of the British peasantry:

> For I appeal to common sense whether to affirm that the Slaves are as well off as our Peasantry, be not the same as to assert that our Peasantry are as bad off as Negro Slaves – and whether if the Peasantry believed it there is a man amongst them *who [would] not rebel? and be justified in Rebellion?*[54]

Thus Coleridge's lecture 'on' rather than 'against' the slave trade strategically avoided a discussion of the slaves themselves; rather, it centred upon a discussion of the concept of luxury and the sufferings of the English peasantry, and hinted at the threat which he felt had been posed to his creative 'empire' by the females of 'pretended sensibility'. Yet despite its shortcomings, Coleridge's *Lecture* provides ample evidence of the poet's awareness and involvement in abolitionist activity. It was, however, within the 'conversation poems', composed during the late 1790s, that the poet presented a sensitive exploration of the conditions of estrangement, captivity and liberty, and in so doing, revealed the influence of the discourse of radical dissenting Protestantism on his own contribution to Romantic poetry.

COLERIDGE'S DISCOURSE OF THE SPIRIT: THE 'CONVERSATION POEMS'

During the period of his closest friendship with Wordsworth, Coleridge composed a letter to Thomas Poole (6 February 1797), the first in a series of five autobiographical letters written at Poole's request. In that letter the poet expressed his admiration for the power of the spiritual autobiographies composed by dissenting Protestants, published by *The Gospel Magazine and Theological Review*, which had made its first appearance the year before:

> I could inform the dullest author how he might write an interesting book – let him relate the events of his own Life with honesty, not disguising the feelings that accompanied them. – I never yet read even a Methodist's 'Experience' in the Gospel Magazine without receiving instruction & amusement: & I should almost despair of that Man, who could peruse the Life of John Woolman without an amelioration of Heart.[55]

Although there is no further evidence to confirm Coleridge's detailed knowledge of these or any other spiritual autobiographies by radical dissenting Protestants, Coleridge's reference to the Quaker-abolitionist and spiritual autobiographer, John Woolman, suggests that his interest in such autobiographies emerged from an antislavery context. Likewise, evidence of his borrowings from the Bristol Library between 1793 and 1798 reveal the poet's thorough investigation of antislavery accounts: in March 1795 Coleridge borrowed the third volume of the library's *Miscellaneous Poems* which contained Hannah More's *Slavery: A Poem* (1788) and Ann Yearsley's *Poems on the Inhumanity of the Slave Trade* (1788).[56] Between March and August 1795, Coleridge also borrowed Raynal's *Philosophical and Political History of the Settlements* (1776), Clarkson's *Essay on the Impolicy of the Slave Trade* (1788), Wadstrom's *Essay on Colonisation* (1794–1795) and Edwards' *The History, Civil and Commercial, of the British Colonies in the West Indies* (1793–1794).

On the front page of the first volume of *The Gospel Magazine*, the editor introduced 'A Word to those Lovers of Truth' in 'these days of blasphemy, rebuke, infidelity, heresy and error' and adamantly claimed that the narratives (including the 'Memoirs of the Life of John James Claude', the 'Remarkable Passages in the Life of Mr Vavasor Powel', and the 'Singular Experience and Great Sufferings of Mrs Agnes') which followed were valid examples of 'sterling truth, in all its brilliancy and glory'.[57] Over two decades earlier, the abolitionist Quaker, John Woolman (1720–1772) had published his *Journal of the Life, Gospel Labours, and Christian Experiences of that Faithful Minister of Jesus Christ, John Woolman* in Philadelphia in 1774, in London in 1775 and in Dublin in 1776. In this *Journal*, the narrative of Woolman's deliverance from the 'depths of misery' by the 'inward principle' demonstrated his concern for the inhuman and iniquitous practice of slavery:

> I was so afflicted in my mind, that I said, before my master and the friend, that I believed slave-keeping to be a practice inconsistent with the Christian religion.[58]

Likewise, in his tract, *Some Considerations on the Keeping of Negroes* (1754), Woolman had declared to his Quaker Friends in words not unlike those contained within Coleridge's *Lecture*, that it was their duty as 'creatures accountable to our Creator, to employ rightly the understanding which he hath given us'.[59] Moreover, Woolman had identified the 'spirit which breathes peace and good will' as the agent which would bring about their philanthropic ambitions.[60]

In keeping with the narrative framework of Woolman's text and those contained within the *Gospel Magazine*, Coleridge elucidated in his letter to Poole his own plans for a similar autobiographical project. This, he suggested, would trace the progress of his life with all its 'charms of variety: high Life, & low Life, Vices and Virtues, great Folly & some Wisdom'.[61] Such a 'task' would prove to be invaluable in his effort to 'renew and deepen' his reflections of the past and thereby reveal the 'many untoward circumstances' which had concurred to form those 'weaknesses and defects of his character'.[62] Coleridge's interest in the discourse of radical dissenting Protestantism may have been provoked by his despair at the news of his brother Frank's suicide in 1792, the deaths of six members of his immediate family between 1780 and 1792 and his own feelings of hopelessness following his secret enlistment in the King's Light Dragoons on 2 December 1793: 'Shall I profess an abhorrence of my past conduct? . . . I am lost in the labyrinth, the trackless wilderness of my own bosom'.[63] The fact that Coleridge's father was vicar of the parish church at Ottery St Mary (where Joanna Southcott was baptised) in Devon and that Coleridge visited him and his brother there on a fairly regular basis, suggests that he may have been familiar with reports of the spiritual teachings advanced by Southcott and Wesley. Likewise, his running away after a quarrel with his brother Frank in the autumn of 1779 and his subsequent night spent by the banks of the River Otter during a storm suggests that he would have responded sympathetically to the narratives of salvation and despair presented within spiritual autobiographies, by John Newton, William Cowper and the slaves.

Whatever the actual source of his awareness of this literary trope, the poet's interest in 'spiritual autobiography' occurred alongside his deliberate withdrawal from the sociopolitical, and indeed, abolitionist, sphere. As he explained in his letter to J. P. Estlin, by the summer of 1797 he had become, or so he claimed, 'wearied with politics even to soreness'. One year later, in a letter to his brother of March 1798, Coleridge announced that he had completely detached himself from any consideration of 'immediate causes'. Rather, he announced that he would turn his attentions towards the composition of a style of poetry which he believed would 'elevate the imagination & set the affections in right tune by the beauty of the inanimate impregnated as with the living soul, by the presence of Life'. The works composed during this period, however, reveal a subtle continuation of the concepts of spiritual liberty and self-autonomy, characteristic of both the language of radical dissenting Protestantism and abolitionist discourse. Likewise, according to Bernard Martin, it was very possible that Coleridge had read Newton's *Authentic Narrative* or had had it brought to his attention by William or Dorothy Wordsworth between 13 November 1797 and 23 March 1798.[64] Indeed it seems that Wordsworth was making use of John Newton's *Authentic Narrative* (most likely the episode in which Newton becomes a slave to a man named Clow on the Guinea Coast of Africa) at the same time that Coleridge was composing 'The Rime of the Ancient Mariner' (1797).[65]

Thomas Clarkson had introduced Coleridge to the Quaker, John Broadhead, and during his time at Leeds, Coleridge reread the works of many of his favourite Quaker authors, including George Fox, William Penn and John Woolman, amply demonstrating the intertextual transatlantic connection between nonconformist religious sentiment, abolitionist ideology and Romantic concerns.[66] Both Coleridge's and Wordsworth's work denotes an important metamorphosis of the captivity and liberationist genre in which the concept of spiritual impregnation, as recorded by Wesley and other radical prophets, is subtly translated into the power of poetry and identified as imagination's power to impregnate and thereby liberate the 'living soul', hence inaugurating (or rather confirming) the poet/prophet's spiritual role. And yet whilst structurally and ideologically these poets continue the trope of liberationist, individual determinism advanced by such spiritual autobiographies, they also determine a severance from and erasure of overt references to abolitionism. Coleridge's 'conversation poems' skilfully establish a composite continuation of, and departure from the discourse of spiritual autobiography articulated within the paradigm of radical dissenting Protestantism.[67]

Dedicated to Sara Fricker, whom Coleridge had married on 4 October 1795, four months following his *Lecture on the Slave Trade*, the first of these 'conversation poems', 'The Eolian Harp' (1795), presented a transformation of Wesley's image of the 'breath of the spirit' as a metaphor delineating the workings of an 'intellectual breeze' which stirred the mind into consciousness:

> And what if all of animated nature
> Be but organic Harps diversely fram'd,
> That tremble into thought, as o'er them sweeps
> Plastic and vast, one intellectual breeze,
> At once the Soul of each, and God of all?[68]

Sara's mild reproof cautions the poet against too scientific a rationale of the 'incomprehensible', that which one 'inly feels'. Yet the poem's authentication of the powers of the spirit (that 'indeterminate breeze' which impregnates all things) and its complex interrelationship with self-knowledge, remains unchallenged. It is a breeze, which like Wesley's breath of the spirit enlivens, animates and in a sense 'reveals' the self. Coleridge's use of the language of radical dissenting Protestantism forges a link with that employed within the slave narratives, yet in Coleridge's version, the self is mapped on to a mode of discourse severed (or seemingly so) from socioeconomic or historical specificity – a self prescribed *by* the self. In the editorial amendments to the poem of 1817, this source of liberation is redetermined as a power, no longer originating exclusively from without, but as a power which emerged from *within* the self: 'O! the one Life within us and abroad, / Which meets all motion and becomes its soul, / A light in sound, a sound-like power in light, / Rhythm in all thought, and joyance every where'.[69] Although the difference is subtle, the implications of this transformation are great: in Coleridge's hands, narratives of spiritual liberation and self-authorisation become centred around the concept of the imagination and the individual, rather than the collective self.

Coleridge's poem, 'This Lime-Tree Bower My Prison', composed in June 1797, inscribes a model of redemption similarly expounded in the auto-biographical narratives of spiritual salvation. More importantly perhaps, in this poetical model of deliverance, the powers of the spirit are unambiguously replaced by the liberating powers of the poet's own imagination. His friends William, Dorothy and Charles Lamb are free to wander as they please, yet Coleridge envisages himself as 'imprisoned' within the perimeters of the lime-tree bower, an image which reflects the decrepit or 'stagnant' powers of his own powers of creativity: '...I have lost / Beauties and feelings, such as would have been / Most sweet to my remembrance even when age / Had dimm'd mine eyes to blindness!'[70] Whereas the magnificent external landscape revives the 'gentle-hearted' Charles (whose insane sister had stabbed their mother to death ten months earlier), Coleridge's inner self is impregnated by a power that emerges from within. It is a power which enables him to imagine himself liberated from the constraints of his present condition and reunited with his friends: 'A delight / Comes sudden on my heart, and I am glad / As I myself were there!'[71] As with Wesley's resonant utterances of the spirit's revitalising power of 'new birth', the restorative power of the imagination liberates the anguished poetical self from physical and mental confinement and achieves an hypostatic state of illuminated bliss. In this state, akin to sanctification, the bower is transformed from an image of imprisonment and exile to that of 'transparent' and therefore unbinding, luxurious foliage. Hence the poet glimpses a prophetic state of being in which he is able to discover ('gaze', 'perceive'), acknowledge ('henceforth I shall know') and partake in that which is usually unavailable to man ('And sometimes . . . contemplate with lively joy, the joys we cannot share'); a participation within manifestations of infinitude (space) and eternity (time):

> . . . So my friend
> Struck with deep joy may stand, as I have stood,
> Silent with swimming sense; yea, gazing round

On the wide landscape, gaze till all doth seem
Less gross than bodily; and of such hues
As veil the Almighty Spirit, when yet he makes
Spirits perceive his presence.[72]

As the poet is 'blessed' with a disclosure of the realm inhabited by the 'Almighty Spirit', he is endowed with a mystical power of articulation which enables him to speak of salvation and which fuses his own text with a manifestation of divine logos, the Word.

COLERIDGE'S 'LETTER TO SARA HUTCHINSON'

In line with the early 'conversation poems', Coleridge's 'Letter to Sara Hutchinson' remains distinctly informed by the schema of spiritual autobiography in its elucidation of the poet's acute sense of melancholy, his depressed state of delusion and inactivity, and his subsequent 'deliverance'. Composed on the evening of 4 April 1802 after hearing the first four stanzas of Wordsworth's *Ode: Intimations of Immortality*, the original version of the 340-line verse 'Letter to Sara' underwent a significant series of revisions and deletions over a six month period, the final variant of which (entitled *Dejection: An Ode*) presents a far less autobiographical, less personalised and less critical text. In this subsequent published version, dedicated to Wordsworth under the pseudonym 'Edmund' and printed in the *Morning Post* (4 October 1802) on both Wordsworth's wedding day and the seventh anniversary of Coleridge's own wedding, the earlier references to Sara Hutchinson (sister of Wordsworth's fiancée with whom Coleridge had fallen in love) and to his disastrous relationship with Sara Fricker were carefully omitted.[73]

In the original form of the 'Letter to Sara', the poet's depressed state isolates him from any solace arising from the soothing landscape and its enigmatic evening sunset: hence he gazes 'in this heartless Mood' with 'how blank an eye!'[74] Identifying himself with the hero of Milton's *Samson Agonistes*, Coleridge's 'genial spirits' fail to deliver him from this state of spiritual malaise or from the erosion of his innate creative powers effected by the oppressive 'smoth'ring Weight' of his 'coarse domestic life' (experiencing no 'mutual mild Enjoyment of its own') with Delilah/Sara Fricker: 'All this long Eve, so balmy & serene, / Have I been gazing on the western Sky . . . / I see them all, so excellently fair! / I see, not feel, how beautiful they [clouds] are!'[75] This 'burden' of a grief 'without a pang', 'stifling, drowsy and unimpassioned', constitutes an emotional and spiritual sterility ('Void, dark, drear') which the poet suffers alone, unconsoled by external forms which, according to him, remain 'lifeless shapes': 'I may not hope from outward Forms to win / The Passion & the Life, *whose Fountains are within!*'[76]

Coleridge's search for spiritual liberation takes him on a retrospective journey through time towards the memory of his younger self, a being similarly 'cloistered in a City school', who gazes with 'secret yearnings' towards an hypothetical maiden, 'a kind of Vision to me!' who exists beyond the boundaries of his imprisonment.[77] Having 'established' a continuum through time between his past and present self, the poet projects a future 'vision' of Sara, whose gaze he imagines as coalescing with his own yearning for spiritual and emotional liberation. As the boundaries of space and time are transcended, the poet's metaphorical blindness is miraculously 'cured' amidst an ecstatic moment of spiritual awakening and emotional deliverance which leaves his spirit 'awe-stricken with the Excess / And trance-like Depth of it's brief Happiness'.

> I feel my spirit moved –
> And wheresoe'er thou be,
> O Sister! O Beloved!
> Those dear mild Eyes, that see
> Even now the Heaven, *I* see –
> There is a Prayer in them! It is for *me* –
> And I, dear Sara – *I* am blessing *thee*![78]

In accordance with the structural framework of former confessional narratives and spiritual autobiographies by radical dissenting Protestants, Coleridge's poetical 'Letter to Sara' underscores the distinction between his former 'blessed' self and his present despairing self: 'For Hope grew round me, like the climbing Vine . . . / But now Ill Tidings bow me down . . .'.[79] However, despite his emotional wretchedness and anguished inactivity, the poet's text expounds a new-found faith in his own 'shaping Spirit of Imagination'; that gift which, it is claimed, nature gave him at his birth, a powerful and innate capacity to transform his captivity into a condition of liberation.[80] This intense release from emotional deadlock inaugurates a deliverance from spiritual dead(wed)lock and advances instead a phase of confident, self-authorised mobility: 'I too will crown me with a Coronal'.[81] Denying the basis of his earlier belief in the passive role played by the mind (and indeed, the soul), the poet proclaims his new-found faith in the creative potential of the 'shaping spirit' of imagination:

> Ah! from the Soul itself must issue forth
> A Light, a Glory, and a luminous Cloud
>   Enveloping the Earth!
> And from the Soul itself must there be se[nt]
> A sweet & potent Voice, of it's own Bir[th],
> Of all sweet Sounds the Life & Element.[82]

Accordingly the poet imagines a superior 'marriage' between mind and nature which liberates him from his previous state of domestic captivity (the marriage between two 'unequal minds, two discordant wills') and his desperate condition as a *tongueless* (and hence, creatively 'flightless') poet/ Philomel. Hence his text celebrates the impregnating power of the mind itself: 'O Sara! we receive but what we give, / And in *our* Life alone does Nature live. / Our's is her Wedding Garment, our's her Shroud'.[83]

As the powers of the 'spirit' and the poet's imagination merge into one, Coleridge's poem presents a prophetic vision of regeneration which resonates with the apocalyptical language of the Book of Revelation. As 'joy' is identified as the dowry which emerges from this imagined 'wedlock', Coleridge endeavours to expound a purely spiritual, unerotic embrace which transcends the conditions of the physical, or indeed 'sensual' world, and 'satisfies' the condition of Sara's continued physical absence:

> JOY, Sara! is the *Spirit* & the Power,
>   That wedding Nature to us gives in Dower
> A new Earth & new Heaven
> Undreamt of by the Sensual & the Proud!
> Joy is that strong Voice, Joy that luminous Cloud –
>   We, *we ourselves rejoice!*[84]

Interestingly, Coleridge's 'Letter' establishes an important shift away from the voyeuristic Book of Revelation ('And I saw the holy city, new Jerusalem, coming down out of heaven from God, prepared as a bride adorned for her husband')[85] and denotes instead a personalised account of the poet's own spiritual marriage as a reciprocation of that between God/Israel and the New Jerusalem: 'A new Earth & new Heaven / Undreamt of by the Sensual & the Proud!'[86] Although the poet's claims for a resolutely unerotic 'spiritual' embrace signifies an unambiguous severance from the overtly erotic tone of the Old Testament Song of Songs around which it revolves ('My beloved is mine and I am his . . . Upon my bed by night I sought him whom my soul loves'), nevertheless such a division sits problematically amidst the distinctly physical paradigm of the earlier stanzas.[87] In an effort to complete this process of de-erotisation, Sara is transformed into a maternal (rather than sexualised) image of the Holy Spirit ('mother Dove'), who, with wings 'blessedly outspread', manifests the promise of divine possibility, corresponding to the poet's imaginative potential. Furthermore, as the confessional 'Letter to Sara Hutchinson' advocates the poet's own 'spiritual' liberation from emotional and domestic slavery, the poetical ego emerges 'victorious' with a newly formed (de-eroticised) sense of self, ultimately freed (or rather, almost freed) from any overt relationship with either the discourse of the spirit or the language of abolitionism.

Thus Coleridge's poetical schema prescribes both a revival and revision of spiritual autobiography established by radical dissenting Protestantism, and reveals the subtle relationship between the emergence of antislavery ideology and the development of the Romantic genre. The discourse of the spirit, with its connotations of liberationist ideology and identity configuration, had a distinct influence upon a body of writing which we have come to know as 'Romantic'; as well as the body of lesser-known work referred to as the slave narratives. Yet, as I shall discuss below, although the Romantic poet, William Wordsworth continued the liberationist and self-authorising dialogue advanced by radical dissenting Protestantism, his poems also paradoxically witnessed a deliberate severance from specific tenets of abolitionism and overt manifestations of spiritual discourse.

WORDSWORTH'S SPIRITUAL AUTOBIOGRAPHY

According to Abrams' *Natural Supernaturalism*, Wordsworth's *Prelude* traced a harmonic secularisation of the Judaeo-Christian myth, framed within the parameters of epic biography and thereby described the poet's emergence as a self-elected prophet:

> Wordsworth's is a secular theodicy . . . which translates the painful process of Christian conversion and redemption into a painful process of self-formation, crisis, and self-recognition, which culminates in a stage of self-coherence, self-awareness, and *assured power* that is its own reward.[88]

Likewise, in his book, *Wordsworth's 'Natural Methodism'* (1975), Richard Brantley argued that the poem's emphasis upon self-mastery, spiritual renewal and confessional introspection determined Wordsworth, not only as a 'definable moral and religious poet', but established the connection between Wordsworth's work, Evangelical Anglicanism and Evangelical nonconformism.[89] In an expansion of the ideas put forward by M. H. Abrams and Geoffrey Hartman, Brantley suggested that Wordsworth's faith was strategically influenced by the broad and reverential evangelicalism of the 'first' Evangelical, John Wesley, and the Evangelical philanthropist and abolitionist, William Wilberforce. Indeed, in the lengthy letter which praised Wilberforce's *Practical View of the Prevailing Religious System of Professed Christians Contrasted with Real Christianity* (1798) and which accompanied a complimentary copy of the *Lyrical Ballads*, Wordsworth claimed to be a 'Fellow-labourer' with Wilberforce 'in the same Vineyard'.[90] However, as I shall discuss below, although the poet's praise of Wilberforce suggested an intimate liaison with both the discourse of dissenting Protestantism and abolitionist ideology, Wordsworth's relationship with these movements was deeply ambiguous.

Whilst at Cambridge, Wordsworth encountered concepts of evangelical-ism both formally and informally through the activities and beliefs of his friends, Thomas Middleton (later Bishop of Calcutta), John Gisbourne (a convert to Methodism), William Mathews (son of a London Methodist preacher) and the fervent Evangelical ministry of Charles Simeon (vicar of Holy Trinity during the 1780s).[91] Likewise, the poet's appropriation and revision of spiritual discourse and liberationist ideology may have been influenced by Coleridge's plans to develop the autobiographical style of the Methodist narratives and the philanthropic interests and concerns of the poet's sister, Dorothy. In fact, the nature of Dorothy's close friendship with the parliamentary abolitionist, William Wilberforce, prompted Jane Pollard, one of Dorothy's closest friends, to predict a likely marriage between them, an hypothesis adamantly denied by Dorothy in her self-deprecating reply of 30 April 1790:

> Your way of accounting for my apparent absence of mind diverted me exceedingly. I will set forward with assuring you that my heart is perfectly disengaged and then endeavour to shew you how very improbable it is that Mr W. would think of me ... Mr W. would, were he ever to marry, look for a Lady possessed of many more accomplishments than I can boast.[92]

During his stay at her uncle's parsonage, Wilberforce had introduced Dorothy to a variety of 'Great Awakening' texts, including Philip Doddridge's *Family Expositor* (1739–1756).[93] Wordsworth's discussions with Dorothy over the concerns of the 'soul' described in Francis Wrangham's *Thirteen Practical Sermons: Founded on Doddridge's 'Rise and Progress of Religion in the Soul'* (1800) appear to have had a pervasive influence on his poetical compositions, in terms of their emphasis upon intense self-examination, emotional crisis and spiritual illumination.[94] Indeed Wordsworth had met Francis Wrangham *c.* 1795 when Basil Montagu, the bastard son of the fourth Earl of Sandwich and friend to Godwin, had introduced them. Dorothy's role as mediator between William and various sociopolitical and dissenting discourses of the 1790s may be confirmed by her response to the defeat of Wilberforce's Bill proposing the Abolition of the Slave Trade: 'I was indeed greatly mortified on hearing of Mr W.'s bad success, every friend to humanity must applaud his zeal and lament that it failed in its effect'.[95] In a letter of 8 May 1792, Dorothy persuasively and deter-minedly urged Jane Pollard to participate in the antislavery debate: 'I hope you were an *immediate* abolitionist and are angry with the House of Commons for continuing the traffic in human flesh so long as till 1796 but you will also rejoice that so *much* has been done. I hate Mr Dundas'.[96] Dorothy Wordsworth's transcription of an extract from letter V of Newton's *Authentic Narrative*, was made sometime between 1798–1799 and

273

provides the source of Book VI of Wordsworth's own *Prelude* of 1805: 'And as I have read of one by shipwreck thrown . . . who having brought to land a single volume and no more' (VI, 160–5). Wordsworth was most likely referring to the passage of the *Authentic Narrative* in which Newton had described his ill-treatment at the hands of his master's African mistress:

> Though destitute of food and clothing, depressed to a degree beyond common wretchedness, I could sometimes collect my mind to math-ematical studies. I had bought *Barrow's Euclid* at Plymouth . . . it was the only volume I brought on shore; it was always with me, and I used to take it to remote corners of the island by the seaside, and draw my *diagrams* with a long stick upon the sand. Thus I often beguiled my sorrows, and almost forgot my feeling.[97]

This 'relationship' between Newton's and Wordsworth's texts, as with those of Southey and Coleridge discussed above, suggests a process of intertextuality between these authors. Given the captivity motif which provides the overall framework for Wordsworth's *Prelude*, it seems difficult to imagine that Wordsworth was unaware of Newton's subsequent debates over slavery.[98] Moreover, as I shall elucidate, Wordsworth's poetical spiritual autobi-ography bears a marked resemblance to the first literary articulations by black slaves.

In the 1798 draft version of the *Prelude*, the poet identified the natural and spiritual forces which he believed had shaped his early years and nourished his poetical propensity. The 'divine' visitations of the spirit are hence translated, in Wordsworth's schema, into a tableau of privileged election, identifying him as one 'chosen' by the 'spirit of nature': 'was it for this / That one, the fairest of all rivers, loved / To blend his murmurs with my nurse's song . . . / And from his fords and shallows, sent a voice / To intertwine my dreams?'[99] As the poet's salvation is presented in terms of his restored sense of purpose, the opening lines of the 1805 version of the *Prelude* refer not only to the concluding lines of Milton's *Paradise Lost*, but (as with the slave narratives) to the Israelites' escape from Egyptian bondage related in Exodus 13:3:

> A captive greets thee, coming from a house
> *Of bondage, from yon city's walls set free,*
> *A prison where he hath been long immured.*
> *Now I am free, enfranchised and at large,*
> *May fix my habitation where I will . . .*
> Joyous, *nor scared at its own liberty,*
> I look about, and should the guide I chuse
> Be nothing better than a wandering cloud
> I cannot miss my way.[100]

Wordsworth discerns these spiritual visitations as manifestations of the 'sweet breath' from heaven which, like Coleridge's 'intellectual breeze', 'saturates' his body with a 'vital breeze'.[101] Wesley's 'discourse of the spirit' had, of course, similarly presented images describing the 'breath' of heaven and its blessed visitations, but Wordsworth appropriates this spiritual framework in order to determine himself as a prophet, not only graced with the power of divine tongues, but with the ability to transcribe such oral utterances into text, the written word: 'To the open fields I told / A prophesy; poetic numbers came / Spontaneously, and clothed in priestly robe / My spirit, thus singled out, as it might seem, / For holy services'.[102] For this reason, the 'conviction of sin' episode (an essential tenet of the 'conversion narrative') presented in the *Prelude* identifies the poet's time at Cambridge as a period of transgression from which he must be saved. As with Cowper's poem *The Task*, it describes an indulgence in erring dreams rather than visionary prophecy – 'I was the dreamer, they the dream; I roamed / Delighted through the motley spectacle'.[103] 'Sealed' by the attributes of divine election, however, such lapses fail, or so he claims, to inflict any permanent damage upon his poetic destiny as 'a chosen son'; rather, they serve to confirm his conviction in his own holy powers.

Three further references in the *Prelude* complete the narrative of the poet's spiritual deterioration: his encounter with the 'Babel din' ('barbarian and infernal – 'tis a dream Monstrous in colour, motion, shape, sight, sound') of the city of London; his carefully disguised 'testimony' of *sexual* transgression (which revolves around his encounter with Annette Vallon and the conception of his illegitimate child); and finally, his abandonment of spiritual truths by his embracement of Godwin's philosophical rationalism, his ruthless 'probing' into one of 'Nature's holiest places'.[104] Yet despite these 'lapses', Wordsworth's ultimate self-restoration, disclosed in the final book of the 1805 *Prelude*, represents a magnificent reworking of dissenting Protestantism's model of apocalyptical sanctification – a witness of divine spirit ('a spirit / Living in time and space, and far diffused')[105] which simultaneously obliterates and confirms the poet's identity:

> For instantly a light upon the turf
> Fell like a flash. I looked about, and lo,
> The moon stood naked in the heavens at height
> Immense above my head, and on the shore
> I found myself of a huge sea of mist,
>
> . . . and it appeared to me
> The perfect image of a mighty mind,
> Of one that feeds upon infinity,
> That is exalted by an under-presence,
> The sense of God, or whatsoe'er is dim
> Or vast in its own being – above all.[106]

In accordance with the autobiographical framework of the conversion narratives, therefore, Wordsworth's discourse of spiritual ecstasy, divine witness and ethereal illumination discloses a process of self-engendered ecstasy that continues and revises the traditional schema of spiritual salvation. Indeed, as with Coleridge's texts, Wordsworth's *Prelude* advances a discourse of spiritual 'under-presence' which illuminates and exalts, and more importantly, is both 'God-given' and *self*-initiated. In this way, the creation of matter from the void described in the biblical account of the holy spirit in Genesis, is envisaged by the poet as similarly informing his *own* powers of creative imagination.[107] As 'the perfect image of the mighty mind' reveals the union of God's and the poet's identity, Wordsworth's 'word' is figured within a syncretic collusion with that Word which animates the universe. Accordingly, the power to assimilate, transform and illuminate is described as having been appropriated by the poet himself: 'Imagination! . . . / Like an unfathered vapour, here that power, / In all the might of its endowments, came / Athwart me'.[108] Recovering from the self-erasure, self-obliteration and spiritual excess typical of spiritual autobiography, Wordsworth's text recognises not the power of the divine, but the ethereal powers of the individual's mind over the dimensions of space and time:

> Tumult and peace, the darkness and the light,
> Were all like workings of one mind, the features
> Of the same face, blossoms upon one tree,
> Characters of the great apocalypse,
> The types and symbols of eternity,
> Of first, and last, and midst, and without end.[109]

Drawing upon the tenets of autobiography popularised by radical dissenting Protestantism, Wordsworth's *Prelude* confirms the interrelationship between Romanticism and the discourse of the spirit advanced by the confessional narratives of conversion. As with Coleridge's 'conversation poems', Wordsworth's work maintains the liberationist rhetoric of spiritual autobiography, yet reveals a discernible severance from the abolitionist activities of the late eighteenth-century transatlantic forum, especially in his address to the slave insurrectionist, Toussaint L'Ouverture.

WORDSWORTH AND THE SLAVES

On 2 February 1803, *The Morning Post* published the following sonnet by Wordsworth, 'To Toussaint L'Ouverture', the addressee of which was one of the principal commanders of the violent slave uprising of August 1791. During this insurrection (which was celebrated in Southey's 'To the Genius of Africa') approximately 20,000 former slaves abandoned the slave estates of the French owned colony of St Domingue, the largest and most productive slave colony in the Caribbean:

> TOUSSAINT, the most unhappy man of men!
> Whether the whistling Rustic tend his plough
> Within thy hearing, or thy head be now
> Pillowed in some deep dungeon's earless den; –
> O miserable Chieftain! where and when
> Wilt thou find patience! Yet die not; do thou
> Wear rather in thy bonds a cheerful brow:
> Though fallen thyself, never to rise again,
> Live, and take comfort. Thou hast left behind
> Powers that will work for thee; air, earth, and skies;
> There's not a breathing of the common wind
> That will forget thee; thou hast great allies;
> Thy friends are exultations, agonies,
> And love, and man's unconquerable mind.[110]

Toussaint L'Ouverture, whose pseudonym registered his belief in his own self-appointment as 'one who makes an opening' (that is, the source of hiatus or fissure in the sociopolitical and linguistic order) had seen himself as Napoleon Bonaparte's counterpart and had thus referred to himself as 'the First of the Blacks' in a letter addressed to the latter, 'the First of the Whites'.[111] Wordsworth's reference to the 'Chieftain's' confinement within some 'deep dungeon's earless den' alluded to the slave insurrectionist's detention within the icy dungeons of the Fortress of Joux in the Jura mountains where he died after a ten-month imprisonment in April 1803. Toussaint's imprisonment was similarly described in Marcus Rainsford's *Historical Account of the Black Empire of Hayti: Comprehending a View of the Principal Transactions in the Revolution in Saint Domingo* (1805):

> He who had been the benefactor of white people in a country where their enormities had provoked hatred, whose power was never stained by malevolence, and who was greater in his fall, than his enemies in their assumed power, was kept in a *damp and cheerless prison*, without the comfort of a single friend, without trial or even examination ... This prison may be considered the sepulture of Toussaint. France forgot awhile the habits of a civilized nation, to entomb one she should have graced with a public triumph; and England ... *should have guarded from violation the rights of humanity in its person*.[112]

Wordsworth's sonnet conclusively marks the translation of the slaves' insurrectionist demands (and indeed, the discourse of abolitionism) into Romanticism's claims for the liberationist powers of the mind. It situates the attributes of the black military leader within a schema that avoids any discussion of race and determines the indiscernible spiritual workings of the natural elements as inseparable from the 'natural' progression of man's 'unconquerable mind'. The poet's homage to L'Ouverture, as one of those 'who will not forget thee', consequently presents the great revolutionary leader as a manifestation of that expansionist, 'intellectual' power, the 'unconquerable mind', and as an individual now fused with the spiritual 'breathings of the common wind'. Likewise Wordsworth's conviction that despite his defeat and imprisonment, the slave rebel should retain a 'cheerful brow', reinscribes Addison's belief in the power of the imagination described in *The Spectator* of 21 June 1712:

> By this Faculty [the imagination] a Man in a Dungeon is capable of entertaining himself with Scenes and Landscapes more beautiful than any that can be found in the whole Compass of Nature.[113]

Wordsworth's sonnet provides an important example of the appropriation and concealment of abolitionist discourse contained within Romantic poetry, via its gradual withdrawal from its original focus, the great slave rebel, and its subsequent prioritisation of the symbolic emblem of Romanticism – the power of 'man's unconquerable mind', the imagination. This withdrawal from a sociohistoric figure of non-western specificity was similarly described in the *Prelude* by the poet's account of his conscious detachment from the momentum of the abolitionists' caravan 'towards Liberty' which, by the time of his return from France in 1792, had spread its influence across England: 'a contention ... raised up / Against the traffickers in Negro blood'.[114] During his absence, public support for the Society of the Abolition of the Slave Trade (founded in 1787) had steadily gained momentum and although Wilberforce's Abolition Bill was defeated in 1791, the 'virtuous feeling' of the antislavery campaign continued to escalate. In 1792, 519 petitions bearing almost half a million signatures were presented to Parliament demanding a cessation of the trade. The Bill providing for a gradual abolition of the trade was finally passed in the House of Commons by a narrow margin of 151 to 132 votes and in the House of Lords in 1807.[115]

Conversely, however, in his own autobiographical text, Wordsworth strategically endeavours to sever himself from any overt identification with the abolitionist movement: 'For me that strife had ne'er / fastened on my affections' (Book 10, lines 218–19). Indeed, he suggests, somewhat dubiously, that the progressive force which had inspired revolutionary France would similarly generate a 'natural' cessation of the slave trade:

> My sorrow, having laid this faith to heart,
> That if France prospered good men would not long
> Pay fruitless worship to humanity,

And this most rotten branch of human shame
(Object, as seemed, of a superfluous pains)
Would fall together with its parent tree.[116]

The poet's faith in 'natural progression' underscores his allegiance to gradual rather than immediate abolition and moreover, indicates his reluctance to consider colonial insurrection as an appropriate model of sociopolitical reform. Likewise, his reference to the 'natural' decay of Milton's 'rotten tree' in *Paradise Lost*, offers an inherently western epistemological response to the 'problem' of the trade, an image which attempts to conceal Britain's past role in nurturing the trade and which fails to acknowledge the insurrectionist efforts of the slaves themselves. By positing the French Revolution as a precursor *to* rather than descendant *of* the liberationist ideology promoted by abolitionists (and slaves), Wordsworth's poem demonstrates a shift away from antislavery activities within the colonies (the non-west) and focuses instead upon the revolutions of the western world. This shift suggests a reluctance to consider the parasitic relation between Great Britain and the colonies and reverses the proposals set out in the pro-rebellion pamphlet by James Stephen, Wilberforce's brother-in-law.[117] Whereas the 1789 revolution in France, despite the poet's subsequent disappointment, could still be celebrated as a praiseworthy event, references to the slave insurrections in St Domingue (1791), Jamaica (1795–1796), Grenada (1795–1797) and Virginia (1800) were carefully excluded from his text and its subsequent revisions.

According to Mary Jacobus, Wordsworth's silence about the material conditions upon which his poems and his culture were ultimately founded, indicate the poet's endeavour to maintain the 'fictive representation of the providentially self-shaped mind' within the autobiographical project.[118] This silence may also have been connected to the colonial activities undertaken by the poet's own relatives and the material benefits received by him from participants in the slave trade. In a letter to Jane Pollard of 28 December 1788, Dorothy Wordsworth noted that her brother, John, had embarked on a trip to Barbados, a fact reiterated in her letter of 27 January 1789.[119] Again, in January 1790, Dorothy noted John's involvement in the famous East India Company and his impending voyage to either America or the West Indies.[120] In July 1795, it was agreed that Wordsworth should become a non-paying tenant of Racedown Lodge, a house in North Devon which was owned by the wealthy Bristol merchant and sugar plantation owner, John Pretor Pinney.[121] And according to Dorothy's letter of 1808, another of Wordsworth's relatives, Henry Hutchinson, had been captured whilst travelling on a slave ship.[122] Not surprisingly therefore, Book 12 of Wordsworth's *Prelude* dismissed Adam Smith's *Inquiry into the Nature and Causes of the Wealth of Nations* (1776) as a work of 'utter hollowness', an example of 'plans without thought' founded upon 'false thought and false philosophy'.[123] His vehement rejection of Smith's critique of colonial slavery on sociopolitical and economic terms suggests in particular that his concealment of abolitionist discourse and his reluctance to partake in abolitionist activities stemmed from a complex web of personal loyalties and competitive creativity. The poet's resolute detachment from abolitionism is even more intriguing when one considers that during the composition and subsequent revisions of the *Prelude*, Wordsworth had become close friends with both Coleridge and Thomas Clarkson, the co-founder of the Abolition Society and the author of *The History of the Rise, Progress and Accomplishment of the Abolition of the African Slave Trade* (1808).[124]

This process of 'self-erasure' from abolitionist dialogue is most revealing in Wordsworth's sonnet, 'To Thomas Clarkson, on the Final Passing of the Bill for the Abolition of the Slave Trade, March 1807'. In this poem, the poet presents an egotistical trope of (personal and collective) self-referencing which strategically endeavours to override both Clarkson's success and the issue of slavery *per se*.[125] Hence when Wordsworth refers to Clarkson's parliamentary successes, the latter's achievements are conveniently mapped on to an image of national victory which duplicates images of the poet's own triumphant ascent, described in the (unpublished at this time) *Prelude*: 'CLARKSON! It was an obstinate hill to climb'.[126] In addition, the poet's response to Clarkson's concern for L'Ouverture's relatives, the three black exiles – Madame Christophe and her daughters – generates a satirical, explicitly racist version of Ben Jonson's sonnet, 'Queen and Huntress, Chaste and Fair' which plays, condescendingly and immaturely, upon concepts of enlightenment and excessive black sexuality:

> Queen and Negress chaste and fair!
>
> Shine for Clarkson's pure delight
> Negro Princess, Ebon Bright!
>
> Hayti's shining Queen was made
> To illumine Playford Hall
> Bless it then with constant light
> Negress excellently bright![127]

Wordsworth's attitude towards abolitionism suggests a disturbingly ambivalent stance, problematised by familial obligation and influenced by the poet's reluctance to accept antislavery ideologies based on concepts of black (spiritual and physical) equality. For him, the schemas of self-determination and 'imaginative' liberation presented within his own autobiographical texts were not interchangeable with the slaves' demands for political emancipation; nor did he envisage that England's responsibility to its subjects necessitated its participation in any emancipatory role. In this respect, Wordsworth's attitude towards slavery was very different from that of other first generation poets and artists, most especially William Blake.[128] Nearly three decades after the composition of Wordsworth's sonnet to Clarkson, in a letter to Benjamin Dockray (25 April 1833), Wordsworth's conservatism was confirmed by his criticism of the British public's endeavours to bring about an end of the slave trade. In this letter, the poet pledged his support for the rights and powers of the plantocrats and for what he considered the permanent and 'unalterable' nature of English law:

> Fanaticism is the disease of these times as much or more than of any other; fanaticism is set, as it has always been, whether moral, religious, or political, upon attainment of its ends with disregard of the means. In this question there are *three* parties, – the slave, the slaveowner and the British people ... *But by no means does it follow*, from this ... that the *third* party, the people of England, who through their legislature have sanctioned and even encouraged slavery, *have a right to interfere for its destruction* by a sweeping measure, of which an equivalent to the owner makes no part. This course appears to me unfeeling and unjust.[129]

In the same letter, the poet declared that although he believed that the principle of slavery was indeed 'monstrous', it was not, according to him, 'in itself' or 'under all circumstances' to be deplored. Wordsworth's attempted isolation from the abolition movement was similarly indicated when, in a letter to Benjamin Haydon of 10 September 1840, he identified demands for emancipation on socioeconomic (as Smith had done) rather than moral terms: 'Tho' from the first I took a lively interest in the Abolition of Slavery ... I was too little a Man of business to have an active part in the Work'.[130]

WILLIAM BLAKE: SPIRITUALISM AND ABOLITIONISM

William Blake's tripartite position as a key Romantic artist and poet, as a perceptive critic of colonialist and slave ideology, and as an adamant proponent of the value of the spiritual world confirms his stature in the development of spiritual discourse and abolitionist polemic. Moreover, his expansion of the lineaments of physical, psychological and sexual enslavement presents sophisticated explorations of the complex configurations of individual and national identity, sexuality and subjectivity. Born the son of a London shopkeeper in November 1757, William Blake's initial apprenticeship as an engraver to James Basire was followed by a studentship at the Royal Academy, which began in October 1779 under the tutelage of George Michael Moser, its keeper. In 1791, Joseph Johnson, patron to William Cowper and publisher of Mary Scott's *The Female Advocate* (1774), Stedman's *Narrative, of a Five Year's Expedition* (1796) (see Chapter 4 below) and William Wordsworth's *Descriptive Sketches* (1793), agreed to publish Mary

Wollstonecraft's *Original Stories from Real Life: With Conversations Calculated to Regulate the Affections, and Form the Mind to Truth and Goodness* (1791), which included six illustrations by Blake that Johnson had commissioned.[131] In addition to Blake's connection with the writings of Coleridge, Wordsworth and Wollstonecraft, it is probable that he had direct knowledge of the works of African writers then living in London. As Lauren Henry and Paul Edwards note, Blake was a good friend of the painter Richard Cosway. Cosway's house servant was the former slave, Ottobah Cugoano (a member of the Fanti people), who published his abolitionist text, *Thoughts and Sentiments on the Evil and Wicked Traffic of the Slavery and Commerce of the Human Species* in 1787.[132] It is possible therefore, that Blake had direct contact with Cugoano, or even his friend Gronniosaw (another former slave – see Chapter 6 below), or at least had been introduced to their narratives by the Cosway household.[133]

In 1787, after the death of his brother, aged nineteen, Blake claimed to see his brother's spirit rise to heaven, a spirit which he later claimed revealed a method of illuminated printing to him in a dream:

> Thirteen years ago. I lost a brother & with his spirit I converse daily & hourly in the Spirit. & See him in my remembrance in the regions of my Imagination. I hear his advice & even now write from his Dictate – Forgive me for expressing to you my Enthusiasm which I wish all to partake of Since it is to me a Source of Immortal Joy even in this world by it I am the companion of Angels.[134]

Blake's elaboration upon the language of dissenting Protestantism, as advanced by the evangelicals John Wesley and George Whitefield, was in part influenced by the visionary accounts of the mystic theologian Emmanuel Swedenborg (1688–1772). In 1789, Blake and his wife Catherine became members of the Great Eastcheap Swedenborg Society in London. Inspired by Swedenborg's belief in the spiritual symbolism of the material world and his corresponding interpretation of the Bible, Blake's poetical and visual compositions redefined the church as a form of spiritual wisdom. Likewise, his letters and prophetic books presented explorations and illuminations of symbolic insight predicated upon individualist mythology.[135] According to Swedenborg, the world of spirits was neither a form of heaven nor hell; rather it was 'a middle place or state between both; for thither man first comes after death'.[136] Swedenborg had defined the spiritual world as 'the vision of God', a state which he believed the biblical prophets had access to.[137] Blake's annotations to Swedenborg's *Wisdom of Angels Concerning Divine Love and Divine Wisdom*, attested to their mutual belief in spiritual wisdom:

> [Swedenborg] Hence it may appear, that Man from a *merely natural* Idea cannot comprehend that the Divine is every where, and yet not

in Space; and yet that Angels and Spirits clearly comprehend this;
consequently *that Man also may*, if so be he will admit something of
Spiritual Light into his Thought;
[Blake] *Observe the distinction here between Natural & Spiritual as seen
by Man* . . . [Swedenborg] The Negation of God constitutes Hell, and
in the Christian World the Negation of the Lord's Divinity.
[Blake] *the Negation of the Poetic Genius.*[138]

In his letter to Thomas Butts of 25 April 1803, Blake celebrated his return to
London from Felpham in Sussex, where he had taken up residence in 1800,
in terms of the spiritual freedom it provided: there he believed he could pursue
his visionary studies 'unannoyed', converse with his friends in Eternity and 'See
Visions, Dream Dreams, & prophecy & speak Parables unobserv'd & at liberty
from the Doubts of other Mortals'.[139] On 11 December 1805 Blake wrote in
similarly spiritual terms to William Hayley, thanking him for his support
during what he described as 'the Darkest Years that ever Mortal Sufferd':

> I speak of Spiritual Things. Not of Natural. Of Things known only
> to Myself & to Spirits Good & Evil. but Not Known to Men on
> Earth. It is the passage thro these Three Years that has brought me
> into my Present State. & *I know* that if I had not been with You
> I must have Perish'd – Those Dangers are now Passed & I can see
> them beneath my feet It will not be long before I shall be able to
> present the full history of my Spiritual Sufferings to the Dwellers
> upon Earth. & of the Spiritual Victories obtained for me by my
> Friends.[140]

In addition to the prophetic writings of Swedenborg, the work of the
sixteenth-century German cobbler and mystic, Jacob Boehme, had an even
greater influence upon Blake's thinking. In particular, Boehme's work insti-
gated Blake's subsequent reexamination and critique of Swedenborg's
doctrines, most especially his condemnation of Swedenborg's belief in
predestination. Boehme's initial influence upon Blake can most easily be
detected in two illustrated prints created in 1788 – 'There is No Natural
Religion' and 'All Religions are One' – texts which denounced the failings
of the established church and the invidious doctrine of rationalism, and
advocated instead a belief in the 'Poetic or Prophetic character':

> Conclusion. If it were not for the Poetic or Prophetic character, the
> Philosophic & Experimental would soon be at the ratio of all things
> & stand still, unable to do other than repeat the same dull round
> over again.
> Application. He who sees the Infinite in all things sees God. He who
> sees the Ratio only sees himself only.[141]

Blake's employment and systematic revision of the symbolic and mystical schemas advocated by Swedenborg and Boehme, present constantly shifting narratives which resist chronology and thereby reflect eternal states of visionary transformation. At once unsettling, episodic and disjunctive, Blake's prophetic writings demand an active, visionary mode of perception and readership. This ambiguity and instability reflect the subversive nature of Blake's work, as it both verifies and undermines preconceptions brought to it by its readers.

Subtitled 'The Voice of One Crying in the Wilderness', Blake's 'All Religions are One' (1788) dissolved the boundaries between religious and cultural differences and located the origins of spiritual and prophetic illumination within man himself. According to Blake, the Poetic Genius was the 'True Man', the source of all religions: 'The Religions of all Nations are derived from each Nations different reception of the Poetic Genius which is every where call'd the Spirit of Prophecy'.[142] For him, the doctrines of future reward prescribed by natural religion (deism) and the orthodox church, not only propounded a pernicious control of the individual but also implicated a denial of the eternal, spiritual world. Blake's prophetic stance hence pronounced a gospel of revolution which negated the traditional Christian dichotomy between body and soul. Consequently, Blake's *The Marriage of Heaven and Hell* (engraved *c.* 1790) promoted a balanced dependence upon spiritual and physical perception, a stance informed by Blake's belief in 'eternal delight' or energy:

(1) Man has no Body distinct from his Soul for that calld Body is a portion of Soul discerned by the five Senses. the chief inlets of Soul in this age.
(2) Energy is the only life and is from the Body and Reason is the bound or outward circumference of Energy.
(3) Energy is Eternal Delight.[143]

Fashioned ostensibly as a parody of Swedenborg's 'Memorable Relations' of his visions of Eternity, Blake's text preserved Swedenborg's concept of the Divine Humanity in which human form figured as a vital index of perfection. In an endeavour to restore 'energy' within a world dominated by Reason, Blake employed the figure of Satan as the representative of 'infernal wisdom' or energy:

Without Contraries is no progression. Attraction and Repulsion, Reason and Energy, Love and Hate, are necessary to Human existence . . . God is the passive that obeys Reason. Evil is the active springing from Energy.[144]

As this revised Satanic figure challenged the limits upon perception defined by reason, the 'Proverbs of Hell' reinstated the importance of impulse, imaginative creativity, sensual passion and vision:

> Prudence is a rich ugly maid courted by Incapacity.
> He who desires but acts not, breeds pestilence . . .
> The lust of the goat is the bounty of God . . .
> The nakedness of woman is the work of God.[145]

Furthermore, Blake's revision of Swedenborg's text traced the historical and psychological moment of segregation from God's existence and human experience ('Thus men forget that All deities reside in the human breast') and called for a reintegration of the divine with mankind.[146] Man's inclination to restrain imaginative vision and repress energy is seen by the poet as a contradiction of the prophets of Israel's prioritisation of the Poetic Genius as the 'first principle'. According to Blake, the restoration of infinity 'will come to pass by an improvement of sensual enjoyment', and it was this co-alignment of the sensual and the spiritual which distinguished Blake's work from the restrictions enforced by some of Wesley's successors.[147] As a text thoroughly opposed to the limitations of rationalism and empirical philosophy, Blake's *Marriage of Heaven and Hell* presented a gospel of unorthodox revolution, intense spirituality and imaginative impulse which identified the mind as an active spiritual agent, an expansive agent of consciousness of individuality which struggled against the oppressed or sealed condition of the rational man.

In the prophetic text, *Jerusalem: the Emanation of the Giant Albion* (printed in 1804), the poet recounts the development of the human consciousness from what he calls 'Eternal Death' (or what we call 'life') to authentic life in Eternity: 'Of the Sleep of Ulro! and of the passage through Eternal Death! and of the awaking to Eternal Life'.[148] Having rejected the imaginative realm signified by Jerusalem (the emanation of Albion), Albion falls into a spiritual stupor. Los, the personification of the imaginative spirit, struggles to resist Albion's perverted vision, yet he becomes afflicted by the imbalance in Albion and is separated from his emanation, Enitharmon.[149] Blake's poem locates the various efforts to reunite Albion with Jerusalem within a context of repressive moralistic and religious epistemologies: 'Jerusalem replied. I am an outcast: Albion is dead! I am left to the trampling foot & the spurning heel! A Harlot I am calld'.[150] Rebellion, embodied by the figures of Los and Vala, incorporates a declaration of self-assertion and revolt against forms of enslavement prescribed by the dominant culture: 'I know of no other Christianity and no other Gospel than the liberty both of body & mind to exercise the Divine Arts of Imagination'.[151] In Plate 52 (subtitled 'To the Deists') of this complex but beautiful poem, the true pathway towards

spiritual enlightenment, taken by the Methodists and the poet himself, is juxtaposed with the repressive regimes advocated by Voltaire and Rousseau:

> Deism, is the Worship of the God of this World by the means of
> what you call Natural Religion and Natural Philosophy, and
> of Natural Morality or Self-Righteousness, the Selfish Virtues of
> the Natural Heart. This was the Religion of the Pharisees who
> murderd Jesus. Deism is the same & ends in the same. Voltaire
> Rousseau Gibbon Hume. charge the Spiritually Religious with
> Hypocrisy! but how a Monk or a Methodist either, can be a
> Hypocrite: I cannot conceive . . . The Glory of Christianity is, To
> Conquer by Forgiveness. All the Destruction therefore, in Christian
> Europe has arisen from Deism, which is Natural Religion.[152]

Blake's defence of Whitefield in the section entitled 'To the Deists' at
the beginning of Chapter 3 of *Jerusalem* ('Foote in calling Whitefield,
Hypocrite: was himself one: for Whitefield pretended not to be holier than
others') is followed by a description of the exploitation of human resources
within the market economy reminiscent of accounts detailing the slaves'
transportation on to slave ships – 'We were carried away in 100s from
London . . . in ships clos'd up'.[153] Calling for the transformative and inspirational power which Los possesses and which the poet believes will achieve
a restoration of Albion: 'Teach me, O Holy Spirit, the Testimony of Jesus',
the concluding chapter of *Jerusalem* addresses those Christians who have
rejected the tyrannies of institutional and natural religion and celebrates
Albion's forthcoming spiritual awakening:

> Awake! Awake Jerusalem! O lovely Emanation of Albion
> Awake and overspread all Nations as in Ancient Time
> For lo! the Night of Death is past and the Eternal Day
> Appears upon our hills.[154]

Blake's poem 'The Little Black Boy' in *Songs of Innocence and Experience*,
composed as early as 1789 (the same year that he joined the Swedenborg
Society) confronts colonial ideology and cultural difference within a simple
yet effective spiritual framework:

> My mother bore me in the southern wild,
> And I am black, but O! my soul is white;
> White as an angel is the English child:
> But I am black as if bereav'd of light . . .
>
> Thus did my mother say and kissed me,
> And thus I say to the little English boy.

When I from black and he from white cloud free,
And round the tent of God like lambs we joy:

I'll shade him from the heat till he can bear,
To lean in joy upon our fathers knee.
And then I'll stand and stroke his silver hair,
And be like him and will then love me.[155]

By drawing parallels between black and white, lamb and Christ, Blake's poem counters pro-slavery discourse and introduces a poignant moment between mother and son, tenderness alongside a clear articulation of racial and spiritual equality. Anne Mellor has argued that Blake's poem affirms the ideological construction of the African as one who benefits from Christianity, but as his antagonistic relationship with institutionalised religion confirms, Blake's concept of Christianity is radically individual.[156]

Between 1788 and 1789, John Caspar Lavater, the lifelong friend of Henri Fuseli, published his *Essays on Physiognomy*, a work which examined the relationship between cranial proportion and character. One edition of Lavater's work contained four plates which were engraved by Blake and attest to an encounter with the science of physiognomy which must have challenged Blake's belief in racial equality. Less than a year later, Blake engraved sixteen plates for John Stedman's *Narrative of a Five Years' Expedition* (1790), described in Chapter 4 below. Blake's engravings included disturbing illustrations of colonial and slave ideology, such as his 'Execution of Breaking on the Rack' and The Flagellation of a Female Samboe Slave', which sought to replace typical depictions of black inferiority and sexual excess with unsettling representations of sufferings endured under the command of white masters. Given the sociopolitical context of the time and the fact that Stedman's text does not negate the necessity of the slave trade nor criticise the violent suppression of a slave insurrection in Dutch Guiana, Blake's illustrations were radically uncompromising. Designed to shock and educate, the intentions behind Blake's visual supplements to and departures from Stedman's *Narrative* were clearly presented at a time when other abolitionist texts remained cautious and circumspect in their approach. As Richard and Sally Price have noted, during the mid-1790s the relationship between Stedman and Blake was fairly close: the two corresponded, dined and sent gifts to each other frequently.[157] Yet Stedman adamantly refused to sign abolition petitions and when he left for Holland he did not free his personal slave but transferred him to another owner.[158] Conversely, Blake's financial contribution of £10 (approximately £1000 in today's terms), despite his impecuniosity, to the London Abolition Society demonstrated his antipathy toward slave ideology. Under Stedman's instructions, Blake engraved an emblematic representation of the interdependence between Africa, America and Europe. In this revised version of the 'Three Graces', entitled 'Europe Supported by Africa and America', Europe, a white female decorated in pearls, stands supported by her colonially and racially oppressed 'sisters', the enslaved African and the marginalised native American. In Blake's hands, the symbol of harmonious colonial venture and intercultural exchange becomes a sinister emblem of debasement and exclusion.[159]

Significantly influenced by Mary Wollstonecraft's *A Vindication of the Rights of Woman* published the previous year (see above), Blake's *Visions of the Daughters of Albion* (1793) questions the permanency of existing power structures. In its attack against the evils of slavery, sexual inequality, colonial expansionism and repressive cults of virginity, Blake's poem examines the conditions of psychological, sexual and racial enslavement prescribed by the ideologies and practices of mystery, idolatry and cultural superiority: 'Stampt with my signet are the swarthy children of the sun: / They are obedient, they resist not, they obey the scourge'.[160] As David Erdman notes, love and slavery prove to be the 'two poles' guiding the axis of the poem.[161] The unresolved debate between Oothoon, Theotormon and Bromion provides a poetic counterpart to the parliamentary and editorial debates of 1789–1793 which centred upon the Bill for the Abolition of the Slave Trade. Like those gradual reformists who deplored the slave trade but could not subscribe to an open condemnation of slavery itself, Theotormon remains locked in a psychological impasse. On the poem's frontispiece, Oothoon (the representative of liberty – 'the soft soul of America') is enveloped by the restraining manacles of Bromion, rapist and slaver, whilst Theotormon's 'jealous waters' form a chain 'round the adulterate pair, bound back to back in Bromion's caves':

> The voice of slaves beneath the sun,
> and children bought with money.
> That shiver in religious caves beneath the burning fires
> Of lust, that belch incessant from the summits of the earth
> Oothoon weeps not: she cannot weep! her tears are locked up;
> But she can howl incessant writhing her soft snowy limbs.[162]

In Plate 4 Oothoon soars upwards but is held down by a chain as Theotormon sits rigidly, his hands over his face, 'shut up in cold despair', degraded by his misguided ethics:

> The moment of desire! the moment of desire! The virgin
> That pines for man; shall awaken her womb to enormous joys
> In the secret shadows of her chamber; the youth shut up from
> The lustful joy, shall forget to generate, & create an amorous image
> In the shadows of his curtains and in the folds of his silent pillow.[163]

Blake's rendition of Theotormon's psychological impasse exposes one of the most significant flaws in the British constitution. In the light of French revolutionary idealism, the defeat of the Bill in Parliament under pressure from the anti-Jacobin attacks staged by Edmund Burke, Lord Abingdon and various slave agents, determined Britain's continuing involvement in colonial and racial slavery at a deplorable and fundamentally regressive stage. Likewise, the announcement in the *London Chronicle* of February 2, 1792 which disassociated the Abolition Society from any desire to bring about 'the Emancipation of the Negroes in the British Colonies' and claimed instead that the Society sought merely to bring an end to the 'trade of the slaves', highlighted the paralysis at the heart of Britain's parliamentary and 'moral' centre. As a fused embodiment of America, Africa and Europe, Oothoon coalesces with, yet also departs from the ideological parameters prescribed by Wollstonecraft and Stedman. Theotormon's love for the 'gentle' Oothoon appears to be a coded reference to Stedman's account of his love for the slave 'Joanna'.[164] However, the fact that Oothoon is not freed, nor able to articulate her anger, nor transform her visions into realities suggests that Blake was presenting an intertextual critique of Wollstonecraft's rationalised arguments for female equality. For Blake, colonial ideology, possessive morality and sexual oppression were all fundamental forms of the pernicious enslavement which corrupted the visionary potential of England.[165]

Blake's concern with physical and spiritual enslavement is thus developed into a sophisticated exploration of psychological enslavement and repression. His extension of the spiritual legacy of radical dissenting Protestantism is reworked on his own terms to provide an all-embracing philosophy of redemption and equality for mankind. Advocating his belief in the potential harmony of mind, body and spirit within all individuals, Blake propounds his conviction in man's ability to experience imaginative vision and achieve eternal life. With radical and absolute egalitarianism, Blake celebrates a state of being in which the evils of cultural difference, based on the injustices of racism, the subordination of women and the pernicious effects of materialism and power abuse, are rejected. As a political activist, unafraid to illustrate the brutality and degradation endured by slaves, as a free thinker and as a radical visionary, Blake avoids the strictures of moral and Christian polemic, beyond the confines of material wealth and concepts of ownership towards a state of intense spiritualism. Unfettered by religious doctrine or utilitarian ethics, Blake occupies a crucial position within the development of the discourse of the spirit. Yet Blake's concern with the spiritual is not at the expense of the physical – as his sensual celebration of the human body demonstrates. Whilst Blake's rejection of eighteenth-century rationalist and empiricist epistemology distinguishes him from the line of argument propounded by Mary Wollstonecraft, his artistic and poetic enjoyment of the physical links his work with that of the Scotsman, John Stedman (discussed below).

In their complex interaction with the language of radical dissenting Protestantism and abolitionist demands prevalent in England at the time, the poetical works by Coleridge, Wordsworth and Blake reveal the transient and protean nature of spiritual discourse and its compelling dynamics of (self-)liberation from servitude. A similar appropriation and transformation of this mercurial discourse was likewise articulated both within the narratives by ex-slaves, published contemporaneously during the late eighteenth and early nineteenth century, and within Stedman's semi-autobiographical account of the insurrectionist negroes in Surinam. Chronologically, Stedman's *Narrative of a Five Years' Expedition against the Revolted Negroes of Surinam* (1790) predates some of the earlier work by the Romantic poets examined above. Its place within this discussion reflects its significant departure from traditional forms of spiritual autobiography and its status as a pivotal text which describes an important translation of the discourse of the spirit (and indeed, the corresponding confessional genre) into a schema of *physical*, rather than purely spiritual, redemption. In so doing, Stedman's text corresponds to some of the most important strategic motives behind the slave narratives – emancipation from slavery and liberation from theories of racial difference and inferiority, which had been used to justify and continue the abhorrent trade. In its account of morganatic marriage Stedman's text presents an interesting parallel with Blake's ideas of sexual freedom, yet extends this to provide an enigmatic autobiographical form of colonial narrative which demonstrates the problematics involved in interracial (sexual) encounters between European men and African women. As a consequence, Stedman's text offers a significant narrative of cross-cultural contact and thereby provides a fitting precursor to the discussion in the subsequent chapters of this book of the 'creolised' schema contained within the slave narratives and the legislative prohibitions of miscegenation in the eighteenth century.

Notes

1 For a comprehensive overview of the development of Romantic Studies see Marilyn Butler, *Romantics, Rebels and Reactionaries: English Literature and Its Background, 1766–1830* (Oxford: Oxford University Press, 1981); Stephen Copley and John Whale, eds, *Beyond Romanticism: New Approaches to Texts and Contexts, 1780–1832* (London: Routledge, 1992); Paul de Man, *Blindness and Insight: Essays on the Rhetoric of Contemporary Criticism* (New York: Oxford University Press, 1971); *idem, The Rhetoric of Romanticism* (New York: Columbia University Press, 1984).

2 Mary Favret and Nicola Watson, eds, *At the Limits of Romanticism: Essays in Cultural, Feminist, and Materialist Criticism* (Bloomington: Indiana University Press, 1994) 3.

3 Mary Jacobus, *Romanticism, Writing and Sexual Difference: Essays on the 'Prelude'* (Oxford: Clarendon Press, 1989) 69–97; Marjorie Levinson, *Keats' Life of Allegory: The Origins of a Style* (Oxford: Basil Blackwell, 1988); *idem, Romanticism and Feminism* (Bloomington: Indiana University Press, 1988); Ann Mellor, *Romanticism and Gender* (London: Routledge, 1993); Helen Vendler, *The Odes of John Keats* (Cambridge, Mass.: Harvard University Press, 1983).

4 Favret and Mary Watson, *At the Limits of Romanticism*.

5 Jerome McGann, *The Romantic Ideology: A Critical Investigation* (Chicago: Chicago University Press, 1983).

6 Alan Richardson and Sonia Hofkosh, eds, *Romanticism, Race, and Imperial Culture* (Bloomington: Indiana University Press, 1996) and Tim Fulford and Peter Kitson, eds, *Romanticism and Colonialism* (Cambridge: Cambridge University Press, 1998).

7 In her study, *Romanticism, Writing and Sexual Difference*, Jacobus identified Wordsworth's *Prelude* as a site of historical repression and argued that the invisible relationship between Wordsworth's poem, Newton's conversion and slavery marked one of the most crucial chapters in eighteenth-century economic history: see 69–97.

8 Lauren Henry, 'Sunshine and Shady Groves: What Blake's "Little Black Boy" Learned from African Writers', *Romanticism and Colonialism*, ed. Fulford and Kitson, 67–86, 70–1.

9 Wordsworth and Coleridge, *Lyrical Ballads with a Few Other Poems* (London, 1800).

10 Wordsworth, *The Prelude, 1799, 1805, 1850: Authoritative Texts, Context and Reception, Recent Critical Essays*, ed. Jonathan Wordsworth, M. H. Abrams and Stephen Gill (New York: Norton, 1979) x–xi. Likewise, William Blake sold very little of his work and his exhibitions were ill-attended.

11 Samuel Taylor Coleridge, *The Collected Letters of Samuel Taylor Coleridge*, ed. E. L. Griggs, 6 vols. (Oxford: Clarendon Press, 1956–1971) vol. ii, 790–801.

12 M. H. Abrams, ed., *Norton Anthology of English Literature*, 2 vols. (London: Norton, 1993) vol. ii, 18.

13 See Lauren Henry, 'Sunshine and Shady Groves', 69.

14 Mary Wollstonecraft, *A Vindication of the Rights of Men, in a Letter to the Right Honourable Edmund Burke Occasioned by His 'Reflections of the Revolutions in France'* (London, 1790) 71.

15 Anne Mellor, *Romanticism and Gender*, 66–7.

16 Wollstonecraft, *Rights of Men*, 121–2.

17 Moira Ferguson, *Subject to Others: British Women Writers and Colonial Slavery, 1670–1834* (London: Routledge, 1992) 188.

18 Wollstonecraft, *Rights of Men*, 121–2.

19 William Godwin, *An Enquiry Concerning Political Justice and Its Influence on General Virtue and Happiness*, 2 vols. (London, 1793).

20 Mary Wollstonecraft, *A Vindication of the Rights of Woman: With Strictures on Political and Moral Subjects* (London, 1792).

21 *Ibid.*, x–xi.

22 Anne Mellor, 'Am I Not a Woman, and a Sister?': Slavery, Romanticism, and Gender', *Romanticism, Race, and Imperial Culture*, ed. Richardson and Hofkosh, 311–329.

23 Katherine Rogers, *Feminism in Eighteenth Century England* (Sussex: Harvester Press, 1982).

24 Wollstonecraft, *Rights of Woman*, 73.

25 *Ibid.*, 90.

26 Mellor, 'Am I Not a Woman?', 318.

27 Wollstonecraft, *Rights of Woman*, 92.

28 Mary Wollstonecraft, *The Works of Mary Wollstonecraft*, ed. Janet Todd and Marilyn Butler, 7 vols. (London: William Pickering, 1989) vol. vi, 234.

29 Moses Roper, *A Narrative of the Adventures and Escape of Moses Roper, from American Slavery*, ed. Revd T. Price (London: Darton, Harvey and Darton,

1837); Mary Prince, *The History of Mary Prince, a West Indian Slave As Related by Herself with a Supplement by the Editor to Which is Added, the Narrative of Asa-Asa, a Captured African*, ed. T. Pringle (London: Westley and Davis, 1831).

30 Wollstonecraft, *The Works of Mary Wollstonecraft*, vol. vii, 100–1.

31 Coleridge, *Lectures 1795 on Politics and Religion*, ed. Lewis Patton and Peter Mann (London: Routledge and Kegan Paul, 1971) 231–52; 'On the Slave Trade', *The Watchman*, ed. Lewis Patton (London: Routledge and Kegan Paul, 1970) 130–140. These editions of Coleridge's *Lectures 1795* and *The Watchman* form volumes one and two of *The Collected Works of Samuel Taylor Coleridge*, 6 vols., ed. Kathleen Coburn (London: Routledge and Kegan Paul, 1983).

32 Deirdre Coleman, 'Conspicuous Consumption: White Abolitionism and English Women's Protest Writing in the 1790s', *English Literary History* 61 (1994): 342.

33 See Eric Williams, *Capitalism and Slavery* (1945; London: Andre Deutsch, 1964) 195. Coleridge's poem also referred to the slaves' epistemological belief in the world of the spirits.

34 Coleridge, *Lectures 1795*, 235, n.3, 240, n.4.

35 Thomas Clarkson, *An Essay on the Implicity of the African Slave Trade in Two Parts*, 2 vols. (London, 1788) 110.

36 Ferguson, *Subject to Others*, 127, 129. Mary Scott, *The Female Advocate: A Poem Occasioned by Reading Mr. Duncombe's Feminead* (London: Joseph Johnson, 1774); Mary Deverell, *Miscellanies in Prose and Verse, Mostly Written in the epistolary Style*, 2 vols. (London, 1781).

37 Carl Bernhard Wadstrom, *An Essay on Colonisation, Particularly Applied to the Western Coast of Africa, with Some Free Thoughts on Cultivation and Commerce* (London, 1794) 3, 4.

38 *Ibid.*, 4, 5.

39 Coleridge, *Lecture on the Slave Trade*, 236.

40 *Ibid.*, 235.

41 Coleman, 'Conspicuous Consumption', 344.

42 David Hartley, *Observations on Man* (London, 1749).

43 Coleridge, *Lecture on the Slave Trade*, 235.

44 *Ibid.*, 235; my emphases except the word 'real'. Mark Akenside, *The Pleasures of Imagination. A Poem in Three Books*, 3rd edn. (London, 1744); *The Spectator*, 21 June 1712. William Hazlitt defined Coleridge's discourse as the type of 'angelic wings': 'He was the first poet I ever knew . . . His genius at that time had angelic wings, and fed on manna. He talked on for ever . . . And shall I, who heeded him then, listen to him now? Not I! . . . That spell is broke; that time is gone for ever'. Hazlitt, 'Lectures on the English Poets', *The Complete Works of William Hazlitt*, ed. P. P. Howe, 21 vols. (London: J. M. Dent, 1930–1934) vol. v, 167.

45 Coleridge, *Lecture on the Slave Trade*, 238.

46 *Ibid.*, 233.

47 *Ibid.*, 241; my emphases.

48 I am grateful to Alan Richardson for highlighting the correspondence between these poems.

49 Southey, 'The Sailor Who Had Served in the Slave Trade', *Poems, by Robert Southey* (London: Longman and Rees, 1799) 103–8, lines 101–4.

50 Southey was also the author of *The Life of Wesley*. See Robert Southey, *The Minor Poems of Robert Southey*, 3 vols. (London: Longman, Hurst, Rees, Orme and Brown, 1823).

51 See James Walvin, *Black Ivory: A History of Black Slavery* (London: Harper Collins, 1992) 16–22; Fryer, *Staying Power: The History of Black People in Britain* (London: Pluto Press, 1984) 127–30; Potkay and Burr, eds, *Black Atlantic Writers of the Eighteenth Century: Living the New Exodus in England and America* (Basingstoke: Macmillan, 1995) 165; Gilroy, *Small Acts: Thoughts on the Politics of Black Cultures* (London: Serpent's Tail, 1993) 81–5.

52 See also Turner's painting 'Slavers Throwing Overboard the Dead and Dying: Typhoon Coming On' (1840).

53 William Fox, *A Short Account of the African Slave Trade, and an Address to the People of Great Britain on the Propriety of Abstaining from West Indian Sugar and Rum* (Sevenoaks, 1791). Coleridge, *Lecture on the Slave Trade*, 248–9.

54 Coleridge, *Lecture on the Slave Trade*, 251; my emphasis.

55 Coleridge, *Collected Letters*, vol. i, 302.

56 George Whalley, *The Bristol Library Borrowings of Southey and Coleridge, 1793–1798* (London: The Bibliographical Society, 1949) 119.

57 *The Gospel Magazine and Theological Review* (1796) vol. 1, i; 'The Memoirs of the Life of John James Claude', *The Gospel Magazine* vol. 1, 152–7; 'The Remarkable Passages in the Life of Mr Vavasor Powel, Minister of the Gospel in Wales, Written by Himself', *The Gospel Magazine* vol. 1, 217–21; and 'The Singular Experience and Great Sufferings of Mrs Agnes', *The Gospel Magazine* vol. 1, 297–305.

58 Robert Woolman, *A Journal of the Life, Gospel Labours, and Christian Experience of that Faithful Minister of Jesus Christ, John Woolman, to Which Are Added His Works* (Dublin, 1776) v, 8, 15.

59 John Woolman, *Some Considerations on the Keeping of Negroes* (Philadelphia, 1754) included in *A Journal of the Life*, 251–325; 277.

60 John Woolman, *Some Considerations*, 305.

61 Indeed, Coleridge's later project, *Biographia Literaria* (1817) presented an enigmatic form of autobiographical self-examination. See Coleridge, *Biographia Literaria: Or, Biographical Sketches of My Literary Life and Opinions*, ed. James Engell and W. Jackson Bate, 2 vols. (Princeton: Princeton University Press, 1983).

62 Richard Brantley, *Wordsworth's 'Natural Methodism'* (New Haven: Yale University Press, 1975) 38.

63 See Frank Coleridge's suicide note, 19 Dec. 1791 and Coleridge, *Collected Letters*, vol. i, 63, 68.

64 Bernard Martin, *The Ancient Mariner and the Authentic Narrative* (London: Heinemann, 1949) 37–8.

65 *Ibid.*, 37.

66 For more on Coleridge's relation with the Quakers see Deirdre Coleman, *Coleridge and the Friend, 1809–1810* (Oxford: Clarendon Press, 1988).

67 For further discussion of these poems see Lucy Newlyn's *Coleridge, Wordsworth and the Language of Allusion* (Oxford: Clarendon Press, 1986); Kathleen Wheeler, *The Creative Mind in Coleridge's Poetry* (London: Heinemann, 1981) and Kelvin Everest, *Coleridge's Secret Ministry: The Context of the Conversation Poems, 1795–1798* (Hassocks: Harvester Press, 1979).

68 Coleridge, 'The Eolian Harp', *Poetical Works*, ed. Ernest Hartley Coleridge (Oxford: Oxford University Press, 1969) 102, lines 44–8.

69 *Ibid.*, 101, lines 26–9.

70 Coleridge, 'This Lime-Tree Bower My Prison', *Poetical Works*, 178–9, lines 2–5.

71 *Ibid.*, 180, lines 43–5.

72 *Ibid.*, 180, lines 37–43.

73 See Newlyn, *Language of Allusion*, for an excellent discussion of Coleridge's and Wordsworth's exchange of ideas. In the intervening versions of Coleridge's poem, the addressee underwent several gender transformations, changing from Sara, William, then Edmund, and finally ending with the 'Lady' of the 1817 *Sybilline Leaves* version.

74 Coleridge, 'Letter to Sara', *Collected Letters*, vol. i, 790, line 23; vol. i, 790, line 34.

75 *Ibid.*, 791, lines 31–2, 42–3. I am grateful to Jonathan Wordsworth for his suggestions about this poem.

76 *Ibid.*, 791, lines 50–1; my emphasis.

77 *Ibid.*, 791, line 73. Coleridge had in fact been born in rural Devonshire (Ottery St Mary) but with the death of his father was sent to school at Christ's Hospital, London.

78 *Ibid.*, 793, lines 109–10; 792, lines 92–8.

79 *Ibid.*, 796, lines 236–8.

80 *Ibid.*, 796, line 242.

81 *Ibid.*, 793, line 136.

82 *Ibid.*, 798, lines 302–7.

83 *Ibid.*, 797, lines 296–8.

84 *Ibid.*, 798, lines 315–20; my emphases.

85 Rev. 21:3.

86 Coleridge, 'Letter to Sara', 798, lines 317–18.

87 *Song of Songs* 2:16, 3:1.

88 Meyer Howard Abrams, *Natural Supernaturalism: Tradition and Revolution in Romantic Literature* (London: Oxford University Press, 1971) 95–6; my emphasis.

89 Brantley, *Wordsworth's 'Natural Methodism'*, xi.

90 William Wilberforce, *A Practical View of the Prevailing Religious System of Professed Christians Contrasted with Real Christianity* (London, 1798); Wordsworth to Wilberforce, *The Letters of William and Dorothy Wordsworth: The Early Years, 1787–1805*, 2nd edn., ed. Chester Shaver; gen. ed. Kathleen Coburn, 10 vols. (Oxford: Clarendon Press, 1967) vol. i, 685.

91 Brantley, *Wordsworth's 'Natural Methodism'*, 15–20.

92 Dorothy Wordsworth to Jane Pollard, *Letters of William and Dorothy Wordsworth*, vol. i, 28.

93 Philip Doddridge, *The Family Expositor: Or, a Paraphrase and Version of the New Testament*, ed. J. Orton, 6 vols. (London, 1739–1756).

94 Brantley, *Wordsworth's 'Natural Methodism'*, 24; Doddridge, *Rise and Progress of Religion in the Soul: Illustrated in a Course of Serious and Practical Addresses* (London, 1745); Francis Wrangham, *Thirteen Practical Sermons: Founded upon Doddridge's 'Rise and Progress of Religion in the Soul'* (London: J. Mawman, 1800) 23, 26, 59: 'You must be fully aware of your guilt . . . It is no *small matter* to have transgressed the laws of your Maker . . . *To you is the word of salvation sent'*.

95 Dorothy Wordsworth to Jane Pollard (26 Jun. 1791), *Letters of William and Dorothy Wordsworth* vol. i, 54.

96 Dorothy Wordsworth to Jane Pollard (8 May 1792), *ibid.*, vol. i, 75. Dundas had strongly opposed Wilberforce's first Abolition Bill, 18 Apr. 1791.

97 Martin, *The Ancient Mariner*, 38; Newton *Authentic Narrative*, 82.

98 Cf. Brantley, *Wordsworth's 'Natural Methodism'*, 37–8; Jacobus, *Romanticism, Writing, and Sexual Difference*, 79–82; Duncan Wu, *Wordsworth's Reading, 1770–1799* (Cambridge: Cambridge University Press, 1993).

99 Wordsworth, 'MS JJ, October 1798', *The Prelude: 1799, 1805, 1850*, 487, lines 1–3, 5–6. All subsequent references will be from this edition.
100 Wordsworth, 'Prelude of 1805', 28, Book 1, lines 6–10, 16–19; my emphases.
101 *Ibid.*, 30, Book 1, lines 41–4.
102 *Ibid.*, 32, Book 1, lines 59–63.
103 *Ibid.*, 92, Book 3, line 28–9.
104 *Ibid.*, 233, Book 7, line 157; 262, Book 7, 661–2; 406, Book 10, line 878. See Jonathan Wordsworth, 'Versions of the Fall', *William Wordsworth: The Borders of Vision* (1982; Oxford: Clarendon Press, 1984) 231–78.
105 Wordsworth, 'Prelude of 1805', 306, Book 8, lines 763–4.
106 *Ibid.*, 460–2, Book 13, lines 39–43, 68–73.
107 See William Hazlitt, *Complete Works*, vol. v, 156, 163: 'Mr. Wordsworth is the most original poet now living . . . His powers have been mistaken by the age, nor does he understand them himself . . . He tolerates only what he himself creates . . . He see nothing but himself and the universe'.
108 Wordsworth, 'Prelude of 1805', 216, Book 6, lines 526–9.
109 *Ibid.*, 218, Book 6, lines 567–72.
110 Wordsworth, 'To Toussaint L'Ouverture', *Poetical Works*, ed. Ernest de Selincourt (Oxford University Press, 1969) 242–3. Although it first appeared in the *Morning Post*, 2 Feb. 1803, the poem was probably written between 1 and 29 Aug. 1801.
111 Robin Blackburn, *The Overthrow of Colonial Slavery, 1776–1848* (London: Verso, 1990) 163, 218, 240. For a more detailed account of the slave insurrection see C. L. R. James, *The Black Jacobins: Toussaint L'Ouverture and the San Domingo Revolution* (1938; London: Allison and Busby, 1980).
112 Marcus Rainsford, *An Historical Account of the Black Empire of Hayti: Comprehending a View of the Principal Transactions in the Revolution in Saint Domingo; With its Antient and Modern State* (London: James Cundee, 1805) 323–4; my emphases.
113 Joseph Addison, *The Spectator*, ed. Donald Bond, 5 vols. (Oxford: Clarendon Press, 1965) vol. iii, 537.
114 Wordsworth, 'The Prelude of 1805', 370, Book 10, line 217; 368, Book 10, lines 205–6.
115 Blackburn, *Overthrow of Colonial Slavery*, 144–6.
116 Wordsworth, 'The Prelude of 1805', 370, Book 10, lines 221–226.
117 Cited in Blackburn 252. See also James Stephen, *Crisis of the Sugar Colonies: Or, an Enquiry into the Objects and Probable Effects of the French Expedition to the West Indies and their Connection with the Colonial Interests of the British Empire to Which Are Subjoined, Sketches of a Plan for the Settling of the Vacant Lands of Trinidad* (London: L. J. Hatchard, 1802) 195–7; *The Opportunity: Or, Reasons for an Immediate Alliance with San Domingo* (London: C. Whittingham, 1804) 47.
118 Jacobus, *Romanticism, Writing and Sexual Difference*, 72, 74.
119 Dorothy Wordsworth to Jane Pollard, 27 Jan. 1789: 'My Brother John has set sail for Barbados. I hope, poor Lad! that he will be successful and happy, he is much delighted with the profession he has chosen. How we are squandered abroad!', *The Letters of William and Dorothy Wordsworth*, vol. i, 16, 21.
120 Dorothy Wordsworth to Jane Pollard (25–6 Jan. 1790), *The Letters of William and Dorothy Wordsworth*, vol. i, 25.
121 Stephen Gill, *William Wordsworth: A Life* (Oxford: Clarendon Press, 1989) 92.
122 Frank Prentice Rand, *Wordsworth's Mariner Brother* (Amherst, Mass.: Newell Press, 1966) 13–14.

123 Wordsworth, 'Prelude of 1805', 440, Book 12, lines 75–6.
124 Clarkson, *The History of the Rise, Progress and Accomplishment of the Abolition of the African Slave Trade by the British Parliament*, 2 vols. (London: Longman, Reas and Orine, 1808).
125 Wordsworth, 'To Thomas Clarkson, on the Final Passing of the Bill for the Abolition of the Slave Trade, March 1807', *Poetical Works*, 248.
126 Wordsworth, 'To Thomas Clarkson', 248, line 1.
127 Forlarin Shyllon, *Black People in Britain, 1555–1833* (London: Oxford University Press, 1977) 70–1.
128 William Blake, *The Complete Poetry and Prose of William Blake*, ed. David Erdman (New York: Doubleday, 1988) 665. In his annotations to Wordsworth's Poems of 1815, Blake commented: 'I see in Wordsworth the Natural Man rising up against the Spiritual Man Continually and then he is No Poet but a Heathen Philosopher at Enmity against all true Poetry or Inspiration'.
129 Wordsworth, *The Letters of William and Dorothy Wordsworth*, vol. v, 605–6.
130 *Ibid.*, vol. iv, 108–9. See also Norman Lewis Shelley, *The Abolitionist Movement in Sheffield* (Manchester: Manchester University Press, 1934) 15–17.
131 See Anne Mellor, 'Sex, Violence and Slavery: Blake and Wollstonecraft', *Huntington Library Quarterly* 58: 345–360.
132 Ottobah Cugoano, *Thoughts and Sentiments on the Evil and Wicked Traffic of the Slavery and Commerce of the Human Species, Humbly Submitted to the Inhabitants of Great Britain, by Ottobah Cugoano, a Native of Africa* (London, 1787).
133 Lauren Henry, 'Sunshine and Shady Groves', 83; Paul Edwards, *Unreconciled Strivings and Ironic Strategies: Three Afro-British Authors of the Georgian Era: Ignatius Sancho, Olaudah Equiano, Robert Wedderburn* (Edinburgh: Edinburgh University Press, 1992) 181.
134 Blake to William Hayley, 6 May 1800, *The Complete Poetry*, 705.
135 Mona Wilson, *The Life of William Blake* (Hertfordshire: Grenada, 1971) 56–8.
136 Emanuel Swedenborg, *New Jerusalem Tracts* tract 4, 1 in *The True Christian Religion*, 2 vols.
137 *Idem, The True Christian Religion, Containing the Universal Theology of the New Church, Foretold by the Lord* (New York, 1912) 146.
138 Blake, 'Annotations to Swedenborg's *Divine Love and Divine Wisdom*' (London, 1788) *The Complete Poetry*, 603. Blake's annotations are in italics.
139 Blake to Mr. Butts, 25 April 1803, *ibid.*, 728.
140 Blake to Hayley, 11 December 1805, *ibid.*, 767.
141 *Ibid.*, 3; Blake, 'There is No Natural Religion', *ibid.*, 3.
142 Blake, 'All Religions are One', *ibid.*, 1.
143 Blake, Plate 4, 'The Marriage of Heaven and Hell', *ibid.*, 34.
144 Blake, Plate 3, *ibid.*, 34–6.
145 Victor Paananen, *William Blake* (Boston, Mass.: Twayne, 1977), 50.
146 Blake, Plate 11, *ibid.*, 38.
147 *ibid.*, 39.
148 Blake, 'Jerusalem', 146; Paananen, *Blake*, 141.
149 Bernard Nesfield-Cookson, *William Blake: Prophet of Universal Brotherhood* (England: Crucible, 1987) 342.
150 Blake, 'Jerusalem', *The Complete Poetry*, 212.
151 *Ibid.*, 231.
152 *Ibid.*, 201.
153 *Ibid.*, 201.
154 Blake, 'Jerusalem', Plate 97, lines 1–4, *ibid.*, 256–8.

155 Blake, 'The Little Black Boy', *ibid.*, 9. Mellor, *Romanticism and Feminism*, 94.

156 Mellor, 'Sex, Violence, and Slavery: Blake and Wollstonecraft', 345–62; 360.

157 Richard and Sally Price, 'Introduction', *Stedman's Narrative*, xii. See also Hugh Honour, *Representations of Black People in Western Art* (Cambridge Mass.: Harvard University Press, 1989).

158 Joan Baum, *Mind-Forg'd Manacles: Slavery and the English Romantic Poets* (New Haven, Connecticut: Archun, 1994) n.35, 187.

159 Mellor argues that Blake's visual assimilation of the black female body to the classical western white body is either an attempt to 'humanise' the African or a reflection of his neoclassical artistic training. Mellor, 'Sex, Violence, and Slavery: Blake and Wollstonecraft', 358.

160 Blake, *Visions of the Daughters of Albion*, lines 21–2 *The Complete Poetry*, 46.

161 David Erdman, *Blake: Prophet Against Empire: A Poet's Interpretation of the History of His Own Times* (New Jersey: Princeton University Press, 1977) 228–30.

162 Blake, *Visions of the Daughters of Albion*, lines 8–12, *The Complete Poetry*, 46.

163 *Ibid.*, Plate 7, lines 3–7, 50.

164 Joan Baum, *Mind-Forg'd Manacles*, 14.

165 *Ibid.*, 228–30.

Part 5

SCIENCE, MEDICINE, AND ECO-CRITICISM

30

OF HEARTACHE AND HEAD INJURY: MINDS, BRAINS, AND THE SUBJECT OF *PERSUASION*

Alan Richardson

Source: *British Romanticism and the Science of the Mind* (Cambridge: Cambridge University Press, 2001), pp. 93–113, 205–8.

The intellectual attraction of the new, brain-based theories of mind for a poet coming of age around 1798 could only have been heightened by their distinctly avant-garde tinge. The brain science being disseminated throughout the 1790s in the writings, lectures, and laboratories of iconoclasts like Darwin, Beddoes, Thelwall, and the youthful Davy came charged with a Jacobin frisson, redolent of religious dissent and political radicalism, and inspiring accusations of dangerous skepticism at best, godless materialism at worst. Despite a growing climate of reaction, the "radical science" of the mind continues well into the early nineteenth century, reaching a crisis point with the Lawrence controversy in the late 1810s, when it moves "underground" to find oblique expression in the works of a new generation of avant-garde intellectuals typified by the Shelleys.[1] But at the same time, in a subtler but equally significant fashion, key tenets of the new psychology were seeping into the mainstream, helping to transform notions of subjectivity, of culture, and of character. Charles Bell gave the imprimatur of the scientific establishment and the aura of the Established Church to physiological conceptions of mind, esthetics, and human development that overlapped significantly with the ideas of radicals like Darwin and revolutionaries like Cabanis. The relentless critical attention devoted to Gall and Spurzheim in the major reviews guaranteed that at least the basic elements of the new brain-based psychologies were widely known; "no speculations have engaged more attention, or have more frequently afforded a topic for conversation," acidly remarks a reviewer in 1817, "since the time of Joanna Southcote."[2] Medical men in particular were avidly discussing, and selectively embracing, the innovative ideas and challenging findings of Galvani, Bell, and the craniologists.[3] New scholarship on the medical education of John Keats suggests that a number of "radical" scientific developments, including Gall and Spurzheim's new brain anatomy, had become part of the standard London medical curriculum by the time that Lawrence gave his outspoken lectures to the Royal College of Surgeons.[4]

The novel, too, was beginning to take up (and in some ways extend) the brain-based approaches to mind and personality being aired by the materialist–vitalist debates and popularized by the phrenology movement. Jane Austen is often thought of as a novelist working primarily from the empiricist standpoint of an experientially constructed subject, and a succession of critics have paid careful and rewarding attention to the education, socialization, and cultural predicaments of her heroines. In her last novel, *Persuasion*, however, Austen anticipates Victorian novelists in looking to biological and innate aspects of mind and character, in tune with and in some ways ahead of the brain science of her time. Moreover, Austen's famously innovative style for conveying the heroine's impressions in *Persuasion* speaks as much to a new psychological appreciation of unconscious mental life and embodied cognition as to a new esthetic mode for representing the flux of conscious experience.

DUCTILE MINDS, ORGANICAL BRAINS

The shift within Romantic-era discourses on mind and character from environmental to biological approaches to psychological behavior and subject-formation emerges most starkly, perhaps, in the changing views of William Godwin. In the 1790s, Godwin presents a rigorous and influential social constructivist account of mind, one obviously indebted to Locke and Hartley. The "actions and dispositions of mankind," he writes, are the "offspring of circumstances and events, and not of any original determination that they bring into the world"; "innate principles" and "original differences" of physiological "structure" have no role in shaping mind or character. Education in particular, and the effects of social and political life – institutions and ideologies – in general, become all-important in shaping and imprinting the mind's initially "ductile and yielding substance" for good or ill.[5] By 1831, however, in *Thoughts on Man*, Godwin has become convinced that "Human creatures are born into the world with various dispositions" most likely rooted in the "subtle network of the brain." Contrary to the claim of Helvétius (and, by implication, his own earlier view) that the human character "depends upon education only, in the largest sense of that word," Godwin now maintains that innate "temper" significantly shapes psychological development. "He must have been a very inattentive observer of the indications of temper in an infant in the first months of his existence, who does not confess that there are various peculiarities in that respect which the child brings into the world with him."[6]

Godwin's conversion to a psychology of individual differences, human "peculiarities," and innate predispositions reflects the considerable influence of the new brain-based theories of mind, particularly Gall's "organology." A later essay in *Thoughts* is devoted to the "extraordinary vogue" for phrenology, dismissing its precise division of the mind into "twenty-seven compartments" but accepting some of its basic premises: that the "thinking principle" is located in the brain, the "great ligament which binds together" body and mind; that the sensory "nerves all lead up to the brain" and that acts of volition initiate "in the brain itself"; and that the brain is modular, with "one structure of the brain better adapted" for a given discrete "intellectual purpose" than another. Although craniology has not discovered it, a method for identifying these structures is probably an attainable science, one that will help discriminate those "attributes and propensities" that "a human creature may bring into the world with him" from those others that are the "pure growth of the arbitrary institutions of society."[7]

As Godwin's early reliance on Hartleyan associationism attests, Hartley's pioneering physiological psychology was thoroughly compatible with a sensationalist, "blank slate" conception of mind. But as biological approaches to physiology came to displace mechanistic ones, brain-based models of mind began to feature, in Herder's phrase, the "innate, organical, genetic" aspects of mind (*Outlines* 179). Herder takes for granted that "diseases and features, nay that tempers and dispositions, are hereditary," a fact known "to all the world" (*Outlines* 183). Darwin, despite his strong associationist bias, writes of hereditary temperaments in *Zoonomia*, defining temperament in psychopathological terms as "a permanent predisposition to certain classes of diseases" (*Z* 1: 354). Cabanis sets out to update Galen's theory of temperaments, arguing that the innate organization of each brain and nervous system profoundly shapes experience, and that "congenital" inclinations cannot be effaced though they can be modified by education (*R* 1: 267, 306, 2: 259). Gall similarly argues that innate dispositions can be modified, though neither destroyed nor produced, by education, holding that mental characters are "transmitted from family to family" by means of neural "organization" and explicitly condemning, with Cabanis, "tabula rasa" accounts of mental development such as Locke's and Hartley's (*FB* 1: 135, 185). In thus emphasizing the innate and hereditary aspects of character, the new biological psychologies were reasserting a dominant medical and philosophical view of "temperament" as old as the Greeks, while giving scientific credibility to a common folk view of the time.[8]

The novel of the Romantic era made its own contribution to this profound discursive shift regarding character, individuality, and temperament. The radical or "Jacobin" novel of the 1790s offers a fleshed-out version of the Lockean constructivist approach, showing in vivid detail how, as Mary Hays writes in *Emma Courtney*, "We are all the creatures of education."[9] In place of the anecdotal childhood episode or two, revealing innate bias of character, supplied by earlier eighteenth-century novelists such as Fielding, detailed accounts of childhood and early education became the norm. Novelists learned to elaborate basic fairytale plots to set off the "advantages of education" by contrasting the fortunes of one of three daughters (or cousins) in Cinderella fashion (as in Austen's *Mansfield Park*), or one of two sisters (or friends) in the tradition of the "Kind and Unkind" tale type (as in *Sense and Sensibility*). Needless to add, the heroine with the best education – the one who has most thoroughly internalized moral principles and developed habits of self-regulation – wins out.[10]

As the example of Susan Ferrier's *Marriage* (1818) shows, however, notions of innate bias, if they ever disappeared entirely, were returning to at least complicate fictional representations of character by the time of the Lawrence controversy. Anticipating the later use of twin studies to explore issues of nature and nurture, Ferrier invents twin sisters, Mary and Adelaide, raised in different families according to markedly different principles. Mary, the sister whose more careful education has produced a "well-regulated mind," ends up (predictably enough) rising from her Cinderella status to marry happily and well, while her vacuous twin Adelaide (like Maria in *Mansfield Park*) marries a wealthy "fool" before ruining her reputation with an adulterous elopement. Complicating an otherwise schematic plot, however, is the twins' cousin, Emily, who is raised in the same fashion and environment as Adelaide, but whose native intelligence and generosity assert themselves in a "noble" though "wild" character, lacking Mary's exemplary self-control, to be sure, but also remarkably free of Adelaide's meretriciousness and short-sighted egotism.[11] Within another decade, novelists begin to take innate biases of character explicitly into account, using them to balance or at least qualify environmental influences on development. As Mary Shelley puts it in *The Last Man* (1826): "We are born; we choose neither our parents, nor our station; we are educated by others, or by the world's circumstances, and this cultivation, *mingling with our innate disposition*, is the soil in which our desires, passions, and motives grow."[12] Whether or not *Frankenstein* represents the extreme expression of a socially constructed mind, Shelley's later work anticipates the growing influence of phrenological and other physiological theories of personality informing the novels of Charlotte Brontë and later Victorian writers.[13]

NERVOUS SENSIBILITY IN AUSTEN'S LATE STYLE

Austen's portrayal of character in relation to experience has been seen as thoroughly Lockean in spirit, though unusually deft in execution.[14] Her novels include some of the most inventive and subtle reworkings of traditional tale-types to display the effects or contrasting upbringings and the habits of self-scrutiny and discipline they instill – or fail to instill, as

Sir Thomas finds to his grief in contrasting Fanny to her favored but miseducated elder cousins at the end of *Mansfield Park*. In *Persuasion* (1818), Austen's last novel, a Cinderella plot is again deployed to set off the virtues of an undervalued sister, Anne Elliot, to the detriment of her spoiled siblings, the status-conscious, superficial Elizabeth and the plaintive, self-involved Mary. Austen varies this traditional plot by making Anne the middle, rather than youngest, sister, as well as by introducing still another folk character type, the "false heroine," in the person of Louisa Musgrove. As in many a folktale, the false heroine in *Persuasion* functions to delay the eventual union of the true heroine with her "object" (Frederick Wentworth) by temporarily displacing Anne and claiming Frederick for herself.[15] As in many a domestic novel, Anne and Louisa are contrasted in terms of the quality of their upbringing and the degree of their self-discipline. Louisa is more "fashionable" and adept at superficial "accomplishments" while Anne is "more elegant and cultivated," showing modesty and self-restraint where Louisa appears willful and flirtatious, a combination that proves nearly fatal at the novel's crisis point.[16]

That crisis – Louisa's mistimed leap towards Frederick's arms and her headfirst fall onto the paving stones of a massive sea-wall – introduces a further and more startling contrast, this time one without precedent. For while Anne's character has been shaped over her twenty-seven years of often painful experience, most notably her mother's death (when Anne is fourteen) and her youthful break with Frederick (five years later), Louisa's character is "altered," remarkably and apparently for life, by a single incident, a severe knock on the head (223). Once "happy, and merry" and rather giddy (67), Louisa is, as a consequence of head injury, "turned into a person of literary taste, and sentimental reflection," sedentary and neurasthenic. "The day at Lyme, the fall from the Cobb, might influence her health, her nerves, her courage, her character to the end of her life, as thoroughly as it appeared to have influenced her fate" (178).

Critics of *Persuasion* have not known quite what to make of the connection Austen poses here between nerves and character, head trauma and mental alteration, and sometimes they have simply made fun of it. "True, she has fallen on her head," writes one, "but it had never been a good one, and the blow seems to have cleared it."[17] To read what another calls the "zany incident at Lyme" as slapstick, however, fails to do justice to what has been aptly described as the "most sensational moment of physical violence in Austen's work."[18] It also fails to bring out the truly remarkable implications of Louisa's character change. At the very least, the fall and its consequences serve, in John Wiltshire's phrase, as a "graphic reminder that human beings are bodies as well as minds."[19] In the context of Romantic-era speculation on the brain and nerves, however, it also suggests that the relation between bodies and minds is of more consequence, at least in *Persuasion*, than critics of Austen have wanted to acknowledge.

Wiltshire offers his account of the body's salience in *Persuasion* to counterbalance readings that he worries may have exaggerated its "historicist
dimension."[20] But Austen's portrayal of an embodied mind – most remarkably in relation to Louisa's fall but in quieter ways throughout the novel –
has an important historicist dimension of its own. Head injury, strange as
it may seem in retrospect, was a politically loaded topic at the very time
Austen was writing *Persuasion*. From Hartley to Lawrence, proponents of
physiological accounts of mind cite the effects of "Blows upon the Head"
among other reasons to locate the mind in the brain – a notion that was still
considered unproven, unorthodox, and ideologically subversive in Austen's
time.[21] Concussions serve, along with visual illusions, somnambulism, and
intoxication, as favorite examples of what might be called in retrospect the
neuropathology of everyday life. Particularly loaded are instances in which
(as Andrew Combe writes) the "temper and moral sentiments have . . . been
entirely changed, in consequence of certain injuries to the brain, while the
intellect remained unimpaired," suggesting that not only cognition but
character is physiologically based.[22] Some of these instances are evocative
of Louisa's transformation, including Hartley's claim that "concussions"
have sometimes resulted in a "Melancholy" temperament, or Gall's "lady
of fine talents" who falls, striking the "back part of her head against the
mantel-piece," and comes to lose "all of her brilliant qualities" as a result
(*FB* 2: 119).[23] Gall mentions more exotic cases as well. A split brain subject
"continually heard insults against him" on his left side only, causing him to
turn "his eyes that way, although, with the right side, he distinctly perceived,
that these sounds came from no other source than a derangement in the left
side of his head" (*FB* 2: 164). A man who suffered a fall could no longer
remember proper names, though otherwise intact; another, after a similar
accident, "lost the memory of nouns" (*FB* 2: 285–86). Still another case
reads like a Romantic-era version of Phineas Gage (whose reconstructed
head injury forms one of the central illustrations for Damasio's *Descartes'
Error*).[24] After having his skull "broken in by a blow from a stone," a man
once known as a "peaceful citizen" becomes "quarrelsome" and contentious:
"people saw with surprise that his character was wholly changed." Gall
managed to procure the cranium for his collection, which plainly showed
"by mere inspection, how much the brain had suffered" (*FB* 2: 119–20).

The ideological threat that such accounts represented is clear from the
response they generated in establishment journals, conservative and liberal
alike. A few months before Austen began work on *Persuasion* (in August,
1815), in fact, the *Edinburgh Review* had devoted a long article to countering the implications of an essay on localized brain injury published the
year before in the Royal Society's *Philosophical Transactions*. The author,
Sir Everard Home, was not the ready object of ridicule presented by the
phrenologists and most of their allies, but rather something of a medical
icon: Fellow of the Royal Society, sergeant-surgeon to the king, professor at

the College of Surgeons, protégé and executor of John Hunter, and baronet. In his "Observations on the Function of the Brain" Home avoids "general deductions," instead cataloguing all of the cases he has encountered of brain injury to help "procure accurate information respecting the functions that belong to individual portions of the human brain."[25] Nevertheless, the implications of Home's attempt to connect "still more closely the pursuits of anatomy with those of philosophy" were hard to miss: an intimate relation (if not identity) between mind and brain, a physiological account of mental function, and a brain-based, modular conception of mental behavior distinctly related to Gall's organology, if far more scientifically respectable.

Rather than attack Home directly, the reviewer in the *Edinburgh* instead compiles an imposing list of counter-examples, intended to prove that brain injury need not disrupt mental functioning and, ultimately, that mental life can go on in the entire absence of a brain. Some of the examples approach surrealism in the nonchalance with which they treat head wounds and other neural insults. "VESLINGIUS found the end of a stilletto in the brain of a woman, who had been wounded by it five years before, but who had complained of nothing in the mean while but occasional head-ach; and . . . LACUTUS mentions a case, in which the half of a knife remained in the brain of a man for eight years, without his being at all incommoded."[26] Five pages of such examples are given not as evidence of neural plasticity (which Cabanis discusses from a neuropsychological perspective [*R* 1: 140]), but rather to dismiss altogether any necessary connection between the mental act of "Sensation" and "*particular*" parts of the brain (445). The reviewer then goes on to produce examples in which "the *whole* brain has been destroyed without loss of sensibility" (446) though, as one might imagine, these are not very satisfying. ("We have found indeed, several instances of children born without a brain who lived for a short time; but the state of the sensibility in these, is not quite unequivocally ascertained" [447–48].) Nevertheless, the essay concludes that, despite the cases evidenced by a "person of SIR EVERARD HOME'S reputation," there are "very strong grounds for believing, that the brain is not at all concerned in the changes which precede Sensation" (448), and if not in sensation, than not, "*mutatis mutandis*," in the "phenomena of Thought and Volition" 440).

Home's paper on brain function and the response in the *Edinburgh Review* are worth noting in this context not, of course, as possible "sources" for *Persuasion*. They are valuable, rather, for underscoring the tense co-existence, in Austen's day, of two diametrically opposed yet equally credible notions of mind–body relations, one unabashedly dualistic and in line with orthodox notions of the soul, the other aligning mental acts with discrete brain functions and open to a materialist interpretation. These rival conceptions seem initially to correspond, in an odd way, to the contrasting subjectivities of the rival heroines of *Persuasion*: one shaped by mental and emotional experience, able to transcend bodily discomfort, and exemplifying

Frederick's ideal of a "strong mind" (87), the other "altered" by an insult to the brain and even before that deficient (again according to Frederick) "in a point no less essential than mind" (192). One living with the pangs of a broken heart, the other with the lasting effects of a cracked head. Though the episode on the Cobb is not meant to elicit laughter, these rival systems for representing subjectivity do collide comically later in the novel. When Anne, overwhelmed with emotion, struggles to compose herself after reading a passionate letter from Frederick, Louisa's mother, apparently converted to a brain-based psychology, needs reassurance that "there had been no fall in the case; that Anne had not, at any time lately, slipped down, and got a blow on her head; that she was perfectly convinced of having had no fall" (241). But Anne's very confusion, here and elsewhere in the novel, suggests that the comic disparity in this passage between mind and brain, heart and head, is something of a red herring. For the characterization of Anne touches, in its own way, on the embodied notion of mind, the fragmentation of the subject, and the greater appreciation of unconscious mental life all characteristic of the new Romantic psychologies.

Mrs. Musgrove's comic mistake reasserts the contrast between Anne and Louisa while also emphasizing that this is a moment when, as Wiltshire puts it, Anne's "body takes over."[27] Not that Anne becomes even remotely comatose at such times; rather, her periods of dislocation mark the collision of conscious awareness with unconscious thoughts and feelings and the intense physiological sensations that accompany them. Anne may be prized for her "rational" demeanor, yet she also proves highly susceptible to influxes of feeling from sources not always consciously present to Anne herself, registered instead in the body, in ways that at times become so pressing as to overwhelm the conscious subject.[28] "The absolute necessity of seeming like herself produced then an immediate struggle; but after a while she could do no more. She began not to understand a word they said" (240–41). The "struggle" between rational control and passionate feeling, conscious volition and the physiological rush of intense inner emotions, manifests not a split between mind and body but the impossibility of ever teasing them apart. The illusory unity of the conscious subject is punctured by the actions of an embodied mind that often finds unconscious action and expression more expedient, working in despite of the conscious subject if need be. "Mary talked, but [Anne] could not attend . . . she began to reason with herself, and try to be feeling less . . . Alas! with all her reasonings, she found, that to retentive feelings eight years may be little more than nothing" (85).

Underlying such passages is a view of mind as sensibility, less reminiscent of Locke than of Herder – "It's vibrating fibres, it's sympathizing nerves, need not the call of Reason: they run before her, they often disobediently and forcibly oppose her" (*Outlines* 100) – or of Darwin, Gall, or Cabanis. Austen grants the "inward" senses (never discussed by Locke) the central role given them by brain-based Romantic psychologies, necessarily acknowledging the subject's fragmentation in the process. "For a few minutes she saw nothing before her. It was all confusion. She was lost; and when she had scolded back her senses, she found the others still waiting for the carriage." The intimation of a divided subject ("scolded back her senses") builds to the acknowledgment of a fundamental split between a superintending conscious self and a potentially unruly, desiring, unconscious other: "Why was she to suspect herself of another motive? . . . One half of her should not always be so much wiser than the other half" (185). In related passages, equally in keeping with the emphasis on unconscious mental life found throughout Romantic brain science, Anne performs complex behaviors in an explicitly "unconscious" manner, playing at the keyboard (a prominent example of non-conscious cognition in Darwin's *Zoonomia* [1: 190–94]) and even conversing "unconsciously" (96, 113). Anne can make music and make conversational sense equally well without the benefit of conscious awareness, though her unconscious life emerges more spectacularly in those moments when she seems, for a time, altogether senseless.

Anne's periods of "confusion," episodes lasting up to "several minutes" when internal sensations crowd out external ones, rendering her unseeing and inattentive, bear an uncanny resemblance (seen from the outside) to Louisa's deeper passage into unconsciousness after her fall. Louisa's head injury serves to call attention, in sensational fashion, to the mind's embodiment, a condition that is shown in more subtle ways to be shared by the characters around her. The chapter that recounts the accident is generally seen as the novel's dramatic hinge, limning the contrast between the two rivals by juxtaposing Louisa's "heedlessness" with Anne's display of the "resolution of a collected mind" (244). Yet the scene at the Cobb also serves to soften that very contrast, as one character after another succumbs to emotional and cognitive overload, lapsing into various mental states that appear not so very different from Louisa's; even Anne acts as much from blind instinct as from conscious reason. The indirect cause of the accident is Louisa's love of "sensation" – "In all their walks, he had to jump her from the stiles; the sensation was delightful to her" – a richly complex feeling that confounds the temporary disorientation of an inner sense (proprioception) with the heightening of an external one (touch), connected in turn with the sexual thrill of a kind of robust physical contact ordinarily forbidden to genteel unmarried couples. No wonder Louisa, after being "jumped" once down to the lower level of the Cobb, wants to do it again. The second, more precipitate jump, ironically, leaves her insensible: though by no means farcical, or (given the real horror of the accident) quite so "zany" as sometimes described, the episode is written throughout with a tactful, but in its own way rather remorseless, wit. The immediate reactions of those around her bring the other characters into physiological and even cognitive conditions reflecting back the "corpse-like figure" of Louisa. Frederick looks at her "with a face as pallid as her own"; Charles is rendered "immoveable";

Henrietta, "sinking under the conviction, lost her senses too, and would have fallen on the steps" (129–30). Overcome with genuine shock and horror, one character after another becomes, like Louisa, a prone or otherwise inert body.

Austen underscores the parallel in various ways as the episode continues to unfold. When Anne proposes to send Benwick for a doctor, "Every one capable of thinking felt the advantage of the idea," a formula that groups the fainting Henrietta and the "hysterical" Mary with the unconscious Louisa. Harville's arrival is described in terms that in context weirdly reduce him to a physiological specimen: "Shocked as Captain Harville was, he brought senses and nerves that could be instantly useful" (130–31). Even the "thinking" characters, that is, are portrayed as organic assemblages of nerves and senses under duress. Frederick, though remaining sentient, becomes automaton-like, responding as mechanically as any Hartleyan association network when Anne mentions a surgeon: "He caught the word; it seemed to rouse him at once, and saying only, 'True, true, a surgeon this instant,'" he begins rushing away when Anne reminds him that only Benwick "knows where a surgeon is to be found." Even Anne, foremost among the minority who remain "rational," preserves the situation through the "strength and zeal, and thought, which instinct supplied" (130). Appearing just at this point in the episode, Austen's choice of "instinct" does not seem casual. At a time when writers like Coleridge adamantly distinguish between the "instinct" of beasts and the "higher" intuitions of human beings (*SW* 2: 1390), countering "materialists" like Darwin who view instinctive human responses as a crucial animal inheritance and a key manifestation of the adaptive "inner" senses, "instinct" is a loaded term, one that early brain scientists like Cabanis and Gall had only recently reasserted in the teeth of Locke's dismissal. In this context, Anne's most heroically "rational" episode could be placed on a continuum with, rather than directly opposed to, her automatic, non-rational, but quite natural responses elsewhere in the novel at times of heightened emotion.

Marked by a "strong sensibility" from her adolescence, Anne is represented not as some eviscerated or denervated rational agent, but as an emotive, embodied subject, uncommonly reasonable and also uncommonly sensitive (165). She can become "speechless" from "nervous" sensations or "fixed" by powerful emotions (103–4, 111) and, at her most intense, feels things "in a nervous thrill all over her" (235). But in a novel that asks women to be treated as "rational creature" not "fine ladies" (94), Anne's exquisite sensorium does nothing to diminish or otherwise qualify her exemplary strength of mind. The continuity suggested throughout between reason and emotion, "instinct and judgment, conscious and nonconscious mental activity sets *Persuasion* apart both from the eighteenth-century "sentimental" novel, which aligns enhanced powers of feeling and empathy with the irrational and the effeminate, and from Austen's earlier novels as well.[29] Although *Sense and Sensibility* (1811), to cite the inevitable example, does not oppose feeling and reason quite so schematically as its title might suggest, it does pointedly contrast Elinor's "coolness of judgment" with Marianne's "excessive sensibility" (42). Marianne's unbridled sensibility, moreover, erupts in an extended "nervous complaint" that equates sensitive feelings, the female body, and illness (234). In *Persuasion*, "senses and nerves" become positively revalued along lines remarkably consonant with the new biological psychologies, integrated within a neurocognitive system that does not always require conscious awareness to function rapidly and effectively, although it remains vulnerable (like the rest of the body) and subject to breakdown as well.

Anne's blend of superior rationality and heightened sensibility, her susceptibility to surges of emotion with their marked cognitive and physiological effects, and the mental splitting or fragmenting she regularly manifests, together find voice in the stylistic innovation critics have noted in *Persuasion*. A. Walton Litz first called attention to Austen's "move away from the Johnsonian norm" in her last novel, with its "rapid and nervous syntax designed to imitate the bombardment of impressions upon the mind."[30] Marilyn Butler similarly describes Austen's "experiment with a new kind of subjective writing," marked by a "high-wrought nervous tension" in conveying a particular consciousness (Anne's) for which "the senses have a distinct advantage over reason and fact."[31] It is appropriate that both critics use the term "nervous" to evoke the quality of Anne's subjectivity and the prose that conveys it, for in this novel mind cannot be disentangled from the central nervous system that enacts it. Austen's new subjective style is all the more innovative for prominently including the gaps and disruptions in the represented flux of consciousness, what Wiltshire calls "invasions of feeling."[32] Unconscious mental events are shown in a complex and frequently adversarial relation with conscious ones, and feeling is often known through its mark on the body before it can be registered in conscious awareness. "No, it was not regret which made Anne's heart beat in spite of itself, and brought the color into her cheeks when she thought of Captain Wentworth unshackled and free. She had some feelings which she was ashamed to investigate" (178). Anne's shame here reminds us that the domestic novel, considered as an extension of the literature of female conduct, implicitly enjoins such inner splitting by insisting that "proper" young women feel desire for their future husbands – marry for love – *without* acknowledging such desire too soon, even to themselves.[33] Yet the deft interplay in passages like this between thought and feeling, physiological expression and conscious introspection, signals not just another elaboration on the modest blush but a new, "Romantic" sense of mind–body relations.

Terms like "flow of consciousness" or "interior monologue" cannot entirely do this new style justice.[34] Even if they allow for some shading from unconscious impulses or bodily intrusions upon introspective awareness, they tend to evoke a conscious, integral Cartesian subject, the central self that oversees the conscious flow or articulates the internal monologue. As represented through the "nervous" sentences of *Persuasion*, however, subjectivity seems corporate rather than monologic, unconscious feelings and ideas become as important as conscious ones, and the division between interior and exterior is regularly breached. "Shudder," for example, should be read as a simultaneously physical and psychological reaction in the passage that describes Anne's semi-conscious acknowledgment of her temporary interest in her wealthy cousin, William Walter Elliot: "Anne could just acknowledge within herself such a possibility of having been induced to marry him, as made her shudder at the idea of the misery which must have followed" (216). It is left suggestively unclear whether "within herself" refers to Anne's conscious or unconscious mind, or even whether the "shudder" represents Anne's act of acknowledgment rather than her reaction to it, such that she discovers the nature of her feelings partly through reading their bodily manifestations. The plot owes much of its tension, in fact, to the ongoing threat that feelings which can only be read indirectly can always be misread: Frederick will continue to overvalue his feelings for Louisa, Anne will be "induced" to display feelings for Mr. Elliot, neither Frederick nor Anne will correctly gauge their renewed feelings for one another. Frederick makes this dilemma explicit in an acknowledgment of his own: "Thus much indeed he was obliged to acknowledge – that he had been constant unconsciously, nay, unintentionally; that he had meant to forget her, and believed it to be done" (244). In a novel of the 1790s generation, the claim to have been constant "unintentionally" would be transparently absurd, the statement of a cad; the sort of thing that Darnford, in Mary Wollstonecraft's *Maria*, might be expected to come up with. In *Persuasion*, however, the claim, self-serving as it obviously is, can nevertheless be considered sincere. Unconscious motives can contradict and even come to outweigh conscious ones, feelings that are "believed" to be forgotten can have been present, in retrospect, all along. A "Romantic" novel indeed: one that takes up and extends, in its innovatory syntax, characterization, and narrative style, the embodied approach to human subjectivity being worked out concurrently by Romantic poets like Coleridge and Keats and Romantic brain scientists like Gall and Bell.[35]

Persuasion also bears comparison to Romantic brain science in its emphasis on extrasemantic, bodily communication, unexpected though this may be in a novel that depends on a hastily written letter for its resolution. Characters frequently communicate by non-verbal expression alone ("a look between him and his wife decided what was to be done" [131]) – or reveal by expression what their words are intended to conceal.[36] "There was a momentary expression in Captain Wentworth's face at this speech, a certain glance of his bright eye, and curl of his handsome mouth, which convinced Anne, that instead of sharing in Mrs Musgrove's kind wishes, as to her son, he had probably been at some pains to get rid of him" (92). Some of the novel's most impassioned moments are wordless, as when Anne, having read Frederick's letter, conveys her response with her eyes and is answered by Frederick's flushing skin. "He joined them; but, as if irresolute whether to join or to pass on, said nothing – only looked. Anne could command herself enough to receive that look, and not repulsively. The cheeks which had been pale now glowed, and the movements which had hesitated were decided" (242). (Frederick, no less than Anne, is capable of looking "quite red" [185]; neither has quite "outlived the age of blushing" [75].) In the canceled chapter that records Austen's first attempt at resolving the plot, Anne and Frederick come to an understanding through a "silent but a very powerful dialogue" conducted entirely through "expression" (259). If subjectivity cannot be disentangled from physiology in this novel, neither can communication.

TEMPERAMENTAL SUBJECTS

The concurrence between Austen's late style and emergent biological notions of the subject would not, of course, necessarily commit her to viewing character or temperament as even partly shaped by heredity. Even if one believes that a significant change in brain physiology (such as the neurological effects of a particularly severe head injury) could bring about a change in temperament, one need not agree with Gall or Cabanis that certain patterns of neurophysiological organization associated with specific temperaments or character traits can be passed down within families like a snub nose or a predisposition to hemophilia.[37] Physiological psychology and a renewed interest in the hereditary transmission of character traits do, however, generally go together in Romantic-era brain science and it is significant that, in *Persuasion*, Austen seems to pose a similar connection.[38] Again, the most overt example in the book concerns a relatively minor female character who functions as yet another foil to Anne, her former school-friend Mrs. Smith. Smith's experience has been much harsher still than Anne's: marriage to a spendthrift husband, early widowhood, relative poverty ("unable even to afford herself the comfort of a servant"), and illness (165). Yet, as Anne wonderingly observes, "in spite of all this . . . she had moments only of langour and depression, to hours of occupation and enjoyment. How could it be?" (167) How could temperament so thoroughly belie the effects of experience? Mrs. Smith exemplifies, Anne decides, that "elasticity of mind, that disposition to be comforted, that power of turning readily from evil to good, and of finding employment which carried her out of herself, which was from Nature alone" (167). Here, at least, is one character not altogether shaped by experience, but with a pronounced (and, one could add, adaptive) native "disposition."

Anne herself initially seems another case altogether. Psychoanalytical critics of *Persuasion* argue that Anne's particular temperament is precisely what one would expect of a girl effectively abandoned by her mother at 14, a traumatic and formative experience that makes a history of heartbreak and melancholy seem to follow as a matter of course. As Anita Sokolsky writes, "Anne's tendency to melancholy emerges in reaction to the death of a mother whose attachment to her home and daughters had, terribly, made it 'no small matter of indifference to her to leave this life'".[39] Austen, however, does suggest that Anne's temperament may owe as much to a biological as to a psychological relation to the mother. Later in the same chapter in which Anne speculates on Mrs. Smith's elastic "disposition" (a key term for Gall and his adherents), Lady Russell remarks that Anne is "her mother's self in countenance and disposition" – that she has inherited her mother's temperament along with her physical features (172). Lady Russell's judgment is evidently one of long standing: in the novel's first chapter, her early preference for Anne reflects her sense that "it was only in Anne that she could fancy the mother to revive again" (37). A paragraph above, Sir Walter's contrary preference for his eldest daughter, Elizabeth, is similarly explained on the basis of physical and temperamental resemblance to a parent: "being very handsome, and very like himself, her influence had always been great." Few readers would disagree with Sir Walter's assessment; throughout the novel, Elizabeth reacts and behaves in a manner all too like her father's. Physiology may not be destiny in *Persuasion*, but it seems to play no small role in character formation.

The links implied here between character and physique, heredity and fate, raise the issue of how sexual differences are perceived to shape differences in mind – an issue that Austen will raise herself toward the end of the book (237). In a novel that, in various ways, "upsets conventional conjunctions of ideas about gender," it might seem that appeals to embodied notions of mind and hereditary notions of "disposition" could only serve to reassert those same conjunctions.[40] Both Janet Oppenheim and Sally Shuttleworth have demonstrated how, in the Victorian era, the new biological psychologies were invoked to "bear witness against women's brains" and to reassert conventional oppositions between male self-control and female helplessness, male rationality and female sensibility.[41] As John Elliotson (a radical materialist and early proponent of phrenology) puts it in *Human Physiology* (1835), the "male is formed for corporeal and intellectual power; the female for gentleness, affections, and delicacy of feeling."[42] These tendencies, though much exaggerated over the course of the nineteenth century, are certainly present already in the work of pioneers like Cabanis and Gall. Cabanis holds that women have "softer" brains than men, and remain, in some respects, "children all their lives" (*R* 1: 183, 227); Gall illustrates the power of instinct by observing that the "little girl reaches out her hand for the doll, as the boy, for a drum or sword." "The whole physical constitution of woman," he continues, "combines with her moral and intellectual character, to prove that she is destined, more particularly than man, to take care of children" (*FB* 3: 272). For Lawrence the mind is "male or female, according to the sex of the body" (*LPZ* 94).

Yet as readily the new physiological discourse on the mind lent itself to supporting the received dichotomies of the gender system, it could also serve to unsettle those same oppositions and, at least in principle, to destabilize the traditional system of evaluations. Hazlitt, in a critique of phrenology, complains that Gall's organology weakens the distinction between men and women by localizing it, limiting it to relative differences between only several among the numerous brain "organs." "Women in general," Hazlitt counters, "have more softness and flexibility both of mind and body than men – they have not the same strength and persever-ance, but they take their revenge in tact and *delicacy*: Shall we suppose this marked and universal difference which runs through the whole frame and through every thought and action of life, to proceed from a particular bump or excrescence of the skull, and not to be inherent in the principle (whatever that may be) which feels, and thinks, at all times, and in all circumstances?" (*HW* 20: 253). By fragmenting the mind and disrupting the continuity of the thinking "principle," the new physiological psychologies not only threaten orthodox notions of the soul but throw the system of absolute gender differences into question.[43] If sex-specific mental differences can be localized, moreover, those local differences can be further eroded by the effects of accident and experience. Men, for example, come equipped with the same mental predisposition (and accompanying brain organ) for child-rearing as women, but in a much less pronounced manner; through exercise, however, that organ can be developed and the original difference can be "repressed" (*FB* 3: 263, 275). A thoroughly "domestic" man like Captain Harville would fit readily into Gall's system, but would seem aberrant within Hazlitt's (120). The propensity for sexual behavior, on the other hand, is generally stronger in men but by no means always. For Gall, despite his commitment to basic gender differences, there are no absolute or unalterable distinctions.

In terms of their larger implications, the emergent brain-based psychologies of the era threatened to destabilize received notions of gender in more per-vasive ways. Discussing the ambivalent relation of women writers to scientific discourse in the Romantic era, Marina Benjamin remarks on the "masculine character of scientific epistemologies" that align the opposition of masculine to feminine with "dichotomies like rational/emotional, deductive/intuitive, objective/subjective." But the biological psychologies of Darwin, Cabanis, and Gall were engaged in undoing those very dichotomies, at a time when (again quoting Benjamin) the "cognitive role of the passions, imagination, sensation, and individual experience" was being fundamentally rethought.[44] In giving an expanded and often leading role to unconscious cognition, instinctive behaviors, "inward" sensations, emotional reactions, and bodily sensation within mental life, Romantic brain science threw traditional valuations of reason over passion and mind over body into crisis. More-over, although women were still seen as more emotional and "softer" than men, men were nevertheless fully implicated within a changing vision of the human, one that displaced the rational, disembodied, male-coded ideal sub-ject with an embodied model of human subjectivity, forcing a revaluation of traditionally feminine prerogatives like sensibility and intuition.

Here too one finds unexpected convergence between Austen's experiments with representing character and subjective life in *Persuasion* and the physiological psychologies of her time. Another of the features supporting a "Romantic" reading of the novel (such as Litz's) is its revaluation of ration-ality and emotion, one that cuts across gender lines. The heroine, after all, is one who, famously, "had been forced into prudence in her youth" and "learned romance as she grew older" (58), while Frederick too must learn to respect the wisdom of his unconscious and even involuntary feelings by the novel's close. The novel's most systematically "rational" characters – Lady Russell and William Walter Elliot – are the very ones who cause the most pain and give the worst counsel (42, 173). Frederick's great advantage over Mr. Elliot, in fact, resides in his characteristic "ardour" (58), a trait that is at once psychological and physical, described elsewhere as "glowing" (86). Indeed, Frederick's "sanguine temper" is said to have contributed to his successful career, "command[ed]" his "proper path" (56, 58). All of the sympathetic naval characters share this quality of "warmth" (120), one singularly lacking in Frederick's rival. "Mr Elliot was rational, discreet, polished, – but he was not open. There was never any burst of feeling, any warmth of indignation or delight" (173). Or, in Mrs. Smith's harsher terms, Elliot is a "cold-blooded being," a "man without heart" (206). This last phrase relies on the most conventional of figures, but in a novel that so insistently reevaluates the claims of the body, metaphors like "heart" ask to be taken quite seriously. In conjunction with terms like "warmth" and "ardour," "heart" functions metaphorically just at the uncertain borders between psyche and soma, where character traits are indistinguishable from the "glowing" physical sensations that make them known – to the self as well as to others. (The very notion of "temperament," a term obviously allied to "temperature," ultimately relies on the same basic metaphorical pattern.)[45] Harville is "warm-hearted" not just metaphorically but in the concrete way he experiences his own body, and thus knows his own mind (119). After expressing his love for his wife and children "in a tone of strong feeling," he adds, "'I speak, you know, only of such men as have hearts!' pressing his own with emotion" (238). Men who fail to speak from feeling and to feel from the body are not to be trusted in *Persuasion*.

Not that feelings, sensations, vocal tones, and physiological displays can be trusted in any simple way, either. Austen's turn to an embodied epistemol-ogy in *Persuasion* introduces new complications of its own, such as the difficulties both Anne and Frederick encounter first in consciously perceiving, then in fully acknowledging, their "unconscious" desire for one another. Sensations can be misinterpreted and feelings under- or overvalued, as in the case of Benwick, whose broken heart heals sooner than anyone, least of all himself, could reasonably suppose. Mrs. Musgrove, who rekindles feelings for a son's death that she seems not really to have felt at the time, and whose "substantial" physical bulk is said to belie her feelings of "tenderness," functions as an icon of such misprision (92). This is still a Jane Austen novel. It is, however, a Jane Austen novel like no other, and its difference owes a great deal to its affinities with the biological psychologies just then becoming notorious through the debates on phrenology and the materialist-vitalist controversy. Although it has been claimed that Austen "all but erases" the body in her novels – and that a body reconstructed from her lexicon would have no thighs, no "intestines, wombs, or navels," not even fingers or toes – the body is crucial to character, plot, and subjective life in *Persuasion*.[46] The skin that glows or goes pallid, the heart that swells or goes "cold," the "susceptible" nerves and the brain that, once injured, must be "set to rights," all speak of a mind that has no location or meaning apart from the body (144, 181).

In representing an embodied, nervous sensibility, Austen takes brilliant advantage of the novel's capacity to move rapidly among various perspectives (both internal and external to different characters and sometimes hovering in an uncertain middle ground) and to shuttle between passages of description and snatches of indirect discourse in order to convey, not just the flow of consciousness, but its ebbs as well. The phrase recounting Louisa's condition during her extended period of recovery – "intervals of sense and consciousness" (138) – could provide an apt starting point for a characterization of Austen's late style. Consciousness plays only a limited role in defining the heroine's impressions – and conveying her expressions. At times the body speaks eloquently in a language of its own. "Her eyes were bright, her cheeks glowed, but she knew nothing about it" (194). More noteworthy still are those moments during which emotional, cognitive, and physiological impulses engage in a complicated dance of action and reaction, as when Anne learns that Frederick does not love Louisa. "Anne, who, in spite of the agitated voice in which the latter part had been uttered, and in spite of all the various noises of the room, the almost ceaseless slam of the door, and ceaseless buzz of people walking through, had distinguished every word, was struck, gratified, confused, and beginning to breathe very quick, and feel an hundred things in a moment" (193). The disquisitions of brain scientists like Darwin and Bell can point towards such deft interaction between mind and body, emotion and cognition, but cannot portray it nearly so effectively or so evocatively. The closest analogue to this aspect of Austen's style – surprising as it may seem for a novelist more often compared to Samuel Johnson – may be found in the poetry of John Keats.

Notes

(See Abbreviations following notes.)

1 Edward S. Reed, *From Soul to Mind: The Emergence of Psychology from Erasmus Darwin to William James* (New Haven: Yale UP, 1997), 43–59.
2 M. A., "The Craniological Controversy: Some Observations on the Late Pamphlets of Dr Gordon and Dr Spurzheim," *Blackwood's Edinburgh Magazine* I (1817), 35.
3 Roger Cooter, *The Cultural Meaning of Popular Science* (Cambridge: Cambridge University Press, 1984), 29.
4 See Chapter Five.
5 William Godwin, *Enquiry Concerning Political Justice and Its Influence on Modern Morals and Happiness*, ed. Isaac Kramnick (Harmondsworth: Penguin, 1976), 97–98, 111–12.
6 Godwin, *Thoughts on Man* (London: Effingham Wilson, 1831), 29–30, 41, 32.
7 Godwin, *Thoughts on Man*, 363–65, 370.
8 Jerome Kagan, *Galen's Prophecy: Temperament in Human Nature* (New York: Basic Books, 1994), esp. 1–37; Lawrence Stone, *The Family, Sex, and Marriage in England 1500–1800*, abridged edn (New York: Harper, 1979), 255.
9 Mary Hays, *Memoirs of Emma Courtney*, ed. Gina Luria, 2 vols. (New York: Garland, 1974) 1: 4.
10 Alan Richardson, *Literature, Education, and Romanticism*, 185–202.
11 Susan Ferrier, *Marriage*, ed. Rosemary Ashton (Harmondsworth: Penguin, 1966), 299, 444, 475.
12 Mary Shelley, *The Last Man*, ed. Brian Aldiss (London: Hogarth Press, 1985), 47 (my italics).
13 See Sally Shuttleworth, *Charlotte Brontë and Victorian Psychology* (Cambridge University Press, 1996) and Janet Oppenheim, *"Shattered Nerves": Doctors, Patients, and Depression in Victorian England* (New York: Oxford University Press, 1991).
14 For an extended statement of this claim, see D. D. Devlin, *Jane Austen and Education* (London: Macmillan, 1975).
15 For the role of the "false hero" and "object" see V. Propp, *Morphology of the Folktale*, 2nd edn, trans. Laurence Scott and Louis A. Wagner, ed. Alan Dundes (Austin: University of Texas Press, 1968), 50–62.
16 Jane Austen, *Persuasion*, ed. D. W. Harding (London: Penguin, 1965), 67; hereafter cited in the text.
17 Mary Lascelles, quoted in John Wiltshire, *Jane Austen and the Body* (Cambridge University Press, 1992), 186.
18 Gloria Sybil Gross, "Flights into Illness: Some Characters in Jane Austen," in *Literature and Medicine during the Eighteenth Century*, ed. Marie Mulvey Roberts and Roy Porter (London: Routledge, 1993), 195; Anita Sokolsky, "The Melancholy Persuasion," in *Psychoanalytic Literary Criticism*, ed. Maud Ellman (London: Longman, 1994), 136.
19 Wiltshire, *Jane Austen*, 187.
20 Wiltshire, *Jane Austen*, 196.
21 Hartley, *Observations* 1: 19; cf. Priestley, *Disquisitions*, 27, Lawrence, *Lectures on Physiology*, 6, Robinson, *Some Account*, 27, and Spurzheim, *PS* 137. Thomas Beddoes believed that "blows on the head" could cause insanity by affecting the brain (*Hygëia* 3 [Essay x]: 71–2).
22 Andrew Combe, "On the Effects of Injuries of the Brain upon the Manifestations

of the Mind," *Transactions of the Phrenological Society* 1 (1825); rpt. in George Combe, *A System of Phrenology* (New York: Colyer, 1841), 473.

23 Hartley, *Observations*, 1: 399. Nor is Louisa the only young woman to fall out of love from what appear to be physiological causes. Thomas Brown, in the course of a skeptical view of phrenology, mentions a "young lady, of very good understanding," who married a "person whom she passionately loved" despite "much opposition from her relatives." After a "long illness," however, "she completely lost memory of all the time that had elapsed since her marriage," though her memory was otherwise intact. "From the sight of her child, presented to her as her own, she turned with amazement and horror; and though she now, on the faith and assurance of her friends, consents to consider herself, as a wife and mother, she 'still looks upon her husband, and her child, without being able to conceive, by what magic she has acquired the one, and given birth to the other.'" Review of *A Letter from Charles Villier to Georges Cuvier, Member of the National Institute of France, on a New Theory of the Brain, as the immediate organ of intellectual and moral faculties, by Dr Gall of Vienna, Edinburgh Review* 2 (1803): 152.

24 Damasio, *Descartes' Error*, 3–33; see also H. Damasio *et al.*, "The Return of Phineas Gage: The Skull of a Famous Patient Yields Clues about the Brain," *Science* 264 (1994): 1102–5.

25 Sir Everard Home, "Observations on the Functions of the Brain," *Philosphical Transactions of the Royal Society of London* 104 (1814): 469. Home's essay was also discussed in the *Monthly Review*, 2nd series, 76 (1815): 40.

26 Review of Sir Everard Home, "Observations on the Functions of the Brain," *Edinburgh Review* 24 (1815): 443. Hereafter cited in the text.

27 Wiltshire, *Jane Austen*, 195.

28 Tony Tanner notes, in this novel, the "increased presence of sudden unanticipated and unpredictable inward intensities" in his study *Jane Austen* (Cambridge: Harvard University Press, 1986), 219; Marilyn Butler discusses Austen's representation of Anne's "rich and feeling" "inner life" in *Jane Austen and the War of Ideas*, 2nd edn (New York: Oxford University Press, 1987), 283.

29 For a careful study of the "sentimental" novel in a wider cultural and scientific context, see John Mullan, *Sentiment and Sociability: The Language of Feeling in the Eighteenth Century* (Oxford: Clarendon Press, 1988).

30 A. Walton Litz, "*Persuasion*: Forms of Estrangement," in *Jane Austen: Bicentenary Essays*, ed. John Halperin (Cambridge University Press, 1975), 228.

31 Butler, *Jane Austen*, 277.

32 Wiltshire, *Jane Austen*, 177.

33 Alan Richardson, *Literature, Education, and Romanticism* (Cambridge: Cambridge University Press, 1994), 191–92. For a reading of Austen's *Pride and Prejudice* that emphasizes social significance of blushing and related physiological phenomena, see Mary Ann O'Farrell, *Telling Complexions: The Nineteenth-Century Novel and the Blush* (Durham: Duke University Press, 1997), 13–27.

34 Butler, *Jane Austen*, 290 and Litz, "*Persuasion*," 228.

35 Litz discusses the novel in terms of Austen's "new-found Romanticism" in "*Persuasion*," 227.

36 O'Farrell coins the term "organic mechanics" to describe such wordless, meaningful exchanges between couples in *Persuasion* (*Telling Complexions*, 52).

37 J. F. Blumenbach was an important source for Romantic-era ideas on heredity; his *Essay on Generation* had been translated into English in 1792. James Prichard's *Researches into the Physical History of Man* (1813) was another important source

within the British context. For Lawrence's role in disseminating these and other early notions of heredity, both through his lectures and various encyclopedia articles, see Kentwood D. Wells, "Sir William Lawrence (1783–1867): A Study of Pre-Darwinian Ideas on Heredity and Variation," *Journal of the History of Biology* 4 (1971): 319–61.

38 Spurzheim includes "imbecility" among other examples of how the "same organic constitution of brain" can be "transmitted from parents to children" in his popular *Physiognomical System* of 1815 (*PS* 438–9). It is the more noteworthy, then, that Austen had both a maternal uncle (Thomas Leigh) and an elder brother (George) who were considered mentally "handicapped" and in each case were "boarded out from the family," though remaining near enough for family supervision and visits. It has been surmised that Austen learned the "deaf and dumb alphabet" in order to communicate with George. Whether or not hereditary transmission was suspected, having both a brother and uncle who were considered so mentally "abnormal" as to be brought up insulated from the family might well have inspired a sympathetic interest in "organic" approaches to mind. See William Austen-Leigh and Richard Arthur Austen-Leigh, *Jane Austen: A Family Record*, rev. and enlarged by Deirdre Le Faye (New York: G. K. Hall, 1989), 8, 19–20.

39 Anita Sokolsky, "The Melancholy Persuasion," in *Psychoanalytic Literary Criticism*, ed. Maud Ellmann (London: Longman, 1994), 133. See also Elizabeth Dalton, "Mourning and Melancholia in *Persuasion*," *Partisan Review* 62 (1995): 49–59 and Frances L. Restuccia, "Mortification: Beyond the Persuasion Principle," in *Melancholics in Love: Representing Women's Depression and Domestic Abuse* (Lanham: Rowman & Littlefield, 2000), 17–34.

40 Claudia L. Johnson, *Jane Austen: Women, Politics, and the Novel* (University of Chicago Press, 1988), 151–52.

41 Oppenheim, "*Shattered Nerves*," 185.

42 Quoted in Shuttleworth, *Charlotte Brontë*, 82.

43 In this, the new brain-based psychologies departed not only from vague notions of "universal" sexual difference like Hazlitt's, but from the neurological models of the earlier eighteenth century, which tended to assign "different nervous systems" to men and women. See G. J. Barker-Benfield, *The Culture of Sensibility: Sex and Society in Eighteenth-Century Britain* (University of Chicago Press, 1992), 27.

44 Marina Benjamin, "Elbow Room: Women Writers on Science, 1790–1840," in *Science and Sensibility: Gender and Scientific Inquiry*, ed. Marina Benjamin (Oxford: Blackwell, 1991), 27–28.

45 See Kagan, *Galen's Prophecy*, 34–35 and Sweetser, *From Etymology to Pragmatics*, 28.

46 Carol Shields, "Jane Austen Images of the Body: No Fingers, No Toes," *Persuasions* 13 (1991): 132.

Abbreviations

FB   François Joseph Gall, *On the Functions of the Brain and of Each of Its Parts: With Observations on the Possibility of Determining the Instincts, Propensities, and Talents, or the Moral and Intellectual Dispositions of Men and Animals by the Configuration of the Brain and Head*, tr. Winslow Lewis, 6 vols. (Boston, MA: Marsh, Capen, and Lyon: 1835).

HW   William Hazlitt, *The Complete Works of William Hazlitt*, ed. P. P. Howe, 21 vols. (London, Dent: 1930–34).

LPZ   William Lawrence, *Lectures on Physiology, Zoology, and the Natural History of Man, Delivered to the Royal College of Surgeons* (London: Benbow, 1822).

Outlines Johann Gottfried von Herder, *Outlines of the Philosophy of the History of Man*, trans. T. Churchill (1800; rpt. New York: Bergman, 1966).

R   Pierre-Jean-George Cabanis, *On the Relations Between the Physical and Moral Aspects of Man*, tr. Margaret Duggan Saidi, ed. George Mora, 2 vols. (Baltimore: Johns Hopkins University Press, 1981).

Z   Darwin, *Zoonomia: or, The Laws of Organic Life*, 2 vols. (London: J. Johnson, 1794–96).

31

THE JENNERATION OF DISEASE:
VACCINATION, ROMANTICISM,
AND REVOLUTION

Tim Fulford and Debbie Lee

Source: *Studies in Romanticism* 39 (2000), 139–63.

In 1798, Britain was preparing for invasion by French revolutionary armies. To the government and the press it seemed ill-prepared to defend itself. The navy had recently mutinied at Spithead and the Nore, and pro-French radicals were fomenting discontent amongst the laboring classes. Worse still, France was threatening Britain's colonies in the East and West Indies. Faced with the exigencies of national politics and imperial war, the established powers in London found little opportunity to pay attention to what turned out to be the most significant event of that year—the quiet appearance in print of a medical treatise entitled *An Inquiry into The Causes and Effects of The Variolae Vaccinae, A Disease Discovered in Some of the Western Counties of England . . . and known by the name of The Cow Pox.*[1] This revolutionary work by Edward Jenner, a little-known provincial doctor, outlined the first ever theory of vaccination, making the eventual global eradication of smallpox possible.[2]

Jenner's *Inquiry* was beautiful in its simplicity. It was not rooted in visions of national and international conquest of disease, but in the bodies of those who worked in the English countryside. It was not about global politics but about rural health. It was not derived from scientific authorities but from the oral tradition of Gloucestershire villagers. Just over seventy pages in length, it presented a series of stories about dairy maids, farm hands, paupers, and man servants whose daily, pastoral, activities brought them in touch with cows and cowpox, and thus made them immune to smallpox. The most important case was that of dairymaid Sarah Nelmes. "Infected with the cow-pox from her master's cows," Nelmes's pustulised hand provided the infected matter for Jenner's most crucial experiment. He inserted Nelmes's cowpox into the arm of a "healthy boy, about eight years old" (*An Inquiry* 153). The boy, he discovered, barely took sick and was thereafter immune to smallpox.

Jenner presented Nelmes's hand to the public in the form of an elegant engraving.[3] But his beautifully illustrated story of pastoral healing made little initial impression. The rural simplicity of the story of the dairymaid with a sore hand, like the rustic speech of that other volume of 1798, *Lyrical Ballads*, was too quiet, too bucolic, to find immediate understanding in a metropolis that was alarmed by the threat of invasion and revolution. After three months waiting in London to receive patients, Jenner retired to Gloucestershire. Not a single person had volunteered for vaccination. Jenner, like Wordsworth and Coleridge, needed to promote his work by explaining its innovatory significance—both to men of influence and to the reading public at large. The poets sent their volume to major politicians and added the polemical *Preface*; Jenner, likewise, launched a propaganda campaign designed to convince the socially powerful that Britain would benefit from the healing power of nature that he, a doctor who had "sought the lowly and sequestered paths of life,"[4] had harnessed. This essay tells the story of that campaign. It was a campaign that, from the start, presented science through the medium of poetry. Jenner attracted the services of romantic poets, who lent their verse to his efforts to create the taste by which his discovery might be enjoyed by the people. They helped him make his pastoral medicine seem socially and politically conservative as they sought public approval in a Britain dominated by war with revolutionary France.

Pastoralism and the Body

The taste for Jenner's medicine was affected by the fact that vaccination threatened to break some of the most powerful social and cultural taboos of its time. Jenner's discovery turned the pastoral ideal, long elaborated in polite poetry (including verse by Jenner himself)[5] into a strange reality. It made the life and lore of cowherds and dairymaids, typically portrayed as being of bucolic innocence and ignorance, into the saviors of the lives of their social superiors. Those who owned the land became dependent upon those Burke, in his attack on revolutionary politics, had called the "swinish multitude." Fellow doctors advised Jenner against publishing a theory that relied on "vulgar stories," since "the public opinion of his knowledge and discernment" would "materially suffer."[6] The Royal Society had already begun, in the words of a contemporary, "to suppress all *Jacobin innovations*" in science.[7] It refused to publish Jenner's theories "which appeared so much at variance with established knowledge, and withal so incredible."[8] 1798 was not a good year for a Briton to be challenging the established order.

The *Inquiry* did more than invert the social order: it made the bodies of pastoralists, and ultimately the bodies of cows, essential to the nation's health. Briton's bodies were to be invaded with cow pox matter scraped from the bodies of women such as Nelmes, and from the udders of cows. For vaccination differed from other medical advances: it penetrated the human body with matter derived from the bodies of beasts and, in so doing, it made people sick to make them well.

Jenner asked of people something much more profound than simply to accept that cowpox prevented smallpox. He asked them to accept that cattle and humans had similar constitutions at a time when medical men, philosophers, and politicians alike were drawing lines and creating categories not only between the human and the animal world, but within these worlds.[9] The *Inquiry into the Causes and Effects of the Variolae Vaccinae* emerged from Jenner's training as a comparative anatomist. A pupil of the pioneering surgeon and naturalist, John Hunter, Jenner had long thought that examining the effects of disease on animals "casts a bright and steady light over some of the most obscure parts of human pathology" (quoted in Baron I: 102). He argued that diseases were not just similar in animals and humans, but that they spread from one to the other: "Domestication of animals has certainly proved a prolific source of diseases among men" (quoted in Baron I: 136). Cross-infection was rendered more likely when animals themselves had been cross-bred into hybrids (Jenner himself had conducted experiments to determine whether foxes and dogs would mate and breed). "The wolf, disarmed of ferocity," the *Inquiry* observed, had degenerated into the domesticated dog, often "pillowed in the lady's lap" (153).[10] Such unnatural intimacy between the human and the interbred animal made humans susceptible to a wide variety of diseases.

Animals mutated through crossbreeding to inferior versions of their former selves. Humans, likewise, became vulnerable to disease through degeneration. Through a sort of unnatural crossbreeding with industry and luxury, they were in a constant state of "deviation" from the state in which they were "originally placed by nature" (153). Sounding like Rousseau (regarded as one of the architects of the French Revolution), Jenner identified the causes of human degeneration, as "love of splendour," the "indulgences of luxury," and the association with "a great number of animals" (153). The upper class lady with her lapdog, living a life of ease and luxury, was already to radical writers, not least Coleridge and Wollstonecraft, a symbol of moral degeneracy.[11] She became, in Jenner's theory, a medical danger to the race. The *Inquiry* brought radical suspicion of aristocratic manners home to the body: luxury, Jenner's science suggested, tainted the blood. Pastoral simplicity, on the other hand, protected the body from corruption—and Jenner, as the engraving of Nelmes showed, had the hand to prove it.

Jenner's literalization of the pastoral ideal played to contemporary fears that the ruling classes had become corrupted by the wealth which stemmed from Britain's commercial success. But his pastoralized body bred as many fears as it answered. Fear of English men and women degenerating to cattle became the cornerstone of opposition to Jenner. In 1802 James Gillray published a cartoon imagining the "wonderful effects of the new inoculation": Gillray depicts vaccination as a wild orgy of transformation where a side-glancing doctor vaccinates subjects who then sprout cows from their limbs, buttocks, mouths, and ears. One poor vaccination victim simply grows a giant cowpox pustule from the right side of her face. Satanic horns erupt through the skull of another. The cartoon finds a graphic language to articulate widely-shared anxieties about the power of new science in the hands of an increasingly assertive medical profession. The development of comparative anatomy, like the advances in galvanism and electrochemistry, threatened to invade and transform the human. Dr. Jenner, like the slightly later Dr. Frankenstein, has the power to metamorphose men into grotesque miscreations who are both man and beast.[12]

This vaccination anxiety reached its pinnacle with Dr. Benjamin Moseley, a surgeon to Charles James Fox, who had spent many years treating smallpox in Jamaica. Moseley, like many in the medical profession, had a vested interest in the existing inoculation system, whereby doctors would take "infected matter" from one of the smallpox pustules of a diseased patient, preferably a patient who had a mild case of the disease. They scratched the infected matter into the arms of people who had never had smallpox in the hope it would make them immune. In many cases it did. But the inoculation was risky. The patient could die of smallpox or, more commonly, spread the disease to others and thus amplify the epidemic.[13] Inoculation did not, however, demand the infection of humans from the pustules of animals as did vaccination. Moseley imagined Jenner's patients degenerating into beasts:

> Can any person say what may be the consequences of introducing a bestial humour into the human frame, after a long lapse of years? Who knows, besides, what ideas may rise, in the course of time, from a brutal fever having excited its incongruous impression on the brain? Who knows, also, that the human character may undergo strange mutations from quadruped sympathy; and that some modern Pasiphae may rival the fables of old?[14]

Moseley parodied Jenner's pastoral language and his theory that disease cross-bred from animal into human form. He speculated "that owing to vaccination the british ladies *might* wander in the fields to receive the embraces of the bull."[15] Vaccination had become sexual bestiality, infection a form of impregnation. Pasiphae gave birth to the minotaur: vaccination, in Moseley's allegory, produced monsters, having corrupted the moral character of British gentlewomen from the inside out.[16]

Moseley found allies amongst other doctors who were unconvinced of vaccination's safety and reluctant to lose the income stemming from their professional success as inoculators. Together they launched a noisy pamphlet campaign against Jenner's new science.[17] They attacked him by associating his innovatory science with revolutionary France: "are we to worship—to applaud—or even to submit to *Evil*,—to *Buonaparte*—or to *Vaccination* . . . —No!—Never let us degrade our honour—our virtue—or our consciences—by such servility:—let us contend against them, with all our exertions and might;—not doubting but we shall ultimately triumph, in a cause supported by *truth*, *humanity*, and *virtue*, and which therefore we well know *Heaven* itself must *approve*."[18] Resisting Jenner was like resisting Napoleon, a divinely sanctioned mission against threats to the established order in Britain.

Jenner's opponents struck at the heart of his discovery. They cast doubt on vaccination's safety. "The Holles Street Case" was Moseley's most startling commentary on the subject. In this case, a nine month old boy who was vaccinated began to grow "on his back and loins patches of HAIR, not resembling his own hair, for that was of a light colour, but brown, and of THE SAME LENGTH AND QUALITY AS THAT OF A COW" (Thornton 385). Moseley's hysteric account, like Gillray's cartoon, imagines a cow erupting from the boy's skin in a way even more horrifying than the way smallpox pustules erupted. If this were not enough, Moseley warned against a cowpox conspiracy. "The Cow Pox medical men," he claimed, "were numerous and powerful . . . they had their eye on every person who made observations against the Cow Pox . . . they determined to do all the injury they could to any men, who should make known any cases of mischief, or failure" (Moseley 64). Moseley also suggested that vaccination could cause "Cow Mania," affecting the brain, and in this sense he prefigures the present-day British fear of B.S.E./mad-cow disease:

> Though I am ready to admit that the Cow-pox is not contagious,— yet I know the Cow *Mania* is; and that the malady, whether arising from *empty ventricles of the brain*, or from excessive thickness of the *os frontis*, makes the distempered, to men not steeled against the infirmities of HIS fellow creatures, more objects of pity than of resentment;—more proper,—than any infected from the Levant,— to perform solitary quarantine on beds of straw.
>
> (Moseley, quoted in Thornton 231)

Moseley's remark about the Levant plays on racial fears. It implies that vaccinators leave their subjects like those with diseases caught from Orientals; they infect rather than protect. They degrade the blood just as sexual contact with "beast-like" West Indian slaves did.[19] Yet Moseley's racist reaction to vaccination may have helped Jenner win public acceptance.

Because Moseley articulated the fear of humans turning into cattle in such an extreme way, the medical profession came, after considerable initial doubt about vaccination, to reject opposition to it as irrational prejudice.[20]

Patrons

If the profession and the public came gradually to accept vaccination, it was not by accident. Faced with Moseley's virulent parody of the pastoralism of the *Inquiry*, Jenner had soon realized that he needed powerful supporters. Any radical implications to his theories about luxury were left behind as Jenner set out to cultivate the patronage of royalty and aristocracy. Jenner's neighbor, the Earl of Berkeley, used his influence at Court to gain an audience for the doctor. On 7 March 1800 Jenner was presented to the King, who gave permission for the second edition of the *Inquiry* to be dedicated to him. That same month, he was also received by the Prince of Wales, thus ensuring that vaccination had the public approbation of the man who would succeed as Regent when his father again went mad. The Prince of Wales moved in a younger, more fashionable circle than George III. He also patronized the Whig opposition. By meeting both King and Prince, Jenner had received an injection of patronage that ensured vaccination would spread to all corners of the aristocratic and political elite.

It was through the characteristically eighteenth-century mechanism of patronage that vaccination first took hold in Britain. Jenner was careful to ensure that he cultivated the most influential people—by the end of March 1800 he had also been presented to the Queen, whose eighth son had died of smallpox almost seventeen years earlier. Later he vaccinated the adopted boy of Princess Caroline: approval by the royal mothers was a powerful sanction for the ladies of the aristocracy, who rapidly moved to have their own children vaccinated.

If the ladies of the aristocracy spread vaccination by example, their husbands had more direct power. The Earl of Lonsdale was a Tory magnate with some of the most extensive landholdings in the country. In October 1800 he had Dr. Robert Thornton vaccinate all four hundred inhabitants of the estate-village of Lowther. In the following weeks Thornton vaccinated about one thousand more locals who rented their homes and lands from the Earl. Vaccination was spread from the top down, not by government-organized campaigns but from royalty to aristocracy, and from aristocracy to their tenants. It was disseminated, that is to say, through the existing power-structure of Britain, which depended upon the manipulation of patronage, interest and obligation, on an informal basis, by the landowning elite. Jenner made himself an establishment man, astute enough to secure patronage. Suspicious of radicals such as Tom Paine and William Cobbett,[21] he kept his oppositional politics private[22] and allied his science with high society—in conscious difference from radical scientists such as Erasmus

Darwin and Joseph Priestley.[23] Wordsworth, of course, was to take the same route, accepting the patronage of the Lonsdale family who had pioneered vaccination in Lowther. Both doctor and poet overcame indifference to their versions of pastoral by making alliances with the aristocratic class of which they had first been implicitly critical.

Patronizing a Poet: Jenner and Robert Bloomfield

If Jenner sought patrons, he also acted as one. He encouraged a far more popular rural poet than Wordsworth to write verse praising vaccination. Robert Bloomfield, who termed himself a "writer of Pastoral poetry, and literally a Cow-boy,"[24] was a former farm laborer and shoemaker who had taught himself verse-making after reading Thomson's *The Seasons*. Patronized by Capel Lofft and the Duke of Grafton, Bloomfield had published *The Farmer's Boy* in 1800. It had achieved immediate popular success on a scale made possible by the rapidly expanding book market. Twenty-six thousand copies were sold in fewer than three years, and translations appeared in French, Italian and Latin. To the poetry-reading public, Bloomfield was marketed as an authentic rustic voice, a peasant turned poet, whose pastorals were rooted in his childhood experience of sheep and cowherding. Bloomfield seemed to accept this version of himself, albeit with anxiety, writing that being allowed to remain silent in fashionable company "is no small privilege to a man swung at arm's length into publicity with all his mechanical habits and embarrassments about him. How far such habits are, or ought to be, overcome, is a question upon which I have not decided" (*Poems of Bloomfield* I: ii).

Jenner, himself a poet, showed an astute understanding of the possibilities presented by Bloomfield's success in the burgeoning public sphere addressed by poetry. He encouraged Bloomfield to write on vaccination. After all, Bloomfield was not only the poet in vogue, and not only a former cow-herd, but a rustic who had suffered the effects of smallpox. His father had died of the disease when he was a year old. By July 1802 the gentleman-doctor, accustomed to writing pastoral verse himself, was inviting the laborer-poet to tea, with the intention of directing and correcting his vaccination poem. Bloomfield accepted the hospitality, but worried that Jenner was too pressing a patron:

> This moment a letter from Dr. Jenner invites me to tea this evening. What shall I do—leave 150 lines of an unfinished subject in his hands? I am bound to consult Mr. Lofft and the Duke, and to submit pieces to their judgment, and never will do otherwise; and yet it is hard to say *no* in such cases as this. I wish he would suspend his curiosity six months, and I would take my chance. He is a very amiable man, and perhaps rates my abilities too high. He is an enthusiast, in his pursuit.[25]

Jenner was not a man to let the chance for favorable publicity from a fashionable writer go begging. He pursued Bloomfield until his vaccination poem was published. In 1803 he was writing to Bloomfield "enquiring my determination as to the poem 'On Vaccination,' and expressing great interest in my welfare" (*Correspondence of Bloomfield*, 29 Feb. 1803: 31).

Bloomfield's poem, *Good Tidings; Or, News From the Farm* appeared in 1804, with a dedication to Jenner. True to Bloomfield's public image as "the farmer's boy," the poem spread the gospel of vaccination from the country to the town-based public. The poem begins with a pastoral scene of a kind familiar to today's readers of Wordsworth, Coleridge, and Blake. It focuses on a simple, innocent child of nature at play.

> . . . so admirably fair,
> With guileless dimples, and with flaxen hair
> That waves in ev'ry breeze . . . he's often seen
> Beside yon cottage wall, or on the green,
> With others match'd in spirit and in size,
> Health on their cheeks, and rapture in their eyes;
> That full expanse of voice, to childhood dear,
> Soul of their sports, is duly cherish'd here;
> And hark! that laugh is his, that jovial cry;
> He hears the ball and trundling hoop brush by
> (lines 1–10, *Poems of Bloomfield* I: 100–125)

But this child is blighted by smallpox: "the boy is blind" (22). He is a pathetic figure, an embodiment of rural innocence and natural growth that is tainted by a disease spread from city to country: "When last year's corn was green upon the ground: / From yonder town infection found its way" (48–49).

Bloomfield's poem is a powerful one because it is driven by his rhetorical efforts to resolve a tension which went to the very heart of his poetic authority as a "writer of Pastoral poetry and literally a Cow-boy." It was a tension that affected Wordsworth and John Clare too, for it arose from the attempt to claim that the idealizations inherent in the genre of pastoral poetry were observable in the lives of contemporary rural laborers. When, as was the case for Bloomfield and Clare, the poet's own position as a former laborer was one of the reasons for his fashionable success, the tension became threatening to his commercial prospects and to his sense of identity. Both Bloomfield and Clare suffered declining sales and increasing personal crises.

What is at stake in *Good Tidings* is the very continuance of a rural way of life upon which Bloomfield's poetic authority depends. He had made his reputation as a poet who, by virtue of his peasant upbringing (normally an insuperable disadvantage for a would-be poet), could uniquely root the pastoral ideal in the real. But smallpox threatened to uproot the ideal from the experienced world—to destroy innocence and peace as it wiped out whole families and blasted entire communities. Smallpox threatened Bloomfield's precarious poetic career because it exposed a fatal gap between the real world of farm laborers of which he had personal experience, and the idealized version of it to which his publication as a "pastoral" poet committed him.

Bloomfield's sense of the danger his muse was in is evident in the dedication, which pleads that "the egotism, so conspicuous in the poem . . . ought to be forgiven" (ɪ: 100). In the poem itself, he again apologized for including grim details drawn from his real personal history, for these details undermined the pastoral poetic models to which he (and his readers) wanted to conform. Yet these details constitute the most powerful passage in the poem as smallpox menaces the Bloomfield family's domestic bliss:

> *Home*, where six children, yielding to its pow'r,
> Gave hope and patience a most trying hour;
> One at her breast still drew the living stream,
> And sense of danger never marr'd his dream;
> Yet all exclaim'd, and with a pitying eye
> "Whoe'er survives the shock, that child will die!"
> But vain the fiat,—Heav'n restor'd them all,
> And destin'd one of riper years to fall.
> Midnight beheld the close of all his pain,
> His grave was clos'd when midnight came again;
> No bell was heard to toll, no funeral pray'r,
> No kindred bow'd, no wife, no children there;
> Its horrid nature could inspire a dread
> That cut the bonds of custom like a thread.
> (179–92)

As if anticipating Jeffrey's attacks on the dismal egotism of Wordsworth's rural verse, Bloomfield has his imaginary readers criticize him: " 'Why tell us tales of woe, thou who didst give / Thy soul to rural themes, and bade them live? / What means this zeal of thine, this kindling fire? / The rescu'd infant and the dying sire?' " (201–4). To this the poet replies by trading on the affection readers feel for him as author of *The Farmer's Boy*. He calls the reader a "Kind heart," he terms himself "the lowly minstrel dear to thee" (205, 207). He asks for pity on the basis that his humble origins exposed him to the disease which makes visions of rural peace hard to sustain. If he sinks below the pastoral into "tales of woe" it is because he was the child whose father died: "Though love enjoin'd not infant eyes to weep, / In manhood's zenith shall his feelings sleep?" (211–12). Pathos, it seems, is the device by which Bloomfield will overcome the division between his own experience of rural life and the pastoral terms into which he is expected to translate it.

Pathos is not the poem's final solution to the tensions in Bloomfield's position: Edward Jenner is. Vaccination saved Bloomfield's muse because it made the pastoral ideal seem liveable—at least in one poem. It allowed it again to appear rooted in actual rural life. He said as much explicitly:

> Sweet beam'd the star of peace upon those days
> When Virtue watch'd my childhood's quiet ways,
> Whence a warm spark of Nature's holy flame
> Gave the farm-yard an honourable name,
> But left one theme unsung: then, who had seen
> In herds that feast upon the vernal green,
> Or dreamt that in the blood of kine there ran
> Blessings beyond the sustenance of man?
> We tread the meadow, and we scent the thorn,
> We hail the day-spring of a summer's morn;
> Nor mead at dawning day, nor thymy heath,
> Transcends the fragrance of the heifer's breath:
> May that dear fragrance, as it floats along
> O'er ev'ry flow'r that lives in rustic song;
> May all the sweets of meadows and of kine
> Embalm, O Health! this offering at thy shrine.
>
> (81–94)

The sweet smell of success was the "dear fragrance" of a cow's breath, now revealed not just as a feature of rustic song, but as nature's remedy for diseases bred in towns.

Briefly, Bloomfield's pastoralism offers to become socially radical. Not only is rural life preferred to urban but, as in *Lyrical Ballads*, rustics seem wiser than gentlemen. Jenner, Bloomfield tells us, had been dependent upon rural knowledge, on the local "tradition" known to Gloucestershire pastoralists that contact with cows prevented smallpox infection. But if this seems to make professional medicine secondary to rustic experience, Bloomfield soon suggests that Jenner had raised pastoral lore to the status of scientific truth. In the process, in Bloomfield's heroic portrait, he became godlike, giving healing law to the whole world. By the poem's climax, its pastoralism was neither radical nor levelling: vaccination did not lower men to the level of cattle; Jenner did not simply codify what cowherds already knew. Instead, through Jenner, the cowshed came to command the international stage:

> Perhaps supreme, alone, triumphant stood
> The great, the conscious power of doing good,
> The power to will, and wishes to embrace
> Th' emancipation of the human race;

331

A joy that must all mortal praise outlive,
A wealth that grateful nations cannot give.
Forth sped the truth immediate from his hand,
And confirmations sprung in ev'ry land;
In ev'ry land, on beauty's lily arm,
On infant softness, like a magic charm,
Appear'd the gift that conquers as it goes;
The dairy's boast, the simple, saving Rose!

                                          (115–26)

In the image of the rose Bloomfield made the blister raised in the vaccinated arm into a symbol of natural beauty and fertility. Jenner, scattering vaccine roses, had become a romantic hero—a godlike genius who harnessed the hidden virtue of nature. Vaccination killed the "foul serpent" contagion and allowed villagers to "Love ye your neighbours" without fear of infecting their own children (237, 243). In other words, it restored Eden and allowed God's commandments to be lived out on earth. Jenner's "victory" over smallpox was an apotheosis of the pastoral life which Bloomfield declared himself uniquely fitted to celebrate:

Victory shall increase
Th'incalculable wealth of private peace;
And such a victory, unstain'd with gore,
That strews its laurels at the cottage door,
Sprung from the farm, and from the yellow mead,
Should be the glory of the pastoral reed.

                                          (365–70)

Jenner saved Bloomfield's pastoralism (at least in the short term) by allowing him to maintain the idealizations that his gentlemanly public expected. In return, Bloomfield helped Jenner's publicity drive, assistance which Jenner relished. After the poem was recited to a special meeting of the Royal Jennerian Society, he rewarded Bloomfield with a silver inkstand. Later, he sent a silver tea-caddy for Mrs Bloomfield.

The Doctor as Romantic Genius: Jenner, Coleridge and Southey

As university-educated gentlemen, Coleridge and Southey were not to be so easily patronized as Bloomfield. Yet as enthusiasts for the healing power of nature and subscribers to Rousseau's idealization of childhood innocence, they were ready converts to the cause. As a father, Southey found ample reason to praise the discoverer of vaccination. In 1802 he declared "My little girl has taught me some new feelings: I have learnt to see beauty in that total absence of all thought and all feeling in an infant's face. As soon as

332

there is good matter in town, she is to be inoculated for the cow-pox. I begin to think Dr. Jenner has not been rewarded as he deserves—that the sum was not enough for such a discovery—nor for a great nation to bestow."[26] Coleridge agreed and gathered evidence from his reading to help Jenner prove his case for the "the identity of the Small & cow pox."[27] Southey also used his pen to aid the cause. He reviewed *Good Tidings* favorably, taking the opportunity to publicize vaccination.[28]

Like Bloomfield, the Bristol-based poets elevated Jenner to the status of scientific genius. In so doing, they viewed him in romantic terms derived from their own experience of medical experimentation. It was in Bristol that they had become involved with Dr. Thomas Beddoes, who was pioneering new forms of treatment (with Jenner's help) at his Pneumatic Institution and who became a strong supporter of Jenner.[29] Beddoes was a radical democrat, who pamphleteered against war with France and criticized aristocratic corruption in Britain's government.[30] His medicine had radical elements too, for like Jenner he speculated that disease was caused by the fashionable and luxurious lifestyles of the rich. "Fatal indolence" amongst the leisured classes weakened their constitutions, leaving them vulnerable to consumption.[31] Like Jenner, Beddoes proposed a remedy that seemed levelling in its social implications, for he too had been putting pastoral lore to experimental test. Interested in the tradition that "stable-boys and grooms . . . are . . . but little liable to consumption," Beddoes sought to develop the healing powers of cows.[32] He had consumptive patients housed in cowsheds, hoping that the atmosphere produced by the cattle's breath and manure would effect a cure. Joseph Priestley's daughter was one who endured this "stabling." She wrote from her "Cow-House" that despite the "nauseous" stench and the "successive generations of flies" she had become "more than ever a friend to the cows" (quoted in Porter 106). Others were less enamored, complaining of the "disgrace" of being a "fellow-lodger with the cows" (quoted in Porter 106). Beddoes lamented one young lady who had died after refusing to spend a second winter closeted with cattle.

Beddoes' cowshed method exposed him to "ridicule" because it reduced well-to-do patients to the level of peasants living alongside beasts. Beddoes offered the alternative of introducing "vessels" containing cattle manure into the patient's apartment (quoted in Porter 106). But this only rubbed respectable noses, already offended by Beddoes' politics, in the dirt. Beddoes found the reputation of his medicine tainted by the way it violated the taboos on which the social and political hierarchy depended. Still worse, it did not work as the Bristol poets came to realize. Southey wrote in 1800, "This is a place of experiments. We have consumptive patients, in cow-houses some, and some in a uniform high temperature—and the only result seems to be, that a cure may sometimes be effected, but very rarely" (*Southey Letters* I: 93).

Beddoes' cowshed method failed in practice, but so, argued Jenner's opponents, did vaccination. And in 1800 epidemiology was not capable of understanding theoretically how either would work. Based on rural tradition, the remedies of the West Country doctors seemed not only similar in origin, but similarly untested and unfounded on medical authorities. William Rowley attacked Jenner and Beddoes together—cow-pox madness had infected a medical profession that was already "Gas and vital air mad," "Electricity and galvanism mad." Jenner's medicine was like the "fanciful and extravagant celestial visions" of the "illuminati" (the mystical secret society suspected of fomenting political revolution).[33]

Jenner and his supporters drew lessons from such attacks. Not only did Jenner steer clear of Beddoes' radical politics, but his publicists gradually replaced the levelling implications of his cow medicine with an emphasis on the doctor as a genius of nature. Coleridge and Southey had another Bristol scientist in mind as they made that emphasis—the young Humphry Davy, Beddoes' assistant. Coleridge wrote that he had "never met so extraordinary a young man" as Davy, and Southey encouraged him to write poetry as well as develop his science.[34] Davy responded with verse that embraced the idea of the discoverer as genius:

> To scan the laws of Nature, to explore
> The tranquil reign of mild Philosophy;
> Or on Newtonian wings sublime to soar
> Through the bright regions of the starry sky.
>
> From these pursuits the Sons of Genius scan
> The end of their creation; hence they know
> The fair, sublime, immortal hopes of man,
> From whence alone undying pleasures glow.[35]

Davy put his fine words into practice: it was by intervening in nature that he revealed previously unknown aspects of Creation and justified, in the eyes of his peers, the title of genius.

With Jenner vaccinating in Gloucestershire and Davy developing nitrous oxide in Bristol the West Country was suddenly at the forefront of science. In this heady atmosphere, it was the notion of genius that the poets created for Davy (and that he embraced) which they began to apply to Jenner too. Coleridge wrote directly to Jenner in 1811, telling the doctor that he congratulated himself that he had known men whom "Providence has gifted with the power to acquire" true fame by doing "what I could most have wished to have done" (*Coleridge Letters* 6.1025). Amongst these men he named Humphry Davy and Jenner himself. They were benefactors of mankind who would be justly revered by future generations. Jenner had gained a place in the romantic Pantheon of creative geniuses. According to Coleridge's excited theories, scientist and poet were engaged in a similar, prophetic, pursuit— harnessing the powers of nature by their imaginations, and so blessing mankind. Davy was a "man who *born* a Poet first converted Poetry into Science and *realized* what few men possessed Genius enough to fancy."[36]

If scientific thought was a kind of realization of poetry, poetry could be an exaltation of science. Convinced of Jenner's genius, Coleridge declared that he would lend his own poetic powers to the vaccination cause: "I have planned a poem on this theme, which after long deliberation, I have convinced myself is capable in the highest degree of being poetically treated, according to our divine bard's own definition of poetry, as *simple, sensuous* (i.e. appealing to the senses, by imagery, sweetness of sound, &c.) *and impassioned*" (*Coleridge Letters* 6.1025). He never wrote the poem, but his enthusiasm for vaccination was sincere enough (he had also seen his family menaced by smallpox). He was well aware that enthusiasm would promote the spread of vaccination, if published in influential places. He told Jenner that he intended to write articles on the discovery in *The Courier* as it was "the paper of widest circulation, and, as an evening paper, both more read in the country, and read more at leisure than the morning papers" (*Coleridge Letters* 6.1025). Jenner responded appreciatively to the prospect of such favorable publicity: "his offer to me was very important" (Fisher 156).

Poetic Conquest: Jenner as Military Hero

Coleridge ceased writing for *The Courier* before he could write his articles praising Jenner. But he had by then already singled the doctor out as an example to the nation. In his journal, *The Friend*, he wrote, "Pronounce meditatively the name of Jenner, and ask what might we not hope, what need we deem unattainable, if all the time, the effort, the skill, which we waste in making ourselves miserable through vice, and vicious through misery, were embodied and marshalled to a systematic War against the existing Evils of Nature?" (*The Friend* 2.69). Jenner's science had become holy war: his conquest of evil offered an example, in Coleridge's moralizing scheme, to redeem Britons, high and low, from lethargy and viciousness.

John Williams agreed. His "Ode to the Discoverer of Vaccination" saw Jenner's work in heroic terms as a biblical battle against evil:

> A fearful plague whose black envenomed breath
> Loads the pure air with misery and death,
> Dire as the pest that smote Thy servant Job,
> Hath long run riot round this motley globe.
> On beauty's native sweets profanely trod.
> And marred, with cruel joy, the handiworks of GOD.[37]

Jenner came to believe in the truth, as well as the propaganda value, of publicity of this kind: by 1807 he saw himself as an inspired benefactor who deserved greater reward by the nation.

With Britain at war with Napoleonic France throughout the period in which Jenner was actively promoting vaccination, images of battle and conquest were not only current but patriotic. Portraying vaccination as a holy war ensured that Jenner's medicine appeared to the public as a cause for national pride. Bloomfield declared that, through Jenner, "England strikes down the nation's bitterest foe" and, "amidst the clangor" of Europe's war, ensures "new germs of life sprung up beneath the sword" (312–18). Jenner had become a military hero to make the nation proud of itself because it could fight the life-giving fight of vaccination as well as the life-destroying war with Napoleon. Vaccination became evidence of the value of the British civilization which was currently being menaced by the French. Coleridge told Jenner that he thought the idea of vaccination had been "inspired into you by the All-preserver, as a counterpoise to the crushing weight of this unexampled war" (*Coleridge Letters* 6.1025).

Coleridge and Bloomfield were not the only poets who portrayed vaccination as God's gift to Britain and Jenner as a native genius worth fighting for. Christopher Anstey's "Ode to Jenner" actually viewed the feared French invasion as an epidemic. The paternal Jenner could offer Britain victory over one disease, but not over the pestilence of Napoleonic imperialism:

> But what, alas! avails the blooming boy,
> His father's pride, his mother's only joy,—
> The lovely virgin, or the well-earn'd fame,
> And all the glories of the British name,—
> If Heav'n has doom'd the downfall of the state,
> And thy [Jenner's] protection but retards our fate
> If France pursues her infamous career,
> To spread the pest of her dominion here;
> And if the blood of innocence must flow;
> To grace the triumphs of a Gallic foe?[38]

War-imagery of this kind performed two functions at once. It promoted Jenner's medicine by elevating him to the status of heroic victor (a peaceful conqueror in contrast to the warlike conqueror Napoleon). It gave Britons motives to fight France—the civilization which produced and was protected by Jenner needed preserving from foreign political diseases. Vaccination thereby became enlisted as a key part of a nationalistic call-to-arms. Paradoxically, its very peacefulness became a cause for war. In the process, the patriotic loyalty of poet and doctor was established beyond doubt—a matter of no small importance for both Coleridge and Jenner because their past association with the democratic Dr. Beddoes left them vulnerable to charges of pro-French Jacobinism.

Southey had also been a democrat in his Bristol years. After 1800 he also wished to live down his reputation for radicalism. And he also used

336

vaccination to do so. Where Anstey saw revolution as an infection threatening to spread from France, Southey viewed it as a disease that had already become endemic in Britain's laboring classes. He wrote in 1816 that

> revolutions in the state are like the eruption in the small pox—the consequence of the disease pre-existent in the system—the body politic has been successfully inoculated for it, & the inoculation has taken;—the disease exists; & if it should not run the same course as in France, it will be because government can depend upon the army, & the Gentry of the country, Whigs & all, would rally round it in danger. But as far depends upon the opinion of the multitude, the work is done.[39]

Here the actual success of vaccination in protecting against smallpox makes it a reassuring political metaphor for those afraid of a revolution by the disenfranchised. If revolution is an infectious disease, the immunization of the "body politic" (i.e. the enfranchised, gentlemanly classes) suggests that it can be contained. Here vaccination assuages Southey's political alarm and gives an air of scientific certainty to his hopes that revolution will be put down. It is an imaginative means of stemming political change. Southey, that is to say, uses Jenner to save the political status quo that he had himself earlier hoped to destroy. Vaccination, in Southey's reactionary prose, protects the political health of the nation.

Jenner was both topicalized and made respectably anti-democratic by Southey's politicization of vaccination. By 1815 Southey was Poet Laureate, the voice of the establishment. In this capacity he portrayed Wellington's victory at Waterloo as a divinely sanctioned victory of British good over Napoleonic evil. Later he celebrated Jenner in similar terms. In *A Tale of Paraguay* (1825) Jenner is a soldier against smallpox: he waged a "war ... against the miseries which afflict mankind."[40] He and the Duke of Wellington are warriors who "triumph'd once again for God and for the right" (*Proem* to *A Tale of Paraguay*, line 23). Fighting smallpox is here like fighting the ultimate enemy of British power: Napoleon and the revolutionary politics with which he threatened Britain and its colonies. Jenner is made a hero. He becomes a national savior as important, and as respectable, as the Iron Duke.

Vaccination and the Fighting Forces

Publicizing vaccination as a form of holy war would, of itself, have converted few to the cause had it not been so badly needed in the actual military campaigns Britain was launching against France. In 1797, Dr. Thomas Trotter issued a pamphlet called *Medicina Nautica: An Essay on the Diseases of Seamen*, where he wrote:

> The ravages which this fatal disease have made . . . in our fleets and armies, are beyond all precedent: the insidious mode of attack, the rapid strides at which it advances to an incurable stage, point it out as one of the most formidable opponents of medical skill. It has offered the severest obstacle to military operations, which the history of modern warfare can produce.[41]

Like its close cousin, yellow fever, smallpox was a contagion whose reputation arose from Britain's experience of war—particularly in the tropics, where deaths from disease exceeded deaths in battle by a ratio of eight to one. In the early part of the eighteenth century, doctors had believed that people contracted smallpox through inevitable changes to the "innate seeds," which formed a part of every human's anatomy. As the period wore on, military doctors observed at close hand the circumstances in which it spread.[42] Smallpox and other diseases, they concluded, resulted instead from atmospheric changes or from small particles penetrating the body (perhaps an early version of germ-theory). Smallpox went from being a disease inside of the body, to one outside of it. This shift in perception turned the personal body political, and turned the purely medical, military. When pestilence stemmed from the body, people self-destructed. When it came from the earth and air, people were the victims of the environment. Military doctors branded it as an enemy whose methods for attack seemed beyond normal wartime decorum. Jenner himself referred to it with military terminology, as "that formidable foe to health."[43]

In fact, smallpox had waged its own biological warfare in the recent political past. In 1779, the French and Spanish sought to attack Britain in what historians refer to as the closest France had ever come to successful invasion. The French and Spanish fleets had lined up in the English Channel and dominated it for three days. When the time for attack came, however, neither the French nor the Spanish troops could move a muscle. The crews were weakened by smallpox. So much so, that bodies reportedly piled up in the Channel at such an alarming rate that villagers would not eat the harbor fish for over a month. The remaining crews turned home in defeat (Hopkins 73–74).

It was not only foreign troops who were weakened by disease. During the Napoleonic wars the British military was desperate to recruit more men. The navy found it almost impossible to keep ships' crews at full strength, despite constant use of the press-gang. Naval captains warned parliament that the war would be lost unless Britain's fleet could fight with a full and fit complement of men. The army, likewise, needed soldiers after losing whole expeditions to disease in the West Indies. The Commander-in-Chief of the army was Jenner's patron, the Duke of York. Here the campaign to convert the powerful to the vaccination cause had direct results: the Duke ordered the compulsory vaccination of regiments in 1800. In the same year, Gilbert

Blane, formerly Physician to the Fleet and currently Physician-in-Ordinary to another of Jenner's patrons—the Prince of Wales—introduced vaccination into the navy. In the armed forces, patrons rapidly translated Jenner's desire to make war on smallpox into action. Vaccination first became institutionalized by the state in the hierarchical structure of the military, as part of reforms designed to impose mass hygiene on the ranks.[44] Winning the war against smallpox helped win the war against Napoleon and Jenner was praised for both.[45] In 1822 Blane remembered

> those lately at the head of the navy and army, with that vigilant wisdom and humanity which become those who direct the affairs of a great and enlightened nation, recommended and enforced the practice of vaccination in both these departments, to the great furtherance of the public service. Their example has by no means been followed among the civil population of England.[46]

The Power of Jenner's Example

Blane's words reveal both Jenner's power and its limits. By 1815 Jenner's campaign had been successful. He was no longer an obscure provincial doctor, but a man acknowledged as a benefactor to mankind and rewarded by parliament. He had overcome objections that vaccination was revolutionary and defeated Moseley and the campaigns who had accused him of lowering humans to the level of beasts. His discovery had been adopted by the military and spread round the globe.

Yet the civil population of Britain had not offered their arms to Jenner's lancet. In part, their reluctance was a result of the way in which the vaccination campaign was organized. Jenner and his publicists had preached to the educated reading public. They had allied vaccination with the ruling classes —royalty, aristocracy and gentry. Here they had been successful: by 1815 vaccination was widespread amongst these classes. But although these classes had the power of patronage, this itself had limits. In the country, the laboring classes were tied to the lords and squires by relationships of deference. In the burgeoning cities, this was not the case, as Jenner complained in 1805: "in London my practice is limited to the higher orders of Society— In the Country, I can always find little Cottagers on whom I can introduce vaccine Virus in any form" (Fisher 147). Like Wordsworth, Jenner found the metropolis alienating because its social fluidity meant that his rustic vision was ineffective there. The lower classes in London could simply not be grasped, even when Jenner's notable patrons funded the Royal Jennerian Society to bring the benefits of vaccination to London's poor. By March 1805 it had performed only 6924 vaccinations in London; by roughly the same period 145,840 people had been vaccinated in Madras. The Society had failed to vaccinate on a mass scale because it expected candidates for vaccination to conform to a bureaucratic discipline of form filling and regular attendance at specified centers. Workers were reluctant or unable to meet these conditions: the Society's expectations were simply alien to the lives of those it set out to help.

Jenner never won the hearts of Britain's laboring classes—ironically enough since it was with rural laborers that he had begun. In the later Victorian period parliament created a centralized state bureaucracy through which vaccination could be imposed on the population as a whole. Vaccination was made compulsory and fines and imprisonment were the punishments for those who refused. But compulsion only bred resistance and a campaign to take "the parliamentary lancet out of the national arm,"[47] involving street protests and mass rallies, was successful by 1908. Vaccination had become the epitome of established, state control. It was resisted as an infringement of civil liberties by those on whom the government tried to impose it by force.

The seeds of vaccination's later history were sown by Jenner's publicity campaign. He had sold his discovery to the existing political elite and had relied on their influence and patronage to spread it. He had addressed that elite in person, but also through publicists writing for the press. Those publicists had aligned it with the anti-Jacobin politics of much of that elite— a politics that, in Southey's hands, revealed a deep need to impose order on the laboring classes (a need Jenner had come to share).[48] After 1800, then, vaccination was no longer simply imagined in the pastoral terms of the 1798 *Inquiry*. It was given a new public image as the divinely inspired discovery of a specifically British genius and as a holy war against infection— natural and political. It acquired a changed status in response to the need of Jenner and his allies to promote it (and to vindicate themselves) in a time of national and imperial strife with the forces unleashed by the French Revolution. With the aid of the poets, vaccination had become a remedy for multiple "infections." Its discoverer had become a hero, to be revered (but also, by some, resisted) for his "Jenneration" of both nature and politics.[49]

Notes

1 (London, 1798). All subsequent quotations from the *Inquiry* are taken from *The Harvard Classics*, ed. Charles W. Eliot: *Scientific Papers. Physiology Medicine Surgery Geology* (New York: P. F. Collier and Son, 1897) 153–80.

2 The World Health Organization has recently announced that polio will soon become the second disease to be eradicated.

3 The plate faces page 32 of the 1798 *Inquiry*.

4 Jenner's letter of 29 September 1798, quoted in Paul Saunders, *Edward Jenner, The Cheltenham Years 1795–1823. Being a Chronicle of the Vaccination Campaign* (Hanover and London: UP of New England, 1982) 72. Jenner's presentation of himself in pastoral terms is evident not only in comments such as this but in his refusal of the chance to cement his fame either by living in London or by exploring the Pacific with Captain Cook.

5 Jenner was an accomplished minor poet, whose pastoral verse in the Thomsonian tradition benefits from the detailed observation he practiced as a natural historian. These lines from "The Signs of Rain" are typical: "The boding shepherd heaves a sigh, / For see! a rainbow spans the sky. / The walls are damp, the ditches smell / Clos'd is the pink eye'd pimpernel" (lines 7–10), quoted in John Baron, *The Life of Edward Jenner*, 2 vols. (London, 1838) 1: 23.

6 Dr Haygarth, letter of 15 April 1794, quoted in Baron, *The Life of Edward Jenner* 1: 134.

7 James Watt, Jr., quoted in Jan Golinski, *Science as Public Culture: Chemistry and Enlightenment in Britain, 1760–1820* (Cambridge: Cambridge UP, 1992) 163.

8 Baron, summarizing a conversation with the Royal Society's President, in *The Life of Edward Jenner* 2: 168.

9 The period saw the elaboration of comparative anatomy, which compared the bodies of animals with those of humans from different races in order to make "scientific" distinctions between them. According to the categorizations elaborated by William Lawrence, Petrus Camper and J. F. Blumenbach, black Africans were more "degenerate," and nearer to the apes, than whites: see *The Works Of The Late Professor Camper: On The Connexion Between The Science Of Anatomy And The Arts Of Drawing, Painting, Statuary* (London, 1794), William Lawrence, *Lectures on Physiology, Zoology and the Natural History of Man* (London, 1822), J. F. Blumenbach, *A Manual of the Elements of Natural History*, tr. R. T. Gore (London, 1825) 37. Other theorists argued that blacks were a separate, inferior, species from whites. See Charles White, *Regular Gradation in Man, and in Different Animals and Vegetables* (London, 1799) and Edward Long, *History of Jamaica*, 3 vols. (London, 1774), 2: 51–83, 383.

10 Here Jenner explicitly followed what he advertised as Hunter's discovery.

11 Jenner's suspicion of aristocratic luxury echoes a widespread eighteenth century fear, expressed forcibly by Gibbon, Cowper, and Thomson amongst others. See John Sekora, *Luxury: The Concept in Western Thought, Eden to Smollet* (Baltimore: Johns Hopkins UP, 1977). Mary Wollstonecraft symbolized the corruptions of luxury in the figure of the lady of fashion in *Vindication of the Rights of Woman* (London: Penguin, 1985) 254–59; Coleridge did so in his lectures on the slave trade of 1795. The lap dog is treated as a symptom of upper class women's diseased sensibility in Sarah Scott, *The History of Sir George Ellison* (London, 1766) and Jonas Hanway, "Remarks on Lap-dogs," in *A Journal of Eight Days' Journey* (London, 1756) 69–70. For the medical argument that luxury was a danger to the body see George Cheyne, *The English Malady. Or, A Treatise of Nervous Diseases Of All Kinds* (London, 1733).

12 On the influence of the new science on *Frankenstein* see Anne K. Mellor, *Mary Shelley: Her Life, Her Fiction, Her Monsters* (New York and London: Routledge, 1988), chapter 5.

13 Inoculation was introduced to Britain from Turkey in 1721 by Lady Mary Wortley Montagu, and helped to control a disease which, during the eighteenth-century, killed six European monarchs and an annual average of 300 per 100,000 persons in Britain.

14 Moseley, *Treatise on the Lues Bovilla; or Cow Pox*, 2nd edn. (London, 1805) 214.

15 Quoted in Robert Thornton, *Vaccinae Vindicia; or, Defence of Vaccination* (London, 1806) 4–5.

16 The new botany was also depicted by conservatives as an unleashing of female sexuality which undermined the social order. See Richard Polwhele, *The Unsex'd Females: A Poem* (London, 1798).

17 Details of the campaign, in which fifteen doctors joined Moseley in anti-Jenner pamphleteering, can be found in Paul Saunders (see note 4 above).

18 Mr. Stuart, quoted in "Review of Pamphlets on Vaccination," *The Edinburgh Review*, 15 (January, 1810): 322–51 (343).

19 Benjamin Moseley's association of black slaves with wild beasts is apparent in his *A Treatise on Sugar With Miscellaneous Medical Observations*, 1st edn. (London, 1799) 169–80 and 2nd edn. (London, 1800) 167–68. His racist views are also apparent from his comments on Edward Long (see note 9 above), whom he called "the father of correct English-West-Indian literature" (2nd edn., 171).

20 By 1810 *The Edinburgh Review* was able to sum up the debate conclusively in Jenner's favor: "Review of Pamphlets on Vaccination" 15 (January, 1810): 322–51.

21 In 1819 Jenner declared "I wish Cobbett would change places with Tom Paine [whose bones Cobbett had brought from America in a box]—I would travel many a mile in the snow to put him in the Box." Quoted in Richard B. Fisher, *Edward Jenner 1749–1823* (London: Andre Deutsch, 1991) 277.

22 In a letter of 29 April 1802 to his trusted friend, Henry Hicks, Jenner drew a caricature of Pitt with a forked tongue below these verses "And gentle Reader woulds't thou know / What curs'd, what most malignant star, / Produced the Income Tax and War / Look at that Fellow's head below" (MS 5236 item 2, Wellcome Trust).

23 On Darwin see Alan Bewell, "'Jacobin Plants:' Botany as Social Theory in the 1790s," *The Wordsworth Circle* 20 (1989): 132–39; on Priestley see Simon Schaffer, "Priestley and the Politics of Spirit," in *Science, Medicine and Dissent: Joseph Priestley 1733–1804*, eds. R. G. W. Anderson and Christopher Lawrence (London: Wellcome Trust and Science Museum, 1987) 39–53.

24 From the Preface to *The Poems of Robert Bloomfield*, 2 vols. (London: Vernor, Hood and Sharpe and others, 1809) 1: ii.

25 Letter to George Bloomfield, 21 July 1802; in *Selections from the Correspondence of Robert Bloomfield, The Suffolk Poet*, ed. W. H. Hart (London: Spottiswoode, 1870 [facs. rpt. Walton-on-Thames, 1968]) 29.

26 *Selections from the Letters of Robert Southey*, ed. John Wood Warter, 4 vols. (London, 1856) 1: 208.

27 *The Collected Letters of Samuel Taylor Coleridge*, ed. E. L. Griggs, 6 vols. (Oxford: Oxford UP, 1956–71) 2.852.

28 In the *Annual Review for 1804*, 3: 574. The *Monthly Magazine* said of the poem, "Mr. Bloomfield's genius burns with undiminished lustre. Nature marked him for a poet in his cradle" 18 (1804): 594.

29 Jenner had speculated that tuberculosis might "arise from our familiarity with an animal that nature intended to keep separate from man"—the sheep (see F. Dawtrey Drewitt, *The Notebook of Edward Jenner in the Possession of the Royal College of Physicians of London* [London: Oxford UP, 1931] 41). He passed his experimental evidence to Beddoes, who incorporated it in his publications on using gases to treat tuberculosis. Jenner, that is to say, influenced Beddoes' cow-house cure by communicating his findings, as well as by example. Beddoes rapidly became a convert to vaccination and campaigned for Jenner to be given a greater reward by parliament.

30 See *An Essay on the Public Merits of Mr. Pitt* (London, 1796) and *Alternatives compared: or, What shall the rich do to be safe?* (London, 1797).

31 Quoted in Roy Porter, *Doctor of Society: Thomas Beddoes and the Sick Trade* in *Late-Enlightenment England* (London and New York: Routledge, 1992) 103.

32 Thomas Beddoes, *Essay on the Causes, Early Signs, and Prevention of Pulmonary Consumption For the Use of Parents and Preceptors* (Bristol, 1799) 60.

33 William Rowley, *Cow-pox Inoculation no security against small-pox infection* (London, 1805) 5.

34 Quoted in Trevor H. Levere, *Poetry Realized in Nature: Samuel Taylor Coleridge and Early Nineteenth-Century Science* (Cambridge, Cambridge UP, 1981) 21.

35 "The Sons of Genius," quoted in Trevor H. Levere, "Humphry Davy, 'The Sons of Genius,' and the Idea of Glory," in Sophie Forgan, ed. *Science and the Sons of Genius: Studies on Humphry Davy* (London: Science Reviews, 1980) 33–57.

36 *Coleridge Letters* 5.309. See also *The Friend*, ed. Barbara E. Rooke, 2 vols. (London and Princeton, N.J.: Routledge and Princeton UP, 1969) 1.471.

37 John Williams, *Sacred Allegories . . . to Which is Added an Anacreontic: An Ode on the Discovery of Vaccination* (London, 1810).

38 J. Ring, *A Translation of Anstey's Ode to Jenner* (London, 1804) 10–11.

39 Quoted in Mark Storey, *Robert Southey. A Life* (Oxford and New York: Oxford UP, 1997) 248.

40 Volume 7, Canto 1, stanza 2, in *The Poetical Works of Robert Southey, collected by himself*, 10 vols. (London, 1837–38).

41 (London, 1797) 322.

42 Donald R. Hopkins, *Princes and Peasants. Smallpox in History* (Chicago and London: U of Chicago P, 1983) 9–13.

43 Jenner, *A Continuation of Facts and Observations Relative to the Variolae Vaccinae, or Cow Pox* (London, 1800), in *Harvard Classics*, ed. Eliot 231.

44 Blane and Thomas Trotter introduced vaccination to the navy as part of reforms instituted by Admiral St. Vincent designed to impose sanitation on the fleet. It was through these reforms that doctors and surgeons increased their status in the navy, as they became officially responsible for inspection and supervision of crews. This official responsibility for imposing health through discipline anticipated the development of a similar role by civilian doctors. On the institutionalization of health discipline in the navy see Christopher Lloyd and Jack L. S. Coulter, *Medicine and the Navy 1200–1900, vol. 3: 1714–1815* (Edinburgh and London: E & S Livingstone, 1961) 165, 349–52.

45 Thomas Alston Warren told his parishioners that "our brave Seamen and Soldiers could successfully ply the ropes, direct the cannon, and handle the musket, whilst undergoing this new Inoculation. Our enemies did not like this at all." In *An Address from a Country Minister to his Parishioners on the Subject of the Cow-Pox, or Vaccine Inoculation* (Oxford, 1803) 7. In parliament, Admiral Berkeley and General Tarleton agreed that vaccination was helping to win the war: Tarleton declared that "in future ages, the glory of DR. JENNER's fame will be superior to the trophied urn of the most renowned of warriors" (Charles Murray, *Debates in Parliament Respecting the Jennerian Discovery* [London, 1808] 5, 78).

46 Sir Gilbert Blane, *Select Dissertations on Several Subjects of Medical Science* (London, 1822) 354–55.

47 Hansard 146 col 722, quoted in R. M. MacLeod, "Law, Medicine and Public Opinion: The Resistance to Compulsory Health Legislation 1870–1907," *Public Law* (1967): 107–28; 189–211 (211).

48 By 1819 Jenner had espoused an authoritarian paternalism with regard to the rural laborers that echoes Southey's and Wordsworth's later opinions. During the unrest of that year he declared "fortunately they have no leader—so that if tens of thousands were embodied they must be considered merely as a Mob. . . . However they would do a vast deal of mischief before the Corps of Hangmen had finish'd the business" (quoted in Fisher 278).

49 Words used by the Victorian Anti-Vaccination League, quoted in MacLeod 124.

32

'CHOLERA CURED BEFORE HAND': COLERIDGE, ABJECTION, AND THE 'DIRTY BUSINESS OF LAUDANUM'

Alan Bewell

Source: *Romanticism* 4 (1998), 155–73.

Like the current AIDS epidemic, cholera in 1831–32 produced an epidemic of signs, as the disease intensified class anxieties that were already high in the period leading up to the passage of the Reform Bill on 4 June 1832. The framing of cholera was a public debate, much of it taking place, R. J. Morris notes 'by handbill as well as by press report and letter', where cholera produced 'appeals, denials and derision' (pp. 115–16). Henry Gaulter went so far as to claim that the flood of handbills posted to local hoardings was itself playing a major role in the promulgation of the epidemic: 'Without any adequate counterbalance of benefit, these systems committed the capital offence of setting and keeping at work, through a whole community, that agitation and fear which, as we have seen, render the human frame most capable of being acted upon by the cause of cholera. The perpetual appearance of fresh placards headed by this dreadful word – the daily parade of reports . . . all this ostentation of pestilence was most pernicious' (p. 137). Cobbett saw the epidemic as a fiction disseminated by health authorities, a 'hobgoblin' (p. 515) that gave them 'powers wholly unknown to *English law*!' (p. 513). He cites approvingly a placard recently posted in Lambeth:

> CHOLERA HUMBUG! – Inhabitants of Lambeth, be not imposed upon by the villainously false report that the Asiatic Cholera has reached London. A set of half-starved doctors, apothecaries' clerks, and jobbers in the parish funds, have endeavoured to frighten the nation into a lavish expenditure; with the Government they have

succeeded in carrying a bill which will afford fine pickings. A ruinous system of taxation, starvation, and intemperance, has been long carried on; it has now arrived at its acme, and disease is the natural result.

(p. 523)

Cobbett's view was not unjustified, for the conditions of the urban poor were so bad that this new disease, if it really existed, was the least of their worries.[1] He shrewdly recognised that cholera was primarily a middle-class anxiety, and that current efforts to assist the poor might stem from self-interest: 'the *danger to themselves* has now awakened their compassion' (p. 514). Nevertheless, even if the disease existed only in the '*alarming paragraphs*' (p. 516) produced by the Health Board, 'an imaginary may be just as effectual as real pestilence' (p. 517) if it encouraged efforts to improve conditions. Middle-class reformers, especially those of the Sanitary movement, also hoped that the epidemic might prove socially beneficial. James Kay (later, Kay-Shuttleworth), in *The Moral and Physical Conditions of the Working Classes* suggests that 'the ingression of a disease, which threatens, with a stealthy step, to invade the sanctity of the domestic circle; which may be unconsciously conveyed from those haunts of beggary where it is rife into the most still and secluded retreat of refinement . . . ensures that the anxious attention of every order of society shall be directed to that, in which social ills abound' (p. 12). Until the mid-1840s, Kay's was a minority position. Nevertheless, the consequences of the medical framing of the labouring classes as a *health threat* not only to themselves but to others were enormous. Class anxieties were now very much structured along epidemiological lines. Working-class districts – 'the precincts of vice and disease' (p. 4) – were seen as a general source of continuing infection, the portals through which foreign diseases entered British society. For middle-class conservatives, such as Rev. Newton Smart, it was not only cholera but the aspiration toward democratic rights that was contagious: 'pestilence' was even to be preferred to 'the horrors of revolution and anarchy' (p. 382). Robert Southey thought that cholera might assist the anti-reform movement, as 'a more effectual ally in aid of the constitution' (IV, p. 230). Working-class radicals joined middle-class reformers in seeing the numerous proclamations of the Board of Health as part of a larger conspiracy 'to frighten people out of their wits, and thus set up Cholera as a rival to Reform' ('Cholera in the Gazette').

The contemporary engraving *John Bull Catching the Cholera* encapsulates the middle-class association of the politics of Reform with the cholera epidemic. The broadsheet turns the anxiety of 'catching' the disease into an assertion of the superiority of the British nation. Cholera, depicted as an emaciated Indian, blue from the disease, has been caught sneaking through a break in 'The Wooden Walls of England' separating England from the colonial world. He should have known better, for two signs, one inscribed 'Beware the Bull', the other, 'Board of Health', mark this territory as being guarded by nationalism and medicine. With one hand holding a club inscribed 'Heart of Oak', while the other grabs this outsider by the throat, John Bull asks, 'Now you rascal where are you going to'? Cholera answers, 'I am going back again'. Meanwhile the disease reaches for the broadside entitled 'Reform Bill', which he apparently has brought along with him to assist in his invasion of England.

In July 1832, Coleridge entered this political fray with a poem entitled 'Cholera cured before hand'.[2] His attitude toward the Reform Bill was unambiguously conservative. Even as he believed in the need for social reform, and was critical of the degrading commercialism of the age, he feared the consequences of extending political power beyond its traditional limits. To the American H. B. McLellan, he remarked that 'care like a foul hag sits on us all . . . things have come to a dreadful pass with us, we need most deeply a reform, but I fear not the horrid reform which we shall have; things must alter, the upper classes of England have made the lower persons, *things*; the people in breaking from this unnatural state will break from their duties also' (*Table Talk*, I, pp. 281–82). In the letter to J. H. Green in which he included 'Cholera cured before hand', Coleridge draws out the analogy between the cholera epidemic and the politics of Reform, writing: 'I am jealous of the Glory of this new-imported Nabob, from the Indian Jungles, his Serene Blueness, Prince of the Air – lest he should have the presumption – for there is no bounds to the arrogance of these Oriental Imports – to set himself up in Hell against Lords Grey, Durham & the Reform-Bill'. Cholera, it appears, is likely to win more Hellish followers than the Reform Movement, though Coleridge doubts whether 'filling the Church-yard [can] be reckoned an equal service with stripping and emptying the Church!' (*Collected Letters*, VI, p. 916).

'Cholera cured before hand' is an unusual text for Coleridge because it appears to be addressed to the working class. In 1816, he had planned to write three *Lay Sermons* addressed respectively to the upper class, the higher and middle classes, and the working class, but the last of these was never written. The poem can be seen, therefore, as a belated gesture in this direction. It is not, however, written in Coleridge's voice, but instead under the pseudonym of a working-class reformer. The first version, signed 'Demophilus Mudlarkiades' (*Collected Letters*, VI, p. 917), suggests that the poet is both a democrat or 'lover-of-the-people' and a 'mudlark', a *Dunciadic* singer in/of dirt. *Mudlark* was slang for a hog, but also referred to people who scavenged in rivers, bays, and harbours at low water for old ropes, iron, and so on. Describing himself as 'the People's, loyal Subject', he ends the poem by shouting the populist slogans:

> Vivat Rex Popellus!
> Vivat Regina Plebs!
> Hurra! 3 times 3 thrice
> repeated. –Hurra! –

The two other versions also emphasise the poet's affiliation with Catholicism and the sovereignty of the 'Plebs', but now he signs himself

> Philodemus Coprophilus,
> Physician prophylactic to their
> Majesties, the He and She People.[3]

Here the 'lover-of-the-people' is a 'lover-of-dung': the poet-physician who would claim to treat the poor also reduces them to filth and to the Yahoo 'He and She People'.

Like Swift's satires, it is difficult to establish Coleridge's attitude toward this fictional 'doctor of the people'. Clearly, however, the parody is directed less towards the working class than its democratic pamphleteers, aimed at suggesting that these people degrade those they would claim to help. In a notebook entry of 1816, he writes: '[T]he Cobbetts & Hunts address you (– the lower Ranks) as Beasts who have no future Selves – as if by a natural necessity you must *all* forever remain poor & slaving. But what is the *fact*? How many scores might each of you point out in your neighbourhood of men raised to wealth or comfort from your own ranks' (III, entry 4311). 'Cholera cured before hand' undercuts working-class democratic discourse by arguing that it is itself the disease, as it produces and feeds upon the degradation of the poor, turning them into 'He and She People' in order to justify the need for a political cure. As Carl Woodring notes, the poem invents 'a contemptible persona as author of a transparently ironic set of verses' (p. 229). The poem is not patterned upon literary texts, but instead on the deluge of 'handbills' that were produced by local health authorities as they sought to control cholera by giving the working class information about the new disease and how to avoid it. The title draws attention to its status as a pastiche: 'CHOLERA CURED BEFORE HAND: Premonitory promulgated *gratis* for the use of the useful Classes, specially those resident in St Giles's, Saffron Hill, Bethnal Green, &c – and likewise, inasmuch as the good man is merciful even to the Beasts, for the benefits of the Bulls and Bears of the Stock Exchange'. Coleridge provides instructions that this 'premonitory' should be 'so printed as to secure a facile legibility to a current eye'. He even suggests that 'a number of Copies [might be] struck off, pasted to parallelograms of Deal, and sent abroad as Placards Ambulant'. By way of 'attracting notice and giving authority to the thing, I would have each superscribed in red Capitals, THE BOARD OF HEALTH'. To the epidemic of signs produced by cholera and the Reform Bill, Coleridge added his own politico-medical broadside.

That Coleridge did not actually publish the poem in the newspapers or as a handbill, but instead distributed it to three physicians, suggests that its real audience was not the working class or its spokespersons, but the 'clerisy' whom he believed should play a key role in the governing of the nation. With so many 'ligneous' ('woody' or 'mad') Doctors using hoardings to give advice, 'a few additional Doctor Lignums cannot fairly be complained [of]', he writes. In the letter to J. H. B. Williams, he argues that one sign of the 'malignity' of cholera is that it 'called into notoriety so many ligneous Doctors'. He further writes that the poem was 'as much activated by indignation as by philanthropy . . . at the presumptuous folly of sundry cholerophobists' (in the letter to H. N. Coleridge, they are a 'herd of Cholerophilists'). Coleridge thus uses the cholera epidemic to focus upon the failure of political authority that has given rise to both cholera and Reform. The poem is a *tour de force* pastiche, a rough parodic satire, not only of the deluge of cholera literature produced during the 1820s and 1830s, but also of the 'woody' authorities (both Cholerophobes and Cholerophiles) that were producing it.[4] In 'Cholera cured before hand', another ligneous doctor enters the political arena offering advice to the poor. Through him and his 'iatrognomonic prophylactic Anthro[po]philous Doggrel', Coleridge parodies the contemporary political framing of cholera.

Coleridge was well positioned to write such a pastiche for he had a substantial knowledge of contemporary medical theory and was well read in the cholera literature.[5] Along with the consensus of contemporary physicians in the 1830s, he understands cholera to be a poison produced by the physical environment that under certain conditions can become virulent. In a letter of 24th February 1832, he suggests that the English ague, malaria, and cholera differ only as 'Grades of intensity':

I think, however, that I could give the theory with an important competing adjunct, and so fill up the whole line of transit and connection from an Essex Ague thro' a Pontine Marsh-fever to the present Malignant Cholera – and explain the super-induction of the *epidemic* on the two latter – the reason, I mean, why they are likely to be modified by aerial influences in unlucky states of the atmosphere – tho' of the three Factors of the Disease, viz. the Predisposition of the Patient, the unknown Virus, and the predisposing Circumstances, in which word I include quaecunque stant circum circa, state of atmosphere, soil, air, temperature condition of the Habitat, &c – it is on the *first* that the *third principally* acts.
(VI, pp. 887–88)

Disease depends upon the 'Predisposition of the Patient' (general health, diet, age, behaviour, etc.) as it is acted upon by 'predisposing Circumstances' (factors such as filth, overcrowding, lack of ventilation). During the early

348

history of cholera, British and colonial physicians, especially those connected with the Sanitarian Movement, drew many of their ideas about cholera from what was already known about the behaviour of 'fevers', especially epidemic typhus. Pelling notes, for instance, that under the direction of Chadwick, the Board of Health in 1848 left in doubt 'whether typhus, plague, scarlatina, influenza, yellow fever, and cholera depended on peculiar and specific causes or on one common agent modified by circumstances; and then stated that, regardless of the answer to this, these diseases were all fevers, all dependent upon certain atmospheric conditions, all obedient to similar laws of diffusion, all infesting the same sorts of localities, all attacking the same classes and age groups, and all increased in severity by the same sanitary and social conditions' (pp. 64–65).[6] Referring to 'Virus' in its Latin meaning of 'poison' or 'slime', Coleridge asserts that one need not suppose 'a specific *Virus* for the different diseases' (*Collected Letters*, VI, p. 887).

Since epidemics are produced by the action of 'predisposing circumstances' on 'predisposed populations', the premonitory is addressed to the population who were generally believed most likely to fall victim to it, the poor living in the 'Cholera districts' – 'St Giles's, Bethnal Green, Saffron Hill, &c'. The handbill provides a typical list of dietary and behavioural recommendations:

> Pains ventral, subventral,
> In stomach or entrail
> Think no longer mere prefaces
> For Damns, Grins and Wry Faces;
> But off to the Doctor, fast as ye can crawl:
> Yet far better 'twould be not to have them at all.

> Now to 'scape inward aches
> Eat no plums nor plum-cakes;
> Cry, Avaunt, New Potato!
> And don't drink, like old Cato.
> Ah beware of Dis Pipsy,
> And therefore don't get tipsy!
> For tho' Gin and Whisky
> May make you feel frisky,
> They're but Crimps to Dis Pipsy:
> And nose to tail with this Gypsy
> Comes, black as a Porpus,
> The Diabolus ipse
> Call'd Cholery Morpus:
> Who with Horns, Hoofs and Tale croaks for Carrion to feed him,
> Tho' being a Devil, nobody never has see'd him.

Since stomach ills (dyspepsia) were believed to predispose one to cholera, the poem recommends that the working class 'Eat no plums nor plum-cakes', avoid the 'New Potato', and later, beware of 'Hot drams and cold Sallads'. Dietary recommendations, however, express moral attitudes. Like *The Methodist Magazine* which emphasised that cholera seeks out 'the dissipated, dissolute, profane, and intemperate', this pseudo public-health notice warns of the dangers of drink.[7] 'Gin and Whisky' are 'Crimps' to dyspepsia, the means by which the dissolute among the working class are forced against their will to serve 'this Gypsy'. Wherever she goes, cholera, described as a 'black porpus' (the 'hog-fish'), follows her 'nose to tail'.

The representation of cholera as a companion of Gypsies suggests the manner in which British ideas of this new disease conveyed attitudes toward gender, sexuality, vagrancy, and colonial otherness. England is here shown to be threatened not by the India over there, but the 'E-gyptians' who live within it, a threatening nomadic population associated with sexuality, poverty, and disease. The gypsy 'Dis Pipsy' (her name, punning on 'dyspepsia', 'hell', and the colloquial word for a minor ailment *'pip'*) serves a similar purpose, as she embodies heightened middle- and lower-class anxieties about the new populations produced by colonialism – immigrants. Dr. Samuel Busey expresses the dominant nineteenth-century viewpoint: 'In the cities, those direful and pestilential diseases, ship fever, yellow fever, and small pox, are almost exclusively confined to the filthy alleys, lanes, and streets, and low, damp, filthy and ill-ventilated haunts, which are exclusively tenanted by *foreigners*' (p. 125). On 23 July 1832, the New York City *Evening Post* describes the local red-light district, The Five Points, as being 'inhabited by a race of beings of all colours, ages, sexes, and nations, though generally of but one condition, and that . . . almost of the vilest brute. With such a crew, inhabiting the most populous and central portion of the city, when may we be considered secure from pestilence. Be the air pure from Heaven, their breath would contaminate it, and infect it with disease' (qtd. in Rosenberg, pp. 33–34). Cholera was a disease especially associated with harbours and the dockyards, places where foreign populations promiscuously associated with one another. It was here too that the 'mudlarks' carried on their business, sometimes being accused of robbing ships as they unloaded their goods.

The British middle-class emphasis upon female propriety was profoundly shaped by colonial experience. Female colonists' 'temperate' behaviour and their greater concern for hygiene were seen as making them less susceptible than men to tropical disease. In an England increasingly worried about the possibility of epidemics being introduced from elsewhere, female propriety took on a new meaning: it was now seen as one of the primary means of safeguarding the health of the nation. By the 1850s, as Florence Nightingale became a cultural icon, women were increasingly seen as having a social responsibility in employing female virtue to defend against 'foreign' disease. The first major health act to deal with contagious diseases, the Contagious Disease Act (1864), focused upon prostitutes, whose 'improper' behaviour was now seen as being not only immoral, but a threat to society. Judith R. Walkowitz observes that pollution assumes a 'heightened scatological significance in a society where the poor seemed to be living in their own excrement . . . Literally and figuratively, the prostitute was the conduit of infection to respectable society' (p. 4). During the first cholera outbreak much was made of the fact that cholera seemed to have a special liking for prostitutes. Charles E. Rosenberg notes that newspapers in the United States drew attention to the fact that 'Of "fourteen hundred lewd women" in one street in Paris . . . thirteen hundred had died of cholera' (p. 41).

The next stanza of 'Cholera cured before hand' draws upon these concerns as it focuses on working-class women, the 'She people' associated with the 'gas-light[ed]' world of the urban metropolis and with prostitution:

> Ah! then, my dear Honeys!
> There's no Cure for you
> For Loves, nor for Moneys –
> You'll find it too true!
> Och! the halloballoo!
> Och! och! how ye'll wail
> When the offal-fed Vagrant
> Shall turn you as blue
> As the gas-light unfragrant
> That gushes in jets from beneath his own Tail:
> Till swift as the Mail,
> He at last brings the Cramps on,
> That will twist you, like Sampson.

Mention of Sampson suggests that a lower-class woman is a Delilah, the harlot ('For Loves . . . for Moneys') hired by the Philistines to betray Sampson. The disgust that abjects an Other is intense in this stanza, as working-class women's sexuality is seen as a threat to the integrity of the male body. 'Bring the Cramps on', the speaker seems to say, as if the physical sign of female sexuality – menstruation – also links her to disease and pollution; the punishment, the spasms of cholera, suits the crime. Kristeva notes that 'menstrual blood . . . stands for the danger issuing from within the identity (social or sexual); it threatens the relationship between the sexes within a social aggregate and, through internalisation, the identity of each sex in the face of sexual difference' (p. 71). Sex is abjected as a sickness. 'There is no Cure for you', the premonitory declares, as it takes a grotesque pleasure in the traditional language of the incurability of the prostitute. Abjection, the ridding by the self of all that threatens its autonomy,

351

produces its own pleasures, especially as sexual anxiety is expelled violently by the speaker, 'swift as the Mail'[e]. He describes how 'the offal-fed Vagrant' will turn these 'dear Honeys' as 'blue' as 'the gas-light unfragrant/That gushes in jets from beneath his own Tail'. The disgust created by cholera, sexuality, and working-class women is heightened as the handbill, seeking to see into the bottom of cholera, describes the very fundament of evil. The poetics of cholera is, indeed, a poetics of filthy doggerel.

Richard Evans has observed that in Europe the high incidence of cholera among working-class women was frequently seen as a sign or their failure to maintain the cleanliness of the home (ironically, it was through cleaning that they frequently became sick) (*Death*, pp. 450–65). The 'premonitory' affirms this domestic ideology as it employs cholera as a demon to punish women who ignore their place in the home to seek the pleasure of the streets. Cholera is gendered as a male demon, a Sampson or 'Son of Sam' who 'twists' his female victims, and a 'Vagrant' who feeds on 'offal'. In this late poem of the Romantic period, the link between colonialism and vagrancy is given its darkest interpretation. Vagrants were commonly viewed as a primary means of the spread of cholera (among other diseases), and urban health authorities established policies to control their movement. The personification of cholera as an 'offal-fed Vagrant' powerfully condenses contemporary knowledge of the link between this disease and filth, yet it also heightens the reader's disgust by collapsing the distinction between food and excrement. Cholera is a dirty business that confuses the two, collapsing the boundaries that preserve the body. Yet disgust is also the means by which boundaries are re-established. The premonitory spits out what *is not* 'me' in an anxious effort to establish what *is* 'me'.

The final stanza turns from lower-class women to their male partners:

> So without further Blethring,
> Dear Mudlarks! my Brethren!
> Of all scents and degrees
> (Yourselves with your Shes)
> Forswear all Cabal, Lads!
> Wakes, Unions and Rows;
> Hot Drams and cold Sallads;
> And don't pig in Styes that would suffocate Sows!
> Quit COBBET's, O'CONNEL's and BELZEBUB's banners,
> And White-wash at once your Guts, Rooms, and Manners.

Here the advice is explicitly political. Echoing the popular belief that 'white-wash' was an effective means of disinfecting streets and dwellings, the speaker extends this recommendation to the diet and manners of the working class: 'white-wash at once your Guts, Rooms, and Manners'. Burke's

'Swinish multitude' – already suggested in previous references to hogs – is given its strongest echo in the suggestion that the poor live worse than pigs: 'Don't pig in Styes that would suffocate Sows'. Unusual here is the employment of *pig* as a verb. The *OED* indicates that it means 'to huddle together in a disorderly dirty, or irregular manner; to herd, lodge, or sleep together, like pigs'. Few words capture as powerfully how the life of the poor in cholera districts was being described. The *Ecclesiologist*, for instance, speaks of 'the six-and-thirty Irish families who pig in the adjoining alley' (*OED*). As if this were not enough, these are also the people most likely to want democratic reform. To cure cholera beforehand requires that the working class 'Quit Cobbet's, O'Connel's, and Belzebub's Banners'. Coleridge has his Cobbett-like doctor condemn himself in his own words.

Mention of the noted Irish statesman Daniel O'Connell, who founded the Catholic Association in 1823, and succeeded in getting the Catholic Emancipation Act passed in 1829, indicates that the poem is specifically directed toward the Irish poor, an immigrant population that was often blamed for the spread of epidemics, especially typhus and cholera.[8] A contemporary reader would hardly miss the inclusion of the 'Potato' in the list of foods to be avoided. In James Kay's *The Moral and Physical Condition of the Working Classes*, the Irish are portrayed as having taught a 'pernicious lesson' to the labouring classes of England, having shown them how to survive even the meanest of social conditions: 'The system of cottier farming, the demoralization and barbarism of the people, and the general use of the potato as the chief article of food, have encouraged the population in Ireland more rapidly than the *available* means of subsistence have been increased' (p. 21). The recommendation that these 'dear Mudlarks' forswear 'Wakes, Unions, and Rows' draws attention to the wave of rioting that occurred in primarily working-class Irish districts in March–April 1832 when Public Health authorities attempted to bury cholera victims before they had been given a proper burial. Since the Irish poor frequently needed time to find the money necessary for a burial and were rarely able to bury their dead until the Sabbath day, when they were free from work, British Public Health regulations, which insisted on burial within twenty-four hours of death in quicklime (normally reserved for criminals), produced violent ethnic conflicts, especially in London and Liverpool.[9] For a people whose lives were often so miserable that their one hope was for a decent burial, the middle-class insistence on quick burials without a 'Wake' was a focal point of resistance.

Doctor Mudlark obviously claims to speak for the working class, for he refers to his ostensible audience as 'my brethren'. Grammar, spelling, and crude imagery mark the handbill as a pastiche of working-class language and culture. Words like 'frisky' and 'hullabaloo' are vernacular. 'Never has see'd him' is not only ungrammatical, but also powerfully captures Cobbett's view that the cholera scare is humbug. Probably most disturbing is the misspelling of 'Cholera Morbus' as 'Cholery morpus', which not only links the disease to coal-miners through the pun on *'colliery'*, but also suggests that the speaker has little medical training at all. Most obvious to a contemporary audience would have been the frequent appearance of Scottish and Irish dialect. 'Och', the Irish or Scottish mode of exclamation is scattered throughout this poetic handbill. 'Blethering' is a Scottish word meaning senseless talk, which appears in Burns's *Tam O'Shanter*: 'A bletherin, blusterin, drunken blellum' (II, p. 55). The use of 'Honeys' as a term of endearment was almost exclusively an Irish and Scottish idiom.

As in Swift's satires of the Irish poor, Coleridge's adoption of the voice of a working-class Democrat was not a neutral, distanced activity. On a general level, one might note the satire is directed against both the ruling and the working classes, one for its failure to govern effectively, and the other for its assertion of the right to play a role in government, each side deriving its claims not from religion and tradition, but from rationalistic economic and political theory ('the Bulls and Bears of the Stock Exchange'). The idea of linking politics with contagion came easy to hand, for Coleridge regularly drew this analogy, as in his argument in *The Statesman's Manual* that 'The histories and political economy of the present and preceding century partake in the general contagion of its mechanic philosophy, and are the *product* of an unenlivened generalizing Understanding' (p. 28). Yet this abstract account of the origins of the poem does not adequately address the extent to which its vitriolic energy, at times almost out of control, largely derives from the disgust produced by Coleridge's adoption of the language of Reform, the language of those who would employ the cholera epidemic for political purposes. The poem is essentially an act of abjection. Coleridge consumes the language of those he disliked in order to spit it out; feeding on 'offal' produces the disgust that cures. The cholera handbill is thus a form of poetic inoculation, not so much against the miserable conditions of the working class, as against the unsuitability of allowing this class to play a role in governing the nation. Thus, despite his own sympathy for working class people, Coleridge nevertheless sees them as being *abject*. By adopting their voice in its most degraded form (in the representations and the words of an Irish Dr Mudlark), Coleridge seeks to produce a social cure. The two voices in the poem – that of the pseudonymous doctor and Coleridge – in their mutual antagonism and contradiction drive the poem forward. 'As much activated by indignation as by philanthropy', Coleridge takes into himself the abject Other from whom he seeks to separate himself.

Coleridge's health during the period leading up to the passage of the Reform Bill further complicates the interpretation of the poem. Oddly, one of the most popular remedies of the period – opium – is missing from his handbill. Since one of the first signs of cholera was a 'premonitory diarrhoea', physicians often prescribed laudanum as an anti-diarrhoeal to stop its progress. The following notice posted by the Central Health Board of London in 1832 is typical:

> Cholera Districts. – Looseness of bowels is the beginning of cholera; thousands of lives may be saved by attending in time to this, a complaint which should on no account be neglected by either old or young. In places where the disease prevails, when cramps in the legs, arms, or belly are felt, with looseness or sickness at the stomach, when medical assistance is not at hand, three tea-spoonsful of mustard-powder, in half a pint of warm water, or the same quantity of warm water with as much common salt as it would melt, should be taken as a vomit, and after the stomach has been cleared out with more warm water, 25 drops of laudanum should be taken in a small glass of any agreeable drink . . .
>
> (Cobbett, pp. 520–21)

There can be little doubt that Coleridge knew about the anti-choleric aspects of opium, for in the Crewe manuscript he indicates that 'Kubla Khan' was 'composed, in a sort of Reverie brought on by two grains of Opium, taken to check a dysentery, at a Farm House between Porlock & Linton, a quarter mile from Culbone Church, in the fall of the year, 1797' (*Complete Poems*, p. 525). Addicted to opium most of his life, the poet had had many lessons in its anti-diarrhoeal powers. On his return from Malta, he was so constipated that he resorted to requesting the Captain to use an instrument specifically designed to remove the obstruction in his bowels. On 18 November 1811, he writes that 'Truly for 8 days together the Trunk of my poor Body was or seemed to be a Trunk which Nature had first locked, and then thrown away the Key' (*Collected Letters*, III, p. 347). On 14 May 1814, he remarks: 'I used to think St James's Text, "He who offendeth in one point of the Law, offendeth in all", very harsh; but my own sad experience has taught me it's aweful, dreadful Truth . . . I have in this one dirty business of Laudanum an hundred times deceived, tricked, nay, actually & consciously LIED' (*Collected Letters*, III, p. 490). In 'Cholera cured before hand', he appears to have been caught between two kinds of dirtiness – opium and cholera. Both were Eastern imports, both caused a loss of self-control, and both were understood as poisons that attacked the bowels, one causing constipation, the other extreme diarrhoea. Thus, even as the poem participates in the public debates connected with Reform, which Coleridge not surprisingly refers to as a 'huge tape-worm *Lie* of some 3 score & ten joints' (*Collected Letters*, VI, p. 902), it is also a culminating personal statement about more than thirty years of what the poet described as 'intestine conflict' (VI, p. 589).

This conflict came to a crisis in the months immediately preceding the passage of the Reform Bill. Over the previous decade, if it were not for ongoing bronchial problems and erysipelas on the legs, Coleridge had suffered from an 'all-absorbing Bowel-Complaint' (*Collected Letters*, VI, p. 845). As if the East and the West were fighting it out for control of his body, whenever the bowel problems subsided, those of the bronchia would reappear. 'As my intestinal Canal has subsided into a Calm', Coleridge writes, 'the Bronchia have set to work, all hands or glands rather, in the production and excretion of phlegm' (*Collected Letters*, VI, p. 870). In October 1831, just as the epidemic was gaining a foothold in England, Coleridge believed that he had suffered a 'retrocession of the morbid action to the intestinal Canal in a type resembling Cholera' (*Collected Letters*, VI, p. 874)[10] In February 1832, after eating two pork chops, Coleridge had an almost fatal bout of diarrhoea: 'from Noon till past six o'clock I never *once* sate down, but continued pacing to the tune of my prayers & groans from the window of my own to that in the room opposite' (*Collected Letters*, VI, p. 886). He probably did not actually contract epidemic cholera – though this possibility cannot be dismissed. Nevertheless, in a context in which the difference between modern cholera and the cholera morbus was not clear, his belief that the widely publicised epidemic was repeatedly victimising him was not unreasonable.

Coleridge was also seeking at this time to be rid of his opium dependency even though his physician, James Gillman, warned against the effort, given his diarrhoeal state and the prevailing epidemic. In a letter to J. H. Green, 23 March 1832, Coleridge expresses his ambivalence in striking terms: 'By the mercy of God I remain quiet, and far from any craving for the poison that has been the curse of my existence, my shame and my *negro-slave* inward humiliation and debasement, I feel an aversion, a horror at the imagining: so that I doubt, whether I could swallow a dose without a resiliency, amounting almost to a convulsion' (*Collected Letters*, VI, p. 892). Here, the addiction to opium is described as a 'curse', 'shame', 'humiliation', and 'debasement'. As someone who justifiably claimed that he had been 'an ardent & almost life-long Denouncer of Slavery' (VI, p. 940), Coleridge's suggestion that these feelings make him like a 'negro-slave' derive from a deep sympathy for the oppressed. One month later, at a time when it appeared that he had, indeed, conquered his addiction, he speaks of the miracle of 'a sudden emancipation from a 33 years' fearful Slavery' (VI, p. 901). Nevertheless, it is also obvious that the 'slave' represents a state of abjection that Coleridge was seeking to surmount. The situation where he found himself unable to let laudanum pass his lips, his feeling that he would vomit if he were to allow it to enter himself, verges on the condition Kristeva calls the 'abjection of self': that moment when the subject discovers that what it denies 'constitutes its very *being*, that it *is* none other than abject' (p. 5). Opium was a figure of his own abjection, his own unwilling participation in the dirtiness of life. In rejecting laudanum, therefore, Coleridge was seeking to reassert his own autonomy by separating his own abject, enslaved self from the Others that embodied this abjection. Yet as he rid himself of one Eastern poison (laudanum), the other Eastern poison (cholera) took its place. The abjection of one 'new-imported Nabob' allowed the entrance of another. Less than a week after first announcing his decision to renounce opium, Coleridge writes that he continues to suffer from 'a sad trial of intestinal pain and restlessness; but thro' God's Mercy, without any craving for the Poison, which for more than 30 years has been the guilt, debasement, and misery of my Existence' (*Collected Letters*, VI, p. 894). Despite this apparent improvement, however, an extraordinary change appears simultaneously to have been taking place in his outward appearance, or at least in how he saw himself. Gillman assured him that he was healthier, but 'when I look at myself in the Glass, I see almost the contrary'. Harriet Macklin, a servant, confirmed his opinion, for when she saw him she exclaimed, 'Sir! your face has not the same expression of Pain, Anxiety, and the being worn out by pain; [but] it is yellower, or brown and yellow, m[ore] than I have ever seen it' (*Collected Letters*, VI, p. 892). As Coleridge struggled to emancipate himself from the slavery of opium, his body seemed to be making him more like a 'negro-slave'.

On 17 May 1832 Coleridge suffered another bout of cholera. His health seemed improved, and he had enjoyed an afternoon in 'high spirits' demolishing 'a large number of incendary 1/2d & penny flying sheets' supporting the Reform Bill and eulogising Lord Grey, when, like the keelman William Sproat, he ate a mutton chop, which had an effect on his system equivalent to a 'narcotic poison' (*Collected Letters*, VI, p. 907). Gillman prescribed morphine and mercury. Salivation occurred, but then Coleridge's head began to swell. 'I will answer for it', Coleridge writes to J. H. Green, 'that out of the foul Ward of a Hospital even you have never seen a Head so swoln, or a physiognomy so frightfully deformed as that of your poor friend at this moment. I have very nearly lost the voluntary power of ejecting the mucus from my Throat – & as to eating, it is impracticable . . . I do not feel the slightest wish or craving for the Laudanum; nor do I believe, that it would even alleviate my sufferin[g]s. But yet I grieve for the too apparent failure of the experiment' (VI, p. 908). No longer able either to eat or to expel phlegm, Coleridge's mastery over opium seems to have come at the cost of losing control over the upper part of his body and seeing his head become monstrous. The next day, he provides a clearer picture of his physical appearance. His brother James came to visit him, but Coleridge refused him admittance. 'I would not expose him to the fatigue of getting out of his Carriage, & climbing 5 flights of Stairs, in order to behold a Mask of Syphilis, as a Venus *sub* Medicis et Mercurio, when he had expected to see the Son of his Father' (*Collected Letters*, VI, p. 909). Coleridge's likeness to his family has disappeared, nor is it even clear that he is any longer male. Instead of seeing the 'Son of his Father', James would have encountered 'a Venus *sub* Medicis et Mercurio' – his face that of a syphilitic woman taking mercury. The poet's assertion in 'Cholera cured before hand', 'My dear Honeys! / There is no Cure for you' would thus have had a deeply personal meaning for Coleridge, who only months before had seen himself as inhabiting the body of a syphilitic, cholera-ridden prostitute. By 10 June the poet's condition had improved. The 'Virus Hermaphroditicum' was on the wane. His gums were no longer like 'hillocks of sponge', the 'bigness' and 'aching' of his head had diminished, the salivation had stopped and his breath was no longer fetid. He writes that now, when he looks in the mirror, 'I no longer behold in my glass a Hottentot Venus sub medicis, with the characteristic Feature transplaced' (*Collected Letters*, VI, p. 913).

Whether one sees Coleridge's illness as physical or psychological, it nevertheless suggests that he believed that he had undergone the state of abjection that he associated with slavery and the working class. In 'The Hottentot and the Prostitute', Sander Gilman has suggested the degree to which nineteenth-century notions of female sexuality were read across the iconography of race, prostitution, and disease, as European doctors, searching for physical signs of sexual deviancy in Blacks and prostitutes, associated the Hottentot Venus Sarah Bartmann's characteristic feature, her protruding buttocks or steatopygia, with excessive sexuality. In an even stranger contribution to the psychopathology of disease, Coleridge outdoes Bartmann, seeing himself not only as a Hottentot Venus, but one whose buttocks have been transplanted to his face. In a situation in which the physicality of the lower stratum seems to have displaced his head and face, Coleridge has only to look into the mirror in order to see into the bottom of cholera – its link to dirt, slavery, blacks, and sexuality. 'Cholera cured before hand', written six weeks after Coleridge had recovered from this illness, is in many ways a highly personal document of his response to the extraordinary events taking place not only in the nation but in his personal life. In *Confessions of an English Opium Eater*, De Quincey magnified his own struggle with opium into an epic battle between East and West whose locus is the opium-eater's imagination. Coleridge fought a similar battle, only on multiple terrains: East/West, male/female, Irish/English, black/white, middle-class/working-class, head/bowels. A poem that ultimately addresses the question of government, a subject that for more than thirty years had been a source of personal embarrassment for the poet, his pastiche of a working-class medical text constitutes a complex articulation of a special kind of middle-class hybridity, which struggles with feelings of dependency and vulnerability by abjecting them onto Others. Having only just recently gained control over opium (thus allowing him to govern himself), and having recently inhabited a body that he himself would have excluded from universal suffrage, Coleridge must have wondered what else the conflict between his bowels and opium had in store for him.

Notes

* This essay is drawn from my forthcoming book entitled *Romanticism and Colonial Disease*. [*Romanticism and Colonial Disease*, Baltimore: Johns Hopkins UP, 1999.]

1 See Pelling: 'As the cause of death and debility in mid-nineteenth-century England, cholera was surpassed among epidemic diseases by 'common continued fever' (chiefly typhoid, relapsing fever, and some typhus), scarlet fever, smallpox, and measles, and accounted for only a very small proportion of the area of highest mortality, which occurred among infants and young children' (p. 4).

2 Three versions of the poem exist in separate letters, one to Coleridge's physician friend J. H. Green, 26 July 1832, VI, pp. 916–18; the second, to Henry Nelson Coleridge, 28 August 1832, VI, pp, 922–25; and another, dated 5 September 1832, to the surgeon J. H. B. Williams (not published in the *Collected Letters* but available in Stephens). Unless otherwise indicated, I will be referring to the version sent to H. N. Coleridge. The poem appeared in Coleridge's *Political Works* in a group entitled 'Jeux d'Esprit'.

3 The September version is signed 'Philodemus Coprophilus, Physician extraordinary to their sovereign Majesties, the People'.

4 J. R. de J. Jackson notes that the NCSTC CD-ROM produces 305 titles with the word 'cholera' in them between 1820 and 1832.

5 For Coleridge's knowledge of contemporary medicine, see Harris; Levere, pp. 36–57, 201–21; H. Jackson, 'Kings Evil' and 'Coleridge's Collaborator'; and Vickers.

6 In a marginal comment on the fly-leaf to John Walker's *A Dictionary of the English Language, answering at once the purposes of rhyming, spelling, and pronouncing* . . . (London: 1775), written sometime around 1815, Coleridge writes: 'Contagious Typhus – originates, at least is always aggravated by impure air – especially human Effluvia – General treatment, applicable to all cases – Cleanliness, Ventilation, plentiful dilution-partial fomentation, friction' (see *Marginalia*, VI, forthcoming). Anthony Harding has drawn my attention to a passage from *Notebook* 49 (BM add. MS 47544) in which Coleridge, referring to James Welsh's *Military Reminiscences, from a Journal of nearly forty years' Active Service in the East Indies* (1830), reflects on the puzzling selectivity of cholera in its victims and its apparent disregard for environmental barriers: 'When we read so often (& who that read military history can do otherwise of the Fevers, Cholera Morbus &c &c evidently occasioned by particular states of the Atmosphere, sometimes in connection with the Soil – marsh or swamp-land – but often, where no such accessory influences can be traced – as where the Disease tacks & veers its mysterious Course from India to Russia, over soils & lands of the most various & opposite conditions & characters – how forcibly does not the sense of the dependence of our Lives on a directing Providence present itself to the Mind!'

7 *Wesleyan Methodist Magazine*, 11, 3rd series (1832), pp. 204–05.

8 In a letter to Henry Coleridge, Coleridge describes 'O'Connel, and the gang of Agitators' as but symptoms of the popular unrest of the 'agitated Mass'. O'Connell fares better than does Joseph Hume, leader of the radical party, who is described as being 'more mischievous', as 'a *fermenting* Virus' (VI, p. 885). For discussion of the popular association of the Irish with the spread of disease, see A. Kraut, pp. 31–49.

9 Lord Greville notes that 'furious contests have taken place about the burials, it having been recommended that bodies should be buried directly after death, and the most violent prejudice opposing itself to this recommendation' (II, p. 79). See also R. J. Morris, pp. 104–14; Durey, pp. 163–70.

10 Thomas Poole notes that Coleridge suffered 'two very severe attacks of the pre-
    vailing cholera, & suffered dreadfully under them' (*Collected Letters*, VI, p. 874n).

Works cited

Burns, Robert, *The Poems and Songs of Robert Burns*, ed. by James Kinsley, 3 vols
(Oxford: Clarendon Press, 1968).

Busey, Samuel S., *Immigration: Its Evils and Consequences*. (1870); New York: Arno
Press, 1969.

'The Cholera in the Gazette', *New Monthly Magazine*, 31 (1831), p. 490.

Cobbett, William, 'Cholera Morbus', *Cobbett's Weekly Political Register* 75, 9 (25
February, 1832), pp. 513–23.

Coleridge, Samuel Taylor, *Collected Letters of Samuel Taylor Coleridge*, ed. by Earl
Leslie Griggs, 6 vols (Oxford: Clarendon Press, 1956–71).

——, *The Complete Poems*, ed. by William Keach (London: Penguin, 1997).

——, *Lay Sermons*, ed. by R. J. White, *The Collected Works of Samuel Taylor
Coleridge* (Princeton, N.J.: Princeton University Press, 1972).

——, *Marginalia*, ed. by Heather Jackson and George Whalley, *The Collected Works
of Samuel Taylor Coleridge*, 6 vols (Princeton, NJ.: Princeton University Press,
1980–).

——, *Notebooks of Samuel Taylor Coleridge*, ed. by Kathleen Coburn (Princeton,
N.J.: Princeton University Press, 1957–).

——, *Table Talk*, ed. by Carl Woodring, *The Collected Works of Samuel Taylor
Coleridge* (Princeton, N.J.: Princeton University Press, 1990).

Durey, Michael, *The Return of the Plague: British Society and the Cholera 1831–2*
(Dublin: Gill and Macmillan, 1979).

Evans, Richard J., *Death in Hamburg: Society and Politics in the Cholera Years
1830–1910* (Oxford: Clarendon Press, 1987).

Gaulter, Henry, *The Origins and Progress of the Malignant Cholera in Manchester*
(London: Longman, 1833).

Gilman, Sander L., 'The Hottentot and the Prostitute: Toward an Iconography of
Female Sexuality', *Difference and Pathology: Stereotypes of Sexuality, Race, and
Madness* (Ithaca: Cornell University Press, 1985), pp. 76–108.

Greville, Charles, *The Greville Memoirs*, ed. by Henry Reeve, 2 vols (New York:
D. Appleton, 1875).

Harris, John, 'Coleridge's Readings in Medicine', *The Wordsworth Circle*, 3
(1973), pp. 85–95.

Jackson, H. J., 'Coleridge on the King's Evil', *Studies in Romanticism*, 16 (1977),
pp. 337–47.

——, 'Coleridge's Collaborator, Joseph Henry Green', *Studies in Romanticism*, 21
(Summer 1982), pp. 161–79.

Kay-Shuttleworth, James, *The Moral and Physical Conditions of the Working Classes*
(2nd ed., 1832; New York: Augustus M. Kelley 1970).

Kraut, Alan M., *Silent Travellers: Germs, Genes, and the 'Immigrant Menace'* (New
York: Basic, 1994).

Kristeva, Julia, *Powers of Horror: An Essay on Abjection*, tr. Leon S. Roudiez
(New York: Columbia University Press, 1982).

Levere, Trevor, *Poetry Realized in Nature: Samuel Taylor Coleridge and Early Nineteenth-Century Science* (Cambridge: Cambridge University Press, 1981).

Morris, R. J., *Cholera 1832: The Social Response to an Epidemic* (London: Croom Helm, 1976).

Pelling, Margaret, *Cholera, Fever and English Medicine 1825–1865* (Oxford: Oxford University Press, 1978).

Rosenberg, Charles E., *The Cholera Years* (Chicago: University of Chicago Press, 1962).

Smart, Rev. Newton, 'The Duty of a Christian People under Divine Visitations', *The British Critic*, 11 (1832), pp. 375–90.

Southey, Robert, *Selections from the Letters of Robert Southey*, ed. by John Wood Warter, 4 vols (London: Longman, 1856).

Stephens, Fran Carlock, 'An Autograph Letter of S. T. Coleridge', *Review of English Studies*, 33 (1982), pp. 298–302.

Vickers, Neil, 'Coleridge, Thomas Beddoes and Brunonian Medicine', *European Romantic Review*, 8 (1997), pp. 47–94.

Walkowitz, Judith R., *Prostitution and Victorian Society: Women, Class, and the State* (Cambridge: Cambridge University Press, 1980).

Woodring, Carl R., *Politics in the Poetry of Coleridge* (Madison: University of Wisconsin Press, 1961).

33

CHAOS AND EVOLUTION:
A QUANTUM LEAP IN
SHELLEY'S PROCESS

Hugh Roberts

Source: *Keats-Shelley Journal* 45 (1996), 156–94.

I

In a recent reading of Shelley's *Defence of Poetry*, Jean Hall attempts to come to terms with one of its most troubling aspects: the ease with which so many of its most stirring and memorable phrases can be assimilated to a straightforwardly "Romantic"—transcendental, redemptive—theory of poetry.[1] This is problematical for what is increasingly coming to be the dominant reading of Shelley in contemporary criticism, one that owes a great deal to Hall's own *The Transforming Image*. The most comprehensive statement of this reading is to be found in Jerrold E. Hogle's massive *Shelley's Process*, to which my title alludes. This "decentering," or "nontranscendental" version of Shelley—to use Hogle's and Hall's terms, respectively[2] —sees him as an insistently skeptical subverter of all stable signification, metaphorically "transforming" and "transferring" meaning so as to undermine any claims to eternally valid "truths."

There is much in the *Defence* to support the "decentering" approach: notably the insistence upon poetry's annihilatory force, which "makes us the inhabitants of a world to which the familiar world is a chaos,"[3] and the concomitant imperative that it "creates anew" in the ensuing void (p. 505). But Hall must work hard to account for Shelley's claims that "A Poet participates in the eternal, the infinite, and the one" (p. 483), or that all poets contribute to "that great poem, which all poets, like the co-operating thoughts of one great mind, have built up since the beginning of the world" (p. 493).

One of the best readings of Shelley's theory of poetic language as outlined in the *Defence* is William Keach's, which finds its chief problematic in this opposition between what he reads as competing visions of the nature of language.[4] On the one hand, Keach argues, Shelley sees language as a divine "spark," a "mirror" which has the unique capability of reflecting the pure truth underlying the distorted surfaces of reality; and on the other, it is seen as itself a distorting "veil," or smothering layer of "ashes," which falls between the poet's original conception and the poem's readers, robbing them of the force and perfection of the poet's initial, complete inspiration. This opposition is, *mutatis mutandis*, the familiar one between Shelley's "skepticism" and his "idealism"; indeed Keach describes it as "an underlying linguistic skepticism" (p. 22) opposed to a Romantic conception of poetry as incarnation of a higher truth. For Keach, this is also a struggle between pessimism and optimism; a struggle which pessimism, or skepticism, wins: "in the end the veil of language remains as evidence of 'the limitedness of the poetical faculty,' in spite of Shelley's wondrous capacity to make a virtue of that limitedness" (p. 33).

But need we accept this view that the *Defence* is one more schizophrenic argument between an Enlightenment Shelley and his Romantic alter ego? Hall argues that we need not, that Shelley's skeptical transformations inform even his apparent aspirations toward the absolute: Shelley's one "great poem" is "not an object but a collective text embodying potential that must be activated if it is to be of any use."[5] Her argument is similar to that of Hogle, who accounts for Shelley's apparently idealist allusions to the "One Mind" of all humanity with a theory of the "transferential One," a vast clearing-house of infinitely transposable "mythographs" which comprises the "Great Memory," or the sum total of human thought.[6]

The problem with this solution is that it either means too much or too little, especially if we consider the political implications of the "decentering" approach. Radical transference is politically "radical" in so far as it grants to literature a negative capacity: the power to undo oppressive ideological structures. But if the Great Memory is no more than the aggregative total of what-has-been-thought-so-far then this skeptical capacity threatens to be politically incoherent. If Shelley's poetry converts mythograph to mythograph in an arbitrary will-to-transference, it might be true that it will help topple tyranny; it will be equally likely, however, to help topple any society we might recognize as human. Consequently, there is a constant temptation among the skeptical, "decentering" critics to make the negativity of Shelley's poetry a negation of the negation; Shelley's "skepticism" becomes a *via negativa* to a curious second-order idealism which guarantees that the only changes it brings about are ones that bring us closer to a fuller expression of our essential (collective) humanity.

Hogle succumbs to this temptation in his reading of the Shelleyan "One." The "Great Memory" proves to be more than just an aggregate: it is revealed to have a coherent tendency. This suggests affinities with Hegelian World History which make the transferential poet a World Historical Spirit blindly fulfilling the "cunning of Reason." Consider Hogle's reading of the role of Demogorgon in *Prometheus Unbound*, particularly as it relates to his deposition of Jupiter:

> This shifting from old methods of retraction and repression to more productive yet related constructs that drag down their predecessors: this sequence is history's enactment of Demogorgon's "nature." In that sense it/he is, as he later claims (III.i.52), the "Eternity" in the process of time, the perpetual impulse bringing about the ideologies of the past, the present, and the future.[7]

"'Eternity' in the process of time" cannot but make us think of Coleridge's idealist definition of the symbol as "Above all . . . the translucence of the Eternal through and in the Temporal."[8] If Demogorgon represents Hogle's transferential principle operating in the historical world, he must also represent just such a Providential Absolute acting to bring about the redemption of the "One" that has fallen into division. How else to explain that this supposedly amoral and atelic transference is always towards "more productive . . . constructs?" "Incessant transformation," Hogle insists a little after this (reading the figures of act III), "is humankind's best hope for future equality, free development, and social justice."[9] It is only so, I would argue, because an unconsciously presupposed idealism acts as a kind of safety net ensuring that the most nihilistic disruptions of meaning ultimately betray a therapeutic import. Similarly, Hall's supposedly open-ended, uncontainable "transformation" has in fact a final goal, although the quest for it can be constantly renewed. It is one familiar to readers of Schiller, Schelling, and Coleridge: a "universal fusion," or reconciliation of mind and world, achieved in the creative act: "the poet [by writing a poem] changes the world into an image of his ideal self."[10] It is not difficult to see her reading of the "great poem" as a "collective text" awaiting actualization as another version of the "Great Memory" as World-Historical *Begriff*.

For Shelley, "memory"—what we owe to it, how we can escape from it—was central to the political problematic of his time. The amnesiac disjunctions of the French Revolution which had, in Tocqueville's words, "bris[è] tout à coup le lien des souvenirs,"[11] posed the problem of "memory" very clearly. Like Hegel in Germany, Shelley's Romantic precursors, Wordsworth and Coleridge, had decided that Burke's prophetic account of the Revolution's excesses had also suggested the antidote to this "fury of destruction"[12]—the "consecration" of the state as an organic "body."

> To avoid therefore the evils of inconstancy and versatility, ten thousand times worse than those of obstinacy and the blindest prejudice, we have consecrated the state, that no man should approach to look into its defects or corruptions but with due caution . . . that

he should approach to the faults of the state as to the wounds of a father, with pious awe and trembling solicitude. By this wise prejudice we are taught to look with horror on those children of their country who are prompt rashly to hack that aged parent in pieces, and put him into the kettle of magicians, in hopes that . . . they may regenerate the paternal constitution and renovate their father's life.[13]

This organicism is important for two reasons. The first is its insistence upon memory, and our duty to preserve and maintain what we remember. Applying an organic logic to the process of social reproduction makes all innovation implicitly seem an inorganic assault upon the organism; incomplete or "amnesiac" reproduction is literally monstrous. The second reason is the organic inherence of the part in the whole, an aspect of Burke's political thought which became the keystone of Romantic idealism, most familiar to us in the form of the Coleridgean symbol. If every part instantiates and mystically embodies the whole, then any political change, no matter how slight its scope, becomes, according to Burke, unthinkable:

Our political system is placed in a just correspondence and symmetry with the order of the world, and with the mode of existence decreed to a permanent body composed of transitory parts; wherein, by the disposition of a stupendous wisdom, moulding together the great mysterious incorporation of the human race, the whole, at one time, is never old, or middle-aged, or young, but in a condition of unchangeable constancy, moves on through the varied tenour of perpetual decay, fall, renovation, and progression.

(*Reflections*, p. 120)

When Burke does consider change, even admittedly necessary and ameliorative change, this reproductive logic overrides all other considerations: "I would not exclude alteration neither; but even when I changed, it should be to preserve. . . . In what I did, I should follow the example of our ancestors. I would make the reparation as nearly as possible in the style of the building" (*Reflections*, p. 375).

This therapeutic response to the fragmentation and disjunctive change of the Revolution—"therapeutic" because it sought to restore the organism to "health" by recuperating its disjoined "parts" and restoring them to collective unity—was both attractive and problematic for Shelley. It was attractive because the philosophical anarchism which had been the logical result of the application of Enlightenment skepticism to social and political thought was clearly inadequate to account for the political events of the Revolution. It had not proven possible to simply ignore the past and the claims of memory as skeptical anarchism had suggested: "If the Revolution had been in every respect prosperous, then misrule and superstition would lose half their claims to our abhorrence, as fetters which the captive can unlock with the slightest motion of his fingers, and which do not eat with poisonous rust into the soul."[14] The past was too much with the revolutionaries, in a way for which a skeptical critique of causality could not account, any more than can, now, the "free transference" and "transformation" of the "decentering" critics.

But Burke's kind of response was also problematic for Shelley, because to accept the entire reproductive logic of philosophic organicism is to negate the possibility of successful resistance to the *status quo*. Even if we did not believe ourselves or others to be oppressed by that *status quo*, the organic world of "unchangeable constancy"—like the world of Hogle's "Great Memory"—would be a world without genuine creativity, without the possibility of surprise. Shelley's problem was to discover how change emerges from a world in which memory, and socio-political reproduction premised upon memory, are demonstrably operable. What he required was a way of understanding poetry as revolutionary thought—"revolutionary" not in the sense that it would automatically bring about what we would recognize as a political revolution, but that it would open a conceptual space within which genuine change could emerge within the cycles of mnemonic reproduction, a conceptual space in which "Each part *exceeds* the whole" (*Epipsychidion*, line 181; my emphasis).

The therapeutic idealism of Coleridge and Wordsworth does not accept the possibility of an opposition between the text and its sociopolitical context of production; for them the text must function symbolically as an "expression"[15] of that context, as the part which reflects and instantiates the whole. Ironically, this way of reading the text's relationship to its social and political context, a way which strips it of any active political significance, has been, and remains, the standard model for "political" literary criticism. "Historicist" critics, old and New, in large part due to the Hegelian legacy within Marxist thought, seek to make all "parts" representative of the "whole," to read all texts as "typical" expressions of a given socio-political form. To find this "revolutionary" possibility within Shelley's theory of poetics, then, is not merely to reinterpret Shelley, but to challenge our own understanding of the political nature of the text.

II. Chaos and Evolution

To begin with, we need a new basis on which to address this oldest and toughest of critical chestnuts, the relationship of Shelley's "skepticism" to his "idealism." Every generation of Shelley critics has tried to settle this problem, but Shelley will not come into focus as either a "pure" skeptic or a "pure" idealist. On the other hand, Shelley was too consciously the inheritor of the Enlightenment tradition of skeptical materialism and the Romantic idealism of Coleridge and Wordsworth, and was too aware of the deep political and philosophical divisions between these positions, for us to suppose that he could be long content drawing on both simultaneously—as he does in such early poems as *Queen Mab*, *Alastor*, and *The Revolt of Islam*. I suggest that what has long gone unrecognized in Shelley's thought is the active, and ultimately successful, pursuit of a third position from which to critique the epistemological and political failings of both these inherited "traditions." That position finds its closest affinities in recent thought with the new sciences of complex dynamics popularly known as "chaos theory."[16]

Chaos theory, the study of "determinate indeterminacy," provides us with a model with which we can conceptualize the flux and indeterminacy so central to the "skeptical" Shelley without having to abandon a deterministic universe. From the standpoint of chaos theory, the limits to our ability to know the world have less to do with epistemology than with the hitherto unsuspected complexity—the "fractal" complexity—of the world itself. To trace the path back from effects to causes through the feedback cycles of nonlinear dynamic systems (which is to say virtually all natural dynamic systems including the "organic" autoreproductive systems of Burke's metaphor) becomes infinitely complex, not because of Hume's discrediting of the principle of causality itself, but because "sensitive dependence on initial conditions" means that the determining "initial conditions" of the system will escape any arbitrarily accurate attempt at definition. The chaotic world is an entropic world: information is constantly lost from it because nature itself is unable to conserve infinite accuracy in its own interactions. It is not only practically, but theoretically impossible to project a causal chain backwards in a chaotic system and deduce its origin from its current state. A chaotic system is irreversible, unlike the world as seen by classical science; to describe it, we must resort to a radically empirical history of its unpredictable, and unrepeatable, evolution.[17] This empiricism is "radical" because it renounces, unlike conventional empiricism, the ultimate appeal to, or theoretical possibility of, an organically cohesive "narrative" or "plot" within which empirically observed phenomena take their ultimately predictable place. It accepts, bucking the trend of centuries, even millennia, of Western thought, the possibility of genuine novelty and innovation in an inherently surprising world. To observe a system in the process of evolution is to be brought to that same state of "modesty" which Tocqueville found appropriate in the face of the Revolution: "car il n'y eut jamais d'événements plus grands, conduits de plus loin, mieux préparés et moins prévus."[18]

That the Revolution was a "logical" consequence of the history which preceded it goes without saying—although the proponents of the "radical transference" argument, at least in their more "skeptical" mood, might not agree. The "evolutionary" point, which amounts simply to taking history seriously, is that other "logical" consequences are always equally conceivable at any given moment. In Stephen Jay Gould's *Wonderful Life*, a study of the Burgess Shale, an unparalleled find of detailed fossils of very early animal species, he proposes as a metaphor for this errant creativity the replaying of "life's tape." He asks us to envision life as a videotape that we wind back to the time of the Burgess Shale organisms, and then allow to play forward again. The "therapeutic," organicist assumption, which is also the assumption of classical science, is that the story will unfold more or less as it did before, that evolutionary history must have some internal teleology which tends, ultimately, to produce creatures like us. Gould argues, however, that

> the reconstructed Burgess fauna, interpreted by the theme of replaying life's tape, offers powerful support for . . . [a] different view of life: any replay of the tape would lead evolution down a pathway radically different from the road actually taken. . . . [T]he divergent route of the replay would be just as interpretable, just as explainable *after* the fact, as the actual road. But the diversity of possible itineraries does demonstrate that eventual results cannot be predicted at the outset. Each step proceeds for cause, but no finale can be specified at the start, and none would ever occur a second time in the same way, because any pathway proceeds through thousands of improbable stages. Alter any early event, ever so slightly and without apparent importance at the time, and evolution cascades into a radically different channel.[19]

That Shelley's view of the world is "evolutionary" has been noted before, but what this means has been distorted in the light of the "skeptical"/ "idealist" dilemma. Either, like Kenneth Neill Cameron, one saw Shelley as an "evolutionist" in the Marxist/Hegelian sense—society "evolves" through a predetermined course of "stages"[20] —or, as for the "decentering" critics, "evolution" becomes a synonym for purely indeterminate transference. Shelley did not live to read *On the Origin of Species*, but he read and re-read throughout his life the work which accounts for the surprising frequency with which evolutionary theories are proposed in the eighteenth century, the work which underlay Erasmus Darwin's evolutionary theory, Lucretius' *De Rerum Natura*.

Michel Serres has shown in detail how much of contemporary chaotic dynamics—and that other revolutionary discovery of irreversible evolution in the physical world, quantum physics—are prefigured in the work of Lucretius. The much derided *clinamen* has been reinstated as a brilliant intuition of the impossibility—with an arbitrary degree of precision—of absolutely determining trajectories in the complexities of real world interactions. The *clinamen* marks the fact of entropy in our world, the inevitable erasure of "initial conditions" as information is lost in the flux of time. It is not to be confused with Harold Bloom's oedipal "revisionary ratio" of the same name,[21] nor with Hogle's and Hall's "transformation." The evolutionary "swerve"—which indeed performs a "transformation" upon the development of the system in which it occurs—is neither a desperate imposition of innovation upon the juggernaut of "influence," nor an effortless teleportation from one corner of the Great Memory to any other. It is an inevitable, constant deformation of a globally reiterative dynamic.

Lucretius describes the "greatest joy of all" as being "to stand aloof in a quiet citadel . . . and to gaze down from that elevation on others wandering aimlessly in a vain search for the way of life. . . ."[22] The point of contact between the Enlightenment's scientific ideal and Romantic idealism is the belief that from some sufficiently elevated position (the position occupied by Laplace's "demon") the flux of the world would resolve itself into an ordered, systematic totality. This is the belief Shelley draws upon, with Baron Holbach's help, in *Queen Mab*, when Ianthe gazes down from sufficient height upon our mortal storm to realize that "No atom of this turbulence fulfils / A vague and unnecessitated task" (VI, 171–72). But Lucretius' point is that the observer in the citadel realizes that the search for the "way of life"—a "plot," or *fil conducteur* to life's history—is futile; the *clinamen* introduces an inevitable degree of contingency into the causal chains of the world.

Lucretius insists, however, that this entropic deformation is the key to the negentropic creativity of our world. The *clinamen* may be an "error," but it is an error which gives birth to the universe. Evolution is premised upon disorder: death, natural disaster, mutation. Gould has shown that the sheer contingency of evolutionary development is the key to its unpredictable creativity.[23] As each contingent "error" is caught up in the nonlinear cycles of organic reproduction, it becomes, through constant reiteration and proliferation, part of the "essence" of future generations. Chaotic creativity is a constant process of error becoming essence. "Reparation" is never quite "in the style of the building," and what we take to be its "style" at any given moment is a product of a long history of errant reparations. It is a tenet of chaos theory that if a "system ever does reach equilibrium," in the manner of Burke's "unchangeable constancy," "it isn't just stable. It's dead."[24] Or as James Gleick puts it: "Chaos [is] the creation of information":

> As the system becomes chaotic . . . strictly by virtue of its unpredictability, it generates a steady stream of information. Each new observation is a new bit. This is a problem for the experimenter trying to characterize the system completely. "He could never leave the room," as Shaw said. "The flow would be a continuous source of information."[25]

It is this that makes irreversibility the basis of a "nouvelle alliance" between humanity and the world, according to Ilya Prigogine and Isabelle Stengers. A chaotic world is an endlessly destructive one, but it is also an endlessly creative, and endlessly engaging one:

> Aucun langage . . . ne peut épuiser la réalité du système; les différents langages possibles, les différents points de vue pris sur le système, sont *complémentaires*. . . . Ce caractère irréductible des points de vue sur une même réalité, c'est très exactement l'impossibilité de découvrir un point de vue de survol [cf. the "view from the citadel"], un point de vue à partir duquel la totalité du réel serait simultanément visible. . . . [L]a réalité . . . est trop riche, . . . ses reliefs sont trop complexes pour qu'un seul projecteur puisse l'éclairer dans sa totalité.[26]

The essence of fractal organization is that any "part," at whatever scale, is itself comprised of equally non-integral and potentially oppositional "parts." Each "part" (or "seed") resists recuperation into a determining whole, and is potentially a new departure point, or bifurcation, in an errant history before which, like the scientific experimenter unable to leave the room, we can maintain only a radical empiricism. Far from cementing a political or aesthetic conservatism, memory, in Lucretian terms, is the motive force of a permanent revolution; in *De Rerum Natura*, the daughters of memory *are* the daughters of inspiration.

III. Evolutionary Thought in the *Defence of Poetry*

If we return to the problems of Shelley's *Defence of Poetry*, we can now see that many of the apparent paradoxes of its argument disappear from this Lucretian perspective. While it is impossible, and undesirable, to reduce all the complications of the *Defence* to variations on a single theme, it is possible to see both veil and mirror, spark and ashes, as aspects of a single problematic. The key passage for Keach's argument is this description of the nature of Dante's poetic language, whose affinities with the passage from the *Nouvelle Alliance* quoted above are immediately striking:

> His very words are instinct with spirit; each is as a spark, a burning atom of inextinguishable thought; and many yet lie covered in the ashes of their birth, and pregnant with a lightning which has yet found no conductor. All high poetry is infinite; it is as the first acorn, which contained all oaks potentially. Veil after veil may be undrawn, and the inmost naked beauty of the meaning never exposed. A great Poem is a fountain for ever overflowing with the waters of wisdom and delight; and after one person and one age has exhausted all its divine effluence which their peculiar relations enable them to share, another and yet another succeeds, and new relations are ever developed, the source of an unforeseen and an unconceived delight.
>
> (p. 500)

370

"New relations are ever developed, the source of an unforeseen and an unconceived delight": there are two radical claims being made here. The first is that a text will never be finally and completely "understood"; through time, it will continue to be interpreted and re-interpreted *ad infinitum*. The second is that what is new in each new reading is, at least sometimes, absolutely so. Different readings do not develop out of each other in an organic unfolding through time of a unitary truth; rather, they arrive "unforeseen" and above all "unconceived." This is to say that no matter how closely we read the text *now*, we shall be unable to determine within it the seeds of its future interpretations. Strictly speaking, the hermeneutic history of the literary work of art is, Shelley is claiming, erratic, irreversible, and chaotically creative of information; the critic is reduced—or exalted—to a radical empiricism with respect to the unfolding of the text's history of consumption.

Shelley has touched here upon one of the central problems of all hermeneutic endeavours—their interminability. This is something of which, as critics, we are all aware, but rarely acknowledge directly. It is difficult, within the dominant Western *episteme*, to escape the feeling that if the disjunctive sequence of undrawn veils never comes to an end, or does not, at the very least, converge upon some final revelation, literary criticism's claims to "knowledge" will have suffered a formidable blow. Knowledge should be final and absolute; if "chatter about books" can never be resolved—if interpretation, like analysis, is interminable—what use is there in continuing?

Keach's interpretation, for example, seeks to avoid this discomfort. When confronted with this passage in the *Defence*, he reads the "veils" as an infinite number of partial barriers which lie between the reader and a truth which is somehow "there," despite the fact that it is never finally revealed. For Shelley, Keach argues, the spark of "pure" inspiration lies covered in the ashes of poetic realization, which it is our (infinite) task to remove, piece by piece. With this reading, Keach is able to account for Shelley's apparent celebration of what would seem to be an admission of interpretive defeat: thus Shelley "sets about transmuting an apparent limitation into a strength."[27] Shelley's position would then be the archetypal Romantic-ironic one of celebrating progress over achievement. As Schiller puts it in his *Naive and Sentimental Poetry*: "the absolute achievement of a finite" is less rewarding than an "approximation to an infinite greatness" because "only the latter possesses *degrees* and displays a *progress*. . . ."[28]

Keach, however, is too good a reader of the *Defence* not to realize that this reading doesn't fit Shelley's many explicit statements concerning what we might call entropy. Meaning in the *Defence* rarely has a constant, incremental drive to plenitude; rather, it seems often to turn awry and, ultimately, to become erased. Poetic inspiration—the fleeting revelation of the absolute truth that underlies the deceptive phenomenal world—is "a fading coal" (p. 504). For Keach to maintain his argument that Shelley ultimately posits a final and absolute truth that somewhere underlies the poem, he must read

Shelley's veils as curtains which the poet uses almost wilfully, initially to obscure, and eventually to completely eclipse that truth. It is not hard for Keach to find passages in the *Defence* that appear to suit this reading:

> Few poets of the highest class have chosen to exhibit the beauty of their conceptions in its naked truth and splendour; and it is doubtful whether the alloy of costume, habit, etc., be not necessary to temper this planetary music for mortal ears.
>
> (p. 487)

> [Poetry] arrests the vanishing apparitions which haunt the interlunations of life, and veiling them or in language or in form sends them forth among mankind.
>
> (p. 505)

In Keach's view, when Shelley's pessimistic skepticism gets the better of him, this protective "tempering" becomes a nearly complete, and quite inevitable, betrayal of the original "naked truth and splendour." The clearest statement of that pessimism, he suggests, is the "fading coal" passage: "when composition begins, inspiration is already on the decline, and the most glorious poetry that has ever been communicated to the world is probably a feeble shadow of the original conception of the poet" (p. 504).[29] The words that comprise poetry are subtly transformed here, Keach argues, from divine sparks covered with the ashes of a given period's interpretive blindnesses, into being themselves ashes that bury the spark of inspiration that prompted the poem. Despite the generally confident and celebratory tone of the *Defence*, Keach feels that it is this pessimistic view which ultimately prevails. If it were not for the inadequacy of words—specifically poetic words—we might be able to attain to the truths that they obscure. This then is a first "structural" answer to the "dynamic" problem of infinite interpretive renewal, and a very disturbing one; poetry's inherent obscurity makes it ultimately undecidable; one reader's guess is as good, or bad, as another's.

Keach's argument that Shelley attempts to save an "inmost naked beauty of the meaning" at the high price of accepting that we have no adequate tools with which we can reach that meaning calls to mind an earlier attempt to deal with interpretive interminability by one of the most influential interpreters of this century, Freud's "Analysis Terminable and Interminable." The impossibility of establishing, in theory or in practice, a definite end-point at which analysis can be said to have been "completed" was—and still is—as much of an embarrassment for therapeutic psychoanalysis as for literary criticism, and for the same reasons; if the process produces no definite solutions, we suspect that it is at some level arbitrary and artificial, the problems which it addresses either entirely fanciful or else unstable epiphenomena of some misrecognized underlying problem. Freud's solution,

372

like Keach's, is to accept a pragmatic limitation upon the effectiveness of psychoanalytic practice as the price to pay for leaving its theoretical claims to scientific accuracy inviolate. Some nuts, Freud concludes, are simply too tough to crack; feminine penis envy, for example, and masculine "repudiation of femininity" render the subject incapable of properly submitting to the therapeutic situation. Still more telling, however, is his concession that even when therapy is "successful" the therapist's decision to terminate analysis is always more or less arbitrary, a matter for the practitioner's judgment.[30]

An alternative to ascribing the interpretive dilemma to an imperfect world of obscure, "veiling" words and ultra-defensive egos is proposed in Jacques Derrida's essay "My Chances/*Mes Chances*." Derrida finds in Freud's *Psychopathology of Everyday Life* a comparison between the interpretive stance of the psychoanalyst and that of the "superstitious man" who finds deep significance in the most minor phenomena of life. Both are resolved, Freud writes, "not to let chance count as chance but to interpret it."[31] Naturally, Freud does not admit to being indistinguishable from the "superstitious man"; he even tells a complex tale in order to demonstrate the difference—an incident which the superstitious person would regard as full of obscure portent, but which he accepts as mere chance—but just as in "Analysis Terminable and Interminable," the boundaries he establishes are purely pragmatic. It may be that "sometimes a cigar is just a cigar," but the option of reading it as more is always open.[32]

Derrida argues that Freud's unsuccessful attempts to find some principle upon which to rest the distinction between superstitious paranoia and hermeneutic tenacity are based upon a classic misrecognition of the nature of meaning. Derrida argues that it is an error to think of meaning as something stable, an "inmost naked beauty" which is difficultly won by diligent hermeneutic endeavour; rather, meaning tends to proliferate endlessly in the promiscuous iterability of the "trace" or "mark." Derrida's argument is explicitly a re-emergence of the atomism of Democritus, Epicurus, and Lucretius. The promiscuity of the mark is a function of the "*atomystique* of the letter,"[33] its liability to an atomistic deviation or *clinamen*. The "Freudian slip" is simply another *clinamen*; Freud's failure to determine an absolute difference between the "true" or "significant" slip, and the mere accident is entirely predictable; there is none. This does not mean either that a cigar is never more than a cigar, or that it is always a phallus; rather, the boundaries between cigar and phallus, chance and meaning, error and essence, are fluid. The insatiability of the hermeneutic compulsion, and the interminability of the hermeneutic process, is not the product of a world that is niggardly of grist to the hermeneutic mill (veiling words and defensive egos), but one that is riven with an infinitude of "chances," or *clinamines*, any of which can defensibly be taken as a starting point for hermeneutic activity.

If we return to Shelley's description of the ever-renewed source of unforeseen and unconceived delight in Dante's poetic language with Derrida's argument in mind, we are immediately struck by the Lucretian provenance of his imagery. There is the characteristic combination of flux ("fountain," "effluence") and atomistic punctuality ("burning atom," "spark"), the latter most tellingly represented by the meteorological indeterminacy of the lightning awaiting its imprevisible conductor: Serres shows that Lucretius uses all such "meteors" as definitive examples of the chaotic indeterminacy of the *clinamen*.[34] Lucretius is particularly fascinated, as Shelley will be, by the lightning which falls *nunc hinc, nunc illinc* (II.214): a description immediately picked up in the passage on the *clinamen*, which strikes at *incerto tempore, incertisque locis* (II.218–19). There is also the evolutionary imagery of reproductive generational iteration (the acorn which promises a succession of oaks; the sequence of social contexts or "peculiar relations" which "succeed" one another in the same generational rhythm) that nonetheless veers into innovation ("new relations are ever developed, the source of an unforeseen and an unconceived delight"). But the image we have thus far been concentrating on—the "veil after veil" which "may be undrawn and the inmost naked beauty of the meaning never exposed"—is the most interesting. Although Lucretius does not actually use the word "veil," it is a small step from Shelley's veils that are constantly being "undrawn" to Lucretius' *membranae:* "a sort of outer skin perpetually peeled off the surface of objects and flying about this way and that through the air."[35] These are the *simulacra*, those images comprised of an atomthin outer layer being thrown off by all objects in a constant stream which are the medium of sight, and which, in their deformed versions, are the basis of occult visions, hallucinations, and dreams.

We know from the nightmare vision of "Mask after mask" (cf. "veil after veil") that "fell from the countenance / And form of all" (lines 536–37) that closes the *Triumph of Life* that Shelley was struck by this feature of Lucretian physics. Serres (who, incidently, calls them "voiles invisibles") reads the *simulacra* as an image for the infinitesimal limits to the precision with which we can define any physical object. For him, they are virtual objects that symbolize the arbitrary, but always significant, limit to our ability to define the difference between a curve and a tangent to that curve; the difference in which the *clinamen* performs its entropic erosion of initial conditions:

> Les tuniques volantes sont les bords fluctuants, et les superficies des limites. *Summo de corpore*. Les simulacres se détachent des choses comme en leur traitement infinitésimal. Il s'en détache autant qu'on veut. Chaque objet devient source d'une infinité d'enveloppes. La vue est aussi rigoureuse que la méthode mathématicienne. Or, comme tout objet n'a pu être produit que part et dans un tourbillon, ou dans un spirale, c'est la turbulence comme telle qui devient Èmettrice de ses enveloppes.[36]

374

"Il s'en détache autant qu'on veut"; "veil after veil can be undrawn": arbitrary degrees of precision always leave room for error, or the atom-*clinamen* of significant difference. Every object has a virtual border of possible "envelopes"—possible definitions—no one of which exhausts the reality of that object. This creates a fractal coastline of infinite complexity:

> *Les formes idéales de la géométrie ne sont pas transparentes, invariantes et vides, elles sont denses et compactes*, pleines presque à saturation, d'un tissu complexe, *et recouvertes, sur les bords, de voiles invisibles et que permettent de les voir*, de limites infinitaires et qui pourtant sont là.[37]

In the *Defence of Poetry*, Shelley is proposing a theory of the text as a hermeneutic fractal of this nature. In a very precise sense he regards the literary text as infinitely detailed: "All high poetry is infinite." Thomas McFarland quotes this line as an affirmation of the Romantic drive to the Absolute,[38] but he has missed Shelley's point; like the Lucretian object presented to the eye, the literary text never appears twice in exactly the same way, revealing new meanings/veils in the light of the "peculiar relations" of its context of consumption. Any one reading of the text is a "veil" which may conform more or less adequately to the "reality" of the text, but which always leaves room for an infinite number of other "veils," other valid descriptions of the work.

Shelley's veils do not stand *between* the reader and the work's "meaning": they are all there is of meaning in the literary work of art. The "inmost naked beauty of the meaning" is never revealed because there is no such thing; Shelley's celebration of the "unforeseen and unconceived delights" offered by poems each time we reread them is not *faute de mieux* or paradoxical, as Keach implies. The veils do not represent an endless deferral of the "real meaning" but a perpetually renewed succession of "meanings," each as real as the next.

Perhaps the closest existing analogue of this theory of interpretation is Lyotard's concept of *enchaînement*, expounded principally in his *Le Différend*. The similarity is unsurprising: Lyotard proposes his theory as a first step in bringing our approach to language into conformity with the "révolution relativiste et quantique" in modern Physics, the same "revolution[s]" that Serres, Prigogine, and others, see founded in the physics of *De Rerum Natura*, and intimately connected with the most dramatic implications of contemporary chaos theory. Quantum theory is the crucial blow to the Laplacean dream of an infinitely predictable world; it is the discovery, in the physical world, of "atomism" in the Lucretian sense: an ineradicable and potentially entropic degree of uncertainty in our most refined descriptions of physical trajectories.

Lyotard, like Shelley, wants to expand this uncertainty—this *clinamen*—to the world of literary meaning. He proposes a hermeneutic analogy with the Heisenberg principle of indeterminacy, but not in the all-too-familiar form of a simplistic relativism. What he observes is that meaning, the response to meaning, and the production of new meanings in response to that response does not form a stable, homeostatic cycle in which errors are progressively eliminated through repeated iterations, as hermeneutic theorists, drawing on the pervasive organicism of their post-Kantian forbears, have assumed. Rather, it is best understood as an evolutionary chain, each of whose links represent a moment of partial indeterminacy and potential errance. This could be described as a quantum theory of meaning: meaning is not amenable to infinite precision; you can describe a range (or "envelope") of possible trajectories for it, even suggest which are more statistically probable, but you cannot determine its course with finality. A chain is an apt image for the irreversible historical flux that Lucretius derives from the constantly renewed, and constantly defeated, attempt at reproduction in physical and human systems. A chain appears to be linear, but is comprised of nonlinear elements: it demonstrates that the cyclic can generate the "progressive." Each "link" in the chain represents the decisive evolutionary moment of contingency, a logical development from what precedes it, but which *might*, with equal logic, have been otherwise. The iterative impulse of hermeneutic endeavour operates in practice in the same way as the feedback loop of nonlinear chaotic creativity. (Chains feature prominently in Shelley's poetry as an image for the disjunctive association of ideas [most notably at *Prometheus Unbound*, iv.394], and in the *Defence* as an image for the evolving, transgenerational linkage of poet to poet through time: a linkage that is never "entirely," though implicitly partly, "disjoined" [p. 493]).

Lyotard also uses the image of a conversation. All cultural pursuits can be understood as contributions to the continuing "conversation" a society embodies and enacts. This has long been a favorite metaphor for Ordinary Language philosophers and philosophical Pragmatists (such as Richard Rorty), who judge each contribution to the conversation as successful or unsuccessful ("happy" or "unhappy," to use J. L. Austin's terms[39]) depending on whether or not it successfully enacts and reproduces that ineffable hermeneutic totality Wittgenstein called a "form of life." Wittgenstein's model of socialization, and indeed of all learning, is learning "how to go on," how to join in and continue a language-game already in progress: each "happy" contribution to the conversation must in fact maintain it; there can be no "happy" contribution that throws the conversation into entirely unexplored territory. The rules, therefore, are constantly reinforced and a "form of life" is perpetuated in "organic," Burkean fashion.

Lyotard calls all of this into question. For each "turn" in the cultural "conversation," he suggests, there are innumerable ways to respond— *enchaîner*—and each response diverts the course of the conversation relative to the other possibilities: "il faut enchaîner, mais le mode d'enchaînement n'est jamais nécessaire."[40] Each *enchaînement* is retrospectively (empirically) explicable, and different *enchaînements* may be more or less statistically probable, but none is ever fully predictable. Language is not a Totality which excludes all but "happy" contributions; it is a series of indeterminate, quantic, decisions—a fact with directly political implications: "la politique consiste en ce que le langage n'est pas un langage mais des phrases. . . ."[41] These atomistic *phrases* are so many potential sites for the *clinamen*, so many potential sites of revolution, or political dispute, where the part (*phrase*) can overthrow the whole (*langage*): "Tout est politique si la politique est la possibilité du différend à l'occasion du moindre enchaînement."[42] That possibility is what makes "all high poetry" infinite and it is this infinitude that I am describing as fractal. Poetry as a response to its context of production (or consumption) opens up the possibility of such a "*différend*" —or evolutionary diversion within the reproductive cycles of the social "conversation"—whenever it enters that cycle. Above all, this evolutionary logic allows Shelley to see poetic texts as functioning in *opposition* to their context of production, as being the "seeds"—a characteristically Shelleyan word which is also one of Lucretius's words for "atoms"—of some unimaginable future state.

The advantage of this version of the political significance of poetry over the "decentering" critics' "transformation" is that while still allowing poetry a genuine negative power to disrupt the reproductive cycles of Custom, it does not make oppressive social institutions mere will-o'-the-wisps within the grab-bag of the Great Memory, or suggest that poetry operates magically to reinvent the world *in toto*, thereby making a nonsense of political struggle. The possibility for poetry to act as an evolutionary *clinamen* within the *enchaînement* of social reproduction does not deny the power of "Custom's lawless law" to struggle successfully against this erosion of the *status quo*, to "eat with poisonous rust into the soul." Nor does it deny the possibility of a coherent political response to oppression, although it suggests, as history amply confirms, that the outcome of such responses will rarely be quite what was envisaged.

IV. "The Witch of Atlas"

But what, then, is poetry's, and the poet's, relationship to "the eternal, the infinite, and the one?" An answer, as well as a general corroboration of my reading of the *Defence*, can be found by turning to one of Shelley's poetic meditations on the role and nature of poetry: "The Witch of Atlas." The Witch, whether or not she is supposed to be identified with that of "the still cave of the witch Poesy" ("Mont Blanc," line 44) seems to represent poetry, or at least its effects. Her cave holds "Visions swift, and sweet, and quaint" (line 161) which she visits inconstantly upon humanity.

The word "quaint" is interesting; not one of Shelley's favorite adjectives, it seems reasonable to wonder if he doesn't have in mind that other witch of his, the "quaint witch Memory" from the "Letter to Maria Gisborne." The very least one could say of this poetic Witch's relationship to Mnemosyne is that it is "quaint." She herself is a poet: "All day the wizard lady sate aloof . . . broidering the pictured poesy . . . upon her growing woof" (lines 249–53). The poetry she writes and represents is of the kind described in the *Defence*: a deeply playful re-invention of normal hierarchies of oppositions and values. While she writes, a fire burns in her hearth:

> Men scarcely know how beautiful fire is—
> Each flame of it is as a precious stone
> Dissolved in ever-moving light, and this
> Belongs to each and all who gaze upon.
> The Witch beheld it not, for in her hand
> She held a woof that dimmed the burning brand.
>
> (lines 259–64)

Shelley rediscovers and re-invents here the image of radically negative poetry as "words of flame" found in *The Revolt of Islam* (VII.vi.6). Fire is entropy—the dissipation of heat—made visible. The purely evanescent beauty of flame is a negentropic dissipative structure dependent upon that entropic dissolution; as such, it defeats both the appeal to a noumenal *ens* and the absolute restrictions of property which are its capitalist counterpart, creating a democratic, promiscuous beauty which belongs, unlike the "precious stones" it rivals, to "each and all" (see line 261, above). The Witch's poetry is even more insubstantial—or, rather, insubstantiating—than the fire; her poetic "woof" has all the beauty and entropic, revolutionary potential of the Lucretian lightning/*clinamen* awaiting its conductor. The Witch accordingly is an atelic prankster seeking to subvert "all the code of Custom's lawless law" (line 541), wreaking havoc among all the structures of state power (Church, Court, Army, and Family respectively, in stanzas lxxiii–lxxvi). She is always at one step removed from the world, aloof, unwilling to treat as necessarily real and present the hypostatized forms of Custom's lawless laws which are "Written upon the brows of old and young" (line 542): "little did the sight disturb her soul" (line 545), says Shelley.

The Witch, and the "Witch," pose starkly for us the problem of poetry's relationship to the amnesiac negativity of genuine change and its putatively "eternal" verities. On the one hand, the Witch is strongly associated, in the poem, with the meteorological imagery whose Lucretian associations we have already established. Her mother, after being impregnated by Apollo, runs through a (neg-)entropic series of metamorphoses, "dissolv[ing] away" (line 64) into a "vapour" (line 65), "then into a cloud" (line 66), "then into a meteor" (line 69), and lastly into an asteroid (lines 71–72). This *clinamen*-ridden career sets the pattern for the Witch's own history. She herself is constantly associated with Shelley's habitual meteorological pyrotechnics:

her ministering thoughts "Cloth[e] themselves or with the Ocean foam, / Or with the wind, or with the speed of fire" (lines 211–12); her boat moves "like a cloud / Upon a stream of wind" (lines 369–70); her troops of "ministering Spirits" emblazon their merits on "meteor flags" (lines 459, 462). "Ofttime" she "Follow[s] the serpent lightning's winding track [perhaps a reference to Lucretius' *nunc hinc, nunc illinc*]. . . laugh[ing] to hear the fireballs roar behind" (lines 485–88); and to her eye, "the constellations reel and dance / Like fire-flies" (lines 269–70), defying the clockwork order of a Newtonian universe with a Dionysian revel.

Her direct actions connect her even more closely to Shelley's Lucretian poetic than these associations: Shelley had a complex theory of the proper attitude toward evil, believing that to take it too seriously, to treat it as too real, was to hypostatize it, making it an immutable *ens* rather than an ultimately defeasible *substantia*.[43] The Witch's attitude, therefore, is playful, subverting oppositions in accordance with the *Defence*'s poetic principle of "yok[ing together] all irreconcilable things" (p. 505), such as the fire and snow she kneads together to create the hermaphrodite, a figure who disrupts in turn the stability of sexual difference. The hermaphrodite is the Witch's only "child" (and a reproductive *clinamen* at that), the Witch herself being a "sexless bee / Tasting all blossoms and confined to none" (lines 589–90)— an affirmation of the disruptive *jouissance* of sexuality over its reproductive role. In the Witch's dealings with "those who were less beautiful" (line 618)—Shelley's apparently circumlocutory phrase for "evil" or "wicked" people is actually a careful avoidance of hypostatization—Shelley returns to a favorite image of entropic, atomistic erasure to describe the way the Witch, as the principle of revolutionary poetic negation, makes "All harsh and crooked purposes more vain / Than in the desert is the serpent's wake / Which the sand covers" (lines 620–22). A re-shuffling of, or aggregation of *clinamines* in, the atomistic order that maintains the trace in the sand obliterates it completely: information is lost irretrievably, and revolutionary innovation enters by the same door, in the familiar chaotic pattern of entropy engendering negentropic evolution. In the "Ode to Liberty," Shelley had used this same atomistic/entropic imagery when wishing that "the impious name / Of KING" be written in the dust like "a serpent's path, which the light air / Erases, and the flat sands close behind" (lines 211–12, 24–15). In the *Defence*, he writes of poetic inspiration as a "wind over a sea" which leaves fugacious "traces . . . on the wrinkled sand which paves it" (line 504), confirming this connection between poetry, politics, and atomistic entropy.[44]

Above all there is the structure of the poem itself, or rather its anti-structure. It begins logically enough with the Witch's conception, but after that it is motivated by sheer narrativity-without-narrative (peripeteia without plot, *substantia* without *ens*) like the democratic art of the fire dazzling us with ephemeral verbal pyrotechnics. In terms that set the tone of nearly all subsequent criticism, both hostile and appreciative, Mary Shelley calls it "wildly fanciful," "a brilliant congregation of ideas," and "abstract and dreamy."[45] This is true as far as it goes, and the phrase "congregation of ideas" is particularly shrewd, identifying as it does the structural principle on which the poem is based as atomistic constellation rather than "organic" inherence of each in all. But "abstract and dreamy," which inevitably comes to our ear with a flurry of luminous wings beating vainly and ineffectually in the void, is misleading. The verse impels us forward; thirty of the poem's seventy odd stanzas begin with the word "And," imparting a marked narrative urgency to the poem ("And then . . . and then . . ."). This narrative drive is ironic, however, because the poem subverts the concept of the organic Aristotelian "plot" by being a largely contingent sequence of sheer events: it "tell[s] no story, false or true" (line 4). The insistently repeated "and" throughout the poem is merely the trace, or scar, of the suturing which has brought these diasparactive narrative elements together.

In every way, the poem is a deliberate affront to the Romantic-organic drive to narrative absolutism. As in Shelley's "The Triumph of Life," one is forced to respond to the poem empirically as a series of "unforeseen and unconceived" events; one is never quite sure what any given part of the poem "remembers" of what has gone before. The poem's parts cannot help but exceed a whole which can never be identified. The poem's "ands" are as much disjunctions as conjunctions, moments of evolutionary *enchaînement* in Lyotard's sense. The Witch's "story" is a chain of digressions, each of which leads only to a new digression (or *clinamen*) and never back to the "main" story; it is a series of atomistic *phrases* rather than *un langage*. This digressive, disjunctive sequence of events—none of which build predictably upon preceding ones, although they sometimes inherit certain things from them—comes to no resolution. The poem ends with the entropic collapse which terminates so much of Shelley's poetry (e.g., "Julian and Maddalo," *Prometheus Unbound*, the "Ode to Liberty," "Mont Blanc"): the narrator suddenly leaves off with secrets still in his (or her?) possession:

> what she did to Sprites
> And Gods . . .
> . . . .
> I will declare another time; for it is
> A tale more fit for the weird winter nights
> Than for these garish summer days, when we
> Scarcely believe much more than we can see.
> (lines 666–72)

Shelley's endlessly digressive and centerless narrative mounts an assault on our concepts of identity. As Charles Taylor argues, it is imperative for the Romantic idealist approach to be able to confidently ground notions of personal identity in an assertion of narrative totality: we "understand ourselves inescapably in narrative," he argues, because we seek a "meaningful unity" in our lives, grounded upon the "a priori unity of a human life through its whole extent."[46] What is it, in the rarely-used "name" Witch (actually a descriptive label) or the more frequently employed personal pronoun "she," that guarantees to us the continuity of the Witch's identity through the amnesiac string of incidents in which "she" figures? These unnarrativizable incidents in Shelley's poem are best described by Derrida's Lucretian definition of "events" in "My Chances/*Mes Chances*":

> there are those of us who are inclined to think that unexpectability conditions the very structure of an event. Would an event that can be anticipated and therefore apprehended or comprehended, or one without an element of absolute encounter, actually be an event in the full sense of the word? . . . [A]n event worthy of this name cannot be foretold.[47]

Taylor, or any philosopher who wants "the future to 'redeem' the past,"[48] cannot allow the possibility of an event in this sense. The truly unpredictable, or irreversible, is always, in Edmund Burke's sense of the word, sublime; it creates a revolutionary discontinuity in what should be the "unchangeable constancy" of organic auto-reproduction.[49] Any such "event," in Burke's world, amounts to a revolution because it defies the organic totality which claims all events as representative elements of a predetermined plot; Shelley's Witch is, in this sense, a "revolutionary," although an entirely non-oedipal one; she converts the army of "king Amasis" to pacifism, and liberates his political prisoners (stanza 75) but establishes no alternative power-structure in his place.

This is not to imply that Shelley naively imagined that a genuine political revolution would not necessarily impose some institutional power-structure of its own—a power-structure which could in turn become oppressive. No reader of *The Revolt of Islam* or the *Philosophical View of Reform* could believe that. The Witch represents not "revolution," but "poetry" as part of the enabling conditions of revolution. One of the more curious conventional misreadings of Shelley is that which holds him to be a wild-eyed visionary painting portraits of ideal societies, but short on practical proposals for how to bring them into being. In fact, Shelley very rarely gives any positive detail of what he imagines to be the good future society, unlike Godwin who elaborates visions of the anarchic society ordered by the strict *a priori* laws of reason. Typical of Shelley's attitude are the much-discussed "negative forms" in his *Prometheus Unbound*. Consider the description by the Spirit of the Hour of the new "paradise gained" of the post-revolutionary society (III.iv.190–97) that closes the third act, and was originally the end of the drama. Structurally, if this poem were an example of utopian "Poetry of Idealism," this would be the place for a rousing evocation of the Ideal City. It is interesting, in contrast, to compare how much is positively asserted as achieved and how much negatively described as overcome: "Man" is now "Sceptreless . . . uncircumscribed . . . un-classed, tribeless, and nationless, / Exempt from awe, worship, degree. . . ." Shelley's vision of change, even at the moment of triumph, remains profoundly negative, and radically empirical. As I have suggested, Shelley's problem was how to understand our ability to change *at all* in an intellectual climate which read change as either impossible or disastrous. For Shelley the question of what form future societies would take was self-evidently foolish; the unforeseen and unconceived future would necessarily contain rewards and problems unimaginable in our present situation.[50] The issue is how to rid ourselves of a system or part of a system which actively oppresses us: "It remains to know, / . . . and those who try may find / How strong the chains are which our spirit bind; / Brittle perchance as straw . . ." (*Julian and Maddalo*, lines 179–82).

The Witch represents poetry which although a product of a given socio-political system is yet not fully "of" that system. She represents poetry as an evolutionary, conceptual *clinamen* which enables us to become conscious of the chains which bind our spirits. Her "revolution" is an *enchaînement*, an "and" added to a conservative socio-political order that was premised upon the abolition, or the permanent suspension, of the possibility of adding an "and" to the "unchanging" and "eternal" order. Her contingent "and" announces both the (partial) erasure, or supersession, of that old order and the inevitability of change and evolutionary innovation. What directly "political" response we make to this new understanding of our world is not a question which this poem addresses.

The insecurity of the Witch's identity, the chaotic creativity with which her career develops, and the necessity for the reader to adopt a radically empirical approach to her wholly irreversible history all find their counterparts in the *Defence*'s concept of a poetry which removes "veil after veil" but of which the "inmost naked beauty of the meaning" is never revealed. The Witch, of course, is also veiled: "Light the vest of flowing metre / She wears" (lines 37–38). Her vest/veil is "light," but not lightly to be removed: "If you unveil my Witch, no Priest or Primate / Can shrive you of that sin, if sin there be / In love, when it becomes idolatry" (lines 46–48). Keach uses the first of these two quotations as further evidence of Shelley's belief in the unfortunate necessity of "clothing or veiling . . . thought in language."[51] The second is less helpful for this argument, however, because Shelley here not only confirms our understanding that the removal of "veil after veil" is never an unveiling *per se*, but also reasserts in only half-playful terms what he had already implied in his sonnet "Lift not the Painted Veil": that the attempt to find the "inmost naked truth," which we assume or hope lies behind the painted veil, is not only delusive, but a "sin."

The nature of that "sin" is made clear to us by the contrast Shelley draws between the Witch's light robe and Peter Bell's "looped and windowed raggedness" (line 40). To strip Peter of his poetic "veil" is all too easy; the arras of poetic *substantia* in Wordsworth's didactic fable is woven for the sole purpose of disclosing the "universal," Christian *ens* that lurks behind it. In Shelley's opinion, this is not poetry, the anti-essential essence of which is to "tell no story, false or true" (line 4), but "leap and play . . . / Till its claws come" (lines 6–7). In the words of the *Defence*: "A Poet . . . would do ill to embody his own conceptions of right and wrong, which are usually those of his place and time, in his poetical creations, which participate in neither" (p. 488). The attempt to so embody his "own conceptions of right or wrong" leads Wordsworth, in Shelley's view, to shut his poetry off from its true sources of "unforeseen and unconceived delight": the infinitely complex and endlessly changeable "vest of *flowing* metre" that is poetry's *substantia*-without-*ens*. In place of this, so to speak, profound superficiality, Wordsworth has opted for a superficial profundity: the Romantic idealist desire to move above the flux of process to an Absolute that in Shelley's view is merely infinite redundancy. This is "Hell's hyperequatorial climate" (line 42), the same inhabited by the "dead and damned" Peter Bell the Third. In both cases, the emptiness of their pretensions to transcendence, of their claims to see "beyond the bottom . . . / Of truth's clear well" (*Peter Bell the Third*, lines 539–40), are the death of true poetic creativity; Peter is "hardly fit to fling a rhyme at" ("Witch," line 43) because Wordsworth has attempted to sacrifice the fractal multiplicity and complexity of his text, and the joyful processual flux of the world, to the hollow ideal of an eternally self-same noumenal *ens*.

Shelley's strictures against didacticism have drawn much ironical comment, ever since Claire Clairmont's astute comment about "Shelley's three aversions, God Almighty, Lord Chancellor and didactic Poetry."[52] Shelley's claim that a poet's "creations" have no part in the poet's "place and time" could be quoted to illustrate Shelley's commitment to an ideal of "transcendental" poetic values, indicating that his denunciations of poetic didacticism stem from a commitment to "eternal truths." This would undermine my reading of Shelley's condemnation of Wordsworth's "sin": perhaps Wordsworth's didacticism is wrong because it is too much concerned with the ephemeral, and too little with the eternal and unchanging?

This brings us to that other aspect of the Witch which makes her such a useful figure for thinking the relationship between poetry's ephemerality and its eternal "truths." The Witch appears to draw a sharp distinction between herself and the entropic world she inhabits. When the "Ocean-Nymphs and Hamadryades, / Oreads and Naiads" (lines 217–18) sue to "live forever in the light / Of her sweet presence" (lines 223–24) she replies "This may not be" because she cannot tolerate their ephemerality:

"The fountains where the Naiades bedew
Their shining hair at length are drained and dried;
 The solid oaks forget their strength, and strew
Their latest leaf upon the mountains wide;
 The boundless Ocean like a drop of dew
Will be consumed—the stubborn centre must
Be scattered like a cloud of summer dust—

XXIV
"And ye with them will perish one by one—
 if I must sigh to think that this shall be—
if I must weep when the surviving Sun
 Shall smile on your decay—Oh, ask not me
To love you till your little race is run;
 I cannot die as ye must . . . over me
Your leaves shall glance—the streams in which ye dwell
Shall be my paths henceforth, and so, farewell!"

(lines 226–40)

This is the portrait of a world caught in that "storm / Which with the shattered present chokes the past" (*Epipsychidion*, lines 211–12) familiar to us from so many of Shelley's poems. The obvious question is what we are to make of the Witch's relationship to that atomistic, entropic flux? Why is she apparently not a part of it, and if she in some way represents the revolutionary force of poetry, what does that mean for poetry's own relationship to the "storm of time"?

One answer would be to argue that the Witch has attained Baron Holbach's version of the "view from the citadel" of a world whose flux of mutability can be re-interpreted as a coherent narrative with a providential "plot." As such she would represent a sort of constant derivative of the world's geometric rate of change; this is what Jerrold Hogle has in mind when he makes her embody his "transferential One"—the only possible *ens* of his diasparactive world, the principle of the interchangeability of all signs become an endless, universal I AM, or "Great Memory."[53] In support of such a reading one could cite the Witch's apparent access to a world

                              beyond the rage
Of death or life, while they were still arraying
In liveries ever new, the rapid, blind
And fleeting generations of mankind.

(lines 613–16)

This is where she hides "those she saw most beautiful" (line 593) when she steals them from the grave to restore them to a strange kind of suspended

384

animation. Reading the Witch as an allegory of Poetry, we could then argue that indeed, poetry is the eternal Absolute that arises from a world of error when it is stripped of its delusive veils, vests, and "liveries ever new."

Jean Hall has recently revived Harold Bloom's argument, though in a "decentering" vein, that the Witch represents a purely autarchic and autonomous alterity which challenges our capacity for imaginative transcendence of our everyday world of mutability and error. Hall cites the passage we are examining here to prove that there is no point of contact between the Witch and the mutable world inhabited by the Naiades, which is, of course, our world.[54] She equates this passage with two others in the poem: one, quoted above, which follows the Witch's speech to the Naiades— "All day the wizard lady sate aloof . . . broidering the pictured poesy . . . upon her growing woof" (lines 249–53)—and one preceding that speech in which the Witch, realizing that her beauty has noxious effects upon those who gaze upon it, weaves "a subtle veil . . . / A shadow for the splendour of her love" (lines 151–52). Hall argues that this implies a dualism which we would express in our terms as one between the Witch as transcendent, absolute *ens*, and our world of mutable *substantia*. For the transcendent to be perceived in our fallen world, it must undergo a process of *kenosis*, and wrap itself in mortal form; in this case the Witch's veil.

But such a reading—apart from "sinning" against Shelley's injunction not to seek to unveil his Witch—struggles to account for the Witch's actual behavior in the poem. Despite renouncing contact with the Nymphs, her period of sitting "aloof" (line 249) seems indeed to last but a "day" (line 249). The corpses she reanimates might lie "age after age / Mute, breathing, beating, warm and undecaying / Like one asleep . . ." (lines 609–11), but she herself lives emphatically in the present; not rising above the world, but moving on with it; not only caught up in the turbulent flow of the world's transient events, but actively adding to that turbulence. She cannot bear to love the rapid, blind, and fleeting generations of mankind, but she can bear to tease, subvert, and revolutionize them.

If we return to the Witch's speech to the Naiads, however, we see that what the Witch is really claiming there is not the power to become a transcendental representative of all these myriad acts of mutability; rather, she claims the power of forgetting:

> If I must sigh to think that this shall be—
> If I must weep when the surviving Sun
>   Shall smile on your decay—Oh, ask not me
> To love you till your little race is run;
>   I cannot die as ye must. . . .

"*If*" the Witch must remain attached to the past, *if* she must "sigh" and "weep" for each entropic loss, *then* she refuses to love the passing forms of the world. The figure that hovers behind this speech, and particularly in the line "I *cannot* die as ye must," is the Sybil, whose enchainment to memory and the past makes a mockery of her immortality. The Sybil "wants to die" because her world has been reduced to the redundant world of absolute and unalterable memory: no information is lost, and therefore no evolution—no life, no growth, no creation—can take place. The Witch, however, chooses to sacrifice the claims of memory in order to perpetuate the possibility of love; she "tast[es] all blossoms" but is "confined to none." She maintains her fierce enjoyment of the world's catastrophic career by claiming the Olympian right of a near total indifference to its fate, past and future; little does any "sight disturb her soul." This is not to say that she is, like the Sybil, indifferent to the world *per se*—far from it; rather, her radically empirical approach to the world simply breaks the chains that would tie her, futilely, to loss. She overcomes her eternity by becoming eternally contemporary. Only those rare few "most beautiful" can penetrate her unconcern, and the dubious immortality she bestows upon them says more of the limitations of her devotion to what is past—and the limitations of the efficacity of that devotion—than of its intensity.[55]

This amnesiac capacity makes it impossible for her to subsume the chaotic flux of events into an Absolute "view from the citadel." That flux is her element; nothing in her transcends its entropic powers of erasure. To call the Witch immortal suggests that there is some irreducible *ens* which persists through all her transformations, and lies beneath all her infinite veils. We have seen that the Witch is not a "character," however, but a prosopopoeia of the principle of the inescapability of change. Her "immortality," her so-called inability to die, is actually an openness to "death" (in the form of the *clinamen*, or *enchaînement*) so constant and complete that no moment can be singled out as "her death." She escapes from death as it is understood in the hermeneutic tradition: a moment of narrative closure that withdraws the veil to reveal the secret unity of all that preceded it.

It is true, as Hall points out, that we do see the Witch "weaving" her own "veil" to shelter mere mortals from the glory of her beauty, and that this is a venerable metaphor of the necessarily oblique manifestations of the divine in our profane world. In such an avowedly playful poem, however, the very venerability of the image should alert us to the fact that Shelley may not be using it straightforwardly. The game Shelley is playing is made clear by bringing together the two quotations Hall uses to support her reading of the speech to the Naiades. The Witch weaves a "subtle veil" out of "three threads of fleecy mist, and three / Long lines of light" and "As many star-beams " (lines 146–47, 149) and cloaks herself in it; but when, at line 249 she "sits aloof" to weave her "pictured poetry" (line 252), we learn that she does so upon a "growing woof" (line 253) that can only be a continuation of the "subtle veil" already commenced. The Witch, then, has "veiled" herself in poetry. But the Witch, if she can be said to "be" anything (we might recall Milton Wilson's comment that Shelley's poems "may mean [but], I doubt if they can be said to be"[56]) is "poetry." She has veiled herself in herself. To remove the Witch's veil is always to find another, and yet another; it is an endless play of unforeseen and unconceived delights which yields us no constant derivative which can be presented as the changeless essence of the process. What could be less an "*ens*" than the entropic, fugitive substances from which she weaves her veil?[57] As for the "divine" beauty of the unveiled (or "pre-veiled") Witch, a second reading of Shelley's language in describing the state of those who gaze upon it reveals that they are not a lucky few to have gained access to the unchanging One which underlies the Many— a "One" which, to Shelley, means only sterility and death. Rather, like Rousseau with his brain become as sand before the "Shape all light" in the "Triumph of Life," *they* are the deluded ones, natives of Peter Bell's "hyperequatorial climate" "betrayed" by the hunt for a chimerical *ens* into an incapacity to see the beauty in our "bright world" and its "fleeting images," in the "world so wide" and its "circling skies":

> For she was beautiful—her beauty made
> The bright world dim, and every thing beside
> Seemed like the fleeting image of a shade:
> No thought of living spirit could abide—
> Which to her looks had ever been betrayed,
> On any object in the world so wide,
> On any hope within the circling skies,
> But on her form, and in her inmost eyes.
>
> (lines 137–44)

This is the only "immortality" possible in a world that operates on the entropic principles that Shelley sets out in the very first stanza of the poem proper, when he refers to "those cruel Twins, whom at one birth / Incestuous Change bore to her father Time, Error and Truth" (lines 49–51). This playful mythic cosmogony sums up with remarkable precision the Lucretian principle of chaotic creativity. It is a mythologized sketch of a "chaotic attractor" which establishes the inevitability of error, or the unavoidability of the *clinamen*, which is both the condition and the result of the Witch's madly fanciful career. *Change* is the daughter of Time: this is a comment on the inevitability of change—the inevitability of decay, which is also growth— but it is more, it is an acknowledgment of the constant, and general, assertion of continuity within time, and its necessary defeat. Change is the *daughter* of time: the flux of time is a reproductive flux, a reiterative one. It is just that it is never quite successful in its attempt at reproductive continuity; Time produces Change, and Change in turn produces the "Twins" Error and Truth. No Truth without Error (there can be no reproduction without innovation) but no Error without Truth—how could we find delight in what is "unforeseen and unconceived" if nothing could be foreseen, and nothing came to fruition from a prior conception? Shelley makes it clear that he is not asserting the absolute transferential equivalence of all signifiers. For there to be information there must be both order and disorder, Error *and* Truth. This is a world, in short, that demands a stance of radical empiricism, a world in which the past cannot be preserved for long before it is obliterated by accumulated errors, a world in which consciousness must live, like the Witch, in the eye of that storm "which with the shattered present chokes the past," a world in which one must delight in ruins, and learn to accept the limitations of memory.

What, then, does this mean for poetry—above all for a *soi-disant* "political" poetry? If the Witch represents poetry, are we to assume that Shelley thought that poetry should be indifferent to the world—that it should find little in it to "disturb its soul?" Such a finding seems counter to Shelley's own poetic practice and political aspirations, and counter to our hopes of what poetry can be for us.

That it does seem so is a measure of how "natural" it has become for us to understand a text's political force in the terms of a hermeneutic, expressivist historicism that seeks to bind the text to a "form of life." Like Mary Shelley, we distrust a poem like "The Witch of Atlas" that "leap[s] and play[s]," "tasting all blossoms and confined to none." We seek an authenticity of utterance within a specific socio-political context which makes the text seem truly "committed" to the political juncture of its context of production. We seek the genuine "speech act" which momentarily instantiates, and crystallizes, all the rules and conditions of its appearance. We seek the part that incarnates the whole. What "The Witch of Atlas" shows us, however, is that when Shelley argues, in the *Defence*, that poetry "participates in the eternal, the infinite, and the one" (p. 483), or that "A Poet ... would do ill to embody his own conceptions of right and wrong, which are usually those of his place and time, in his poetical creations, which participate in neither" (p. 488), he is arguing for a radically different conception of the political role of poetry, not that poetry should be politically irrelevant. The "Witch of Atlas" shows us that poetry's "eternity" and "infinity" need not imply its abstraction from, or synthesis of, the flux of events. Poetry is "eternal" in the same way the Witch is: it is eternally contemporary. Like the Witch, poetry must choose between the ability to continue loving the world—to continue its urgency for the world, its political relevance— and memory, its dedication to the conditions that originally called it forth. A poem that could only speak "authentically" within the "peculiar relations" of its context of production—that could, in other words, be only one "happy" speech act—would be a poetic Sybil without the gift of prophecy, a withered relic only "alive" enough to make us conscious of its affinity with the dead.

The only partial exception to this rule is poetry's ability to preserve in memory the deeds and thoughts of "the Wise, / The great, the unforgotten" ("Triumph of Life," lines 208–9), those heroes and heroines whose names recur as touchstones in Shelley's prose and poetry. It is this function of poetry that Shelley has in mind in the Witch's peculiar suspended animation of "those she saw most beautiful." The limitations of the Witch's powers indicate the limitations of poetry's purely mnemonic capacity; a very few names from the past can be "kept alive" by poetry (which, in Shelley's sense of the word, includes history), but only poetry itself continues to live. Homer is nothing but a name to us, Hector and Achilleus live and evolve. We must not be fooled by the poet's ability to use real people as the starting point for the creation of poetic characters. Shakespeare's Richard III, Tolstoy's Napoleon, Plato's Socrates; these may help "keep alive" the name of the historical characters whose names they share, but their vitality, their richness, their challenge are all their own. The historical Socrates is a subject of academic debate; Plato's creation is a living, and therefore changeable, presence.

To say that poetry "participates in neither" the place nor the time of the poet is not to say that it transcends place or time; indeed, "the alloy of costume, habit, etc. . . . [is] necessary to temper [poetry's] planetary music for mortal ears" (p. 487); "a poet considers the vices of his contemporaries as the temporary dress in which his creations must be arrayed . . ." (p. 487). This "temporary dress" is not one eventually to be shucked off to reveal the unchanging *ens* that lies behind: "after one person and one age has exhausted all of its divine effluence which their peculiar relations enable them to share, another and yet another [veil / dress] succeeds, and new relations are ever developed, the source of an unforeseen and an unconceived delight." If poetry is veiled, it is, like the Witch, veiled in itself; the work of the critic is not to "strip" the poem, to move from veil to revelation, *substantia* to *ens*, but to join in on the poem's own terms in its endlessly provocative, endlessly enticing, endlessly delightful dance of veils. The poem, like the Witch "tasting all blossoms, and confined to none," belongs to all contexts and to none; but it can only exist *for* us within the veils of "place and time"— within our "peculiar relations," our particular consumptive context.

It is this insistence upon the Witch's continuing presence in and response to the world which marks the distance between Shelley's position and that which the "decentering" critics impute to him. The power of poetry to enable us to re-invent and "create anew" depends upon its attachment to and presence within the world. The "chaotic creativity" of evolutionary process demands the incorporation of poetry within the reproductive cycles of social action. Poetry must be read in a given context, and carries with it some mnemonic associations with its context of production. Poetry is not a "wormhole" within the socio-political fabric or "Great Memory," it does not allow us to jump arbitrarily from one political situation to another quite unrelated one. But within each context of consumption poetry acts as an evolutionary *clinamen*, opening up a quantic moment of indeterminacy which makes it possible to *enchaîne* a previously unimaginable—though retrospectively and empirically explicable—future.

On the other hand, poetry's continuing relevance and power across time are dependent on its ability to "exceed the whole," to exceed its context of production and any future context of consumption and continue in its eternal renewal of chaotic creativity—"unforeseen and unconceived delight." Poetic "immortality," then, is premised on the very revolutionary sublimity to which it seemed to be in paradoxical opposition. Poetry is "immortal" because it is always dying, just as its negentropic effects on its readers result from its constant entropy, and just as its amnesiac powers are dependent upon its mnemonic function.

Shelley's strictures against "didactic poetry" are an attempt to make us recognize the greatest political power of the poem. The poem that participates in neither its time nor its place is the promiscuous text that by virtue of that negativity can revolutionize all contexts in which it is consumed; it is poetry that eternally applies Pound's dictum, "make it new," both to itself and to its context of consumption; it is the part that always exceeds the whole. This is the kind of poetry of which he writes in the *Defence*: "it is a strain which distends, and then bursts the circumference of the hearer's mind, and pours itself forth together with it into the universal element with which it has perpetual sympathy" (p. 485). This is poetry that has the capacity to break us free from the narrow circles of thought "blunted by reiteration" (*Defence*, p. 506) that define, at any given moment, the poet's context of production and the readers' context(s) of consumption and give us a "perpetual[ly renewed] sympathy" with a universe in becoming.

Notes

1 Jean Hall, "The Divine and the Dispassionate Selves: Shelley's *Defence* and Peacock's *The Four Ages of Poetry*," *Keats-Shelley Journal*, 41 (1992), 139–63.

2 Jerrold E. Hogle, *Shelley's Process. Radical Transference and the Development of his Major Works* (New York: Oxford University Press, 1988), p. vii. Jean Hall, "Shelley's *Defence*," p. 152. Hall gives a useful thumbnail sketch of the history of "nontranscendental" readings of the *Defence* (p. 152n15). See also Hall, *The Transforming Image: A Study of Shelley's Major Poetry* (Urbana: University of Illinois Press, 1980).

3 Unless otherwise noted, quotations from Shelley's works are taken from *Shelley's Poetry and Prose*, ed. Donald H. Reiman and Sharon B. Powers (New York: Norton, 1977).

4 William Keach, *Shelley's Style* (New York: Methuen, 1984), pp. 22–33.

5 Hall, "Shelley's *Defence*," p. 163.

6 "The 'One' in the Later Works: 'Thought's Eternal Flight,'" chapter six of Jerrold E. Hogle's *Shelley's Process*, pp. 263–342; see pp. 176ff. for Hogle's use of Yeats's "Great Memory" and the term "mythograph."

7 Hogle, *Shelley's Process*, p. 189.

8 Samuel Taylor Coleridge, *The Statesman's Manual*, in *Lay Sermons*, ed. R. J. White (London: Routledge and Kegan Paul, 1972), p. 30.

9 Hogle, *Shelley's Process*, p. 197.

10 Hall, *The Transforming Image*, pp. 104, 165.

11 "Suddenly broken the tie of memory" (my trans.): Alexis de Tocqueville, "Ètat Social et Politique de la France Avant et Après 1798," in *L'Ancien Régime et la Révolution* (Paris: Flammarion, 1988), p. 44.

12 G. W. F. Hegel, *The Phenomenology of Spirit*, trans. A. V. Miller (Oxford: Clarendon Press, 1977), p. 357.

13 Edmund Burke, *Reflections on the Revolution in France and on the Proceedings in Certain Societies in London Relative to that Event* (Harmondsworth, U.K.: Penguin, 1969), p. 194.

14 Shelley, "Preface" to *The Revolt of Islam*, in *Shelley: Poetical Works*, ed. Thomas Hutchinson, corr. G. M. Matthews (Oxford: Oxford University Press, 1970), p. 33.

15 I am using the term in Charles Taylor's sense. See *Sources of the Self: The Making of the Modern Identity* (Cambridge: Harvard University Press, 1989), and *Hegel and Modern Society* (Cambridge: Cambridge University Press, 1979).

16 The best short general outline of chaos science I know of, though it is now a little dated, is James P. Crutchfield *et al.*, "Chaos," *Scientific American*, 225. 6 (December 1986), 46–57; James Gleick's *Chaos: Making a New Science* (New York: Penguin, 1987) offers an excellent book-length survey for the non-scientist; John Briggs' and F. David Peat's *Turbulent Mirror: An Illustrated Guide to Chaos Theory and the Science of Wholeness* (New York: Harper and Row, 1989) is a useful general introduction. Ilya Prigogine's and Isabelle Stengers' *La Nouvelle Alliance: Métamorphose de la Science* (Paris: Gallimard, 1979, 1986) is a work I have drawn on heavily for my own understanding of the wider philosophical implications of chaos theory; Michel Serres's *La Naissance de la Physique dans le Texte de Lucrèce* (Paris: Les Editions de Minuit, 1977) gives the best account of the Lucretian roots of chaos theory. N. Katherine Hayles, *Chaos Bound: Orderly Disorder in Contemporary Literature and Science* (Ithaca: Cornell University Press, 1990), and Alexander J. Argyros, *A Blessed Rage for Order: Deconstruction, Evolution, and Chaos* (Ann Arbor: University of Michigan Press, 1991), have produced the only book-length works, so far, applying chaos theory to literary studies. Hayles has also edited a useful and suggestive collection of articles on chaos and literature: *Chaos and Order: Complex Dynamics in Literature and Science* (Ithaca: Cornell University Press, 1991).

17 See Argyros, *A Blessed Rage for Order*, and Stephen J. Gould, *Wonderful Life: The Burgess Shale and the Nature of History* (New York: Norton, 1989), for two contrasting accounts of the relationship between chaos and evolutionary theory.

18 "For never was any such event, stemming from factors so far back in the past, so inevitable yet so completely unforeseen" (Tocqueville, *L'ancien régime*, p. 97; trans. Stuart Gilbert, *The Ancien Régime and the French Revolution* [Fontana, 1966], p. 33).

19 Stephen Jay Gould, *Wonderful Life*, p. 51.

20 See Kenneth Neill Cameron, "The Social Philosophy of Shelley," *The Sewanee Review*, 50.4 (October–December 1942), 457–66, and *Shelley: The Golden Years* (Cambridge: Harvard University Press, 1974), pp. 131ff.

21 See Harold Bloom, *The Anxiety of Influence* (London: Oxford University Press, 1973).

22 Lucretius, *On the Nature of the Universe*, trans. R. E. Latham (Harmondsworth U.K.: Penguin, 1951), p. 60.

23 Gould, *Wonderful Life*, pp. 284–304.

24 M. Mitchell Waldrop, *Complexity: The Emerging Science at the Edge of Order and Chaos* (New York: Simon and Schuster, 1992), p. 147.

25 Gleick, *Chaos*, p. 260.

26 "No single language . . . can exhaust the reality of a system; the different possible languages, the different points of view about the system, are *complementary*. . . . This irreducible character of the multiple possible points of view on a single reality represents precisely the impossibility of discovering an overview, a point of view from which the totality of the real would be simultaneously visible. . . . Reality . . . is too rich, . . . its contours are too complex for a single light source to be able to illuminate it in its totality" (Prigogine and Stengers, *La Nouvelle Alliance*, p. 313; my translation).

27 Keach, *Shelley's Style*, p. 28.

28 Schiller, *Naive and Sentimental Poetry and On the Sublime: Two Essays*, trans. Julius A. Elias (New York: Frederick Ungar, 1966), pp. 112–13.

29 Keach, *Shelley's Style*, pp. 26, 29, 32.

30 Sigmund Freud, "Analysis Terminable and Interminable," in *The Standard Edition of the Complete Psychological Works of Sigmund Freud, Vol. XXXIII*, ed. James Strachey (London: Hogarth Press, 1964), pp. 249–50.

31 Quoted in Jacques Derrida, "My Chances/*Mes Chances*," in *Taking Chances: Derrida, Psychoanalysis, and Literature*, ed. Joseph H. Smith and William Kerrigan (Baltimore: Johns Hopkins University Press, 1984), p. 22.

32 Freud's story that divides him from the superstitious person, for example, involves a coachman who delivers him to a wrong, but significant, address. Freud concludes that this significance is only apparent, however, because the coachman could not have known the circumstances that made it seem portentous to Freud. Freud overlooks the possibility, however, that he might have absentmindedly (Freudian slip) given the wrong address to the coachman—an unverifiable possibility which instantly returns these "chance" events to the domain of psychological significance.

33 Derrida, "My Chances," p. 10.

34 See for example Serres, *La Naissance*, pp. 11, 13ff., 95, 97.

35 Lucretius, *Nature*, IV, p. 131.

36 "The flying tunics are fluctuating borders, the surface as it approaches its limit. *Summo de corpore*. The *simulacra* detach themselves from things as in an infinitesimal calculation. As many can be removed as one wishes. Each object becomes a source of an infinite number of envelopes. Sight is as rigorous as the mathematical method, Now, as all objects are produced from and within a vortex, or in a spiral, it is turbulence itself which becomes the emitter of its own envelopes" (my translation): Serres, *La Naissance*, p. 129.

37 "*The ideal forms of geometry are not transparent, invariant, and empty, they are dense and compact*, full almost to saturation, of a complex tissue, *and their borders are covered with invisible veils which allow them to be seen*, with infinitesimal limits which nonetheless are there" (my translation): Serres, *La Naissance*, p. 130.

38 Thomas McFarland, *Romanticism and the Forms of Ruin* (Princeton: Princeton University Press, 1981), p. 28.

39 J. L. Austin, *How To Do Things With Words* (Cambridge: Harvard University Press, 1962, 1975), pp. 14ff., 133ff.

40 "It is necessary to link up, but there is never a necessary way to link up" (my translation): J.-F. Lyotard, *Le Différend* (Paris: Les Editions de Minuit, 1983), p. 52.

41 "Politics results from the fact that language is not 'a language' but is made up of sentences" (my translation): Lyotard, *Le Différend*, p. 200.

42 "Everything is politics if politics is the possibility of a *différend* on the occasion of even the most minor *enchaînement*" (my translation): Lyotard, *Le Différend*, p. 201.

43 The best statement of this idea is Orsino's speech in *The Cenci*: "self-anatomy shall teach the will / Dangerous secrets. . . . / Since Beatrice unveiled me to myself . . . / [I] Show a poor figure to my own esteem, / To which I grow half reconciled" (II.ii.110–18). I draw the opposition of poetic *ens* to poetic *substantia* from McFarland, *Romanticism and the Forms of Ruin*. The poem's *ens* corresponds to the Hegelian *Begriff*, or Notion. It is its total ideal which the fragmentary ("diasparactive") *substantia*—the poem as real, imperfect, object—attempts to realize.

44 See also "The Sensitive Plant" (1.102–5) and "The Triumph of Life" (lines 405–10).

45 Mary Shelley, "Note on the Witch of Atlas," in *Shelley, Poetical Works*, pp. 388–89.

46 Taylor, *Sources of the Self*, p. 51.

47 Derrida, "My Chances," p. 6.

48 Taylor, *Sources of the Self*, pp. 50–51.

49 See Burke, *Reflections*, p. 120.

50 A good example can be found in the "Even Love is Sold" note to *Queen Mab*, where, after tentatively beginning to debate what new system may develop after the abolition of marriage, Shelley stops and writes: "But this is a subject which it is perhaps premature to discuss. That which will result from the abolition of marriage will be natural and right; because choice and change will be exempted from restraint.

In fact, religion and morality, as they now stand, compose a practical code of misery and servitude . . ." (*Shelley: Poetical Works*, p. 808).

51 Keach, *Shelley's Style*, p. 182.

52 Claire Clairmont's journal, 8 November 1820; quoted in Newman Ivey White, *Shelley*, 2 vols. (London: Secker and Warburg, 1947), II, 602n63.

53 Hogle, *Shelley's Process*, pp. 217ff.

54 See Jean Hall, "Poetic Autonomy in *Peter Bell the Third* and *The Witch of Atlas*," in *The New Shelley*, ed. G. Kim Blank (New York: St. Martin's Press, 1991), 204–19, 259n1, 209.

55 Both Hall ("Poetic Autonomy," 209 ff., 215) and Richard Cronin (*Shelley's Poetic Thoughts* [New York: St. Martin's Press, 1981], p. 67) state the opposite case powerfully. Hall sees the Witch as "autonomous because she is perfect and immortal" (209), and therefore inhuman, while Cronin argues that her "power is contingent on her remaining abstracted from any personal relationship with transient beings" (p. 67). If they are right, the Witch would then become a self-sufficient autarchic philosopher, either Platonist, Stoic, or Epicurean. That argument could only be made on the grounds that the portrait is deliberately ironic, and designed to show us that such a position is untenable. Otherwise it is difficult to account for the fact that the Witch is so constantly engaged with the petty details of the lives of "transient beings." The Witch, as she is shown in the poem, is not remotely "autonomous" or autarchic; rather, she is constantly assuaging desires that are as continually renewed ("tasting all blossoms yet confined to none").

56 Milton Wilson, *Shelley's Later Poetry: A Study of His Prophetic Imagination* (New York: Columbia University Press, 1959), p. 39.

57 This passage has leant itself to a wide range of interpretations. Richard Cronin rightly mocks the more abstruse allegorizations of this passage as misdirected and over-serious, but he errs on the other side in reading it as nothing more than

a collection of "tongue-twisters" and deliberately ridiculous images (*Shelley's Poetic Thoughts*, p. 65). Their fragility and improbability is precisely what makes the Witch's ability to "weave" them into the veil/poetry miraculous. The obvious comparison is to *Prometheus Unbound*, I: "But from these create he can / Forms more real than living man, / Nurslings of immortality!" (lines 737–51). The "over-serious" readings of these lines prove Shelley's point; the most insubstantial materials can be woven by the poet into "nurslings of immortality."

34

LIVING WITH THE WEATHER

Jonathan Bate

Source: *Studies in Romanticism* 35 (1996), 431–47.

I had a dream, which was not all a dream.
The bright sun was extinguish'd, and the stars
Did wander darkling in the eternal space,
Rayless, and pathless, and the icy earth
Swung blind and blackening in the moonless air;
Morn came, and went—and came, and brought no day,
And men forgot their passions in the dread
Of this their desolation; and all hearts
Were chill'd into a selfish prayer for light;
And they did live by watchfires—and the thrones,
The palaces of crowned kings—the huts,
The habitations of all things which dwell,
Were burnt for beacons; cities were consumed,
And men were gathered round their blazing homes
To look once more into each other's face;
Happy were those who dwelt within the eye
Of the volcanos, and their mountain-torch:
A fearful hope was all the world contain'd;
Forests were set on fire—but hour by hour
They fell and faded—and the crackling trunks
Extinguish'd with a crash—and all was black.[1]

I first encountered Byron's poem "Darkness," of which these are the opening lines, in the early 1980s, when I heard it quoted by the then leader of the Labour Party, Michael Foot. The party was avowedly in favor of unilateral nuclear disarmament; membership of the Campaign for Nuclear Disarmament was at its highest ever; the women's peace camp at Greenham Common, Fortress UK's principal base for American Cruise missiles, was yoking gender politics and defense policy as never before; E. P. Thompson had just written *Protest and Survive*; and scientists were telling us about something called "nuclear winter"—the dust blasted into the stratosphere by the

SCIENCE, MEDICINE, AND ECO-CRITICISM

explosion of the ICBMs would blot out the sun for three years, destroying all but the most resilient forms of organic life upon the planet. Michael Foot quoted from the close of the poem, hailing Byron as a prophet who foreknew that war would ultimately lead to global winter:

> The world was void,
> The populous and the powerful—was a lump,
> Seasonless, herbless, treeless, manless, lifeless—
> A lump of death—a chaos of hard clay.
> The rivers, lakes, and ocean all stood still,
> And nothing stirred within their silent depths.

The romantic in me was uplifted by Foot's futuristic reading. The critic in me was more skeptical: the poem could not *really* be about nuclear winter, so what *was* it about?

In 1986, there arose with the publication of volume four of the Oxford edition of Byron's *Complete Poetical Works* the possibility of "Darkness" being elucidated. That edition's headnote to the poem consists principally of a catalogue of possible literary sources: *The Last Man*, which was an anonymous translation (published in 1806) of a French novel by Cousin de Grainville; "various apocalyptic passages in the bible"; Burnet's *Sacred Theory of the Earth*; "various commonplaces of Enlightenment science," to be found in Buffon and Fontenelle; the conclusion to the *De rerum natura* of Lucretius; and "M. G. (Monk) Lewis, who came to Diodati on 14 August 1816 and who helped to shift the conversations with the Shelleys, Polidori, and B[yron] on to grim subjects."[2] This is a rich list, but does it not evade the poem every bit as much as Foot did? The politician's rhetorical appropriation propels the poem into its future; the scholar's elucidation of sources fossilizes it in its past. Its present, its significance in 1816, is in neither case addressed. Neither the politician nor the scholar has an answer to the obvious questions: what led Byron to write a poem about the extinction of sunlight in the summer of 1816 and what would have come to the minds of his readers when the poem was published with *The Prisoner of Chillon* later that year?

The Oxford edition pins the poem's date of composition down to the five weeks between 21 July and 25 August 1816. I propose that the key which unlocks it is an apparently flippant remark in a letter of Byron to Samuel Rogers, dated 29 July 1816: "we have had lately such stupid mists—fogs—rains—and perpetual density—that one would think Castlereagh had the foreign affairs of the kingdom of Heaven also—upon his hands."[3] The summer weather around Lake Geneva is always variable, but in 1816 Byron found it particularly irksome. A month earlier, he had complained in a letter to John Murray of the "stress of weather" (*Letters* 5.81).

This, it seems to me, is where "Darkness" begins: with the stress of weather. The poem opens, "I had a dream, which was not all a dream. / The bright sun was extinguish'd." Does it stretch credulity too far to suppose that the first clause of the second sentence follows from the second clause of the first sentence? That the extinguished sun was not all a dream? Might the origin of the poem not be the absence of sunshine in June, July and August 1816?

It rained in Switzerland on 130 out of the 183 days from April to September 1816. The average temperature that July was an astonishing 4.9 degrees Fahrenheit below the mean for that month in the years 1807–24.[4] As Byron shivered in Geneva, so did his readers back home. In London it rained on eighteen days in July 1816 and on only one day did the temperature reach 70 degrees; during the same month the previous year, the temperature was over 70 degrees on nineteen days and it only rained three times. 70 degrees was recorded on only two days in August, whereas the figure for the previous year was thirteen. At noon on 1 September 1816, the temperature in London was 47 degrees; the average noon temperature in the first half of the previous September had been 63 degrees.[5]

The pattern was the same across Europe and the United States. Consult the meteorological reports and you will find that 1816 was the worst summer ever recorded; indeed, it became popularly known as "the year without a summer." The bad weather led to failed harvests. To continue with the example of Switzerland: annual harvests for that country have been graded by economic historians on a scale of one to six, according to yield. 1816 achieved a minimal one. As a result of the poor harvests, there was a hemispheric subsistence crisis, marked by violent price fluctuation, basic food shortage and concordant public disorder.

What caused the bad weather? In the popular imagination it was frequently associated with the unusual visibility of sun spots. The darkening of the sun led to fears of apocalypse—the exact situation of Byron's poem. More precise observers noted a consistently dense haze permanently on the horizon—"It had nothing of the nature of a humid fog. It was like that smoking vapour which overspread Europe about thirty years ago," wrote Dr. Thomas D. Mitchell in the *New York Medical Repository*.[6]

"Smoking vapour" is a good intuition. Benjamin Franklin had observed similar atmospheric conditions back in 1784 and suggeste that the cause might have been volcanic vapor.[7] There is an unintentional irony in the lines in which Byron says that those who live close to volcanoes are lucky because they are accorded at least some light and warmth in the darkened world, for as it happens the eruption of Tambora volcano in Indonesia in 1815 killed some 80,000 people on the islands of Sumbawa and Lombok. It was the greatest eruption since 1500. The dust blasted into the stratosphere reduced the transparency of the atmosphere, filtered out the sun and consequently lowered surface temperatures. The effect lasted for three years, straining the growth-capacity of organic life across the planet. Beginning in 1816, crop failure led to food riots in nearly every country in Europe. Only in 1819 were there good harvests again. The index for the Swiss harvest that year shot up to a maximal six.

Editors have a tendency to explain literary works with reference to other literary works. The Oxford headnote to "Darkness," with its network of sources, treats the poem as a purely textual weave. Because a poetic composition is a cultural phenomenon, it is related to other phenomena in the culture. It is not explained in terms of nature.

But Byron does not set culture apart from nature. What is striking about both the remark in the letter to Rogers and the poem itself is Byron's easy yoking of politics and nature. The letter jokingly blames the ministry of Castlereagh for the bad weather; "perpetual density" is taken to be simultaneously a meteorological and a socio-political condition. The poem darkly narrates a history in which war temporarily ceases as humankind pulls together in the face of inclement weather but is then renewed on a global scale as a result of the famine consequent upon the absence of sunlight. The global struggle for subsistence leads ultimately to the extinction of mankind. In 1815, Byron and his public witnessed the cessation of a European war which had lasted for more than twenty years; in 1816, they endured the year without a summer. The poem is as contemporary as it is apocalyptic. It seems to me that the first referent for any reader of the poem in 1868 would be not Lucretius or de Grainville's novel *The Last Man*, but the sunless summer they had just undergone and the fear of famine brought with it.

But contemporary as it was, the poem remains powerfully prophetic: how far away the nuclear forebodings of the Cold War seem now, how near the vision of a world seasonless, herbless, treeless, the rivers, lakes and oceans silent. When Michael Foot read "Darkness" we had in our minds the Mutually Assured Destruction of the Cold War. When we read "Darkness" now, Byron may be reclaimed as a prophet of ecocide.[8] What, I want to ask here, is the legacy of romanticism in our age of eco-crisis?

The ideologically-inflected literary criticism of the 1980s taught us to take our romanticism with a large pinch of historical salt. Even the most rarefied, aesthetically "pure" romantic poems, such as the odes of John Keats, were to be read in the context of their social setting. In his influential essay, "Keats and the Historical Method in Literary Criticism," Jerome J. McGann turned his severely historicized gaze upon what had traditionally been read as the quintessence of romanticism, "To Autumn." By means of a reading of the poem's publication history, and its relations to the fine arts and the contemporary social scene, romantic idealism was transformed before our eyes into romantic ideology. Keats's poem, it was argued, served to foster the illusion that all autumns are the same; it did so in order to draw the reader away from the hard economic fact of bad autumns, poor harvests and the resulting food riots. "This is the reflexive world of Romantic art . . . wherein all events are far removed from the Terror, King Ludd, Peterloo, the Six Acts, and the recurrent financial crises of the Regency."[9]

McGann was explicit about his reason for reading "To Autumn" as he did: it was "because of the prevailing anti-historical climate of opinion epitomized in [Geoffrey] Hartman's [influential] essay [on the poem]" (54). The sentence about romantic art which I have just quoted could, then, be rewritten on the following lines: "This is the reflexive world of Yale criticism . . . wherein all poems are far removed from Vietnam, Watergate, Reaganomics, right-wing appointments to the bench of the Supreme Court, and the recurrent financial crises of successive administrations which have led to the degradation of welfare, education and health-care." Any body of literature maintains its life through a process of mutation whereby it is reconstituted by the forces of later culture. Romanticism has remained a living legacy because, like a fit Darwinian organism, it has proved singularly adaptable to a succession of new environments, whether Victorian mediaevalism, *fin de siècle* aestheticism, new critical Urn-wrighting, Hartmanesque phenomenology, or the counter-reading of 1980s ideologism.

McGann could react in the early 1980s against "the prevailing anti-historical climate of opinion" among romanticists. But in the mid-1990s would he able to use the metaphor of a *climate* of opinion so casually? I suggest that we are now in a period of Kuhnian paradigm-shift. It is a shift which could be described in various ways. Perhaps: a New Geographism is replacing the New Historicism. Or, to locate it in a wider context: Cold War Criticism is dying, Global Warming Criticism is about to be born.[10]

Let me try to prove that this paradigm-shift is occurring. I take the key paragraph in McGann's treatment of the poem to be the following:

> "To Autumn" asks us to believe—to willingly suspend our disbelief —that all autumns are the same. We must imagine them to be, universally, the "season of mists and mellow fruitfulness." But Keats asks us to believe this because he knows, as we know, that it is not true. Such an autumn of perfect harvests and luxurious agricultural abundance is an autumn in the mind. City people, industrialized communities, do not know of these autumns except in the memories of art; and in the country such abundance is rare indeed, particularly in the early nineteenth century. In fact, 1819 brought in a good harvest in England, and the year was notable for its abundance precisely because of the series of disastrous harvests which characterized many of the years immediately preceding.
>
> (57–58)

The question we then have to ask is *why* does Keats imagine autumn thus in the autumn of 1819? The paradigm inhabited by McGann forced him to find an answer in terms of a series of oppositions: the country versus the city, personal tranquility versus political unrest, old world charm versus the tide of historical change. McGann summed this up in terms of the associations of Winchester (where the poem was written) versus the associations of Peterloo (where the militia had recently ridden into a peacefully protesting crowd). The paradigm of Cold War Criticism was such that the thought-cluster "weather, harvests, abundance or scarcity of grain" was considered in relation to its *effect*. McGann asked: what was the effect of the series of disastrous harvests in the years immediately preceding 1819, and came up with the answer, food riots and social unrest. Because he was locked within the Cold War paradigm it did not occur to him to consider the thought-cluster in relation to its *cause*. To ask *what was the cause of the bad harvests in the years 1816 to 1818*? was not a meaningful question within this paradigm.

Why was it not a meaningful question? Because Cold War criticism, for all its Althusserian flourishes, was interested in human agency. McGann was excited by such agencies as the radical press (Leigh Hunt's *Examiner*, say) because they offered an appetizing model of writing as social intervention, harbinger of change. If we had asked McGann the question in the early 1980s, he would probably have said something like: "The cause of the bad harvests in the years 1816 to 1818 was the bad weather and I'm not interested in bad weather because we can't do anything about it—what interests me is the price of grain, the Corn Law, the stuff of real politics." The Cold War paradigm had no answer to the question, *what is the cause of bad weather?* In the face of this question, it was as baffled as King Lear when he cries "is there any cause in nature which makes these hard hearts?"

Why did it not have an answer? Because the Cold War paradigm was a product of the modern critical stance which sought to "establish a partition between a natural world that has always been there, a society with predictable and stable interests and stakes, and a discourse that is independent of both reference and society"; it participated in what Bruno Latour calls "the work of purification" which "create[d] two entirely distinct ontological zones: that of human beings on the one hand; that of nonhumans on the other."[11] For Latour and his master Michel Serres, eco-crisis sounds the death knell of the "modern Constitution," inaugurated by Bacon and Descartes, which effects these separations. Serres writes in *Le contrat naturel*:

> Question: Who, then, inflicts this damage on the world, the objective yet common enemy, the damage we hope is still reversible, the petroleum spilled into the sea, the millions of tons of carbon oxides evaporated into the air, acids and toxic products that rain back down on us? where does this waste come from that suffocates our children and spots our skin? Who, beyond the individual or the public? Who, beyond the huge cities: a simple number, or a simplex, of causes? [Answer]: Our tools, our armaments, our efficacy, finally, our reason, of which we prove to be legitimately vain: our mastery and our possessions.

Mastery and possession: the master concepts announced by Descartes at the birth of the scientific and technological age when our Occidental reason went in conquest of the universe. We dominate and appropriate: that is the underlying philosophy common both to industrial enterprise and to the science said to be impartial—in this sense the two are undifferentiable. Cartesian mastery redresses the objective violence of science in a well-ordered strategy. Our fundamental relationship with objects is summed up by war and property.[12]

Mastery and possession are the driving forces not only of science but also of capitalism. Karl Marx added his signature to the modern Constitution when he claimed that man was superior to the animals by virtue of his "working-over of inorganic nature."[13] So too did Cold War literary criticism, locked as it was into a model of inter-cultural conflict.

The Lisbon earthquake of 1755 gave the direst affront to post-Cartesian aspiration precisely because it was a reminder that man was not master of nature. Bad weather was a scandal to the modern Constitution. As Serres has remarked, the Enlightenment was one long attempt to repress the weather, to dispel the clouds of unknowing: "the eighteenth century can be defined quite simply, in both its epistemology and its history, as the erasure of 'meteors.' "[14] But, as the Lisbon earthquake shows, we cannot master nature, erase the meteors. The earth has its way of striking back, most drastically with earthquakes and volcanic eruptions, but more often with plain old bad weather. This is what the Global Warming paradigm knows. It is a paradigm that is no less political than the Cold War one, but its politics are global in the proper sense. The Global Warming paradigm does not confine itself to local politics, to Corn Laws and the moral economy of the rioting crowd. It asks for the cause of flooding in Bangladesh and finds the answer in the deforestation of the Himalayan foothills; it looks at starvation in Africa and discovers that imperialism has always been accompanied by ecological exploitation.[15]

The modern Constitution presupposed a Newtonian concept of order in nature. It is not a coincidence that James Thomson's poem in praise of Newton was published with *The Seasons* in 1730: Thomson celebrated the variety of the seasons, but the thrust of his argument was that the weather itself had a fundamental order, a concord in its discord; disorder resided in the morality of the observer and was accordingly a matter of human agency.[16] The constancy of nature was something against which to measure the vicissitudes of culture. Hence interpretations which regard the romantic preoccupation with nature as a symptom of reaction against revolutionary cultural change. But nature is not stable. Weather is the primary sign of its mutability. The Chaos theory of the 1990s puts disorder back into nature. It can be demonstrated mathematically that a small intervention upon the environment in one part of the world can have a massive effect on the other side of the world. Chaos theory has been able to explain the unpredictability of the weather as Newtonian theory could not.

The modern Constitution was above all premised on a strict separation between culture and nature. Montesquieu's analysis of the spirit of the laws of different societies in relation to their respective *climates* is by this account strikingly anti-modern. We who claim to be modern have taken the Cartesian Constitution for granted and ignored Montesquieu's insistence that ideology may be determined by the weather. Because they work indoors in their air-conditioned libraries, the modern analysts of ideology—like Enlightenment scientists enclosed in their laboratories—have forgotten about the weather.

McGann's failure to read Byron's "Darkness" and Keats's "To Autumn" as weather-poems was not personal but symptomatic. The blindness was not his, but the Constitution's; the blindness is that of all who have signed the social contract but refused to draw up a natural contract. Post-1989 we have to come out of the hermetically-sealed laboratory: the experiment of planned socialism has failed, the confidence of science has been shaken. We are learning to attend once more to the weather: to read the signs of the times in the signs of the skies, as our ancestors did. The Global Warming paradigm has the answer to the question which the Cold War paradigm could not ask, the question of why there were bad harvests in the years 1816 to 1818. The answer is a simple one: the eruption of Tambora.

The weather is the primary sign of the inextricability of culture and nature. Serres points out in *Le contrat naturel* that peasants and sailors know the power of the weather in ways that scientists and politicians do not. Romanticism listens to the wisdom of sailors and peasants—of the Mariner and Michael. It challenges the moderns' separation of culture from nature. Romanticism knows that, in Latour's phrase, a delicate shuttle has woven together "the heavens, industry, texts, soul and moral law" (Latour 5).

A living reading of "To Autumn," in the age of global warming must begin with the knowledge that we have no choice but to live with the weather. As the meteorological reports for July 1816 are the key context for Byron's "Darkness," so our understanding of "To Autumn" should begin with the knowledge that the weather was clear and sunny on 38 out of the 47 days from 7 August to 22 September 1819, and that in the week of 15–22 September temperatures were in the mid-sixties, whereas in the correspond-ing week in each of the three previous years they had been in the mid-fifties. Remember the meteorological and consequent agricultural pattern: the terrible summer and failed harvest of 1816, bad weather and poor harvests continuing in 1817 and 1818, then at last in 1819 a good summer, a full harvest, a beautiful autumn.

"To Autumn" is not an escapist fantasy which turns its back on the ruptures of Regency culture; it is a meditation on how human culture can only function through links and reciprocal relations with nature. For Keats, there is a direct correlation between the self's bond with its environment and the bonds between people which make up society. The link is clear in the letters he wrote around the time of the composition of "Autumn." At the end of August 1819, he writes to Fanny Keats:

> The delightful Weather we have had for two Months is the highest gratification I could receive—no chill'd red noses—no shivering— but fair Atmosphere to think in—a clean towel mark'd with the mangle and a basin of clear Water to drench one's face with ten times a day: no need of much exercise—a Mile a day being quite sufficient—My greatest regret is that I have not been well enough to bathe though I have been two Months by the sea side and live now close to delicious bathing—Still I enjoy the Weather I adore fine Weather as the greatest blessing I can have.[17]

The measure of human happiness, Keats suggests, is not a matter of government decree, is not determined by the high politics of Fat Louis and Fat Regent, to whom he refers dismissively later in the same letter. There are more basic necessities: good weather, clean water to wash and bathe in, unpolluted air in which to exercise. Keats's residence in Margate and the emergent discourses of sea-bathing and ozone are crucial here.[18]

Then on 21 September 1819 in his journal-letter to George and Georgiana Keats (2.208–9) he moves easily from human bonds ("Men who live together have a silent moulding and influencing power over each other— They interassimilate") to the bond between self and environment ("Now the time is beautiful. I take a walk every day for an hour before dinner and this is generally my walk"). The walk is described: it traces a path from culture to nature, from cathedral and college to meadow and river. Between theorizing about interassimilation and describing his walk in the fresh autumn air, Keats writes "I am not certain how I should endure loneliness and bad weather together." Life depends on sociability and warmth: in order to survive, our species needs both social and environmental networks, both human bonds and good weather.

"To Autumn" is a poem about these networks. That it is a weather poem is manifest from the passage describing its genesis in the other famous letter which Keats wrote on Tuesday, 21 September 1819, to J. H. Reynolds:

> How beautiful the season is now—How fine the air. A temperate sharpness about it. Really, without joking, chaste weather—Dian skies—I never lik'd stubble fields so much as now—Aye better than the chilly green of the spring. Somehow a stubble plain looks warm —in the same way that some pictures look warm—this struck me so much in my sunday's walk that I composed upon it. I hope you are better employed than in gaping after weather. I have been at different times so happy as not to know what weather it was.
>
> (*Letters* 2.167)

The consumptive has no choice but to gape after weather. I believe that the key context for this passage is the poor air quality of the years 1816–18— Byron's "perpetual density," the effect of Tambora. Health, wrote Keats in his late letters, is the greatest of blessings, the cornerstone of all pleasures (2.289, 306). When his body was finally opened by Dr. Clark, Dr. Luby and an Italian surgeon, "they thought it the worst possible Consumption—the lungs were intirely destroyed—the cells were quite gone" (Severn to Taylor, *Letters* 2.379). Air quality is of the highest importance for the weak of lung. Keats was killed less by the reviewers than by the weather. I suspect that when he refers to the "different times" at which he was "so happy as not to know what weather it was," he is thinking nostalgically of the time before the bad weather of the immediate post-Tambora years which tragically coincided with the first taking hold of his pulmonary tuberculosis. The good summer and clear autumn of 1819 very literally gave him a new lease of life.

"To Autumn" itself is a poem of networks, links, bonds and correspondences. Linguistically, it achieves its most characteristic effects by making metaphors seem like metonymies. Mist and fruitfulness, bosom-friend and sun, load and bless, are not "naturally" linked pairs in the manner of bread and butter. One would expect the yoking of them to have the element of surprise, even violence, associated with metaphor. But Keats makes the links seem natural: the progression of one thing to another through the poem is anything but violent or surprising. The effect of this naturalization within the poem is to create contiguity between all its elements.

The world of the poem thus comes to resemble a well-regulated ecosystem. Keats has an intuitive understanding of the underlying law of community ecology, namely that biodiversity is the key to the survival and adaptation of ecosystems.[19] Biodiversity depends on a principle which we might call *illusory excess*. In order to withstand the onslaught of weather an ecosystem needs a sufficient diversity of species to regenerate itself; species which serve no obvious purpose in one homeostasis may play a vital role in changed environmental circumstances. Their superfluousness is an illusion; they are in fact necessary. The wild flowers in the second stanza of "To Autumn" are an excellent example: in terms of the agricultural economy, the flowers which seed themselves in the cornfield are a waste, an unnecessary excess, but under different environmental conditions they could be more valuable than the corn. The wild-flower which Keats names is the poppy. I believe that this is chosen not only for aesthetic effect—the red dots contrasting with the golden corn, as in Monet's *Wild Poppies*—but also as a reminder of medicinal value. "The fume of poppies" makes us think of opiates against pain and care. Spare the next swath with your reaping-hook, says Keats, and you might just gain medical benefit; spare the remaining rainforests, say ecologists, and you might just find a vaccine against AIDS among the billions of still unstudied plant species you would otherwise annihilate.

The ecosystem of "To Autumn" is something larger than an image of agribusiness. Agribusiness sprays the cornfields with pesticides, impatient of poppies and gnats. Agribusiness removes hedgerows, regarding them as wasteful; "To Autumn," in contrast, listens to hedge-crickets. The poem is concerned with a larger economy than the human one: its bees are there to pollinate flowers, not to produce honey for humans to consume ("later flowers for the bees," not bees for human bee-keepers).

But the imaginary ecosystem of the text is also something larger than a piece of descriptive biology. There are not only links within the biota— flower and bee, the food-chain that associates gnat and swallow—but also links between the discourses which the modern Constitution sought to separate out. The poem not only yokes external and internal marks of biological process (the visible bending of the apple tree, the invisible swelling of the gourd), it also yokes community and chemistry (bosom-friend and sun), physics and theology (load and bless), biology and aesthetics (a link which we may express through the two halves of the word which describes the closing images of the poem: bird-song). And crucially, it refuses to sign the Cartesian constitution which splits apart thinking mind and embodied substance. In contrast to Keats's earlier odes, there is no "I" listening to a nightingale or looking at an urn: the self is dissolved into the ecosystem. In his journal-letter, Keats wrote of his ideal of interassimilation between men; in the poem he is interassimilated with the environment. Indeed, environment is probably the wrong word, because it presupposes an image of man at the center, *surrounded by* things; ecosystem is the better word exactly because an ecosystem does not have a center; it is a network of relations.

Insofar as the poem does have a center and does anthropomorphize, it is distinctively female. The human figures in the central stanza—winnower, reaper, gleaner and cider-presser—embody traditional woman's work. Yet they are not in process of "working over inorganic nature" in the manner of Marxian man. They are suspended, immobile. The winnower's hair is balanced in the wind, the gleaner balances herself in equilibrium with the eddies of the brook, the reaper is asleep under the influence of the poppy, the cider-presser is winding down in entropic rhythm with the oozings.

In contrast to those feminists who seek to denaturalize traditional images of masculinity and femininity, ecofeminists reappropriate and celebrate the idea of woman's closeness to the rhythms of mother earth. A line of work beginning with Sherry Ortner's "Is Female to Male as Nature is to Culture?" and best exemplified by Carolyn Merchant's *The Death of Nature*, posits direct links between Enlightenment science, masculinity and technology on the one hand, the exploitation of women and the exploitation of the earth on the other.[20] Keats's images of wise female passivity and responsiveness to nature are prototypically ecofeminist.

If we return to the letter to Reynolds with this in mind, we will notice that it offers more than a weather report. It mediates between meteorology and

405

mythology. The unblemished sky is compared to Diana, mythical goddess of chastity. This allusion fits with the poem's feminized relationship with nature. Keats would have read in Lemprière's *Classical Dictionary* that the poppy was sacred to Diana. Several of the goddess' traditional functions and associations suggest that she may be regarded as a spirit of ecological wholeness: she was supposed to promote the union of communities; she was especially worshipped by women; she seems originally to have been a spirit of the woods and of wild nature who was subsequently brought into friendly accord with early Roman farmers. But this latter shift also reveals the illusion upon which the poem is based. Diana, with her associations of woodland, chase and pool, is preeminently the presider over a pre-agrarian world. The meadows in which she runs are never harvested. Chastity is an ancient image of untouched—virgin—land. It might be said that a more appropriate presider for the poem would be one of Diana's opposites, the fertile Cleopatra: "he ploughed her and she cropped," says Enobarbus of Caesar and Cleopatra. The male farmer ploughs, the female land is cropped.

In both letter and poem, Keats celebrates the stubble, that which remains after the cropping and the gathering. This land is worked-over, not virgin. The aestheticized still-point of the poem occurs at the moment when humankind has possessed and emptied the land. But where in the "Ode on a Grecian Urn" the objective correlative is a human artwork which is celebrated precisely because it transcends time, "To Autumn" offers only a momentary suspension upon the completion of harvest. At the close of the poem, the gathering swallows and the full-grown lamb are already reminding us of the next spring. Famously, Keats gives up on the earlier odes' quest for aesthetic transcendence, embracing instead the immanence of nature's time, the cycle of the seasons.

"Accidentally or knowingly," writes Serres, "the French language uses only one word, *temps*, to speak both of the time that ticks by or flows, and of the weather produced by the clime and by what our ancestors called meteors" (*Le contrat naturel* 1; trans. McCarren). "To Autumn" is a poem of both time and the weather. In this respect, it mediates between exterior and interior ecologies. Ecosystems evolve in time through the operation of weather; the ecology of the human mind is equally dependent on the two senses of *temps*. Our moods are affected by the weather. Our identities are constituted in both time and place, are always shaped by both memory and environment. Romantic poetry is especially concerned with these two constitutions. It is both a mnemonic and an ecologic. Weather is a prime means of linking spatiality and temporality—this, I suggest, is why so many major romantic poems are weather poems. A romantic poem is a model of a certain kind of being and of dwelling; whilst always at several removes from the actual moment of being and place of dwelling in which it is thought and written, the poem itself is an image of ecological wholeness which may grant to the attentive and receptive reader a sense of being-at-home-in-the-world.

Let us read "To Autumn" backwards. The poem ends with an at-homeness-with-all-living-things (swallow, robin, cricket, sheep, willow, gnat). The final stanza's river and distant hill are not virgin ecosystems, but they are less touched by humankind than is the intermediate farmed environment of the middle stanza. Where the poem has begun is with an intensively managed but highly fertile domestic economy in a cottage-garden. The movement *of* the poem is thus like that of the inspirational walk out of Winchester: from culture to nature. But the movement *through* the poem, with its intricate syntactical, metrical and aural interlinkings, is not one which divides the culture from the nature. There is no sense of river, hill and sky as the opposite of house and garden. Rather, what Keats seems to be saying is that to achieve being-at-homeness-in-the-world you have to begin from your own dwelling-place. Think globally, act locally.

With its thatch-eves, mossed cottage-trees and morning mistiness, Keats's imaginary dwelling-place is built upon the Nether Stowey cottage-home described by Coleridge in "Frost at Midnight." The verbal echoes sound from the closing section of "Frost":

> Therefore all seasons shall be sweet to thee,
> Whether the summer clothe the general earth
> With greenness, or the redbreast sit and sing
> Betwixt the tufts of snow on the bare branch
> Or mossy apple-tree, while the nigh thatch
> Smokes in the sun-thaw; whether the eave-drops fall
> Heard only in the trances of the blast,
> Or if the secret ministry of frost
> Shall hang them up in silent icicles,
> Quietly shining to the quiet Moon.[21]

At the micro-political level of ideology, "Frost at Midnight"'s celebration of snug (though surely not smug) domestic virtue may be related to a Burkean defense of "home" against French revolutionary innovation during the invasion-fear of 1798; at the macro-political level of ecosophy it is a meditation on the relationship between being and dwelling, achieved through a subtle interplay of what Serres calls *les deux temps*.

The secret ministry of the frost (weather) is the exterior analogue for the equally secret interior ministry of the memory (time). As the frost writes upon the window-pane, so memory writes the poet's identity. By the end of the night both the environment of the cottage and the ecology of the poet's mind will have subtly evolved. The poet has learnt to dwell more securely with himself, his home and his environment. But the structure of the evolution is that of a topological network, not a Newtonian sequence of action and reaction. The distinction I have in mind here is one made by Serres in his *Éclaircissements.* If you take a handkerchief and lay it flat to iron it, you can define fixed distances between points on it: this is the geometry of the classical age. But if you crumple up the same handkerchief to put it in your pocket, two points that were far apart can be near together or even superimposed on one another: this is the topology of networks. For Serres, both time and the weather are structured according to this kind of topology.[22]

Chaos theory has a name for these relationships: they are fractal. I believe that as Keats had an intuitive knowledge of the importance of illusory excess as a principle of community ecology, so Coleridge had an intuitive knowledge of the fractal structure of time and weather. How may we measure the motions of "Frost at Midnight"? The pattern of the frost; the flickering of the flame and the flapping of the film on the grate; the flowings of breeze, wave, cloud, thaw-steam, eve-drop and icicle? They are fractal. The poet's abstruser musings have dim sympathy with these motions because they have a similar structure, in that the poem's temporal structure is not classically sequential, but crumpled like Serres' handkerchief in such a way that it makes manifest neighborings ("voisinages" [*Éclaircissements* 93]) which are invisible to the modem Constitution.

The temporal structure may be simplified as present-past-future-present. In its imagining of the baby Hartley's future, the poem proposes an ideal mode of dwelling in which the human subject is set into a new relationship with the objects of nature:

> But *thou*, my babe! shalt wander like a breeze
> By lakes and sandy shores, beneath the crags
> Of ancient mountain, and beneath the clouds,
> Which image in their bulk both lakes and shores
> And mountain crags.

The child is imagined as becoming like the weather, the breeze which plays across both land and water. But, more than this, the Enlightenment form of spatial perception is shattered: the parallelism of "beneath the crags" and "beneath the clouds" breaks down the rigid distinction between solid and vaporous matter, while the image of the mountains and clouds imaging the lakes reverses the classical structure of substance and shadow (real mountain above, illusory image reflected in water below). The dislocation— the *pliage*—is such that it no longer seems appropriate to talk about human subject and natural object. The Cartesian subject/object distinction is made to vanish.

The imagined relationship between Hartley and nature is like the articulated relationship between Samuel and Hartley. The italicized *thou* strives to replace the dialectic of subject and object with an intercourse of I and thou. Where the subject/object relationship is one of power, the I/thou is one of love. Bond and tie replace mastery and possession. An ecofeminist language of nurture and care, as against male technological exploitation, is again apposite. What is truly radical about "Frost at Midnight" is Coleridge's self-representation as a father in the traditional maternal posture of watching over a sleeping baby. In ecofeminist terms, this realignment of gender roles clears the way for a caring as opposed to an exploitative relationship with the earth.

Michel Serres asks: "In politics or economics, by means of the sciences, we know how to define power; [but] how can we *think fragility?*" (*Le contrat naturel* 71; my trans. and emphasis). I ask myself: what might be the legacy of romantic poetry for us now? And it occurs to me that the answer to Serres' question is the answer to mine: romantic poetry can enable us to think fragility. Byron's "Darkness" proposes that when ecosystems collapse, human bonds do so too. Keats's "To Autumn" and Coleridge's "Frost at Midnight" are thinkings of our bonds with each other and the earth, thinkings of fragile, beautiful, necessary ecological wholeness. Serres presides over this paper, so he may be given the last word:

> In our exclusively social contracts, we have dropped the bonds that attach us to the world, those that bind temporality to temperature, time to weather, those that put social sciences and physics, history and geography, law and nature, politics and physics, into relation; the bond that directs our language to silent, passive, obscure things that because of our excesses take back their voice, presence, activity, light. We can no longer neglect it.
>
> In the disquieting lull before the second deluge, can we practice a religion diligent of the world?
>
> It is said that certain organisms disappeared from the surface of the Earth because of their tremendous size. It still surprises us that the biggest things are the most fragile, like the entire Earth, humans in the megalopolis, or an all-being, God. Having taken pleasure at the death of these fragile giants for so long, philosophy today takes refuge in the little details that give it security.
>
> Whose diligent shoulders can support, from now on, this huge, fissured sky which we fear will, for a second time in a long history, fall on our heads?
>
> (*Le contrat naturel* 19; trans. McCarren)

Notes

An abbreviated version of this paper was delivered as the opening plenary lecture of the third annual conference of the North American Association for the Study of Romanticism at the University of Maryland, Baltimore County, July 1995. I would like to thank James McKusick and the organizing committee for their invitation. Research for the paper was undertaken during the tenure of a British Academy Research Readership, for which I am deeply grateful.

1 Lord Byron, *The Complete Poetical Works*, ed. Jerome J. McGann, vol. 4 (Oxford: Clarendon P, 1986) 40–41.

2 *Poetical Works* 4.459–60. The main substance of the note is taken from R. J. Dingley's "'I had a dream . . .': Byron's 'Darkness,'" *The Byron Journal* 9 (1981): 20–33, an article that is strong on literary sources but silent on meteorology.

3 *Byron's Letters and Journals*, ed. Leslie A. Marchand, 12 vols (London: John Murray, 1973–82) 5.86.

4 John D. Post, *The Last Great Subsistence Crisis in the Western World* (Baltimore and London: Johns Hopkins UP, 1977) 21, 9. Post is also my source for more general remarks about the weather at this time.

5 Figures from W. Cary's monthly Meteorological Tables in *The Gentleman's Magazine*.

6 "Atmospheric Constitution of New York, from March to July 1816," *New York Medical Repository*, NS, 3 (1817): 301–7 (301).

7 Franklin, *Works*, ed. Jared Sparks, 10 vols (Boston, 1836–40) 6.456–57.

8 Though he does not mention the weather, Timothy Morton sees "Darkness" as "demonstrating an ecological consciousness of famine as the death of nature and of cultural, political order"—*Shelley and the Revolution in Taste: The Body and the Natural World* (Cambridge: Cambridge UP, 1994) 220–21.

9 McGann, *The Beauty of Inflections* (Oxford: Clarendon, 1985) 61.

10 On Cold War criticism, see chap. 3 of Karl Kroeber, *Ecological Literary Criticism: Romantic Imagining and the Biology of Mind* (New York: Columbia UP, 1994).

11 Bruno Latour, *We have never been Modern*, trans. Catherine Porter (Cambridge, MA: Harvard UP and Hemel Hempstead: Harvester Wheatsheaf, 1993) 10–11.

12 Michel Serres, *Le contrat naturel* (Paris: François Bourin, 1990; rpt. Flammarion, 1992) 57–58, quoted from Felicia McCarren's trans. of chap. 2 of this book in *Critical Inquiry* 19 (1992): 1–21.

13 Karl Marx, *Selected Writings*, ed. David McLellan (Oxford: Oxford UP, 1977) 82.

14 Arden Reed, *Romantic Weather: The Climates of Coleridge and Baudelaire* (Hanover and London: UP of New England, 1983) 38, citing Serres, *Hermès IV: la distribution* (Paris: Minuit, 1977) 229. See also Serres, *La naissance de la physique* (Paris: Minuit, 1977) 86. Reed's book is an attempt to reintroduce unstable weather into the discourse of romanticism, but for a deconstructive purpose. His favorite weather is mist and cloud, which serve as metaphors of *aporia* and hermeneutic *abyme*. My reading of romantic weather, in contrast, begins from actual meteorological conditions at a particular historical moment.

15 See Alfred W. Crosby, *Ecological Imperialism: The Biological Expansion of Europe, 900–1900* (Cambridge: Cambridge UP, 1986).

16 See especially *Spring*, lines 272 ff. On Newton's mastery: "Nature herself / Stood all subdued by him, and open laid / Her every latent glory to his view" ("To the Memory of Sir Isaac Newton," lines 36–38)—Nature here is female, passive, open to possession.

17 *The Letters of John Keats*, ed. Hyder E. Rollins, 2 vols (Cambridge, MA: Harvard UP, 1958) 2.148.

18 It was at Margate that Dr. A. P. Buchan practiced and wrote his seminal book on the healthy atmosphere of the Thanet peninsula, *Practical Observations concerning Sea-Bathing* (1804). See further, Alain Corbin, *The Lure of the Sea: The Discovery of the Seaside 1750–1840*, trans. Jocelyn Phelps (London: Penguin, 1995) 62, 71–72.

19 See Edward O. Wilson, *The Diversity of Life* (Cambridge, MA: Harvard UP; rpt. London: Penguin, 1994), especially chap. 9.

20 Ortner's essay was published in *Women, Culture, and Society*, ed. Michelle Rosaldo and Louise Lamphere (Stanford: Stanford UP, 1974) 67–87; Merchant, *The Death of Nature: Women, Ecology, and the Scientific Revolution* (San Francisco: Harper and Row, 1980). But see also the critique in Janet Biehl, *Rethinking Ecofeminist Politics* (Boston: South End P, 1991).

21 Coleridge, *Poms*, ed. John Beer (London: Everyman, 1993) 190. The influence on "Antumn" has often been noted; see for example, Miriam Allott's notes to her edition of Keats's *Complete Poems* (London: Longman, 1970) 651–54.

22 Serres, *Éclaircissements: cinq entretiens avec Bruno Latour* (Paris: Bourin, 1992; rpt. Flammarion, 1994) 92–93.